Environment and Development in a Resource-Rich Economy

Malaysia
under the
New Economic Policy

HARVARD STUDIES IN INTERNATIONAL DEVELOPMENT

Other volumes in the series include:

Reforming Economic Systems in Developing Countries
edited by Dwight H. Perkins and Michael Roemer, 1991

The Challenge of Reform in Indochina
edited by Börje Ljunggren, 1993

Macroeconomic Policy and Adjustment in Korea, 1970-1990
by Stephan Haggard, Richard N. Cooper, Susan Collins, Choongsoo Kim, and Sung-Tae Ro, 1994

Framing Questions, Constructing Answers: Linking Research with Education Policy for Developing Countries
by Noel F. McGinn and Allison M. Borden, 1995

Industrialization and the State: The Korean Heavy and Chemical Industry Drive
by Joseph J. Stern, Ji-hong Kim, Dwight H. Perkins, and Jung-ho Yoo, 1995

Moving to Market: Restructuring Transport in the Former Soviet Union
by John S. Strong and John R. Meyer, with Clell G. Harral and Graham Smith, 1996

The Strains of Economic Growth: Labor Unrest and Social Dissatisfaction in Korea
by David Lindauer, Jong-Gie Kim, Joung-Woo Lee, Hy-Sop Lim, Jae-Young Son, and Ezra F. Vogel, 1997

Between a Swamp and a Hard Place: Developmental Challenges in Remote Rural Africa
by David C. Cole and Richard Huntington, with Francis Mading Deng, 1997

Getting Good Government: Capacity Building in the Public Sectors of Developing Countries
edited by Merilee S. Grindle, 1997

Assisting Development in a Changing World: The Harvard Institute for International Development, 1980-1995
edited by Dwight H. Perkins, Richard Pagett, Michael Roemer, Donald Snodgrass, and Joseph J. Stern, 1997

Volumes published jointly with the International Center for Economic Growth:

Markets in Developing Countries: Parallel, Fragmented, and Black
edited by Michael Roemer and Christine Jones, 1991

Progress with Profits: The Development of Rural Banking in Indonesia
by Richard Patten and Jay K. Rosengard, 1991

Green Markets: The Economics of Sustainable Development
by Theodore Panayotou, 1993

Building Private Pension Systems: a Handbook
by Yves Guérard and Glenn Jenkins, 1993

Asia and Africa: Legacies and Opportunities in Development
edited by David L. Lindauer and Michael Roemer, 1994

Green Taxes and Incentive Policies: An International Perspective
by Glenn Jenkins and Ranjit Lamech, 1994

Industrialization and the Small Firm: Patterns and Policies
by Donald R. Snodgrass and Tyler Biggs, 1996

Harvard Studies in International Development

Environment and Development in a Resource-Rich Economy

Malaysia
under the
New Economic Policy

Jeffrey R. Vincent and *Rozali Mohamed Ali*

with

Chang Yii Tan

Jahara Yahaya

Khalid Abdul Rahim

Lim Teck Ghee

Anke Sofia Meyer

Mohd. Shahwahid Haji Othman

G. Sivalingam

Harvard Institute for International Development
Harvard University
Distributed by Harvard University Press

Published by the Harvard Institute for International Development

Distributed by Harvard University Press

Editorial management: Don Lippincott
Editorial assistance: Jolanta Davis
Design and production: Northeastern Graphic Services, Inc.

Library of Congress Cataloging-in-Publication Data

Environment and development in a resource-rich economy : Malaysia
    under the new economic policy / Jeffrey R. Vincent and Rozali
    Mohamed Ali with Chang Yii Tan . . . [et al.].
        p.   cm.—(Harvard studies in international development)
    Includes bibliographical references and index.
    ISBN 0-674-25852-5 (cloth).—ISBN 0-674-25853-3 (paper)
    1. Sustainable development—Malaysia. 2. Environmental policy—
Economic aspects—Malaysia. 3. Natural resources—Malaysia.
4. Malaysia—Economic policy. 5. Malaysia—Economic conditions.
I. Vincent, Jeffrey R. II. Rozali, Mohamed Ali. III. Chang, Yii
Tan. IV. Series.
HC445.5.Z9E544   1997
333.7'09595—dc21   97-21937
                                                           CIP

Printed in the United States of America

To Liz and Ben,
for sharing wonderful times in Kuala Lumpur

To Kim and Hafiz,
always sources of joy, for their unfailing support

Contents

Foreword   xi

Preface   xiii

Acknowledgments   xix

1 **Natural Resources and the Environment in the Malaysian Context**   1

Malaysia: key features   3
Natural resources and development during the colonial period   8
The New Economic Policy   10
Trends in natural resource utilization and environmental
     quality during the NEP period   15
Institutional aspects of natural resource and environmental
     management   23
Questions for research   27

2 **Natural Resources and Economic Sustainability**   29

Introduction   29
Resource rents and sustainability   30
Resource depletion and economic sustainability in Malaysia   40
Conclusions   50
Appendix 2.1: Mineral consumption allowances   58
Appendix 2.2: Timber consumption allowances   61
Appendix 2.3: Capital consumption allowances   68

vii

3 **Petroleum**   **73**

Introduction   73
Basic analytics of oil contracts   78
Development of institutional arrangements in the oil sector   80
Economic analysis of production-sharing contracts   89
Conclusions   98

4 **Forests**   **105**

Introduction   105
Basic concepts in forest economics   109
Deforestation   113
Timber depletion   124
Conclusions   141
Appendix 4: Deforestation regressions   146

5 **Agricultural Land**   **151**

Introduction   151
Emergence of the idle land issue   154
The extent of idle land   160
The policy response to idle land   163
Socioeconomic and institutional explanations for idle land   170
Conclusions   173

6 **Marine Fisheries**   **181**

Introduction   181
Fundamental concepts of fisheries economics   185
Development of west coast fisheries during the 1970s
    and 1980s   189
Economic analysis of catch and effort in west coast fisheries
    during the 1980s   210
Conclusions   223
Appendix 6: Bioeconomic model of west coast fisheries   227

7 **Freshwater**   **233**

Introduction   233
Economics of water resource development   237
Water resource development in Malaysia   244
Conclusions   261

8 **Pollution and Economic Development**   **267**

Introduction   267
Cross-country studies of the pollution/development
   relationship   269
The pollution/development relationship in Malaysia   274
Conclusions   285
Appendix 8: Analysis of ambient environmental quality
   and development   287

9 **Air Pollution and Health**   **295**

Introduction   295
Valuing lives saved   298
Development of air pollution policies in Malaysia   303
Mortality-related benefits in urban areas in Malaysia in 1991   308
Conclusions   314

10 **Water Pollution Control**   **319**

Introduction   319
The economic approach to pollution control   322
Palm-oil effluent charges in Malaysia   328
Cost savings of the effluent charges in the Sungai Johor basin   337
Conclusions   341
Appendix 10: Estimation and solution of the simulation
   model for CPO mills on the Sungai Johor   344

11 **Conclusions**   **351**

What were the links between natural resources and
   economic growth?   351
Were natural resources managed to maximize net benefits?   352
What were the links between economic development and
   environmental quality?   359
Was environmental quality managed to maximize net benefits?   360

Bibliography   **365**

Contributors   **401**

Index   **403**

Foreword

Malaysia's economic performance in recent decades is surprising in light of the experience of much of the rest of the developing world. Three of the country's defining characteristics in the 1970s were impediments to economic growth in many other developing countries: ethnic heterogeneity, a large public sector, and a reliance on natural resource exports. Yet, from the 1970s until the present, Malaysia has had one of the fastest-growing economies in the world.

This book is the first of two volumes that seek to provide a deeper understanding of the Malaysian development experience. They are the product of a collaborative research project that the Harvard Institute for International Development (HIID) and the Institute of Strategic and International Studies (ISIS) in Malaysia launched in late 1992. Focusing on the period of the New Economic Policy (the 1970s and 1980s), the books closely examine the key policy decisions that influenced Malaysia's economic take-off. In this volume, Dr. Jeffrey Vincent, a Fellow at HIID, and Dr. Rozali Mohamed Ali, former Director of ISIS's Center for Environmental Studies, examine the interrelationships among natural resources, environmental quality, and economic development. The second volume will probe issues concerning management of economic development in a setting of ethnic heterogeneity.

HIID and ISIS were among the first research institutes in the world to recognize the need for a better understanding of the environmental dimension of development, which directly and indirectly affects the well-being of vast numbers of people in developing countries. Since the 1980s, both institutes have conducted numerous studies on environmental themes, including several book-length treatments. This is the first time, however, that either institute has produced a scholarly work that addresses, from an economic perspective, a broad set of natural resource and environmental issues in a single country. This book is among the few such studies that exist for any country in the world.

Another notable feature of the HIID-ISIS project—and one that is testimony to Malaysia's market-orientation and the remarkable increase in its standard of living—is that it was primarily funded by Malaysian private-sector sources. The project was conceived in the course of discussions with Tun Daim Zainuddin, former Malaysian Minister of Finance, who was a visiting scholar at HIID during the 1991-92 academic year. Tun Daim was instrumental in arranging financial support for the project from several Malaysian companies—Magnum Foundation, Pan Malaysia Pools, Petronas, Resorts World Bhd., and Sports Toto Malaysia—as well as securing the full cooperation of the Malaysian government. The project would not have occurred without Tun Daim's efforts on its behalf. Both of our institutions are deeply grateful to him.

The manner in which the project was designed permitted Dr. Vincent's full-time residency at ISIS during 1992-93, an arrangement that greatly facilitated collaboration between HIID and ISIS. Such residencies are a hallmark of both HIID's and ISIS's approach to international collaboration. In coming years, we hope to take full advantage of modern information technology to continue the research relationships that this study forged, even when long-term residencies are not possible.

Ptolemy produced the oldest known map showing lands that are today part of Malaysia. He referred to those lands as the "Golden Peninsula." Although Malaysia is much-changed, it remains a rich land today, nearly two thousand years later. Thanks to the efforts of Drs. Vincent and Rozali and their collaborators, those who read this book will gain a better understanding of economic development in this fast-growing, resource-abundant economy. The lessons of Malaysia's development experience are important for developing countries throughout the world.

Jeffrey Sachs
Director, HIID

Noordin Sopiee
Chairman, ISIS

Preface

Economists conducting research on natural resource and environmental policy issues in developing countries typically face three obstacles. First, pertinent literature is difficult to identify and obtain. Studies by local researchers are often not published in widely circulated journals, especially not international ones, and access to government reports and memos is often restricted under confidentiality rules. Lack of knowledge of the local language often complicates these difficulties for foreign researchers.

The second obstacle is the difficulty of obtaining data for empirical analysis. Data on natural resources and environmental quality are usually excluded from developing countries' general statistical bulletins. Hence, they are excluded as well from standard international publications used by economists, such as those of the World Bank and International Monetary Fund. When they are included, typically they cover just a few, recent points in time. Compiling time-series data requires the tedious piecing together of information from individual departmental reports. The data often exist only in raw form, as the budgets of natural resource and environmental departments are usually among the slimmest within the government.

Third, because there has been little research on natural resource and environmental policies in developing countries, complete and accurate descriptions of key policy reforms generally do not exist. What happened, and when, are questions whose answers are either not formally recorded or are scattered among internal memos, annual departmental reports, and newspaper articles. The absence of policy histories makes it difficult to identify the most critical natural resource and environmental issues, to place them in the context of a country's overall development experience, and to understand how institutional factors have shaped the responses of economic agents to new or modified policies.

General accounts by economists of the development experience of individual countries, and surveys of development economics, have neglected natural resource and environmental issues until very recently. Dasgupta and Mäler (1991) cited two survey articles from the late 1980s, each nearly one hundred pages in length, that contained exactly one sentence each on natural resources and the environment. They also pointed out that the initial two volumes of the *Handbook of Development Economics* (Chenery and Srinivasan 1988) did not contain a chapter on natural resources and the environment.[1] It was not until 1992 that the World Bank devoted a *World Development Report* to the interface between development and environment.

A principal reason for writing this book was to create a reference volume that would help other researchers overcome these obstacles and facilitate further research on Malaysian natural resource and environmental policy issues, for there are useful lessons to be drawn from the Malaysian experience. In conducting research for the book, the authors made a special effort to identify all relevant material, whether published or unpublished, in English or Bahasa Malaysia, available inside and outside Malaysia. The Malaysian complexion of the research team, a fifteen-month residency in Kuala Lumpur by the principal non-Malaysian researcher, the generous cooperation of Malaysian authorities, and the willingness of policy makers and other individuals to be interviewed facilitated this effort. These factors have made it possible, for the first time, to bring between two covers an economics-oriented discussion of major natural resource and environmental policy developments in Malaysia during what is arguably the most important period in the country's development, the New Economic Policy period of the 1970s and 1980s. This was a period of profound socioeconomic changes, heavy utilization of natural resources, and the emergence of serious air and water pollution problems.

Despite the inclusion of historical information on policy developments, the book is not intended to be a history book. Instead, it attempts to place the economic analysis of natural resource and environmental policy issues in a historical context. It is concerned with the process of development, and how that process affects the economics of managing natural resources and the environment. It attempts to determine how public policies have influenced the contribution of natural resources and the environment to economic development, and the impacts of development on natural resources and the environment.

The book has three specific objectives. The first is to convey, to as broad an audience as possible, an economic approach to analyzing natural resource and environmental policy issues in a particular, and particularly interesting, developing country. The book is not written for academic theoreticians. In light of the limited attention that economists have paid to natural resource and environmental issues in developing countries, most chapters in the book include short pedagogic sections explaining the relevance of economic concepts to the issues discussed therein. To further increase the book's readability, concepts are presented solely in words and diagrams. All equations and all but the most essential technical terms are relegated to notes and appendices. If Stephen Hawking's *A Brief History of Time* was able to present cosmology without the crutch of higher mathematics, it seemed that a book on natural resource and environmental economics ought to be able to do so too. Notes and citations direct the academically minded reader to more advanced concepts and analyses.

The authors hope that the level of discourse in the book will increase its usefulness for undergraduate and graduate courses in universities in developing countries. No Malaysia-specific textbook on natural resource and environmental economics exists. Although this book is not a textbook, it can perhaps serve as a link between foreign textbooks and the local research literature until one becomes available.

The second objective is to capitalize on the unprecedented access to data that the researchers enjoyed by extending existing empirical analyses of Malaysian natural resource and environmental policy issues. Quantitative economic analysis of these issues is relatively rare—in fact, nonexistent for several of the issues covered in the book. Some of the existing analysis is also so divorced from an institutional context that the simple crunching of numbers has led researchers to incorrect or incomplete inferences. All chapters, aside from the first and last, therefore contain new empirical analyses of key policy issues. The purpose is not to extend economic theory, but to extend its application in the Malaysian context.

Although the purview of the book is the 1970s and 1980s, the analysis in it is intended to provide useful lessons for current and future policy makers. This is the book's third objective. The book is not purely retrospective. It contains forward-looking recommendations for both specific sectors and overall economic management.

These three objectives shape the structure of the book and the chapters in it. In the interest of making the book more accessible to individuals who are not familiar with Malaysia, Chapter 1 provides an overview of essential aspects of the country's development experience, highlighting those relevant to natural resources and the environment. This overview also frames the broad research questions addressed in subsequent chapters. Those chapters are divided into two groups, with Chapters 2 through 7 focusing on natural resources and Chapters 8 through 10 on environmental quality (in particular, air and water quality). The initial chapter in each group provides, by way of introduction, a macro perspective. Subsequent chapters present issues at a sectoral level and have a similar format. An initial section presents the main issue addressed in the chapter, describing its general features and explaining its policy relevance in the Malaysian context. The second, third, and fourth sections present key concepts, policy history, and new empirical analysis. The fifth and final section draws out sector-specific policy implications from the analyses in the third and fourth sections. The final chapter, Chapter 11, distills policy lessons at an aggregate level.

This is by no means the first book to address natural resource and environmental issues in Malaysia. The most comprehensive single work to date is probably *Development and Environment in Peninsular Malaysia*, by Aiken et al. (1982), which offers a geographer's perspective. It reviews policy developments and is a useful source of quantitative information up to the end of the 1970s. A similar perspective has been provided more recently for Sabah and Sarawak by Cleary and Eaton (1992) in *Borneo: Change and Development*. Sham Sani's (1993) *Environment and Development in Malaysia* updates much of the information in Aiken et al., with particular emphasis on air pollution, and it also reviews Malaysia's role in international environmental activities. Papers by Goh (1982), Ong et al. (1987), Abdul Rahman (1993), and several chapters in Brookfield (1994) provide similar, though more concise, reviews of the sort of information in Aiken et al. and Sham Sani. *Key Environments: Malaysia*, edited by the Earl of Cranbrook (1988), is an excellent source of information on physical aspects of the natural environment in Malaysia.

What is new about this book is its emphasis on economics as a source of concepts and methods for analyzing the country's natural resource and environmental policies. Two recent policy-oriented documents contain some of the first information available on the economics of natural resource and environmental management in the country at a macro level. These are *Economic Policies for Sustainable Development* by the Asian Development Bank (1990), which contains a chapter on Malaysia prepared by the Malaysian Institute of Economic Research,[2] and the country's *National Conservation Strategy* (Economic Planning Unit 1993; prepared by World Wildlife Fund Malaysia under contract with the government's Economic Planning Unit, the agency responsible for preparing the five-year Malaysia Plans and evaluating economic development projects). Their scope and the depth of their analysis, however, are necessarily much more limited than this book's.

The emphasis on economics does not imply that the authors believe that economics provides the only useful perspective for analyzing natural resource and environmental issues. The book simply attempts to demonstrate that economics can provide helpful information for understanding environmental problems and formulating policy responses. Work by researchers in other disciplines is essential for generating the information that economists need for their analyses and policy makers need for their decisions.

As an initial effort on issues that have received scant attention from economists in Malaysia, and as the product of a research process that was limited in time and funds, the book is necessarily selective. It covers issues that satisfied three basic criteria: they were important from a policy standpoint; they were ones for which existing information, in particular quantitative information, was adequate for relatively in-depth analysis; and they provided an opportunity to involve local economists with relevant research experience. The book omits several important issues. Tin, for example, had a major impact on the economic, spatial, and social development of Malaya, but it is no longer an economically important commodity. For an economic history of tin in the Peninsula, see Yip (1969). Plantation tree crops remain economically important, but researchers have written extensively about them already. For information on environmental aspects of rubber and oil-palm plantations, see Vincent and Yusuf (1991, 1993) and the references therein. Other obvious omissions include population growth (although Chapter 8 presents some information on its aggregate environmental impacts), energy,[3] protected areas,[4] urban environmental issues related to congestion, household sewage, and solid and hazardous wastes,[5] and Malaysia's role in global environmental issues related to climate change, ozone depletion, and loss of biodiversity. This list, and the table of contents, indicates that the book's coverage of environmental quality issues (just three chapters) is much less complete than its coverage of natural resource issues (six chapters). This is due to the smaller amount of information that was available on the former.

In conclusion, the book attempts to make a constructive contribution to a complex area that is receiving increased attention from policy makers. It is intended as a starting point for the economic analysis of natural resource and environmental issues in Malaysia, not the final word. The authors hope that the book will stimulate further serious research in the field, and that the information contained in it will assist other researchers in plugging the numerous gaps that remain. Above all, the authors hope that it will help to lay the foundations for effective policies to address critical natural resource, environment, and development issues in coming years.

NOTES

1 This omission was rectified in volume 3A (Behrman and Srinivasan 1995).

2 See also the full report by the Malaysian Institute of Economic Research (1990).

3 Chapter 3 contains some pertinent information on the supply side of the energy sector.

4 We initiated research on the recreational value of Taman Negara, the country's oldest

national park, with Wan Sabri Wan Mansor and Ahmad Shuib of Universiti Pertanian Malaysia, but unfortunately we had to discontinue it due to time constraints.

5 The report of a World Bank mission conducted while the research for this book was in progress is the best source of economic information on these issues. See World Bank (1993).

Acknowledgments

Many individuals and organizations contributed to the creation of this book. We begin by thanking the seven individuals who co-authored particular chapters with us: Anke Sofia Meyer (Chapter 3), Mohd. Shahwahid Haji Othman (Chapter 4), Lim Teck Ghee (Chapter 5), Jahara Yahaya (Chapter 6), G. Sivalingam (Chapter 7), Chang Yii Tan (Chapter 9), and Khalid Abdul Rahim (Chapter 10). In the absence of these experts' detailed knowledge of the sectors concerned, we would have overlooked key information and important features of the Malaysian policy environment. Some of these individuals, as well as Chamhuri Siwar and Frank Harrigan, also prepared background papers that helped us initiate the research. Kam Suan Pheng, Ku Izhar Ku Baharudin, K. Zulkifli, Sandra Brown, and Louis Iverson provided technical support related to GIS (geographic information systems) analyses in Chapters 4 and 5.

Participants in the ISIS-HIID Conference on the Malaysian Economy (June 1-3, 1992), the 1993 ISIS Environmental Conference (September 1-2, 1993), and seminars sponsored by the Persatuan Ekonomi Malaysia and the Harvard Club of Malaysia (June 16, 1993), the Sabah Institute for Development Studies (September 27, 1993), and the Sarawak State Planning Unit (September 30, 1993) provided constructive comments on the scope of the research, research methods, and preliminary findings during the field portion of the project (August, 1992-October, 1993). Subsequently, several individuals kindly reviewed drafts of one or more chapters as we completed them: Anjum Altaf, Peter Ashton, Abu Bakar Jaafar, Harry Cheah, John Dixon, Jaya Gopal, John Hartwick, Jack Knetsch, Lin Mui Kiang, Ma Ah Ngan, Karl-Göran Mäler, S.T. Mok, Theodore Panayotou, Salleh Mohd. Nor, Peter Rogers, Thomas Selden, Charanpal Singh, Daqing Song, Jack Spengler, Jomo K. Sundram, C. Peter Timmer, Louis T. Wells, Jr., Dale Whittington, Larry Wong, and three anonymous referees.

Although we were fortunate to have excellent collaborators and reviewers, very little of the research reported in this book would have been possible in the first place without the assistance of Malaysian government agencies. Those agencies provided essential data and documents, helped us understand the development of institutions and policies, and helped us interpret our research results. Many government officials, including the Honorable Dato' Seri Dr. Mahathir bin Mohamad, the Prime Minister of Malaysia, and several cabinet ministers and department directors, kindly consented to be interviewed for the project. Unfortunately, space does not permit us to list all these individuals by name. Instead, we note the following agencies that were particularly helpful: at the federal level, the Prime Minister's Department, Ministries of Finance, Trade and Industry, Agriculture, and Primary Industries, Economic Planning Unit, Bank Negara Malaysia, Departments of Statistics, Agriculture, Forestry (Peninsular Malaysia Headquarters), Fisheries, and Environment, Federal Land Consolidation and Rehabilitation Authority, Rubber Industries Smallholders' Development Authority, Fisheries Development Authority of Malaysia, Palm Oil Research Institute of Malaysia, and Forest Research Institute Malaysia; in Sabah, the Ministry of Tourism and Environmental Development, Forestry Department, Geological Survey, Sabah Foundation, and Sabah Borneo Development Corporation; in Sarawak, the State Planning Unit, Ministry of Natural Resource Planning, and Departments of Forestry, Fisheries, and Environment. We also thank WWF Malaysia, the Sabah Institute for Development Studies, Angkatan Zama Mansang (AZAM) Sarawak, and, outside Malaysia, the World Bank.

Many individuals provided technical and administrative support for the project. At ISIS, Zamros bin Dzulkafli and Rozi bin Muda were tireless research assistants; Zarinah bt Ab Wahid, Fauziah bt Daud, and Yassin Affandi bin Salman Halili provided reliable secretarial assistance; and Frank Yong, Wan Portiah Wan Hamzah, and Zahir bin Ismail made substantive contributions while working full-time on other projects. At HIID, Ann Grover served as Vincent's backstopper during his residency at ISIS, and she, along with Brandi Sladek, Selena Rose, Jennifer Watts, Phil Krall, Jolanta Davis, Elena Patino, Sarah Newberry, and Katherine Yost helped immensely in preparing the book manuscript. Joy Sobeck was a careful copy editor, Diane Benison developed the index, and Don Lippincott shepherded the manuscript through the publication process with aplomb. The ISIS and HIID administrations were also unstinting in their support, especially the late, and much-missed, Michael Roemer.

Lastly, we thank our colleagues on other components of the ISIS-HIID project on Malaysian economic development, in particular Ismail Muhd. Salleh, Zainal Aznam Yusof, and Donald Snodgrass, for their willingness to help us place our findings in the broader context of the Malaysian development experience. The Vincent family thanks Donald and Anne Snodgrass for being such good neighbors during our year together on Jalan Ledang.

1

Natural Resources and the Environment in the Malaysian Context

Malaysia provides an ideal case for examining the relationships among natural resources, environmental quality, and development from an economic perspective. To begin, it is one of the most resource-rich countries in the world. In this regard it stands in contrast to the East Asian "tigers" (South Korea, Taiwan, Hong Kong, and Singapore) that are often cited as models of successful economic development, and it is more similar to the rest of the developing world. Land and mineral resources were the basis of the country's economy when the Federation of Malaysia was formed in 1963. The relative importance of resource-based sectors has declined since, but they remain important in absolute terms. Indeed, GDP in primary sectors—mining and quarrying, agriculture, forestry, and fishing—was larger by a factor of more than two in real terms in 1990 than in 1970 (Figure 1.1). So were exports of primary commodities (Figure 1.2).[1]

During most of the 1970s and 1980s, Malaysia was the world's largest producer and exporter of tin, tropical timber, natural rubber, and palm oil. The rapid total GDP growth shown in Figure 1.1 stands in marked contrast to the experience of most other resource-rich countries, which have tended to grow less rapidly than countries with fewer natural resources (Sachs and Warner 1995). Gaining a better understanding of the role of natural resources in Malaysia's exceptional economic performance is therefore important not only from a research standpoint but also for practical policy making, both within the country and elsewhere.

As elsewhere, economic growth in Malaysia has been accompanied by

1

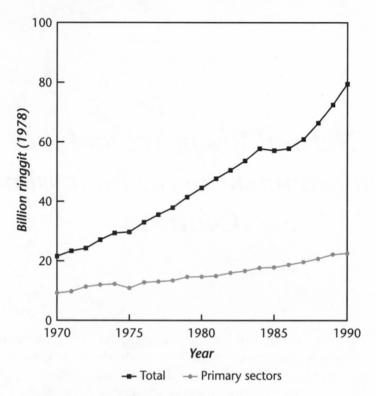

Figure 1.1   GDP: total and primary sectors

serious pollution problems in industrialized and urbanized areas. Unlike most developing countries, however, Malaysia began monitoring these problems in the early stages of industrialization. It established a national system of monitoring stations for air and water quality in the late 1970s. The combination of its rapid economic growth and the existence of abundant, high-quality data on trends in environmental quality creates an unusually good opportunity for studying the relationship between economic development and pollution. The results of such analysis could be useful not only for predicting future environmental trends in the country, but also for determining, in a more general sense, whether a trade-off between growth and environmental quality is inevitable. Malaysia might offer a valuable reference case for other countries where industrialization is less advanced.

Malaysia therefore merits a closer look by environmental economists outside as well as inside the country. This chapter begins the examination of the

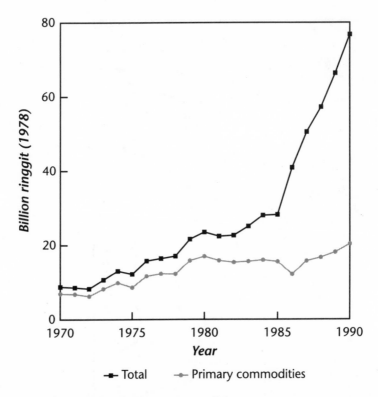

Figure 1.2 Exports: total and primary commodities

Malaysian experience at a general level. Its purpose is twofold: to provide essential background information for readers who are not very familiar with the country, and to identify the broad research questions that will be the subject of more detailed analysis in the remainder of the book.

MALAYSIA: KEY FEATURES

Malaysia is located in the humid tropics in Southeast Asia. Geographically, its two parts are separated by more than 500 kilometers of the South China Sea (Figure 1.3). One part, Peninsular Malaysia, borders Thailand and extends south from the land mass of Asia. The other, composed of the states of Sabah and Sarawak, extends along the northern coast of the island of Borneo. The

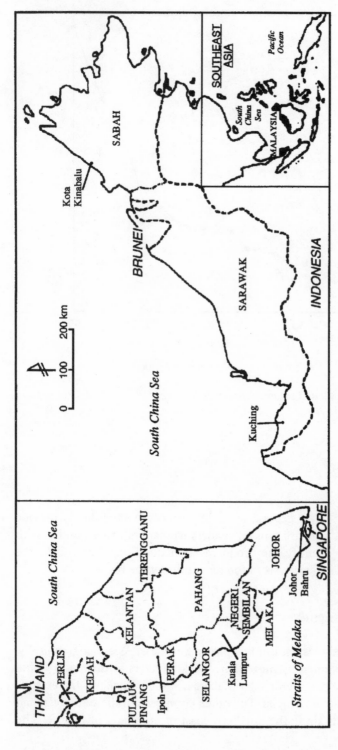

Figure 1.3   States and major cities of Malaysia.

Borneo states cover somewhat more area, 198,160 km² (124,449 km² for Sarawak and 73,711 km² for Sabah²) compared to 131,598 km² for Peninsular Malaysia.

The country's peninsular/insular composition gives it a long coastline. Consequently, marine resources—in particular, offshore oil and gas, and marine fisheries—are economically important. Plains many kilometers wide extend along most coasts. The soils in these lowland areas are generally nutrient poor, but they have good physical properties. Hence, agricultural development, primarily for perennial tree crops, has been extensive. Table 1.1 shows estimates of land use in the three major regions of the country over time.

Forests were the largest single land use in all three at all points in time, but the area in agriculture expanded substantially. Because rainfall is abundant year-round in most of the country,³ agriculture is primarily rain fed, except in the northern peninsular states that form the country's rice bowl. The interior of the country is rugged—the highest peak in Southeast Asia, Gunung

Table 1.1 *Land use by region (in thousands of hectares)*

Region and use	1966[a]	1974[b]	1981	1990[c]
Peninsular Malaysia				
Agriculture	2,736	3,565	4,085	4,244
Forest[d]	10,034	8,843	8,460	6,270
Urban	134	199	251	—
Other	311	430	448	—
Sabah				
Agriculture	313			693
Forest	6,949			4,437
Urban	9			—
Other	118			—
Sarawak				
Agriculture	2,814	3,206		4,045
Forest	9,433	9,032		8,301
Urban	12	15		37
Other	136	72		62

Sources: For Peninsular Malaysia, Wong (1971) for 1966, Economic Planning Unit (1980) for 1974, Kementerian Pertanian (1992) for 1981, and Kementerian Pertanian (1992) and Kementerian Perusahaan Utama (1992) for 1990. For Sabah, Kementerian Pertanian (1992) for 1970 and Seksyen Banci and Perangkaan, Bahagian Ekonomi Pertanian (1990) for 1990. For Sarawak, Kementerian Pertanian (1992) for 1976, and Jabatan Pertanian (various issues) for 1966 and 1991.

[a] 1970 for Sabah.

[b] 1976 for Sarawak.

[c] 1991 for Sarawak.

[d] Broadly defined, to make estimates comparable across years. Includes dryland forests, swamps and swamp forests, scrub forests, and grassland. The 1990 estimate for Peninsular Malaysia is more narrowly defined.

Kinabalu at 4101 meters, is in Sabah—and heavily forested, due to the difficulty of developing agriculture (although vegetables are grown in some highland areas).

Malaysia is one of the least densely populated countries in Asia, and Sabah and Sarawak are particularly sparsely populated (Table 1.2). The population is multi-ethnic in all parts of the country. Malays, who are Muslim and traditionally dwelled in coastal and rural areas, form the largest group. Next largest are the Chinese, who began to settle in coastal areas of the Peninsula as early as the fifteenth century but did not immigrate in large numbers until the late 1800s and 1900s, during the commercial development of the country's tin resources. Indians, mainly Tamils from south India, form the third largest group. Indian influence reaches back centuries (Hinduism preceded Islam as the Malays' religion), but most Indians came to Malaysia as workers on rubber estates during the first half of the twentieth century.

The ethnic mosaic is more complicated in Sabah and Sarawak where, in addition to these groups, there are numerous indigenous groups including the Iban, Bidayuh, Melanau, Kenyan, Kayan, and Penan in Sarawak (the Iban are the largest of all ethnic groups in the state), and the Kadazan, Bajau, and Murut in Sabah (the Kadazan, who are unusual in Malaysia in being predominantly Christian, are Sabah's largest ethnic group). In Peninsular Malaysia, there is a very small population of aboriginal groups, collectively termed the *Orang asli*. Groups considered to be indigenous to the country, which are

Table 1.2 *Population, population density, and population growth rate by region*

Region	1970	1980	1991
Peninsular Malaysia			
Population ('000)	8,809.5	11,426.6	14,797.7
Density (per km²)	66.9	86.8	112.4
Growth rate (%/yr)	—	2.6	2.4
Sabah			
Population ('000)	653.6	1,011.0	1,863.6
Density (per km²)	8.9	13.7	25.3
Growth rate (%/yr)	—	4.5	5.7
Sarawak			
Population ('000)	976.0	1,307.6	1,718.4
Density (per km²)	7.8	10.5	13.8
Growth rate (%/yr)	—	3.0	2.5
Malaysia			
Population ('000)	10,439.4	13,745.2	18,379.7
Density (per km²)	31.7	41.7	55.7
Growth rate (%/yr)	—	2.8	2.7

Source: Khoo (1995).

generally all those other than of Chinese, Indian, or European descent, are termed *bumiputera*. Table 1.3 shows ethnic composition by region according to the 1991 census.

Politically, Malaysia is a federation of thirteen states and two federal territories (the capital city of Kuala Lumpur, and the island of Labuan off Sabah). Until 1957, Peninsular Malaysia (Malaya), Sabah (North Borneo), and Sarawak were administered as separate British colonies. Malaya gained its independence in 1957, and the Federation of Malaysia was formed in 1963. The Federation, which included Singapore until 1965, is a constitutional monarchy, with the *Yang di-Pertuan Agong* (king) as head of state. The *Agong* serves a five-year term and is selected from among the sultans of the nine peninsular states with royal families: Johor, Kedah, Kelantan, Negeri Sembilan, Pahang, Perak, Perlis, Selangor, and Terengganu.[4]

The federal government is a parliamentary system headed by a prime minister, with government agencies headed by ministers (chosen from among members of Parliament) and staffed by professional civil servants. Most political parties are defined on the basis of ethnicity. Core parties in the National Front (*Barisan Nasional*), the coalition that has held power since independence, are the United Malays National Organization, the Malaysian Chinese Association, and the Malaysian Indian Congress. The lead opposition party, the Democratic Action Party, is predominantly identified with the

Table 1.3   *Population of ethnic groups by region, 1991*

Region and group	Number ('000)	Percentage
Peninsular Malaysia		
Bumiputera	8,433.8	58.3
Chinese	4,251.0	29.4
Indian	1,380.0	9.5
Others	410.5	2.8
Sabah		
Bumiputera	1,003.6	71.7
Chinese	218.2	15.6
Others	177.1	12.7
Sarawak		
Bumiputera	1,209.1	71.1
Chinese	475.8	28.0
Others	15.1	0.9
Malaysia		
Bumiputera	10,646.5	62.0
Chinese	4,945.0	28.8
Others	1,572.2	9.2

Source: Khoo (1995).
Note: Includes Malaysian citizens only.

Chinese community. Dr. Mahathir Mohamad was the prime minister at the time of writing, a position he has held since June 1981.

At the state level, the government consists of state assemblies and chief ministers. Much decision-making authority is vested in the chief ministers, who head the states' Executive Councils. These function as state-level cabinets and have particular authority over natural resources, especially land and timber.

NATURAL RESOURCES AND DEVELOPMENT DURING THE COLONIAL PERIOD[5]

Natural resources have played an important role in the country since well before the colonial period. Malaysia's natural wealth, combined with its location along maritime routes linking the Indian subcontinent and East Asia, has made international commerce an important feature of its economy for centuries. Minerals such as gold and tin, and forest products of bewildering variety, formed the basis of economic activity at the beginning of its recorded history. They led to the formation of a thriving trading regime centered in Melaka, which reached its zenith in the 1400s. But the foundations of natural resource and environmental management were most firmly established during the colonial era, which began with the fall of Melaka to the Portuguese in 1511. This was followed by Dutch and later British rule.

The natural harbors at Pulau Pinang and Singapore led to their use as shelters and ports by the British for ships plying the trade routes between India and Canton. They also formed the initial staging point for natural resource exploitation. The colonial trading system was based on the exploitation of natural resources to supply raw materials to industries in the Western world. Pulau Pinang, Singapore, and later Melaka (collectively, the Straits Settlements) formed part of the regional network of enclaves of the British Empire in the Far East, functioning as administrative centers for export-oriented economic development. Initially these enclaves were collecting and gathering points for various spices such as gambier,[6] nutmeg, and pepper. By the late 1800s, the increasing demand for these products, as well as for tapioca, sugar cane, and cloves, spurred the introduction of plantation agriculture in areas adjacent to the enclaves.

The cultivation of these crops required clearing of primary forests and was ecologically very destructive. Planters exploited the temporary fertility of the fresh forest soil and abandoned the land for new clearings when fertility declined. This practice of commercial shifting cultivation caused substantial deforestation in certain parts of the western coastal plain of the

Peninsula. In Negeri Sembilan, tapioca planting had completely denuded the Gemencheh area and turned the Rembau area into a largely *lalang*[7] plain by 1890. Sugar cane plantations in the southern part of Seberang Prai (the coastal strip of Pulau Pinang) and in the neighboring Kerian district of Perak resulted in the clearing of large tracts of mangrove and freshwater swamp. Cultivation of coffee cleared substantial tracts of forest in Perak, Selangor, Negeri Sembilan, and Johor. In Pulau Pinang, forests on steep slopes were cleared to make way for plantations, to capitalize on the good soil quality and constant moisture.

The development of commercial deposits of tin in the second half of the nineteenth century triggered a major change in the pattern of resource exploitation. Economic activity moved inland, and immigrants from China were brought in to work the mines. Concentrations of Chinese immigrants in tin-rich areas formed the nuclei for urbanization in many parts of the Peninsula, including Kuala Lumpur. As tin became an important export commodity, the colonial government invested in physical infrastructure linking tin mines to ports. Railroads were built linking Taiping to Port Weld (Kuala Sepeting), Kuala Lumpur to Port Swettenham (Port Klang), Tapah Road to Telok Anson (Telok Intan), and Seremban to Port Dickson. These were joined by an interstate line in 1903, which was subsequently extended to Johor and Singapore in the south and Pulau Pinang and Kedah in the north. The colonial government concurrently invested in road networks, whose density and complexity reflected the level and nature of economic activity in each state.

Institutional and administrative arrangements to support large-scale, resource-based activities were also developed. The government encouraged foreign investment in agricultural plantations and tin mining, and introduced a land tenure system that allowed private ownership. Rising government revenues from resource-based taxes made possible the continued expansion of road and rail networks as well as investment in other public works, such as irrigation and drainage. In response to these and other policies, the alienation of land for agriculture and mining accelerated.

Around the turn of the century, coconut and especially rubber plantations began spreading rapidly across the western coastal plain of Peninsular Malaysia, first in the form of large foreign-owned estates and soon after in smallholdings. This expansion initially depended on the infrastructure financed earlier by the tin industry, but it soon became in its own right a major driving force of the spatial development pattern.

By the early twentieth century, the small foreign enclaves in the Straits Settlements had been transformed into relatively large urban centers with many industries of considerable size, and they had been joined by others in Ipoh, Taiping, and Kuala Lumpur. This urban growth increased the demand for food, particularly rice. In response, traditional subsistence agricultural activities expanded to produce a modest surplus for sale to urban areas. Through this process a form of dualism developed in the economy, in which both advanced and traditional sectors operated in the domestic market.

Development efforts in Peninsular Malaysia under the colonial administration focused on areas with ready access to available infrastructure: mainly areas west of the Main Range between Pulau Pinang in the north and Singapore in the south. The northwestern states of Kedah and Perlis were outside this ambit. The Main Range acted as a barrier to the extension of infrastructure to the east coast, and this hindered expansion of the modern economy into those areas. Access was particularly difficult for Kelantan and Terengganu. The east coast remained economically detached from the rest of the Peninsula until the 1960s. The pace of development was even slower in Sabah and Sarawak, which were far from potential export markets and, with their sparse and scattered populations, did not offer large work forces or domestic markets to potential investors.

The New Economic Policy[8]

Independent Malaysia inherited a colonial economic system that was highly dependent on exploitation of natural resources for export. Primary sectors were the major component of the economy: 37 percent of GDP, 53 percent of employment, and 89 percent of exports in 1965 (*Mid-Term Review of the First Malaysia Plan 1966–1970*). Given the well-developed commodity sectors, early development plans adopted a fairly straightforward strategy of modernizing the economy within the established colonial trading system.

A decade of this strategy failed to provide many benefits to the traditional economy, however. Rural/urban income disparities widened as income rose rapidly in the advanced sectors of the economy and slowly, if at all, in traditional sectors. The political consequences of this imbalanced growth were magnified by economic aspects of the country's ethnic composition. Historically, the different ethnic groups could be as easily distinguished by their economic activities as by their religion, customs, language, and appearance. Malays were smallholder farmers and fishermen; Chinese were tin miners and controlled most commercial enterprises; Indians were rubber tappers; and the other non-European groups were farmers and forest dwellers. Most Chinese lived in cities and towns and earned higher incomes; most members of other groups lived in rural areas and suffered high rates of poverty. Malays, due to their longer time in the country, their superior numbers, and the sultanates, held political power.

In May 1969, latent ethnic tensions, sparked by opposition parties' unexpectedly strong showing in parliamentary elections, erupted in racial riots that left hundreds dead. In the aftermath, the government formulated the New Economic Policy (NEP), which had two objectives: "to eradicate poverty among all Malaysians, irrespective of race," and "to restructure Malaysian society so that the present identification of race with economic function and geographical location is reduced and eventually eliminated" (*Mid-Term Review of the Second Malaysia Plan 1971–1975*, p. 61). The NEP set numerical targets for raising the *bumiputera* stake in the economy. For example, it aimed at raising the ownership of share capital by *bumiputera* from 2 percent in 1970 to 30 percent in 1990. To achieve the dual objectives of the NEP, the government established numerous new agencies, became more directly involved in the economy through state-owned enterprises, and aggressively pursued the purchase of controlling interests in foreign-owned companies.

The economy expanded rapidly during the NEP period. Per capita GDP was only RM1,999 in 1970 (1978 price levels), but it more than doubled to RM4,411 by 1990. The average annual growth rate in real per capita GDP during that period was 3.7 percent,[9] which was among the highest rates in the world.

Changes in the economy's structure were as impressive as its growth. Malaysia began the 1970s as dependent on primary commodity exports as other lower-middle-income countries, but by 1990 it had diversified its export bundle tremendously. Table 1.4 shows the percentage of merchandise exports accounted for by primary commodities in Malaysia, neighboring countries in Southeast Asia, the "tigers,"[10] and other developing countries classified as lower-middle-income by the World Bank in 1990. Only ten countries of the thirty-three listed had a higher percentage than Malaysia in 1970. Malaysia's percentage at that point in time was comparable to Indonesia's, the Philippines', and Thailand's and much higher than those of the "tigers." In contrast, by 1990, the percentage had fallen more than in most on the list, as only ten countries had a lower percentage. It remained much higher than those of the "tigers."

Rapid growth in the manufacturing sector explains this transformation and the sharp divergence between total exports and exports of primary commodities after 1985 (Figure 1.2). The manufacturing sector rose from 14 percent of GDP in 1970 to 27 percent in 1990, while the share of manufactured goods in total exports rose even more sharply, from 12 percent to 59 percent. Much of the initial growth in manufacturing occurred in export processing zones, the first of which was established in Pulau Pinang. Foreign investors who set up operations in the zones benefitted from lower taxes and tariffs. Industrial capacity also rose due to government investment in heavy

Table 1.4 *Primary commodities as a percentage of merchandise exports*

Country	1970	1990
Ecuador	98	97
Peru	98	84
Mauritius	98	70
Indonesia[a]	98	64
Bolivia	97	96
Papua New Guinea[a]	97	95
Iran	96	99
Panama	96	80
Chile	95	90
Cote d'Ivoire	94	90
Algeria	93	96
Malaysia[a]	**93**	**56**
Philippines[a]	93	38
Cameroon	92	74
Colombia	92	74
Thailand[a]	92	36
Paraguay	91	90
Syria	91	62
Turkey	91	32
Morocco	90	53
Argentina	86	66
Jordan	83	55
Senegal	81	78
Dominican Rep.	81	76
Tunisia	81	27
Costa Rica	80	74
El Salvador	72	78
Guatemala	72	76
Congo	71	97
Singapore[a]	70	27
Jamaica	47	42
South Korea[a]	24	7
Hong Kong[a]	4	4

Source: World Bank (1992, 1994).
[a] Country in East or Southeast Asia or Oceania.

industries such as steel and automobiles. Foreign investment in manufacturing increased particularly rapidly after the mid-1980s when, in response to the country's worst recession since independence, the government liberalized foreign investment regulations. The recession had been triggered by the collapse of most commodity prices, in particular oil. The more liberal investment regime prompted a quadrupling of the annual rate of proposed investment in approved manufacturing projects. By the early 1990s, three areas of the country, all on the west coast of Peninsular Malaysia, were heavily industrialized: the Klang Valley, which encompasses the corridor from Kuala Lumpur to the country's main port, at Klang on the Straits of Melaka; Pulau Pinang in the

Table 1.5 *Percentage of urban population by region*

Region	1970	1980	1991
Peninsular Malaysia	28.8	37.3	54.4
Sabah	16.9	19.9	33.2
Sarawak	15.5	18.0	37.6
Malaysia	26.8	34.2	50.7

Source: Khoo (1995).

northwest; and Johor Bahru, across from Singapore in the south. Industrialization remained much more limited on the east coast of the Peninsula and in the Borneo states.

Although the country became increasingly industrialized—and consequently increasingly urbanized (Table 1.5)—the government by no means ignored the agricultural sector during the NEP period. Given the concentration of both poverty and Malays in rural areas, much government expenditure was allocated to land development schemes, the objectives of which were to provide land to landless households and households with uneconomically sized holdings, and to facilitate the modernization of the smallholding sector. The lead federal agency, the Federal Land Development Authority (FELDA), had been established in 1956 and had been responsible for substantial land development during the 1960s. The pace of public sector land development accelerated with the adoption of the NEP (Figure 1.4).

Developed area more than doubled under the *Second Malaysia Plan 1971–1975*, while expenditure did the same under the *Third Malaysia Plan 1976–1980*. Land development schemes emphasized oil palm, which the government had promoted as a means of reducing the agricultural sector's dependence on rubber since an influential Ford Foundation report in 1963. Much land in existing private rubber estates was also converted to oil palm. The government also extended support to padi rice farmers in the form of price supports, fertilizer and pesticide subsidies, and irrigation works. Similar assistance was extended to traditional fishermen.

Due to these and other programs, spending by the federal government rose rapidly during the first decade of the NEP period, from about 5 billion ringgit (1978 prices) in 1970 to more than 20 billion in the early 1980s. By 1981, total federal government expenditure was nearly half (47 percent) of GDP, generating a fiscal deficit of 19 percent of GDP and a current-account deficit of 10 percent of GDP. The government took aggressive corrective action by embarking on a fiscal austerity program. It reduced or eliminated various subsidies, and reduced its direct involvement in the economy by fully or partly privatizing state-owned enterprises and some other government entities, such as the electricity and telecommunications utilities. In real terms, total federal

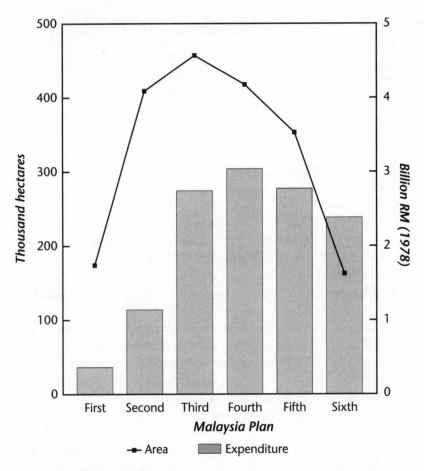

Figure 1.4   Public-sector land development in Malaysia

expenditure was held between 20 and 25 billion ringgit for most of the 1980s. Development expenditure (public sector investment) actually declined.

Malaysia did not achieve all of the NEP targets, but it made impressive progress toward most. Corporate ownership by *bumiputera* reached 20 percent in 1990, and the poverty rate, which had been 49 percent in 1970, fell to 17 percent. The NEP was succeeded by the National Development Policy (1991–2000), which aims at the same general goals but places less emphasis on specific numerical targets and direct government intervention in the economy. In a speech before the Malaysian Business Council in December 1991, Prime Minister Mahathir affirmed the government's commitment to economic growth, calling for Malaysia to become a "fully developed country" by the year 2020.

TRENDS IN NATURAL RESOURCE UTILIZATION AND ENVIRONMENTAL QUALITY DURING THE NEP PERIOD

Production of most natural resources expanded during the NEP period, albeit less rapidly in most cases than output of the manufacturing sector (Figure 1.5). The annual timber harvest doubled, and the annual fish catch tripled. The most dramatic rise occurred in the hydrocarbon sector. Crude oil production rose by a factor of more than thirty times, and production of liquefied natural gas (LNG) nearly quadrupled between 1983 (the first year of production) and 1990.[11] Among major extractive resources, only tin experienced a decline in output during the period, falling by about 60 percent as low-cost deposits were exhausted.

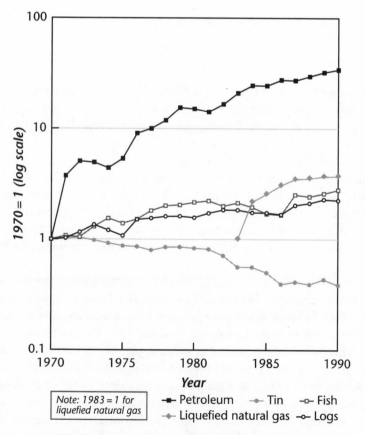

Figure 1.5   *Production indices for major natural resource commodities*

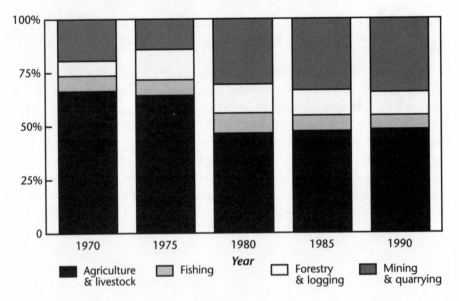

Figure 1.6   *Composition of primary sector GDP*

These changes were reflected in a rising share for mining and quarrying (which includes petroleum and natural gas) in the primary portion of GDP, offsetting a declining share for agriculture and livestock (Figure 1.6), and a rising share for petroleum in primary commodity export earnings, offsetting declining shares for tin and rubber (Figure 1.7).

Primary sectors remained more important in Sabah and Sarawak than in Peninsular Malaysia. In fact, the primary-sector share of GDP rose slightly in the Borneo states, while it fell sharply (by nearly half) in the Peninsula (Figure 1.8). This difference reflected not only the more rapid industrialization of the Peninsula, but also a substantial increase in resource extraction in the Borneo states.

Annual timber harvest fluctuated around 10 million m³ in Peninsular Malaysia, but this amount was exceeded until the late 1980s by Sabah's and after the early 1980s by Sarawak's (Figure 1.9). The combined harvest in the two Borneo states more than doubled between 1970 and 1990. Oil production also rose rapidly in the Borneo states, as well as in Peninsular Malaysia (Figure 1.10). The increases in both regions reflected the development of offshore fields.

The higher levels of resource utilization were driven by rising demand both internationally and domestically. The latter was particularly important for energy and water. Primary energy consumption quadrupled during the period, from just over three billion tonnes of oil equivalents per year in 1970 to

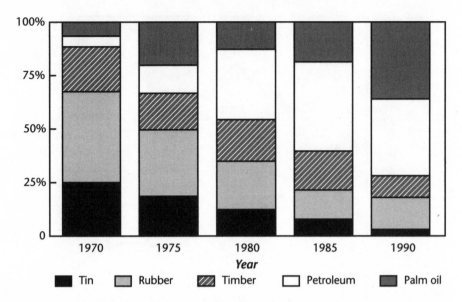

Figure 1.7   Composition of primary commodity exports

just over 13 billion tonnes in 1990, while water consumption increased more than sixfold, from under one billion liters per day in 1970 to nearly five billion liters per day in 1990. Domestic consumption of more tradable goods like timber products and fish also increased significantly.

Various forms of water and air pollution rose along with higher levels of resource extraction, industrialization, urbanization, and energy use. Evidence of local environmental stress began to surface in the mid-1970s. A chapter titled "Environment and Development" in the *Third Malaysia Plan 1976–1980* observed with some prescience that "more explicit attention will need to be given to the management of the environment as economic development progresses."

Pollution of water courses by agro-based industries was an early area of concern. According to the 1980 *Environmental Quality Report* of the Department of Environment (DOE 1981), only 5 percent of the readings at the DOE's river monitoring stations in Peninsular Malaysia were classified as "clean," while about 25 percent were classified as worse than "slightly polluted." Thirty rivers or stretches of rivers were identified as "moderately" or "grossly" polluted. These ratings were based on the DOE's water quality index, which reflected the combined effects of five indicators of water quality: biochemical oxygen demand (BOD), an indicator of organic pollutants from industrial and domestic effluents whose decomposition depletes the dissolved

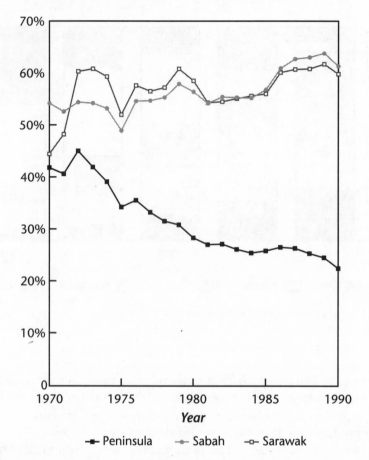

Figure 1.8   Primary-sector share of GDP, by region

oxygen found naturally in freshwater; chemical oxygen demand (COD), an indicator of inorganic pollutants from industrial effluents that also have oxygen-depleting effects; ammoniacal nitrogen, an indicator of contamination by domestic sewage, animal wastes, and fertilizer runoff; suspended solids, which indicate "muddiness" caused by soil erosion; and pH, which indicates the degree of acidity or alkalinity and affects the ability of freshwater to support aquatic life and be used for irrigation and municipal needs.

The main sources of water pollution were palm oil and rubber mills, manufacturing industries of various kinds, inadequate sewage systems, livestock operations, and land development activities. Water quality was generally higher in Sabah and Sarawak than in the Peninsula, and higher on the east

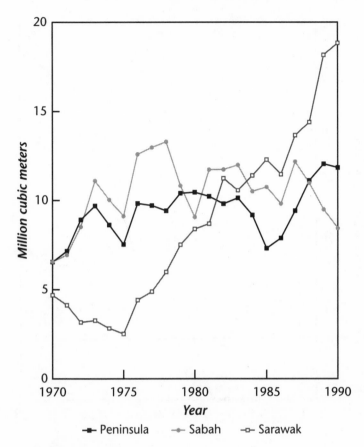

Figure 1.9   Timber harvest, by region

coast of the Peninsula than on the west coast, where industry and urban centers were concentrated. Table 1.6 compares average annual readings for the five water quality parameters in the Sungai Kelang (Klang River), which runs through the country's major urban-industrial region, to proposed interim national water-quality standards developed by the DOE.

Readings for BOD, COD, and suspended solids generally violated the standards for even class III rivers, indicating that the river was suitable for no higher use than irrigation; readings for ammoniacal nitrogen and pH indicated that it was not suitable for even this use. Trends in the indicators were mixed. Levels of BOD and suspended solids were especially high initially but improved considerably over time, while COD rose in the late 1980s after an

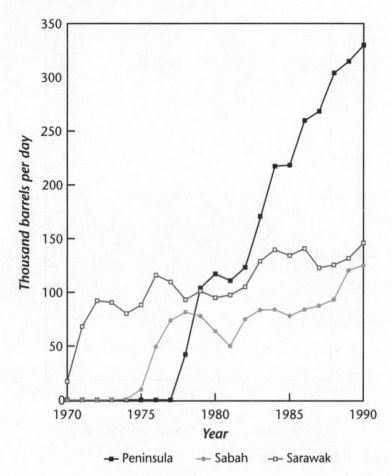

Figure 1.10   Crude oil production, by region

initial improvement. The river became more acidic (i.e., pH fell) during the first half of the period but less so toward the end. Ammoniacal nitrogen rose fairly steadily during the entire period (aside from a freak high value in 1979).

The DOE announced an overall improvement in water quality in the 1984 *Report,* but in 1990 it reported that "river quality . . . on the whole experienced a slight deterioration." In 1993, it reported that 28 percent of the 116 rivers it monitored were "clean." This was higher than in 1980 but still low in absolute terms.

Violations of proposed standards also drew attention to air pollution. The annual average concentration of total suspended particulates (TSP) regularly exceeded the recommended standard of 90 µg/m^3 at monitoring stations oper-

Table 1.6 *Average annual levels of principal water quality parameters in the Sungai Kelang*

Year	BOD[a]	COD[b]	Ammoniacal nitrogen	Suspended solids	pH
	mg/l	mg/l	mg/l	mg/l	
1978	13.5	110.8	3.9	1676	6.9
1979	14.6	99.4	16.9	1480	6.8
1980	11.3	63.0	3.0	602	6.4
1981	6.8	55.2	1.8	492	3.9
1982	8.0	60.7	2.7	708	4.3
1983	8.4	46.6	4.8	505	4.9
1984	8.3	38.5	5.4	392	4.3
1985	6.2	39.0	4.2	405	4.0
1986	7.5	41.7	4.1	270	6.5
1987	7.5	39.9	4.8	166	6.1
1988	6.7	31.6	3.0	180	4.1
1989	5.7	41.8	4.1	194	4.6
1990	9.8	52.2	6.9	136	5.5
1991	5.7	50.4	5.5	216	6.1

[a] Biochemical oxygen demand.
[b] Chemical oxygen demand.
Source: Raw data provided by Department of Environment.

Note: Proposed interim national water quality standards (units same as in table):

River class	BOD	COD	Ammoniacal nitrogen	Suspended solids	pH
I	1	10	0.1	25	6.5-8.5
IIA	3	25	0.3	50	6.5-9.0
IIB	3	25	0.3	50	6.5-9.0
III	6	50	0.9	150	5.0-9.0
IV	12	100	2.7	300	5.0-9.0
V	>12	>100	>2.7	>300	<5.0, >9.0

Class I: practically no treatment required for water supply; very sensitive aquatic species.
Class IIA: conventional treatment required for water supply; sensitive aquatic species.
Class IIB: recreation use with body contact permissible.
Class III: extensive treatment required for water supply; tolerant aquatic species present.
Class IV: irrigation use.
Class V: none of above uses possible.

ated by the DOE and the Malaysian Meteorological Service in major urban areas.[12] Particulates are generated primarily by the combustion of fuels; the burning of municipal, industrial, and agricultural wastes; and the conversion of sulfur dioxide and other sulfur oxides into sulfates.[13] Inhalation of particulates can raise the risk of premature death. The DOE reported in the 1983 *Environmental Quality Report* that "ambient air quality over 80 percent of the areas monitored in 1983 failed 50 percent or more of the time to comply with the proposed standard for total suspended particulate matter," and that "the quality of the air in 40 percent of these areas continued to deteriorate" (DOE 1984). Figure 1.11 shows annual average TSP readings for all DOE monitoring stations in the Klang Valley. Only one station, which was on the campus of the University of Malaya, had readings within the standard in every year.

The DOE began monitoring ambient levels of fine particulates, or PM_{10}, in 1990. PM_{10} represents respirable particles (diameter no greater than 10 microns), which are of prime concern because of their potential adverse effects on human health. The DOE found that PM_{10} levels exceeded the recommended standard at all four monitoring stations, which were located mainly in residential areas.[14] Dustfall readings also exceeded the recommended standard,[15] particularly in residential and commercial locations.

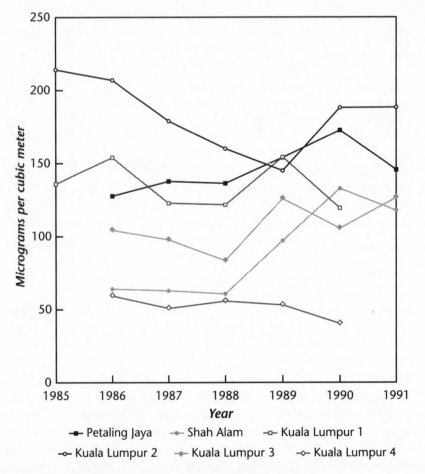

Figure 1.11   Annual average TSP readings in the Klang Valley

Data are much more limited for gaseous pollutants, but the available data suggest that pollution levels rose in urban and industrial locations, especially in the most recent years. Perhaps the most important gaseous pollutant is sulfur dioxide (SO_2), which is generated by power plants and other facilities that burn high-sulfur fossil fuels. SO_2 contributes to acid rain, which can accelerate the weathering of buildings and other structures and adversely affect agriculture, forestry, and fisheries. It has also been linked to respiratory disorders in children, the elderly, and asthmatics. Other important gaseous pollutants include nitrogen oxides (NO_x), which are generated by various industrial processes, impair visibility (they are a principal source of smog), and contribute to acid rain; and carbon monoxide (CO), which results from the incomplete combustion of fossil fuels (especially by motor vehicles), interferes with the uptake of oxygen by red blood cells, and can cause severe illness, even death.

SO_2 levels were within the World Health Organization's (WHO) recommended ambient standard in 1980. The 1992 *Environmental Quality Report* commented that "gaseous pollutants such as carbon monoxide, oxides of nitrogen, and sulphur dioxide still remained at safe levels" (DOE 1993). Just the following year, however, the *Report* drew attention to "the seriousness of air pollution," noting that a new study had determined that hourly measurements of SO_2, nitrogen dioxide, and CO in Kuala Lumpur, Petaling Jaya, and Shah Alam exceeded the recommended Malaysian standards during peak pollution periods (DOE 1994).[16]

Data for airborne heavy metals are even more limited. One of the most important heavy metals is lead, which can impair the neurological and mental development of children. Available data indicate that concentrations of lead decreased over time. Average annual concentrations greater than the recommended ambient standard of 1.5 $\mu g/m^3$ occurred in the central business districts of Kuala Lumpur and Georgetown (Pulau Pinang) in 1984, but they had fallen to less than 0.5 $\mu g/m^3$ by 1992.[17] The improvement was due to a reduction in the lead content of gasoline, and the introduction of unleaded gasoline.

INSTITUTIONAL ASPECTS OF NATURAL RESOURCE AND ENVIRONMENTAL MANAGEMENT

Concerns about resource depletion and environmental degradation resulted in a host of government actions from the mid-1970s onward. The *Third Malaysia Plan 1976–1980* asserted that "environmental improvement and protection will receive the full attention of the government in the planning and implementation of programmes." The legislative and policy framework

that emerged was fundamentally influenced by the allocation of powers between federal and state governments.

The Ninth Schedule of the federal constitution contains three lists of
legislative powers: the State List, the Federal List, and the Concurrent List.
Most natural resources, including land, onshore minerals, agriculture, forests,
riverine fishing, and turtles, are on the State List. Under the Tenth Schedule
of the constitution, revenues from lands, mines, forests, and water supplies,
including water rates, accrue to the states.[18] Consequently, natural resources
are an important source of revenue in most states. They are especially important in Sabah, where forestry fees accounted for a median value of 70 percent
of annual state revenue from 1971 to 1987; and Sarawak, where forestry fees
and petroleum and natural gas royalties were equally important, at median
values of 25 percent and 26 percent of annual state revenue, respectively
(Umikalsum 1991). Petroleum and natural gas royalties became more important to state governments in all three regions after the early 1970s.[19]

The figures in Umikalsum (1991) do not include all forms of resource-
based revenue collected by the states. The constitution provides that states
receive at least 10 percent of the export duty on tin, and states may receive a
prescribed proportion of the export duty on other minerals, too. Special
provisions in part V of the Tenth Schedule apply to Sabah and Sarawak,
granting the two states additional (though not necessarily complete) authority over resource-related taxes. These include import and excise duties on
petroleum products, export duties on minerals other than tin (provided that
the total royalty and duty does not exceed 10 percent), and export duties on
logs and other forest products.

Marine and estuarine fisheries (excluding turtles) are on the Federal List.
The most important resources under federal control are offshore oil and gas
deposits, which were transferred from state to federal control by the 1974
Petroleum Development Act. Consequently, most revenue from oil and gas
accrues to the federal government, either directly or through the national oil
company, Petronas. Oil and gas revenue was a major source of total federal
revenue during the 1970s and 1980s, reaching nearly a third in the mid-1980s,
although its share fell during the manufacturing boom of the late 1980s. It
played an essential role in financing the increased government expenditures
that occurred during the NEP period.

Protection of wild mammals and birds, and national parks, are on the
Concurrent List. A supplement to the Concurrent List, applicable to Sabah
and Sarawak, includes water power and agricultural and forestry research.
Legislative powers for items on the Concurrent List can be exercised by either
parliament or state assemblies. Notwithstanding this division of power, the
constitution states that "if any State law is inconsistent with a federal law, the

federal law shall prevail, and the State law shall, to the extent of the inconsistency, be void." Article 76(1) of the constitution also empowers Parliament to make laws affecting items on the State List under certain circumstances, but this provision has seldom been invoked.

These constitutional arrangements translate into a mix of federal and state agencies in the natural resource and environmental sectors, with state agencies being particularly strong in the Borneo states. Key federal agencies include the Departments of Mines and Forestry under the Ministry of Primary Industries, the Departments of Agriculture and Fisheries under the Ministry of Agriculture, and the DOE under the Ministry of Science, Technology, and Environment. Most have state-level offices, which are typically staffed by federal officers or sometimes a mix of federal and state officers. Exceptions include the Forestry Departments in Sabah and Sarawak and the Fisheries Department in Sabah, which are purely state agencies.

State policies often comply fairly closely with guidelines suggested by federal legislation, even for items on the State List. The 1966 Land Use Capability Classification Act introduced criteria for allocating land among competing uses; it gave the highest priority to mining, followed by agriculture and then forestry. The 1978 National Forestry Policy established a Permanent Forest Estate to ensure that the country would maintain a minimum area under forest cover, and the 1984 National Forestry Act introduced various associated regulations. The country's first Fisheries Act, legislated in 1963, was replaced by a new act in 1985, which placed more emphasis on the need to control fishing to prevent depletion of the resource. To varying degrees, official state policies are consistent with the principles enunciated in these pieces of federal legislation.

Aside from wildlife and national parks, none of the three lists specifies protection of environmental quality, which is covered by over forty separate pieces of federal and state legislation. Many had their beginnings in sector-specific legislation, for example the Federated Malay States Waters Enactment of 1920 and the Mining Enactment of 1929. These enactments were initially formulated to promote and enforce sound production practices and utilization-oriented resource conservation, but over time they have been amended and supplemented by new legislation in order to take into account broader environmental quality concerns.

Malaysia's 1974 Environmental Quality Act was one of the first framework environmental laws in the developing world. It complemented sector-specific legislation, but also represented a major reorientation of environmental management by encouraging an integrated approach. A federal law, it was conceived as a comprehensive piece of legislation that would provide the basis for coordinating all activities related to environmental management throughout the country. It established the DOE, which is responsible for monitoring environmental quality, estimating the environmental impacts of new projects, designing environmental regulations, and enforcing regulations approved by the government. The act mandates environmental impact assessment as a preventive procedure prior to project approval and implementation, and pollution control as a curative measure. It has spawned fifteen sets of regulations, with the most recent ones including regulations related to the generation, storage, treatment, transportation, and disposal of toxic and hazardous wastes.

The passage of the Environmental Quality Act was prompted in part by the global rise in environmental awareness that followed the 1972 United Nations Conference on the Environment held in Stockholm. Global concern about the environment rose again in the late 1980s and early 1990s, as evidence accumulated that deforestation and species loss were accelerating, that global temperatures were rising (due to the buildup of carbon dioxide and other greenhouse gases in the atmosphere), and that the earth's protective ozone layer, which screens out ultraviolet radiation, was becoming thinner (due to the buildup of chlorofluorocarbons, which are common industrial chemical compounds, in the stratosphere). As the focus of environmental concern widened from local and national environmental problems to the global impacts of human activity, Malaysia, as a major producer of tropical timber, came under intense scrutiny by international environmental organizations for the management of its tropical forests. The country increasingly played a leadership role with regard to international environmental issues, actively participating in the negotiation of the Conventions on Climate Change and Biodiversity and the preparatory meetings for the 1992 United Nations Conference on Environment and Development (UNCED; the "Earth Summit") held in Rio de Janeiro. The viewpoints of the "South" were articulated at preparatory meetings hosted by Malaysia, first at a meeting of the Commonwealth heads of government in Langkawi in 1989 and then at a meeting of leaders of developing countries in Kuala Lumpur in 1991. The declarations of those meetings helped to delineate the issues and lines of debate that featured prominently at the Rio meeting. Nongovernmental organizations, including some active in Malaysia, played a major role in the preparatory meetings and at UNCED itself. This both reflected and stimulated higher levels of public environmental awareness within the country.

Following UNCED, Malaysia was elected chair of the Commission on Sustainable Development, which was established to implement the recommendations contained in Agenda 21, the principal document generated by UNCED. Research for this book began at about the same time.

QUESTIONS FOR RESEARCH

The preceding overview raises four issues worthy of more detailed investigation. The first pertains to Malaysia's better-than-average performance compared to other resource-rich countries. Obviously, such success must have much to do with macroeconomic policies, which are not the focus of this book.[20] What is within the scope of this book is an analysis of *the links between natural resources and economic growth.* How important were natural resource rents—economic surpluses—as a source of development capital that fueled the country's rapid growth? And considering the rapid increase in resource utilization during the 1970s and 1980s, can the country sustain the level of consumption that this growth has made possible? The differences in economic structure between the Borneo states and the Peninsula indicated in Figure 1.8 suggest that these questions need to be examined at the regional level as well as the national level.

The analysis in this book starts with this broad yet concrete issue in Chapter 2. Subsequent chapters in the first half of the book then address, at a sectoral level, a second, related issue: *were natural resources managed to maximize net benefits?* Although Malaysia's economic growth rate was high, and even if its consumption level was sustainable, it is possible that inefficient resource policies prevented both from being as high as possible. Chapters 3 through 7 analyze the efficiency of resource policies during the 1970s and 1980s for one nonrenewable and four renewable resource sectors: oil, timber, agricultural land, marine fisheries, and fresh water.

Evidence of high and rising pollution levels during the 1970s and 1980s raises parallel issues with regard to environmental quality. At the macro level, *what were the links between economic growth and pollution?* Did the latter necessarily rise in lock step with the former, or was the relationship more complex? Malaysia's unusually abundant environmental monitoring data, and the regional differences in level of industrialization, make it possible to analyze these questions empirically rather than merely speculate. Chapter 8 introduces the second part of the book by presenting the results of such an analysis. At the sectoral level (in this case, environmental as opposed to economic sectors), *was environmental quality managed to maximize net benefits?* This issue has two aspects: whether policies and regulations focused on aspects of environmental quality that were economically most important, and whether those policies and regulations achieved target levels of environmental quality at the lowest cost (cost-effectiveness). Ideally, one should examine both aspects for a given environmental sector. Unfortunately, limited information made this impossible. Instead, Chapter 9 focuses on the benefits side for the case of air pollution, with some information presented on the cost side, while Chapter 10 focuses exclusively on the cost side for the case of water pollution.

NOTES

1 Figure 1.2 includes tin, petroleum, rubber, palm oil, and timber (logs and sawn wood).
2 Including the island of Labuan, which is a federal territory.
3 There is a distinct dry season only in the extreme northwest of the Peninsula and on the east coast of Sabah. Heavy rains from the northeast monsoon occur only on the east coast of the Peninsula and in Sarawak and Sabah.
4 Melaka, Pulau Pinang, Sabah, and Sarawak have civilian governors as their titular heads.
5 Good sources of information on Malaysian development during the colonial period include Chai (1964), Courtenay (1972), Lim (1967), and Lim (1973).
6 *Uncaria gambir*, a climbing plant of considerable importance to the tanning industry. It is also used locally as an ingredient in betel nut chewing.
7 *Imperata cylindrica*, a tall grass that grows in unmanaged land and is notoriously difficult to eradicate.
8 Good sources of information on economic development during the postindependence period, including the New Economic Policy, include Bruton et al. (1992), INTAN (1994), Jomo (1990), Snodgrass (1980), Young et al. (1980), and a forthcoming book that is a companion to this volume, *Managing Economic Development in an Ethnically Diverse Society*, by Donald R. Snodgrass, Zainal Aznam Yusof, and Ishak Shari.
9 This growth rate is the logarithmic average (determined by regression) of all values during the period, not a point-to-point growth rate.
10 Taiwan is excluded due to a lack of data.
11 Some of Malaysia's natural gas reserves are associated with oil deposits, while others are nonassociated. Before 1983, when an LNG plant began operating in Sarawak, associated gas was usually flared.
12 The recommended standard also called for daily averages not to exceed 260 $\mu g/m^3$.
13 Descriptive information on this and other air pollutants is drawn primarily from World Resources Institute (1992).
14 The recommended standard was an annual average of 50 $\mu g/m^3$, with daily averages not exceeding 150 $\mu g/m^3$.
15 An annual average of 133 $mg/m^2/day$.
16 For SO_2, a daily average of 40 parts per billion (ppb), an hourly average of 130 ppb, and a ten minute average of 190 ppb. For NO_2, an hourly average of 170 ppb. For CO, an eight hour average of 9 parts per million (ppm), and an hourly average of 30 ppm.
17 See also Table 4.2 and Figure 4.1 in the 1991 *Environmental Quality Report* (DOE 1992).
18 Parliament may, however, prohibit or restrict mineral royalties levied by states.
19 In Peninsular Malaysia, only Terengganu collected oil and gas royalties, as it was the only producing state.
20 See the companion volume by Snodgrass et al. mentioned in note 8.

2

Natural Resources and Economic Sustainability

INTRODUCTION

Malaysia and other countries that are generously endowed with natural resources would seem to have a nature-given advantage in economic development. Yet some of the fastest growing economies are those with virtually no natural resources. Singapore and Hong Kong are well-known examples. Moreover, many resource-rich developing countries have achieved little more than transient "resource booms." Their economies expand rapidly while there are resources to exploit, but they contract once the resources are exhausted. An oft-cited example is the Pacific island nation of Kiribati, where phosphate production mined much of the nation out of existence (Ward 1982, Stauffer 1986, Repetto et al. 1989).

An example that illustrates this last point, though in a less extreme way, can be drawn from within Malaysia itself. Historically, much of the country's tin was mined from the fertile alluvial deposits of the Kinta Valley in Perak. In 1970, Perak accounted for half of the country's output in the mining and quarrying sector, which was dominated by tin. Thereafter, due to exhaustion of the best deposits and, in the 1980s, a slump in prices that occurred in spite of a government attempt to intervene in the market (Jomo 1990), tin production began a decline that has continued until today. The decline in output revealed that the great value of tin that had been extracted during the preceding hundred years did not put Perak in an advantageous economic position compared to other states in the country. From 1970 to 1990, Perak's per capita GDP grew more slowly than any other state's. It fell from second highest among the thirteen states in 1970 to ninth in 1990.

Natural resources have been, and continue to be, economically important in Malaysia, but their stocks are lower today than two decades ago. What are the implications of this depletion for the country's long-run growth? Is Perak's subpar performance something that might be repeated at the national level? This chapter addresses these and related questions. It argues that the reason why resource-rich countries are often unable to sustain economic output has less to do with the physical depletion of natural resources than the use of rents (economic surpluses) generated when resources are exploited. The chapter has two main parts. The first part, *Resource rents and sustainability*, presents concepts related to the linkage between resource rents and economic sustainability, and it reviews empirical efforts to apply these concepts in other countries. The second part, *Resource depletion and economic sustainability in Malaysia*, applies the concepts to Malaysia. Along the way the chapter evaluates the adequacy of GDP, the most popular measure of macroeconomic performance, for measuring economic welfare and sustainability. A final section comments on the policy implications of the Malaysian analysis.

RESOURCE RENTS AND SUSTAINABILITY

Hartwick's Rule

Natural resources typically earn a return over and above the opportunity costs of labor and capital used to exploit them. This return, or resource rent,[1] is an economic surplus that countries can potentially use to finance either investment or consumption, or a mix of the two. The fundamental question is, How does the allocation of rents between investment and consumption affect economic sustainability?

Hartwick (1977) identified the theoretical condition linking resource rents to economic sustainability. He considered the hypothetical case of a country with only nonrenewable resources and no source of investment funds other than resource rents (there are no savings from earnings in other industries). He demonstrated that even a country in such an extreme situation can maintain a constant level of per capita consumption in perpetuity, as long as it invests a certain portion of the rents in reproducible, physical (human-made) capital. This simple but striking result has become known as Hartwick's Rule.

Figure 2.1 illustrates Hartwick's Rule for the case of a nonrenewable resource. Incremental production costs are given by an upward-sloping marginal cost curve: costs per unit of output escalate as production rises. For most ordinary goods, the optimal production level is determined by the intersection of price and the marginal cost curve. For natural resources, however, the

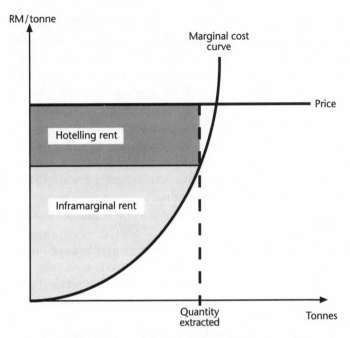

Figure 2.1   Components of resource rent (Hartwick's Rule)

optimal production point falls to the left of this point, because a resource producer must take into account not only direct production costs but also the opportunity cost associated with forgoing production in future periods: extracting a unit of the resource today precludes the extraction of that particular unit in the future. This opportunity cost is termed the *user cost*. In Figure 2.1, it equals the vertical distance between price and marginal cost at the optimal production level.

Total resource rent is the shaded area above the marginal cost curve, below the price line, and left of the production level. The user cost divides this area into two parts. The rectangle given by the product of the user cost and the amount produced is the total Hotelling rent, and the remainder is the inframarginal rent.[2] The total Hotelling rent is the portion that Hartwick's Rule says must be invested to sustain consumption. The inframarginal rent can be consumed. To achieve higher consumption over time, a country must invest more than the Hotelling rent by forgoing consumption of some of the inframarginal rent. This should be the strategy of developing countries, assuming that they desire to raise standards of living. Hartwick's Rule indicates the minimum amount of investment required to prevent a fall in the standard of living, not the optimal amount for achieving development objectives.

The logic of Hartwick's Rule may be explained as follows. The value of any capital good, whether physical or nature-given, is the sum of its discounted future net returns. In the case of a unit of a nonrenewable natural resource, these returns simply equal its discounted future net price (price minus extraction cost). This is the technical definition of the user cost. It follows that the reduction in capital value when a resource is depleted—the value of the change in the resource stock[3]—equals the user cost times the physical amount depleted, i.e., the total Hotelling rent. By investing this amount in physical capital, a country maintains its total capital stock—natural capital plus physical capital—and therefore its consumption possibilities (Solow 1986).

In simple terms, the rule says that a country must use resource rents to finance economic diversification into activities that are relatively more dependent on labor and physical capital than on natural resources. These activities sustain the economy as the stock of natural resources dwindles. Casual observation suggests that this conversion of natural wealth to other forms of wealth was an important factor in the development of many countries that are today highly industrialized. Prime examples are the United States and Canada, where the production of minerals, timber, and other natural resources accounted for a large share of national output in the nineteenth and early twentieth centuries.

In his seminal article Hartwick defined reproducible capital simply as physical capital: equipment, structures, and infrastructure. He did not include skills, technology, knowledge, and other forms of human capital. He also assumed a constant population and labor force. His rule has since been shown to apply in more complicated, realistic situations, including ones involving renewable resources, technological progress, and a growing population (Solow 1986).[4]

In deriving their results, Hartwick and Solow assumed that other forms of capital are highly substitutable for natural resources.[5] That is, they assumed that declining inputs of natural resources can always be offset by greater reliance on physical capital and improvements in technology. For example, as fossil fuels are depleted, energy can be derived from sources that are more capital- and technology-intensive, such as nuclear and solar power. At the extreme, natural resources can be synthesized, as in the case of industrial diamonds. Hartwick and Solow recognized that substitutability is a critical assumption.[6] Mäler (1986) has emphasized that "we simply do not know" the extent of its empirical validity. For this reason, the investment of total Hotelling rents might not prevent an eventual economic bust after all.

Anticipating this criticism, Solow (1992) argued that Hartwick's Rule is nevertheless "a better-than-average rule of thumb" that provides "a way of constantly reminding ourselves that there are considerations other than immediate utility [short-run consumption] to be taken into account." Reinvesting rents might not necessarily yield a consumption level that can be permanently maintained, but it is more likely to do so than using rents to boost current consumption. Solow expressed the hope that greater awareness of the rule might prevent policy makers from succumbing to the latter temptation, which he likened to the Sirens calling to Ulysses.

Applying Hartwick's Rule

Hartwick's Rule suggests a way to determine whether a country is investing enough to maintain its consumption: to check whether net investment, defined as the difference between all additions to and all subtractions from all forms of capital, is nonnegative. Additions should include not only gross investment in physical capital but also increases in stocks of human capital and natural resources. For example, they should include growth of renewable resources. Subtractions should include reductions in all types of capital: depreciation of physical capital, depletion of natural resources, and so on. Net investment thus defined indicates directly whether a country's total capital stock is rising or falling: the stock is rising if net investment is positive, and falling if it is negative.[7]

In practice, the measurement of human capital is extremely difficult. A partial but more practical measure of net investment is one that includes only net changes in physical and natural capital: gross investment in physical capital, minus depreciation of physical capital and the depletion value of natural resources. This partial measure is likely to be biased downward in most countries, as it ignores increases in human capital due to better education and greater literacy.

Most countries publish macroeconomic estimates of gross investment in physical capital, usually under the heading *gross fixed capital formation* or *gross fixed investment.* A few also report aggregate depreciation of physical capital, which is usually termed the *capital consumption allowance.* No country, however, routinely calculates the capital value of changes in its natural resource stocks. This quantity may be termed the *resource consumption allowance,* by analogy with the capital consumption allowance. One would expect this allowance to be an especially important component of net investment in economies dominated by primary sectors, like Malaysia's into the early 1980s.

Estimating the resource consumption allowance is the focus of "natural resource accounting." Following Figure 2.1, for nonrenewable resources the allowance should be calculated by multiplying the amount extracted times the user cost. In practice, two factors complicate this calculation. The first is the estimation of the user cost, which is a function of the discount rate and future prices and costs. Fortunately, if markets for nonrenewable resources are efficient, the user cost equals the current marginal net price (Hotelling 1931): price minus extraction cost for the last unit of resource extracted in the current period. The reason for this equivalence is production arbitrage between current and future periods. If current marginal net price exceeds discounted future marginal net price, the net present value of aggregate resource rents can be increased by raising current extraction. The opposite is true if current marginal net price is below discounted future marginal net price. Extraction levels adjust until current and discounted future marginal net prices are equal, that is, until current marginal net price equals the user cost.[8]

Note that marginal, not average, costs must be used in calculating current net price (Hartwick 1990, Dasgupta and Mäler 1991, Mäler 1991). Production arbitrage equalizes the present values of marginal, not average, net prices across time. Average net prices overstate user costs, and therefore the resource consumption allowances, because average costs are less than marginal costs in resource-extractive industries.[9]

The second complication has to do with the fact that natural resource stocks are never known with certainty, especially in the case of subsurface minerals. In calculating resource consumption allowances, Landefeld and Hines (1985) and Repetto et al. (1989) subtracted discoveries and revisions of reserves from the amount extracted to calculate a broader measure of "net depletion."[10] But the economic justification for this adjustment is weak. These changes reflect not physical changes in resource stocks, but rather changes in information about stocks. Bartelmus et al. (1993, p. 116) argued against including discoveries on the basis that "the increase in natural capital is not the result of economic production." The United Nations Statistical Division, in its forthcoming *Handbook on Integrated Environmental and Economic Accounting*, shares this view.[11]

Discoveries and revisions do indeed affect the resource consumption allowance, but they do so through the amount extracted and the current marginal net price. For example, the discovery of large oil deposits would be expected to cause producers to increase current production. Assuming that marginal extraction costs increase with production level (as in Figure 2.1), current marginal net price would fall. The resource consumption allowance could either rise or fall, depending on the relative magnitudes of the rise in production and the fall in current marginal net price.

Adjustments to the amount extracted do indeed need to be made for renewable resources, whose stocks, unlike those of nonrenewable resources, can regenerate. For renewable resources, the resource consumption allowance is calculated by multiplying current marginal net price times net depletion, which is the difference between amount extracted and growth. If growth is large enough, the resource consumption allowance can be negative, which implies that natural capital has accumulated. This could make net investment larger than gross fixed capital formation.

In summary, the resource consumption allowance can be calculated by multiplying the user cost, which equals current marginal net price, times the negative of the net change in the stock of the resource, or net depletion. For nonrenewable resources, net depletion simply equals the amount extracted. Not surprisingly, natural resource accounting studies often refer to this procedure as the *net-price method*.

Previous studies

Stauffer (1986) demonstrated the feasibility of the net-price method by calculating allowances for petroleum depletion in Kuwait from 1977 to 1980 and in Norway from 1978 to 1981. He found that the allowances were equivalent to 60 to 70 percent of GDP in Kuwait and 2 to 8 percent in Norway. He did not use the allowances to estimate net investment, however, so the implications of these large allowances for sustainability are not clear. He did remark, however, that Kuwait has invested so heavily overseas that it "has almost become a true *rentier* in the strict sense of the term as applied to someone living off of, but not invading, his capital." This was graphically illustrated during the 1991 Gulf War when Kuwait continued earning income despite a collapse in oil production following the Iraqi invasion. He also used average net prices instead of marginal net prices, so even if he had analyzed net investment, the results would have understated the prospects for sustainability.

In a study of Indonesia, Repetto et al. (1989) used average net prices to calculate allowances for petroleum, timber, and agricultural soils from 1971 to 1984. They found that the aggregate resource consumption allowance was equivalent to about a quarter of GDP. They also calculated a partial measure of net investment, by subtracting the resource consumption allowance from gross fixed capital formation.[12] They found that partial net investment was much smaller than gross investment during most of the period. In fact, it was actually negative in two years. Aggregated over the entire period, however, it was positive. This is an encouraging finding from the standpoint of sustainability, even more so when one considers that Repetto et al., like Stauffer, overestimated the resource consumption allowances by using average net prices. One cannot be sure that Indonesia's total capital stock increased, however, without making the additional deduction for the capital consumption allowance.

Repetto et al. (1991) did this in a follow-up study on Costa Rica for the period 1970–1989. They again included allowances for timber and soils, and they added an allowance for fisheries resources. They excluded petroleum because Costa Rica is not a producer. They found that net investment rose rapidly during the 1970s but then stagnated during the 1980s, when a high rate of deforestation increased the resource consumption allowance. The difference between gross and net investment was large in every year. This led Repetto et al. to conclude pessimistically that "Costa Rican decision-makers [have been led] farther and farther from development choices that would have been economically . . . sustainable" (p. viii).

This conclusion was not supported by their results, however. The test of sustainability is not the level of net investment relative to gross investment, but rather the absolute level of net investment: whether it is positive or negative. Net investment was positive in every year, which implies that Costa Rica's total capital stock rose: the accumulation of physical capital more than offset the depletion of Costa Rica's natural capital stocks. While it may be true that "the economic 'development' programs carried out to date [in Costa Rica] have sacrificed [its land, its forests, and the surrounding seas]" (p. 8), the sacrifice apparently enriched the country by building up other forms of capital. Moreover, the sacrifice was overstated in economic terms, as Repetto et al. again used average net prices instead of current net prices.

Two of the most recent studies were conducted by the United Nations and the World Bank in Papua New Guinea (Bartelmus et al. 1993) and Mexico (van Tongeren et al. 1993),[13] to gain experience in implementing proposed revisions to the U.N. System of National Accounts. The study in Papua New Guinea found that the net increase in physical capital from 1985 to 1990 exceeded natural resource depletion in every year, but it estimated resource consumption allowances only for minerals and used average net prices in doing so. The study in Mexico found that net investment was positive in the only year analyzed, 1985, after accounting for both depreciation of physical capital and resource depletion. Its estimate of the latter included oil, timber, and land, but it too was based on average net prices.

Net national income

Analyzing net investment is the most direct means of putting Hartwick's Rule into practice. Results in a paper by Weitzman (1976) suggest an alternative but theoretically equivalent approach, which provides more information on changes in economic welfare as resources are depleted. This approach uses data on national income.

Economists have long recognized that net domestic product (NDP) provides a better measure of national economic welfare than GDP. Assuming trade is in balance, GDP equals the sum of (final) consumption and gross investment.[14] Conventional NDP is calculated by deducting the capital consumption allowance from GDP. Hence, conventional NDP equals consumption plus net investment in physical capital.

Weitzman argued that a true measure of NDP should reflect changes in other capital stocks as well, a point echoed by Dasgupta and Heal (1979, pp. 244–246) and Solow (1986). Specifically, he stated that natural resources "ought to qualify as capital," as should "states of knowledge resulting from learning or research activities" (human capital). His key finding was to demonstrate that true NDP equals the maximum consumption level that a country can permanently maintain, given its capital stocks at that point in time. Solow (1986) provided an intuitive explanation of this finding. By definition, NDP equals consumption only if net investment equals zero. If this is the case, then a country's total capital stock does not change from one period to the next. The country cannot consume any more without causing its total capital stock, and therefore the output of goods and services available for consumption, to fall. In effect, NDP represents interest on a country's total capital stock. A country that consumes more than NDP is eating into its principal.

Weitzman's finding was elaborated by Hartwick (1990), Dasgupta and Mäler (1991), and Mäler (1991, 1993), who demonstrated that NDP can be interpreted as a national benefit-cost measure:[15] changes in NDP reflect the net welfare impact of changes in the economy, including future impacts. Hence, a country can determine whether its long-term welfare level is rising, falling, or remaining constant by examining the trend in NDP. Sustainability requires that the trend be nonnegative. Long-run welfare can increase, instead of merely remaining constant, only if the trend is positive.

Both studies by Repetto et al. used the resource consumption allowances to estimate NDP. In the case of Indonesia, Repetto et al. estimated a partial measure of NDP by subtracting just the resource consumption allowance from GDP. They found that partial NDP was positive, but grew only about half as rapidly as GDP, 4.0 versus 7.1 percent per year. In the case of Costa Rica, they obtained data on the capital consumption allowance, and used it to calculate a more complete estimate of NDP. In contrast to Indonesia, Costa Rica's NDP[16] actually grew slightly faster than its GDP, 4.1 versus 3.9 percent per year (based on analysis of data in Table I-2 in their report). In both cases, partial NDP was generally much smaller than GDP.[17] Differences are to be expected, given that one measure is net and the other gross. The salient point is that NDP rose, indicating that, insofar as the analysis captured all significant changes in capital stocks, development in both countries was not only sustainable but promised increased well-being for future Indonesians and Costa Ricans.

Adjusting GDP

Both studies by Repetto et al. severely criticized GDP as a measure of the sustainability of economic output. Indeed, NDP is superior for this purpose, particularly when it is compared to consumption. But GDP's omission of the value of resource depletion does not reveal an intrinsic flaw. It simply reflects the fact that GDP is not a net measure of aggregate economic performance. By definition, a gross measure should not be adjusted for capital depreciation and resource depletion.

Adjusting GDP is warranted for other reasons, however. Devarajan and Weiner (1990) pointed out that conventional GDP overstates the level of GDP consistent with long-run welfare maximization when natural resources are not exploited efficiently. They proposed a correction, based on the difference between actual resource rents and hypothetical rents associated with optimal utilization.[18] When they applied this procedure to soil erosion in Mali and Thailand, they found that the magnitude of the correction was on the order of 1 to 2 percent of GDP. The allowance (Repetto et al. 1991) for the depletion of open-access fisheries in Costa Rica was a conceptually similar adjustment.

Application of Devarajan and Weiner's formula is complicated by two practical difficulties: first, in determining whether or not resources are being utilized optimally, and second, in quantifying the differences between actual and optimal rents. Moreover, economic behavior is surely suboptimal in many economic sectors, not just those related to natural resources. Distortions in resource-based sectors could be minor compared to other distortions affecting GDP. If one is concerned about distortions in the measurement of GDP, should one necessarily address resource-related distortions first?

A second reason for adjusting GDP relates to nonmarket aspects of the environment. The environment has value beyond being a potential source of investment funds. In particular, environmental quality can affect human well-being directly. For example, air pollution can cause losses in amenity values by obscuring scenic views, and deforestation can cause the extinction of valued species.

GDP accurately reflects gross economic welfare only if consumption is defined as including the direct welfare impacts of changes in environmental quality (Dasgupta and Mäler 1991, Mäler 1991). Conventional GDP is not defined in this way, for a practical reason: unlike minerals, timber, and other natural resource commodities, environmental values are not explicitly priced in markets.[19] GDP therefore overstates the benefits of economic growth when environmental degradation directly reduces the quality of life, and it understates the benefits when improvements in environmental quality directly raise welfare. Since NDP is derived from GDP, it is also biased by the omission of these effects.

Nordhaus and Tobin (1972) attempted one of the first, and still best-known, efforts to adjust GDP for the welfare value of changes in environmental quality. They developed a measure of national income for the United States which they termed *MEW*, for "measure of economic welfare." MEW included an adjustment for the "disamenities" of urban life. They estimated that this adjustment was equivalent to 5.6 percent of GDP in 1965. Tentative efforts to value aggregate environmental degradation in developing countries include the U.N./World Bank studies in Papua New Guinea and Mexico (Bartelmus et al. 1993, van Tongeren et al. 1993). In the former case, the value of environmental degradation was estimated to be 2.0 to 10.4 percent of conventional NDP, depending on the year and valuation method employed; in the latter case, 7.5 percent.

Dasgupta and Mäler (1991) and Mäler (1991) have shown that two other frequently proposed adjustments to GDP are inappropriate. The first is an adjustment for the impacts of environmental degradation on current production. For example, when air pollution raises the number of days of work lost due to illness, it might seem sensible to reduce GDP to reflect this cost. But as long as the illnesses are temporary ones that do not decrease workers' long-run health and productivity, GDP does not need to be adjusted. This is because it is already lower due to the workers' lost output. The impacts of the air pollution are not costed explicitly by the market, but they do affect market outcomes. On the other hand, if production-related impacts are persistent, in that they reflect degradation of some component of the country's capital stock, then they should be included in the resource consumption allowance and thereby reflected in NDP, though not in GDP. Permanent productivity losses due to incapacitating environmental illnesses, and increased mortality due to exposure to air pollutants (see Chapter 9) provide examples.

The second inappropriate adjustment relates to expenditures to prevent or remedy environmental degradation. Some economists have proposed that so-called defensive expenditures by households and the government should be deducted from GDP (El Serafy and Lutz 1989, Repetto et al. 1989). The correct procedure is not to deduct defensive expenditures, but rather to deduct the value of direct welfare losses, as discussed above. Defensive expenditures provide economically valuable services and therefore should be included in GDP. Only under special circumstances does their cost equal the value of environmental degradation (Mäler 1991).

Some, but not all, proposed adjustments to GDP are therefore theoretically valid. In practice, these adjustments are more difficult than the calculation of resource consumption allowances, because they require information on optimal resource extraction rates and the value of changes in environmental quality. For this reason, most natural resource accounting studies have focused on adjustments to NDP for natural resource depletion. The analysis of Malaysia in the following section is no exception.

Resource Depletion and Economic Sustainability in Malaysia

In light of the differences in economic structure among Peninsular Malaysia, Sabah, and Sarawak discussed in Chapter 1, we investigated resource depletion and sustainability not only for Malaysia as a whole but also separately for the three regions. Lack of data prevented us from conducting the analysis for individual states in the Peninsula. We estimated resource consumption allowances for two natural resource sectors: minerals and timber. We used these estimates to calculate net measures of investment and domestic product annually for the years 1970 to 1990. The estimates represent revised versions of earlier ones presented in EPU (1993). Unfortunately, data limitations prevented us from including changes in human capital. We will return to this and other limitations of the analysis in the section *Conclusions*.

All economic values discussed below are expressed in ringgit. They are in real (inflation-adjusted) terms, converted to 1978 price levels using the GDP deflator. In most cases the values are expressed on a per capita basis, to take into account the effects of population growth. The analysis therefore indicates whether the consumption level of the average Malaysian is sustainable. This approach ignores distributional issues: not all Malaysians have equal access to or control over the country's capital stocks (natural as well as physical) and the returns they generate. The analysis provides no information on whether the country's growth path leads to greater or lesser socioeconomic disparities. In the final section of the chapter, we do discuss some distributional issues related to petroleum and timber rents.

Estimating resource consumption allowances

A fundamental shortcoming of the empirical studies reviewed in the section *Previous studies* is the use of average costs instead of marginal costs in calculating net prices. This causes them to overstate the economic value of natural resource depletion. They therefore contain a pessimistic bias with regard to economic sustainability. Our analysis of Malaysia avoided this bias by converting estimates of total resource rents, based implicitly (in the case of minerals) or explicitly (in the case of timber) on average costs, to estimates of Hotelling rents. The following paragraphs explain in general terms how we did this. Appendices 2.1 and 2.2 contain additional technical details.

The resource consumption allowance for minerals covered all minerals, not just petroleum and natural gas. We estimated total resource rent according to a procedure suggested by Stauffer (1986). We first obtained data on value added, salaries and wages, and value of fixed assets in mining and stone quarrying industries from the Department of Statistics' annual *Industrial Surveys*. The *Surveys* cover most but not all firms in the sector. We then subtracted salaries and wages from value added to calculate the combined rents to physical capital and natural resources. In a competitive economy, the payment to physical capital equals the product of the capital stock times the opportunity cost of capital. We set the former equal to the value of fixed assets in the mining and stone quarrying industries and the latter equal to the average rate of return on fixed assets in manufacturing industries, and we subtracted the product of the two from combined rents to obtain total resource rent. Finally, we scaled this survey-based estimate to the national level by multiplying it times the ratio of GDP in Sector 2, "Mining and Quarrying," to the value added figure in the *Surveys*. We allocated the resulting national estimate across regions in proportion to regional GDP in Sector 2.

We converted estimates of total resource rent to Hotelling rent by using a formula similar to one proposed by El Serafy (1989). In Figure 2.1, one can see that Hotelling rent comprises a larger share of total resource rent as production declines. Declining production is indeed what one would expect over time for optimal resource depletion in the simple situation depicted in Figure 2.1. The arbitrage process between current and future periods described in the section *Applying Hartwick's Rule* implies that the marginal net price rises over time at the rate of discount (Hotelling's Rule). With price fixed, this can occur only if marginal cost, and therefore production, falls. El Serafy proposed that the share of Hotelling rent could be predicted by a formula involving the discount rate and the ratio of mineral stock to annual production, which provides a rough estimate of the number of years until exhaustion. Hartwick and Hageman (1993) demonstrated, however, that El Serafy's formula yields correct estimates only in the special case when total resource rent is constant over time. This shortcoming reflects an implicit assumption that the marginal cost curve is infinitely elastic (see Appendix 2.1). It can be overcome by modifying the formula to include the elasticity of the marginal cost curve. We made this modification and used the resulting formula to convert estimates of total resource rent to Hotelling rent. We assumed that the discount rate was 10 percent, which is between the estimates for the 1970s and 1980s reported by Veitch (1986), 8 percent and 13 percent respectively,[20] and that the elasticity of the marginal cost curve was 0.15, which is implied by information in Chapter 3 (see Appendix 2.1).

Calculating the resource consumption allowance was more complicated in the case of timber. To begin, net depletion does not equal the amount of timber harvested, for two reasons. First and most fundamentally, timber resources are renewable. Net depletion estimates must take into account the growth of the resource. Second, various factors in addition to harvesting can deplete timber stocks. For example, even careful logging inevitably damages some standing timber, and some commercially valuable timber may be destroyed when forests are converted to other uses. We therefore first developed an internally consistent system of physical accounts that provided annual estimates of the various additions to and subtractions from timber stocks in each region. These accounts were based on data published or specially provided by the Forestry Departments in the three regions. They covered natural forests only,[21] and they were divided into sections on virgin (unlogged) and logged-over forests. In the case of Sarawak, there were separate accounts for hill forests and swamp forests.

The accounts summarized changes in commercial timber stocks due to one factor that increases stocks—growth—and five that decrease them—harvest; logging damage; defect (felled timber volume that is not merchantable); deforestation; and, in Peninsular Malaysia and Sabah only (see Appendix 2.2), miscellaneous adjustments necessary to reconcile the accounts with timber inventory data. Net depletion was defined as the sum of the latter five factors, minus growth. The accounts reflect a crude model of forest dynamics—in particular, they assume that growth per hectare is constant, regardless of the age of the forest—but they are probably sufficiently accurate for our purposes. Most timber harvesting in Malaysia from 1970 to 1990 occurred in virgin forests, where growth was insignificant, and the length of time analyzed, twenty years, is short compared to the time it takes for timber to grow to commercial size in logged-over forests.

As discussed in the section *Applying Hartwick's Rule*, the general expression for the resource consumption allowance is net depletion times user cost, which generally equals current marginal net price. For timber, net price is termed *stumpage value*, and it is calculated by subtracting logging costs from log price. We adjusted the stumpage value downward to avoid overstating the user cost when some amount of logging damage and defect is inevitable. Because available data on logging costs in Malaysia were for average, not marginal, costs, we performed an adjustment similar to that for the mineral allowance. Appendix 2.2 provides details on the formula we used to do this. The formula assumed a discount rate of 10 percent, as in the case of the mineral allowance, and a marginal cost elasticity of 3, based on Vincent (1990).

The cumulative values of the two resource consumption allowances from 1970 to 1990 were almost identical, at 25 billion ringgit (1978 prices). Resource rents were a substantial portion of value added in the mining and quarrying sector, an average of 51 percent during the period, which was even larger than the portion for imputed returns to physical capital, 39 percent. Hotelling rents were about half of resource rents on average. A principal reason the timber allowance was equal in magnitude to the mineral allowance, despite timber being a renewable resource, is that timber harvests were not the only cause of depletion of timber stocks. From 1970 to 1990, 598 million m³ of timber were harvested according to official figures, but another 595 million m³ were apparently lost to logging damage and defect, 656 million m³ to deforestation, and 632 million m³ to miscellaneous causes. In contrast, cumulative growth totaled only 319 million m³. These figures suggest that the country lost significant potential rents from timber production.[22]

Figure 2.2 shows the estimated allowances on an annual basis. The allowance for minerals rose significantly during the 1980s. This reflects both the rapid

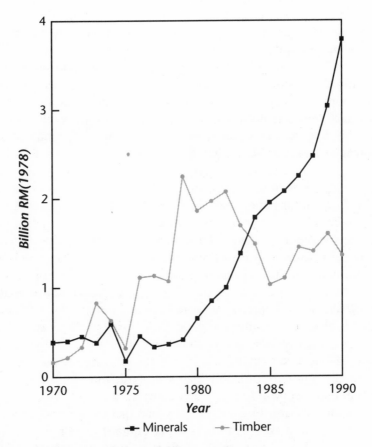

Figure 2.2   Resource consumption allowances, Malaysia

expansion of petroleum production and the rising share of Hotelling rent in total resource rent. The timber allowance rose until 1979-80 but declined thereafter, though not to levels as low as in the early 1970s. This pattern mirrors changes in stumpage values (see Appendix 2.2), which peaked in 1979–80 during the global commodity price boom. The decline in stumpage values in the 1980s offset the effects of rising harvests and a rising Hotelling rent share. The timber allowance was generally greater than the mineral allowance before the mid-1980s, but by 1990 it was only a third as large.

National analysis

Figure 2.3 shows trends in gross investment (gross fixed capital formation) and total resource rents (not resource consumption allowances). Resource rents are defined in this figure as the sum of mineral rents (calculated as described in the previous section) and the aggregate stumpage value of ex-tracted timber (unit stumpage value times timber harvest). Aside from a sharp drop during the recession of the mid-1980s, gross investment generally rose during the period, and so did resource rents. On average, rents were equivalent to about one-third of gross investment. The share showed no overall trend during the period, which indicates that rents were as important a potential source of capital at the end of the period as at the beginning. Whether they were actually invested cannot be determined, as they are fungible. But this does not matter for sustainability. What is important is that net investment in reproducible capital, financed from all sources, is at least as large as the economic value of resource depletion.

Figure 2.4 provides information on this issue. The top line shows per capita gross fixed capital formation, based on the same data as in Figure 2.3, while the second line shows per capita conventional net investment, determined by subtracting the capital consumption allowance from the top line. Calculating conventional net investment was complicated by the fact that no Malaysian agency estimates the capital consumption allowance.[23] We developed our own estimates by using data on depreciation from the Department of Statistics' annual *Report of the Financial Survey of Limited Companies*. Appendix 2.3 provides details. The definition of depreciation used in the *Financial Survey* is based on the tax code, which assumes rates of depreciation that are prob-ably more accelerated than actuals. Hence, the estimates of the capital con-sumption allowance are probably biased upward, and the estimates of net investment (and net product) are biased downward.

Despite this probable bias, Figure 2.4 shows that conventional net invest-ment was positive in every year. Hence, per capita stocks of physical capital increased. Per capita adjusted net investment[24]—conventional net investment

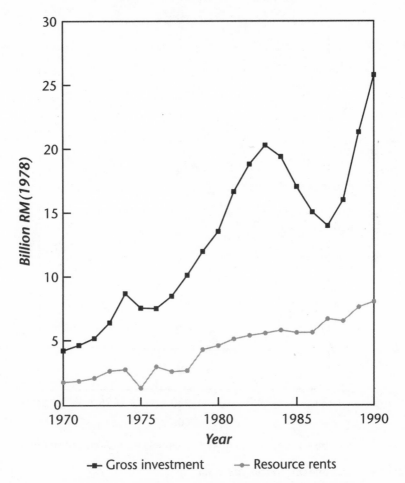

Figure 2.3   Resource rents relative to gross fixed capital formation, Malaysia

minus the resource consumption allowance—is literally the bottom line in Figure 2.4. Only if this quantity was nonnegative did the country maintain its per capita total capital stock and, according to Hartwick's Rule, put itself in a position to sustain per capita consumption. Figure 2.4 shows that the value of per capita adjusted net investment was positive in all years but one. Hence, per capita total capital stocks increased in Malaysia during the 1970s and 1980s, despite the depletion of the country's mineral and timber resources. On this basis, per capita consumption levels appear to be more than sustainable. The country did better than Hartwick's Rule.

Analysis of trends in NDP provides a check on this finding. If adjusted net investment was truly positive, then per capita NDP should have risen.

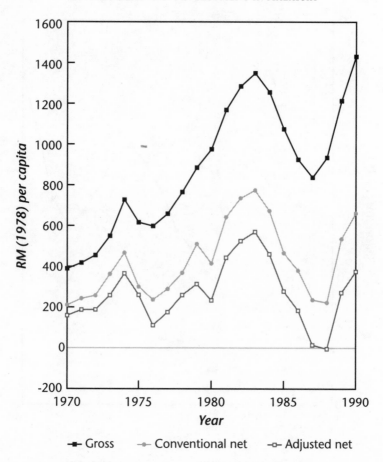

Figure 2.4   Per capita investment, Malaysia

If this was not the case, then the estimates of per capita adjusted net in-vestment in Figure 2.4 are probably biased upward. This could occur if not all investments were in fact productive ones. Figure 2.5 shows per capita values of GDP, conventional NDP (only the capital consumption allowance deducted), and adjusted NDP (the resource consumption allowance de-ducted as well).[25]

Results are as expected: per capita NDP rose over time. Hence, the econ-omy apparently grew in a sustainable fashion. The average annual growth rate for per capita adjusted NDP was, however, considerably less than for per capita GDP: 2.9 percent compared to 3.7 percent. True income did not grow nearly as rapidly as GDP indicates, but it did grow.

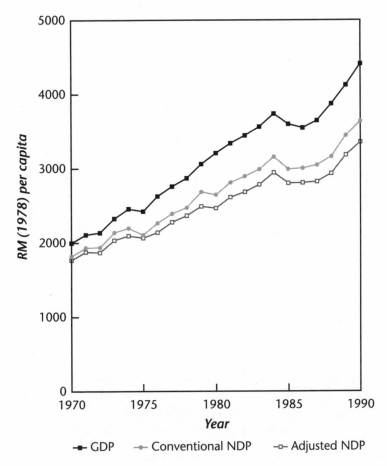

Figure 2.5   Per capita income, Malaysia

Regional analysis

Per capita gross investment rose in all three regions into the early 1980s. It then declined, until the country began recovering from the recession of the mid-1980s. It was lowest in Sarawak in most years, but in fact it might have been even lower in Sabah. The so-called transient population is especially large in Sabah, due to immigration from the Philippines and Indonesia. This population is not fully reflected in census figures. Hence, per capita estimates for Sabah could be biased upward substantially.

As at the national level, conventional net investment was only about half as large as gross investment in all three regions, but it was still positive. Hence,

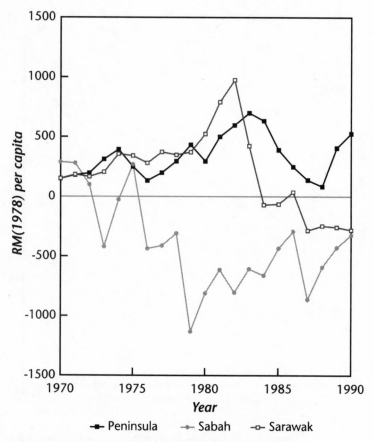

Figure 2.6　Per capita adjusted net investment, by region

all regions increased their per capita stocks of physical capital. The "bottom lines" for the regions, however, shown in Figure 2.6, indicate important differences with regard to total capital stocks. Per capita adjusted net investment was positive in Peninsular Malaysia in all years, but it was negative in every year after 1975 in Sabah and in every year but one after 1983 in Sarawak. The two Borneo states depleted their natural capital more rapidly than they built up stocks of physical capital in the 1980s, with the depletion being particularly large in Sabah. The implication is that consumption levels at the end of the period were more than sustainable in Peninsular Malaysia, but not sustainable in Sabah or Sarawak.

Figure 2.7 shows corresponding results for per capita adjusted NDP. Re-

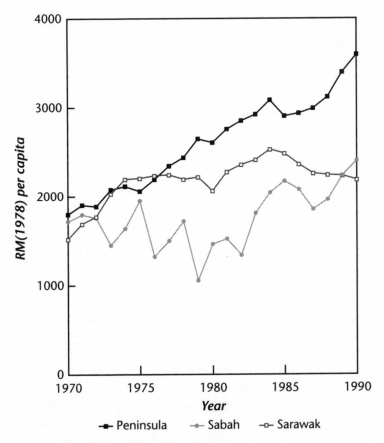

Figure 2.7 Per capita adjusted NDP, by region

sults for Peninsular Malaysia were consistent with those just mentioned: per capita adjusted NDP grew at a statistically significant, positive rate. The rate was, however, less rapid than for per capita GDP, at 3.2 percent per year versus 3.8 percent per year. For Sabah and Sarawak, at first glance the results appear to contradict those from the analysis of per capita adjusted net investment. Per capita adjusted NDP grew at a statistically significant rate in both states: in Sabah, at 1.6 percent per year, and in Sarawak, at 1.4 percent per year. The apparent discrepancy might be explained by a downward bias in the estimates of conventional net investment, due not only to exaggerated capital consumption allowances but also to incomplete data on gross fixed capital formation. Pang (1993) has criticized official Malaysian investment data for excluding certain types of agricultural investments, which are relatively more important in the Borneo states than in the more industrialized Peninsula.

Examined more closely, however, the overall positive growth rates for per capita adjusted NDP in Sabah and Sarawak are not very reassuring. The rates are much less than for per capita GDP, which grew at 2.9 percent per year in Sabah and 3.4 percent per year in Sarawak. Moreover, although Sabah's per capita adjusted NDP recovered during the 1980s from a substantial decline during the 1970s, it was scarcely higher at the end of the period than at the beginning, and then only at the very end. Per capita adjusted NDP rose in fits and starts in Sarawak up to 1984, but it declined thereafter, even as per capita GDP rose. At the end of the period, it had fallen to levels typical of the mid-1970s.

In sum, both analyses indicate that prospects are brighter for Peninsular Malaysia than for the Borneo states. For Peninsular Malaysia, both point toward the region having successfully used resource rents and other sources of investment funds to build a diversified base of sustainable economic activities. The region depleted its natural resources but accumulated more than an equivalent amount of physical capital. In the case of Sabah and Sarawak, only the analysis of per capita adjusted NDP offers much evidence that consumption levels can be sustained, and that evidence basically suggests that the consumption levels that can be sustained are those toward the beginning of the period, not the end. In the case of Sarawak, both analyses point toward unsustainability at the end of the period. There appears to be little risk of an economic decline following the resource boom of the last two decades in Peninsular Malaysia, but the odds are much less favorable for Sabah and Sarawak.

CONCLUSIONS

Resource-rich countries can sustain their consumption levels only if they accumulate stocks of reproducible capital at a rate that matches the depletion of natural capital. Overall, Malaysia appears to have done this, and more. Adjusted net investment, calculated by deducting capital and resource consumption allowances from gross fixed capital formation, was positive in every year but one in the period from 1970 to 1990. Adjusted NDP, calculated similarly by deducting capital and resource consumption allowances from GDP, grew at a statistically significant positive rate, albeit not as rapidly as GDP.

Several features of the analysis should be borne in mind in interpreting this favorable conclusion. To begin, the analysis implicitly treated production levels of minerals and timber as optimal. If production levels and other aspects of resource management were not in fact optimal, then the long-term increases in consumption that Malaysia apparently achieved were not as large as they could have been. Subsequent chapters examine the optimality of resource management in more detail, with Chapter 3 focusing on oil and Chapter 4 on timber.

Three other features suggest that Malaysia's performance was even better than the analysis indicated. One is the probable understatement of the increase in physical capital stocks, due to the upward bias in the capital consumption allowance and the incompleteness of gross investment data noted by Pang (1993). The second is that the analysis implicitly focused on the sustainability of domestic economic activity, by using gross fixed capital formation as the measure of investment and GDP as the measure of income. This ignores the reality that overseas investments and employment can make important contributions to financing national consumption. Overseas investments are a better use of resource rents and other sources of investable funds when they earn higher returns than domestic investments. Small oil-rich states like Kuwait and Brunei have built their development strategies around diversified portfolios of overseas investments. A natural resource accounting study for these countries that focused on domestic investment and domestic income would overlook the essential role of such investments in sustaining the countries' economies. Fortunately, this chapter's focus on the domestic economy probably did not distort the analysis much, as Malaysia was not a significant net exporter of capital or labor services during the 1970s and 1980s. But this situation is changing, particularly in regard to capital. Follow-up studies should use more inclusive measures of national investment and national income, i.e., GNP instead of GDP.

The third feature is that the analysis ignored changes in the country's human capital stock, which was much greater in 1990 than in 1970. Public investment in education in Malaysia has been substantial. It accounted for 23 percent of operating expenditure and 12 percent of development expenditure in the federal budget for fiscal year 1993, and it was at similar levels in previous years (Ministry of Finance 1992). Due to such investments, the percentage of Malaysians of school age enrolled in secondary education rose from 28 percent in 1965 to 59 percent in 1989, and the adult illiteracy rate fell to 22 percent by 1990, better than average for lower-income countries (World Bank 1992). The exclusion of human capital surely introduced a significant downward bias into the analysis.

Two other features created a bias in the opposite direction. The first is that the analysis ignored depletion of all natural resources other than minerals and timber. For this reason, it surely understated the depletion of natural capital.

Minerals and timber may be the most important natural resource commodities at a national level, but they are not the country's only natural resources. Perhaps the three most important excluded resources are marine fisheries, agricultural land, and freshwater. Subsequent chapters analyze these resources in considerable detail, but not in a way that permits explicit linkage to the national accounts. Some comments can be made here, however, on the impact of their exclusion from the analysis.

Like timber, fishery resources are renewable, but, as Chapter 6 explains, there is ample evidence that they were excessively depleted, particularly in the 1970s. At the national level, however, fisheries accounted for under 3 percent of GDP in 1986 (Department of Statistics 1988). Hence, their exclusion probably did not affect the analysis much.

The exclusion of agricultural land is potentially more serious. Nutrient depletion and soil erosion can deplete the productive capacity of soils, and hence their capital value. Repetto et al. (1989, 1991) found that resource consumption allowances for soil degradation were large in Indonesia and Costa Rica. Malaysia's soils are an essential input for the production of rubber, palm oil, and other important agricultural commodities. Rubber and palm oil accounted for 39 percent of the country's total export earnings in 1970 and 9 percent in 1990.[26] In contrast to Indonesia and Costa Rica, however, most agricultural land in Malaysia is in perennial crops. These crops protect the soil better and require fewer nutrients than annual crops. Malaysia's tree-crop plantations are recognized as one of the technically most sustainable forms of agriculture in the humid tropics (see Vincent and Yusuf 1993 and the references therein). One would therefore expect depletion allowances for agricultural soils to be relatively small in Malaysia. This is indeed what EPU (1993) found in a preliminary analysis.

Soil erosion is not the only factor that can reduce the capital value of agricultural land. Another is inefficiencies due to market and policy failures. During the 1970s, a significant portion of the land in rice and rubber smallholdings in Peninsular Malaysia began to be left idle. Chapter 5 assesses whether this phenomenon indeed represented underutilization of valuable land resources. It turns out that much of the idle area was probably simply an inevitable consequence of the country's modernization, so the reduction in the capital value of land was probably small relative to the mineral and timber allowances.

The flow nature of freshwater resources (other than groundwater), and Malaysia's location in the humid tropics, would seem to imply that depletion issues are unimportant for freshwater. But the utilization of freshwater requires substantial investments in physical capital, whose value, and thus the value of the total capital stock, can be diminished by inappropriate policies.

Chapter 7 investigates whether this was the case in Malaysia. The analysis concludes that there were indeed significant inefficiencies associated with water policies, but it does not quantify those inefficiencies at the national level.

The second feature is that the analysis used official estimates of GDP, which exclude direct consumption values related to the environment, in calculating adjusted NDP. To the extent that economic growth in Malaysia reduced these values, the estimates of NDP were biased upward, with the bias greater at the end of the period. This means that the estimates of adjusted NDP in Figure 2.5 overstate sustainable consumption levels and long-run increases in welfare. Chapters 8 through 10 provide some insight into the magnitude of environmental degradation associated with economic growth during the 1970s and 1980s. It turns out that one form of environmental degradation, increased particulate air pollution, had economic consequences in 1991 that were not much smaller than the average values of the mineral and timber allowances (separately) in the years from 1970 to 1990.

These features apply to the regional analyses as well. Their net impact on the pessimistic findings for Sabah and Sarawak is unclear, as some suggest that the analysis of net investment exaggerated decreases in the two states' total capital stocks, while others suggest that long-run welfare did not increase as rapidly as the NDP analysis indicated. To be on the safe side, the two states probably should consider ways of increasing their total capital stocks. How can they do this? The broad answer is to raise investment. Paraphrasing Solow (1992), the problem the states face is not depletion of natural resources, but overconsumption of resource rents. A discussion of policies for raising investment in the states is beyond the scope of this book, but some comments on the relationship between resource rents and public and private investments can be made. Although these comments refer to Sabah and Sarawak, they probably apply to resource-dependent states in the Peninsula as well, as Perak's relatively poor economic performance since 1970 suggests.

As discussed in Chapter 1, state governments in Sabah and Sarawak derive the bulk of their revenue from resource-based royalties, export duties, and other taxes and charges that capture a portion of resource rents. The state governments are not only much more dependent on resource-based revenue than the federal government, but they have also tended to invest a smaller proportion of the rents they capture.

Figure 2.8 shows the ratio of development expenditure, which provides a reasonable proxy[27] for public investment,[28] to resource-based revenue. At the federal level, the ratio was greater than one in all years: the federal government invested more than the value of the resource rents it collected.[29] In contrast, except in the early 1970s, the state governments in both Sabah and Sarawak

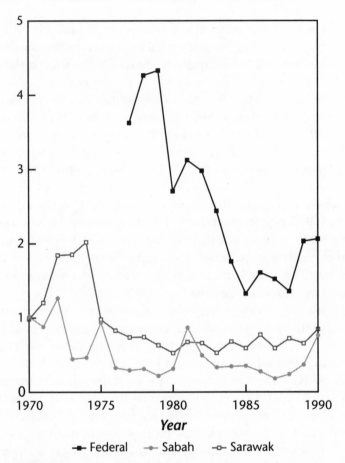

Figure 2.8   Ratio of development expenditure to resource-based revenue

consumed much of the rents. They were not the only state governments to do so: during 1971–87, development expenditure was below resource-based revenue in 10 of the 17 years in Pahang and 8 of the 17 years in Terengganu.[30]

A first step for the state governments would therefore be to direct more of their expenditure toward public investments. They also have great scope for boosting public investment funds by capturing a greater portion of timber rents. Revenue from timber accounts for most of the Borneo states' resource-based revenue (see Chapter 1), while revenue from petroleum accounts for most of the federal government's. Many studies have demonstrated that timber fees capture only a small portion of the resource rent of harvested timber in all parts of the country, with the possible exception of Sabah (Teo 1966; Sulaiman 1977; Gillis 1988; Vincent 1990, 1991; Vincent et al. 1993).

Table 2.1 summarizes estimates of state governments' capture of timber rents during the past two to three decades.[31] State rent capture was less than about a quarter in Peninsular Malaysia, less than half in Sarawak, and around one-half to two-thirds in Sabah. In contrast, evidence presented in the next chapter indicates that federal and state governments captured most of the available petroleum rents, with the federal government capturing more.

The states could also conceivably boost their investment funds by lobbying for a greater share of the petroleum rents captured by the federal government. The allocation of petroleum revenue between federal and state governments has been a contentious issue. From 1971 to 1987, the federal government collected RM36.0 billion in petroleum-related revenue from production throughout the country. Using output shares for crude oil to allocate this total among the states, the federal government captured approximately RM7.5 billion in petroleum rents in Sabah and RM15.0 billion in Sarawak. During the same period, Sabah and Sarawak received federal grants totaling only RM1.4 billion and RM1.0 billion, respectively (Umikalsum 1991, Table 5.51). On this basis, it would appear that there has been a net resource outflow from the states. However, this calculation overlooks federal development expenditures in the states, the federal share of operating expenses for certain government agencies in the states, and the value of national defense and other national responsibilities financed by the federal government. The federal government also offers the state governments loans at concessional rates (Umikalsum 1991, p. 186). We know of no comprehensive analysis of the net flow of financial resources between the two levels of government.

Even if the state governments captured more of the timber and petroleum rents, sustainability would not be promoted unless they invested the rents, and did so efficiently. Their historical tendency to allocate too little resource-

Table 2.1 *Estimates of government rent capture from timber harvests*

Region	Study	Period	Percentage [a]
Peninsular Malaysia	Vincent (1990)	1966–85	23
	Vincent (1991)	1966–89	15–23
	Vincent et al. (1993)	1989	9–49[b]
Sabah	Gillis (1988)	1979–83	70–93
	Vincent (1990)	1966–85	49
	Vincent (1991)	1966–89	53–64
Sarawak	Vincent (1990)	1966–85	25
	Vincent (1991)	1966–89	35–69

[a] Government revenue from royalties and other timber charges (including export taxes on logs) divided by stumpage value of harvested timber.

[b] The wide range is due to the fact that the estimates, eight in total, were for individual concession compartments (annual cutting blocks). Six of the estimates were below 25 percent.

based revenue to development expenditure is a worrisome sign. There is also evidence that many state investments have not been productive. Public enterprises are involved in numerous commercial activities in both states, and many have been consistently unprofitable. In Sabah, expenditure on statutory bodies responsible for public enterprises accounted for 18 to 57 percent of annual development expenditure from 1970 to 1986 (Pang 1989). The outstanding loan balance for these bodies at the end of 1986 was 30 percent of state GDP. According to Pang (1989, p. 115), "Most . . . were unable to pay even the interest due." More recently, Khalil (1992) reported that the state government spent RM6.0 billion on public enterprises and associated agencies from 1980 to 1990, and that their arrears on repayments of principal and interest had reached more than RM800 million by December, 1990. In Sarawak, statutory bodies accounted for about 20 percent of development expenditure from 1989 to 1992 (Abang Helmi 1993). Less information is available on their performance than in Sabah, although Abang Helmi (1993) reported that taken together, four of the largest showed a net surplus during 1990 and 1991. Financial problems are not unique to public enterprises in Sabah and Sarawak; Ismail (1993) estimated that more than half of all federal and state enterprises in Malaysia were not managed profitably.

Of course, investment need not be by the public sector. Timber rents are captured by various private parties, including concessionaires, logging contractors, and individuals with political connections (Kumar 1986, Pura 1990, Hendrix 1990, Sesser 1991, *The Star* 1991). No data are available on the degree to which these parties invest the rents or, if they do, whether it is within the states or elsewhere. In interviews, state officials and individuals in the timber industry claim that most of the rents captured by the private sector flow abroad. Rents should not necessarily be invested within Malaysia—they should be invested in the highest-yielding opportunities, wherever they exist—but if they are not, and if they are not distributed equitably, then most of the Malaysian public will receive little long-run benefit from the exploitation of the country's timber resources.

The outflow of timber rents from Sabah and Sarawak is in some ways reminiscent of the outflow that occurred in the tin sector in Peninsular Malaysia after European-owned companies came to dominate the sector in the early 1900s (Yip 1969). Before this happened, "most of the profits from early tin mining were reinvested within the domestic economy . . . and it was through this that the early tin mining industry exercised some of its most important developmental effects on the Malayan economy" (Yip 1969, p. 121). Subsequently, however, "Over time, an increasing proportion of . . . the output of the area was transferred to the outside world as interest, profits and dividends, contributions to private pension reserves, and the family remittances of alien [expatriate] businessman and their alien employees" (Golay 1976, p. 373). The transfers apparently included resource rents, and not just normal returns on the foreign capital invested in the industries.

In contrast to the outflow during the colonial era, however, which reflected the imposition of foreign rule, the outflow from Sabah and Sarawak during the 1970s and 1980s was voluntary. If resource rents captured by the private sector tend to flow out of Sabah and Sarawak, one should wonder whether the states are intrinsically attractive locations for investment. Both are in remote locations, have small populations, and have terrain that makes infrastructural investments costly. Nothing in economic theory suggests that it is efficient to sustain economic activity in all locations. Historically, outmigration has followed resource depletion in resource-based economies in many regions of the world. Although this process is socially disruptive, it might be inevitable and in fact economically efficient when resource-extractive industries are the only viable ones in a region. Whether this is the case for Sabah and Sarawak is an issue beyond the scope of this book, but it is a possibility that policy makers should not overlook.

Appendix 2.1: Mineral Consumption Allowances

The text summarized the procedures used to calculate mineral allowances. Here, we add detail on four issues: payments to physical capital in the mining and stone quarrying sectors, the treatment of missing data, the formula for converting total resource rents to Hotelling rents, and regional estimates of the allowances.

Payments to physical capital

If capital is allocated efficiently in the economy, it should earn the same rate of return across sectors after adjusting for differences in investment risk. We ignored the risk factor, due to lack of data. We assumed that the rate of return in the manufacturing sector represented the opportunity cost of capital invested in mining and stone quarrying industries. Value added in manufacturing consists solely of payments to labor and capital. Hence, the average rate of return in manufacturing equaled value added minus salaries and wages, divided by the value of fixed assets. Payments to physical capital in the mining and stone quarrying industries were then calculated by multiplying this rate of return times the value of fixed assets in mining and stone quarrying.

Missing data

The Department of Statistics conducted *Industrial Surveys* in all years from 1970 to 1990, except 1980 for manufacturing industries, 1970–71 for stone quarrying industries, and 1980 and 1982 for mining industries. The rate of return on fixed assets in manufacturing industries in 1980 was set equal to the average in other years. The ratio of resource rents to value added in 1970–71, 1980, and 1982 was set equal to the average of values in the years before and after.

Converting total resource rents to Hotelling rents

The conversion formula was derived as follows. Suppose the marginal cost of producing q_t tonnes of a nonrenewable resource in period t is given by $MC_t = \alpha q_t^\beta$. The remaining stock of the resource at the beginning of period t is S_t, the price of a tonne of the extracted resource is constant over time at p, and the discount rate is i. Under an optimal extraction program, marginal cost equals average cost at the instant the stock is exhausted (terminal-time transversality condition). The period when this occurs is denoted by T. For the marginal cost specification given above, average cost equals $MC_t / (1+\beta)$, which can equal MC_t only if $q_t = 0$, as MC_t then equals zero as well. This implies that marginal rent in period $T (= p - MC_T)$ equals simply p. Then by Hotelling's Rule we have:

$$p = (p - MC_t)(1+i)^{T-t}$$

which after rearrangement yields:

$$MC_t = p[1 - (1+i)^{t-T}]. \tag{A2.1}$$

The ratio of Hotelling rent to total resource rent equals the ratio of marginal rent to average rent, or:

$$(p - MC_t)/[p - MC_t/(1+\beta)].$$

Substituting equation (A2.1) for MC_t, this equals:

$$(1+\beta)/[1 + \beta(1+i)^{T-t}].$$

If we approximate the number of years until terminal time by $S_t/q_t - 1$ (we subtract 1 because $q_T = S_T$), this becomes:

$$(1+\beta)/[1 + \beta(1+i)^{S(t)/q(t) - 1}]. \tag{A2.2}$$

This equals El Serafy's formula in the special case when β is infinite. Regardless of the value of β, it equals 1 when the resource is exhausted, and it is less than 1 in preceding periods.

Mineral consumption allowances by region

The mineral consumption allowances were estimated using expression (A2.2). β was set equal to 0.15, which is implied by the development cost function for oil given in Chapter 3. That function relates total development cost to size of an oil field (R):

$$C = 40 \times R^{0.85}.$$

This implies that the development cost for a marginal field is:

$$MC = 34 \times R^{-0.15}. \tag{A2.3}$$

Note that marginal development cost declines with field size. Assuming, as is likely, that the largest fields are discovered and developed first, this implies that increases in production are associated with declining marginal field size and rising marginal development costs. Operating costs do not vary with field size, and so the overall marginal cost elasticity equals the marginal development cost elasticity. That elasticity is given by:

$$\beta = dMC/dR \times dR/dQ \times Q/MC.$$

Substituting equation (A2.3), and assuming that $R = \gamma/Q$,[32] this yields a value of 0.15.

The conversion formula was first applied to oil depletion at the national level, under the assumption that the stock of oil at the beginning of 1970 equaled 4.9 billion barrels (the estimated oil "originally-in-place" in Malaysia; see Chapter 3). This yielded the values shown in Figure A2.1.

These values were then multiplied by the annual resource rent estimates for Sabah and Sarawak to obtain Hotelling rent estimates for those states. The use of national Hotelling rent shares for oil is an appropriate approximation for the Borneo states, as oil rents dominated mineral rents in the two states, and oil reserves in the two states were depleted at about the same rate as aggregate national reserves. The values in Figure A2.1 were modified before being

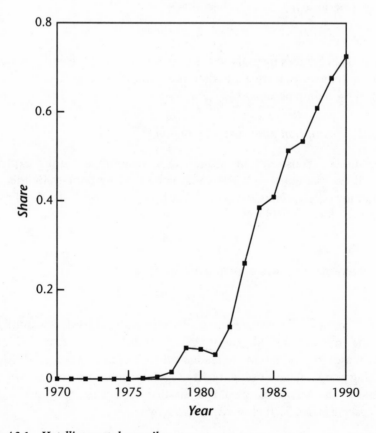

Figure A2.1   Hotelling rent share, oil

applied to Peninsular Malaysia, where tin accounted for a significant, albeit declining, share of mineral rents into the mid-1980s. All values before 1986 were set equal to 0.5, the assumed weighted average of the Hotelling rent shares for tin and oil.

Estimated regional mineral allowances were highest in Peninsular Malaysia and lowest in Sabah in all years. They rose in all regions during the period, especially during the 1980s. The allowance in Peninsular Malaysia rose sharply after 1978, when production of oil from the fields off the coast of Terengganu began. The increasing divergence in allowances between Sabah and Sarawak over time was caused by an increasing divergence in production not only of oil but also of natural gas: Sarawak accounted for more than half of the country's gas production in every year during the 1970s and 1980s (see Chapter 1). Combined allowances for Sabah and Sarawak were tiny compared to Peninsular Malaysia's allowance in 1970, but they rose to about four-fifths of Peninsular Malaysia's allowances during the 1980s.

Appendix 2.2: Timber Consumption Allowances

The text indicated that estimation of the timber consumption allowances required the development of both physical accounts for timber and a formula for converting the resource rent value of net timber depletion to a Hotelling rent counterpart. This appendix discusses the latter issue first.

Hotelling rent in the case of forestry

Forests in Malaysia consist of both virgin (primary) forests and logged-over (secondary) forests. Denote harvests from the former by q^P and harvests from the latter by q^S. Under sustained-yield management, harvest equals growth in logged-over forests: $q^S = gA$, where g is the per hectare growth rate and A is the area of logged-over forest. The change in area of logged-over forest is given by $(1 - d)q^P/v$, where d is the deforestation rate and v is the per hectare harvest in the virgin forest. In practice, all these variables can vary over time, but we suppress subscripts for time to simplify notation.

Under these assumptions, the current-value Hamiltonian for optimal forest harvesting (maximization of the discounted sum of resource rents) is given by:

$$\mathcal{H} = p(q^P + gA) - C^P(q^P) - C^S(gA) - \lambda^P q^P + (1 - d)\lambda^A q^P/v$$

where C is a logging cost function and λ is an adjoint variable. The timber consumption allowance is equal to the sum of the last two terms. The control variable is the harvest in the virgin forest, q^P. The first-order condition for this variable is:

$$\lambda^P = p - C^{P\prime} + (1 - d)\lambda^A/v.$$

This allows us to rewrite the Hamiltonian without the adjoint variable for area of logged-over forest:

$$\mathcal{H} = p(q^P + gA) - C^P(q^P) - C^S(gA) - (p - C^{P\prime})q^P.$$

The timber consumption allowance is now given by just the last term, $(p - C^{P\prime})q^P$, which is marginal stumpage value times harvest in the virgin forest.

If the marginal stumpage value in virgin forests approximately obeys Hotelling's Rule (i.e., it rises over time at the rate of discount), then the conversion formula derived for minerals can also be applied to timber. That is, the timber consumption allowance equals expression (A2.2) multiplied by the aggregate stumpage value of timber harvested in the primary forest, $(p - AC^P)q^P$, where AC^P is average logging cost. The adjoint equations for the timber stock in virgin forests and the area of secondary forest are, respectively:

$$d\lambda^P/dt = i[(p - C^{P\prime}) + (1 - d)\lambda^A/v]$$
$$d\lambda^A/dt = i\lambda^A - g(p - C^{S\prime}).$$

If logging cost varies little with harvest level, integrating the latter yields $\lambda^A = g(p - C^{S\prime})/i$. Substituting this into the former yields:

$$d\lambda^P/dt = i[(p - C^{P\prime}) + (1 - d)g(p - C^{S\prime})/i/v].$$

The marginal stumpage value in virgin forests approximately obeys Hotelling's Rule if the second term in the bracket is small relative to the first. This is likely in Malaysia. For example, in Peninsular Malaysia from 1970 to 1990, $d = 0.40$, $g = 2.2$ m³/ha, $i = 10$ percent, and $v = 114$ m³/ha (the first, second, and fourth values are based on the physical accounts described below). The value of these variables as combined in the second term is just 0.12. Hence, the second term is large relative to the first only if the marginal stumpage value in logged-over forests $(p - C^{S\prime})$ is very large relative to the marginal stumpage value in virgin forests $(p - C^{P\prime})$, which is unlikely.

As discussed in the text, the stock of timber in virgin forests in Malaysia decreased during the 1970s and 1980s for reasons other than just harvest, and not all the reduction was of commercial timber. Under these conditions, expression (A2.2) should be multiplied by the aggregate stumpage value of the reduction in the commercial timber stock, given by the sum of harvest and other reductions and net of defective and unavoidably damaged timber. As mentioned in the text and described in detail below, the adjustment for defect and damage was made indirectly, via the stumpage value estimates. This is equivalent to making the adjustment directly, but it was more convenient given the structure of the timber accounts. In applying expression (A2.2), we assumed a discount rate of 10 percent, as in the case of the mineral allowance, and a marginal cost elasticity of 3, based on Vincent (1990).

Overview of the physical accounts for timber

The physical accounts for timber keep track of both areas of forest and stocks of timber, because changes in areas affect changes in timber stocks. Areas and stocks are recorded separately for virgin and logged-over forests. Areas are measured in thousand hectares (ha), and stocks in thousand cubic meters (m³).

We defined timber stocks as the volume of wood in standing trees of commercial species with a diameter at breast height (1.5 m above the ground) greater than or equal to a specified minimum value. Volumes were gross, that is, inclusive of defect (for example, hollow trunks), in Peninsular Malaysia and Sabah, but net in Sarawak. The minimum diameters differed between the regions due to differences in available data, but in all cases they were set as low as possible, to provide estimates of aggregate growing stocks. Given the differences in gross and net volumes and in minimum diameters between the regions, the estimates of timber stocks are not directly comparable across regions.

The accounts were based on the following general assumptions about changes in areas and stocks. The area of virgin forests declines due to logging.[33] Following logging, virgin forests are either converted to nonforest uses or reclassified as logged-over forests. Unlike virgin forests, the area of logged-over forests can expand, if the area added through logging of virgin forests exceeds the area of existing logged-over forests that are converted to other uses.

When a hectare of virgin forest is logged, only a portion of the timber stock on it is harvested. Some of the timber cannot be harvested because it is defective, and some is lost due to logging damage. What remains is added to the stock of logged-over forests if the hectare is not converted. It is lost if the hectare is converted.

The stock of timber in logged-over forests can increase for two reasons: residual timber in newly logged virgin forests that are reclassified as logged-over, and timber growth that occurs in existing logged-over forests. As in virgin forests, timber stocks decrease during logging due to harvest, defect, and damage, and they also decrease when forests are converted.

Data on aggregate stocks were available for more than one point in time for Peninsular Malaysia and Sabah. The accounts for these regions therefore also included a miscellaneous adjustments category to reconcile the estimates. The miscellaneous adjustments were always negative, indicating that an unexplained reduction in stocks occurred. This might reflect illegal timber extraction.

Peninsular Malaysia: data and accounts

For Peninsular Malaysia, published data were available from the Forestry Department on the total quantity of timber harvested and domestic log prices in each year, and on average logging costs in 1985 and 1990 (RM60 and RM64 per m³, respectively). Logging costs from 1986 to 1989 were interpolated between these estimates; logging costs in earlier years were set equal in real terms (1978 price levels) to the 1985 logging cost (which was virtually identical in real terms to the 1990 cost). Thang (1986, 1987) provided estimates of the gross growth rate for commercial timber (2.2 m³/ha/yr), the defect rate (30 percent), and the damage rate (20 percent).[34]

Forest Inventories I and II provided data on virgin and logged-over timber stocks and forest areas in the middle of 1972 and at the beginning of 1982 (FAO 1973; Ibu Pejabat Perhutanan, Semenanjung Malaysia 1987). The accounts treated data from Forest Inventory I as referring to the beginning of 1972. Timber stocks were defined using a minimum diameter of 15 cm. They included only commercial species (as defined in Forest Inventory II). The accounts used the revised estimates of forest areas from Brown, Iverson, and Lugo's (1991) GIS (geographic information system) analysis of the original inventory maps. This analysis provided additional information on the total areas of virgin and logged-over forests deforested between the inventories. An estimate of total area of forest, virgin and logged-over combined, was also available for 1990 from a Ministry of Primary Industries statistical compilation, *Statistics on Primary Commodities: Forestry*.

Harvests were allocated between virgin and logged-over forests by assuming that the shares were proportional to the timber stocks in each type of forest. By definition, the area of virgin forest logged in a given year equals harvest volume divided by the harvest per hectare (the harvest intensity). Areas logged were calculated by determining the harvest intensity that reconciled the point estimates of areas from the inventories: that is, so that the cumulative area logged from 1972 to 1981 equaled the actual change in area as given by the inventories. The value of the harvest intensity was 21 percent of the standing stock per hectare.

Similarly, annual areas of logged-over forest that were deforested were calculated by determining the deforestation rate that balanced the logged-over forest areas. This rate was 2.7 percent per year.

In a completely analogous way, the inventories' point estimates of timber stocks were reconciled via a miscellaneous adjustments term, which was made proportional to timber harvest. This term indicated that for every m³ of timber harvested in virgin forests, stocks decreased by an additional 2.5 m³ not accounted for by defect, damage, deforestation, and reclassification as logged-over forests. In logged-over forests, the factor was 0.06 m³ per m³ of timber harvested.

Sabah: data and accounts

The accounts for Sabah included data only for dipterocarp (high) forests. As in Peninsular Malaysia, data were available from the Sabah Forestry Department on the total quantity of timber harvested and log prices (export unit values) in each year. Estimates of average total logging costs in 1983 and 1988, RM66 and RM100 per m³, were taken from the Forestry Department's royalty formula. The gross growth rate for commercial timber and the logging damage rate were set equal to the estimates for Peninsular Malaysia. The estimate of the defect rate, 40 percent, was taken from Sabah Forestry Department materials.

A forest inventory carried out from 1969 to 1972 provided data on virgin and logged-over timber stocks and forest areas at the beginning of 1972. We decreased the stock estimates by 20 percent, a factor taken from Sabah Forestry Department materials, to exclude noncommercial species. An additional estimate of forest areas was available for the beginning of 1987; partial information on timber stocks was available for this year as well. Timber stocks were defined using a minimum diameter of 17.5 cm (FAO/UNEP 1981).

The harvest intensity that balanced the estimates of virgin areas was 19 percent of standing timber. The deforestation rate that balanced the estimates of logged-over areas was 8.8 percent per year. Since complete stock estimates at two points in time were not available, the miscellaneous adjustments term could not be calculated directly. Instead, the factors calculated for Peninsular Malaysia were used. Their inclusion in the accounts yielded stock estimates consistent with the partial 1987 estimates.

Sarawak: data and accounts

For Sarawak, separate accounts were generated for hill dipterocarp and swamp (excluding mangrove) forests. Data on the total quantity of timber harvested, total area logged, and log prices (export unit values) were available from the Forestry Department for each forest type in each year. Estimates of logging costs in each forest type were available for years 1979 to 1981 from a paper by Chung (1984)—RM74.40 to RM94.07 per m³ in hill forests and RM44.03 to RM53.54 per m³ in swamp forests—and for 1990 from an unpublished study by the department—RM129 per m^3 in hill forests and RM66.75 per m^3 in swamp forests. Estimates of total forest areas for each type at the beginning of 1966 (from the 1962 to 1966 Sarawak land use survey) and the beginning of 1985 (from unpublished Forestry Department data based on aerial photographs and satellite imagery) were used to calculate average deforestation rates (in thousand ha/yr). Additional data were available on areas of logged-over forests at the beginning of 1989 for hill and swamp forests.

Timber growth rates were taken from FAO/UNEP (1981). The values were 1.7 m^3/ha/yr in hill forests and 1.5 m^3/ha/yr in swamp forests. These estimates are lower than in Peninsular Malaysia and Sabah because they are net of defect. Damage to residual timber was assumed to equal 32.3 percent in hill forests, a rate taken from FAO/UNEP (1981). A rate half as large was used for swamp forests, based on information provided by the Sarawak Forestry Department.

Timber stocks in virgin forests were determined by multiplying virgin forest areas by FAO estimates of per hectare growing stocks (FAO/UNEP 1981, citing earlier FAO studies). Growing stock was defined as the volume of net—not gross, as in Peninsular Malaysia and Sabah—industrial stemwood per hectare in trees with a minimum diameter of 10 cm. FAO's estimates were reduced by 20 percent to deduct noncommercial species.

Timber stocks in logged-over forests in 1972 were determined in the same way. In other years, they were determined endogenously by the accounts by adding growth and subtracting harvest, damage, and deforestation. Miscellaneous adjustments were excluded because the data on stocks were so limited.

Estimates of regional timber consumption allowances

As discussed in the section *Estimating resource consumption allowances,* factors other than harvests are important in explaining the stock reductions that occurred in the three regions. In Peninsular Malaysia and Sabah, harvests accounted for only 20 to 30 percent of net depletion in all forests (not just virgin forests) in most years. Defect in felled trees, damage to other trees, deforestation, and miscellaneous adjustments all accounted for large reductions in standing volumes. In Sarawak, harvests were apparently much larger relative to net depletion, but this probably reflects differences in the structure of the accounts more than differences in actual harvest behavior.[35]

Average stumpage values were lowest in Sarawak, due to lower log prices and higher logging costs.[36] Values in all regions fluctuated considerably from year to year. The fluctuations reflect constraints on adjusting short-run log output to desired levels, due to government policies (regulation of annual areas opened for logging) and capacity constraints related to the extent of forest roads and stocks of logging equipment. They imply that current stump-age values provide only approximate estimates of long-run user costs.[37]

Average stumpage values suffer two additional shortcomings as user cost estimates. The first is that they overstate user costs in the presence of logging damage and timber defect.[38] They must be adjusted downward, or else the resource consumption allowance overstates the value of timber depletion. Consider the case of logging damage. The following model is simpler than the one presented at the beginning of the appendix, but it serves to make the point. Suppose that a country has a stock, S, of a renewable resource. The country's harvest is given by q. For every unit harvested, an additional f units are lost to damage. Growth is proportional to the stock and is given by gS. Total harvest costs are $C(q)$, and a unit of the resource sells for p. The current-value Hamiltonian for this resource allocation problem is:

$$\mathcal{H} = pq - C(q) + \lambda[gS - (1+f)q]$$

where λ is the user cost. If q is chosen optimally, then the user cost equals the marginal net price divided by one plus the damage rate:

$$\lambda = (p - C')/(1+f).$$

A similar result can be obtained for defect. Adjusting stumpage values in this fashion is, as mentioned earlier, equivalent to deducting the physical amounts of damage and defect from net depletion, and reducing physical amounts related to growth, deforestation, and miscellaneous adjustments so that they exclude timber that cannot be commercially realized.[39] The size of the adjust-ment depends on the magnitude of damage and defect. In Peninsular Malay-sia, the adjusted stumpage values (user costs) were, on average, 42 percent as large as actual stumpage values from 1970 to 1990; in Sabah, 39 percent; and in Sarawak, 46 percent for hill forests and 92 percent for swamp forests.[40]

The second shortcoming, of course, is that average stumpage values are indeed average, not marginal, values. As discussed in the first section of this appendix, this shortcoming can be addressed by applying expression (A2.2). Figure A2.2 shows the resulting estimates of the Hotelling rent shares for reductions in commercial timber stocks in virgin forests. The share rose most rapidly in Sabah, where virgin forests were depleted most rapidly.

The estimated timber allowances, calculated by multiplying the gross re-duction in virgin timber stocks times the adjusted stumpage values and the Hotelling rent shares, were largest in Sabah and smallest in Sarawak. Sarawak's harvests were the highest in the 1980s (see Chapter 1), but its stumpage values were the lowest. This demonstrates that the economic value of resource depletion is not necessarily proportional to the physical level of resource extraction.

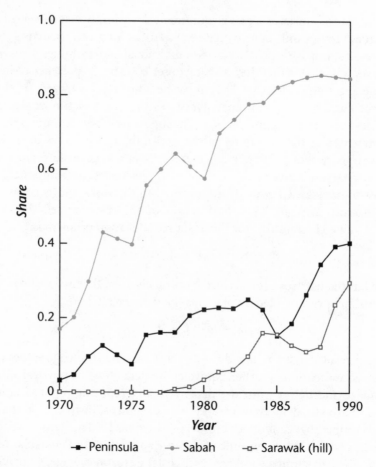

Figure A2.2   Hotelling rent share, timber

APPENDIX 2.3: CAPITAL CONSUMPTION ALLOWANCES

To estimate national and regional capital consumption allowances, we first calculated physical capital stocks at the national level. We obtained annual data on gross capital formation during 1960-90 from the IMF *International Financial Statistics* (IMF 1992). We assumed that the ratio of the country's capital stock to its GDP in 1960 was the same as in 1955: 1.3 according to early national income accounts. To estimate capital stocks in succeeding years, the only additional data we needed were annual estimates of depreciation rates, so that we could apply the identity,

$$K_t = (1 - \delta_{t-1})K_{t-1} + I_{t-1}.$$

where K is capital stock, I is gross investment, and δ is the depreciation rate.

We set the national depreciation rate equal to the annual depreciation rate for limited companies. These companies accounted for over half of national value added (GDP) in 1990. The Department of Statistics' annual *Report of the Financial Survey of Limited Companies* provides extensive data by type of industry, including data on value of depreciation and value of fixed assets. We calculated the aggregate annual depreciation rate across industries by dividing the aggregate value of depreciation by the aggregate value of fixed assets. The resulting rate ranged from 6.6 to 12.0 percent, depending on the year. We set the rate for 1960 to 1969 equal to the 1970 rate. Sensitivity analysis determined that the estimated capital stocks were relatively insensitive to the value of the depreciation rate employed.

We estimated capital stocks in each region in 1970 by assuming that the regional ratios of capital stock to GDP were the same in that year as at the national level. We then estimated capital stocks from 1971 to 1990 by substituting the national depreciation rate and regional data on gross fixed capital formation into the capital stock identity. Finally, we calculated regional capital consumption allowances by multiplying the regional capital stock series times the national depreciation rate. The national allowance was then given by the sum of the three regional estimates.

NOTES

1 Resources may not earn a rent if they suffer from a "tragedy of the commons." Open-access pasture lands and fisheries are classic examples of this problem. See Chapter 6, on marine fisheries.

2 Inframarginal rent is akin to producer surplus for an ordinary good.

3 Mäler (1991) and Dasgupta and Mäler (1991) have emphasized that this is not the same as the change in the value of the stock, which includes capital gains and losses. Capital gains occur when, for example, the price of crude oil rises, causing the value of a country's oil reserves to rise. Landefeld and Hines (1985) and Peskin (1989) proposed including capital gains and losses in the resource consumption allowance, but Stauffer (1986) argued against it. Vincent, Panayotou, and Hartwick (1995) have demonstrated that resource consumption allowances do indeed need to be adjusted for exogenous changes in resource prices, but not for ordinary changes in net prices (resource price minus marginal extraction cost) that occur according to Hotelling's Rule.

4 In the presence of population growth, technological progress must be sufficiently rapid to offset the rise in population.

5 Technically, the elasticity of substitution between the two is one.

6 Solow (1992) remarked, "Without this minimal degree of optimism, the conclusion might be that [the] economy is like a watch that can be wound only once.... In that case there is no point in talking about sustainability, because it is ruled out by assumption; the only choice is between a short happy life and a longer unhappy one."

7 This statement may not hold under some definitions of the total capital stock. Solow (1974)

presented a model in which mineral price is endogenous (there is a downward-sloping derived demand curve) and extraction costs are zero. If the capital value of the mine is defined as the discounted sum of resource rent, which in this model equals gross revenue, then zero net investment is associated with a rising total capital stock. On the other hand, if the capital value of the mine is defined as the discounted sum of the area under the demand curve (gross revenue plus consumer surplus for resource users), then zero net investment again implies a constant total capital stock.

8 In practice, current marginal net prices might approximate user costs on average over time, but they are likely to deviate in particular periods due to market imperfections and short-run supply constraints. Prices for natural resources are notoriously volatile and, in Solow's (1992) words, "cannot be accepted as indicating 'true' values [of user costs]." EPU (1993) dealt with this problem by setting user costs equal to trend values of net prices.

9 See Figure 3.1 in Hartwick and Olewiler (1986).

10 *Net depletion* is Solow's (1992) term.

11 Hartwick and Hageman (1993, p. 227) offered analytical support for excluding discoveries from the resource consumption allowance. They commented, "If we assume instantaneous capitalization of discoveries in market prices so that the [mining] firm immediately extracts the newly optimal amount, we can use current marginal profit [net price] and quantity extracted in the usual THR [Total Hotelling Rent] calculation and never register economic appreciation." Since discoveries are never fully anticipated, however, they can be associated with significant price decreases, which imply that prediscovery marginal net prices over-stated postdiscovery user costs. Hartwick and Hageman suggested smoothing out the price profile as a means of obtaining approximately correct estimates of user costs. As stated in note 9, EPU (1993) did this in preliminary natural resource accounting work in Malaysia.

12 Data were apparently not available on the capital consumption allowance.

13 Two cross-country studies that came to our attention after the work on this chapter was completed are Pearce and Atkinson (1993) and World Bank (1995).

14 This assumes that consumption and investment are defined as including both private and public sector components.

15 Technically, for this to be true, NDP must be calculated using shadow prices that indicate marginal economic values along an optimal economic development path (Mäler 1993).

16 What Repetto et al. term *adjusted NDP*.

17 In Indonesia, partial NDP was actually higher than GDP in some years, due to Repetto et al.'s inclusion of discoveries in the resource consumption allowance for petroleum.

18 Building on Mäler's (1993) point about shadow prices and NDP, an alternative approach would be to make the adjustment to NDP by valuing the actual, albeit suboptimal, level of resource utilization at its shadow net price rather than the actual net price. But this approach breaks down when the divergence between actual and optimal utilization levels is great.

19 Market outcomes can, however, reflect market values. For example, property values may be lower when air pollution obscures scenic views.

20 A discount rate of 10 percent might strike some as high, but it is plausible in a fast growing economy like Malaysia's. The social discount rate is the weighted average of the social rate of time preference (the supply side of the capital market) and the marginal opportunity cost of capital (the demand side). In turn, the former is given by the sum of the pure rate of time preference and the consumption discount rate, which is the product of the elasticity of marginal utility and the rate of change in consumption. Markandya and Pearce (1988) report estimates of 0–2 percent for the pure rate of time preference and 1–2 for the elasticity of marginal utility. Applying these to Malaysia, which had a per capita GDP growth rate of 3.7 percent per year during 1970–80, yields an estimated social rate of time preference of 3.7–9.4 percent. The marginal opportunity cost of capital was surely far in excess of 10 percent during most of the period, making a weighted average of 10 percent or greater entirely possible.

21 Significant areas of timber plantations were established in Malaysia only recently, and timber harvests in them are insignificant compared to those in the natural forest. Moreover, the species grown in plantations are different from those in natural forests and produce wood that sells at a substantially lower price. The accounts also excluded rubberwood, which is an increasingly important timber.

22 Some of the timber volume included in the miscellaneous category could represent illegal logging. In this case, the government is losing revenue, but the country is not losing rents. The rents are simply being captured entirely by timber concessionaires and logging contractors.

23 In the 1960s, the Department of Statistics published estimates of the capital consumption allowance for Peninsular Malaysia, calculated crudely by assuming that the allowance equaled 6 percent of GDP. It has not published estimates since then. Table 4-11 of *The Mid-Term Review of the Second Malaysia Plan 1971-1975* contained estimates of conventional net investment in 1970 and projections for 1975, 1980, 1985, and 1990. The ratio of conventional net investment to gross investment was 0.71–0.72, depending on the year. The method for estimating conventional net investment is not clear from the plan, but it probably involved an assumption similar to the Department of Statistics' assumption about the capital consumption allowance.

24 *Adjusted net investment* is Repetto et al.'s (1991) term.

25 *Adjusted NDP* is Repetto et al.'s (1991) term.

26 The decrease was due to increases in other exports, in particular exports of manufactured goods. In real terms (1978 price levels), exports of rubber and palm oil were higher in 1990 (RM5.5 billion) than in 1970 (RM4.1 billion).

27 At the national level, consolidated public sector development expenditure from 1987 to 1992 was within 12 to 20 percent (depending on the year) of public gross fixed capital formation. (Ministry of Finance 1992, Table 2.1 and 4.1).

28 Development expenditure is best viewed as a proxy for public investment in physical capital. Investment in human capital, through expenditure on education, is included in operating expenditure.

29 The ratio is not plotted for years before 1977, because it is off the scale. A ratio greater than one does not necessarily indicate that the actual ringgits derived from resource rents were invested, as revenues are fungible once they arrive at the Treasury. Some information on this issue is, however, available for oil rents captured by the national oil company, Petronas. On the positive side, in 1985 the government established the National Trust Fund, which is intended to reserve some of the country's oil and gas revenues for future use. As of the early 1990s, Petronas was the only contributor, providing some RM200 million annually. This was equivalent to about 3 percent of total federal revenue from the oil sector. Other uses of Petronas's earnings have been criticized. Most controversial was its purchase, at the government's request, of an 86.7 percent stake in Bank Bumiputera in 1984 (Hough 1986, Foo and Ramasamy 1991, Toh 1991). This bailed out the bank but prompted a civil suit against the federal government. The suit was dismissed after the government eliminated its legal grounds by amending the Petroleum Development Act.

30 These figures are based on data in Tables 5.18 ("Forest taxes," "Lands and mines," "Royalties"), 5.27 ("State government expenditures"), and 5.30 ("Development expenditure as a per cent of total expenditure") in Umikalsum (1991). Development expenditure exceeded resource-based revenue in almost every year in three other resource-rich states in the Peninsula, Johor, Kelantan, and Perak.

31 The estimates exclude rent that might be captured via the corporate and personal federal income taxes on logging companies and timber concessionaires. Available evidence suggests that little of the rent is captured this way, due to tax evasion (World Bank 1991). In the 1970s, the Income Tax Department instituted a supplemental Timber Profits Tax on unusually high profits in the logging industry. The tax was suspended in 1986 because it generated

so little revenue: only RM40.5 million from 1977 to 1985. During the same period, timber harvesting generated resource rents worth billions of ringgit (Vincent 1990; see also Chapter 4).

32 Although some rough information on the size distribution of oil fields is available (see the section *Economic analysis of production-sharing contracts* in Chapter 3), the same is not true for output by field size. This forced us to assume a functional form for the relationship between Z and Q.

33 The accounts assume that virgin forests are always logged before being converted to non-forest uses.

34 The values of the defect and damage rates are the values for trees with a minimum diameter of 60 cm, which historically has been the size class that accounts for most of the harvest.

35 As discussed above, stock estimates in Sarawak were based on net volumes, not gross volumes as in other regions. Moreover, the lack of data on standing volumes at more than one point in time meant that the Sarawak accounts excluded a miscellaneous adjustments term, which indicated large, unexplained reductions in the other two regions.

36 Stumpage values would have been even higher in Peninsular Malaysia if the region had not restricted log exports since the early 1970s. The restrictions have depressed domestic log prices by a substantial amount (Vincent 1992). This implies that some of what appears to be value added in local wood processing industries is simply displaced resource rents. For further discussion of this point, see Chapter 4.

37 EPU (1993) addressed this issue by using smoothed stumpage values.

38 To be precise, when defect is present and logging damage is controlled up to the point where the marginal benefits of more careful logging just equal the marginal costs.

39 Even after making such adjustments, net depletion as we calculated it could conceivably overstate actual depletion of economically valuable timber. In Malaysia, particularly in Peninsular Malaysia, deforestation is driven primarily by an organized land development process (see Chapter 4). The Forestry Department permits intensive harvesting of forests (clear-felling) before they are converted. It is reasonable to infer that some of the timber that the accounts record as destroyed during deforestation is not in fact commercially valuable; otherwise, it would have been harvested. The bottom line is that estimates of reductions in timber stocks used in calculating timber consumption allowances should exclude noncommercial timber.

40 Most of Sarawak's log production comes from hill forests, so the aggregate adjustment factor was similar to those in Peninsular Malaysia and Sabah.

Petroleum

INTRODUCTION

Had this book been written thirty years ago, this chapter would be about tin, not petroleum. Oil was discovered in Malaysia in the late 1800s, but its economic contribution remained insignificant compared to tin's, and that of most other nonrenewable resources as well, until the 1970s. The *First Malaysia Plan 1966–70* listed tin, iron ore, bauxite, and gold as the country's "minerals of importance" (pp. 127–128). The *Plan*'s forecast for nonrenewable resources was pessimistic—"The overall picture for the mining sector, at least in the short run, is . . . quite bleak" (p. 128)—although it tempered this view by noting that discoveries of new deposits could change the situation. By the *Second Malaysia Plan 1971–75*, oil was listed as one of the country's top four mineral resources, but it still ranked behind tin, iron ore, and bauxite. In 1970, oil's shares of GDP and export earnings were only 1 percent and 4 percent, respectively, compared to 4 percent and 20 percent for tin.

Two events combined to boost oil's importance. The first was the discovery of offshore fields in Sarawak in the mid-1960s, and subsequent discoveries off Sabah and Terengganu in the 1970s. Two hydrocarbon basins are in Malaysian territory: the Northwest Borneo basin, which straddles the coast of Sabah, Sarawak, and Brunei and is mainly offshore; and the Malay basin, which extends into the South China Sea from the southern end of the Gulf of Thailand and is entirely offshore. Until 1968, the Miri Field in Sarawak, an onshore portion of the Northwest Borneo basin, accounted for all of the country's oil production, but offshore fields quickly surpassed it.[1] In the early 1990s, slightly more than half of production was from twelve offshore fields in Peninsular Malaysia, slightly more than a quarter was from nine in

---

Anke Sofia Meyer was a coauthor of this chapter.

Sarawak, and a fifth was from nine in Sabah. These production proportions roughly mirrored the distribution of measured reserves among the regions: 48 percent in Peninsular Malaysia, 34 percent in Sarawak, and 17 percent in Sabah (Rozali 1992).[2]

Second, in a marvelous stroke of good fortune, at virtually the same time the first OPEC "oil shock" tripled world prices for crude oil. Although Malaysia was not (and is not today) a member of OPEC, it benefitted nevertheless from the higher export prices for oil.[3] The price rise also enhanced the economics of oil production, particularly because oil production is characterized by economies of scale. Most fields in Malaysia are medium sized (production between 15,000 barrels per day [bpd] and 50,000 bpd) or small (production below 15,000 bpd; Arief and Wells 1985). Mean field size, in terms of recoverable reserves, is just 60 million barrels, with a median of about 28 million barrels. Most of the fields discovered in the 1980s were in the range of 20 to 30 million barrels.

The upward trends in production and prices made oil the country's most important nonrenewable resource. Oil production rose by a factor of about 90 relative to tin production from 1970 to 1990, while oil prices rose by a factor of 6 to 8 relative to tin prices. In 1990, oil's shares of GDP and export earnings were 8 percent and 13 percent, respectively, compared to less than 1 percent of each for tin. Oil's export earnings surpassed those of tin and palm oil in 1976, timber products in 1979, and finally rubber in 1980, making oil the country's leading export. Oil held this position until being overtaken by manufactured goods later in the decade.

The magnitude of the contribution oil could potentially make to the country's development was recognized by the time of the *Mid-Term Review of the Second Malaysia Plan 1971–75*, which was being completed just as the first oil shock hit. The *Mid-Term Review* stated (p. 162), "The development of the petroleum industries will not be restricted merely to the extraction of oil. Vertical integration will be stimulated. . . . To enable Malaysians, particularly Malays and other indigenous people, to participate fully in this expanding sector of the economy, training programmes will be instituted." Given that the *Mid-Term Review* was the document that introduced the New Economic Policy, it is not surprising that it emphasized *bumiputera* participation. The *Third Malaysia Plan 1976–1980* elaborated on these points, calling for a "new and strategic role" for oil. It announced five objectives for the sector (p. 327):

1. . . . to serve national needs by making available adequate supplies at reasonable prices to meet domestic consumption including the requirements of power, industry and agriculture;
2. [to] enhance the favorable investment climate of the country by opening up new opportunities for the establishment of heavy energy-using and petrochemical industries both for the domestic and the export market;

3. [to] take advantage of the option of increasing revenue and export earnings by the export of oil . . . to overseas markets;

4. [to] ensure that Malaysians are adequately represented in terms of ownership, management and control in all phases of petroleum operations . . . ; and

5. [to] effect an optimal social and economic pace of exploration . . . taking into account the need for conservation of these depletable assets and the protection of the environment.

The government recognized that "oil exploration and extraction are highly capital intensive operations" (p. 325) and thus did not list employment among these objectives.[4]

Statistics indicate that great progress was made toward these objectives during the 1970s and 1980s. Both production and exports of crude oil rose almost without a break after the mid-1970s, from around 100,000 bpd in both cases to more than 600,000 and 400,000 bpd, respectively, in 1990. A comparison of production and export levels to the levels forecast in the *Malaysia Plans* indicates that the sector's performance generally exceeded the government's expectations, especially for export earnings.[5] The difference between production and exports, which is the portion of apparent domestic consumption met by domestic production (the first objective), increased by a factor of about five from the mid-1970s to 1990. Thanks to the expanded production, expenditure on imports of crude oil was 50 percent lower (in real terms) at the end of the 1980s than at the beginning of the 1970s. The country would have imported even less if Malaysian crude oil did not have a low sulfur content and a low gravity. Due to these physical characteristics, it must be mixed with heavier Arabian crudes to produce diesel, kerosene, bitumen, and other heavy refined products to suit the domestic demand mix (Meyanathan and Wells 1982). On the other hand, these same characteristics enable Malaysian crude to command a premium in export markets (Subramaniam 1982, Arief and Wells 1985, Rozali 1992). Hence, every barrel of exported Malaysian crude finances the import of more than a barrel of heavier crude.

The increase in domestic crude oil consumption partly reflected increased output of refined oil products and petrochemicals (the second objective).[6] The output of domestic refineries nearly doubled from 1974 to 1983, from 87,000 bpd to 151,000 bpd (Arief and Wells 1985). Total refining capacity was 210,000 bpd in 1990, with an additional 200,000 bpd in the planning stage (Rozali 1992).[7] Federal government revenue and export earnings from oil (the third objective) rose even more dramatically than production and exports, at least until the mid-1980s when they reached more than 4 billion and 6 billion ringgit (1978 prices), respectively. A key reason was the sharp increase in oil prices in 1973–74 and 1979–80 due to the two oil shocks. Oil-based revenue rose from 8 percent of federal government revenue in 1975 to about 27 percent in 1990. Oil-based revenue was also important at the state level, rising from 5 percent in Sarawak and nil in other states in 1971 to 14 percent in Sarawak, 5 percent in Sabah, and 76 percent in Terengganu in 1987 (Umikalsum 1991, Tables 5.15 and 5.19). The Malaysian role in ownership, management, and control (the fourth objective) was asserted strongly by the 1974 Petroleum Development Act, which established the national oil company, Petronas.

Of the five objectives, the fifth is obviously the most essential. If exploration is unsuccessful, there is no oil to satisfy domestic demand, to provide raw materials for industry, to generate government revenue, or to earn foreign exchange. Exploration activities in Malaysia during the 1970s and 1980s were complicated by the institutional structure of the sector. The country owned the oil fields, but international oil companies provided most of the investment and technology. The government faced the difficult challenge of negotiating contracts that captured as much of the rent from extracted oil as possible, while creating incentives for investment in exploration and development. If the terms were too lenient, oil companies would earn a higher return than necessary to operate profitably, and rents would flow out of the country. On the other hand, if the terms were too harsh, companies would invest little in the sector, and production would not achieve its full potential.

At first glance, the increases in production, exports, and federal revenue since the mid-1970s seem to suggest that Malaysia addressed the contracting problem effectively. This conclusion also appears to be supported by rising estimates of the country's measured (proven) oil reserves: reserves were larger in 1985 than in 1975, according to estimates by both Petronas and international sources, despite the great increase in production that occurred in intervening years (see Figure 3.1).[8]

This positive assessment bears closer scrutiny, however. Production has certainly expanded rapidly, but the pace of investment in the sector was not necessarily optimal. Figure 3.2 shows that investment in exploration and development declined substantially in the 1980s. This is despite the fact that the country had a better-than-average exploration discovery rate: according to Energy Information Administration (1984), 22 percent of exploration wells drilled from 1951 to 1982 found oil or natural gas, while Arief and Wells (1985) reported a rate of 1 in 6. Both rates are substantially better than the international average, 1 in 10. While the decline in oil prices in the 1980s is an obvious candidate for a proximate cause of the decline in investment, the fact that investment declined mainly before the sharp price drop in 1986 and rose afterwards suggests that other factors were at work.

Figure 3.1   Estimates of measured petroleum reserves

This chapter examines institutional factors related to oil contracts. It looks in detail at the interrelated issues of government rent capture and investment. The section *Basic analytics of oil contracts* presents useful economic concepts pertinent to oil contracts. *Development of institutional arrangements in the oil sector* then traces the development of institutional arrangements in the Malaysian oil sector, focusing on the emergence of production-sharing contracts. *Economic analysis of production-sharing contracts* presents the results of an analysis of the effectiveness of production-sharing contracts in capturing rent for the government while creating incentives for exploration and development. Finally, *Conclusions* comments on opportunities to improve contractual arrangements in the oil sector.

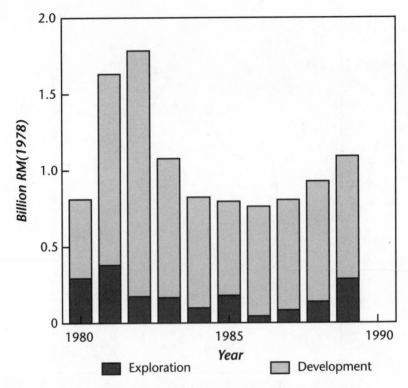

Figure 3.2   Investment in oil exploration and development

Basic Analytics of Oil Contracts

Figure 3.3 illustrates basic features of the contractual problem in a simplified, dynamic context. This figure is a more complicated version of Figure 2.1. The price of oil is p. *MPC* shows the monetary cost—the marginal production cost—of producing an incremental barrel of oil. It includes exploration, development, and production costs. In effect, it ranks, in order of increasing cost, the amount of oil that can be produced in a given period from the country's oil fields. $MPC + MDC$, the full marginal cost,[9] adds to this curve the marginal depletion cost, or user cost: the net return (discounted unit rent) that is sacrificed by pumping a barrel of oil today instead of waiting to do so until the next period. The optimal production level, q^*, is determined by the point where price intersects full marginal cost (point B). Production at this level maximizes, from a long-run perspective, the resource rent generated by oil production. Oil fields with costs higher than point E on *MPC* are not economically viable in the current period.

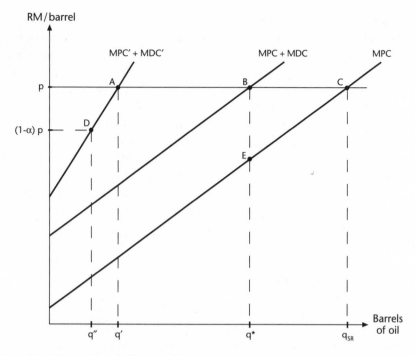

Figure 3.3 Economics of oil extraction

If oil contracts are long-term and secure, and if the government does not impose any taxes or other fiscal obligations on oil companies, a profit-maximizing oil industry would produce at the optimal level.[10] But violating either of these assumptions typically results in suboptimal behavior, leading to oil being produced either too rapidly or too slowly. Contract risk causes the oil industry to discount the returns to future production more heavily. That is, it causes the industry to place less weight on the user cost: the difference between $MPC+MDC$ and MPC diminishes. In the extreme, the industry produces as much oil in the current period as it can while covering just its marginal production costs: it produces at q_{SR}, where p intersects MPC (point C). Rent is lost due to the overproduction of oil in the current period.

But overproduction results only if investment is already in place. In the more general case, oil companies take risks into account *before* investing in exploration, development, and production. They require a higher expected rate of return to invest in riskier countries. Risk increases their capital costs (Emerson 1985), causing MPC to shift upward, say to MPC'. This upward shift can more than offset the decrease in the user cost (note that $MPC' + MDC'$ is higher than $MPC+MDC$). Hence, production is lower, at q', as this is the production level where p and $MPC' + MDC'$ intersect (point A).

Taxes and other fiscal instruments instituted by the government to capture rent typically reduce production further. Suppose that the government levies an ad valorem royalty of α on each barrel of oil produced or, equivalently, requires oil companies to surrender α of the oil produced (production sharing). This reduces the price received by the oil industry to $(1-\alpha)p$. The long-run optimal production level for the industry is now q'' (note that $(1-\alpha)p$ and $MPC' + MDC'$ intersect at point D).[11] Production is lower than in the absence of the fiscal regime. "High-grading" occurs: oil fields that are economically viable in the absence of the fiscal regime are not developed. This reduces the size of the revenue base—it is not profitable for oil companies to develop smaller, more costly fields or to explore to find such fields—and thereby creates the possibility that higher royalties or production shares could generate lower revenue.

DEVELOPMENT OF INSTITUTIONAL ARRANGEMENTS IN THE OIL SECTOR

Arief and Wells (1985) provide a concise history of the oil industry in Malaysia. This section draws extensively from that source, supplemented by others as indicated.

Developments up to 1974

The first recorded oil production in Malaysia dates to July 31, 1882, when the British resident advisor in Baram, Sarawak, wrote in his diary that oil (*minyak tanah*, or "ground oil") had been discovered in wells dug by local people. The following resident, Charles Hose, conducted further explorations. Several years later, the Anglo-Saxon Petroleum Company, a London-based member of the Royal Dutch Shell Group and the precursor of Sarawak Shell, obtained Hose's maps and samples and sent its chief geologist to investigate. It received a mining lease in 1909, and on December 22, 1910, it struck oil a few miles outside of Miri. It began commercial production the next year.

Early exploration efforts in Sabah were less successful. A prospecting lease was granted as early as 1889 to the Central Borneo Company, but it and subsequent leases (to Shell in 1989, to the Labuan Exploration Company in 1918, and to Shell again in 1934 and 1952) did not result in the discovery of commercial onshore deposits.

Production from the Miri Field peaked in 1929 and declined after World War II, as no new onshore fields were discovered. Exploration moved offshore in the late 1950s, prompted by discoveries off Brunei (Foo and Ramasamy 1991). Shell conducted marine seismic surveys off Sarawak in 1954 and Sabah in 1955, and it received an offshore operating license in 1957, when it built fixed offshore drilling platforms in both Sabah and Sarawak. Neither, however, struck oil. Starting in 1960, it brought in mobile offshore rigs. Those rigs found oil off Sarawak, first at the Patricia and Tamana Fields in 1962. The West Lutong Field, discovered in 1966, was the first to start producing, in 1968. Offshore discoveries followed in Sabah, with the Erb West Field in 1971 and the Semarang Field in 1973.

Exploration activities started later in Peninsular Malaysia. Siddayao (1978, p. 28) referred to Peninsular Malaysia as "a classic example of how changing technology and economic conditions can alter the petroleum potential of a country." A 1959 U.N. report (ECAFE 1959, cited on pp. 28–29 in Siddayao 1978) had concluded that, "Although a large proportion of the area of the Malay Peninsula has not been mapped geologically in detail, it is evident from what is already known that the prospects of finding large workable reserves of petroleum at depth to be [sic] very remote." The introduction of offshore exploration changed this situation. Esso and Continental Oil received exploration leases for areas off the East Coast in 1968, and Mobil received an exploration lease in the Straits of Malacca in 1971. Esso discovered oil off Terengganu in 1973 (EPU 1993).[12]

At the formation of the Malaysian federation, individual states' mining enactments governed oil exploration and production. In 1964, the federal government commissioned Walter Levy to review the country's oil policies. Based on recommendations in Levy's report, it passed a series of acts. The Continental Shelf Act (1966) asserted Malaysia's claim to offshore deposits of oil and other resources. Under this act, the country declared "ownership of the natural resources to be found upon or beneath the seabed of the continental shelf beyond its territorial limits up to a water depth of 200 meters or deeper where the superadjacent waters permit exploitation of the natural resources" (Arief and Wells 1985, p. 6). Three subsequent acts pertained specifically to oil. The Petroleum Mining Act (1966) governed oil exploration, development, and production. The Petroleum Income Tax Act (1967) levied a 50 percent tax on oil companies' profits. Previously, oil income was taxed under the general provisions of the 1947 Income Tax Ordinance (Subramaniam 1982). Finally, the Petroleum Mining Rules (1968), promulgated under the Petroleum Mining Act, governed royalties and other charges related to oil production.

This body of legislation established a system based on long-term oil concessions. Oil companies were given ten years for exploration, with a possible five-year extension. To discourage delays, they were required to relinquish 50 percent of the original area at the end of the first five years and another 25 percent at the end of the following five years, unless this made the remaining area too small to develop. In the event of a commercial discovery, they were given thirty years for development and production, which could be extended if both parties agreed.

The concession system provided oil companies considerable autonomy, including complete freedom in making management decisions (e.g., the rate of production) and ownership of all physical assets and any oil produced. Companies were obliged in return to make payments to both state and federal governments. To the state government, they paid a royalty equivalent to 8 to 11 percent of output after the fifth year of production. To the federal government, they paid the petroleum income tax.

The Petroleum Mining Act originally applied only to Peninsular Malaysia. On November 10, 1969, however, in the wake of the May riots, it was extended to Sabah and Sarawak under the Emergency (Essential Powers) Ordinance.[13] This ordinance transferred Sabah's and Sarawak's rights and liabilities associated with existing offshore concessions to the federal government. It also required oil companies to apply to the federal government for exploration licenses in areas three miles beyond the country's territorial waters. States retained licensing rights in other areas.

Arief and Wells (1985, Table 1.1) present information on concession areas leased to oil companies before 1974. Shell was the biggest concessionaire in both Sabah and Sarawak (the only concessionaire in the latter state), while Esso was the largest in Peninsular Malaysia. Sarawak had the greatest concession area, 178,000 km², followed by Peninsular Malaysia at 157,000 km² and Sabah at 61,000 km². All concessions in Peninsular Malaysia were offshore, while those in Sabah and Sarawak were both onshore and offshore.

First-generation production-sharing contracts (FGPSCs)

The Emergency (Essential Powers) Ordinance was the first step in what was to become a dominant federal role in the sector. Next, in 1972, came a revision of the Petroleum Mining Act, which officially extended the act to Sabah and Sarawak. But the major step was the Petroleum Development Act, signed on October 1, 1974. Under section 2(1) of this act, "The entire ownership in, and the exclusive rights, powers, liberties and privileges of exploring, exploiting, winning and obtaining petroleum whether onshore or offshore of Malaysia shall be vested in a Corporation to be incorporated under the Companies Act, 1965, or under the law relating to incorporation of companies." This corporation was Petroliam Nasional Berhad, or Petronas. Under section 8, "The Petroleum Mining Act, 1966, shall not apply to the Corporation." Instead, section 3(2) made Petronas "subject to the control and direction of the Prime

Minister"; under section 3(3), "Notwithstanding the provisions of the Companies Act, 1965, or any other written law to the contrary, the direction so issued shall be binding on the Corporation."

The establishment of Petronas can be viewed as part of the trend in the 1960s and the 1970s for developing countries to establish state-owned oil companies (Siddayao 1980). Indonesia had set up such a company in the 1960s, Pertamina. The interest of the federal government in gaining control over a sector whose importance had risen so sharply needs no explanation. What is less obvious is the reason the state governments would be willing to surrender ownership of their oil resources. There are several explanations. First, although the constitution was quite clear about the ownership of land and onshore resources like tin and forests, ownership of offshore resources was more murky. The Emergency (Essential Powers) Ordinance established a precedent for federal control of most of the offshore area. Second, there was a history of delays in developing nonfuel mineral resources under state mining enactments (Emerson 1985). It was thought that a national oil company could conclude deals with international oil companies more rapidly and thereby speed up the flow of revenue from oil production to both state and federal governments.

Third, and most important, forcing oil companies to negotiate with a single Malaysian owner of the resource, one acting as the agent of the prime minister, made it more likely that the deals would be favorable to Malaysia, the state governments included. If state governments negotiated separately with oil companies, they faced the risk that oil companies would play them off against each other. Finally, to provide some assurance to state governments, section 4 of the act stated, "In return for the ownership and the rights, powers, liberties and privileges vested in it by virtue of this Act, the Corporation shall make to the Government of the Federation and the Government of any relevant State such cash payment as may be agreed between the parties concerned." Reaching agreement with Sabah over the transfer of ownership proved to be the most difficult, but the state government and Petronas concluded an agreement on June 14, 1976.

The establishment of Petronas fundamentally changed the relationship between oil companies and the government. Section 9 called for the drawing up of new contractual arrangements, and quickly: "Any exploration licenses issued and any petroleum agreements entered into pursuant to the Petroleum Mining act, 1966, and any mining leases issued under any written law in force relating to petroleum shall continue to be in force for a period of six months from the date of the coming into force of this Act or for such extended period as the Prime Minister may allow." The Petroleum Regulations of 1974, promulgated under section 7 of the Petroleum Development Act, gave Petronas the authority to replace concession agreements with production-sharing contracts (PSCs). Production sharing was an approach pioneered in Southeast Asia by Pertamina, and the broad features of Petronas's PSCs are similar to Pertamina's. PSCs sharply curtailed the autonomy of oil companies operating in Malaysia. Companies had to submit investment plans and annual work programs and budgets to Petronas for approval. This officially gave Petronas control over the rate of development and the level of production, which it monitored. Companies also had to furnish to Petronas all information they possessed on oil resources, investment, and production. Petronas registered and approved subcontractors, favoring local companies, especially *bumiputera* companies, that met industry standards. To create competition for international oil companies and to reduce the country's dependence on them for production technology (Foo and Ramasamy 1991), Petronas itself entered directly into oil exploration, development, and production by establishing a subsidiary, Petronas Carigali, in 1978.

Equally great were changes in the fiscal regime facing oil companies. The first-generation PSCs (FGPSCs) established various general terms, with individual contracts differing slightly depending on the outcome of the negotiations:

1. *Duration.* Contracts were for 24 years: 5 years for exploration, 4 years for development, and 15 years for production.
2. *Cost oil.* The contractor automatically retained 20 percent of annual gross production of crude oil to recover exploration, development, and operating costs. These costs could be carried forward but not shared between contracts held by the same company. Hence, companies had no means of recovering their investment if exploration and development were unsuccessful. They bore the full risk of failure.
3. *Royalties.* The contractor paid 5 percent of gross production to the state government and another 5 percent to the federal government.
4. *Profit oil.* The remaining 70 percent of oil production was split 70:30 between Petronas and the contractor (hence, 49 percent of gross production and 21 percent of gross production, respectively).
5. *Research cess.* The contractor paid 0.5 percent of its portion of cost oil and profit oil to a Petronas research fund (hence, 0.205 percent of gross production).
6. *Excess proceeds tax.* The contractor paid Petronas 70 percent of any increase in the price of crude oil above a base price, which was set equal to the average value of Malaysian crudes at the time of signing of the contract.
7. *Bonuses.* The contractor paid a signature bonus (about RM1 million), a discovery bonus (about RM2.5 million per commercial discovery), and a production bonus (RM5 million for every 50,000 bpd).

If costs were indeed equivalent to the 20 percent cost-oil share, then provisions 3 and 4 alone imply that the remaining 80 percent, which constituted resource rent, was captured mainly by the government (state and federal governments plus Petronas): 59 percent, versus 21 percent for the contractor.

But the government's share was actually substantially higher, due to the petroleum income tax.[14] If the contractor's chargeable income actually equaled its 30 percent profit oil share,[15] the government's "take," inclusive of income tax paid at the 50 percent rate, was at least 69 percent of gross output, or nearly 90 percent of the rent.[16] This left the contractor with a net return of no more than 10.5 percent of gross output. This was further reduced by the excess proceeds tax and the various bonuses. The Petroleum Income Tax Amendment Act of 1977 reduced the income tax rate to 45 percent (retroactive to April 1, 1975), but this was more than offset a few years later, on April 28, 1980, when the government introduced a petroleum export tax. This tax was set equal to 25 percent of the contractor's profit oil on exported oil.[17] It was prompted by concerns about windfall profits stemming from the second oil shock, as well as by government interest in discouraging the export of crude oil and promoting local refining. It reduced the maximum net return of a contractor who exported all its oil and faced the 45 percent income tax from 11.5 percent of gross output to 9 percent. Table 3.1 summarizes the calculations of the contractor's net "take" under FGPSCs, with and without the export tax.

The fiscal regime under the FGPSCs was certainly much more stringent than under the concession agreements. According to a study by Siddayao (1980, Table 5.5), it was more stringent than in either Indonesia or the Philippines: an oil company's gross "take" (inclusive of cost oil) was only 32 barrels per 100 barrels of output in Malaysia, compared to 47 to 100 barrels in Indonesia and 65 to 78 barrels in the Philippines.[18] Two companies, Continental Oil and Aquitane Petroleum, found Malaysia's fiscal regime too harsh and pulled out of Malaysia (Jasin 1995).[19] Other companies, however, reached agreement with Petronas relatively rapidly. The three largest contractors, Sabah Shell, Sarawak Shell, and Esso, all concluded PSCs by 1976 (Foo and Ramasamy 1991).

The high proportion of rents captured by the government under the FGPSCs was potentially beneficial from a national standpoint, as it reduced the repatriation of rents by oil companies. But the FGPSCs also made development of marginal oil fields less attractive and thereby reduced the aggregate amount of rents generated by oil production. Contractors could not fully recover costs in excess of 20 percent of gross revenues; hence, fields with costs of such magnitude were not worth developing. Even when costs were within the 20 percent limit over the life of the contract, the limit delayed contractors' recovery of their substantial upfront investments in exploration and develop-

Table 3.1 *Oil contractor's net "take" (in barrels) under first-generation production-sharing contracts (FGPSCs)*

Item in fiscal regime	Without export tax	With export tax
1. Production	100	100
Cost oil	−20	−20
Rent	80	80
2. Royalties	−10	−10
Profit oil	70	70
3. Petronas share (70%)	−49	−49
Contractor's share	21	21
4. Export tax (25%)	−0	−5
Chargeable income	21	16
5. Petroleum income tax (45%)	−9.5	−7
Net "take"	11.5	9

ment. The 10 percent royalty and the government's 49 percent profit-oil share amounted to an α of 0.59 in Figure 3.3, discouraging development of all but the largest and lowest-cost fields. Diminished prospects of an acceptable return on developed fields reduced the incentive to explore.

It is therefore not surprising that investment in exploration and development fell off sharply in the early 1980s, when oil prices that had been artificially inflated by OPEC's actions began declining.[20] The *Fourth Malaysia Plan 1981–1985* forecast that oil prices would rise by 16 percent per year from 1981 to 1985, but they went in the other direction instead. Exploration investment was not the only indicator of falling exploration activity. The number of new exploration wells reached a twenty-year peak in 1981 at 61, and fell to 23 in 1982 and 20 in 1983 (Arief and Wells 1985, Table 3.6).[21] Those were the lowest numbers since the 1960s, aside from 1976 and 1977 when contractors were adjusting to the PSC system. Exploration footage fell from 430,649 feet in 1981 to 188,837 feet in 1982, the lowest figure since the early 1970s, aside from 1976 and 1977 (Energy Information Administration 1984, Table 24.)

The decline in exploration activity accentuated growing government concern about the finiteness of the country's oil resources. In the early 1980s, Malaysia's ratio of proven reserves to annual production was only 21 years, compared to 50 years for Saudi Arabia and 140 years for Kuwait (Arief and Wells 1985). As early as the *Mid-Term Review of the Third Malaysia Plan 1976–1980*, the government declared that it would "take steps to ensure that there is a balance between demand and production to safeguard future security of supply in the country" (p. 161); a similar statement was made at the beginning of the mining chapter in the *Fourth Malaysia Plan 1981–1985*. On June 1, 1980, the government took a concrete step by introducing the National Oil Depletion Policy. This provided two means of limiting production. First, it authorized Petronas to postpone the development of major oil fields, which were defined as those having initial reserves of at least 400 million barrels. Under this provision, Petronas delayed Esso's development of the Seligi Field (440 million barrels) for eight years (EPU 1993).[22] Second, it placed an annual limit on total oil production, equal to 3 percent of oil originally-in-place in major fields (*Mid-Term Review of the Fifth Malaysia Plan 1986–1990*).

In sum, although the government succeeded in getting most existing contractors to sign FGPSCs, it was less successful in attracting new investment under the terms of those contracts. This forced it to be concerned not only about the ultimate exhaustion of the country's oil resources, but also about shortfalls in expected production in the near term. Siddayao (1988, p. 615) concluded that Malaysia "had to learn the basics of private sector investment in the petroleum industry the hard way."

Second-generation production-sharing contracts (SGPSCs)

In response to the decreased investment in exploration and development, the government eased up on the terms of the PSCs in the 1980s. A PSC signed by Petronas and Elf Aquitane in 1982 raised the cost-oil share to 30 percent.[23] More generous, across-the-board revisions were announced in 1985 for new PSCs. Under second-generation PSCs (SGPSCs), the following changes were introduced:

1. *Cost oil.* The cost-oil share was raised to a maximum of 50 percent.[24] The actual cost oil that contractors could retain was based on actual costs,[25] which Petronas reviewed.
2. *Profit oil.* A sliding scale was introduced for the first 50 million barrels of oil recovered from the contract area: the first 10,000 bpd were split 50:50 (Petronas:contractor), the next 10,000 bpd were split 60:40, and daily production above 20,000 bpd was split 70:30. All production in excess of 50 million barrels was split 70:30.
3. *Bonuses.* All bonuses were eliminated.
4. *Participation.* A requirement was added that Petronas Carigali must be given a minimum equity of 15 percent (on a carried interest basis) and have the option to participate in the development of any commercial discovery up to the extent of its participating interest (i.e., at minimum, 15 percent).

Table 3.2 compares key features of FGPSCs and SGPSCs.

The government explained the rationale for these revisions as follows (*Fifth Malaysia Plan 1986–1990*, p. 422):[26]

The original production-sharing contract terms were considered stringent, particularly for new contract areas. Together with the falling crude oil prices and the global economic recession, exploration activities slackened. Given the very capital intensive and technologically sophisticated nature of petroleum exploration and exploitation, coupled with the inadequate capacity of PETRONAS in undertaking a wide range of programmes, the terms and conditions of the production-sharing contract have been revised to further encourage the private sector, both local and foreign, to invest in these activities.

The SGPSCs did indeed succeed in attracting new investment to the Malaysian oil sector, despite continued low oil prices (and notably, the March 1986 price collapse). While only seven FGPSCs were signed between 1976 and 1982 (and four were relinquished), twenty-five SGPSCs were signed from 1986 to 1990 (*Sixth Malaysia Plan 1991–1995*).[27] The *Sixth Malaysia Plan 1991–1995* stated that the increase was "a direct consequence of the liberalization of PSC terms" (p. 306). Figure 3.2 shows that both exploration and development expenditure rose steadily from 1986 to 1989.

Petronas did not renegotiate existing FGPSCs after it introduced the SGPSCs. But it did negotiate an SGPSC with Shell when the FGPSC for one of its fields expired. With the exception of that oil field and a field operated jointly by Petronas Carigali and Esso (the Dulang Field), the entire production of crude oil in the early 1990s was still taking place under the terms of the FGPSCs.

Despite the relaxation of the terms, Malaysia's PSCs apparently remained the best in the Asia-Pacific region at minimizing oil companies' "take." Wid-

Table 3.2   *Comparison of first- and second-generation production-sharing contracts (PSCs)*

Contract feature	First-generation PSC	Second-generation PSC
Royalties	10% of gross production	Same
Cost oil	20% of gross production	Up to 50% of gross production
Profit oil split (Petronas: contractor)	70:30	Sliding scale 1. First 50 million barrels • First 10,000 bpd: 50:50 • Next 10,000 bpd: 60:40 • Above 20,000 bpd: 70:30 2. Remaining oil: 70:30
Bonuses	Signature Discovery Production	None
Research cess	0.5% of contractor's cost and profit oil	Same
Participation by Petronas Carigali	None	15% carried interest during exploration phase with 15% option to participate upon commercial discovery

jadono (1993) compared oil contracts in Australia, Brunei, China, Indonesia, New Zealand, Malaysia, the Philippines, and Thailand.[28] All countries except Australia, New Zealand, and Thailand utilized production-sharing contracts. For small fields (36 million barrels), contractors operating under Malaysia's SGPSCs earned a lower rate of return, on the order of 11 to 12 percent, than contractors in all other countries except Brunei (where the rate was just marginally lower) and Indonesia (where the rate was lower only for pre-1984 contracts). This rate is comparable to the marginal economic opportunity cost of capital in Malaysia in the 1970s and 1980s, 8 to 13 percent (Veitch 1986). For large fields (146 million barrels), Malaysia's rates were the lowest at all points in time: although the rate rose from 2 percent for FGPSCs, to 11 to 12 percent for the 1982 Elf Aquitane PSC, to 18 percent for SGPSCs, the last rate was lower than the return earned by contractors in all other countries in the late 1980s. In a global review of fiscal arrangements for oil, Barrows (1995) rated the SGPSCs "very tough," its most stringent rating. *Oxford Analytica Daily Brief* (1995) called them "among the most unfavorable to foreign partners in the world."

A high rate of government rent capture is also indicated by the ratio of petroleum-based federal revenue (the sum of petroleum income tax, export tax, royalties, and petroleum dividend)[29] to value added in the oil sector. Because value added includes not only resource rents but also payments to labor and capital, the ratio actually understates rent capture. Table 3.3 shows that the ratio was at least two-thirds in all years and above one in some.

One can infer that the federal government captured more than two-thirds of oil rents in every year. Total government rent capture was even higher, as the states also collected royalties and Petronas retained residual rents after paying the petroleum income tax, the export tax, and the petroleum dividend.

ECONOMIC ANALYSIS OF PRODUCTION-SHARING CONTRACTS

In this section, we look more closely at three issues related to Malaysia's PSCs: rent capture, high-grading, and risk sharing. The preceding section contained a fair amount of information on the first issue; the main contribution of the analysis in this section is to provide more rigorous estimates, and to relate rent capture to size of oil field. The second issue concerns the effects of PSCs on the production decisions of oil contractors. Specifically, we examine whether it is profitable for an oil company operating under a Malaysian PSC to develop all oil fields that are capable of generating a positive resource rent, or only some. If the latter, the country's revenue base and export earnings are reduced. The third issue concerns the relative abilities of the govern-

Table 3.3   *Ratio of petroleum-based federal government revenue to value added of the petroleum sector*

Year	Ratio
1980	0.78
1981	1.38
1982	1.32
1983	0.83
1984	0.86
1985	0.95
1986	0.83
1987	0.71
1988	0.71
1989	0.67
1990	0.82

Source: Official data.

Note: Petroleum-based revenue includes the Petroleum Income Tax, the petroleum export tax, the federal government's share of the petroleum royalty, and the petroleum dividend.

ment and contractors to bear risks related to fluctuations in oil prices and the costs of oil production.

For each issue we compare FGPSCs and SGPSCs. Given the complexities of the Malaysian PSC system, we perform most of the analysis with the help of a simulation model. The model takes into account geological and cost conditions in Malaysia as well as key features of the Malaysian PSCs. It has the same structure as models by Blitzer et al. (1984) for Ecuador and Meyer (1986) for Peru. It determines the expected net present value (NPV),[30] from both the government's and the contractor's perspectives, of hypothetical oil projects that differ due to field size. The expected NPV is the economic rent that each party expects to capture. It consists of not only the scarcity rent of the exhaustible oil resource (the Hotelling rent in Figure 2.1), but also the inframarginal rent that accrues to nonmarginal, lower-cost deposits. The *government* is defined broadly as the federal and state governments and Petronas; NPVs are not calculated separately for each. The government only captures rent on fields actually developed. A contractor will only develop fields that it expects to yield a nonnegative NPV. Only on such fields does it earn a sufficient return on its investment.

The model involves the following assumptions. The probability that an oil deposit contains recoverable reserves of R million barrels is:[31]

20 percent for $R \leq 10$ million barrels

65 percent for 10 million barrels $< R \leq 100$ million barrels

15 percent for $R > 100$ million barrels.

These probabilities are based on the sizes of fields actually discovered in Malaysia. The project term is 24 years, of which 5 years are for exploration, 4 years for development, and 15 years for production. Exploration costs are US$4 million per year. Development costs depend on the size of the field, with the cost function exhibiting economies of scale.[32] Parameters of the cost function were chosen to generate development costs, on a per barrel basis, of (after converting from dollars to ringgits) RM2.80, RM2.50, and RM2.30 for 50-, 100-, and 200-million-barrel fields, respectively. These values are within the range of estimates reported by EPU (1993) for eight major fields in Malaysia, RM1.19 to RM30.21 (mean of RM5.11, when weighted by reserve size).[33] In each of the first two years of development, 20 percent of development costs are incurred; in years 3 and 4, 30 percent each. Operating costs are US$1.50 per barrel. This is virtually identical to an estimate by Wood Mackenzie, a consulting company specializing in the oil industry, US$1.56 (*Oxford Analytica Daily Brief* 1995), and very close to the weighted mean reported by EPU (1993), US$1.74 (the range was US$0.85 to US$3.66).[34] All costs are constant over time in real terms.

In the base-line case, crude oil price is constant at US$20 per barrel. The discount rate, the opportunity cost of capital invested in the oil sector, is assumed to be identical for the contractor and the government and is set equal to 10 percent.[35] This value implies a low risk premium, which is appropriate given the country's political and economic stability and the higher than average chance of discovery in its offshore territory. The production profile is as follows: 1/10 of the deposit is extracted in each of the first five years, 1/15 in each of the second five years, and 1/30 in each of the last five years.[36] Hence, the field is exhausted at the end of the fifteen-year production period.

In applying the model to the PSCs, some simplifications compared to actual contractual arrangements were made. For FGPSCs, the model includes the 10 percent royalty, the 20 percent cost oil, the 45 percent Petroleum Income Tax, and the 25 percent export tax. Depreciation of capital costs is over ten years on a straight-line basis. For SGPSCs, the only differences compared to FGPSCs are: 1) cost oil is raised to 50 percent, and 2) profit oil is shared on the sliding scale. The model ignores bonuses (which applied only to FGPSCs), the research cess (which applied to both), the excess proceeds tax (which applied only to SGPSCs), and Petronas Carigali's participation (which applied only to SGPSCs). Due to these omissions, the model overstates the contractor's NPV, especially for SGPSCs.

Rent capture

The government's NPV can be compared to the contractor's NPV to assess the effectiveness of FGPSCs and SGPSCs in retaining rents within the country. Table 3.4 shows the results of this comparison, expressed in terms of the percentage of the aggregate NPV captured by the contractor. A higher percentage indicates lower government rent capture. Under FGPSCs (base-line scenario), the contractor captures less than 13 percent of the NPV, depending on the size of the field. The share is quite sensitive to oil price: an increase in the oil price results in a more than proportionate increase in the contractor's share for all fields except the biggest. The contractor's share is much higher under SGPSCs, and more stable. For a wide range of fields, the contractor captures 25–30 percent of the NPV. These results are consistent with the estimates of "take" reported in sections *First-generation production-sharing contracts* and *Second-generation production-sharing contracts*. SGPSCs reduced the government's rent capture from the extremely high levels of FGPSCs, but rent capture remained high in absolute terms.

High-grading

As discussed earlier, one would expect the royalties and production shares and the limit on the cost-oil share to cause high-grading. But how significant are such impacts empirically? To answer this question, we determined the marginal field for FGPSCs and SGPSCs: the field with an NPV of zero from the contractor's standpoint. This field offers a return just equal to the opportunity cost of the contractor's funds. It allows recovery of capital and other costs but does not generate any rent for the contractor.

The marginal field depends not just on contract terms but also on oil prices and the discount rate. Table 3.5 shows the marginal field under varying assumptions. In the base-line case (i.e., price of US$20 per barrel and discount rate of 10 percent), the marginal field is only 6 million barrels when there is no fiscal regime. That is, a contractor who owed no taxes or other payments

Table 3.4 *Contractor's share of NPV under first- and second-generation production-sharing contracts (FGPSCs and SGPSCs), with export tax*

Type of contract	Oil price	Field size (million barrels)					
		25	50	100	200	500	1000
		Percent					
FGPSC	US$15	<0	<0	<0	<0	3.1	6.4
	US$20	<0	<0	4.5	8.5	11.5	12.9
	US$25	<0	6.6	10.8	13.0	14.7	15.5
SGPSC	US$15	0.3	19.8	21.9	23.3	25.6	26.7
	US$20	0.5	23.9	29.7	28.5	28.1	28.9
	US$25	30.0	32.7	30.7	29.9	30.2	30.5

(in cash or in kind) to the government would find it profitable to develop all fields with recoverable reserves of at least 6 million barrels. This provides a reference point for evaluating the relative high-grading induced by FGPSCs and SGPSCs.

FGPSCs increase the marginal field substantially, to 64 million barrels in the base-line case. Abolition of the export tax, which is analogous to a reduction in α in Figure 3.3, decreases the marginal field somewhat, to 51 million barrels. Given that median field size in the Malaysian offshore region is only 28 million barrels, these results imply that more than half of the country's oil fields are unprofitable under FGPSCs, with or without the export tax, under base-line assumptions. The marginal field under FGPSCs is, however, very sensitive to oil price. For example, with the export tax, the marginal field is 12,400 million barrels—nearly thirty times larger than the biggest field ever discovered in Malaysia—when the price falls to US\$10, but it is just 18 million barrels when price rises to US\$30. The big increase in the marginal field as prices fall is consistent with the decline in investment after 1982 (Figure 3.2), when prices began sliding downward. The marginal field is also quite sensitive to the discount rate, with the relationship being the opposite of that for price (as one would expect): an increase in the discount rate increases marginal field size. This is analogous to the shift from *MPC* to *MPC'* in Figure 3.3.

Many more fields have a positive NPV under SGPSCs: the marginal field is

Table 3.5 *Marginal oil fields under first- and second-generation production-sharing contracts (FGPSCs and SGPSCs), with and without export tax*

Scenario	No fiscal regime[a]	FGPSCs		SGPSCs	
		w/tax	w/o tax	w/tax	w/o tax
		Million barrels			
Base-line[b]	6	64	51	13	12
Discount rate 10%, price:					
• US\$10	25	12,400	7,500	230	176
• US\$15	10	314	220	18	16
• US\$25	4	29	25	8	8
• US\$30	3	18	15	6	6
Price US\$20, discount rate:					
• 5%	3	21	18	6	5
• 15%	11	271	203	30	28

Notes:
[a] Contractor not obliged to make any payment, whether monetary (e.g., tax) or in kind (production share), to the government or Petronas.
[b] Discount rate = 10%, price = US\$20 per barrel.

13 million barrels with the export tax and 12 million barrels without. These amounts are smaller than those for FGPSCs under even the most optimistic price and discount rate assumptions. The marginal field is still sensitive to price, but not nearly as sensitive as under FGPSCs. It is also not as sensitive to the discount rate. The impact of the export tax is much less pronounced under all price and discount-rate assumptions.

The internal rate of return (IRR) is another way to analyze the economic viability of investment projects.[37] Table 3.6 shows that the IRR is considerably higher under SGPSCs than under FGPSCs, reaching 26 percent for a 500-million-barrel field developed under an SGPSC. Only fields with an IRR of at least 10 percent (the contractor's discount rate) are profitable to develop. As in Table 3.5, the marginal field is 64 million barrels under FGPSCs and 13 million barrels under SGPSCs.

In sum, the analysis confirms that SGPSCs dramatically increased the number of fields and the amount of oil reserves that could be developed in Malaysia. Although SGPSCs made the government's "slice" of the rent thinner, they made the overall oil "cake" bigger. In practice, because larger fields tend to be found first, fields developed under SGPSCs will probably be smaller on average than those developed under FGPSCs. Thus, the government probably did not give up much rent on individual fields by settling for a smaller share of the NPV, and it surely gained rent in aggregate terms due to the great increase in the revenue base. It also gained stability in its share of the NPV, which varied less under SGPSCs.

Risk sharing

The oil industry is often considered more risky than other industries because it has to cope with exploration and political risks in addition to common commercial risks related to prices, costs, and quantities. Given that offshore exploration in Malaysia has a rather high success rate in international terms, it is not unusually risky from a geological standpoint.[38] International oil companies as well as foreign investors in general rate the business climate

Table 3.6 *Contractor's internal rate of return under first- and second-generation production-sharing contracts (FGPSCs and SGPSCs), baseline assumptions*

Contract	Field size (million barrels)					
	12.5	25	50	100	200	500
	Percentage					
FGPSC	2	6	9	10	12	17
SGPSC	10	14	17	18	20	26

in Malaysia as favorable due to the country's political stability, sound economic policies, educated labor force, good infrastructure, and other factors. Although, as Emerson (1985, p. 50) put it, "the tendency of the government to revise existing fiscal arrangements in times of high oil prices (as demonstrated by the introduction of [the PSCs and] the petroleum export tax) must have a deterring effect upon petroleum exploration," the long-term involvement of the two main contractors, Esso and Shell, suggests that such risks, and other political and institutional ones, are manageable. Uncertainty about future prices and costs therefore seems to be the main concern.

Meaningful comparisons of price variability can be made across sectors only if variability is measured in a unit-free way. In this regard, the coefficient of variation—the ratio of the standard deviation of a price series to its mean—and the correlation coefficient are both useful and appropriate. We estimated these measures for the oil sector and other sectors of the economy from 1970 to 1990, using information on international commodity prices in U.S. dollars, deflated by the U.S. wholesale price index. Results are shown in Table 3.7. Of all commodity prices, crude oil exhibited the greatest variability during the last two decades. Its coefficient of variation was almost a third higher than those for tin and palm oil, and approximately double those for forest products. Oil price was also positively correlated with all other commodity prices, so the expansion of oil exports did not reduce overall price volatility in the commodity sector by diversifying risks. On the other hand, and rather surprisingly, the prices of oil and other commodities were less variable than the price index of all exports taken together. For this reason, the diversification of the economy into manufactured goods and away from commodities, including oil, did not reduce the overall variability of export revenue.[39] After de-trending the data, the value of agricultural and mining exports was less variable from 1970 to 1990 than the value of manufactured goods exports (coefficients of variation were 0.141 and 0.254, respectively).

In sum, the expansion of oil exports increased price volatility in the commodity sector but decreased price volatility in the overall export bundle, because oil price was more variable than the prices of other commodities but less variable than the prices of manufactured goods. In contrast, the variability of the federal government's revenue from the oil sector was much greater than the variability of total federal revenue. The coefficient of variation of the former was 0.759, while that of the latter was 0.382. Part of the variability, however, was due simply to rising trends. In the 1980s, when oil revenue was no longer increasing, its variability was much less pronounced and more similar to total revenue variability (coefficients of variation of 0.173 versus 0.140).

Table 3.7 *Variability of export prices, 1970–90*

Item[a]	Coefficient of variation[b]	Correlation matrix					
		Oil	Tin	Palm oil	Rubber	Logs	Sawnwood
Commodities							
• Oil	0.443	1.00					
• Tin	0.342	0.60	1.00				
• Palm oil	0.340	0.13	0.70	1.00			
• Rubber	0.248	0.23	0.71	0.61	1.00		
• Logs	0.228	0.24	−0.04	−0.31	0.29	1.00	
• Sawnwood	0.195	0.34	0.15	−0.19	0.27	0.53	1.00
All goods	0.488						

[a] Commodity prices are in U.S. dollars, deflated by U.S. wholesale price index.
[b] Standard deviation divided by mean of variable.

Contractors and the government therefore faced considerable variability in oil prices during the 1970s and 1980s, and this variability affected both government revenues and export earnings. Production sharing meant that the government shared price risks to a considerable extent with foreign contractors. We analyzed risk-sharing features of FGPSCs and SGPSCs by incorporating price and cost volatility into the NPV model. We assumed that prices and costs were normally distributed, with mean values equal to the values given earlier and with a positive covariance between the two variables (price and cost tend to rise or fall together).[40] The standard deviation for price was US$6.80, the historical value in Table 3.7: there is a 68 percent probability (1 standard deviation) that price is greater than US$13.20 and less than US$26.80, and a 95 percent probability (2 standard deviations) that it is greater than US$6.40 and less than US$33.60. Similarly, there is a 68 percent probability that cost is within US$0.50 of its mean and a 95 percent probability that it is within US$1.00. Under this formulation, NPVs are also distributed normally.

Table 3.8 shows results of the analysis. In qualitative terms, FGPSCs and SGPSCs allocate risks similarly between the contractor and the government, with the government bearing more of the risk in absolute terms (its standard deviation is larger) and the contractor more in relative terms (its coefficient of variation is larger). The differences between the two parties are narrower under SGPSCs, however. Under FGPSCs, the government bears much more of the risk in absolute terms: the standard deviation for its NPV share ranges from US$36.6 million for a 100-million-barrel field to US$194.1 for a 50-million-barrel field. These values are more than double the corresponding ones for the contractor. But in relative terms, the government bears much less of the risk, because its share of the NPV is so much larger. Its coefficient of variation is only 0.122 for a 100-million-barrel field and 0.124 for a 50-mil-

Table 3.8 *Means, standard deviations, and coefficients of variation for contractors' and government's NPVs*

	50-million-barrel field		100-million-barrel field	
	FGPSC[a]	SGPSC[b]	FGPSC	SGPSC
Contractor				
• Mean	235	518	21	91
• Standard deviation	74	96	17	21
• Coefficient of variation	0.32	0.19	0.82	0.23
Government				
• Mean	1,564	1,282	301	231
• Standard deviation	194	172	37	32
• Coefficient of variation	0.12	0.13	0.12	0.14

Note: Means and standard deviations are expressed in million US$. The coefficient of variation is the ratio of the standard deviation to the mean.

[a] FGPSC—First-generation production-sharing contract.

[b] SGPSC—Second-generation production-sharing contract.

lion-barrel field, versus values of 0.818 and 0.315, respectively, for the contractor. Risk is shared more equitably under SGPSCs, especially in relative terms (because of the approximate tripling of the contractor's share of the NPV). The contractor continues to bear most of the risk in relative terms, however.

In designing a contract system that allocates risks between contractor and government, one must consider which party is better able to bear a particular form of risk. It is usually assumed that countries are risk neutral and companies are risk averse.[41] But developing countries that depend on income from oil or other natural resources often exhibit behavior that makes them appear at as least as risk averse as big international oil companies, which take many steps to pool and diversify risks. Adelman (1986a) argued, in fact, that the government discount rates of small oil-exporting countries, particularly those that depend heavily on oil for revenue and have large public sectors with expenditures that are politically difficult to trim, include a much larger risk premium than the discount rates of international oil companies. In lay terms, oil companies can more easily build up reserves in good times and draw them down in periods of losses than can governments, which commit their revenues more or less completely and face political obstacles in reducing expenditures in times of reduced revenues. When such differences exist, Blitzer et al. (1984) have suggested that it is better for both parties for oil companies to bear more of the risk.

Although Malaysia was less dependent on oil revenue during the 1970s and 1980s than, say, the Persian Gulf states, its dependence was substantial (at least after the mid-1970s), and its public sector was large. Moreover, its efforts to reduce dependence on natural resources and diversify the economy can be interpreted as reflecting risk aversion, even if those efforts apparently had the opposite impact of increasing the volatility of export earnings. For these reasons, oil contractors were probably better able than the government to bear the relatively higher risks that they faced during the 1970s and 1980s under both generations of the PSCs.

CONCLUSIONS

Contractual arrangements played a critical role in the expansion of oil production in Malaysia during the 1970s and 1980s. With the introduction of production-sharing contracts in the mid-1970s, the country succeeded in minimizing the capture and repatriation of rents by international oil companies. Until the mid-1980s, however, it was less successful in structuring the contracts to encourage investment in exploration and development and to minimize high-grading. Revisions introduced in the SGPSCs went a long way toward addressing those shortcomings, without sacrificing much rent.

The stringent terms of the FGPSCs were premised on an assumption, stated explicitly in the *Fourth Malaysia Plan 1981–1985*, that the rapid rise in crude oil prices during the 1970s would continue. As the 1980s unfolded, this proved to be mistaken. Studies by Adelman (1986b, 1990, Adelman and Shahi 1989) and others have demonstrated that the price rises in the 1970s were an aberration, that oil has not become more scarce. Only artificial restraints on supply, like those by OPEC, can generate sustained increases in prices. Over the long term, oil prices have in fact fallen steadily. Nordhaus (1992) noted that real oil prices declined by 1.6 percent per year from 1870 to 1970. Data in his Figure 2 indicate that the trend for 1870 to 1989 was only slightly less steep, at about 1.5 percent per year. The price collapse in the 1980s put oil prices back on their long-term, downward trajectory. Although oil contracts must include provisions to reduce windfall profits when oil prices rise during upturns in the business cycle (the excess proceeds tax in Malaysia's PSCs is an example of such a provision), their basic structure should be such that they encourage investment even in the face of declining prices. The SGPSCs come closer to this structure than do the FGPSCs.

Whether the SGPSCs provide sufficient incentive for actual production is less clear. The study by Wood Mackenzie reported that "none of the oil and gas reserves found [in Malaysia] by foreign oil companies over the last ten years . . . has been put into production," and that the only contractors producing oil were the original two, Shell and Esso (*Oxford Analytica Daily Brief* 1995). At least three aspects of the SGPSCs accentuate the effects of soft oil prices. First, the sliding scale for profit oil creates incentives for the contractor to hold both daily and overall production artificially low, to avoid moving up the scale. The contractor's profit-oil share is cut almost in half (from 50 percent to 30 percent) if daily production rises from less than 10,000 bpd to more than 20,000 bpd or if overall production exceeds 50 million barrels. The daily and overall production limits and the associated profit-oil shares should be reviewed to ensure that they encourage development of and production from the fields involved, as well as capture a high proportion of the rent. The scale itself should be retained, as it makes incremental oil in small fields profitable to develop.

Second, the petroleum income tax imposes a tax burden greater than in other sectors. On theoretical grounds, income other than rents should be taxed at the same rate across sectors. For this reason, Emerson (1985) recommended reducing the Petroleum Income Tax rate to the corporate income tax rate of 35 percent. But since the income tax is the only component of the fiscal regime that is based, if not on rent, at least on net income, its contribution should probably not be diminished. A better option would be to accelerate depreciation of exploration costs. This would delay, but not diminish, tax payments, and it would strengthen incentives for exploration.

Emerson (1985) also proposed, more boldly, replacing the remainder of the fiscal regime with a cash-flow tax. A cash-flow tax is a tax on rent, and therefore it is completely neutral: it does not induce any high-grading. But it has serious implementation problems, and it does not provide a stable revenue flow, because its base is very volatile. If implemented in the form of a straight resource-rent tax (see Garnaut and Clunies Ross 1983), it does not generate any revenue until late in the production phase. For this reason, it is probably not the ideal tax until the country becomes less dependent on oil-based revenue.

Third, the export tax increases high-grading and reduces profits without generating much additional revenue. This tax was introduced as a kind of windfall profits tax following the second oil shock. Considering that: 1) the PSCs already include the excess proceeds tax; 2) Petronas pays about 80 percent of the export tax anyway; and 3) income tax payments would increase (the export tax is tax deductible), elimination of the export tax would have only a minor impact on total revenue, and then probably only in the short run. After taking into account the reduction in high-grading (Table 3.5), revenue might actually increase.

Eliminating the export tax would also help simplify the PSC system. To some extent, complexity and high administrative costs are inherent features of any PSC system, which requires extended negotiations, constant supervision, and so on. However, given that the Malaysian fiscal regime includes not just production sharing but also royalties, the excess proceeds tax, the export tax, the income tax, bonuses (only FGPSCs), and equity participation (only SGPSCs), there is certainly room for streamlining. The export tax is the most obvious candidate for elimination.

Revisions to the PSC system were indeed introduced in 1991 for exploration in deep-water acreage,[42] where risks and costs are higher (*Oxford Analytica Daily Brief* 1995). Barrows (1995) rated geological risks in Malaysia's deep-water acreage as "average," compared to "very low" for regular offshore areas. In effect, the revisions replicated the transition from FGPSCs to SGPSCs by providing higher returns for contractors. Cost oil was raised to 75 percent, and the government's profit-oil share was reduced to 14 percent for the first 50,000 bpd, 18 percent up to 100,000 bpd, 37 percent over 200,000 bpd, and 50 percent once a cumulative production of 300 million barrels has been reached (Barrows 1995). An alternative approach, which might involve less sacrifice of rent, would be for the government to consider sharing more of the risk associated with exploration and development. It could do this by, say, allowing contractors to deduct expenses related to unsuccessful ventures from income generated by other, producing fields. Unlike many resource-rich developing countries, Malaysia may be in a position to afford risk sharing due to its diversified economy, its relatively broad fiscal base, and its technological and management capacity.

As of the early 1990s, only slightly more than a third (1.8 billion barrels) of the oil originally-in-place in the country's measured reserves (4.9 billion barrels) had been extracted. Hence, there is still a considerable resource to manage, even without allowing for the discovery of deep-water reserves. Aside from the specific contractual points discussed in the preceding paragraphs, at least one broad policy issue merits greater attention by the government. This issue is relevant to other nonrenewable resources as well, in particular natural gas.[43] The issue is, as the *Fourth Malaysia Plan 1981–1985* put it, "the Government's policy of maintaining a balance between revenue maximization from oil and its products and conserving this depleting and irreplaceable natural resource" (p. 315). Revenue maximization is not inconsistent with rent maximization,[44] the economic interpretation of resource conservation, as long as the time frame for revenue maximization is consistent with the time horizon of oil ventures. There is some evidence, however, that in the 1980s the government's time horizon for revenue maximization was very short-term, certainly less than the twenty-four-year duration of PSCs. Both Arief and Wells (1985, p. 36) and Emerson (1985, p. 43) attributed increases in oil production during the *Fourth Plan* period to an intentional effort by the government to offset the drop in crude oil prices. While some increase may have been justified to maintain macroeconomic stability,[45] rent is inevitably sacrificed when oil production is increased during temporary periods of low prices, instead of being decreased to reserve oil for production after prices recover.

In this light, the lack of action by the government in the 1990s to revise SGPSCs to stimulate oil production might be justified. The risk, however, is that declining prices are a permanent, not temporary, feature of oil markets. In this case, failure to stimulate production could sacrifice not only revenue but rents, as decling prices cause the value of the oil in the ground to depreciate.

NOTES

1 The Miri Field was closed on October 1, 1972. The country's second onshore field, the Asam Paya Field in Sarawak, was discovered In the late 1980s. (EPU 1993).

2 According to Siddayao (1980, p. 177), "reserves" comprise "oil . . . that has been discovered and is producible at the prices and technology that existed when the estimate was made." "Discovered" refers to "oil . . . whose presence has been physically confirmed through actual exploration drilling" (p. 175). Reserves do not include oil that has been discovered but is uneconomic (i.e., is not recoverable). *Measured reserves* refer to "reserves contained primarily in the drilled portion of fields. The data to be employed and the method of estimation are specified so that the average error will normally be less than 20 per cent [*sic*]" (p. 176). Two other categories of reserves are *indicated reserves*—"Known oil . . . that is currently producible but cannot be estimated accurately enough to qualify as proved" (p. 174)—and *inferred reserves*—"Reserves . . . [whose] presence is based upon limited physical evidence and considerable geologic extrapolation. This places them on the borderline of being undiscovered" (p. 175).

3 Higher oil prices were a mixed blessing in the short run: the greater cost of oil imports triggered a short recession.

4 Although the oil industry's capital intensity and enclave character limit its employment impact, it is an important local source of jobs and income in the parts of Sabah, Sarawak, and Terengganu where its activities are concentrated.

5 See Auty (1990) for a critical discussion of Malaysia's pursuit of resource-based industrialization in the petroleum sector. On a scale of 0 (low risk of failure) to 1 (high risk), he gave Malaysia's resource-based industrialization strategy a score of 0.53. That placed Malaysia in the middle among the eight countries he examined (Bahrain, Cameroon, Indonesia, Malaysia, Nigeria, Saudi Arabia, Trinidad and Tobago, and Venezuela).

6 Arief and Wells (1985) observed that there was significant excess capacity in Malaysia's refineries. For example, the capacity utilization ratio was only 0.51 in 1974 and 0.73 in 1983. They reported "national security and prestige" as political justifications for expanding refining capacity, particularly through Petronas, but they observed that such projects are expensive and create few jobs (p. 68).

7 Despite the great increase in oil's economic importance, Malaysia did not become nearly as dependent on oil as did most oil-exporting countries. Auty (1990, Table 10.4) calculated an "oil dependence index" for eight countries (Bahrain, Cameroon, Indonesia, Malaysia, Nigeria, Saudi Arabia, Trinidad and Tobago, and Venezuela) in 1981 by taking the mean of the percentage share of oil in GDP, exports, and government revenue. Malaysia had by far the lowest value, 26 percent. Next was Cameroon, at 48 percent. Highest was Saudi Arabia, at 86 percent.

8 EPU (1993) suggested that the discrepancy between the two sets of estimates might be due to international oil companies underreporting reserves to Malaysian authorities for tax reasons. A more innocuous reason could be differences in estimation methods. Siddayao (1980) noted that mathematical and geologic (volumetric) methods yield different estimates.

9 This is the full marginal cost only if environmental damage associated with oil production is negligible. If such damage is not negligible, then the marginal cost curve should include a third component, the marginal environmental cost, as well.

10 This also assumes that oil companies' discount rates equal the government's discount rate. See Adelman (1986a) for a discussion of reasons why these rates diverge in practice.

11 To be completely correct, the $MPC' + MDC'$ curve in Figure 3.3 should shift down when the royalty is introduced, as the royalty reduces net returns per barrel of oil in not only the current period but future periods as well. We have ignored this shift to keep the figure simple.

12 Other sources place the discovery of oil off Peninsular Malaysia earlier. Energy Information Administration (1984) stated that the Tapis Field was found in 1969, a date also reported in Arief and Wells (1985).

13 Subramaniam (1982) lists the date as November 8, not November 10.

14 See Subramaniam (1982) for a detailed description and analysis of the Petroleum Income Tax.

15 The petroleum income tax is actually levied on chargeable income, not profit oil.

16 Petronas also paid the petroleum income tax.

17 The export tax was also levied on Petronas, with an allowance for the royalty portion of its oil. Since 1981, Petronas has also paid a petroleum dividend to the federal government.

18 Table 4.1 in Siddayao (1980) provides a useful summation of contractual terms in nine countries in Southeast Asia (Brunei, Burma, Cambodia, Indonesia, Laos, Malaysia, the Philippines, Thailand, and Vietnam), as of June 1, 1978.

19 Petronas Carigali took over Continental Oil's operating area.

20 See Adelman (1986b) for a prescient analysis of the importance of factors other than scarcity in causing increases in world oil prices after 1973. In a later paper, Adelman (1990) provided information on long-run trends in development costs, which bolsters the case that oil has not become more scarce.

21 The number also declined after 1981 because Shell and Esso reached the end of the exploration phase of their PSCs at the end of that year.

22 Subramaniam (1982) reported that the policy was used to delay production in smaller fields as well (the Guntung and Palas Fields).

23 Segal (1982) argued that other provisions of the PSC offset the higher cost-oil share.

24 The increase accelerated contractors' recovery of exploration and development costs. For example, based on the assumptions in the text, exploration and development costs for a typical 100-million-barrel field would take fourteen years to recover under an FGPSC but only four years under an SGPSC.

25 Making cost oil conditional on actual costs could induce contractors to make unnecessary expenditures in order to reduce their income tax liability ("goldplating"). The alternative, however, which is to grant the cost oil automatically as under the FGPSCs, runs the risk of excessive loss of revenue in lower-cost fields.

26 The government's concern about the level of exploration activity is also indicated by other statements in the *Fifth Malaysia Plan 1986–1990*, that "the thrust for the development of the sector will be directed towards encouraging more intensive prospecting" (p. 413), and in the *Mid-Term Review* of that plan, which stated that "Efforts will continue to be undertaken to attract more foreign oil companies to invest in the upstream sector, particularly in encouraging greater inflow of risk capital in exploration activities" (p. 171).

27 Data in EPU (1993, Table 3) indicate that twenty-eight PSCs were signed during this period, not twenty-five.

28 Widjadono (1993) ignored the issue of whether the contracts generated home-country tax credits.

29 In 1990, shares of these were 37 percent, 25 percent, 8 percent, and 30 percent, respectively, according to Ministry of Finance (1991).

30 Net present value is the difference between the sum of discounted benefits of a project, expressed in monetary terms, and the sum of discounted costs, also expressed in monetary terms. Discounting adjusts for the time value of money. Hence, 1 ringgit of income received one year from now is worth less than 1 ringgit received today, as a ringgit received today can be invested at an interest rate of r percent to yield $1+r$ ringgit in one year.

31 The probability distribution used in the model is a log-normal distribution, with a mean of 3.335 and a standard deviation of 1.226. The underlying normal distribution has a mean of 59.5 million barrels and a standard deviation of 111 million barrels.

32 The development cost function was: $C = 40 \times R^{0.85}$. Under this specification, marginal development cost declines with reserve size: $MC = 34/R^{0.15}$.

33 On the other hand, the mean and median of annual estimates for Malaysia from 1973 to 1985 extrapolated by Adelman and Shahi (1989) from U.S. data were RM7.28 and RM7.09 (based on Adelman and Shahi's "adjusted" values).

34 Adelman and Ward (1980) reported a hypothetical estimate of US$0.18 per barrel for offshore wells in countries other than the United States.

35 This is within the range of estimates of the marginal opportunity cost of capital in Malaysia in the 1970s and 1980s reported by Veitch (1986), 8–13 percent. See Adelman (1986a) for a discussion of reasons why discount rates normally vary between oil companies and governments.

36 This is a "rule-of-thumb" extraction profile. We assume that it is approximately optimal for the average oil field in Malaysia. The actual optimal extraction profile varies among fields depending on their size, their cost characteristics, and contractors' expectations about future oil prices.

37 The IRR is defined as the rate of return at which the NPV equals zero.

38 This statement is not true for Malaysia's largely unknown deep-water acreage. As of the early 1990s, this area was estimated to contain 400 million barrels of potential oil reserves (50 percent probability).

39 This finding contradicts the common assumption that manufactured goods lower the instability of gross export earnings. See, for example, Bank Negara Malaysia (1991 pp. 56–59). ·

40 This follows the procedure in Conrad, Shalizi, and Syme (1990). The observed price in a given year, p_t, is given by:

$$p_t = E(p_t) + \mu_t$$

where $E(p_t)$ is the expected price (US$20) and μ_t is the price shock. The latter is distributed normally, with a mean of 0 and a standard deviation of US$6.80. Operating costs are given by:

$$c_t = \{1 + w[p_t/E(p_t)-1]\} \times [E(c_t)+v_t]$$

where w is a parameter relating price to cost (set equal to 0.5) and v_t is the cost shock. The latter is distributed normally, with a mean of 0 and a standard deviation of US$0.50.

41 A risk-averse economic agent is one that prefers a certain return to an uncertain return having the same expected value.

42 Regular SGPSCs were also revised to raise Petronas Carigali's participation option to 25 percent (Barrows 1995).

43 Malaysia's measured reserves of natural gas are the second largest in Asia and the sixteenth largest in the world, totaling 10.1 billion barrels of oil-equivalents as of 1990. This was three

times larger than measured oil reserves. About 20 percent of the gas reserves are associated with oil reserves. For more information, see World Bank (1991).

44 We are referring here to maximization of rents, not maximization of rent capture.

45 The impossibility of increasing production sufficiently to offset the collapse of oil prices in March 1986 was one cause of the subsequent deep recession.

4

Forests

INTRODUCTION

The federal Forestry Department in Peninsular Malaysia began the 1970s confronting several issues from an unexpectedly turbulent first decade of independence (*Malayan Forester* 1983). The 1958 *Forest Administration Report* by the chief conservator of forests had been upbeat about the possibilities for forestry in the new nation (quoted in *Malayan Forester* 1960a, p. 1):

Thus it comes about that the present time is one where there has been a culmination of three factors vital and favourable to the future of forestry in Malaya. Firstly, the "tools" for the essential job of converting the nation's forests to a higher yielding type have been evolved. Secondly, after eighteen years of delay resulting from the war and the Emergency,[1] it has now become possible to put the tools to work. And, thirdly, the machinery now exists, under a strong Federal Government, for developing a practical Federal Forest Policy before it is too late.

The "tools" refer to the Malayan Uniform System (MUS), a system for harvesting lowland rain forests[2] to ensure regeneration of the most desired species.

The optimism soon gave way to grave concern about a higher priority of state and federal governments: agricultural development (*Malayan Forester* 1960b, *Malayan Forester* 1960d, *Malayan Forester* 1962a).[3] Although 72 percent of the Peninsula was forested in 1960, two-thirds of this amount was in stateland forests, which were intended for conversion (see Setten 1962, Appendix II). Most of the remainder was in forest reserves,[4] which were less secure

---

Mohd. Shahwahid Haji Othman was a coauthor of this chapter.

than the name implies.[5] Forestry is a state matter under the constitution, and state governments had the unilateral authority to excise areas from forest reserves for development. State and federal governments shared an interest in promoting agricultural development more aggressively than had the colonial administration. Indeed, there was some sentiment that "forest regulations . . . have been imposed by an alien government and are regarded by the local inhabitants as oppressive regulations" (*Malayan Forester* 1960a, p. 82).

Led by land development schemes administered by the Federal Land Development Authority (FELDA), agricultural area expanded—and forest area shrank—at a rate not witnessed since the great rubber boom of the first third of the century (Vincent and Yusuf 1993). More than 400,000 hectares of lowland rain forest were converted to rubber and oil-palm plantations during the 1960s. Land development showed no sign of slowing down at the start of the 1970s; in fact, the case was quite the opposite, particularly after the introduction of the NEP and its emphasis on alleviating rural poverty. Deforestation caused by rapid land development was the first major issue still confronting the Forestry Department in 1970.

The second issue was a perceived imbalance between timber supply and timber demand. The Forestry Department believed that timber stocks in the country's virgin (old-growth) forests were being depleted too rapidly. Its goal was to manage the country's forests on a sustained-yield basis. It prescribed harvesting an "annual allowable coupe" equal to one-seventieth of the timber-producing forest area every year (*Malayan Forester* 1960a), as its studies indicated that the rotation age (the age of timber maturity) under the MUS was seventy years. Forest conversion threw off this tidy calculation. Great amounts of timber were felled when forests were cleared for land development schemes. Land development also indirectly contributed to increased timber production by improving access to formerly remote areas. Timber harvests tripled between 1960 and 1970.[6]

The additional production found ready markets both locally and abroad, enabling log exports and the domestic processing industry, particularly sawmilling, to expand rapidly. Domestic consumption was increasing due to population growth and rising income (Setten 1962, *Malayan Forester* 1964c). Even greater was the increase in export demand. International consumption of tropical timber had been low before World War II (*Malayan Forester* 1963a, 1965b, 1967b), but it expanded greatly in the postwar years due to the worldwide construction boom, technological developments that made it possible to make plywood from Southeast Asian timber (and to pressure-treat it), and the introduction of chainsaws, caterpillar tractors, and other mechanized equipment, much of it salvaged from World War II, which raised logging efficiency (*Malayan Forester* 1963a; Aiken and Leigh 1992, p. 69).[7] Malaysia's competitiveness was enhanced by the exhaustion of low-cost supplies from West Africa and the Philippines (Kumar 1986, Vincent 1992b). An additional advantage over Africa (and, for that matter, Latin America) was that most timber-sized trees in Malaysia's forests, and other forests in insular Southeast Asia west of the "Wallace Line,"[8] were members of a single plant family, the *Dipterocarpaceae*. Nearly all dipterocarps offer good quality and relatively homogeneous timber. This makes marketing considerably easier, as the wood of several species is sufficiently similar to be marketed under a single trade name. The discrepancy between the logging rate and the annual allowable coupe, combined with the rapid conversion of forests to agriculture, cast doubt on the Peninsula's long-run ability to supply logs to the growing wood processing industry (*Malayan Forester* 1962b, 1968a; Lian 1966).

The third issue was uncertainty related to the regeneration of logged-over forests spared from conversion. The MUS had been designed specifically for dipterocarp forests in the lowlands, and it had been the culmination of some fifty years of research (*Malayan Forester* 1970b). The first forest research officer had been appointed in 1918, and construction of the Forest Research Institute in Kepong began in 1929 (Menon 1976). The rapid conversion of lowland forests shifted the country's long-term timber base to hill dipterocarp forests—steepland forests with ridges dominated by the dipterocarp *Shorea curtisii* (seraya), generally found at elevations above 300 m[9]—where the MUS was untried and silvicultural knowledge was almost nonexistent[10] (*Malayan Forester* 1965b, 1968a). Worse, most hill forests were on the east side of the Main Range, where even the most basic information about forest resources was absent until a reconnaissance survey was completed in the late 1960s (*Malayan Forester* 1968a).

Research on hill forest silviculture was hampered by understaffing of the Forestry Department and the Forest Research Institute. At independence, most forestry researchers were expatriates. A "Malayanisation" policy called for replacing expatriate research officers as they retired with Malaysians. The last expatriate research officer retired in 1965, but his and many other positions remained unfilled due to a shortage of candidates (*Malayan Forester* 1964a, 1965b). This included all full-time silvicultural positions (*Malayan Forester* 1968a). FELDA and other agencies associated with land development were viewed as more attractive employers, ones leading the development charge.[11] The staffing problem was not limited to research; there was also a shortage of on-the-ground foresters, which limited the department's ability to supervise logging and to ensure that seedlings and saplings, the source of the next crop under the MUS, were protected (*Malayan Forester* 1970c, 1971c).[12] An early 1970s report by the U.N. Food and Agriculture Organization (FAO) referred to logging "as an entirely *ad hoc* activity in which [logging] subcontractors were virtually unsupervised" (cited in Kumar 1986, p. 97).

The forestry situation was quite different in Sabah and Sarawak. To begin, the two states had their own Forestry Departments and, under the constitution, were independent of the federal government insofar as forestry matters were concerned. They were more lightly populated, and so were not the focus of land development schemes. Export-oriented logging expanded in Sabah in the 1960s, but processing remained limited for a variety of reasons, including the state's poor infrastructure and small work force. Logging grew modestly in Sarawak, and processing almost not at all. Harvests were small relative to timber resources in both states. In sum, forestry issues in the Borneo states appeared much less pressing than in Peninsular Malaysia at the start of the 1970s.

It is evident from this review that forestry issues are more complicated than the oil issues discussed in the previous chapter. As in the case of oil, there are issues related to depletion of the resource, but in addition there is the issue of regeneration (as forests are renewable resources) and competition with other uses (as forests grow on land that may be valuable for agriculture, settlement, etc.). There is also the issue of multiple outputs: forests produce not just timber, but nontimber benefits as well, including watershed protection, wild-life habitat, and so on. An oil field produces a single product, crude oil (with natural gas sometimes associated), whose characteristics are predetermined by its chemical composition, while a forest can provide a range of benefits, which are not necessarily complementary, depending on the way it is man-aged. In the case of Malaysia, national forestry policy is further complicated by the economic, social, and political differences among Peninsular Malaysia, Sabah, and Sarawak, as well as the constitutional issue mentioned above.

For these reasons, a comprehensive treatment of forestry policy issues in Malaysia during the 1970s and 1980s is beyond the scope of this chapter. Such a treatment would require a book; indeed, a book that provides thorough coverage into the early 1980s does exist (Kumar 1986). Our approach in this chapter is instead a selective one: we focus on issues related to deforestation and timber depletion in natural forests in Peninsular Malaysia. Adopting this focus enables us to address the two issues in reasonable depth and to draw out some of their interrelationships.

The focus on natural forests is justified because plantation efforts were relatively minor during the period[13] and, in any event, natural forests are an important and complex resource in their own right. The issue of regeneration is important—indeed, it is of paramount importance from the standpoint of sustainability—but it involves a number of technical, silvicultural issues that are outside the competence of economists and beyond the scope of this book.[14] There are, of course, economic aspects to silvicultural interventions, which affect physical outputs of the forest and are not costless. We will address some of these issues in passing, as they relate to deforestation and timber depletion.

Regarding the regional focus, we selected Peninsular Malaysia for a number of reasons. Competition between forestry and land development was more intense in the Peninsula than in the Borneo states during the 1970s and 1980s, log production was higher than in Sarawak during the 1970s and Sabah at the end of the 1980s, and mills in the Peninsula consistently accounted for the bulk of the country's output and exports of processed wood products. In addition, information is more complete for the Peninsula. For example, while two forest inventories were conducted in Peninsular Malaysia during the 1970s and 1980s, a complete forest inventory still did not exist for Sarawak at the time of writing. The only comprehensive information on forest cover in that state dates from an unpublished land use survey conducted from 1962 to 1966. A complete forest inventory was conducted in Sabah in the early 1970s, but it was only partially updated in the late 1980s. Finally, while it is true that the forest sector is relatively more important to the economies of Sabah and Sarawak than to the Peninsular economy, the principal policy implications of this were addressed in Chapter 2, and more details are available in an outstanding recent study on the political economy of logging in the two states, by Ross (1996).

The chapter has the following sections. *Basic concepts in forest economics* presents some basic concepts in forest economics, which provides the analytical framework for discussions in subsequent sections. *Deforestation* and *Timber depletion* then deal in turn with the issues of deforestation and timber depletion. Both sections include the results of new quantitative analyses. Finally, *Conclusions* summarizes the findings and draws out their implications for future forestry policy, taking into account nontimber values.

Basic Concepts in Forest Economics

Tropical deforestation has attracted tremendous global attention since the early 1980s. Its causes and consequences, and potential policy responses, have been debated at numerous conferences, perhaps most notably at the U.N. Conference on Environment and Development in Rio de Janeiro in 1992. Even its definition is controversial. Some favor a strict definition: the complete or nearly complete removal of tree cover. Others favor a broader definition, which encompasses human actions that change the structure of a forest without necessarily eliminating tree cover. For example, Myers (1980) considered the logging of virgin forests to be a form of forest conversion, even when logging is selective and leaves a residual stand of trees.

In this chapter, we will follow the strict definition. Deforestation in this sense is usually the consequence of an intentional process to convert forestland to alternative uses, principally agriculture (FAO/UNEP 1981). It may be preceded by logging when commercially valuable timber is present, but it is driven by demand for land. In some cases, this demand is manifested as large-scale, state-sponsored land development schemes (as in Peninsular Malaysia); in other cases, it appears as "spontaneous" clearing of small plots by farmers acting independently or as part of small communities.[15] Conversion to nonagricultural uses can be locally important, especially in and around urban areas, but at a national level it usually affects a small area compared to agricultural conversion.

Figure 4.1 illustrates the economic fundamentals of deforestation. The horizontal axis indicates land area in a region, organized according to quality (capability class): highest quality land is at the left end of the axis, and lowest quality land is at the right end. The vertical axis indicates land rent, in ringgit per hectare. Land rent is defined here as the discounted sum of resource rents generated by the land. It is given by the difference between the discounted sum of revenue from the sales of products of the land, whether crops, timber, or something else, and the discounted sum of the costs of labor and other inputs used to produce those products. It represents the long-run economic value generated by the land as a factor of production. It is the asset value of the land to its owner.[16]

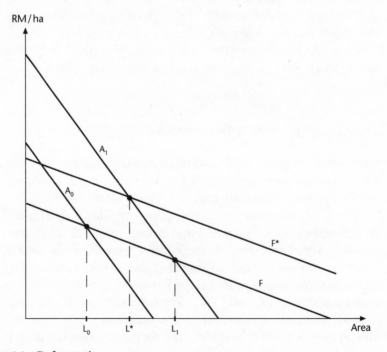

Figure 4.1   Deforestation

To make the concept of land rent clearer in the case of timber production, consider the following example, which is based on figures comparable to those in Peninsular Malaysia in the late 1980s. Suppose that the price of sawnwood is RM600/m³, and that processing costs related to labor, capital, energy, and materials total RM400/m³. Then the value of logs delivered to the mill is given by the difference, RM200/m³. This is the maximum amount the mill would be willing to pay for logs in the mill yard. If harvest and delivery costs are RM60/m³, the value of timber in the forest—the stumpage value—is the residual, RM140/m³. This is the maximum amount a logging contractor would be willing to pay for the right to harvest the timber. If the contractor harvests 50 m³/ha, then the rent generated at the time of harvest is the product of this quantity times the stumpage value, or RM7,000/ha. In present-value terms, this value is RM401/ha for a rotation of 30 years and a discount rate of 10 percent.[17] That is, a harvest of 50 m³/ha of timber 30 years from now is worth RM401/ha today. This is the land rent for a single harvest cycle. For a perpetual series of cycles, the value is of course higher; it turns out to be RM426/ha.[18]

Two implicit aspects of this calculation are worth highlighting for the sake of later discussions. First, rent is reduced if the rotation age is either too long or too short from an economic perspective. What is most important from this perspective is the percentage growth rate of timber compared to the discount rate. The former falls as the forest ages, thus decreasing the return from leaving timber in the forest to grow for another period. At some point, this biological rate of return falls below the rate of return on outside investments (the discount rate). The forest should be harvested before this point is reached, even if timber volume has not yet been maximized.[19]

Second, payments to labor and capital employed in sawmilling and other forms of processing—that is, the value added in processing—are not part of the value of the forest. In fact, at a given sawnwood price, an increase in value added reduces the value of the forest, which is determined residually. As long as labor and capital can be employed at the same wage in other industries, wood processing does not generate any additional economic surplus (resource rents plus value added) for the economy. If labor and capital are not fully employed, then policies to promote wood processing by, say, reducing the domestic price of wood, increase economic surplus only if the additional value added associated with labor and capital inputs that would otherwise be unemployed is greater than the loss of resource rent resulting from the reduction in stumpage value.

Figure 4.1 includes rent gradients for two land uses, agriculture (A_0, A_1) and forestry (F, F^*).[20] A rent gradient shows the relationship between rent and land quality. In each case, the gradient slopes downward: lower-quality land generates lower rents. The gradients for agriculture are higher than those for forestry on better land (e.g., lowland areas), but lower on poorer land (e.g., upland soils). Agriculture is economically superior to forestry in some, but not all, areas.

The two gradients for agriculture pertain to different stages of development. A_0 pertains to the earliest stage of development, when traditional subsistence agriculture dominates the sector. Assume for the moment that the relevant gradient for forestry is F, which includes only commercial timber values. Then the optimal area of land in cultivation is given by L_0, the point of intersection between A_0 and F.[21] All land up to L_0 generates a higher rent in agriculture than in forestry. Land of lower quality, however, generates a higher rent in forestry. Because A_0 is relatively low, most of the land in the region remains in forest.

The net returns to agriculture rise as it is transformed from a subsistence activity to a commercial venture. The agricultural gradient shifts outward, causing cultivated area to expand. Hence, deforestation occurs. But it is not necessarily the case that deforestation will proceed until no forest is left. With continued development, the economy diversifies into manufacturing and other nonagricultural sectors. This causes the opportunity cost of agricultural labor to rise, which reduces the outward shift of the gradient.[22] Ultimately, the gradient shifts only up to A_1, which implies an optimal, long-run cultivated area of L_1. At this point in development, deforestation ceases, forest area stabilizes, and the agricultural frontier is closed.

The total area of forest lost due to agricultural expansion is given by L_0-L_1. The economic cost of deforestation is the lost rent from timber production, which is given by the area between L_0 and L_1 and under F. But the economic benefit of deforestation—the rents from agricultural production, the area between L_0 and L_1 and under A_1—is even greater. The region is better off having converted L_0-L_1 hectares of forest to agriculture. Deforestation is "good," as long as it proceeds no further than L_1.

This exposition implies that deforestation bears an inverted U-shaped relationship with development, rising early on and falling later.[23] This relationship is in fact what industrialized portions of the world like North America and Europe have experienced (Clawson 1979; World Resources Institute 1992, p. 294). Several empirical studies have investigated whether this relationship also holds in developing countries, using per capita GDP as the measure of development. The findings have been mixed. Several of the studies analyzed cross-country data at the national level. The first such study, by Allen and Barnes (1985), failed to find evidence of a statistically significant relationship between deforestation and per capita GDP, as did later, more statistically rigorous studies by Shafik and Bandyopadhyay (1992) and Cropper and Griffiths (1994).[24] On the other hand, Rudel (1989) and Bilsborrow and Geores (1991) found that higher per capita GDP was generally associated with higher deforestation rates. Panayotou and Sungsuwan (1989) obtained the opposite result when they analyzed data at the provincial level in Thailand: higher per capita GDP was associated with less deforestation. For cross sections of both developing countries alone and developed as well as developing countries, Panayotou (1993, 1995) found that the inverted U-shaped relationship did indeed hold, with turning points of US$823 in the former sample and US$1,200 in the latter. Based on these studies, support for the U-shaped hypothesis appears weak. However, this may simply reflect the fact that all studies other than Panayotou's restricted their samples to developing countries. The samples they analyzed simply may not have included countries beyond the turning point.

When forests yield values in addition to timber, or when agriculture generates off-site environmental damage (for example, from fertilizer or pesticide runoff), some of the deforestation that occurs up to L_1 is not economically justified. F^* is the forest gradient after adding nontimber values. Once these other values are taken into account, the optimal area of cleared land is only L^*. Ignoring nontimber values leads to excessive land conversion. As many nontimber values are not priced in markets (e.g., watershed protection services and biological diversity), the risk of excessive conversion is great. Similarly, the optimal area of cleared land would be even lower if the agricultural gradient were reduced to reflect off-site environmental damage caused by agriculture.

DEFORESTATION

The National Forest Policy

For decades the Forestry Department had been pressing for a federal forestry policy that would establish a truly permanent forest estate. State forestry directors had agreed on an Interim Forest Policy as far back as 1952 (Salleh 1972, Menon 1976). The core of the Interim Policy was the following objective (Menon 1976, p. 18):

To reserve permanently for the benefit of the present and future inhabitants of the country forest land sufficient
(i) to ensure the sound climatic and physical condition of the country, the safeguarding of water supplies and soil fertility, and the prevention of damage by flooding and erosion to rivers and padi and other agricultural land; such reserves are known as PROTECTIVE RESERVES,
(ii) for the supply in perpetuity at reasonable rates, of all forms of forest produce which can be economically produced within the country and required by the

people for agricultural, domestic and industrial purposes; such reserves are known as PRODUCTIVE RESERVES.

Hill forests were expected to comprise the former category, and lowland forests the latter (*Malayan Forester* 1970b, p. 124). The department was interested not simply in enhancing the security of existing forest reserves, but in increasing the area of productive reserves by about fifty percent through the incorporation of stateland forests (*Malayan Forester* 1960c). The federal government did not act on the Interim Policy after independence because, as the minister of agriculture and cooperatives explained to a meeting of state forest officers in November 1963, "it has to take into consideration other land development policies of the country" (A.M.b.Hj.M.S. 1963, p. 298).

The department next placed its hope in a national land-use planning exercise, which it expected would demonstrate forestry's superiority in much of the lowlands (*Malayan Forester* 1960b, 1960d). The government did indeed set up a Technical Sub-Committee on Land Capability Classification within the National Development Planning Committee in 1963 (Lee 1968), but the department's enthusiasm waned when it learned that the classification system would be based on soil quality (*Malayan Forester* 1964d, p. 296): "The conclusion is inescapable, that soil fertility will become the criterion of land-use in Malaya. . . . The corollary to this, unpalatable as it may be, is that a large portion of our present productive lowland forest estate may be surrendered to agriculture, and productive forestry will be confined largely to land unsuited to permanent agriculture—land unlikely to be carrying highly productive natural forest." The Land Capability Classification established five classes of land and recommended economically best uses for each (Lee and Panton 1971). Mining (mainly for tin) and agriculture were deemed more valuable in classes I to III, which comprised the better-quality land in the lowlands and on gentle slopes, while forestry was assigned to the poorest land, in classes IV and V. These two classes covered about 40 percent of the Peninsula, but they were largely restricted to inland freshwater swamps and upland areas, where there was almost no knowledge of forest management. Swamps were later reassigned to class III, leaving forestry with only the uplands (Salleh 1972). In short, the Land Capability Classification provided some assurance of a permanent forest base, but it did not include the forests the department valued most (*Malayan Forester* 1968c, 1978). On the contrary, the department viewed the Land Capability Classification as sanctioning the accelerated conversion of virgin forests (Abdul Ghaffar 1972, Salleh 1972).

The Land Capability Classification was essentially an application of the economic concepts in Figure 4.1. In assigning land uses to capability classes, it focused on the "added value due to the use of the land and did not consider secondary processing industries" (Salleh 1972, pp. 271–272). This was conceptually correct: land-use allocation was determined (in principle) by the magnitude of rents generated by alternative uses of the land, with the rents reflecting the net value of the land's products, whether they were used domestically or exported, or were consumed directly or further processed. According to the classification, forestry did not belong in classes I through III because it generated lower rents than competing uses, but it did belong in classes IV and V, where it generated higher rents. Numerous studies have determined that rubber and oil-palm plantations established during the 1960s and 1970s, including those established by FELDA, did indeed earn acceptable rates of return (Vincent and Yusuf 1993, Tables 6 and 7).

Both the rent-gradient concept and the conclusions it implied were difficult for the department to accept. It argued that agricultural development should occur first on lower-quality land, thus buying time for lowland forests (*Malayan Forester* 1968b). It felt that value added in processing, which was greater for forestry than for mining or agriculture at that time, should also be taken into account. Although the department did not say so explicitly, its statements reveal that it believed that rent was a less important economic criterion than previous investment. For example, it attempted to save regenerated forests from conversion by arguing, "If forests must make way for other forms of land-use, virgin forests should be cleared before regenerated forests, as the latter represents considerable investment in labour and funds which have yet to reach maturity" (*Malayan Forester* 1968b, p. 73). In truth, such investments were sunk costs that should have been ignored; the relevant issue was which type of forest, regenerated or virgin, would generate higher rents in the future, not which type had received the most investment in the past.

The Land Capability Classification was supported by the first comprehensive land use survey ever conducted in the Peninsula. The survey, which had a base year of 1966, was based on aerial photographs and land development records. Results were eventually published in Wong (1971). Although the primary purpose was to estimate agricultural areas, the survey did estimate areas of four forest-related land uses: 1) dryland forests, in both lowlands and uplands; 2) wetland grass and forest associations, which include unforested wetlands as well as mangrove and freshwater swamp forests; 3) scrub forests, which refer to land where more than half the area is covered by shrubs, bushes, and young or dwarf trees; and 4) shifting cultivation. Table 4.1 presents the estimates. According to these estimates, the Peninsula was 73 percent forested in 1966.

The survey's estimates were of limited value to the Forestry Department, which was concerned not only with the aggregate area of forest but also

Table 4.1   *Forested areas in Peninsular Malaysia, according to the 1966 land use survey (in thousands of hectares)*

Type of forest	Area
Dryland forests	7,870
Swamps, marshlands, and wetland forests	1,178
Scrub forests	595
Shifting cultivation	8
Total	9,651

Source: Wong (1971).

with its distribution by elevation and its quality in terms of timber stocks and timber-growing potential. With assistance from the United Nations Development Programme (UNDP) and FAO, the department conducted Forest Inventory I from 1969 to 1972 to generate this information. The inventory was based on both aerial photographs and field surveys, and it provided estimates as of the middle of 1972 (FAO/UNDP 1973). It classified most forests into two broad categories, virgin and logged-over; two additional special categories, mangrove forests and shifting cultivation, accounted for only a small portion of total area.[25] Forests in each of the two broad categories were further classified into dryland and inland swamp subcategories.[26] For the virgin category, dryland forests were also classified according to elevation (above or below 1,000 m) and timber potential (superior, good, moderate, poor). The 1,000-m boundary was chosen because it is approximately the highest elevation at which dipterocarps occur in abundance (Whitmore 1988).

Table 4.2 presents the estimates, as corrected and revised by Brown et al. (1991). The good news for the department was that more than two-thirds of the Peninsula's forests were still virgin. The bad news was that only two-fifths of the virgin forests were in the superior and good categories, which represented most of the lowland rain forests,[27] and that the amount in those two categories was not much larger than the area of forest, most of it originally superior or good, that had been logged but not (yet) converted since 1966. At this rate, the remaining superior and good forests would be logged over in about ten years. Compared to total area in the 1966 land use survey, 15 percent of total forest cover had been lost since 1966, implying an annual deforestation rate of 236,000 ha (hectares), or 2.6 percent. Deforestation was occurring in forest reserves as well as stateland forests. Salleh (1972) noted that some 115,000 ha of forest reserves were excised in 1970 alone.

With the introduction of the NEP, the Forestry Department toned down its public criticism of land development, but it continued to press for a national forestry policy that would protect remaining forest reserves. It gradually, and

Table 4.2 *Forested areas in Peninsular Malaysia, according to Forest Inventories I and II (in thousands of hectares)*

Forest type	Forest Inventory I (1972)	Forest Inventory II (1981)
I. Virgin	4743	3564
A. Dryland	4285	3284
1. Below 1,000 m	4001	3003
a. Superior	845	683
b. Good	1160	916
c. Moderate	1572	1143
d. Poor	424	261
2. Above 1,000 m	284	281
B. Freshwater swamp	458	280
II. Logged-over	3175	3042
A. Dryland	2846	2727
1. Logged before 1966	1615	481
2. Logged after 1966	1231	2246
B. Freshwater swamp	329	315
1. Logged before 1966	152	39
2. Logged after 1966	177	276
III. Shifting cultivation	317	216
IV. Mangrove	155	121
V. Total	8233	6822

Source: Brown et al. (1991).

reluctantly, became resigned that the bulk of such Reserves would ultimately be in the hills (*Malayan Forester* 1970b). In 1971, armed with preliminary results from Forest Inventory I, it began preparing a detailed proposal for a permanent forest estate (Salleh 1972). The proposal called for an area that included not only forests in land capability classes IV and V but also additional forests in better classes.

The federal government took a significant step toward legitimizing the proposal by establishing, in the same year, the National Forestry Council. The council was a high-level forum for discussions on the planning, management, and development of the country's forest resources. It was chaired by the deputy prime minister and included the political leaders of all states (*menteri-menteri besar* and *ketua menteri-menteri*); the federal ministers of finance, trade and industry, primary industries, land development and federal territory, agriculture and rural development, and science, technology, and environment; the attorney general; the director-general of the Forestry Department; and the conservators of forests in Sabah and Sarawak (Menon 1976). The department's proposal provided the basis for discussions in the council about the make-up of the permanent forest estate, and states' willingness to contribute land to it. The council met four times during 1971–77, reaching agreement on final wording of the policy at the fourth meeting, held August 29, 1977. The National Forest Policy was endorsed by the National Land Council on April 10th, 1978 (*Malayan Forester* 1980).

First among several objectives listed in the policy was the following, which was virtually identical to the statement of the core objective of the Interim Policy (source):

1. To dedicate as Permanent Forest Estate sufficient areas of land strategically located throughout the country, in accordance with the concept of rational land use, in order to ensure:
(i)   the sound climatic and physical condition of the country, the safe-guarding of water supplies, soil fertility and environmental quality and the minimization of damage by floods and erosion to rivers and agricultural land; such forest lands being known as: PROTECTIVE FORESTS;
(ii)   the supply in perpetuity of reasonable rates of all forms of forest produce which can be economically produced within the country and are required for agricultural, domestic and industrial purposes, and for export; such forest lands being known as: PRODUCTIVE FORESTS;
(iii) the conservation of adequate forest areas for recreation, education, research and the protection of the country's unique flora and fauna; such forest lands being known as: AMENITY FORESTS.

The policy was a well-crafted document, but it was weak on specifics of how this objective would be achieved. It stated that "A Permanent Forest Estate of sufficient acreage must be determined and its security of tenure assured," but it set no timetables for establishing it and no penalties if states delayed. It offered little assurance with regard to the security of tenure over productive forests. Although it stated that "Protective Forests should never be alienated, save in the most exceptional circumstances and after the most careful objective study," it contained no similar statement for the more fertile, timber-rich productive forests. The Department had hoped that a policy in Selangor, that "an area taken away from a forest reserve [ought] to be replaced by an equal area elsewhere with little or no agricultural or mineral potential" (*Malayan Forester* 1965c, p. 263), would be included in the policy (Salleh 1972), but the states did not accept this either. In the end, the Policy enhanced the permanence of forest areas only in terms of the following distinction, which was accepted in discussions during the fourth council meeting but not stated explicitly in the policy: "Forest Reserves are managed and financed by the State Governments and they can withdraw those areas for other purposes without negotiating with the Federal Government. Regarding the PFE, State Governments should discuss with the Federal Government before issuing any license." In effect, states agreed—though not in writing—merely to consult with the federal government before degazetting areas they had contributed to the Permanent Forest Estate. They did not agree to pay any expense related to establishing the estate. The policy stated, "The Federal Government with contributions from the private sector shall bear all the costs for the development of Permanent Forest Estate."

The weaknesses of the policy were soon demonstrated. Addressing the fifth council meeting, held December 7, 1981, the deputy prime minister stated, "Although the Council accepted and agreed in 1977 to establish a 12.8 million hectare [*sic*; should be acre] PFE in Peninsular Malaysia, several State Governments have breached the agreement within that short span of time and as a result about 700,000 hectares of PFE has [*sic*] been converted for agriculture." At the end of the same year, the department completed Forest Inventory II, which was not published until 1987 (Ibu Pejabat Perhutanan, Semenanjung Malaysia, 1987). Results are shown in Table 4.2. In absolute terms, the deforestation rate since Forest Inventory I, 141,000 ha/yr, was substantially lower than the rate between that inventory and the 1966 land use survey, but it was not much lower in relative terms, 1.9 percent/yr. The percentage rate was much higher than the average rate for Asia in the late 1970s, 0.6 percent per year, according to estimates reported in FAO/UNEP (1981).

A third land use survey was also completed in 1981 (see discussion in Vincent and Yusuf 1993). It updated estimates of agricultural areas from the first survey in 1966 and a second one in 1974–75 (EPU 1980). Total agricultural areas in 1974–75 and 1981 were 3,565,000 ha and 4,101,000 ha, respectively, implying an annual rate of agricultural conversion of 77,000 ha. This is far below the rate of deforestation implied by the forest inventories. The discrepancy would appear to confirm complaints by the Forestry Department that the states were "dereserving large areas of Forest Reserves . . . under the pretext and noble cause of Rural Development," when their actual purpose was the clear-felling of timber (*Malayan Forester* 1970d, p. 281). Although logging supervised by the Forestry Department did not ordinarily result in deforestation (there was some residual tree cover), conversion fellings, which were much more intensive, did. The department charged that "Forests reserved for growing of timber have been de-gazetted, denuded and reverted to forestry!" (*Malayan Forester* 1971b, p. 163). Similarly, Lee (1978, p. 406) claimed, "There had been obvious cases of abuse in that the recipients of alienated land were more interested in removing the timber on the land rather than in its subsequent development," and he supported this claim with data showing that only 58 percent of the land designated for agriculture from 1961 to 1970 was actually developed. This percentage is almost identical to the ratio of agricultural expansion during 1974–81 (from the land use surveys) to deforestation during 1972–81 (from the forest inventories).

The policy was bound to be ineffective in protecting remaining forests as long as it was not backed up by legislation. The legal basis for forestry rules and regulations were various state-level forest enactments and rules, which had been enacted as far back as 1909 in Melaka and Pulau Pinang and the 1930s in the other Peninsular states (*Malayan Forester* 1983). In 1972, with UNDP/FAO funding, the department obtained the services of a legal consultant to review the existing enactments and to propose a "uniform forestry act" (*Malayan Forester* 1983). The National Forestry Council addressed the issue during its fourth meeting in 1977, requesting "that the existing Forest Enactments in the States of Peninsular Malaysia be reviewed, updated and uniformised in order to streamline forest administration and forestry sector development in the country" (*Malayan Forester* 1983, p. 286). Key among the provisions requested by the Forestry Department was the following "no net loss" policy, which, as noted above, it had failed to get included in the National Forest Policy (*Malayan Forester* 1983, pp. 287–88): "Where Permanent Forest Reserves are excised, replacement of such excised land should be undertaken immediately as far as possible taking into consideration the need for sustained yield and environmental factors." The council discussed the draft National Forestry Act further at the fifth through seventh meetings (1981–84), finally reaching agreement at the seventh meeting. The act was sent to Parliament, which passed it on October 17, 1984. By the ninth council meeting on August 20, 1987, the act had been gazetted as state law, a requirement for it to come into force (under section 1 of the Act), by all states in the Peninsula except Perlis, which followed suit soon thereafter.[28]

The act was wide ranging, filling nearly eighty pages. Chapter 1, part III simplified the process for adding forests to the Permanent Forest Estate, a change that the Forestry Department had recommended to accelerate the formation of the estate (*Malayan Forester* 1983). That chapter also included the following sections, however:

11. The State Authority, if satisfied that any land in a permanent reserved forest—

(*a*) is no longer required for the purpose for which it was classified . . . ; and

(*b*) is required for economic use higher than that for which it is being utilised,
     may excise such land from the permanent reserved forest.

12. Where any land is excised under section 11 the State Authority shall, wherever possible and if it is satisfied that it is in the national interest to do so having regard to—

(*a*) the need for soil and water conservation and other environmental consideration;

(*b*) the need to sustain timber production in the State in order to meet the requirements of the forest industry;

(c) the economic development of the State; and

(*d*) the availability of suitable land,
   constitute . . . an approximately equal area of land as permanent reserved forest.

Although section 12 endorsed the replacement ("no net loss") principle, it heavily qualified it. Replacement need not be immediate and was not automatic; rather, the burden was implicitly on the federal government ("the national interest") to convince the states that, on the basis of one of the four grounds listed, replacement should occur. Under section 11, states clearly retained unilateral authority to excise land from the Permanent Forest Estate for development. Note that consultation with the federal government is not mentioned. Item 11(*b*) can be read as an endorsement of the Land Capability Classification and its ranking of mining and agriculture ahead of forestry as "highest and best" uses. From the standpoint of enhancing the security of Forest Reserves, the act represented little progress beyond the policy.

On the positive side, Table 4.3 shows that as of December 31, 1991, the states had contributed 4,413,000 ha to the Permanent Forest Estate (Kementerian Perusahaan Utama 1992). About three-fifths of the area was classified as Productive Forests, most of it hill forest. Another 313,000 ha was in the process of being added. Although the estate's tenure was not very secure, and its area was 10 percent below what the states had proposed at the end of 1978, at least it had been constituted.

Deforestation at the end of the 1980s

States surrendered no real authority in agreeing to the National Forest Policy and the National Forestry Act. Hence, deforestation in the 1980s continued to be driven by perceived returns to agricultural expansion, with the Forestry Department's efforts to prevent conversion providing only minor resistance. If there was a reasonable request to alienate forests for some form of development, the states generally granted it.

The actual amount of forest cover remaining in the early 1990s was un-

Table 4.3   *Area of the Permanent Forest Estate in Peninsular Malaysia (in thousands of hectares)*

Date	Existing	Proposed additions	Proposed excisions	Proposed total
December 1978	3,117	2,655	432	5,340
December 1985	3,277	1,830	3	5,104
December 1988	4,490	447	8	4,929
December 1991	4,413	313	0	4,726

Sources: Unit Ekonomi, Ibu Pejabat Perhutanan (n.d.(a), n.d.(b), n.d.(c)); Kementerian Perusahaan Utama (1992).

known at the time of writing, as Forest Inventory III was still underway. But there was evidence by the late 1980s that the rate of conversion was slowing, as industrialization and urbanization caused the rural labor market to tighten and agricultural returns to fall. Most striking was a statement in the *Sixth Malaysia Plan 1991–1995* (p. 117) that, except for projects in progress, FELDA would develop no additional land during the period covered by the *Plan*. The decline in conversion is consistent with the exposition in the section *Basic concepts in forest economics*, which portrayed the rate of deforestation as rising in the early stages of economic development and falling later. It was noted in that section, however, that previous studies have generally not found support for this relationship in developing countries. It is therefore worth investigating the situation in Peninsular Malaysia more carefully, to determine whether the decline in deforestation in the late 1980s signaled a permanent change or just a temporary pause, perhaps analogous to the slowdown after the first third of the century (Vincent and Yusuf 1993).

The data from Forest Inventories I and II make it possible to test formally whether the loss in forest cover from the early 1970s to the early 1980s followed an inverted U-shaped relationship. The analysis amounted to regressing district-level data for the percentage change in forest cover (the negative of the deforestation rate) upon variables related to income and other likely explanatory factors, such as those related to population.[29] Vincent and Yusuf (1991) found that population provided a statistically significant explanation for the expansion of aggregate agricultural area in Peninsular Malaysia from 1904 to 1988. First, we used a geographic information system (GIS)[30] to calculate forest areas at the district level for each inventory.[31] Then, we calculated the average annual percentage change in forest area between inventories.[32] These district-level rates of change were the dependent variables in the regressions. Because there were just two forest inventories, there was just one observation per district.

The explanatory variables included, among others, population density and income at the beginning of the time period. We calculated population density at the district level. For income, we used estimates of monthly per capita income for the state where the district was located. The estimates were drawn from the Economic Planning Unit's occasional household income surveys, which provide more accurate estimates of household income than does per capita GDP, and were in Malaysian ringgit, at 1978 price levels.[33] Because we analyzed changes in forest areas, we also included the average annual percentage changes in population density[34] and income during the period. That is, we expected that not only the levels of population and income but also their growth rates could affect deforestation rates.[35]

There are also significant inherent differences between districts that might be expected to affect deforestation rates. The most important are probably the amount of land covered by forest—obviously, districts that are completely deforested can experience no further deforestation—and the amount of land suitable for agricultural development. We therefore included as explanatory variables the proportion of the district covered by forest at the beginning of the period and the proportion of the state classified in land capability classes II and III (from data in Wong 1971).[36]

Appendix 4 provides further details, including regression results. The analysis failed to find evidence that the rate of change in forest cover was significantly related to population density, population growth, rate of change in income, or land capability, but it did find that the rate was significantly related to the level of per capita income. The relationship with income had the hypothesized form, and it is plotted in Figure 4.2.[37] Note that the variables

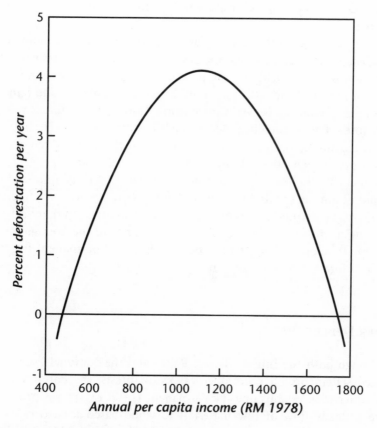

Figure 4.2   Deforestation rate versus per capita income

have been redefined so that the figure shows the rate of deforestation (not the rate of change in forest cover, of which it is the negative) and annual (not monthly) per capita income. The relationship predicts that the rate of deforestation increased as annual per capita income rose to about RM1,100 (1978 price levels), and declined thereafter. The maximum value, just above 4 percent per year, is plausible in view of the aggregate rate of 1.9 percent per year between the inventories: one would expect some districts to have rates higher than 1.9 percent, and others lower.

According to the 1970 Household Income Survey, annual per capita income exceeded RM1,100 in only one state in Peninsular Malaysia, Selangor (which then included Kuala Lumpur). The relationship therefore predicts, correctly, that deforestation was accelerating in the Peninsula at the start of the 1970s. By the time of the 1987 survey, however, per capita income exceeded RM1,100 in all states. The deforestation rate should have been declining throughout the Peninsula at the end of the 1980s. This is consistent with the observed decline in agricultural expansion by public agencies, and with FELDA's declaration that it would develop no new land anywhere in the Peninsula.

These results suggest that Peninsular Malaysia's forest area is indeed on the way to being stabilized by economic development. This is consistent with an observation by Brookfield (1994b, p. 93), that: "What seems unmistakably clear . . . is that the 'gold rush' period in the use of the former and remaining forests of the Peninsula is over. Conversion of forest to agriculture will cease even before it has reached its potential high-cost limits. . . ."[38] He continued, "For the remaining forests themselves, though the threat is not removed, it is less in the early 1990s than at any time in the past 30 years" (p. 94). Judging from data in World Resources Institute (1992, Table 19.1), Peninsular Malaysia could be among the first regions in the tropics to reduce its deforestation rate to zero. This would be a remarkable achievement, given that its deforestation rate in the late 1970s was so much higher than the average for Asia. Economic development appears to be delivering the permanent forest area that direct forestry policies could not.

TIMBER DEPLETION

Although both the Interim Forest Policy and the National Forest Policy included statements on nontimber values of forests, the Forestry Department's interest in establishing the Permanent Forest Estate was primarily to ensure a steady flow of raw materials to wood-based industries, both to maintain self-sufficiency and to generate export earnings (*Malayan Forester*

1959, 1967a, 1970d; Setten 1962; *Malayan Forester* 1978). The number of both sawmills and plywood/veneer mills had increased significantly in the 1960s. The department feared that further investment in processing capacity would not be forthcoming, and existing capacity would collapse, if it could not guarantee long-run wood supply (Malayan Forester 1968c).

In 1968, in the midst of the timber boom, the Forestry Department and FAO launched the Forest Industries Development project. This project conducted a comprehensive forest-sector analysis, examining in detail current and future timber supply and demand. Even at a preliminary stage, it was able to conclude that "the existing industrial capacity in the primary wood processing sector [sawmills and plywood/veneer mills] is well above the optimum in relation to available wood resources" (*Malayan Forester* 1970c, p. 201). Over the next two decades, the Forestry Department attempted to bring long-term timber supply in line with processing capacity through efforts on both the supply and demand sides.

Timber concession policies

On the supply side, the Forestry Department's chief efforts were to stabilize the timberland base by getting the National Forest Policy and National Forestry Act accepted and the Permanent Forest Estate established. The department was nearly as concerned, however, with the rate of logging in forest reserves and stateland forests. Under its policy of sustained yield, it aimed at producing a more or less constant flow of timber. It feared that, even if it succeeded in establishing the Permanent Forest Estate, the high harvests during the 1960s could not be sustained, and timber production would inevitably decrease in once the stateland forests had all been converted.

Even at the start of the 1960s, the Department had a rational plan for making a smooth transition from the drawdown of virgin timber stocks in stateland forests and forest reserves to ultimate dependence on sustained-yield harvesting of second-growth, lowland forests in forest reserves. First, it expected that the management of second-growth forests would boost yields, thus raising production in the long run. Under the MUS, it expected to raise yields by up to four times (*Malayan Forester* 1962c). Second, and in the near term, it hoped to "conserve the economic timber on the State Lands for as long as possible in order to supplement an expected temporary deficiency of timber before the considerably richer new crop on the permanent forest estate materialises. . ." (*Malayan Forester* 1960a, p. 1). In other words, it expected to shift timber production in Forest Reserves gradually from less productive, virgin lowland forests to more productive, second-growth lowland forests, using virgin Stateland Forests to fill any shortfall that occurred before the second-growth forests were mature (*Malayan Forester* 1972c).

As mentioned at the beginning of this chapter, at the start of the 1960s the department based the annual allowable coupe on one-seventieth of forest area. Due to regeneration difficulties and rising management costs, the MUS was modified in the mid-1960s (Ismail 1966), with the rotation length reduced to sixty years (Tang 1987). Then, in the late 1970s, a new management system was introduced for hill forests, the Selective Management System (SMS; see Mok 1977, Thang 1986, 1987). Whereas the MUS relied on seedlings for regeneration and consequently created a stand with trees of more or less the same age, the SMS relied on mid-sized trees for the next harvest and intended to create a stand with two age classes.[39] The rotation age (age to maturity) was the same as that under the modified MUS, but the stand was harvested every thirty years due to the staggering of the age classes. In the 1980s, the rotation for the modified MUS was reduced further, to fifty-five years. The Forestry Department's transition plan therefore involved a weighting of annual coupes based on one-fifty-fifth of the area managed under the modified MUS and one-thirtieth of the area managed under the SMS, with allowance made for the conversion of stateland forests.

The transition plan hinged on the states' willingness: 1) to adopt a gradual approach to conversion of stateland forests; 2) to refrain from logging stateland forests when they had no intention of developing the land; and 3) to harvest forest reserves according to the annual allowable coupe prescribed by the department (*Malayan Forester* 1978). The difficulty was that the Forestry Department had no authority to compel the states to do these things, given the states' constitutional rights. The National Forest Act affirmed these rights, stating that it is the "State Authority" that has the power to grant timber concessions in "any permanent reserved forest or State Land" (section 19).[40] In practice, the "State Authority" is the State Executive Committee, and it faces few restrictions in allocating concessions. For example, it is under no obligation to allocate them on a competitive basis (Kumar 1986).

The reduction in forest area implied by the data in Tables 4.1 and 4.2 indicate that the states did not follow a gradual approach to land conversion, while the Forestry Department claims cited in the section *The National Forest Policy* indicate that the states allowed conversion fellings in situations other than when land development was actually intended. On the issue of compliance with the annual allowable coupe, Kumar (1986, pp. 84–85) stated that "the rate of farming out concessions, although decided by annual allowable cuts . . . is in practice determined by other considerations." This was the case even though the coupes were discussed and accepted by the National Forestry Council. At the ninth National Forestry Council meeting, held August 20,

1987, the Forestry Department reported, positively, that 72,749 ha of the Permanent Forest Estate were logged annually from 1981 to 1985, compared to an annual allowable coupe of 74,869 ha for that period. It also reported, however, that 130,316 ha of stateland forests were logged annually, compared to an annual allowable coupe of 101,175 ha. The overall annual allowable coupe was therefore exceeded by 15 percent.

Overharvesting worsened at the end of the 1980s. At the ninth meeting, the council also agreed on state-by-state annual allowable coupes for 1986–90 totaling 71,000 ha per year for the Permanent Forest Estate and 80,940 ha per year for stateland forests. At the tenth council meeting, held April 4, 1991, the department reported that the actual areas logged (through the middle of 1990) were 121,044 ha per year and 96,651 ha per year, respectively. The overall annual allowable coupe was thus exceeded by 43 percent, with the excess in the Permanent Forest Estate being 70 percent. The council set the annual allowable coupe in the Permanent Forest Estate even lower for 1991–95, at 52,250 ha. At the time of writing, statistical information was not available on whether logging stayed within this limit, but newspapers reported that coupes were exceeded by substantial amounts in some states (Shamsul 1992).

Since the 1960s, the Forestry Department's standard explanation for over-logging was that state governments were excessively interested in revenue from logging (*Malayan Forester* 1969a, 1969b, 1970d, 1971b). States had the sole authority to levy fees on timber, a right affirmed by section 61 of the National Forestry Act.[41] The most important fees were royalties assessed on extracted volume, but there were also area-based fees, or premiums. Auctioning of concession rights was rare, except for conversion fellings in stateland forests. Data in Umikalsum (1991) indicate that timber fees did indeed account for much of state revenue in timber-rich states like Kelantan, Pahang, and Terengganu.[42]

The value of timber concessions increased substantially during the 1970s and 1980s, as more species and smaller-diameter logs became marketable and, in the second half of the 1970s, prices reached record high levels for species that were already marketable. In 1970, over 90 percent of the harvest came from species regarded as well known (i.e., ones named in the Forestry Department's statistics). By 1980, the same species accounted for barely three-fourths of the harvest; by 1990, barely half (Kementerian Perusahaan Utama 1992). Minimum commercial log diameters fell from above 45 cm in the 1960s to below 30 cm in the early 1990s.[43] The real price of red meranti (*Shorea spp.*), the flagship timber of the Peninsula, nearly doubled between 1974 and 1979.

The increase in value boosted the returns to granting concessions. Estimates of rent capture presented in Table 2.1 indicate, however, that the returns were not captured primarily by state treasuries. Because timber fees were administratively determined, and concessions were seldom auctioned, there was no market mechanism to link fees to stumpage values.[44] The discrepancy between fees and stumpage values widened over time. For example, in real terms (1978 prices), royalties on red meranti in Pahang, the major log-producing state in the Peninsula, were only RM7/m^3 in 1978, RM12/m^3 in 1985, and RM11/m^3 in 1989. These values were tiny compared to real log price, which was RM100–200/m^3 during those years. The difference, which ranged from a low of RM116/m^3 in 1985 to a high of RM135/m^3 in 1989, cannot be explained by logging costs, which apparently (based on limited evidence) were constant at about RM44/m^3 during the period (Unit Ekonomi, Ibu Pejabat Perhutanan, n.d.(b), n.d.(c)).[45] Subtracting the estimated logging cost from log prices yields estimated stumpage values of RM124/m^3 in 1978, RM84/m^3 in 1985, and RM135/m^3 in 1989, many times larger than the royalties.

If not captured by state treasuries, the rents must have been captured by other parties involved in the concession system. Not surprisingly, documentation on the identity of those parties is hard to come by, although Teo (1966) and Sulaiman (1977) remarked on the unusually high profit margins in the timber industry. Kumar (1986, p. 86) implied that the rents were captured by both concessionaires and those who granted concessions, as part of state-level political patronage systems: "As the [concession] allocation committee usually meets in closed sessions to consider tenders or applications, it is well placed to bring in political considerations in alienating state land to private individuals or companies. Besides favouring party supporters, this system would appear to make it easy for the party in power to manoeuvre concessions to advantage, especially near an election." Journalistic accounts have included similar statements (*The Star* 1991, *New Straits Times* 1993a, 1993b; Azam 1993a, 1993b; Bernama 1993; Shamsul 1993a, 1993b). Reports of involvement by the royal families were a *cause célèbre* in newspapers in the early 1990s and were used by the federal government to gain public support for its efforts to restrict the power of the royalty (*New Straits Times* 1993c; Hisham 1992, Hisham and Shamsul 1992, Jasin 1992, Juhaidi 1992, Kathirasen 1992).

It is tempting to draw a causal link between the low rate of government rent capture and the rapid rate of logging; indeed, this is the thesis of a major cross-country study on tropical forest management (Repetto and Gillis 1988). But as Paris and Ruzicka (1991), Hyde and Sedjo (1992), Vincent and Binkley (1992), Vincent (1992, 1993), and others have pointed out, this is an incomplete explanation. If a concessionaire captures most of the rent, but expects the rent to be even higher in the future, then he might be expected to delay harvesting. That is, windfall profits do not preclude forward-looking behavior by the concessionaire. What *can* preclude such behavior is insecure concession tenure. States ordinarily granted concessions with a duration of no more than a few years. In effect, concessions were just harvesting licenses (Kumar 1986), with the State Forestry Offices responsible for postlogging management activities. Concessionaires did not have any real option to determine whether to harvest in the present period or to delay. They either harvested the timber in the concession before the end of their (short) contracts, or they lost it. They also had little incentive to minimize damage to the residual stand, as they had no reason to expect they would receive the same concession again when it was due for a second harvest in several decades. Hence, it is not surprising that rates of logging damage were high, with consequent negative impacts on regeneration (for a review, see Appanah and Weinland 1990). The impact of the short length of concessions on concessionaires' time horizons had been noted in the 1950s and 1960s (*Malayan Forester* 1959, 1963b), but the department felt that forestry time horizons were inherently so long that one could not expect the private sector to be interested in more than "direct timber utilization" (*Malayan Forester* 1960b, p. 81).

Where it was present, political patronage introduced an element of uncertainty, which shortened time horizons even more. This resulted not so much from the threat of existing concession contracts being canceled as from uncertainty related to renewal when existing contracts expired. The low rate of government rent capture does indeed provide a plausible explanation for the rapid logging, once it is combined with insecure tenure caused by short and uncertain concession contracts. It is not surprising that logged area exceeded the annual allowable coupe by so much in the late 1980s, when log prices, and therefore windfall profits, rose sharply.

At its fifth meeting, held December 7, 1981, the National Forestry Council requested that the Treasury study the possibility of compensating state governments for the revenue they would lose if they reduced their harvests. At the sixth meeting, held November 27, 1982, it was reported that the Treasury was still studying the idea. In light of the estimated low rates of rent capture shown in Table 2.1, the need for compensation was dubious. States could have reduced their harvests by several times and still collected the same amount of revenue, if only they had captured more of the available rent. The existence of a political patronage system would seem to provide the most plausible explanation for their failure to do so.

In sum, as in the case of deforestation, state-level interests drove timber depletion during the 1970s and 1980s. In the case of deforestation, the interests pertained to returns to land development; in the case of timber depletion, to revenue for the state treasuries and windfall profits for those who captured the remaining rents. By the end of the 1980s, the deforestation situation

looked fairly positive, thanks to economic changes that diminished the returns to agriculture. No such positive outcome was in sight for timber harvests. Indeed, recorded harvests were at historically high levels at the end of
the 1980s, and there was concern that illegal logging was on the rise. Illegal
logging was a major issue discussed at the tenth National Forestry Council
meeting, and it attracted substantial press attention in the early 1990s
(Choong and Kuttan 1992, Khairun 1992, Krishnamoorthy et al. 1993,
Ramayah 1993, Ramayah and Sarifuddin 1993, Sabry and Sufi 1993, Shamsul
1993a, Vijiyan 1993). The National Forestry Act was amended in 1993 to
strengthen the government's enforcement capabilities with regard to this
problem (*Mid-Term Review of the Sixth Malaysia Plan 1991–1995*, p. 84).

From an economic perspective, however, the situation may not have been
as bad as the discrepancy between logged area and annual allowable coupes
suggests. The Forestry Department apparently never considered two basic
questions during the 1970s and 1980s: was the 55- to 60-year rotation age, the
basis of the annual allowable coupe calculation, the age that maximized land
rent, and was compliance with annual allowable coupes based on that rotation
in the states' long-run financial interest? The answer to the first question was
site specific to a large degree, but it can be answered for the average forest by
analyzing data published by the Forestry Department. Strictly speaking, the
analysis in the following paragraphs is for an even-aged silvicultural system
like the MUS, not a dual age-class system like the SMS. But even in the latter
case a rotation age for individual age classes must be determined, so the
results have implications for the SMS as well as the MUS.

Department growth and yield studies indicated that the average annual
growth rates for marketable species were 2.2 m^3/ha/yr in volume terms and
0.80 cm/yr in diameter terms (Thang 1986, 1987).[46] Timber growth is generally thought to be a logistic (S-shaped) function of age. A function that has a
logistic shape and yields a maximum average annual growth rate of 2.2
m^3/ha/yr at age 60 is: $132 \times e^{(1-60/Age)}$. This function predicts the gross volume
of timber in the forest at any age. Net volume is 70 percent of gross volume
for trees with a diameter of at least 60 cm (which would be a seventy-five-
year-old tree at a growth increment of 0.80 cm/yr), and 60 percent for trees
with a diameter below 60 cm (Thang 1986, 1987).

To convert from physical to monetary terms, we need information on log
prices, logging costs, and the discount rate. From the forestry accounts in
Chapter 2 (see Appendix 2.2), the average log price in Peninsular Malaysia for
full-sized logs (logs with a diameter of at least 55 cm, i.e., a sixty-nine-year-old
tree[47]) was constant in real terms from 1970 to 1990, at RM115/m^3 (1978 price
levels). Logs of smaller diameters sold at a discount, which ranged from 97.5
percent of the full price for logs with a diameter of at least 50 cm but less than

55 cm, 85 percent for logs with a diameter of at least 45 cm but less than 50 cm, 70 percent for logs with a diameter of at least 30 cm but less than 45 cm, and 50 percent for logs with a diameter of at least 15 cm (the minimum commercial log diameter) but less than 30 cm.[48] The average logging cost was also constant in real terms, at RM45/m³. We used two discount rates, 4 percent (the approximate real return on fixed accounts in Malaysia) and 10 percent (the rate used by international financial institutions like the World Bank). With this information, we were able to calculate net present values (NPVs) for various rotation ages, for both the single-rotation and infinite-rotations cases (see the example in the section *Basic concepts in forest economics*). The NPVs are biased upward, as we ignored all costs associated with managing and protecting the forest.

Table 4.4 shows the results. The second column shows gross timber volume for ages ranging from 0 to 100 years, by 5-year increments. The third and fourth columns show NPVs at the 4 percent discount rate. For both the single-rotation and infinite-rotations cases, the highest NPV is at a rotation age of 65 years. This is very close to the modified MUS/SMS rotation ages. But

Table 4.4 *Determination of optimal rotation age*

Age	Gross timber volume	NPV^a at 4% discount rate		NPV at 10% discount rate	
		1 rotation	Infinite rotations	1 rotation	Infinite rotations
Years	m³	RM(1978)/ha		RM(1978)/ha	
0	0.0	0	0	0	0
5	0.0	0	0	0	0
10	0.9	−16	−50	−9	−15
15	6.6	−99	−222	−42	−56
20	17.9	61	112	20	23
25	32.6	92	147	23	25
30	48.6	112	162	21	22
35	64.6	123	165	17	18
40	80.1	355	449	38	39
45	94.6	345	416	28	28
50	108.1	324	377	20	20
55	120.5	297	336	14	14
60	132.0	397	439	14	14
65	142.6	449	487	12	12
70	152.3	411	439	8	8
75	161.2	417	440	6	6
80	169.5	360	377	4	4
85	177.1	310	321	3	3
90	184.2	265	273	2	2
95	190.8	225	231	1	1
100	196.9	191	195	1	1

[a] NPV—net present value.

at a discount rate of 10 percent, the optimal rotation age is just 40 years in both cases. The selection of the rotation age therefore turns on the choice of the discount rate. In a study commissioned by the Economic Planning Unit, Veitch (1986) estimated that the discount rate in Malaysia was 13 percent in 1984, and 8 percent in the late 1970s. Hence, the 10 percent discount rate seems more justified. The implication is that a 55–60 year rotation was financially justified in Peninsular Malaysia in the 1970s and 1980s only at unrealistically low discount rates. This is consistent with a study by Mohd. Shahwahid (1985a), which determined that virtually all timber groups in a concession compartment in the Bukit Bertangga Forest Reserve reached financial maturity at much smaller diameters (hence, at younger ages) than the minimum-diameter cutting limits prescribed by the SMS. The period between harvests in both the modified MUS and the SMS was too long; it should have been about two-thirds as long (i.e., a rotation of 40 years for the modified MUS and a cutting cycle of 20 years for the SMS).[49] Had the department prescribed a shorter rotation, it would have produced less wood per hectare, but a greater value. A shorter rotation would also have justified a larger coupe, which suggests that the overlogging problem was in part artificial.[50]

Even at the optimal rotations, and even with the upward bias noted earlier, land rents are extremely low. The highest is only RM487/ha (1978 price levels), and that is at the (unrealistically) low 4 percent discount rate. These low values suggest that the Land Capability Classification's ranking of forestry below mining and agriculture was correct, at least in financial terms. The validity of this conclusion is reinforced if, in practice, growth increments and stocking levels are not as high as the studies by the department suggest. Several Malaysian silviculturists have indeed expressed concerns about these matters (see Appanah and Weinland 1990, Tang 1987, Tang and Wan Razali 1981, Wan Razali 1989, and Wyatt-Smith 1988).

Turning to the second question, trends in stumpage values suggest that states were financially justified in harvesting their virgin forests so rapidly. The financial return to delaying harvest in a virgin forest comes from only one source, the stumpage value, as virgin forests by definition show no net growth in timber volume. Although the stumpage value of red meranti increased in real terms during some intervals from 1970 to 1990,[51] it did not increase during the period as a whole; nor did the average stumpage value estimated for the forestry accounts in Chapter 2 (see Appendix 2.2). Hence, the states did not face an opportunity to earn a higher return simply by delaying harvest. From the narrow perspective of financial returns on timber, the rapid harvests made sense.

Whether the states used the revenue they collected in a way that promoted sustainable development is, however, another issue. In Chapter 2 it was pointed out that public sector investment in Sabah and Sarawak was much lower than the revenue the states collected from natural resources. Although the data are less complete for the Peninsular states, the same appears to be true for them (Umikalsum 1991). Moreover, to the extent that windfall rents were captured by individuals in a political patronage system, any benefits derived from their use were not distributed very widely among the populations of the states.

Promotion of domestic processing

On the demand side, the Forestry Department advocated two policies: the restriction of log exports and the promotion of integrated timber complexes (ITCs). Both were intended to maximize the value added from domestic processing, on the theory that this would reduce the economic impacts of timber scarcity. Log export restrictions reserved a high proportion of the timber harvest for domestic mills, which seemed to make sense in light of the Forest Industries Development project's finding of excess capacity relative to available timber supply. ITCs were public enterprises that included a set of primary and secondary processing facilities linked to a large, long-term concession. They were expected to lead the wood-based industry beyond primary processing activities like sawmilling and plymilling into higher-value added, downstream activities like the manufacture of moldings, blockboard, and chipboard.

Log export restrictions were not new to the Peninsula. Until 1965, only white meranti (*Shorea spp.*), mersawa (*Anisoptera spp.*), and a few unpopular species could be exported (Lian 1966). The policy was reviewed in that year, in light of rising demand for white meranti and mersawa by plywood/veneer mills (Lian 1966).[52] It was revised "to prohibit the export of logs except with special permission in order to ensure a sufficient supply of raw materials for the existing sawmilling industry and the newly expanded plywood-cum-veneer industry in the country" (*Malayan Forester* 1966, p. 54). The new policy gave the government discretion to regulate log exports according to conditions in the domestic log market: if mills were running at high capacity, it could grant fewer export licenses to ensure that there were enough logs to process, but if mills could not process all the logs harvested, it could grant more licenses and allow foreign buyers to purchase the surplus. The government also imposed a 10 percent tax on log exports. This was offset, however, by a 5 percent export tax on sawnwood, veneer, and plywood.

Log exports rose more rapidly than harvests during the 1960s, being about four times higher in 1970 than in 1960, compared to about three times higher for harvests. The explanation was only partly that processing capacity did not keep pace with the great increase in harvest, although this was an issue on the east coast, where processing capacity was limited (Lian 1966). In addition, log exporting was lucrative (Muhammad Jabil 1972), and there was considerable pressure on the government to grant licenses. The unit value of exported logs rose 5.1 percent per year in real terms from 1960 to 1972. The export ban did not apply to shipments to Singapore, and, as Lian (1996, p. 247) commented, "There is no means of keeping track of what happens to all the logs that find their way to Singapore from West Malaysia." It is possible that a significant portion was simply transshipped.

Although data on domestic log prices are not available before 1971, it is reasonable to infer that they followed a rising path similar to that for exported logs, given the looseness of the export restrictions. The domestic price for red meranti did rise sharply (by about 20 percent) from 1971 to 1972. Mills complained that the domestic log market was becoming increasingly tight, and they requested that log exports be curtailed. In "an urgent measure," the government responded by banning the export of ten popular species groups in 1972 (*Malayan Forester* 1973a, p. 2).[53] It also raised the export tax on other species to 15 percent. In response to subsequent lobbying by the industry, it added additional species to the embargoed list in 1973,[54] 1978,[55] and 1979,[56] and it raised the export tax further, to 20 percent. On January 1, 1985, it took the ultimate step, banning the export of all logs except small-diameter ones.

The department strongly supported these measures, stating in an editorial in its journal, the *Malayan* (later *Malaysian*) *Forester*, that "Efforts should be made to ensure that the products exported represent the highest possible value through manufacturing refinement" (*Malayan Forester* 1972b, p. 92).[57] This view was endorsed by the National Forest Policy. The fifth objective listed in the policy was: "to stimulate the development of appropriate wood-based industries with determined capacities commensurate with the resource flow in order to achieve maximum resource utilization, create employment opportunities and earn foreign exchange." Perhaps most important, a large, modern, export-oriented wood processing industry was expected to bolster the department's case that the Peninsula needed a large permanent forest estate to ensure that the jobs and export earnings it generated could be sustained (*Malayan Forester* 1969b). Singapore's ability to develop such an industry despite its utter lack of productive forests gave the department confidence that Peninsular Malaysia could, too (Lian 1966, *Malayan Forester* 1968c).

From an economic standpoint, however, two policy issues are relevant: first, whether government intervention was necessary to promote the efficient development of domestic processing industries, and second, what the consequences of the intervention were. The most common justification for government intervention in industrial development is the infant-industry argument:

that industries need temporary protection when they are first established. This argument is not very convincing in Peninsular Malaysia, given the large number of mills at the start of the 1970s (nearly 500 sawmills, and 18 plywood mills) and the high proportion of the harvest processed domestically. Log exports accounted for only 21 percent of log production from 1970 to 1972, and they declined in absolute terms during this period, despite a marked increase in log production. The main impetus for the processing industry's growth appears to have been comparative advantage: effective rates of protection were −2 percent in 1963, −9 percent in 1965, and −5.5 percent in 1969 (various sources cited in Vincent 1986). While one could justify modifying the tariff structure to reduce its modest discrimination against the industry, the fact that the industry was doing so well in spite of the discrimination undermines the argument that it needed protection. Moreover, as the escalating restrictions between 1972 and 1985 show, the protection was not merely temporary.

The log export restrictions provided protection by reducing increases in domestic log prices. Indeed, this was the intention, to keep logs "affordable" for local mills. The prices of logs exported by Peninsular Malaysia from 1966 to 1972 had not differed significantly from the prices of logs exported by Sabah. From 1973 to 1989, however, following the introduction of the more stringent restrictions, domestic prices in the Peninsula were, on average, 25 percent lower than the prices of logs exported by Sabah (Vincent 1992a). Domestic log prices in Peninsular Malaysia rose only 0.8 percent per year in real terms from 1972 to 1985, versus 3.2 percent per year for logs exported by Sabah (Vincent and Binkley 1992).

It is therefore not surprising that the number of mills increased after 1972. The restrictions helped maintain mills' profit margins by suppressing scarcity signals transmitted by log prices. Sustained profits at acceptable levels maintained investor interest in establishing new mills. Lian (1966) had questioned whether the increase in mills was appropriate, given the evidence of a looming timber shortfall, but the Forestry Department had no control over the licensing of mills. This was, as with concession allocation, a state matter. With log exports restricted, states had an incentive to continue issuing mill licenses in order to maintain log demand and therefore maintain the flow of revenue and rents. Hence, the number of mills rose.

Measured by production and exports of sawnwood and plywood,[58] the log export restrictions were a success. But the department's support of them was a Faustian bargain in several respects. First, as it had acknowledged in the late 1960s, "these industries consume timber at a fantastic rate" (*Malayan Forester* 1967a). From the standpoint of timber depletion, it does not matter whether a log extracted from the forest is exported or processed domestically. The growth of the domestic processing industry increased the pressure to open forest reserves and stateland forests for logging. The pressure was arguably even greater from a political standpoint than it would have been had harvests been intended solely for export, as log exporters could not use the value-added and employment arguments as effectively as could the processing industry. The industry's success in using these arguments is demonstrated by the repeated tightening of the log export restrictions. The existence of the industry may have helped justify the creation of the Permanent Forest Estate, but it was no ally to the Forestry Department in the latter's effort to restrain logging to the annual allowable coupe.

Second, the restrictions also hurt the economics of forest management. Lower domestic log prices meant lower stumpage values, which reduced the rent gradient for timber production and thereby reduced the area where timber production yielded higher financial returns than agriculture (Figure 4.1). As discussed in the section *Basic concepts in forest economics*, the value of a forest is determined not by the value added to the raw materials it yields, but rather by the value of those raw materials themselves. Log export restrictions raised the former at the expense of the latter. The NPVs in Table 4.4 would have been higher had log prices been closer to international levels.

Third, it is not evident that the additional domestic processing stimulated by the restrictions generated net economic benefits. The issue is the trade-off between more consumer and producer surplus in wood processing industries and less producer surplus in logging.[59] Some of the increased producer surplus in the processing industries might have been more apparent than real, i.e., simply displaced resource rents. Vincent (1992a) used an economic model of the Peninsular Malaysia forest sector to examine these issues from 1973 to 1989. The model included domestic and international supply and demand curves for logs and sawnwood; production, consumption, and exports of veneer and plywood were set equal to historical values. The analysis determined that the log export restrictions increased average annual sawnwood production by only about 20 percent; they were not needed to maintain the competitiveness of the core of the industry. In return for this additional 20 percent production, the economy suffered a net loss in social surplus (the sum of producer and consumer surpluses). Each sawmilling job created by the restrictions cost the economy US$6,100 (at 1989 price levels) in economic value added (actual value added minus the loss in resource rent due to lower stumpage values) and US$34,300 in resource rent. For comparison, the average annual wage in sawmills was only around US$2,200 in 1989. Hence, the impact of the log export restrictions was the opposite of what was intended: they reduced value added, and they also reduced forest value.

The impact of the restrictions on export earnings is less clear. Vincent

(1992a) estimated that each sawmilling job created by the restrictions from 1973 to 1989 cost the Peninsula US$16,600 in forgone export earnings, as the increase in earnings for sawnwood was smaller than the loss for logs. In contrast, Mohd. Shahwahid (1989) estimated that the increase for sawnwood from 1972 to 1988 was slightly larger (by just over 1 percent) than the decrease for logs. He also estimated that the increase for plywood and veneer, which Vincent's analysis ignored,[60] was nearly as large as the increase for sawnwood.

Finally, by reducing increases in log prices, the restrictions reduced the incentive for mills to operate efficiently. Recovery rates in the Peninsula were low by Western standards, although that was partially due to the heterogeneity of the tropical logs the mills processed (Kumar 1986). Low recovery was a significant concern of the department, which worried that wastage during processing would worsen the impacts of a timber shortage. Soon after the restrictions were introduced, it cautioned, "Let us work positively towards reducing, if not eliminating this wastage and let us not consider the log ban as a temporary 'reprieve' from having to do so" (*Malayan Forester* 1973a, p. 2). From an economic standpoint, however, the restrictions were indeed a reprieve. Numerous studies have confirmed that the recovery rates of wood processing industries are positively correlated with log prices.[61] Mills, as profit-maximizing enterprises, reduce wastage only if they save money by doing so. Lower log prices due to the restrictions meant that there was less money to save. Lower log prices also enabled inefficient mills to remain in business even though they operated at low capacity utilization rates. Mohd. Shahwahid (1985b, 1986) pointed out the pervasive incidence of low capacity utilization that emerged in the Peninsula after the mid-1970s.

Higher recovery in the woods and in mills was one of the reasons the department had long supported the idea of an integrated wood-based industry. Such an industry, it reasoned, could "absorb the material abandoned in the forest, and the off-cuts and other waste products of subsequent milling" (*Malayan Forester* 1963b, p. 138; see also Ismail and Low 1972). A paper by Chong (1972), which favorably evaluated the prospects for various secondary wood processing industries, was influential in consolidating support for government action to promote ITCs. There were two views on the type of action required. One was that the private sector would invest in ITCs if: 1) the states made available large, long-term concessions that offered potential investors "an assured supply of raw material to justify the necessary capital outlay for establishing the more intensive extraction facilities, industrial plant, and marketing organisation" (*Malayan Forester* 1963b, p. 139; also, *Malayan Forester* 1970a); and 2) the government assisted "through the provision of financial incentives, feasibility studies on product types, market surveys and market promotion" (*Malayan Forester* 1972b, p. 92). The department recognized that the first condition would "involve radical changes in our present system of logging licences. . . ." (*Malayan Forester* 1963b, p. 139).

Others were skeptical that the market would respond, observing that "the local conservative wood industrialist . . . has been so used to the traditional system of confining his business interest and venture to only one type of wood industry" (*Malayan Forester* 1972a, p. 2). They felt that the government needed to take a more direct role, by contributing to the financing of new industrial facilities (*Malayan Forester* 1973b). This view gained support with the introduction of the NEP. Proponents also argued that government-financed ITCs would support the twin NEP objectives of reducing poverty and enlarging the *bumiputera* role in the economy (Ismail and Low 1972, Harun 1976). The shift of logging activities to hill forests east of the Main Range was a shift into states that were both poor and overwhelmingly Malay. There was still enough virgin forest in this frontier region to carve out large concessions, and the lack of local processing capacity meant that logs were either not being salvaged when land was cleared for development schemes (Abdul Ghaffar 1972) or were being sent to Singapore for processing (Lian 1966). Investment in ITCs in the region appeared to offer an excellent opportunity to establish a much-needed processing industry that would be not just modern but Malay (Salleh 1972, Ismail 1974). The assistant director-general of the Forestry Department argued, "Forests being rural based, as most of the Bumiputeras are, this resource undoubtedly offers tremendous potential for Bumiputera participation to be developed to the fullest" (Muhammad Jabil 1972, p. 167).

Previous government efforts to increase the role of *bumiputera* in the forest sector had achieved little success (Muhammad Jabil 1972). Prior to independence, most concessions were granted to non-*bumiputera*, and virtually no mills were owned and operated by *bumiputera*. After independence, concession allocation shifted in favor of *bumiputera*. During 1961–70, some 197,000 ha in Forest Reserves and 1,205,000 ha in Stateland Forests were granted as concessions to *bumiputera*, mainly to individuals (Muhammad Jabil 1972). This policy was undermined, however, by the "Ali-Baba" syndrome, in which *bumiputera* license holders immediately sold their rights to non-*bumiputera* (Muhammad Jabil 1972, *Malayan Forester* 1973b, Kumar 1986). The same problem occurred with licenses for timber transport, log exports, and mills. In 1970, only 13 percent of sawmills were licensed either solely or under partnerships to *bumiputera*, a figure scarcely higher than in 1960 (Muhammad Jabil 1972, Table 2). In practice, the partnerships tended to be dominated by the non-*bumiputera* partner (Muhammad Jabil 1972).

The department expected ITCs to be more successful (*Malayan Forester* 1973b, p. 77): "These complexes will provide ideal opportunities for active and real Bumiputra participation at all levels in various part [*sic*] of the country. "Ali-Baba-ism" must be stamped out ruthlessly. The undesirable factors that lead to the temptation of securing quick profits with little risks, financial commitments or efforts must be totally eliminated." The National Forest Policy, which listed as an explicit objective "to promote effective Bumiputera participation in forest and wood-based industries," commented that "a major aspect of future development will be the establishment of integrated wood manufacturing complexes. . . ." (section E, paragraph 16).

Three ITCs actually preceded the NEP: the Permodalan Perak complex, established in 1965, and the Jengka and Ibam complexes in Pahang, established in 1969 and 1971, respectively (Harun 1976). The first was a special case: it was established to salvage timber from forests that would be inundated by a major hydroelectric project. The two complexes in Pahang were also established in part to salvage timber, from remote land development schemes, but they also had substantial concession areas in Forest Reserves. The Jengka complex was financed entirely by government sources, both state and federal (MARA, the Council of Trust for Indigenous People, which promoted *bumiputera* economic interests). The Ibam complex, on the other hand, was financed partially by an international forest products company (MacMillan & Jardine).

The number of complexes rose quickly after the introduction of the NEP, with five established from 1972 to 1975 (Harun 1976). The number reached eight by the end of 1978 (excluding Permodalan Perak) and twelve by the end of 1985 (Unit Ekonomi, Ibu Pejabat Perhutanan, n.d.(a), n.d.(b)). According to Ismail (1974) and Harun (1976), the complexes had a more or less similar structure, with the key features being: 1) majority ownership by the government, through State Development Corporations and other state or federal agencies; and 2) concessions of at least 20,000 ha, under agreements lasting 25 to 30 years.[62] Government ownership was in line with efforts in other sectors to promote a larger *bumiputera* role in the economy (Muhammad Jabil 1972). As the director-general of the Forestry Department put it, "Motivation for the restructure of industry now lies firmly at the combined initiative of both Government and industry, rather than remaining the sole prerogative of the [private] sector" (Ismail 1974, p. 148).

The long-term agreement areas associated with the complexes covered a substantial area of forest, some 22 percent of Forest Reserves in 1985 (Unit Ekonomi, Ibu Pejabat Perhutanan, n.d.(b)). The direct linkage to modern, industrial investment, most of it done with government funds, placed these areas at less risk of conversion than other parts of forest reserves. From the start, however, the processing component of the complexes encountered numerous difficulties. Financial problems were reported as early as 1972 (Muhammad Jabil 1972). Harun (1976, p. 16) reported that mills at Jengka and Ibam "incur [such] a big operating and maintenance cost that [they] could barely break even on their operations." He blamed inappropriate equipment and inexperienced management,[63] along with several classic problems of public enterprises: overstaffing, a lack of incentives for higher productivity, and, "in some cases, political and social issues [which] affect the recruitment and retrenchment of personnel not to the best advantage of the operation of the complexes" (p. 19). Some ITCs resorted to selling logs to private mills to cover their costs (Harun 1976). For this and other reasons, capacity utilization rates were low, and some proposed processing facilities were never constructed. Due to the problems with management and equipment, and the incomplete set of facilities, recovery rates were low and waste in the forest and the mills remained high (Harun 1976).

Harun (1976) was hopeful that these problems could be overcome, but available information suggests that most were not. Kumar (1986) reported that the production costs of mills in ITCs were higher than for smaller, private sector mills, and that there were still instances of ITCs operating simply as log producers instead of processors. Ismail (1993), in an economy-wide study, found that more than half of public enterprises in Malaysia were not profitable from 1980 to 1988. Although he did not provide detail specifically on ITCs, he did comment that the agricultural and timber sectors had the lowest frequency of profitable public enterprises. Perhaps most telling is the complete absence of any mention of ITCs in the country's *Medium and Long Term Industrial Master Plan for the Wood-Based Industry*, prepared in the mid-1980s by the Malaysian Industry Development Authority and the U.N. Industrial Development Organization (MIDA/UNIDO 1985), in 1991. The government evidently no longer saw ITCs as playing a lead role in modernizing the sector.

One might attempt to justify even profit-losing ITCs on the grounds that they served a broader social purpose, i.e., to bring *bumiputera* into the processing industry. But the facts suggest that whatever catalytic role they played was minor. At the eighth National Forestry Council meeting, held February 16, 1985, it was reported that *bumiputera* held only 17.4 percent of sawmill licenses and 12.5 percent of plywood/veneer mill licenses.

In the end, the main contribution of the ITCs appears to have been to worsen the discrepancy between primary processing capacity and sustained-yield harvest levels. The *Industrial Master Plan* (p. 33) drew attention to "over-investment in the saw milling sector (MIDA/UNIDO 1985)," as did the deputy prime minister in a speech opening the tenth National Forestry Council meeting (National Forest Council 1991). The *Industrial Master Plan* (p. 33) attributed the problem to "the lack of coordination between the private investment community and forest authorities." Along these lines, the states agreed at the tenth Council meeting that wood supply should be considered in reviewing applications for new mills and that licenses for mills that had not been in operation for more than two years should be canceled. These administrative solutions did not address, however, what appears to be the root cause of the problem: government policies to promote domestic processing. Government policies were responsible for a significant portion of the increase in mill capacity in the 1970s and 1980s, indirectly through log export restrictions and directly through investment in ITCs. These policies contributed to the development of a processing industry that maintained pressure on state governments to open forests for logging. Both policies cost the economy: the former due to the establishment of mills that were financially viable at artificially low log prices, but not economically viable, and the latter due to the establishment of mills that were not even financially viable.

Conclusions

Peninsular Malaysia's forest areas and timber stocks were depleted rapidly during the 1970s and 1980s, continuing trends that started soon after independence. The chief cause of deforestation was agricultural expansion, although in some cases forests were denuded by logging that occurred under the guise of conversion fellings for land development. Timber depletion was caused by the combination of conversion fellings on alienated land and logging in permanent forests. Demand for timber was primarily from domestic sawmills and plywood/veneer mills, as log exports were restricted stringently from 1972 forward. Rates of timber production and installed milling capacity were far above sustained-yield levels estimated by the Forestry Department.

State governments were responsible, in an administrative sense, for the rapid deforestation and timber depletion, as they had authority over land alienation and the granting of timber concessions. Perceived high returns to agriculture and wood-based industries, a desire for revenue, and political patronage drove their decisions. The National Forest Policy, National Forestry Act, and related efforts by the Forestry Department to protect remaining forests and to slow the rate of harvest had little impact, as they did not curtail states' authority in any significant way. In fact, other federal policies, such as the Land Capability Classification system, restrictions on log exports, and encouragement of ITCs, accelerated deforestation and timber depletion. Deforestation slowed considerably in the late 1980s, thanks to falling agricultural returns brought about by industrialization and urbanization, but there was no sign of a similar slowdown for timber depletion.

The Forestry Department's concerns about the rapid loss of forests (especially lowland forests) and the persistent overlogging (in the sense of logged areas exceeding annual allowable coupes) are understandable. Our analysis suggests, however, that on financial grounds these processes were not necessarily undesirable. Agriculture offered high returns, while the monetary returns to forestry were very low (Table 4.4). The rotation age selected by the department was too long from the standpoint of maximizing resource rents generated by forestry, and this implies that the prescribed annual allowable coupes were too small. In the particular case of virgin forests, rapid harvesting made financial sense because these forests offered no significant biological return (from net growth) or financial return (from rising stumpage values).

From a public policy standpoint, however, the appropriate perspective is not a financial one, but an economic one: benefits and costs measured in social terms, taking into account nonmarket (unpriced) values as well as market values. For deforestation, the issue is whether the gains from land development—agricultural rents, net of any environmental damage associated with agriculture—are at least as great as the losses—forestry rents, inclusive of nontimber values as well as timber values (i.e., the rent gradient F^*, not F, in Figure 4.1). That tree-crop plantations in the Peninsula were sustainable, high-yielding forms of agriculture was discussed in Chapter 2 and mentioned in the section *The National Forest Policy*.[64] It is equally clear, however, that important nontimber values were sacrificed when forests were converted. Aiken and Leigh (1992) and Brookfield (1994a) provide abundant information on physical, biological, and ecological aspects of nontimber values. From the less to more tangible, these values include: "minor" forest products (rattan, bamboo, game, traditional medicines, miscellaneous fruits, and other edible plant products); genetic resources (biological diversity); recreation and tourism; watershed protection (reduced of erosion, sedimentation, and flooding); coastal stabilization (mangrove forests); and, carbon sequestration (to reduce the risk of global climate change).

The Forestry Department has long recognized these values (*Malayan Forester* 1962b, 1964b, 1965a, 1971a). As an editorial in the *Malayan Forester* proclaimed (Malayan Forester 1971a, p. 83), "the fact that the recreational, watershed, research and education, tourism and other nonwood values are difficult or impossible to measure in dollars and cents does not mean that Malaysia can afford to neglect or ignore them." Taman Negara, the national park, was established in 1938–39 and is one of the largest areas of protected tropical rain forest in the world. It covers 434,000 ha, equivalent to 10 percent of the Permanent Forest Estate (of which it is not a part). Wildlife sanctuaries, many dating back to the first third of the century, covered an additional 211,000 ha in 1991 (Unit Ekonomi, Ibu Pejabat Perhutanan, n.d. (c)). Both the 1952 Interim Forest Policy and the 1978 National Forest Policy called for the inclusion of protective forests in the Permanent Forest Estate. Such forests accounted for two-fifths of the existing Permanent Forest Estate in 1991, some 1,900,000 ha (Unit Ekonomi, Ibu Pejabat Perhutanan, n.d. (c)). The Forestry Department has supported a system of small recreational forests (*hutan lipur*) since 1970. This system included 72 sites in 1991 (Unit Ekonomi, Ibu Pejabat Perhutanan, n.d. (c)). In productive forests, the switch to the SMS was partly motivated by concerns about high levels of erosion under the MUS.

Vincent and Yusuf (1993) reviewed available information on the effects of deforestation in Malaysia on three nontimber values: soil conservation (reduced erosion), protection of water systems (reduced sedimentation, flooding, and pollution), and preservation of biological diversity. They concluded that soil erosion could be significant during the establishment phase of tree-crop plantations but was relatively minor after the trees were established. They reached the same conclusion for sedimentation, which is of course linked to erosion, and for flooding. Pollution impacts were due mainly to effluent from rubber and palm-oil mills, but these impacts were reduced to manageable levels after the government implemented water pollution regulations in the 1970s (see Chapter 10). Brookfield (1994a, p. 277) reached a similar conclusion with regard to these first two values, commenting that "within the fact that a new ecosystem [tree-crop plantations] has been created, the environmental problems . . . are all resolvable."

Vincent and Yusuf (1993, p. 471) concluded that the major impact of deforestation had to do with the third value: "the species-richness [plants and animals] of many of Peninsular Malaysia's remnant patches of lowland forest has diminished as these patches have become increasingly isolated and reduced in size in a landscape dominated by rubber and oil palm." This conclusion is based on ecological principles (island biogeography theory), which predict that a 90 percent reduction in area eventually reduces the number of species by 50 percent (MacArthur and Wilson 1967)[65] and that the loss of species is even greater when area is not simply reduced but fragmented (Harris 1989). The rate at which extinction occurs varies among groups of organisms; the most vulnerable are typically ones with short lifespans and restricted geographical ranges. These include many insects and birds. Although it is unlikely that any tree species have yet gone extinct in the Peninsula, the probable loss of small animals that serve as pollinators and seed dispersers does not bode well. The *National Conservation Strategy*, completed by the Economic Planning Unit in the early 1990s, reported that the number of forest-resident bird species that had gone extinct or were threatened with extinction more than doubled between 1978 and 1988, reaching nearly 5 percent of the original number of species by 1988 (EPU 1993).

The economic cost of the reduced biological diversity is unknown, but the

Strategy pointed out that the loss in genetic resources could limit crop improvement efforts and opportunities to develop new pharmaceutical products. In the case of durian (the fruit tree *Durio zibethinus*), the *Strategy* estimated that the net present value of crop improvements from the introduction of new genes was RM80 million at a 10 percent discount rate (EPU 1993). As biology-based high-technology industries become more important in the global economy, the genetic value of the biodiversity in Malaysia's forests will surely rise. The bulk of the biodiversity is in the lowland forests, whose area has been so greatly reduced by conversion and whose quality (from a conservation standpoint) has been further degraded by logging. For these reasons, the apparent trend toward stabilization of the aggregate forest area of the Peninsula is no reason for complacency.

Regarding other values, "minor" forest products are indeed minor at the aggregate level in the Peninsula. They may be locally important, however, particularly to *Orang asli* communities (Lim 1991; Lim and Jamaluddin 1994; Mohd. Shahwahid 1990, 1992, 1994; Mohd. Shahwahid and Nik Mustapha 1991; Norazlin 1990; Poh 1991; Poh, Mohd. Shahwahid, and Saroni 1994). Mohd. Shahwahid and Nik Mustapha (1991) estimated that the annual flow of "minor" forest products from freshwater swamp forests was equivalent to less than 2 percent of the value of annual timber production on a sustained-yield basis.

Brown et al. (1991) conducted a careful analysis of carbon dioxide emissions from deforestation and degradation in the Peninsula. The amounts were small compared to global emissions (Brookfield 1994a), but the important issue is the benefit Malaysia can expect to derive from reducing emissions. This benefit hinges on the prospect of financial compensation by countries that would suffer from climate change. Krutilla (1991) estimated that the carbon sequestration value of Malaysia's forests was in the thousands of ringgit per hectare. His estimates are strongly influenced, however, by his use of US$28 per tonne as the value of carbon. More recent work by Nordhaus (1994) suggests that the value is much lower, around US$5 per tonne. In some forests, this could still yield aggregate values comparable to those for timber, but the value remains hypothetical unless compensation is actually paid.[66]

A final value, forest-based recreation and tourism, appears to be rising rapidly. The number of visitors, foreign and domestic, at Taman Negara rose from 1,390 in 1978 to 18,710 in 1991, with Malaysians accounting for 11 percent in 1991. Studies of recreational demand indicate that Malaysians are increasingly willing to pay significant amounts for quality recreational experiences in the country's natural areas (Wan Sabri 1987, 1993).

The major nontimber costs of deforestation have therefore probably been losses in biological diversity and losses in amenity values, which in many instances are linked to biological diversity. In a general context, Fisher, Krutilla, and Cicchetti (1972) argued persuasively that one can expect these values to rise relative to commodity values, such as timber,[67] with increases in education, income, and technology. The increase in recreational demand suggests that this is occurring in Malaysia. The implication is that the economic costs of deforestation will be even higher in the future than in the past. While not forgetting the importance of timber, the Forestry Department and state governments need to shift their emphasis increasingly toward the important economic values generated by protective and amenity forests, Taman Negara, and wildlife sanctuaries.

The presence of nontimber values also has implications for the rate of timber depletion. Forests that are mature from a financial (timber only) standpoint are not necessarily mature from an economic standpoint. Hartman (1976) argued that, for the general forestry case, nontimber values rise with the age of the forest. This implies that the rotation age should be longer than the one that maximizes just the NPV of timber production. Hence, the optimal rotation ages in Table 4.4 could be too short. Although one cannot determine how much longer they ought to be without conducting a much more detailed analysis, one can infer how great nontimber values must be to justify a longer rotation and, if one follows a sustained-yield policy (which may not be economically best), a smaller annual allowable coupe. For example, at a 10 percent discount rate, a sixty-year rotation is economically justified only if the NPV (infinite rotations) of nontimber values is at least RM25/ha higher (RM39/ha minus RM14/ha) for a sixty-year rotation than for a forty-year rotation (the rotation that maximizes the NPV of timber values). Although this is a small amount in present value terms, the annual value between ages 40 and 60 years would have to be quite large to offset the impact of discounting.

The uncertainty about the magnitude of nontimber values is not a reason to ignore them. Adopting a slower rate of harvest can be viewed, in sound economic terms, as an insurance policy, a means of "buying time" until more is known about values that could be lost irreversibly. A slower rate of harvest can also be justified on the basis of timber values alone. Practical understanding of the regeneration of hill forests, which were the principal source of timber in the Peninsula by the mid-1980s (*Malayan Forester* 1986), was little greater in the early 1990s than at the start of the 1970s (Appanah and Weinland 1991, Tang 1987). Harvesting these forests at a more conservative rate would provide more time for silviculturists to determine how best to manage them to ensure that they grow back. Neither timber nor nontimber values can be supplied in a sustainable fashion in the absence of adequate regeneration.

Appendix 4: Deforestation Regressions

The relationship between annual rates of change in forest cover and per capita income during the period from 1972 to 1981 was analyzed by estimating the following model:

$$f_i = \alpha + \beta_L L_i + \beta_F F_i + \beta_Y Y_i + \beta_{YY} Y_i^2 + \beta_y y_i$$
$$+ \beta_P P_i + \beta_{PP} P_i^2 + \beta_p p_i + \beta_{YP} Y_i P_i$$

where i indicates administrative district, f is the annual rate of change of forest cover, L is the proportion of the area of a district in land capability classes II and III, F is the proportion of the area of a district covered by forest at the beginning of a period, Y is per capita income, y is the annual rate of change of per capita income, P is population density, and p is the annual rate of change of population. This equation and more restricted forms of it were estimated for the forest inventory data. Results are shown in Table A4.1.

Table A4.1   *Regression results for annual rates of change in forest cover: forest inventory data*

	Full model	Restricted model
I. Coefficient estimates[a]		
Intercept	+0.0599	+0.0761
	(0.0680)	(0.0613)
Land capability	-0.134×10^{-4}	-0.000354
	(0.0361)	(0.0352)
Forest cover	+0.0290	+0.0345
	(0.0222)	(0.0157)**
Per capita income	-0.00245	-0.00278
	(0.00127)*	(0.00119)**
Per capita income^2	$+0.143 \times 10^{-4}$	$+0.150 \times 10^{-4}$
	(0.681×10^{-5})**	(0.646×10^{-5})**
Change in per capita income	+0.00392	-0.0943
	(0.630)	(0.597)
Population density	+0.00426	
	(0.00590)	
Population density^2	+0.000146	
	(0.000171)	
Change in population	-0.0492	
	(0.237)	
Interaction term	-0.945×10^{-4}	
	(0.848×10^{-4})	
II. R^2	0.199	0.178
III. Number of observations	65	65

[a]Standard errors are in parentheses. ***, **, and * indicate that estimates are significantly different from zero at the 1, 5, and 10 percent levels, respectively.

NOTES

1 A period of near-martial law to suppress a communist insurgency, lasting from June 1948 to July 1960 (Menon 1976). According to *Malayan Forester* (1959, p. 188), "The Emergency may be said to be *the* factor which upset the [timber] industry most. It forced the mills into towns, confined logging to certain areas, increased wages of loggers and reduced their working day to about four hours, and prevented adequate supervision."

2 Those found mainly below 300 m elevation (Whitmore 1988). This is the average elevation at which the terrain changes from flat or gently hilly to steep, with ridges dominated by trees of the species *Shorea curtisii* (seraya). The absence of seraya is ecologically a better indicator of lowland forests than elevation.

3 *Malayan Forester* (1961) stands out for the calmness of its remarks on agricultural development.

4 Some was also in Wildlife Sanctuaries and Taman Negara, the national park.

5 "Security" here refers to the risk of legal excision for land development. Illegal forest conversion was not a major problem: in 1969, only 1.5 percent of the area in Forest Reserves was not actually in forest (Salleh 1972, Table 2).

6 Land conversion during the first third of the century did not trigger as large an increase in timber production, because only a handful of species were marketable at that time. Most were heavy hardwoods whose wood was naturally durable and was suitable for railway sleepers and heavy construction uses. Most of the trees that were felled were either used as firewood or charcoal or were burned on the site.

7 The equipment included a vehicle unique to Malaysia, the *san tai wong* or winch lorry (Kumar 1986).

8 The "Wallace Line" runs between Bali and Borneo to the west and Lombok and Sulawesi to the east. It separates Asian flora from Australian flora.

9 According to Whitmore (1988), hill dipterocarp forests are found between approximately 300 m, the boundary with lowland dipterocarp forests, and 750 m, the boundary with the lower montane rain-forest formation. Upper dipterocarp forests, a zone within the lower montane rain-forest formation, extend up to 1200 m.

10 Silviculture is the science (and art) of regenerating and manipulating forests, primarily for timber production.

11 They were also much better funded: the allocation for agriculture (including forestry) under the *Second Malaysia Plan* was RM1,921 million, of which forestry was only RM18 million.

12 In the early 1970s, Finland, which had about the same area of forest as Peninsular Malaysia, had 1,800 professional forest officers and 3,700 forest technicians, compared to 53 and 44 in Peninsular Malaysia (*Malayan Forester* 1971c).

13 The Forestry Department launched the Compensatory Plantation Programme in Peninsular Malaysia in 1983, with funding from the Asian Development Bank. From 1983 to 1990, 45,000 hectares were planted (Kementerian Perusahaan Utama 1992), compared to an area of natural forest of 6,822,000 ha at the end of 1981 (Ibu Pejabat Perhutanan, Semenanjung Malaysia, 1987). For more information on this programme, see *Malayan Forester* (1984), Asian Development Bank (1984), and Kanapathy (1986); for information on the history of plantation efforts in the Peninsula, see Appanah and Weinland (1993). An unexpected new, "artificial" source of timber has been rubberwood, which emerged as an important furniture wood in the 1980s. Its levels of production remained small compared to production from the natural forest even in the early 1990s.

14 There has been a lively debate about silvicultural issues in the Malaysian forestry literature. Key references include Appanah and Weinland (1990, 1991), Cheah (1991), Ismail (1966), Lee (1982), Mok (1977), Tang (1974, 1987), Tang and Wan Razali (1981), Thang (1986, 1987), Wan Razali (1989), and Wyatt-Smith (1988).

15 This was more the case in Sabah and Sarawak. See the chapters on those states in FAO/UNEP (1981).

16 Expressed on an annual basis, land rent is equivalent to rent in the ordinary sense when the rental market for land is competitive. A tenant farmer who paid the full land rent (in the economic sense) to the landowner would retain just enough of the value of farm output to cover the opportunity cost of his labor and other inputs.

17 RM401/ha = RM7,000/ha $\times$ 1.1^{-30}.

18 RM426/ha = RM401/ha $\times$ $[1 - (1.1)^{-30}]^{-1}$.

19 The classic objective of foresters is to maximize the "mean annual increment" of wood volume growth.

20 Gradients could be added for other uses, such as industrial or residential, but this would not change the results of the analysis in any substantive way.

21 Whether actual land markets in developing countries produce the optimal outcome is, of course, another issue. Much land, especially forested land, is held by the public sector in developing countries and is not formally allocated by markets. Where land markets exist, property rights are often severely attenuated. This, along with various types of institutional and policy failures, reduces the chances of an efficient outcome. For a recent review of these issues, see Brown and Pearce (1994).

22 At very high income levels, the agricultural gradient might in fact shift inward, causing agricultural land to be abandoned. Chapter 5 discusses this "idle land" phenomenon in Malaysia.

23 Inverted U-shaped relationships between environmental indicators and measures of development (usually, per capita GDP) have been dubbed "environmental Kuznets curves." The environmental Kuznets curve hypothesis is discussed in detail for air and water pollution in Chapter 8.

24 For countries in Latin America and Africa, Cropper and Griffiths (1994) did find that the rate of growth in per capita GDP (as opposed to the level) was associated with lower deforestation, but the magnitude of the effect was small.

25 Vincent and Hadi (1993) compared the classification system used in the inventories to Whitmore's (1988) ecological classification system.

26 Within the logged-over category, both dryland and inland swamp forests are further classified according to the date of logging (before or after 1966).

27 The 1,000-meter dividing line used in Forest Inventory I was far above the traditional dividing line between lowland and hill forests, 1,000 feet (*Malayan Forester* 1970b, p. 121).

28 Sabah and Sarawak did not enact it.

29 Most cross-country studies on deforestation have found that rising population was associated with declining forest cover, even after controlling for differences in income levels (Allen and Barnes 1985, Bilsborrow 1992, Bilsborrow and Goeres 1991, Palloni 1992, Palo 1987, Rudel 1989, Scotti 1990). Country-level studies by Panayotou and Sungsuwan (1989) in Thailand and Southgate et al. (1991) in Ecuador obtained similar results.

30 Kam Suan Pheng and Ku Izhar of the School of Biological Sciences at Universiti Sains Malaysia performed the GIS analysis. We thank Sandra Brown of the University of Illinois and Louis Iverson of the U.S. Forest Service, who provided the forest inventory data as GIS files.

31 There has been some division of districts over time. To get around this problem, we defined the data as much as possible according to district boundaries at the time of Forest Inventory I.

32 We calculated the rates of change by taking the natural logarithm of the ratio of area in Forest Inventory II to area in Forest Inventory I and then dividing by the number of intervening years.

33 We matched data from the 1970 Household Income Survey to Forest Inventory I, and data from the 1987 Household Income Survey to Forest Inventory II.

34 The annual rate of change in population density is equal to the annual rate of change in population as long as the area of a district does not change. We calculated population growth rates by matching estimates from the 1970 Population Census to Forest Inventory I, and estimates from the 1980 Population Census to Forest Inventory II.

35 Suppose that forest area (F) at any point in time is a function of a constant (α), population density (P), and a polynomial related to income (f(Y)):

$$F = \alpha + P \times f(Y).$$

Then the percentage rate of change in F over time is given by:

$$(dF/dt)/F = [f(Y) \times dP/dt + P \times f' \times dY/dt]/F.$$

The right-hand side includes not only income and population, but also their changes over time. It also includes forest area.

36 Wong (1971) did not provide estimates at the district level.

37 Explanatory variables other than per capita income were set equal to their mean values in order to plot the curve.

38 This is a turnaround from an earlier, more pessimistic view by Brookfield et al. (1990, p. 507), that "It seems not improbable that worse is to come before improvement."

39 Strictly speaking, the SMS creates a forest with two *size* classes. The size classes correspond to age classes only after several cutting cycles, as many of the smaller trees in the virgin forest are small due to slow growth, not youth.

40 The act attached conditions, stating that concessionaires were required to mark the boundaries of their concessions and to prepare management and reforestation plans. It also stated, however, these conditions held "Unless otherwise exempted by the State Authority" (section 20).

41 Chapter 8 of the act required the states to establish Forest Development Funds, which were intended to finance activities related to forest management and reforestation. The funds were financed mainly by a cess on log production. The act set the cess at RM2.80/m³. The Fund was administered by a committee chaired by the state secretary and including the state financial officer and the state director of forestry.

42 The share in Terengganu fell in the 1980s due to the expansion of oil production. See Chapter 3.

43 This statement is based on discussions with individuals in the timber industry.

44 In the 1950s, there apparently had been a conscious effort to reflect differences in stumpage values in the timber fees (*Malayan Forester* 1960a).

45 Costs were higher in steep terrain. Kumar (1986, p. 99) cited an estimate of RM115/m³.

46 Foresters measure tree diameter at "breast height," 1.5 m above the ground.

47 This calculation ignores tree taper. The estimated timber volumes, and thus the forest values, are therefore biased upward.

48 These price adjustment factors are based on information provided by the Malaysian Timber Industries Board.

49 This assumes that the desired trees reach reproductive maturity by age forty. If not, a longer rotation would be needed to ensure adequate regeneration.

50 Another problem with the annual allowable coupe approach is that it ignores fluctuations in timber demand during the business cycle and thereby makes log prices more volatile. In the case of Terengganu, Ismail and Low (1972, p. 161) commented, "The annual acreage of the permanent forest estate to be opened for exploitation is dictated by the management plan and, therefore, cannot and should not, be increased at will or as circumstances may require." This rigid approach results in too much timber being dumped on the market in periods of low demand and too little being provided in periods of high demand. Given that the Forestry Department had so little control over actual areas harvested, however, the annual allowable coupe approach had little impact on prices in the Peninsula.

51 Given that logging cost was constant in real terms, changes in the stumpage value of red meranti were identical to the changes in its price.

52 Mersawa contains silica and is therefore less suitable for sawing.

53 Damar minyak, durian hutan, keruing, mengkulang, merbau, mersawa, nyatoh, red meranti, sepetir, and white meranti.

54 Jelutong.

55 Balau, cengal, and kempas.

56 Sesendok and terentang.

57 In fact, the department was interested in reducing exports not merely of logs, but of rough-sawn air-dried lumber, too (*Malayan Forester* 1972b).

58 Plywood production rose from 335,000 m^3 in 1972 to 1,035,000 m^3 in 1990, while exports rose from 268,000 m^3 to 713,000 m^3.

59 Consumer surplus is the difference between the maximum amount a consumer is willing to pay for an item and the actual price paid. Similarly, producer surplus is the difference between the price received and the short-run marginal cost of production. Producer surplus is equivalent to returns to capital and other fixed factors of production; in effect, profits.

60 In addition to this reason, the results of the two analyses differed due to the modeling approaches involved. Vincent used an integrated supply-and-demand model (that is, sawnwood and log markets were explicitly linked to each other), with the supply of exports by the Peninsula determined by the difference between domestic supply and domestic demand. Exports by competing tropical regions and imports by nontropical regions were also modeled explicitly, and they implicitly reflected linkages between log and sawnwood markets. Mohd. Shahwahid used a simpler approach, modeled after an analysis by Lindsay (1989) for Indonesia: he constructed forecasts of exports of logs, sawnwood, plywood, and veneer, based on the assumptions that unrestricted log exports would have remained constant at 1971 levels and that exports of the three processed products would have been reduced according to their historical shares of domestic log demand, and then he applied estimated import demand elasticities to determine the changes in export prices.

61 Vincent et al. (1992) reviewed these studies, albeit with a focus on labor inputs.

62 Concession size was determined by the area needed to provide a sustained flow of timber to the processing facilities, under the assumption that the SMS, with a 25- to 30-year cutting cycle, would be employed (Harun 1976).

63 Ismail and Low (1972) had warned that this would be a problem.

64 Brookfield 1994b (p. 93), referring to the conversion of forests to developed uses, commented, "The forests of the Peninsula have paid a high price; however, there have been substantial benefits. The national economy, now that of a middle-income newly industrializing country, would not [otherwise] have become so, certainly not in so short a time . . . ."

65 Strictly speaking, the 90 percent to 50 percent relationship applies to small islands. For larger land masses, the loss of species is probably not as great.

66 In the early 1990s, Innoprise Corporation in Sabah did indeed receive a small amount of funding from utilities in the Netherlands and the United States for activities that reduced carbon emissions from Sabah's forest estate.

67 Binkley and Vincent (1987), Sedjo and Lyon (1990), and Vincent (1992b) present evidence indicating that stumpage values are rising in real terms, but at a diminishing rate, with stabilization projected around the middle of the twenty first century.

5

Agricultural Land

INTRODUCTION

The most obvious feature of agricultural land use in Malaysia since independence is the rapid expansion of cultivated area. As discussed in Chapter 4, this is the fundamental cause of the deforestation that has occurred in the country. Table 5.1 summarizes land use information for Peninsular Malaysia, which is where most of the agricultural expansion has occurred.[1] It is also the only part of the country where land use surveys have been conducted on a regular basis.[2]

Agriculture increased from 21 percent of total land area in the Peninsula in 1966, to 26 percent in 1974, to 33 percent in 1984. The average annual rate of expansion was relatively constant in absolute terms between the surveys: 92,000 ha/yr from 1966 to 1974 and 93,000 ha/yr from 1974 to 1984. Table 5.2 shows corresponding estimates from cadastral data compiled by the Ministry of Agriculture (MOA). As in Table 5.1, the rates of expansion were rapid and relatively constant over time, though substantially lower: 67,000 ha/yr during the 1970s and 69,000 ha/yr during the 1980s.[3]

The estimates in Table 5.2 also reveal that significant changes occurred in relative crop areas during the two decades. In particular, the areas of three traditional smallholder crops—rubber, padi, and coconut—decreased. This partially offset increases in the areas of crops that led the expansion, i.e., oil palm and, to a much lesser degree, cocoa.

A full treatment of issues related to agricultural land use during the 1970s and 1980s is far beyond the scope of this chapter, and it would be of little scholarly value anyway. Books on individual crop sectors are already available, although some of the standard references cover only the beginning of the

---

Lim Teck Ghee was a coauthor of this chapter.

Table 5.1 *Land use in Peninsular Malaysia, according to land use surveys (in thousands of hectares)*

Land Use	1966	1974	1984
Urban and mining	134	200	251
Agriculture	2734	3471	4406
Grassland	405	223	199
Scrub forest	595	504	431
Forest	7864	7242	6501
Swamp[a]	1176	1068	935
Newly cleared land	115	349	255
Unused land	63	18	16
Unclassified	133	153	250
Total	13220	13227	13244

Sources: For 1966, Wong (1971); for 1974, Economic Planning Unit (1980); for 1984, statistics provided by the Department of Agriculture.
[a] Includes swamp forests and mangroves.

period (e.g., Barlow 1978 on rubber and Khera 1976 on oil palm).[4] Instead, the chapter focuses on the idle land issue. Starting in the 1970s, the government became increasingly concerned that traditional smallholdings were not simply being converted to alternative crops, but were being worked infrequently or going out of production altogether. The term applied to such land, which has since become the standard term used in official discourse on the subject, was *idle land*. The government's concerns led to aggressive, and expensive, programs aimed at returning the land to production.

The idle land issue provides a useful case for examining the allocation of land as a productive resource, and it complements the discussion of deforestation in Chapter 4. Deforestation pertains to expansion of the agricultural frontier, while idle land pertains to retraction. Figure 5.1 illustrates the economics of the issue. The rent gradients A_0, A_1, and F are identical to those in Figure 4.1. The existence of idle land implies an inward shift of the agricultural rent gradient to A_2, which causes L_1–L_2 hectares to be taken out of production.

Table 5.2 *Cultivated area by crop in Peninsular Malaysia, 1970-1990 (in thousands of hectares)*

Year	Rubber	Oil palm	Padi	Coconut	Cocoa	Other	Total
1970	1,724	222	524	214	3	221	2,918
1975	1,695	569	596	233	18	248	3,359
1980	1,697	907	529	245	42	167	3,587
1985	1,663	1,232	465	220	101	215	3,896
1990	1,534	1,662	465	220	148	215	4,279

Sources: For 1970 and 1975, Prime Minister's Department (n.d.); for 1980, 1985, and 1990, Kementerian Pertanian (1983, 1988, and 1993, respectively).

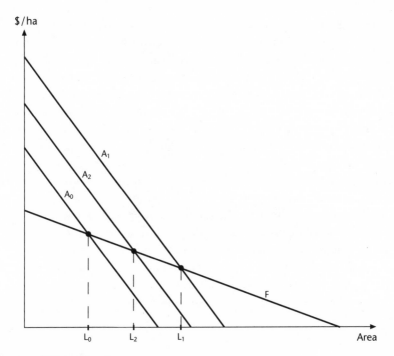

Figure 5.1   Efficient land use

What is important from a policy standpoint is the reason for the shift. There is little evidence that physical factors, such as land degradation due to poor farming practices, were responsible for such a shift in Malaysia in the 1970s. Malaysia's tree-crop plantations are recognized as one of the most sustainable agricultural systems in the humid tropics (Vincent and Yusuf 1993). Pest problems and poor drainage were problems in some padi areas (Fujimoto 1991),[5] but the affected area apparently represented only a minority of the idle land.[6]

A more plausible reason is a continuation of the forces that slowed the rate of deforestation, in particular the rising opportunity cost of agricultural labor. If rising costs caused agricultural rents to fall below zero, or below the rents generated by alternative uses (e.g., industrial development, urban use, or forestry), then the land *should* have gone out of agricultural production. The land might have been technically capable of producing a crop, but it generated no net economic value if farmed. If this was the case, agricultural labor provided more benefits to the economy by being employed in other activities.

Another possible reason, however, is that the land could have generated a positive rent, but it was prevented from doing so by institutional factors. For example, rigidities in the land market could do this, if they prevented smallholdings from adjusting to an optimum size as economic conditions in the agricultural sector changed. If institutional factors were to blame, idleness did indeed indicate that agricultural land was economically underutilized.

The chapter attempts to determine whether idle land represented inefficient utilization of the country's land resources, or whether it was simply an unavoidable consequence of the great socioeconomic changes that occurred in the country during the 1970s and 1980s. The chapter is organized as follows. The section *Emergence of the idle land issue* traces the emergence of government concern about the issue. *The extent of idle land* then reviews evidence on the extent of land considered idle. *The policy response to idle land* assesses the performance of government programs to rehabilitate idle land. This assessment sheds light on the competing hypotheses that idle land was underutilized or uneconomic. The finding that many rehabilitation programs failed, particularly those related to idle padi land, prompts an assessment in *Socioeconomic and institutional explanations for idle land* of underlying factors that the programs did not address adequately. Finally, *Conclusions* discusses implications of the analysis for current and future policy responses to the issue.

EMERGENCE OF THE IDLE LAND ISSUE

Land use in Malaysia as elsewhere is shaped by the interaction of many forces: climatic, physical, economic, social, and political. Idle land has been a phenomenon in the Peninsula since the earliest days of agricultural settlement, when population movements and shifting cultivation left some of the land that had been cleared for agriculture unused for varying periods of time, sometimes permanently. Around the turn of the century, much land was abandoned due to what was essentially large-scale shifting cultivation of tapioca, pepper, and gambier (Barlow 1978, Hill 1982).

Patterns of land use became more complex after British colonial rule was established and a modern land tenure system was introduced. The cultivation of cash crops, the establishment of individual ownership rights to land, and the resulting commercialization of land meant that land use became the outcome of decisions undertaken in a more complex economic environment. Under the land tenure system of colonial Malaya, owners could leave land idle without losing their ownership rights as long as they met certain conditions, such as payment of annual quitrent. In practice, this remains true today, although land that is not cultivated continuously or according to rules of good husbandry is technically liable to action by the state, including repossession, under the National Land Code. This penalty is seldom imposed, however.

Until the late 1970s, official concern over idle agricultural land was generally muted, as the principal concern of agricultural agencies was to expand the area cultivated and to improve the productivity of the smallholder sector in which the majority of *bumiputera* earned their living. Through the *Third Malaysia Plan 1976–1980*, the nation's development policy emphasized agricultural development and improving the socioeconomic status of traditional smallholders. In support of this policy, a two-pronged approach was devised to promote peasant agricultural development. One approach, extensification, involved the opening up of new land for farmers with little or no land of their own. The objective was to enable unemployed or underemployed labor to move into modern agricultural pursuits through large-scale, government-sponsored land development schemes. The second approach, intensification, involved the *in situ* development of existing cropland through the provision of infrastructure (e.g., irrigation), subsidized inputs, and extension services aimed at enhancing farm productivity.

The introduction of the New Economic Policy (NEP) provided new urgency to the task of bringing tangible development benefits to the rural population. As a result of the NEP's focus on poverty eradication and restructuring of the economy to reduce economic disparities between *bumiputera* and non-*bumiputera*, the three principal ministries involved in rural and agricultural development, the Ministries of Agriculture, Land and Regional Development, and Rural Development, undertook a more activist role in development. To accelerate implementation of the NEP, the government established a host of new agencies and entrusted them with specialized tasks in promoting the peasant economy. These new agencies included Bank Pertanian Malaysia (the national farmer's bank), established in 1970; the National Padi and Rice Authority, established in 1971; the Rubber Industry Smallholders' Development Authority (RISDA), established in 1972; and the Farmer's Organization Authority, established in 1973. At the same time, two existing agencies, the Federal Land Development Authority (FELDA), which had been established in 1956, and the Federal Land Consolidation and Rehabilitation Authority (FELCRA), which had been established in 1966, were expanded and given broader mandates. In addition to federal agencies, state governments became more heavily involved in agriculture through various economic, land development, and agricultural development corporations and boards.

Public sector agencies led the land development effort. In the early 1960s, the government virtually stopped the alienation of agricultural land to the private sector, except on a joint basis with the government, and it reserved the clearing and development of new agricultural land almost exclusively for public sector agencies (Barlow 1984). During the twenty years from 1970 to 1990, almost all new agricultural land brought into cultivation was in government land schemes, at federal and state levels. As Figure 1.4 showed, public sector land development peaked in the late 1970s and early 1980s under the *Third Malaysia Plan 1976–1980* and the *Fourth Malaysia Plan 1981–1985*, and public development expenditure for these purposes soared from RM364 million in years 1966 to 1970 to RM2.7 billion in years 1976 to 1980. According to official accounts, the impact of the considerable injection of public funds into peasant agriculture was positive. One observer has commented that "particularly in rubber and oil palm and also in irrigated rice as well as other smallholder crops, public sector investment has enabled the extension of new technologies and improved materials to much of the smallholder sub-sector," and noted that "the impact [of public investment] has generally modernized and structurally transformed a considerable part of the traditional agricultural sector" (Zulkifly 1983, p. 202).

Statistical trends support this claim. Average annual growth in aggregate agricultural output (sectoral GDP) in the country was 5.5 percent from 1971 to 1975 and 5.9 percent from 1976 to 1980 (Shand and Mohd. Ariff 1989, p. 309). Impressive increases were recorded for traditional as well as new crops. For rubber smallholdings outside land development schemes, aggregate latex production grew from 1960 to 1980 at an average annual rate of over 5 percent (Zulkifly 1983, p. 200). Aggregate rice output rose at an average annual rate of about 4 percent from 1960 to 1980, although growth in yield was more modest and averaged about 1.6 and 2.8 percent per year for the main and off-season crops during the same period (Zulkifly 1983, p. 200). The increase in palm-oil production was by far the most impressive, increasing by 112 percent from 1971 to 1975 and 109 percent from 1975 to 1980 (World Bank 1984, p. 3). Much of the increase came from smallholders in land development schemes. The most impressive statistics are those related to poverty. In the agricultural sector, the incidence of poverty fell from more than two-thirds in 1970, 68.3 percent, to less than half by 1980, 45.7 percent (Zulkifly 1989, p. 69).

Despite these encouraging indicators, government officials in agencies related to agriculture and rural development became increasingly concerned about the apparently rising incidence of idle land. The concern led the MOA to conduct a survey in 1978 to estimate the extent of idle land. The survey results were not published directly but rather cited in subsequent papers (for example, Mohd. Helmi 1980; Mustapha 1980; Abdul Rahim 1981; Kementerian Pertanian 1980, 1981; Wan Ibrahim 1982). The survey estimated that there were almost 900,000 hectares of idle land in Peninsular Malaysia. In the same year, the Implementation and Coordination Unit of the Prime Minister's Department completed a separate and also unpublished study, which estimated that there were about 565,000 hectares of idle land in proximity to 5,000 economically backward villages in the Peninsula. Though smaller than the estimate from the MOA's survey—which is not surprising, as the study did not involve a comprehensive survey—the estimate was still large relative to total agricultural area.

Following the survey, a stream of papers on idle land began flowing from the MOA and other agencies. Virtually all the papers advanced the same reasons why the government should be urgently concerned. First, they argued that since land is a productive resource, idle land represented a loss to the economy because the resource was not being fully utilized. For example, a task force established by the MOA estimated that padi farmers suffered an annual loss of RM109.5 million for single-cropped land and RM135 million for double-cropped land (Kementerian Pertanian 1980, p. 2). This concern was linked to the government's interest in promoting self-sufficiency for essential foods, in particular rice. This interest was formalized in the 1984 National Agricultural Policy, which set a goal of 80 to 85 percent self-sufficiency for rice (Cabinet Committee on Agriculture 1984).

Second, they argued that there was a link between idle land and the high incidence of poverty in rural areas. According to the study by the Implementation and Coordination Unit, the villages included in the study had not benefitted from the country's economic development because they lacked basic infrastructure, social services, and other factors necessary for modernizing agriculture and other sectors. With agriculture stagnant and hardly any alternative employment opportunities being created, village youth drifted to urban areas. The resulting reduction in the local agricultural work force forced land out of production. Inaction on idle land, the papers argued, would further increase rural poverty and accelerate rural-urban drift, which in turn would exacerbate the idle land problem. A conviction that "the development of these idle resources, viz. idle padi and other agricultural lands, can and indeed must provide an avenue to augment farm size, productivity, and therefore incomes of low-income farm families" (Zulkifly and Shaik 1985, p. 46), was shared by most writers on the subject during the late 1970s and early 1980s. It was reflected in the National Agricultural Policy, which emphasized provision of subsidies, easy credit, and other means of raising farm income to keep land in production, and public investment in rehabilitation programs to bring idle land back into production. One of the stated objectives of the policy was to "facilitate the retention of productive labour in agriculture" (quoted by Courtenay 1986, p. 183). This objective was appealing to political leaders at the time, many of whom expressed alarm at the lack of interest among young rural *bumiputera* for work in agriculture and were concerned that insufficient jobs were being created in urban areas to absorb them as they migrated.

Finally, and provocatively for the time, some papers pointed out that the existence of idle land cast doubt on the wisdom of continued development of new land. How sensible was it to continue opening up new land at a high cost, when land that was already developed was going out of production? A later paper summarized these doubts in the following, typically cautious, manner: "the development of new land for agriculture should be weighed against productive allocation of land resources through intensification, extensification, and diversification." (Nasaruddin and Zulkifly 1986, p. 86).

One of the most influential papers was written by Burrows (1980).[7] He called for policy measures to achieve three objectives, all of them related to his conviction that land was left idle because landowners did not have "sufficient financial incentives to cultivate their land." The first was to increase the incomes obtained from annual crops, with priority being given to padi. He estimated that a 5 percent increase in average padi yields would boost rural incomes by RM40 million and would "bring far greater benefits to more farmers than all the efforts to promote minor foodcrops." The second was to integrate smallholders better into the modern tree-crop sector. He saw this as the key to both *in situ* and new land development. He argued for a clearly formulated strategy for tree-crop development, appropriate tree-crop development programs to implement the strategy, and an appropriate institutional framework to support the programs. The third objective was to provide smallholders with more land through the rationalization of existing holdings. He recommended a minimum farm size of 20 acres (about 8 ha) and urged the government to prepare for a massive land consolidation program during the 1980s and 1990s to achieve this goal.

Following its survey, the MOA established a special interagency task force to plan for the rehabilitation of idle padi land. Composed of representatives from Bank Pertanian Malaysia, the Malaysian Agricultural Research and Development Institute, the Drainage and Irrigation Department, the Federal Agricultural Marketing Authority, the Department of Agriculture, and the Ministry itself, the task force endorsed an ambitious program to tackle the problem. In its first stage, the program was projected to rehabilitate 31,702 acres from 1980 to 1985 and to cost RM37.5 million for infrastructure and inputs (Kementerian Pertanian 1980, p.88). Besides this program, the Ministry of Land and Regional Development and the Ministry of Rural Development also launched substantial idle land development projects and programs. The National Agricultural Policy formulated at this time illustrates the importance that policy makers attached to the issue: the policy made the rehabilitation of idle land one of the three main components of the country's agricultural modernization program up to the year 2000 (Shand and Mohd. Ariff 1989, p. 312).

Virtually all the papers emanated from government agencies responsible for agricultural development. To the extent that these agencies had a vested interest in additional programs, projects, and funding, it is not surprising that they portrayed the issue as a "problem" and stressed the need for government action. By the late 1980s, a host of new papers and reports appeared, many authored by academics (e.g., Zulkifly and Shaik 1985, Courtenay 1986, Gibbons and Mohd. Ariff 1986, Zulkifly 1989, Amriah 1989, Mohd. Fuad 1989, Mohd. Ghazali and Abdul Aziz 1989, Fujimoto 1991, Pazim 1992).[8] Despite their generally nongovernmental origin, with some being written by international scholars, for the most part they reinforced the official perception of idle land as a major obstacle to agricultural development in the country.

What is surprising about the idle land literature, past and present, official and unofficial, is a general lack of rigorous analysis of several fundamental aspects of the issue: the relative importance of possible causes, the economic consequences of land abandonment, and the benefits and costs of the various rehabilitation projects and programs pursued since the late 1970s. To be sure, the immediate cause of land abandonment was obvious: the outflow of labor from traditional smallholder agriculture to other pursuits. This outflow was not new: Courtenay (1986) observed that the population growth rate in padi-growing districts was lower than the national average from 1947 to 1970, and he attributed the difference to outmigration. But it accelerated during the 1970s and 1980s, with the rapid growth in jobs in manufacturing, services, and the public sector that offered average wages above those in agriculture (International Fund for Agricultural Development 1990, Annex II, p. 2). Pazim (1992), citing other studies, reported that padi farmers in irrigated schemes had become increasingly engaged in more lucrative off-farm employment. The tightening of the rural labor market by the late 1970s was a remarkable turnaround from the situation little more than a decade earlier, when land development was promoted as a key strategy for absorbing surplus rural labor (Gates, Goering, and Keare 1967).

In some cases, migration was within the agricultural sector, as families moved to land development schemes. This was especially true for *bumiputera*, who accounted for the bulk of the traditional agricultural population. Of the 2.4 million people who migrated within Peninsular Malaysia from 1970 to 1980, two out of three were *bumiputera*, and most moved to land development schemes and industrial estates (Mehmet 1986, pp. 79–80). Migration to development schemes naturally left land idle in the areas vacated.

Migration had an impact even when entire families did not move. Many of the migrants were the sons and daughters of farm families. The steady outflow of rural youths caused an aging of the farm population. A study of heads of households in the padi area administered by the Muda Agricultural Development Authority (the Muda scheme)[9] in 1976 showed an average age of 44.4 years, with only 10 percent below 40 years but 30 percent above 60 years. More recently, two nationwide studies found that the mean age of independent smallholders was 49 years during 1982–86 (Jabatan Pertanian 1988), and that farmers over 46 years old comprised more than 64 percent of all farmers from 1990 to 1991 (Jabatan Pertanian 1992). Fadzim (1990) cited mean ages of 55 and 56 years, respectively, for padi farmers in samples drawn from the Muda and Kemubu irrigation schemes.[10] Fujimoto (1991, note 4) commented, "It is my observation in a Kelantan village that not a single youth had entered into the production of rice after 1973." Taking land out of production was one response by farmers to the diminishing household labor pool and their advancing age.[11]

The obvious importance of migration begs the more fundamental question raised earlier, however: Had the returns to agriculture become lower relative to other activities because of inevitable socioeconomic forces, or because of institutional factors that had unnecessarily reduced agricultural returns? In simple terms, was labor pulled out of agriculture or pushed? In the former case, true agricultural land rents had fallen below zero, causing smallholder income to fall below its opportunity cost. In the latter case, rents could theoretically be made positive once the institutional distortions were removed.

Inherent difficulties in approaching the issue have surely hindered economic analysis in previous studies, but attempting such an analysis is important because of its potential implications for current and future agricultural policies. The remainder of this chapter attempts such an analysis.

THE EXTENT OF IDLE LAND

Since the extent of idle land has bearing on perceptions of it as a problem, one must begin by attempting to arrive at an accurate estimate of its extent. Prior to the 1978 MOA survey, official attempts to classify the use of agricultural land in the country made little effort to determine whether cropland was in use. In part this reflected the difficulty of making this determination, particularly for tree crops. For example, one cannot determine whether tree-crop plantations are in use or not by examining aerial photographs.

The first agricultural census after independence, the 1960 Census of Agriculture, estimated the area of uncultivated land, but this was defined as a broad category that included not only abandoned land but also grassland, scrub forest (low *belukar*, or second growth), and primary jungle. The census report cautioned that owners of agricultural estates might leave land temporarily uncultivated for a number of reasons (Selvadurai 1963, p. vii).

Since the 1960 census, the three land use surveys cited in *Introduction* and Table 5.1 have provided information on areas in agricultural use in the Peninsula approximately every ten years. They have not, however, provided much information on idle land. The first survey, which was based on aerial photographs taken in 1966, estimated the area of "Unused Land," but this referred to beaches, mudflats, exposed rocks, cliffs, and other land considered unproductive, not cropland that had gone out of use (Wong 1971). The second survey, for 1974, employed a combination of aerial photographs and cadastral data on alienated land (Economic Planning Unit 1980). It contained a more elaborate categorization of land use, including areas with "senile" (overmature) tree crops: plantations that had exceeded their economic lifespan and were overdue for replanting. The total was just under 300,000 ha: 280,539 ha for rubber, 7,596 for coconut, and 6,972 for oil palm. These estimates may be viewed as indicative of the area of idle tree-crop land, but the survey report was not published until after the MOA survey, in 1980. The third survey, for 1984, eliminated the "senile" categories. A full report on this survey has never been published, although aggregate results are sometimes cited in MOA publications, occasionally anomalously for 1981 (for example, Kementerian Pertanian 1990, p. 31).[12]

The 1978 MOA survey therefore represents the principal source of official data on the extent of idle land. Unfortunately, it does not appear to have been designed and implemented with much rigor. No field enumeration of smallholdings was conducted, nor were farmers questioned about whether their land was in use or not. The survey consisted of a standardized form sent out by the Department of Agriculture to its field staff, who filled in their subjective estimates of the extent of idle land in their districts. The department subsequently tabulated these estimates to produce state and national totals.

Central to the exercise was the issue of how to decide whether land was in use, temporarily idle, or permanently abandoned. To ensure that there was some degree of comparability among the responses of the field staff, the department provided a definition of idle land. Idle land was defined as land with freehold title or a temporary occupation license (pending the issuance of a permanent title) that met *any* of the following criteria:

1. padi land that was not cultivated or used for grazing purposes for three consecutive years;
2. padi land that was provided with the physical infrastructure for double cropping but was single cropped only;
3. padi land that was planted with crops other than padi; and

4. rubber and other tree-crop land that was either abandoned or not fully utilized (e.g., tapped infrequently).

This definition is based on sections 114, 115, 120, and 121 in the National
Land Code, which described circumstances under which the state could take
action against landowners. Note that it applied only to private lands.

The first part of the definition is a straightforward description of land that
can logically be considered "idle." The remaining three parts appear less
justified. In regard to the second and third parts, it is difficult to see why padi
land that is single cropped or planted with other crops should be considered
idle, since it is in fact being used. As for the fourth part, it was (and is) the
customary practice of rubber smallholders to alternate between work on the
farm and other work, depending on the relative returns. Classifying partially
tapped rubber land as "idle" might not match a smallholder's own view of its
status. These excessively broad features of the definition surely contributed to
the survey's estimating such a large area. Yet, no serious objections to the
MOA's definition appear to have been raised at the time of the survey or since.
Even today, the MOA's definition and the associated estimates of the area of
idle land continue to provide the benchmarks cited in governmental and
academic papers on the issue.

According to the survey, 730,060 ha of tree-crop land and 160,940 ha of
padi land were idle in Peninsular Malaysia. These estimates represented 25 to
30 percent of tree-crop and padi areas in the late 1970s (based on figures in
Table 5.2). Reports based on the survey have provided more detailed estimates, though mainly on idle padi land. Table 5.3 shows the distribution of
idle padi land by state and status, as estimated by the survey. Half or more of
the padi land was idle in six states. However, half of the total area was in a
single state, Kelantan, which was the poorest and most agricultural state in the
country. Moreover, most of the "idle" land in that state (three-fourths) was
padi land that was just single cropped. Idle padi land was therefore a "problem" whose incidence varied substantially among the states, and for the most
part it did not take the form of land that was not being worked at all.

The reports contain much less detail on the survey's estimates of idle tree-
crop land. This is unfortunate, considering that this category comprised more
than four-fifths of the total idle area. Two pieces of evidence suggest that the estimate of 730,060 ha was overstated. First, this estimate is hard to reconcile with
the 1974 land use survey. According to statements in the reports, most of the
idle tree-crop land consisted of overmature rubber and coconut smallholdings.
Yet, the 1974 land use survey reported a "senile" tree-crop area of only 295,107
ha. The overmature area could not have more than doubled in just four years.
Second, the MOA estimate is inconsistent with data on rubber replanting col-

Table 5.3 Area of idle padi land in Peninsular Malaysia, 1978 (hectares)

State	Area of padi land	Idle padi land Continuously idle[a]	Idle during off season	Total[b]	
Johor	4,239	1,681	881	2,562	(61%)
Kedah	124,588	4,358	288	4,646	(4%)
Kelantan	84,426	20,009	62,038	82,046	(97%)
Melaka	11,497	3,334	3,334	6,668	(58%)
Negeri Sembilan	14,753	9,386	5,040	14,426	(98%)
Pahang	17,990	9,989	1,632	11,621	(65%)
Perak	50,547	9,026	2,744	11,770	(23%)
Perlis	25,750	—	1,880	1,880	(7%)
Pulau Pinang	18,198	5,633	840	6,473	(35%)
Selangor	20,662	1,427	293	1,720	(8%)
Terengganu	29,136	7,028	10,101	17,129	(59%)
Total	401,786	71,871	89,070	160,941	(40%)

Source: Kementerian Pertanian (1981).

[a] Refers to padi land unused for at least three consecutive years.

[b] Idle land as a percentage of total padi land is in parentheses.

lected by RISDA, the main rubber smallholder agency in the country. The reports do not indicate how the idle tree-crop land was divided between rubber and coconut, but if it was proportional to the total planted area of each crop,[13] then the figure would be about 600,000 ha for rubber smallholdings. But a 1977 survey based on RISDA's census of smallholders estimated that only about 265,000 ha of rubber, a figure remarkably close to the "senile" figure in the 1974 land use survey, had not been replanted by the end of 1977 (RISDA 1983, p. xiii). RISDA's own replanting records gave an even lower figure, only 120,000 ha, as not having been replanted by that date.

THE POLICY RESPONSE TO IDLE LAND

Evaluating the policy response to idle land is not easy for several reasons. One is the fragmentation of administrative responsibility for agriculture and land development among numerous agencies. Projects to rehabilitate idle land have been carried out by FELCRA, RISDA, the Farmers' Organization Authority, agencies administering Integrated Agricultural Development projects, and state agencies. A comprehensive review of these projects would be a daunting exercise. Moreover, rehabilitation efforts were usually part of programs with broader objectives, such as crop diversification, food security, or poverty eradication. Defining these efforts as distinct projects is in many cases difficult.

It is also difficult to determine how *in situ* development programs have affected the incidence of idle land. Public expenditure on *in situ* development programs has included not only rehabilitation, but also drainage and irrigation, replanting, crop diversification, agricultural research, and other activities that certainly had some impact on smallholders' land use decisions. Table 5.4 shows public development expenditure on various *in situ* and related programs to assist smallholders from 1976 to 1990. Programs other than rehabilitation per se accounted for nearly 90 percent of the expenditure.

Evaluating rehabilitation programs that had idle land as their explicit target is a more limited but more feasible objective. The following sections focus on the programs of two agencies: FELCRA, the lead government agency responsible for land rehabilitation, and the MOA, which has specific responsibility for rehabilitating idle padi land.

FELCRA's rehabilitation programs for tree-crop land

FELCRA was established for the express purpose of rehabilitating idle land. Since its inception, it has focused on nonpadi land, mainly tree-crop land. The rehabilitation of independent smallholdings dominated its activities initially, but in 1984 it was directed to address unsuccessful land development schemes

Table 5.4   *Public development expenditure on in situ and related agricultural programs in Malaysia, 1976-1990 (RM million)*

	1976–1980 [a]	1981–1985	1986–1990
In situ development	994.89	2,801.89	2,693.2
IADPs [b]	198.23	476.66	1,021.8
Drainage & irrigation	554.84	1,424.64	200.3
Flood & coastal protection			77.2
Replanting	241.82	396.64	581.2
Rehabilitation [c]	0	503.95	812.7
Support services	393.45	1,082.18	1,011.8
Input subsidies for padi	101.80	430.16	396.8
Agricultural credit, etc.	270.70	576.85	586.1
Extension & other services	20.95	75.17	28.9
Other programs of MOA [d]	162.21	289.49	329.3
Total	1,550.55	4,173.56	4,034.3

Sources: For 1976–80, *Fourth Malaysia Plan* (pp. 290–91); for 1981–85, *Fifth Malaysia Plan* (p. 329); for 1986–90, *Sixth Malaysia Plan* (p. 121).

Note: Estimated actual expenditure, not original or revised allocation. Figures exclude some rural development programs, such as water supply, roads, and health services.

[a] Expenditure was reallocated for IADPs and other programs according to headings in the *Fifth Malaysia Plan.*

[b] IADPs—Integrated Agricultural Development Projects.

[c] Mainly padi land rehabilitation.

[d] MOA—Ministry of Agriculture

sponsored by state governments as well. Data on the area of failed state schemes at that time are not available, but land use surveys suggest that it might have been large. The grassland and scrub forest categories included in the surveys include, *inter alia*, land development schemes that did not proceed beyond the land clearing stage. Table 5.1 shows that the area of this cleared but undeveloped land was comparable to the official estimates of idle cropland: 1,000,000 ha in 1966, 727,000 ha in 1974, and 632,000 in 1984. These statistics provide support for Forestry Department claims, starting in the 1960s, of "unsuccessful land development schemes and neglected holdings" (*Malayan Forester* 1968, p. 73).

FELCRA's usual approach was to reorganize land development schemes as group-farming schemes. In effect, these were government-run estates in which participants were not so much managers of their own land as workers in enterprises administered by FELCRA. As its name implies, it classified the schemes as rehabilitation schemes proper and consolidation schemes. Of the 247,000 ha developed by the agency through 1990, about one-third were in rehabilitation schemes and two-thirds in consolidation schemes. The *modus operandi* in rehabilitation schemes was determined by the area of land available for rehabilitation. Besides the large-scale, group-farming approach, individual smallholdings in villages near an existing FELCRA scheme could be rehabilitated on a farm-by-farm basis by the landowners themselves or by casual labor engaged by FELCRA, with the scheme providing management advice and technical assistance. By the end of 1990, an estimated 38,300 smallholder families were involved in rehabilitation schemes.

In consolidation schemes, FELCRA combined the rehabilitation of idle land with the development of new land. It used several approaches, including consolidation through resettlement and consolidation through village restructuring. Despite the large number of smallholders with inadequate-sized farms, only 8,500 families participated in consolidation schemes in 1990.

Although the number of participants in its programs was relatively small, FELCRA contributed successfully to alleviating rural poverty. According to a report by the World Bank (1990, p. 41), farm incomes in FELCRA's schemes at the end of 1987 were 44 to 100 percent higher than those for comparable smallholdings that had not been rehabilitated. Consolidation schemes provided 20 percent higher incomes than rehabilitation schemes, due to their larger average farm sizes. Whether rubber or oil-palm schemes provided higher incomes depended on crop prices in a given year.

Other evidence also indicates that FELCRA's schemes performed well. The completion report for a five-year project funded by the World Bank, which involved 34,000 ha of smallholdings in 90 group-farming schemes with 12,000 households, reported that crop yields were close to target profiles and estimated that the overall economic rate of return for the project was 13 percent (World Bank 1990, p. ii). The financial rate of return for a representative oil-palm scheme was 21 percent, while that for a rubber scheme was 13 percent (p. 42). For a World Bank project intended to rehabilitate 48,000 ha of idle land (among other objectives) and to improve incomes for 24,000 smallholder families during 1992–95, an appraisal report projected economic rates of return of 12 percent for rubber schemes and 11 percent for oil-palm schemes (World Bank 1992, p. 46).

These appraisals overstated the returns to FELCRA schemes, however, because they typically did not account fully for the agency's substantial overhead costs. FELCRA had a complex bureaucratic structure, consisting of managers and supervisors, agricultural officers and engineers, administrative staff, and officers responsible for social development, marketing, and finance. This bureaucracy was subsidized by government grants, and it became increasingly expensive to maintain. In 1988, 1989 and 1990, government grants for FELCRA's operating expenses amounted to RM81.5 million, RM117.1 million, and RM139.4 million, respectively, out of the agency's total operating expenses of RM192.1 million, RM194.5 million, and RM217.4 million (World Bank 1992, p. 63).[14] The World Bank recommended that FELCRA progressively disengage itself from the management of schemes that had fully repaid their land development costs, and possibly from other schemes that demonstrated good financial performance, and introduce a system of graduated management fees to recoup more of its operating costs (World Bank 1992, pp. 22–23).

The agency's supporters have argued that the high level of subsidy should not be an issue because smallholders' welfare, not economic efficiency, is the main concern of the schemes. The first of FELCRA's stated objectives is "to improve the standard of living of the rural people, and to reduce disparities of income" (FELCRA, n.d., p. 3). Even if this objective is accepted as paramount, it did not provide a very compelling justification for subsidization. This is because the selection procedures for FELCRA schemes did not favor tenant farmers and landowners with the smallest holdings, who were generally the poorest farmers and should be the main target group if redistribution is the objective. State-level committees selected the participants. FELCRA, which sat on the committees, had a set of selection criteria that it recommended to the state governments, but these criteria did not emphasize existing farm size.[15] In the case of rehabilitation schemes, the main criterion was simply that the applicant possess either land or a house in the vicinity of the project area. In the case of consolidation schemes, there were four major criteria: that the applicant be a Malaysian citizen, be married, be more than twenty one years old and less than fifty, and not be a civil servant. A 1977 survey found that the average farm size of poverty-group rubber smallholders was less than 2 ha (RISDA 1983, p. xi), while the average size of smallholdings in FELCRA schemes ranged from 2.43 to 4.05 ha (FELCRA, n.d., p. 22).

In part, the downplaying of farm size reflected economic considerations: economies of scale (particularly with regard to administrative costs) are more easily achieved when individual land holdings are larger. This led, for example, to a bias against locating schemes in densely populated areas, where land holdings were small. However, it also made welfare considerations more vulnerable to being displaced by political considerations, which have long affected land development decisions in the states. Guyot (1971) linked the poor performance of state development schemes to political involvement in land development. She argued that a major reason why schemes were more successful in Johor than Terengganu was that "land is distributed to build political support" in the latter state. According to her, schemes were developed as a short-run means of recruiting and rewarding political supporters; not much importance was attached to the viability of the schemes. In a similar vein, Syed Hussain (1972) claimed that "In both Felda [*sic*] and KSLDA [Kelantan State Land Development Authority] schemes the selection procedure [for settlers] has been so designed that political affiliation becomes the final criterion for determining selection." The Forestry Department also insinuated that some state governments used land development as an excuse to increase the area of forest opened for logging, in order to generate additional revenue for state treasuries (*Malayan Forester* 1970).

MOA's rehabilitation programs for padi land

Although the MOA has been involved in padi land rehabilitation for over a decade, it does not appear to have maintained accessible records on the resources it expended on the programs. There is also a paucity of data on the performance of the programs. Fujimoto (1991, Table VI) compiled MOA data indicating that 12.8 percent (roughly 21,000 ha) of the idle padi land in the country was rehabilitated from 1981 to 1985, but he apparently was not able to compile corresponding data on the costs of the programs and the degree of rehabilitation. Only a handful of studies have managed to obtain sufficient data for evaluating the MOA's programs. Three are reviewed below.

The most ambitious and most expensive padi land rehabilitation program was a project funded by the World Bank and implemented between 1978 and 1982. The major objective was to rehabilitate 60,000 ha of idle padi land in 200 schemes throughout the country. References in a recent World Bank report indicate that the project failed badly (World Bank 1988). Only 111 of the 200 schemes were built, and participation in these schemes was low. Cropping intensity was also low. Cropping intensity would equal 100 percent if all the area in a scheme were single cropped, and 200 percent if all the area were double cropped. On a project-wide basis, average cropping intensity increased during 1981–83 (from 27 percent to 48 percent), but it was below 50 percent in each year. Moreover, according to the report (Annex 1, p. 10), "After six years and an investment of RM 180 million it became apparent that farmer interest had waned. Cropping intensities on completed schemes actually fell from 109% in 1976 to 48% in 1983, ranging from 0% in Selangor to 107% in Perlis, out of a possible 200%." The report estimated that the ex post rate of return on the project was only 3 percent.

Why did so few farmers participate in the project? The principal reason was that they had more lucrative employment opportunities. A survey conducted by the World Bank found that padi accounted for only 4 to 14 percent of household income on schemes in Negeri Sembilan, Perlis, and Melaka.[16] The balance came mostly from off-farm employment and cultivation of oil palm. As these three states had among the highest cropping intensities, the contribution of padi to household income was even lower in other states. Such findings suggest that, in the face of the rising opportunity cost of labor, much of the padi land was no longer capable of generating a positive rent. This conclusion is strengthened when one considers that padi farmers received abundant subsidies: they were furnished, for free or below cost, seeds of high-yielding varieties, fertilizer (free for up to 2.4 ha per household per season, beginning in 1979), irrigation water (see Chapter 7), and price supports (Courtenay 1986, Fujimoto 1991).[17] The World Bank (1988) concluded that "even with the most supportive policy measures, these marginal areas could not be sustained."

Two more recent studies, both conducted by government agencies, have also reported a high failure rate for padi land rehabilitation projects. The Socio-Economic Research Unit (Unit Penyelidikan Sosio-Ekonomi 1988) evaluated thirty-two projects that utilized the "mini-estate" approach. This approach was analogous to FELCRA's group-farming approach, with public or private sector organizations providing centralized management.[18] The study found that ten of the projects, accounting for 32 percent of the total land, had been terminated by the time the study was conducted, which was approximately eight years after the projects were initiated. Most of the terminated projects were managed by private companies that went out of business due to high management costs, pest problems, and inadequate infrastructure. The failures occurred despite the projects having access to subsidies and other forms of assistance beyond what was normally available to padi farmers. The projects that continued were mainly ones operated or supported by government agencies. These projects appear to have been able to continue only because their management costs were subsidized and their losses were absorbed by the government.

The study also attempted a more detailed examination of the economics of four representative projects. It estimated yields, costs, and incomes before and after the projects. It found that yields increased in all projects, by 12 to 60 percent,[19] and that participants' incomes increased as well.[20] All the projects, however, showed net losses after accounting for management and capital costs, which often were the largest components of mini-estates' costs.

The third study, by the Ministry of Agriculture (Kementerian Pertanian 1989), stemmed from a survey conducted by the MOA's Agricultural Economics Division in 1986. This survey had attempted to determine why padi land that had officially been rehabilitated had fallen back into disuse.[21] According to the study, 41 percent of the padi area in forty-seven rehabilitation projects implemented by the Ministry from 1981 to 1985 had reverted to a state of idleness. The study concluded that despite the considerable investment of public resources by agencies involved in the projects—the government had borne most of the development costs of rehabilitation work, besides providing the usual padi-related subsidies—the same factors that had made the land idle in the first place were still present after the schemes were implemented. Chief among them was a shortage of labor.

In the early 1990s, the Farmers' Organization Authority was the lead agency responsible for the Ministry's Padi Land Rehabilitation Programme. Since 1986 it implemented the program through two types of farm management systems, group farming and mini-estates. Under the group-farming system, projects were initiated by the local Farmers' Organization Authority. A manager was appointed to supervise implementation, but participating farmers retained land ownership and responsibility for management. The government provided technical assistance and grants for infrastructure. Under the mini-estate system, private enterprises implemented the projects. Padi farmers leased their lands to the enterprise for a specified period and were given priority to work the land if they so desired. They could also hold shares in the enterprise.

The official position of the authority was that these systems enabled farmers to participate in decisions on activities that affected their land and their livelihoods, but both systems were characterized by highly bureaucratic structures. They were aimed at centralizing farm operations and thereby reducing costs and increasing productivity, but they proved to be high-cost operations dependent on continued government subsidies. From 1986 to 1990, the authority disbursed more grants (RM14.8 million) than loans (RM13.7 million) to rehabilitate 14,000 ha of padi land (Lembaga Pertubuhan Peladang n.d., p. 2; see also Lembaga Pertubuhan Peladang 1991). These amounts do not include the costs of services and inputs provided by other government agencies. The loans were disbursed through the agricultural loan scheme operated by Bank Pertanian Malaysia. No information is available on the loan repayment rate, but it was probably low: Bank Pertanian's overall loan repayment rate from 1986 to 1989 ranged between only 35.2 and 43.9 percent (International Fund for Agricultural Development 1990, Annex III, p. 32). Neither the Authority nor the MOA conducted benefit-cost analyses of the projects, so it is not possible to assess whether the net returns from the RM1,000 to 2,000 per hectare of direct financial assistance and the unquantified costs of management services were positive. The pessimistic findings of the studies by the World Bank (1988), the Socio-Economic Research Unit (Unit Penyelidikan Sosio-Ekonomi 1988), and the Ministry of Agriculture (Kementerian Pertanian 1989), which covered similar projects, make one skeptical.

SOCIOECONOMIC AND INSTITUTIONAL EXPLANATIONS FOR IDLE LAND

Despite heavy subsidization, the MOA's programs to rehabilitate idle padi land achieved little success. FELCRA's tree-crop programs were more successful, but they too involved large subsidies. All of this suggests that under prevailing market conditions and institutional arrangements, idle land was not capable of generating positive agricultural rents. Smallholders who abandoned their land were behaving rationally, as they took up new livelihoods that made them economically better off. To the extent that market conditions were such that smallholding would not have paid off under any conceivable institutional arrangements, short of subsidization, their behavior should not have concerned the government. They were being pulled out of smallholder agriculture by fundamentally more attractive employment opportunities in other sectors. On the other hand, to the extent that smallholders were pushed out by aspects of land tenure and other institutional factors that made smallholding economically less attractive than it could have been, then the government's concern was justified. In this case, policy interventions might have been able to modify the institutional factors and maintain the economic viability of smallholding.

Declining crop prices were a market-related factor that combined with the rising opportunity cost of labor to reduce the economic returns to smallholding. Rubber prices declined more or less continually from 1950 into the early 1970s, even in nominal terms (Vincent and Yusuf 1991, Figure 4). They increased sharply during the 1970s but resumed their long-term declining trend after 1980. This was one of the principal factors that induced estates to initiate large-scale conversion from rubber to oil palm and land development schemes to favor oil palm over rubber after the early 1960s (Vincent and Yusuf 1991; see also Chapter 10). For smallholders whose land was steep (where oil-palm does not do well) or distant from the nearest palm-oil mill (palm-oil fruits must be processed immediately, or else they spoil), leaving the land idle was the only option.

In the case of padi, the National Padi and Rice Board, which was established in 1971, controlled the padi market (Fujimoto 1991, Pazim 1992). It purchased padi from farmers at a guaranteed minimum price, which it reviewed annually.[22] In response to the first oil shock, which caused fertilizer prices to rise sharply (oil is the principal raw material for making nitrogen fertilizers), the government added a price subsidy in 1974. This increased the price received by farmers by about 50 percent. During the next fifteen years, however, the price, inclusive of subsidy, remained virtually constant in nominal terms (Pazim 1992, Table 4). After adjusting for inflation, it of course declined.

Negative price trends for the two crops reflected international market conditions over which the government had little control and which would have decreased the returns to agriculture regardless of institutional arrangements. There is evidence, however, that institutional factors made the squeeze worse. Problems with state governments' approach to land development schemes were mentioned in *FELCRA's rehabilitation programs for tree-crop land*. On private Malay smallholdings, the most important institutional factor was declining farm size resulting from customary (*adat*) and Islamic inheritance laws, under which property is divided among male and female children. All children receive equal shares in the case of *adat* inheritance, but sons receive twice as much as daughters under Islamic law. Constant subdivision of land resulted in fragmentation, eventually making the land held by each heir too small to provide the sole source of household income, at best, or to be farmed at all, at worst (Amriah 1988, pp. 5–12). This forced farm families to pursue off-farm work. If no such work was available locally, they migrated to urban areas or land development schemes. Even after moving they almost always retained ownership of the land: a reluctance to sell or even to mortgage *tanah pusaka*, or inheritance land, is a frequently cited characteristic of traditional Malay culture (Suhaini 1991). In the absence of a pool of land-poor farmers willing to rent the land, the land remained idle. A related consequence was widespread multiple ownership of land (Amriah 1988, p. 11). This impeded investments necessary to increase productivity through replanting of tree crops and crop diversification, because of the difficulty of getting multiple owners to reach agreement.

Small farm size hindered the normal response to rising labor scarcity, mechanization. This was especially true in the padi sector. The Agricultural Census of 1977 reported that only 2 percent of padi smallholders had more than 3 ha; 69 percent had no more than 0.89 ha. Courtenay (1986) compared state-level data on average size of padi holdings and percentage of idle land (defined narrowly as land not cultivated for three or more years) and found that there was an almost perfect negative correlation between the two. Larger farms indeed began using combine harvesters and adopted labor-saving, direct-seeding methods as the rural labor supply shrank (Pazim 1992). This occurred particularly in Kedah, Perlis, and Selangor, where farms tended to be larger (Fujimoto 1991). Note that Table 5.3 indicates that these three states had the lowest incidence of idle land. Smaller farms were less able to mechanize (Pazim 1992, Courtenay 1986). In the case of rubber, mechanization was hindered more by technical obstacles to the development of machinery that could trim, to the right depth and at the right place, the bark on tree trunks that vary greatly in size and straightness. Prospects for mechanization were reduced by the steep slopes of many rubber plantations.

Various government policies also inadvertently raised the incidence of idle land, especially in the padi sector. Crop diversification was hindered by rigid land conversion policies (Perunding Bersatu 1988, p. 59). Conditions in the titles for padi land usually barred its use for other crops (World Bank 1988, p. 11). Since 1917, the Rice Lands Enactment has prohibited state land suitable for wet padi from being alienated for other purposes, and crops other than padi from being grown on Malay-held lands suitable for its cultivation (Courtenay 1986). Where conversion of smallholdings was permitted (e.g., in the case of rubber smallholdings), approval of applications for conversion could take a year or longer. This discouraged owners from pursuing diversification (Perunding Bersatu 1988, p. 37). Padi land rents were controlled under the 1967 Padi Cultivators Act, which was intended to protect tenants' rights. Maximum rents were not raised over time, and this reduced the attractiveness of leasing as an alternative to leaving land idle.

The Malay Reservation Enactment, which prohibited the transfer of ownership of Malay Reserve Land to other races, also distorted land markets and contributed to the creation of idle land. The enactment has been in existence since 1913, and it encompassed most of the country's padi land. Its original intent was to prevent non-Malays from dispossessing Malay peasants. The enactment indeed succeeded in retaining a high proportion of land under Malay control. By preventing non-Malays from purchasing such land, however, it foreclosed options that might have prevented the land from becoming idle. Courtenay (1986) cited evidence that it depressed land values.

Conclusions

Only a minority of the area estimated as idle in Peninsular Malaysia in the late 1970s was not in any agricultural use at all. Most "idle" padi land was in fact cropped during at least one season, and most "idle" tree-crop land was probably utilized at least intermittently. The "problem" was not as big as the MOA's estimate of 900,000 ha implied. Even land that was truly idle may not have represented an economic problem. Land that was idle due solely to socioeconomic forces, such as rising labor costs and declining crop prices, was no longer capable of generating a positive land rent. It could be kept in production only through subsidization, which decreased the country's net economic output by diverting public funds from more productive uses. Land that was idle due to institutional factors, however, was indeed an economic problem: it could have generated a positive rent if those factors were overcome. Chief among the institutional factors were poor design and management of state land development schemes, fragmentation of holdings due to customary and Islamic inheritance laws, and rigidities in the land market due to the Malay Reservation Enactment and other policies. How much land was idle due to institutional factors as opposed to socioeconomic forces is unknown; some land was surely idle for both reasons.

Rehabilitation programs were more successful in eliminating institutional factors in the case of idle tree-crop land than in the case of idle padi land. Some of the tree-crop rehabilitation programs might not have been economically viable, however, if the overhead costs of FELCRA and other agencies involved were taken into account. Distributional considerations did not provide a compelling justification for subsidizing the programs: the participants who benefitted the most were not the hard-core rural poor or the landless, but rather farmers who already owned more than the average amount of land.

Idle land that was a consequence of rural people voluntarily seeking better employment opportunities in urban areas and better (or more) land in development schemes can be viewed as a sign of the country's development success (Sivalingam 1993). A shrinking of the agricultural labor force is a standard feature of economic development (Timmer 1988), and Malaysia is not the only country where this process has been accompanied by large-scale abandonment of agricultural land. In the United States, for example, at least 50 million ha of cropland and pasture were abandoned in the half century between 1920 and 1970 (based on statistics presented in Clawson 1979). This represented about a fifth of the agricultural land at the beginning of the period.

Hart (1968) documented this process in the eastern United States.[23] Large-scale land abandonment began in the second half of the nineteenth century in the northeast, the part of the country where the Industrial Revolution first took hold. It accelerated during the industrial boom years during and immediately after World War II. In less than two decades (1940–1959), cleared farmland in the eastern United States declined by 15 percent (21 million ha).[24] Most of the abandoned land eventually reverted to forest, although a fifth to a third was put into urban use. Hart's descriptions of the process could well refer to Peninsular Malaysia in the 1970s and 1980s:

Individual fields may be abandoned on a farm which continues to operate, or the whole farm may be abandoned; the latter is often associated with the migration of the farm family to another area (p. 418).

Farms and fields are too small. . . . A high proportion of the farmers are older men, with limited management skills and little interest in change or investment in long-range improvements. Many farmers labor under additional handicaps imposed by race or tenure (p. 435).

Among the factors that led to abandonment of cotton fields in the southeastern United States were "small irregular fields, and slopes too steep for effective mechanization" (p. 430); the former sounds like padi fields in Malaysia, the latter like rubber smallholdings. Even the common reaction to abandonment resembled views expressed in writings on idle land in Malaysia: "bringing the land into agricultural production is so deeply engrained in the national mythos of the United States that many Americans refuse even to consider the possibility that land won with such difficulty could ever be abandoned; the very notion seems sinful" (p. 417).

No survey of idle land has been conducted since the 1978 MOA survey, but the area has probably increased, despite the government's rehabilitation efforts. Industrialization has accelerated since the economic reforms of the mid-1980s. The rural-urban drift among *bumiputera* will probably intensify in the years to come. Rising educational standards will place rural youths in a position to take increasing advantage of the opportunities offered by the modernizing economy. The common conception of an illiterate farming population is changing fast. Surveys by the Department of Agriculture of smallholders in 54 districts in 1982 and 1986 revealed that the proportion of smallholders (heads of households) with no formal education dropped from 34.5 percent to 26.2 percent, while the proportion with secondary education almost doubled, from 5.7 percent to 9.4 percent (Jabatan Pertanian 1988). A fifth of family household members (apart from household head and spouse) had either completed or were still pursuing secondary, tertiary, or vocational education. Thanks to governmental campaigns, rural *bumiputera* children are viewed decreasingly as a source of labor whose destiny is tied to their parents' land (Shand and Mohd. Ariff 1989, p. 308).

One sign of a government response to the intensification of these socioeconomic forces is the slowdown in agricultural land development since the peak under the *Third* and *Fourth Malaysia Plans* (see Figure 1.4). The projected area to be developed under the *Sixth Malaysia Plan 1991–1995* was barely half the amount that occurred under the *Fifth Malaysia Plan 1986–1990*. The *Sixth Plan* cited several reasons for the slowdown, including the growing shortage of agricultural labor (p. 114). By 1990, employment in agriculture, forestry, and fishing fell to 28 percent of the labor force (*Sixth Plan*, p. 28). Just as the government has recognized that the country's socioeconomic transformation calls for a slower rate of agricultural expansion, it is time to acknowledge that some land ought to be abandoned and that costly, ineffective rehabilitation programs should be terminated. This view is increasingly accepted. For example, the new National Agricultural Policy for the period 1992 to 2010 reduced the self-sufficiency target for rice from 80 percent to 65 percent (Ministry of Agriculture 1993).

The abandonment of cropland means only that the land ceases to be valuable for agriculture, not that it has no economic value whatsoever. Abandoned cropland and pastures in the United States contributed to a substantial expansion of forest area in that country during this century. Idle land could make a similar contribution in Malaysia. Areas that revert to natural vegetation, whether grassland, scrub, or forest, provide wildlife habitat, protect watersheds, and can serve as sites for recreation. Areas that revert to forest provide a source of future timber harvests. Brookfield (1994a, 1994b) referred to large areas of idle rubber plantations on steep sites having become rubber-dominated secondary forest. In some cases active planting of timber species on idle land might be economically justified. A timber plantation involves a longer waiting period before producing a crop than does a rubber plantation, but on the other hand it is much less labor-intensive. The State Forestry Department in Selangor recently initiated a program to promote the planting of timber species on idle land (Edwin 1993). A recent review of more than sixty years of timber-planting experiments conducted by the Forestry Research Institute Malaysia and other agencies concluded that such efforts are technically feasible (Appanah and Weinland 1993). Idle land also makes a valuable contribution when it is converted to residential and industrial uses, which are the most rapidly rising land uses in the country.

Except for problems related to the design and management of state schemes and to land fragmentation that could be overcome through group-farming approaches, most of the institutional factors responsible for idle land were never seriously tackled by the rehabilitation programs. These factors remain in place. That something must be done is widely recognized. The new National Agricultural Policy calls for consolidation of small farms into more economically sized units. Sivalingam (1993, pp. 44–45) observed, "Given [the] declining trend in agriculture's contribution to the total labour force, it is no use talking of a labour-intensive [agricultural] strategy. Obviously the only way out is to form larger farms, adopt capital-intensive and corporate methods, and run agriculture as a big business." He called for liberalizing land markets and reducing transactions costs related to the buying and selling of land, especially padi land.

Institutional rigidities related to land markets have led to the seeming paradox of idle land existing side-by-side with agricultural land renting to tenant farmers at a high price. Wong (1995) has pointed out that this offers *prima facie* evidence that land markets are not clearing and that economic inefficiencies are occurring. The problem may be most acute among non-Malay farmers living in the vicinity of Malay Reserve Lands. Although no national statistics are available, case studies conducted during the past two decades found that the lack of agricultural land was a serious problem confronting the inhabitants of New Villages, who are predominantly Chinese but also include some Malays and Indians.[25] A 1973 survey of 17 New Villages in Perak and Melaka found that only 23 percent of New Village households had access to agricultural land, even though well over half of the working persons were engaged in agricultural employment (Parti Gerakan Rakyat Malaysia 1986, p. 45). Of those households with agricultural land, about half had 3 acres or less, and another 17 percent had only 4 to 5 acres. Hence, about two-thirds had less than 2 ha. A 1978 survey of 5 New Villages in Melaka found that the majority of the households did not own any agricultural land (Parti Gerakan Rakyat Malaysia 1986, p. 45). Of those who did, land plots were mostly between 2 and 4 acres.

The constraints on New Villagers' access to land have contributed to a proliferation of illegal land clearing and illegal tenancy. A study on land tenure in Pahang stated that "in most new villages that are located next to vacant state land, there is a high probability that it will be developed as an extension to the original site. In many cases it has been developed without approval from the state government" (Perunding Bersatu 1988, p. 30). The study estimated that about 9,515 ha were illegally cultivated in 1987. This was 1 to 2 percent of officially recorded agricultural area in the state (based on statistics in Kementerian Pertanian 1990). There is also anecdotal evidence of a relatively substantial amount of land being used illegally by non-Malay farmers for agricultural activities in other states.[26]

Land hunger has also forced many legal, non-Malay farmers to farm on land held under temporary occupation licenses (TOL). Although the TOL system is legal, insecurity of tenure is inherent in the system, and TOL holders have little incentive to make investments to raise the productivity of their plots. In most cases, they cannot easily secure access to institutional sources of finance, because untitled land cannot be used as collateral. Moreover, TOL holders cannot reap economies of scale because their holdings normally cannot exceed two hectares (Perunding Bersatu 1988, pp. 35–36). Because it carries sensitive racial implications, the hidden economic costs of Malay-held agricultural land lying idle while non-Malay farmers are cultivating land illegally and under TOLs has never been openly discussed, much less properly explored.

Given the racial sensitivities involved, overcoming the rigidities in the land market is a difficult challenge. One proposal that potentially could sidestep the sensitive issue of transfer of ownership is to establish a "land bank." This idea has been mooted by various studies (Gibbons et al. 1981, pp. 189–97; RISDA 1983, pp. 252–54; Courtenay 1986, p. 184). A land bank would buy or rent small parcels from current owners and then resell or sublet land in economically sized parcels. This would help create a market for land held by smallholders who no longer wish to be owners or operators. To some extent the bank could cope with racial aspects of land ownership and land use by operating selectively (limiting its activities to certain areas, types of land, and so on) and emphasizing long-term leases instead of sales. The World Bank (1980, Volume 2, p. 73) commented that the idea "deserved detailed study" and recommended "the establishment of a task force to look into the desirability and feasibility of establishing a land bank as part of the Fourth Plan." The government did not take up this recommendation.

Liberalizing the land market would provide benefits not only to the thousands of genuine farmers lacking access to land but also to the entire economy through more efficient agricultural production. It would benefit current owners by enabling them to lease or sell their land at fair prices, providing them funds they could then invest in other businesses. And it would cost the public less than government rehabilitation programs.

NOTES

1 In 1990, the area under principal crops—rubber, oil palm, padi, coconut, and cocoa—totaled 4.0 million ha in Peninsular Malaysia, compared to less than 0.7 million ha in Sabah and just over 0.5 million ha in Sarawak (Kementerian Pertanian 1993).

2 The data in Table 5.1 are from the same land use surveys that provided the data for Table 4.2.

3 The discrepancy between the land use surveys and the cadastral data probably reflects shortcomings in the cadastral system, which resulted in underrecording of land clearing for agriculture.

4 Sivalingam (1993) has provided a recent, critical survey of economic developments in the smallholder sector.

5 According to Fujimoto (1991), drainage problems were largely due to the design of irrigation systems, which emphasized delivery over drainage. Wong (1995) pointed out to us that a parcel of padi land that went idle for whatever reason could generate agronomic externalities, which compounded the ultimate area taken out of production: idle parcels provided habitat for pests, and they could also interfere with the delivery of irrigation water (Campbell et al. 1985, p. 20).

6 Brookfield (1994a, p. 275) makes the strongest claim in the literature for an ecological explanation of idle padi land, asserting: "The decline of rice cultivation in almost all inland areas [of the Peninsula] since the 1970s . . . may in part reflect a shift of inputs to other activities, but also reflects the severe problems of flooding, a change in the hydrological regime leading to periodic water shortages . . ., and siltation experienced in areas lying downstream of the [land development] conversion areas and the logged forests." He offers no evidence to support this claim, however.

7 Burrows was an agricultural planning advisor in the MOA who had come to Malaysia under the auspices of the UNDP/IBRD State and Rural Development project.

8 Pazim (1992) cited an unpublished Ph.D. thesis that we were unable to obtain, "Land-abandonment in Peninsular Malaysia: a case study of the Malay rubber smallholdings in the district of Ulu Selangor," by Samsudin Hitam (University of Wisconsin-Madison, 1984).

9 This is the largest irrigated padi scheme in the country, covering about 100,000 ha. It is located predominantly in Kedah.

10 The Kemubu scheme is in Kelantan. It covers about 20,000 ha.

11 Some farmers in the Muda scheme were able to keep their farms operating by hiring laborers from southern Thailand (Pazim 1992).

12 We express our gratitude to Dr. K. Zulkifli and the Department of Agriculture, who kindly provided information from the 1984 survey.

13 In 1975, smallholder rubber and coconut areas were approximately 1.13 and 0.22 million ha, respectively (Prime Minister's Department, n.d.), while the areas in 1980 were only slightly larger, 1.20 and 0.23 million ha (Kementerian Pertanian 1983, p. 29).

14 The balance came from payments made by settlers for certain land development costs, such as land clearing and housing construction.

15 The World Bank asked FELCRA to furnish a report proposing modifications to its selection criteria by June 1982. The government argued, however, that settler selection was the prerogative of the state governments, and it requested the Bank to withdraw its request. The Bank did (World Bank 1990, p. 36).

16 Similarly, surveys conducted in 1978 and 1987 by Fujimoto (1991, Tables IX and XI) in two rice-growing areas, Kampung Guar Tok Said in Seberang Prai (Pulau Pinang) and Kampung Hutan Cengal in Kelantan, found that the number of households with farming as the sole occupation declined from 44 to 35 in the former case and 31 to 28 in the latter.

17 World Bank (1988, pp. 5–16) provides a full discussion of government interventions in the padi sector.

18 Of the 32 projects, 15 were implemented by the local Farmers' Association, 9 by private companies, 2 by government agencies, 5 by private individuals, and 1 by a cooperative.

19 This range excludes the increase for one project, which had zero production before the project.

20 Courtenay (1986), reviewing other evidence, concluded that rehabilitation programs raised

yields but had a smaller impact on incomes. He also observed that the incidence of poverty in the padi sector declined less rapidly from 1970 to 1980 than in the economy as a whole, and that it rose after 1980.

21 Unfortunately only the executive summary of the full report was available.

22 The guaranteed minimum price system was introduced in 1949 (Fujimoto 1991).

23 See Hart (1984) for a later discussion of national trends in cropland in the United States.

24 According to more recent statistics (U.S.Bureau of the Census 1989), the area declined another 13 percent (16 million ha) by 1987. The area in 1987 was only three-fourths as large as the area in 1940.

25 The term *New Village* refers to the 480 new settlements set up by the British throughout the Peninsula from 1950 to 1954 to resettle predominantly Chinese squatters and rural workers. The resettlement scheme, which was part of a massive military exercise to deny communist insurgents their support base, affected 1 to 2 million people, about one-seventh of the entire population of colonial Malaya. See Loh (1988, pp. 123–124).

26 For a discussion of land tenure problems of non-Malay livestock farmers, see Lim and Phillips (1992, pp. 25–37).

6

Marine Fisheries

INTRODUCTION

Malaysia's marine fishing industry has "historically [been] among the 10 or 15 largest in the world" (World Bank 1982, p. i). Research on this industry provides the sole exception to the general lack of a substantial body of economic literature on natural resource management in Malaysia. A special 1976 issue of *Kajian Ekonomi Malaysia*, the journal of the Malaysian Economic Association, was devoted to issues related to fisheries development. A bibliography included in that special double issue listed more than 500 references. In the nearly two decades since, the literature has continued to grow. A major monograph on the economics of fisheries development in the states of Pulau Pinang and Kedah was published two years later (Munro and Chee 1978). More recently, Ooi (1990) and Jomo (1991) provided excellent monographs covering the whole of Peninsular Malaysia. As with most other aspects of the country's economic development, the literature is thinner for Sabah and Sarawak. No monograph has yet been written on the fisheries sector in either state.

The attention paid to fisheries issues is not surprising, in light of key features of the Malaysian socioeconomic context. More than timber and other extractive resource sectors, fisheries have a prominent human element. Fishing is a much more labor-intensive activity than logging or mining, and thus it is more obviously linked to important economic issues related to poverty and unemployment. A high level of poverty in the traditional sector, and differences in ethnic composition between the traditional and commercial sectors, make fisheries the natural resource sector that exhibits most obviously the broader development issues that were a central concern of the New Economic Policy (NEP).

Jahara Yahaya was a coauthor of this chapter.

181

Although fishing constituted only around 3 percent of the country's GDP during the 1970s and 1980s (World Bank 1982) and just 1 to 2 percent of employment (*Annual Fisheries Statistics 1980, 1990*; Population Census 1980, 1991), it was a principal source of employment in coastal villages and towns. Labon (1974) remarked that the percentage of the Malaysian labor force employed in fishing in the early 1970s was high by Southeast Asian standards. Households with fishing as their main economic activity have historically comprised a significant proportion of Malaysian households below the poverty line in rural areas. The incidence of poverty among fishermen was 73 percent in 1970, 63 percent in 1976, and 28 percent in 1984, compared to overall averages for rural areas of 59 percent, 48 percent, and 25 percent (*Fifth Malaysia Plan 1986–1990*, Table 3.1).

Poverty is highest among traditional (artisanal) fishermen, who generally fish in shallow, inshore waters within 5 miles of the coast. Traditional gears are labor-intensive, and traditional boats were small and non-motorized until relatively recently. Nearly all traditional fishermen on the east coast, and most on the west coast, are Malay. In contrast, Malaysian Chinese dominate the commercial sector, including the wholesaling and retailing of fish. This sector involves large, motorized boats and capital-intensive gears such as purse seine and trawl nets. Although traditional vessels are more numerous—in 1990, about three-quarters of the number of licensed gears operating in Malaysia were traditional ones (*Jabatan Prikanan* 1990)—the commercial sector is the source of most of the foreign exchange earned by exports of fishery commodities.

A second reason for interest in the sector is its contribution to the country's food supply. Food is more obviously a basic human need than are, say, products made from timber or tin. Fish, unlike pork or beef, is a source of animal protein acceptable to all the major ethnic and religious groups in the country. It is a particularly important source of protein among the poor in coastal Malay villages. Fish was the cheapest source of animal protein in the early 1970s. Labon (1974) estimated that household consumption of fish was twice that of meat. Malaysia's per capita consumption of food fish in 1981, 40 kg, was higher than in Indonesia (10 kg), Thailand (26 kg), and the Philippines (33 kg) (MAJUIKAN 1981).

The sector has attracted the interest of economists for one additional important reason. The country's experience with fisheries development provides a powerful, real-world illustration of a classic natural resource management problem, the "tragedy of the commons." In economic terms, a natural resource provides the greatest benefits to society when it is managed to maximize its net returns, or resource rents. The "tragedy" occurs when property rights over the resource are not clearly defined or are not effectively enforced. In this "open-access" situation, the resource might be exploited so excessively that it yields no rent whatsoever. In lay terms, fisheries tend to become overfished. Fishing grounds are inherently prone to the open-access problem, because they cannot easily be marked out and reserved for sole use. Evidence of overfishing emerged on the west coast of Peninsular Malaysia in the 1960s and 1970s and attracted the interest of economists and, for practical reasons, the Department of Fisheries.

The various reasons for economists' interest in Malaysian fisheries development suggest the challenges involved in setting fisheries management objectives and formulating policies to achieve those objectives. From an efficiency standpoint, the objective is unambiguous: to control fishing effort so that resource rents are maximized. But the resulting level of effort will almost surely not maximize employment, which is important to policy makers for political and social reasons; physical production of fish, which is important for protein supply; and gross revenue, which is important for foreign exchange earnings. These alternative objectives are not always mutually exclusive, but there is no disputing that fisheries managers face several potential objectives that are not necessarily complementary.

Even when there is no dispute over the management objective, determining the most effective means of attaining it is complicated by biological uncertainties related to the population dynamics of fisheries. Malaysia's fisheries, like its forests, contain many species, whose reproductive characteristics, growth rates, and ecological interactions are far from perfectly understood. Simply estimating the stock of fish at a given point in time is much more difficult than estimating the area of forests and the amount of timber in them.

This chapter reviews the factors that have affected the control of fishing effort in Malaysia, and it evaluates the consequences of the level of control that was actually achieved. It analyzes most carefully the 1970s and 1980s (the NEP period), although it covers a good portion of the 1960s too, when several key factors that affected subsequent fishing policies originated. It also provides the first quantitative analysis of the impacts of several major policy changes that were implemented in the early 1980s. These policy changes were a response to intrasectoral conflicts and mounting evidence that fish stocks were being depleted rapidly.

The chapter focuses on the west coast fisheries of Peninsular Malaysia, due to institutional differences among Peninsular Malaysia, Sabah, and Sarawak, the generally greater availability of data and previous studies for Peninsular Malaysia (especially the west coast), and the domination of sectoral input and output by west coast fisheries. At the federal level, management of marine fisheries is the responsibility of the Department of Fisheries within the Ministry of Agriculture. In Peninsular Malaysia, this agency designs policies

Table 6.1   *Number of licensed fishing boats by region in Malaysia*

| Year | Peninsular Malaysia | | Sabah | Sarawak |
	West coast	East coast		
1970	13,908	6,398	4,020	3,537
1975	15,355	6,792	4,236	5,084
1980	22,082	8,438	5,800	7,172
1985	16,696	6,675	6,630	8,932
1990	16,994	6,140	9,200	7,066

Sources: Jabatan Perikanan, various issues.

(which must be approved at higher political levels), enforces regulations, determines the number of licenses to be granted for different fishing gears (though who gets the licenses is determined at the state level), and monitors the sector through the collection of statistics on catch and effort. In Sabah and Sarawak, fisheries matters are on the Concurrent List under the federal constitution. Both states impose regulations in addition to federal ones. Sabah's Department of Fisheries is the most independent. Its officers are paid entirely by the state government, and the federal Department of Fisheries has no say over the licensing of fishing vessels in the state.

Peninsular Malaysia accounts for the majority of fishing effort and fish production in the country. From 1970 to 1990, 60 to 70 percent of the licensed fishing boats in the country were operating off the coasts of the Peninsula (Table 6.1), and landings in the Peninsula were 80–90 percent of total landings in the country (Table 6.2). Within Peninsular Malaysia, effort and landings are greatest on the west coast. The annual number of licensed boats on the west coast was 2.2 to 2.8 times the number on the east coast from 1970 to 1990; the corresponding ratio for landings was 1.6 to 3.8 times. The west coast is where the commercial sector is concentrated, although it also has about half of the traditional Malay fishermen. Its greater stocks of prawns and demersal (bottom-dwelling) fish provide the chief attraction for commercial boats.

Table 6.2   *Landings of marine fish by region in Malaysia (in tonnes)*

| Year | Peninsular Malaysia | | Sabah | Sarawak |
	West coast	East coast		
1970	230,539	63,757	26,000	14,077
1975	270,665	104,570	33,500	63,939
1980	493,495	130,403	34,500	77,070
1985	327,124	135,737	48,600	62,893
1990	510,471	309,432	44,760	78,878

Sources: Jabatan Perikanan, various issues.
[a] Figures for 1970, 1975, and 1985 include landings of freshwater fish.

Demersal fish comprise most landings on the west coast, whereas pelagic (surface-dwelling) and demersal fish are equally important on the east coast. The west coast is where evidence of overfishing has been the strongest and where tensions between the predominantly Malay traditional sector and the predominantly Chinese commercial sector have been the greatest. Consequently, issues on the west coast have been analyzed the most thoroughly and have been the principal driving force behind changes in fisheries policies during the last thirty years.

The chapter is organized as follows. The section *Fundamental concepts of fisheries economics* presents the standard theoretical economic model of fisheries management. This model provides both a reference point for ensuing discussions and the framework for the quantitative analysis later in the chapter. *Development of west coast fisheries during the 1970s and 1980s* provides a historical review of key developments related to the control of fishing effort. It evaluates evidence on overfishing and discusses the government's policy responses. *Economic analysis of catch and efforts in west coast fisheries during the 1980s* presents the quantitative analysis of these policies. The analysis covers both traditional and commercial fisheries. Finally, *Conclusions* summarizes the lessons of the west coast's experience and discusses their relevance to fisheries management elsewhere in the country and in the future.

Fundamental Concepts of Fisheries Economics

Gordon (1954) and Schaefer (1957) developed what has come to be accepted as the basic "bioeconomic" model of fisheries management. Their model pertains to a fishery composed of a single species, and it ignores the age structure of the fish population. These features contrast with the actual characteristics of tropical fisheries in Malaysia, where there are dozens of commercial species, which reach commercial size at varying ages. The model's usefulness as an operational tool in managing tropical fisheries is therefore limited. Nevertheless, it provides a useful framework for understanding the basic economic principles involved in fisheries management.

The Gordon-Schaefer model assumes that annual growth of the fish stock, in tonnes, is related to the level of the stock, also in tonnes, by an inverted U-shaped function. Growth is small when the stock is small, because the breeding population is small. It is also small when the stock is large, because the fishery has a limited carrying capacity. Growth therefore reaches a maximum at an intermediate stock size. Annual catch can be sustained indefinitely as long as it equals annual growth. Then, the fishery is in equilibrium: the stock does not change from one period to the next. Because there is a series of growth points determined by the size of the fish stock, there is also a series of potential sustained-yield catch levels. The maximum sustained-yield (*MSY*) catch level occurs at the stock where growth is at a maximum.

In equilibrium, stock determines growth, growth equals catch, and effort determines catch. Hence, as an alternative to using the relationship between stock and growth to analyze fisheries management, one can equivalently use the relationship between catch and effort. Figure 6.1 depicts this relationship. Catch rises with effort up to the *MSY* point, and declines thereafter as the effect of reductions in the stock outweighs the effect of increased effort. If the catch-effort relationship is known for a given fishery, it can be used to predict the sustained-yield catch level that will result from a given level of sustained fishing effort.

The fishery is said to be biologically overfished if effort exceeds the *MSY* point. This is because the same amount of fish could be caught using less effort. In Figure 6.1, effort at level E_1, which exceeds the *MSY* effort level E_{MSY}, yields a catch of C_1. The same catch, however, could be produced by reducing effort to E_2. At E_2, the fish stock is larger, and thus less effort is

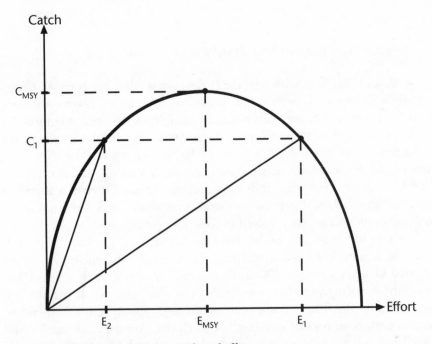

Figure 6.1   Relationship between catch and effort

needed to catch C_1 tonnes of fish. The "catch per unit effort" (*CPUE*) is higher at E_2: $C_1/E_2 > C_1/E_1$.

Geometrically, *CPUE* is given by the slope of a line from the origin to a point on the catch-effort curve. One can see in Figure 6.1 that the slope of the line associated with E_2 is steeper than that of the line associated with E_1. Given the inverted U shape of the catch-effort curve, *CPUE* necessarily declines as effort increases. A declining trend in *CPUE* as fishing effort expands therefore does not indicate biological overfishing, although this is sometimes stated in the Malaysian literature. Beyond the *MSY* point, however, *CPUE* declines increasingly rapidly. This is indeed a sign of biological overfishing.

Maximization of catch might appear to be a sensible objective of fisheries management, but it does not make sense from an economic standpoint. It ignores the costs of catching fish and the revenues from selling them. The appropriate economic objective is to maximize resource rent: the difference between total revenue and total cost. This is the profit earned by the fishery. If the price of fish is unaffected by the level of catch, then the catch-effort curve in Figure 6.1 can be converted to a total revenue curve by multiplying the units on the vertical axis by the price of fish. The resulting total revenue curve is depicted in Figure 6.2. If we also assume that the unit cost of effort

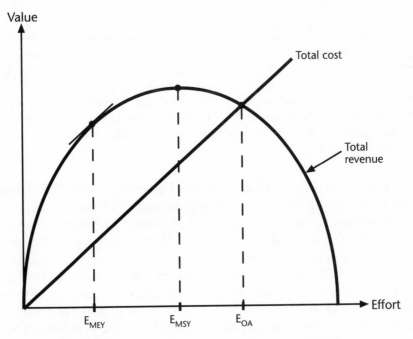

Figure 6.2   Relationship between total revenue and total cost, and effort

is unaffected by the level of effort, then total fishing cost is proportional to effort and can be depicted by a line passing through the origin. The slope of this line equals the unit cost of effort. Rent is maximized at the level of effort where the vertical distance between the total revenue curve and the total cost line is greatest. In Figure 6.2, the maximum economic yield (MEY) occurs at E_{MEY}.

Note that the MEY point occurs to the left of the MSY point. If the fishery were privately owned, the owner would not increase effort beyond the MEY point, because this would diminish his profits. The MEY point is a social as well as a private optimum: the social value of the last fish caught—the marginal revenue, which is the slope of the total revenue curve—equals the social cost of producing it—the marginal cost, which is the slope of the total cost line. Marginal revenue measures society's willingness to pay for fish, and marginal cost measures the opportunity cost of the labor and capital used in fishing. An application of effort beyond the MEY point results in fish "being caught at a cost greater than their value to society" (Ooi 1990, p. 27). Socially as well as privately, raising production to the MSY point is not worth the cost.

In practice, fisheries are seldom privately owned. In the absence of government regulation, they are typically open-access resources open to all with the means to construct or purchase fishing vessels and gear. As Munro and Chee (1978, p. 9) put it:

Since no one owns the fish resource, any rent to the fishery which is generated will appear as additional returns to labour and capital. Thus if the fishery is generating rents, the return to labour and capital will appear to be high in relation to what labour and capital could earn elsewhere in the economy. As a result, more and more labour and capital will be attracted to the fishery. If there are no barriers to entry, labour and capital will continue to flow into the fishery so long as the returns to labour and capital continue to appear to be exceptionally high, i.e. while any rent is generated by the fishery.

Fishing effort will continue to increase until the rent is completely dissipated. At this point, which is labeled E_{OA} (OA = open access) in Figure 6.2, total costs equal total revenue: the value of the catch is no more than the cost of catching the fish. Hence, fishing adds no net value to the economy. Labor and capital earn only their opportunity cost, that is, no more than they do in their next best use. If subsistence or low-wage agriculture provides the principal employment alternative for fishermen, as is often the case, income in fishing communities will be driven down to poverty levels. Fishing can potentially provide a better income, but the lack of control over access prevents it from doing so.

In Figure 6.2, the open-access equilibrium is drawn to the right of the *MSY* point, indicating that both economic and biological overfishing occur. This need not be the case when the unit cost of effort is high.[1] Then, E_{OA} can be between E_{MEY} and E_{MSY}. When open access does lead to biological overfishing, the fishery can collapse altogether: fish stocks can be driven close to zero. This is a particular risk with small pelagic species. The collapse of the California sardine and the Peruvian anchoveta fisheries are well-known historical examples (Ludwig et al. 1993), although the role of fishing pressure as opposed to natural factors in the collapse of these fisheries is a point of some controversy (Aron et al. 1993).

The discussion so far has ignored dynamic issues. In particular, it has ignored discount rates: human beings' preference for receiving economic benefits in the present instead of the future. The dynamics of fisheries management turn out to be quite complicated; discussion of them is beyond the scope of this chapter. One result is worth noting, however: at a positive discount rate, the dynamically optimal level of fishing effort is greater than the static *MEY* level indicated in Figure 6.2 (Munro and Chee 1978). In practice, therefore, the difference between *MEY* and *MSY* is less than Figure 6.2 suggests.

DEVELOPMENT OF WEST COAST FISHERIES DURING THE 1970S AND 1980S

The pretrawling period

Fishing effort is a function of the number of vessels, their fishing power, and the amount of time they spend at sea. Fishing power, which reflects the level of fishing technology, has been a particularly important variable in the effort equation in Malaysia.

The increase in fishing effort in Malaysia was by all accounts a gradual process until the introduction of trawlers in the 1960s. Before World War II, the major technological development was the introduction of the purse seine (Yap 1976), which Chinese immigrants from Thailand brought to Kedah and Perak in the late nineteenth century. By the 1950s and early 1960s, the purse seine had become the most important gear in Malaya, due to increased mechanization of fishing vessels, increased availability of ice and refrigerated storage (which made it possible to store and market larger catches), and government efforts to promote its use (Yap 1976, Ooi 1990). Fishermen using the gear continued to be predominantly Chinese.

Mechanization proceeded relatively slowly in the two decades after the war. In 1959, only one-third of the fishing fleet in Malaya was motorized (Ooi

1990). Mechanization increased fishing effort by reducing fishing boats' dependence on weather conditions (a particular problem on the east coast, due to the northeast monsoon) and increasing their range. An additional technological development that raised fishing effort was the postwar introduction of nets made of synthetic fibers (*First Malaysia Plan 1966–1970*, Ooi 1990). These nets were stronger, easier to operate, and required less repair than traditional nets made of ramie and cotton.

Policies in the 1960s emphasized production. The Fisheries Act of 1963 introduced the licensing of fishing vessels, but otherwise it said little about the control of fishing effort. Fisheries programs under the *First Malaysia Plan* were "aimed at expanding research; training fishermen to be more competent; assisting them to avail themselves of improved equipment, gear and other facilities; helping producers to improve processing and marketing methods; and establishing the necessary infrastructure facilities for large-scale and efficient marine fishing" (p. 113–114). The plan allocated funds for credit programs and subsidies to assist fishermen in purchasing improved gear.

The expansion of trawling

Until 1965, the increase in landings in Peninsular Malaysia reflected mainly increased landings of pelagic species by purse-seiners (World Bank 1982). From 1965 to 1970, however, the increase was due primarily to the expansion of trawling, and it was sharp: landings rose by 50 percent. Trawling made it possible to harvest intensively, for the first time, the demersal fish stocks of inshore waters (World Bank 1982). The adoption and spread of trawling along the northwest coast of the Peninsula was remarkably rapid and was the single most influential factor affecting fisheries management and policies during the 1970s and 1980s.

Gibbons (1976), Munro and Chee (1978), and Ooi (1990) have told the story of the development of trawling particularly well (see also Yap 1973 and Jahara 1977). According to Munro and Chee (p. 24),

The fact that trawling . . . appear[ed] can be traced to the breakdown in Indonesian-Malaysian relations in the 1960s. There had existed a substantial trade between Sumatra and the west coast of West Malaysia carried on by traders employing vessels in the 30 to 50 ton range. With the deterioration in Malaysian-Indonesian relations in the early 1960s, the trade was curbed by the Indonesians and virtually eliminated by 1963. Boat owners with idle vessels looked for other means of employment of their capital.

Ooi continues, "Some of the more enterprising barter traders . . . went to Thailand to learn the techniques of trawling from the fishermen in the Gulf of Thailand. They returned with two types of trawl—the beam trawl and the otter trawl" (p. 7). The converted barter-trade vessels began trawling off the coasts of Pulau Pinang and Perak in March 1963. Their success convinced many owners of purse seine and drift-net boats to convert their boats as well. By 1964, an estimated 900 unlicensed trawlers were operating along the northwest coast (Soong 1964, cited in Ooi 1990).

The trawlers operated primarily in inshore waters no deeper than ten to fifteen fathoms, where the stocks of demersal species were the largest. This was also the zone that historically had been the preserve of traditional fishermen. In response to complaints by traditional fishermen about their gear being destroyed by trawlers' sweeps, the government imposed a temporary ban on trawling. It also initiated a pilot study on the feasibility of trawling in waters more than twelve miles from shore and more than twenty fathoms deep, where competition with traditional fishermen would be minimal (Gibbons 1976). The study, which was conducted off Pulau Langkawi and involved forty-two boats, was considered a success. Consequently, the government legalized trawling in Kedah in 1965 and Pulau Pinang in 1966 (Ooi 1990).

In 1967, Parliament approved the Maritime Fisheries Regulations, which were intended to prevent trawlers from encroaching on inshore waters. The government had already introduced the principal features of the regulations in a directive from the Ministry of Agriculture when it legalized trawling. The regulations limited trawling to members of cooperative trawling societies (Gibbons 1976, Yap 1976, World Bank 1982), to boats larger than fifty gross tonnes (GRT), to waters at least twelve miles from shore or fifteen fathoms deep, and to daylight hours (6 A.M. to 6 P.M.). They also banned the use of the beam trawl, which was designed to operate in shallow inshore waters (Ooi 1990). To reduce the capture of juvenile fish, the regulations required that the mesh size of trawl nets (measured at the cod end) be no less than one inch.

The regulations gave cooperative societies a monopoly over trawler licenses, and they limited the number of licenses each cooperative received. The government expected the cooperatives to ensure that their members abided by the regulations and that traditional fishermen, especially Malays, benefitted from trawling (Gibbons 1976). Cooperatives had the power to choose half the crew of member vessels. Traditional fishermen could join a cooperative society and qualify for a job as a crew member through this mechanism.

The regulations proved to be ineffective at controlling trawling. Unlicensed, illegal trawling continued in waters off Pulau Pinang, Perak, and Kedah. Anderson (1987, p. 331) pointed out the practical difficulties of enforcement along the west coast: "It would have taken a whole navy of utterly uncorruptible and zealous police to oversee the Penang-Perak shore. Fisherman poached regularly, operated at night, bunched together so that a police boat could chase only one at a time while the others saw and escaped, and souped up their engines so that they could (with a fair start) outrun the police boats." When enforcement officers in the Fisheries Department or the Maritime Police succeeded in catching illegal trawlers, Gibbons (1976, pp. 100–101) cited sources who "accused [them] of turning a blind eye toward trawler violations in return for bribes from *towkays* [boat owners] who were said to be reaping huge profits from the illegal trawling."

Cooperatives were likewise ineffective. Gibbons continued (p. 106):

Little needs to be said about the . . . objective of the trawler cooperatives . . . of controlling their number and enforcing the fishing regulations for trawlers. These regulations are violated at every opportunity by trawler boats, and the cooperative societies seem powerless and/or unwilling to do anything about it. In fact, since they enjoy a 5% commission from the catch, they have an incentive to encourage the boats to fish in the bountiful waters, i.e. the in-shore waters.

He also concluded that the cooperatives brought few benefits to their rank-and-file members: "they [cooperatives] are more like cartels of local political and economic elites which enable the latter to ensure that a considerable proportion of the benefits of modernization of the fishing industry in Penang and Kedah have gone to them" (p. 107). Anderson (1987) made similar observations.

The number of licensed trawlers increased from 20 in 1965 to 734 in 1969 (*Second Malaysia Plan 1971–1975*). Nevertheless, the government relaxed restrictions on trawling by amending the regulations in 1971. The amendments allowed boats of less than 25 GRT to trawl as close as 3 miles to the shore, and boats of 25 to 100 GRT to trawl as close as 7 miles (Yap 1976). The 12-mile limit was retained only for boats of 100 GRT and above. The amendments also increased the number of licenses allocated to cooperatives and eliminated the prohibition against night trawling (World Bank 1982).

According to Ooi (1990), the reasons for the amendments were multiple. On one level, the amendments were an admission by the government that it had failed to enforce the 1967 regulations effectively. But more positively, trawling seemed to be an important means of meeting the rising protein needs of the country's growing population, as it tapped the hitherto underexploited demersal resource. Domestic consumption of food fish in Malaysia was approximately 300,000 tonnes in 1970, and Labon (1974) projected that it would rise to 690,000 tonnes by 1995.[2] Moreover, trawling had made fishing a significant source of net export earnings for the first time. It was a highly efficient means of catching not only demersal fish but also prawns, which commanded a high international price. Export earnings from fishing tripled from 1965 to 1971. Finally, the 50 GRT minimum vessel size in the regulations was associated with significant job losses. Many of the licensed trawlers were converted purse-seiners, which were the only 50 GRT fishing boats in existence. Conversion caused many crew members to lose their jobs, as a purse-seiner employed 10 to 22 fishermen and a trawler employed only 2 to 5 (Yap 1976).

Small trawlers proliferated at a phenomenal rate following the Amendments. In the state of Perak alone, 1,709 trawler licenses were issued between February 22 and August 31, 1971 (Yap 1976). Most were granted to "mini-trawlers," vessels of 10 GRT and less (Goh 1976). Yet, traditional fishermen, who were mainly Malay, participated little in the expanding industry. Goh (1976) and the World Bank (1982) cited the fishermen's unfamiliarity with the technology, their conservative nature, and their lack of capital. In a survey conducted in Pulau Pinang and Kedah in 1971–72, Gibbons (1976) found that the owners of nearly all trawlers were not fishermen but rather independent, primarily Chinese, businessmen.

Gibbons also found that only about 10 percent of the traditional fishermen in Pulau Pinang and 20 percent in Kedah had become crew members on trawlers, even though 78 percent of Chinese traditional fishermen and 85 percent of Malay traditional fishermen lived in poverty. A prime reason was that the income of a crew member on a trawler was generally no better than the income earned by a traditional fisherman (Gibbons 1976, Munro and Chee 1978). Moreover, crew members on trawlers worked longer hours, were in port less often (and hence had fewer opportunities to take on second jobs), and had less independence (Gibbons 1976). Consequently, trawlers drew their crews primarily from unemployed or underemployed urban youths, who were predominantly Chinese.

Instead of promoting the adoption of trawling by traditional fishermen, the amendments expanded the fishing population and increased the number of vessels operating in inshore waters. Traditional fishermen resented the intrusion into what they viewed as their waters. They voiced three principal complaints. First, they claimed that trawlers continued to operate, illegally, too close to shore. Second, they claimed that trawlers destroyed their gear. Third, they claimed that trawlers were depleting fish stocks, both directly and by destroying spawning and breeding grounds, and thereby reducing their catch.

There seems to be no doubt that the first two complaints were valid. For example, Gibbons (1976, p. 100) reported that since the introduction of trawling "there had been considerable destruction of in-shore gears, especially bag nets (*pompang*) and drift nets (*hanyut*)." But regarding the third, Munro and Chee (1978) found little evidence of negative impacts on the aggregate catch of traditional fishermen in Pulau Pinang and Kedah, despite anecdotal evidence to the contrary.[3] They noted (p. 18) that "trawling is in *direct* competition with only a limited number of inshore gears," which generally targeted pelagic, not demersal, fish. In the case of Pulau Pinang, three traditional gears that were aimed at demersal fish, the *tuabang, kenka* and *pompang,* "all experienced an increase in the number of units operating since 1965. According to the data, the number of *pompang* units in operation more than doubled between 1965 and 1971. *Hanyut,* a gear which is supposed to have been subject to extensive net and other gear destruction by trawlers, experienced a 40 percent increase in the number of units operating between 1965 and 1971" (Munro and Chee 1978, p. 67). Inshore waters had become more crowded due not only to the expansion of trawling, but also to an expansion in effort by traditional fishermen. Munro and Chee concluded that "one is forced to take the view that there is no clear evidence of trawlers having reduced catches and thus incomes in Kedah inshore gear activities" (p. 60); for Pulau Pinang, they concluded that "trawlers' competitors . . . have seemingly prospered" (p. 67).

Munro and Chee did not study Perak as well, where the conflict was most intense. But aggregate data on number of fishing licenses in Peninsular Malaysia are consistent with their finding for Pulau Pinang of rising traditional fishing effort into the early 1970s. After a sharp decline from 1965 to 1967 (perhaps a statistical artifact), the number of traditional gears rose by about 25 percent up to 1970. It remained more or less constant up to 1974.

Traditional fishermen's complaints about reduced catch were probably valid in the case of prawns, at least in terms of the value of the catch (Munro and Chee 1978). Data from northern Perak showed a decrease in the proportion of the more valuable large prawns (grade I and grade II) in landings after the introduction of trawling. Prawns are most common in waters of three to six fathoms, which occur mainly in the three- to seven-mile zone then open to small trawlers. Trawl nets are an indiscriminant gear and do not catch only demersal fish. In the case of Pulau Pinang, the "percentage of the . . . trawler catch accounted for by prawns [grew] dramatically since the inception of the trawlers," so much so that a U.S. Peace Corps study of the industry referred to trawlers as "prawn boats" (Munro and Chee 1978, pp. 38–39). Mohd. Shaari (1976) presented data showing that the percentage of prawns in the landings of trawlers in Pulau Pinang rose from 4.9 percent in 1968 to 22.2 percent in 1972.

The conflict between traditional fishermen and trawlers often turned violent. According to Goh (1976, p. 18), who headed a task force appointed by Prime Minister Tun Hussein Onn to investigate a particularly nasty conflict in the waters off Krian and Nibong Tebal from 1974 to 1976, "Between 1964 and 1976, a total of 113 incidents involving 437 trawlers and 987 inshore vessels was recorded for the whole of West Malaysia. 45 vessels were destroyed; 62 vessels sunk and 34 lives lost. Perak and, to a lesser extent, Penang proved to be the most sensitive areas. 84% of the incidents occurred in Perak and 11% in Penang." Trawlers often fared the worst in these clashes: Anderson (1987) observed that they were "outnumbered and outgunned" by traditional fishermen. With memories of the May 13, 1969 riots still fresh, the government was concerned that the conflict might evolve from clashes between the operators of competing fishing technologies to a more general confrontation between Malay traditional fishermen and Chinese trawlers. In the mid-1970s, it rescinded several provisions of the amendments (Yap 1976, World Bank 1982). It moved the limit for trawling further offshore, to 7 miles according to Yap and 12 miles according to the World Bank, and it raised the size limit for trawlers, to 25 GRT according to Yap and to boats with at least 40-horsepower engines according to the World Bank. It also froze the number of licenses issued to trawlers and purse-seiners.

Government assistance to traditional fishermen

The conflict between trawlers and traditional fishermen overshadowed the expansion of overall fishing effort. At the same time that the government was trying, with little success, to rein in the trawling industry, it was providing the traditional sector with assistance to modernize fishing vessels and gear. The objective was dual: to raise fish production and to ensure that poor, traditional fishermen benefitted from modern fishing methods.

The government had provided such assistance even before independence. In 1956, it launched the Aid to the Fishing Industry Scheme, which offered assistance in the form of two-thirds loan, one-third grant financing for the purchase of vessels and gear (World Bank 1982). The scheme was aimed primarily at east coast fishermen. Its impact was limited—only 16 percent of east coast fishermen participated—and it was a financial failure: only 2 percent of the loans were repaid.

The next major scheme was the Fishermen's Subsidy Scheme, which was launched in 1972 and was also aimed at the east coast (Jahara 1976). Funding for the scheme was initially a modest RM1.5 million. Fishermen who provided boat hulls were eligible for grants to purchase engines and gear. The grant initially covered 100 percent of the cost of the equipment, but it was reduced to 30 percent for engines in 1973 and 80 percent for gear in 1974, due to rising costs (World Bank 1982). According to Jahara (1976, p. 73), the scheme "has not been very successful in improving the productivity of fishing operations, whether in respect to increasing the income of fishermen or restructuring the fishing community." She attributed its failure to insufficient funds, ineffective administration of loans, fishermen's lack of experience in operating motorized vessels, and inadequate support services. The scheme was suspended in November 1974 (Jomo 1991).

With the increase in public expenditure on NEP programs under the *Third Malaysia Plan 1976–1980*, the scheme was revived at a much higher level of funding (Jahara 1976, Jomo 1991). The *Third Plan* allocated RM72.7 million to the scheme, which was implemented jointly by the Department of Fisheries, Bank Pertanian Malaysia (the national farmers' bank), and a state-owned enterprise, the Fisheries Industry Development Authority (LKIM, for Lembaga Kemajuan Ikan Malaysia; also known as MAJUIKAN), which had been established in 1971. Participation was limited to bona fide traditional fishermen. Fishermen were considered bona fide if they spent more than ninety days a year at sea.

The scheme was aimed at helping non-owner-operators acquire their own vessels and gear, and owner-operators upgrade their equipment. Loans and subsidies for the construction of new vessels were limited to east coast fishermen (with only loans available for building hulls), while west coast as well as east coast fishermen could avail themselves of subsidies to replace inboard engines and gear, to purchase outboard engines for nonmotorized vessels, to convert their vessels to new fishing methods, and to purchase ice boxes and other modern equipment. Subsidy rates ranged from 75 to 100 percent. Fishermen who received assistance for new boats were assured of receiving licenses (Shahrom 1984). The goal was to build approximately 1,580 new vessels on the east coast and to replace 8,000 vessels on both coasts during the *Third Plan* (Jahara 1976, p. 76). The scheme particularly promoted expansion of the east coast fleet because the demersal resources off this coast were considered underexploited (Labon 1974). On the west coast, subsidies for conversion were directed at the owners of minitrawlers (Yap 1976).

From 1971 to 1980, 21,100 fishermen, or 22 percent of the fishermen in the country, received RM50 million in subsidies under the scheme (*Fourth Malaysia Plan 1981–1985*, p. 273). The level of subsidization led the World Bank (1982, p. i) to comment that "the small-scale sector of the Malaysian fishing industry is among the most heavily subsidized in the world." The Bank estimated that subsidies were equivalent to about 14 percent of the value of production, or RM800 per fisherman per year. Within the agricultural sector in Malaysia, the aggregate subsidy for fishermen was second only to that for padi farmers (World Bank 1982).

Several studies published in the early years of the expanded subsidy program warned that, by promoting expanded fishing effort, it could undermine the goal of raising the incomes of traditional fishermen. Yap (1976, p. 15) pointed out that:

Although trawling is not allowed within the seven mile limit, the number of boats operating within this area is not reduced. The use of traditional fishing gear in place of the trawl, the provisions for the purchase of outboard engines and small boats mean that the number of boats within the seven mile zone is continually replaced and added to. To convert from trawling to these gear will merely create over-expansion in the use of another set of fishing gear.

Jahara (1976, p. 75) echoed this warning: "The substantial increase in subsidies to small-scale fisheries [c]ould result in an increase in intensive fishing on already endangered stocks within the 0–7 mile limit."

A few years later, the World Bank (1982, p. 57) concluded that these concerns had been valid:

Subsidization could be justified if it introduced a new technology (e.g. trawling, or use of powered purse-seiners) to an underexploited fisheries resource. Unfortunately, the great increase in subsidy levels during the 1970s mainly encouraged expansion of technologies already well understood and appreciated by Malaysian fisherman, and were indiscriminate enough to be applied vigorously to fish stocks already under considerable pressure.

The subsidy scheme induced existing labor and capital to remain in the inshore fishery and attracted additional resources to it. The number of licensed traditional gears in Peninsular Malaysia doubled during the second half of the 1970s. The number of licensed fishermen rose by about 20,000, an increase of nearly a third (Figure 6.3). Surprisingly, the proportion of motorized vessels did not change significantly between 1975 and 1980, fluctuating within a few percentage points of 80 percent. This suggests that the subsidy scheme was more successful in inducing the owners of motorized boats to increase their engine size, or to switch from outboard to inboard, than in inducing the owners of nonmotorized boats to acquire engines. The proportion of motorized vessels did rise sharply in the early 1980s, however.

Munro and Chee (1978, p. 11) have pointed out that subsidization can be economically justified when unemployment, either open or disguised, is high in the fishery sector:

The consequence of the unemployment will be that the *social cost* of labour used in fishing will be less than the private cost. The true cost to society of the marginal unit of labour employed in fishing is the value of goods and/or services which labour could have produced elsewhere in the economy—the "opportunity cost" to use the economist's terminology. If the only alternative to fishing which many fish-

Figure 6.3   Number of licensed fishermen: Peninsular Malaysia

ermen have is unemployment, then the true cost to society of having these men in fishing is zero. Hence the social cost of labour will be less than the private cost.

In Figure 6.2, the total cost line would rotate downward when adjusted for the lower social cost of under- or unemployed labor. Hence, the *MEY* point would shift to the right: the optimal fishing effort would rise.

Munro and Chee cautioned, however (p. 11), that subsidies are not justified when unemployment extends beyond the fishing sector: "If there is large scale unemployment in the rest of the economy, it may be pointless to shift capital into the fishing sector for the purpose of alleviating unemployment in the fishing sector if the consequence is simply to aggravate the unemployment problem elsewhere in the economy." They also suggested that programs to increase the mobility of fishermen into other economic pursuits might be a less expensive and more permanent solution to any surplus labor problem that existed.

Moreover, subsidization is justified only up to the socially optimal *MEY* point. This point cannot exceed the *MSY* point, as the latter is the point where rent is maximized when fishing costs equal zero. One therefore cannot justify violation of the *MSY* level on the basis of underutilized labor resources. Subsidization to increase employment and expand effort beyond the socially optimal *MEY* point hastens the onset of open-access rent dissipation and results in fishermen earning no more than the opportunity cost of their labor.

In the short run, the incomes of participants in the subsidy scheme did increase. In 1979, the Ministry of Agriculture interviewed approximately 10 percent of the fishermen participating in the scheme (Ministry of Agriculture 1979, cited in World Bank 1982). From 1977 to 1979, their average net monthly fishing income rose from RM275 to RM342 on the east coast and hour RM224 to RM280 on the west coast. The percentage of fishermen below the poverty line (defined as a monthly income of RM250) declined from 68 percent to 30 percent on the east coast and from 75 percent to 55 percent on the west coast.

Long-run impacts are less clear, but the Department of Fisheries appears to have concluded that the subsidy program was counterproductive (Shahrom 1984, p. 323):

The subsidy programmes initiated in the 1970s were based on the reasoning that the promotion of boat ownership is a suitable measure for poverty eradication. There is, however, no clear cut empirical evidence that this is the case. All subsidized units of fishing boats were assured of a licence irrespective of the limitation imposed on fishing effort by the government. This capital-intensive strategy, together with easy entry conditions into the industry, have probably increased labour under-employment and exacerbated the poverty situation. These programmes serve as an incentive for resources to move into or for excess effort and resources to be retained in the marine fisheries sector, thus leading to further depletion of the stocks and lowering of income among inshore small-scale fishermen. The opposite is required if the problem of poverty and over-fishing is to be effectively dealt with.

The department reiterated these views more recently (Shahrom 1992). Anderson (1987) concluded that poor fishermen suffered the most from the failure to resolve the open-access problem, as their economic interests were less diversified than rich fishermen's and their ability move their capital into other activities as returns to fishing declined was more limited.

The government's role in increasing fishing effort was not limited to the Fishermen's Subsidy Scheme. With the establishment of LKIM, the government became directly involved in commercial fishing. Through LKIM, it

hoped to boost fish production in areas considered underexploited, specifically the east coast, and to provide opportunities for traditional Malay fishermen to enter the modern fishing sector. LKIM was intended to prevent a
repeat of the west coast experience, in which the returns to modernization
(trawling) were reaped primarily by nontraditional, predominantly Chinese
fishermen. It was hoped that government involvement would ensure that
Malays benefitted from the expansion of commercial fishing on the east coast.
This direct government involvement was analogous to the government role in
integrated timber complexes, discussed in Chapter 4.

LKIM constructed and launched ninety-eight trawlers during the *Second
Plan* period, mainly in the east coast states of Kelantan, Terengganu, Pahang,
and Johor (*Third Malaysia Plan 1976–1980*). It launched another fifty-four
trawlers and purse-seiners during the *Third Plan* period (*Fourth Malaysia
Plan 1981–1985*). It also built smaller boats, ice plants, fishmeal plants, and
fish processing plants. LKIM increased fishing effort, but it failed to cover the
costs of doing so (World Bank 1982, p. 36):

MAJUIKAN's [LKIM's] direct management of this large fishing fleet is now generally recognized to have been an operational and financial failure. MAJUIKAN itself
estimated its losses on fishing operations at about RM 770,000 from 1974 through
September 1980. As such estimates generally are based only on running costs, and
ignore the much larger costs of depreciation (as well as interest foregone) on vessels, engines, nets, equipment, wharves, etc. (all of which depreciate very rapidly in
unskilled hands), financial losses will eventually be reckoned much higher.

The World Bank (1982, p. 37) attributed LKIM's problems primarily to a
mismatch between the characteristics of the fishing enterprise and the nature
of government agencies: fishing is a "risky and individualistic activity" that is
"not amenable to bureaucratic supervision and control." It noted that private
vessels were able to operate profitably in the same areas.

LKIM's problems also stemmed from excessive optimism about the size of
fishery resources, particularly on the east coast. The World Bank (1982, p. 17)
commented, "Despite consistently optimistic projections . . . the East Coast
demersal fishery has never performed up to official expectations." The more
severe monsoon, deeper and rougher seas, more extensive reefs, and an absence of prawns make the east coast fisheries less suitable for trawling. To the
extent that LKIM's catch contributed to a depletion of fish stocks, it had the
additional negative impact of raising fishing costs for competing, private
vessels.

In recognition of LKIM's failures, the government began dismantling its
fleet in 1979 (World Bank 1982). LKIM transferred ownership of an initial
forty boats to their operators on a trial basis. In December 1980, the Ministry

of Agriculture directed it to provide fishermen with hire-purchase facilities for acquiring not only the remaining boats but also new ones. The objective was "to enable Malay fishermen to own large boats" (Jahara 1981, cited in World Bank 1982, p. 38). From 1981 to 1983, 765 boats were distributed under this Boat Ownership Scheme (*Fifth Malaysia Plan 1986–1990*). Thus the demise of LKIM's fishing operations did not lead to an immediate reduction in effort.

Evidence of overfishing

As a result of the increased commercial and traditional, private and public sector fishing effort, marine fish landings in Peninsular Malaysia doubled between 1967, the year of the Maritime Fisheries Regulations, and 1981, the year of the next major fisheries policy, the Fisheries Licensing Policy. In spite of this spectacular growth, by 1981 there was abundant evidence that fisheries on the west coast were severely overfished. According to Goh (1976, p. 15), "By the 1960s, it was already known that the in-shore waters of the west coast were being over-fished and the marine resources were being fast depleted." But concrete evidence did not become available until the 1970s. The Department of Fisheries conducted its first survey of demersal fish resources in 1970 (Mohd. Shaari 1976). Evidence of overfishing grew stronger during the 1970s as more surveys were conducted.

Conceptually, comparing catch to MSY is the most obvious way of testing for biological overfishing. In practice, uncertainty about the true MSY level makes the comparison difficult, especially in multiple-species tropical fisheries. Ooi (1990, Table 5 and Figure 13) reviewed estimates of annual MSY (and the more vague notion of "potential yield") for the west and east coasts. He found that the estimates diverged widely in both cases. For the west coast, the highest estimate (350,000 tonnes) was nearly three times as large as the lowest estimate (125,000 tonnes); for the east coast, two-and-a-half times (407,000 tonnes versus 164,000 tonnes). Yet, five of the six estimates for the west coast were less than the average catch during 1971–80 (329,000 tonnes), suggesting that biological overfishing did indeed occur. On the other hand, average catch for the east coast (112,520 tonnes) was below all six of the MSY estimates for that region.

A similar comparison in an FAO-sponsored fisheries development plan prepared in the early 1970s had reached similar conclusions, at least for demersal fish (Labon 1974). The plan, citing a preliminary version of a report by Pathansali (1976), reported an estimated MSY of 90,000 to 94,000 tonnes for demersal fish on the west coast. From 1968 to 1971, however, annual catch typically exceeded 100,000 tonnes. In the case of pelagic fish, the plan estimated an *MSY* of 81,000 to 91,000 tonnes, while catch from 1968 to 1972 averaged 77,851 tonnes.

Given the uncertainty in *MSY* estimates, it is advisable to examine other evidence as well. Several studies have cited a declining *CPUE*, expressed as either catch per boat or catch per fisherman, as evidence of biological overfishing. As discussed in *Fundamental concepts of fisheries economics*, however, a declining *CPUE* does not provide a valid indicator of biological overfishing, because *CPUE* should always decline as effort increases in a given fishery, even before the *MSY* point is reached. A better indicator is a decline that accelerates as effort rises. Even then, one must take particular care in measuring effort. Simple measures, such as the number of boats or the number of fishermen, do not reflect important changes in the fishing power of gears and vessels. In fact, both catch per boat and catch per fisherman showed upward trends in the Peninsula from 1965 to 1986 when aggregated across gears and fisheries (Ooi 1990, Figure II). But these aggregate estimates do not control for the introduction of trawling and other technological developments (e.g., increasing motorization). The increase in fishing power could mask depletion in individual fisheries.

It is therefore preferable to examine trends in *CPUE* for a particular gear type in a particular fishery. From 1967 to 1972, the *CPUE* for trawlers on the west coast declined sharply, by a factor of more than five, according to frequently cited data in Pathansali (1977, cited in Khoo 1976). Mohd. Shaari (1976) presented similar data for trawlers in Pulau Pinang, which showed a nearly threefold drop in catch per boat per day, from 877.6 kg in 1966 to 299.7 kg in 1972. Shahrom (1992) reported that succeeding studies found that catch per boat per day for these trawlers fell to 100 to 150 kg by the late 1970s. Ooi (1990, p. 45) cited Elliston (1980), who estimated that "by 1977 . . . [trawlers] required four times as much time and capital to land each ton of fish than was needed in 1968." This estimate is consistent with anecdotal evidence reported by Anderson (1987), that trawlers operating out of a particular fishing village in Pulau Pinang had been forced to increase their daily hauls from one or two in the mid-1960s to four in 1970–71 to catch the same amount of fish. Munro and Chee (1978) found that the gross value of catch per trawler per trip in Pulau Pinang declined by about 40 percent between 1966 and 1971. The decline apparently reflected mainly a declining volume of catch and a decreasing proportion of the most valuable fish (Anderson 1987), not falling prices. Perhaps the most reliable data come from resource surveys conducted by the Fisheries Research Institute. These surveys are conducted using vessels operated under controlled conditions in particular waters. The catch rate of these vessels generally declined, in most cases sharply, during the early 1970s (see data and citations in Jahara 1988, p. 84, and World Bank 1982, p. 18).

One can also investigate trends in total catch. Figure 6.2 predicts that total catch should decline when additional effort is added beyond the *MSY* point. Although marine fish landings in Peninsular Malaysia rose from 1967 to 1981, Ooi (1990) noted that they fell sharply after 1981. The decline from 1981 to 1985 was equivalent to about 30 percent of the 1981 catch. The *Fifth Malaysia Plan* (p. 305) attributed the decline to "depleting fisheries resources, especially in the inshore areas." For the decline to be proof of biological overfishing, however, one must examine trends in effort as well: the declining catch should occur during a period when effort was rising. From 1981 to 1985, the number of licensed fishing boats also fell, by about 25 percent, so the evidence is inconclusive. We will examine this issue in more detail in the next section.

An increasing proportion of trash or manure fish (*ikan baja*), which are used primarily for making fertilizer, is regarded as another sign of biological overfishing. It indicates a relative decline in the stocks of more valuable food fish. Trash fish are often juveniles of commercial species, particularly when the gear is nondiscriminating (as in the case of trawlers) and mesh size is small. This "growth overfishing" interferes with the ability of the fish population to recover from fishing.

The World Bank (1982, p. 12) pointed out that "the remarkable increases in West coast catch during the 1970s largely consisted of huge sustained increases in low-value trash fish taken by trawlers." The trash fish proportion of the trawler catch in Pulau Pinang rose from 27 percent in 1966–67 to 51 percent in 1971–72 (Munro and Chee 1978). For the Peninsula as a whole, the proportion of trash fish rose from the mid-1960s through 1990 for both catch by all gears and catch by trawlers only. Trash fish accounted for about 16 percent of the catch in Peninsular Malaysia during the second half of the 1960s. During the 1970s, however, the proportion ranged between a quarter and a third. The proportion was even higher for trawlers: it rose from about two-fifths in the late 1960s to a high of three-fifths in the mid-1970s.

Immature fish of commercially valuable species did indeed account for much of the trash fish landings (Shahrom 1984, Ooi 1990, Jomo 1991). This perhaps explains why the catch of food fish (excluding prawns) in trawl fisheries in Pulau Pinang in the late 1960s and early 1970s fell not only in relative terms but also in absolute terms: the catch peaked at 7,000 tonnes in 1969 and fell to 4,000 tonnes in 1972 (Munro and Chee 1978). Some commercial species virtually disappeared from the west coast. *Ikan shrumbu* (*Lactarius lactarius*) is an oft-cited example (Ch'ng 1983, cited in Jahara 1988); Anderson (1987) cited two species known only by their Hokkien names, *chi kaq hu* and *kuan im hu*, as having been driven to local extinction.

Munro and Chee (1978) conducted the most careful analysis of evidence that economic, as well as biological, overfishing occurred in the late 1960s and early 1970s. They estimated two versions of the annual rate of return on capital invested in trawling in Pulau Pinang from 1966 to 1971. In one version, they deducted an imputed payment to the boat owner for management of the fishing enterprise; in the other, they treated this management cost as part of the overall return to capital. They also estimated that the opportunity cost of capital invested in trawlers was approximately 16 percent: a risk-free rate of 6 percent that could be earned on a bank deposit, plus a 10 percent premium for the risks involved in trawling. According to their estimates, the return to trawling was initially far in excess of the opportunity cost of capital. For 1966, for example, they estimated an annual rate of return of 51 percent when management costs were included and 55 percent when management costs were excluded. Estimates were similar in 1967, but they fell rapidly thereafter. By 1970, the estimates were well below the opportunity cost of capital, at 7 percent with management costs included and 11 percent with these costs excluded. The rent in trawl fisheries in Pulau Pinang had been completely dissipated, confirming that economic overfishing had occurred.

Policy responses in the 1980s to overfishing

Through the 1970s, the government's fishery policies emphasized production—increasing the catch—even though officers in the Department of Fisheries were aware of the need to control effort to prevent overfishing (Mohamed Mazlan 1972, cited Munro and Chee 1978). The World Bank, in its early 1980s review of the sector, commented that "the conservation and management of the fisheries resource is the quintessential government role in the fisheries sector; paradoxically, it is one which has received little emphasis [in Malaysia], at least in terms of field implementation" (World Bank 1982, p. 55). Ooi (1990, p. 49) has argued that the great speed of expansion of the trawler industry "outstripped the ability of the Fisheries Department to institute controls." Shahrom (1984, p. 320) wrote in the early 1980s that "the management of the fishery resources prior to 1980 had been on a problem-oriented basis, that is, reacting to the problems as they appeared."

Beginning in the early 1980s, the government took a number of steps to conserve fish stocks and to limit fishing effort. To reduce the catch of juvenile fish, the department raised the minimum mesh size for trawl nets from 1 to 1.5 inches (Shahrom 1984). Jahara (1984) found that the proportion of juvenile fish caught by trawlers in Terengganu was indeed lower for larger mesh sizes. Khoo (1980, cited in Ooi 1990) pointed out that a larger mesh size would also reduce trawlers' ability to catch prawns and should dampen their tendency to encroach into the prawn-rich zone 3 to 7 miles offshore.[4] To protect stocks further, under the *Fifth Malaysia Plan* the department and LKIM constructed artificial reefs to create additional breeding grounds. According to Shahrom (1992, p. 7), "by 1990, 67 artificial reefs of tyres, 10 A-reefs of sunken boats and 4 of concrete units had been built." In addition, 22 islands off Peninsular Malaysia were gazetted as Fishery Restricted Areas. The *Sixth Malaysia Plan 1991–1995* called for continuation of these efforts.

Gulland (1974) has pointed out that such supply-side measures alone are inadequate for preventing overfishing. They may succeed in restoring the stocks in a depleted fishery, but once the stocks are restored, additional vessels will be attracted to the fishery. Ultimately, therefore, fishing effort must be controlled. This was a principal objective of the 1981 Fisheries Licensing Policy. Its specific goals were (Shahrom 1984, p. 320):

(a) The elimination of competition and the ensuing conflict between traditional fishermen and mini-trawler fishermen in inshore waters.
(b) The prevention of over-exploitation of the fishery resources in inshore waters.
(c) A more equitable distribution of fishing throughout the waters under the jurisdiction of Malaysia.
(d) The restructuring of the ownership pattern of fishing units in accord with the New Economic Policy.
(e) Promotion of the development of offshore industrial fisheries.

The principal means of achieving the first two goals was to allocate fishing grounds through a zoning cum licensing system. The policy established four zones (Shahrom 1992):

Zone A (0–5 miles offshore): reserved for owner-operated traditional gears.
Zone B (5–12 miles offshore): reserved for owner-operated trawlers and purse-seiners below 40 GRT.
Zone C (12–30 miles offshore): reserved for trawlers, purse seiners, and other Malaysian-owned and operated gears between 40 and 70 GRT.
Zone D (30 miles offshore to outer limit of Exclusive Economic Zone): open to foreign fishing, on a joint-venture or charter basis, as well as domestic fishing, for vessels of 70 GRT and above.

Ooi (1990) has pointed out that zoning alone is not an effective deterrent to overfishing. It restricts the types of vessels and gears that can be used in particular zones, but not their number. In recognition of this, the policy also authorized the department to limit the number of licenses issued in each zone. For the west coast, the department imposed a moratorium on new licenses for all vessels except those of 40 GRT and above. The moratorium was intended to reduce effort gradually in inshore fisheries, as fishermen retired, died, or voluntarily withdrew from the sector.

The license limits and the moratorium encountered both practical and political obstacles. On the practical side, the department was unable to estimate with much confidence the number of licenses to issue in individual fishing areas. Shahrom (1984, p. 321) attributed the difficulty to a lack of information on the relationship between catch and effort: "Adequate information on resources under intensive exploitation and on unexploited resources in areas and sub-areas are [sic] unavailable. Collection of statistics in Malaysia is by sampling at landing points. There is no routine programme to obtain accurate statistics on the fleets' catch and efforts, through requirement of fishing-vessel operators to provide records of their operation." On the political side, the department was frequently pressured to ignore the license limits and to grant licenses to politically favored individuals or communities, especially before elections. In particular, there was strong pressure to grant licenses to the large number of existing illegal trawlers. Khoo (1980, cited in Ooi 1990) estimated that 4,000 unlicensed trawlers were operating in 1978; this was about equal to the number of licensed ones. According to Shahrom (1984, p. 326), there was "a promise of political support for enforcement of a ban on illegal operations subsequent to the legalizing of the present lot." Indeed, several hundred licenses were issued to small trawlers in 1984. In 1989, more than a thousand new licenses were issued for traditional gears on the west coast, mainly sampans with outboard engines, due to political pressures related to the upcoming 1990 general election.

In spite of these obstacles, during the 1980s the number of licensed fishing gears in Peninsular Malaysia did fall dramatically, with traditional gears accounting for most of the decrease. From an all-time peak of some 26,000 in 1981, licensed traditional gears fell to less than 10,000 in 1989. The department's ability to resist political pressures related to licensing was helped by a restructuring of the Ministry of Agriculture, which reassigned agencies related to cooperatives to the Ministry of Land. Fisheries cooperatives were politically well connected, and through the cooperative agencies in the ministry they had been able to pressure the department to issue more licenses.

The World Bank (1982, p. 55) observed that the difficulty of convincing policy makers that effort needed to be controlled was not surprising: "Limiting entry to an activity which can always give short-term profits to the last marginal man or boat (at an unseen cost to all the rest) is bound to disturb many." Shahrom (1984, p. 321) stated that doubts about the necessity of limiting entry existed even within the Department of Fisheries:

The problem here is to be able to convince the political leadership of the necessity for government intervention and of the benefits of such intervention. Although the management measures were accepted by the government, there was still a lack of full comprehension of the unique problem of the common-property fishery resource and the necessity for government intervention. This prevailed not only outside the implementing agency [the Department of Fisheries] itself but also among the officers of the implementing agency. Consequently, the necessary support was not forth-coming. Although there is also a question of taking the line of least resistance in the face of political and social pressure, the nagging doubts of the necessity and benefits of the interventions were uppermost in the mind[s] of these people.

He noted that Fisheries officers "were more attuned to the policy of production rather than management of overcapacity" (p. 325).

The prohibition against non-owner-operated boats in Zones A and B also met with political resistance. According to Jahara (1988), a survey conducted by the Implementation and Coordination Unit of the Prime Minister's Department in 1978 determined that 71 percent of inshore fishermen were operating boats belonging to *towkays*. It was politically impossible to prohibit such a large portion of the industry from operating. The prohibition against non-owner-operated vessels came to be viewed more as a long-term goal, to be achieved gradually through the licensing of new boats instead of by impounding existing boats.

Even without political pressure, Malaysia's long coastline made enforcement of the policy difficult. Before 1980, enforcement was the responsibility of the separate state fisheries directors (Shahrom 1984). Their efforts were not coordinated, nor were they linked to other government enforcement or maritime agencies. In 1980, the Department of Fisheries enlarged its enforcement unit and established four regional centers in Peninsular Malaysia. Between 1979 and 1983, it doubled the number of patrol vessels and speed boats. It also enlisted the support of the Marine Police and the Navy. Shahrom (1984, p. 324) concluded, however, that the "main problem faced in enforcement . . . comes from the lack of political will." He cited the example of 14 trawlers that were seized while operating only 1 to 1½ miles from shore. Political intervention resulted in the guilty parties paying only nominal fines.

The policy was followed in 1985 by a new Fisheries Act, which replaced the 1963 act, by then more than two decades old. The act amounted to a fine-tuning of key features of the policy. It was in part prompted by the 1984 Exclusive Economic Zone (EEZ) Act, which followed the third U.N. Conference on the Law of the Sea in 1980 and formalized Malaysia's claim to waters up to 200 miles offshore. Malaysia's proclamation of its EEZ increased its marine waters by some 114,000 square nautical miles. The act imposed heavy fines (up to RM1 million) against the owners of foreign vessels caught in Malaysia's EEZ (Jahara 1988). It also increased the penalties faced by Malaysian fishermen who violated the zones laid out in the 1981 policy. If caught, such fishermen faced a maximum fine of RM50,000, a maximum jail sentence of two years, or both. Confiscation of vessels and gear was made mandatory upon the third violation. The act changed the licensing requirement so that a license needed to be obtained before building a boat, not simply before putting it into operation. This enhanced the department's ability to prevent fishing by unlicensed boats. The act authorized the Ministry "to specify prohibited fishing areas for all fish or certain species of fish or methods of fishing," which led to the establishment of the Fisheries Restricted Areas mentioned earlier. The act also prohibited the use of explosives, poisons, and electrical devices in fishing.

Ooi (1990) has interpreted the policy and the act as defining distinctly different objectives for inshore and offshore waters. Use of inshore waters is intended to achieve a social objective, employment for traditional fishermen, while use of offshore waters is intended to achieve an economic objective, the production of fish. The country's experience with overfishing on the west coast indicates that neither objective can be achieved on a sustainable basis if effort is not controlled: in the former case, fishermen earn only a poverty-level income and suffer underemployment; in the latter case, production and profits eventually fall as the fishery becomes depleted.

The government appears to have recognized this, at least in the former case. It took additional steps besides zoning and licensing to reduce effort in inshore fisheries. First, it scaled back the Fishermen's Subsidy Scheme in the early 1980s and withdrew a subsidy on diesel fuel in 1983 (Jomo 1991). Shahrom (1984, p. 323) observed that production-oriented subsidies were "not fully rational and consistent with the present management policy." These actions were also motivated by the government's fiscal crisis in the 1980s, which forced it to trim spending wherever possible.

Second, the government promoted nonfishing employment alternatives for fishermen and their families. Goh (1976) had suggested this as a means of curbing growth of the fishing population; the World Bank (1982) had proposed that such an effort could be funded by savings from reductions in subsidies and by taxes on the resource rent generated by fisheries.[5] Gibbons's (1976) survey revealed that, contrary to common belief, fishermen were not highly immobile in either geographical or occupational terms. He found that 29 percent of the traditional fishermen surveyed had lived in places other than their current village. Seventy percent indicated that they would move their families to another fishing village if they could earn more by doing so; 91 percent indicated that they would take up a nonfishing job if it were more remunerative. Eighty-one percent did not want their children to be fisher-men. Ooi (1990, p. 54) cited similar survey results.

To make the pursuit of nonfishing employment more attractive, the government implemented a boat buy-back scheme, under which it paid compensation to boat-owners who gave up fishing. This scheme "brought little result" (Tan 1993). A second scheme was the Fishermen Resettlement Program, which intended to move fishermen and their families to land development schemes. This program was initiated under the *Fifth Malaysia Plan* and was administered by the Department of Fisheries and LKIM, with assistance from land development agencies. Its chances for success seemed good, as many traditional fishermen were part-time farmers. From 1968 to 1981 the settlers on federal land development schemes had already included some 1,000 fishermen (World Bank 1982). No estimates of the number of fishermen resettled under the program are available, and its performance is not clear. Jomo (1991, p. 71) concluded that, "Resettlement schemes [have been] undoubtedly effective in siphoning off surplus labor from fishing." But as one estimate of the cost of resettlement was approximately RM80,000 per family (World Bank 1982, referring to a scheme run by the state of Kedah), he questioned the financial viability of the program. Tan (1993) reported that it "was fraught with obstacles and hardly took off."

Despite the mixed record of the department's programs to reduce the number of fishermen, the *Sixth Plan* (p. 96) reported that the national number declined from a high of 116,500 in the early 1980s to 89,000 in 1990. This decline nearly matched a target set by the Department of Fisheries in the mid-1980s, to reduce the number of inshore fishermen by 30,000 between 1986 and 2000. Virtually all of the decline occurred in Peninsular Malaysia (Figure 6.3). This helps explain the concomitant decline in the number of licensed traditional gears. Most of the decline was evidently voluntary, as fishermen took up jobs in other sectors of the rapidly growing economy (after the end of the mid-1980s recession) or retired and were not replaced by their children, who entered other pursuits. The *Sixth Plan* (p. 96) commented that the decline was "due to outmigration and the preference of fishermen to become farmers." Tan (1993) referred to "the blotter paper effect of the booming economy on surplus labor." In this way the country's economic growth had an unintended, positive impact on fishery management.[6]

In the case of offshore fishing, the government took virtually no steps to control fishing effort. In fact, it quite explicitly promoted increased fishing, on the assumption, reminiscent of the early days of trawling, that fishery resources in distant waters were underexploited. Licenses for deep-sea vessels were subject to fewer restrictions than licenses for smaller vessels, and the government, through LKIM, promoted joint ventures with foreign (primarily

Thai) companies. Jomo (1991) reported that the government offered 100 percent grants for the purchase of engines for deep-sea fishing vessels operated on the east coast; the *Sixth Plan* mentioned credit facilities for building deep-sea vessels and public investment in infrastructure to serve large vessels. The *Sixth Plan* (p. 111) stated that, "Due to the depletion of inshore resources, the future development of the fisheries sector will stress on [*sic*] deep-sea fishing and aquaculture in fresh and brackish water."

The deep-sea catch more than quintupled from 1985 to 1990, from 18,300 to 100,000 tonnes. This explains a good portion of the approximate doubling of total catch during the second half of the 1980s. Rising production from deep-sea vessels helped the country's net trade balance for fishery commodities become positive by the end of the decade, following a deficit during the middle years of the decade.[7] Jomo (1991, p. 19) concluded, however, that available data on fish stocks cast doubt on the prospects for sustaining the expansion:

Resource surveys conducted in offshore waters beyond the present zone of operation have not indicated sufficiently promising fish stock for commercial exploitation. Commercial fishing trials undertaken by Majuikan also suggest relatively low catch rates in waters 12 to 30 miles offshore. Vast areas in the South China Sea are known to have very low fish density, rendering them economically unviable for commercial fishing. Beyond 60 miles, there appears to be a drastic drop in fish density—about 5 metric tonnes per square nautical mile for demersal fish, and 0.28 to 3.03 metric tonnes for pelagic fish.

Studies conducted just a year apart by the Department of Fisheries and the Universiti Pertanian Malaysia reportedly reached opposite conclusions about the viability of the deep-sea industry (Tan 1993). Shahrom (1992, p. 2) observed that "despite [the] recent opportunity to develop off-shore deep-sea fisheries . . . the majority of the fishery—more than 90%—operates in the relatively shallow waters within the 12 mile territorial limit." In 1990, only 586 of the 39,541 licensed fishing boats in the country (1.5 percent) were in the 70+ GRT class (Jabatan Perikanan 1991).

ECONOMIC ANALYSIS OF CATCH AND EFFORT IN WEST COAST FISHERIES DURING THE 1980S

To our knowledge, no one has analyzed the net impact of the various policies and programs of the 1980s. How did they affect effort? Did biological and economic overfishing worsen, improve, or remain about the same? We developed a simple bioeconomic model to address these questions for the case of commercial and traditional fisheries on the west coast of Peninsular Malaysia from 1981 to 1991. The model involved estimating catch-effort relationships corresponding to the one in Figure 6.1. In keeping with the 1981 Fisheries Licensing Policy, we defined the traditional fishery as marine waters within Zone A, and the commercial fishery as marine waters in Zones B and D.[8] We developed indices of catch and effort that took into account the multiple species and variety of gears used in each fishery.

Catch

Both the traditional and commercial fisheries are multispecies fisheries. They produce a great variety of fish, crustaceans (prawns and crabs), mollusks (squid, clams, cockles), and other edible marine organisms. The Department of Fisheries reports data on annual landings by both species and grade. Grade I includes popular species like pomfret (*bawal*), threadfin (*kurau*), grouper (*kerapu*), and Spanish mackerel (*tenggiri*). Grade II includes less expensive species like red snapper (*merah*), shads (*puput-puput*), and giant sea perch (*siakap*). Grade III includes anchovies (*ikan bilis*) and nonfish marine organisms such as squid (*sotong*), crabs (*ketam*), and jellyfish (*ubor-ubor*). In addition to these three grades, there are categories for prawns (*udang*), shellfish (*siput*), and trash fish (*ikan baja*).

We began the analysis of catch by examining aggregate landings in the traditional fishery, defined as the sum of landings by the three most important traditional gears—drift/gill nets (*pukat hanyut*), bag nets (*pukat bakul*), and hooks and lines (*pancing*)—and aggregate landings in the commercial fishery, defined as the sum of landings by trawl nets (*pukat tunda*) and purse seine nets (*pukat tarik*).[9] We excluded landings of shellfish, which are minor in both quantity and value. In both fisheries, landings were found to be higher in the second half of the period than the first. In the commercial fishery, the increase was due mainly to increased landings of Grade III and trash fish, although landings of Grade I and Grade II fish also increased slightly. In the traditional fishery, the increase was due mainly to increased landings of Grade III fish, although landings of trash fish also increased. There was a noticeable decline in landings of grade 1 fish. Hence, the composition of landings shifted toward less valuable species, particularly in the traditional fishery.

We also calculated real (inflation-adjusted) ex-vessel unit values for landings by trawl nets (the most important commercial gear) and drift/gill nets (the most important traditional gear).[10] We converted unit values from a wholesale basis (reported by the department) to an ex-vessel basis by deducting a marketing margin,[11] and then we divided by the Malaysian GDP deflator

(1978 price levels) to convert to real terms. Unit values fluctuated greatly for both gears for all grades except Grade I. They fell dramatically between 1986 and 1987. By the end of the period, unit values had regained their 1981 levels except in the cases of Grade II fish and prawns. The declining unit values for prawns resulted in part from a declining share of the more valuable white prawns (*udang putih*).

These preliminary analyses revealed that both the composition of landings and unit values changed substantially in both fisheries during the 1980s. These changes imply that trends in total landings provide a poor measure of trends in true, economic catch. Catch, in the economic sense, takes into account changes in the shares and unit values of different grades. For example, if landings remain constant over time, but the share of less valuable fish rises, catch declines in economic terms. Hereafter, we will use *catch* to refer to economic catch, and *landings* to refer to the actual physical quantity of fish caught.

We measured catch for each fishery by the divisia quantity index (Jorgenson and Griliches 1971). This index weights landings of different grades by their share of total revenue in the fishery.[12] Calculating this index required data on landings and unit values by gear group:[13] trawlers and purse-seiners for the commercial fishery, and drift/gill nets, bag nets, and hooks and lines for the traditional fishery. We used 1981, the year when the Fisheries Licensing Policy was implemented, as the base year for the index. We set the value of the index in that year equal to total landings in each fishery.

Figures 6.4 and 6.5 compare catch and landings. In the commercial fishery, the increase in landings since 1981 understated the increase in catch by a moderate amount, but the two series were roughly parallel. The comparison yielded a much more surprising result for the traditional fishery. Catch actually *fell* during period, even though landings rose. This reflects the rising share of Grade III fish and the declining share of Grade I fish. Landings data therefore gave a false impression of rising production in the traditional fishery. The estimates of catch shown in Figures 6.4 and 6.5 provided the catch data used in estimating the bioeconomic model.

The divisia quantity index is associated with a companion divisia price index. The latter is calculated by dividing total revenue (landings times ex-vessel unit values, summed across grades) by the quantity index. It provides a measure of fish price at the aggregate, fisheries level. The indices fluctuated less than the prices by grade, but they still declined sharply during 1986–87. Prices per tonne were higher in the traditional fishery, which is not surprising given the smaller share of trash fish in the landings of this fishery. The divisia indices price were used to convert the estimated catch-effort relationship for each fishery into a total revenue curve corresponding to the one in Figure 6.2.

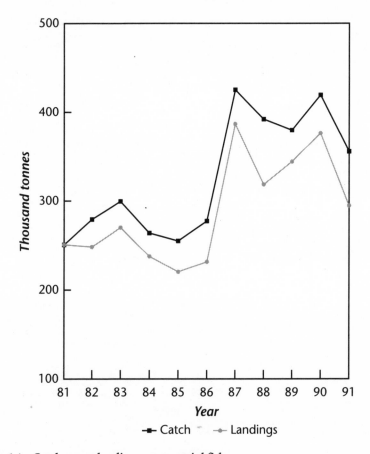

Figure 6.4   Catch versus landings: commercial fishery

Effort

To complete the model, we needed to estimate aggregate fishing effort in each fishery. The total number of licenses declined in both fisheries. The decline was most pronounced in the traditional fishery, although it was partially offset by an increase between 1988 and 1989, when, due to political pressure (1990 was a general election year), the department lifted the moratorium on new licenses. In the commercial fishery, the decline was due entirely to retirement of smaller trawlers and purse-seiners (those under 40 GRT). The number of larger trawlers and purse-seiners actually increased. In

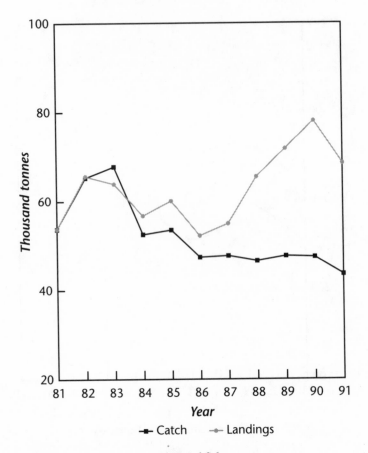

Figure 6.5   Catch versus landings: traditional fishery

the traditional fishery, the number decreased for all gears, with the decline being steepest for the most common gear, drift/gill nets.

As in the case of landings versus catch, such changes imply that the number of licenses provides a poor measure of fishing effort. For example, a smaller fleet can generate greater fishing effort if the average vessel is larger and more powerful. We therefore measured fishing effort by the divisia index approach. Calculating the effort index required annual data on the number of licenses and average total cost for each gear type. Estimates of average total cost served as weights analogous to the ex-vessel unit values in the catch index. Average total cost is the appropriate economic measure of per unit effort, as it gives the opportunity cost of resources that could be employed in other activities. It is superior to purely physical measures of effort, such as the tonnage of boats or the horsepower of their engines: it generally points in the same direction as do the physical measures—bigger boats cost more to purchase and operate—but it is more sensitive to differences in fishing power. Bigger boats command a higher price not because they are bigger, but because fishermen expect them to be more productive and yield higher net earnings.

We included both fixed and variable costs in the measure of total cost. The inclusion of both enabled us to use the model to estimate total rents for the fisheries. Fixed costs were annualized using available information on financing periods, borrowing rates, and depreciation rates. Variable, or operating, costs included fuel, maintenance, ice, labor, and so on. Wage labor was valued at its wage rate, while nonwage labor (owner-operaters) was valued at the rate for fisheries wage labor, the presumed alternative employment option.

Data on costs were drawn from various studies of fishing costs for specific vessel/gear combinations (Institut Penyelidikan Perikanan dan Cawangan Perancang dan Sistem, Maklumat Pengurusan Perikanan, n.d.; Jabatan Perikanan, n.d.; Jahara and Wells 1982; Fredericks et al. 1985; Ishak and Chang 1986; Kusairi and Tai 1988; Jabatan Perikanan 1989; Rabihah et al. 1989). For each gear group, cost estimates were first converted to 1978 price levels using the GDP deflator. Then, they were regressed on gross vessel tonnage and year of the estimate to derive a relationship that predicted annual cost as a function of tonnage and year. Regressions were run separately for fixed and variable costs. Time trends were generally found not to be significant predictors of costs, indicating that costs remained constant in real terms for boats of a given size.[14] As one would expect, estimated costs were greater for commercial boats than for traditional boats, ranging upwards of RM32,790 per year for the former and being no more than RM20,297 for the latter. Within the commercial category, they were greater for purse-seiners and increased with tonnage, reaching a maximum of RM227,290 for purse-seiners of more than 70 GRT.[15]

Figures 6.6 and 6.7 compare the divisia effort indices, based on the data on licenses and the regression-based cost estimates, to number of licenses. The indices used 1981 as a base year, and in that year they were set equal to the total number of licenses in the respective fisheries. Although the number of licenses declined in the commercial fishery, fishing effort was actually higher in 1991 than in 1981. This was due to the increased share of large trawlers and purse-seiners. The declining number of licensed trawlers and purse-seiners therefore gave a false impression of declining effort in the commercial fishery. In the traditional fishery, trends in licenses and effort were virtually identical. Using divisia indices to measure catch and effort instead of data on landings and licenses therefore yielded contrasting results for the two fisheries: in the

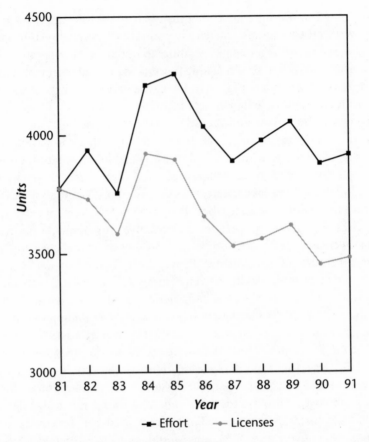

Figure 6.6   Effort versus licenses: commercial fishery

commercial fishery, effort and licenses (Figure 6.6) but not catch and landings (Figure 6.4) diverged; in the traditional fishery, the opposite was true (Figure 6.7 versus Figure 6.5).

Cost per unit of effort, from the divisia price index, is not graphed because it was virtually constant over time for both fisheries, at RM55,220 for the commercial fishery and RM12,478 for the traditional fishery. This is not surprising, given that average total costs were constant over time for all gears (the time trend was insignificant in the regressions). Nor is it surprising that cost was higher in the commercial fishery, which was characterized by much larger boats. These unit cost estimates were used to calculate total cost as a linear function of units of effort, as in Figure 6.2.

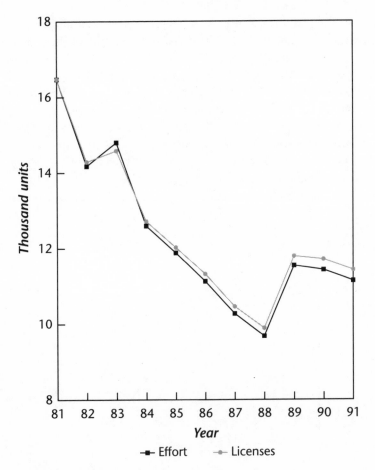

Figure 6.7   Effort versus licenses: traditional fishery

An upward bias in the divisia effort indices must be acknowledged. The indices are based on number of licenses and average total cost by gear group. The estimates of average total cost are for a normal fishing year. The data on licenses were not adjusted for the actual number of days spent fishing, due to insufficient data. Undoubtedly the average number of days spent fishing was less than what is considered a normal fishing year, as not all fishermen are full-time. In fact, it is clear that some licensed gears did not operate at all. The Department of Fisheries has estimated that 2 percent of all licensed gears on the west coast did not operate in 1990 (*Jabatan Perikanan 1991*). The percentage was highest for the traditional fishery: 13 percent of the licensed drift/gill nets, bag nets, and hooks and lines did not operate in 1990. Unfortunately, estimates of the proportion of gear in operation were not available for most earlier years. These factors cause the divisia effort indices to overstate actual effort. Hence, estimates of total cost calculated by multiplying the indices by the corresponding unit costs of effort are also overstated.

Figure 6.8 shows *CPUE* (catch per unit effort), calculated by dividing the data in Figures 6.4 and 6.5 by the data in Figures 6.6 and 6.7. *CPUE* was noticeably higher in the second half of the period for the commercial fishery. It was more or less constant in the traditional fishery after an initial increase between 1981 and 1982, although it declined somewhat after the lifting of the moratorium on new licenses in 1989. Given the difficulty of interpreting *CPUE* trends when the level of effort is not changing at a uniform rate over

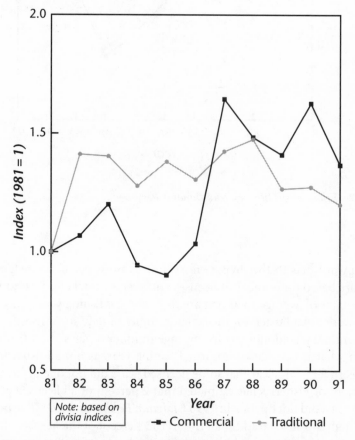

Figure 6.8   Catch per unit effort: commercial versus traditional fishery

time, the implications are not obvious. Overfishing is better analyzed by using catch-effort relationships and total revenue/total cost curves.

Bioeconomic model: results

In the commercial fishery, catch and effort tended to rise during the period, whereas in the traditional fishery, they tended to fall.[16] Do these opposite trends indicate improving or deteriorating management of the two fisheries? In economic terms, management improved if rents increased, and it deteriorated if rents decreased. The bioeconomic model enabled us to answer this question and, furthermore, to estimate the optimal amount of effort in each fishery, that is, the amount that would have maximized rents.

Appendix 6 provides details on the model. In short, it was estimated by regressing the catch data for each fishery on the corresponding effort data.[17] The resulting regression equations are plotted as solid lines in Figures 6.9 and 6.10. Figure 6.1 predicts that catch should increase with effort up to the *MSY* (maximum sustained yield) point, but decrease beyond this point. This is indeed what Figures 6.9 and 6.10 show for both fisheries. In the commercial fishery, the *MSY* point occurs at an effort level of 3,969 units (which equals 3,969 boats at the 1981 composition of the fleet). Catch at this point is 361,974 units (which equals 361,974 tonnes at the 1981 composition of the catch) (Table 6.3). In the traditional fishery, *MSY* occurs at 15,624 units of effort and equals 60,162 units of fish.

Figures 6.9 and 6.10 also show, as asterisks, the actual catch and effort data points for each year. The points do not lie perfectly along the curve for either

Table 6.3 *Catch, effort, and resource rent in west coast fisheries, at 1991 per unit fish values and fishing costs*

Fishery and effort level	Effort	Catch	Rent
	Units[a]	Unit s[b]	Million RM (1978)
I. Commercial			
A. Actual (1991)	3,917	355,725	65.5
B. MSY[c]	3,969	361,974	67.6
C. MEY[d]	3,946	361,178	68.3
II. Traditional			
A. Actual (1991)	11,136	43,543	−16.6
B. MSY	15,624	60,162	−25.9
C. MEY	11,492	51,017	0.4

[a] Divisia index units, which equal number of boats if the fishing fleet has the same relative composition as in 1981, the base year of the index.

[b] Divisia index units, which equal tonnes of fish if landings have the same relative composition as in 1981, the base year of the index.

[c] *MSY*—Maximum sustained yield.

[d] *MEY*—Maximum economic yield.

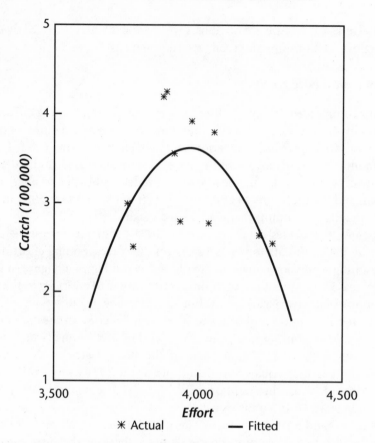

Figure 6.9   Catch versus effort: commercial fishery

fishery, which is to be expected: effort alone does not explain all the variation in catch. Effort exceeded the *MSY* level in five of the eleven years for the commercial fishery, but in only one of the eleven years for the traditional fishery. Hence, the commercial fishery was biologically overfished about half the time, while the traditional fishery was essentially not biologically over-fished at all. The latter finding is consistent with Munro and Chee's (1978) suspicions about fisheries in Pulau Pinang and Kedah.

Effort relative to the *MSY* point is not the relevant issue from an economic perspective, however. As long as the cost per unit of fishing effort is positive, a fishery harvested at the *MSY* level is economically overfished (at least in static economic terms). Resource rent is maximized at a lower level of effort, the *MEY* (maximum economic yield) level. The *MEY* point depends on prices

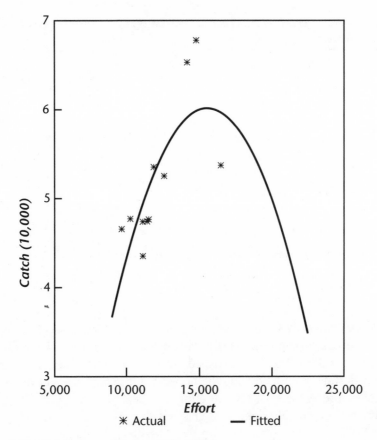

Figure 6.10   Catch versus effort: traditional fishery

and costs and therefore is not constant over time. At the 1991 estimates of prices and costs based on the divisia indices, the *MEY* effort levels were 3,946 units in the commercial fishery and 11,492 units in the traditional fishery (Table 6.3). Hence, *MEY* effort was extremely close to *MSY* effort in the commercial fishery, but substantially lower in the traditional fishery. Actual 1991 levels of fishing effort in the commercial and traditional fisheries, 3,917 and 11,136 units, respectively, were almost identical to the *MEY* levels. It appears that both fisheries were exploited at essentially optimal levels in 1991.

This was not the case during the entire period, however. Table 6.4 shows that the commercial fishery was slightly underfished from 1981to 1983. It became overfished from 1984 to 1986 as the number of large trawlers and

Table 6.4 *Deviation between actual and optimal (MEY) fishing effort in west coast fisheries (percentages)*

	Fishery	
Year	Commercial	Traditional
1981	−4	+44
1982	0	+24
1983	−5	+31
1984	+7	+10
1985	+8	+1
1986	+2	−8
1987	−1	+4
1988	+1	0
1989	+3	+4
1990	−2	+1
1991	−1	−3

Note: A positive deviation indicates that actual effort exceeded optimal effort (economic overfishing).

purse-seiners increased. After that, retirement of smaller vessels reduced the overall level of effort and the degree of overfishing. In contrast, the traditional fishery was indeed heavily overfished during 1981–84. The more or less constant decline in effort during the period (Figure 6.7) brought the fishery extremely close to the *MEY* level of effort by 1985. Since 1986, effort in both fisheries was remarkably close to *MEY* levels.

At 1991 prices and costs, the commercial fishery would generate RM67.6 million annually in resource rent if harvested at the *MSY* level, while the traditional fishery would generate *negative* RM25.9 million annually (Table 6.3).[18] This indicates that reaching the *MSY* level in the traditional fishery would require substantial subsidization and would result in a net loss for the economy. The magnitude of the loss, (RM25.9 million), is probably over-stated, however, due to the upward bias in the divisia effort indices and therefore in total cost. If effort were limited to the *MEY* level, catch in the commercial fishery would fall by only 0.2 percent, to 361,178 units. Consequently, rent would rise only slightly, to RM68.3 million. In the traditional fishery, however, catch would fall by 15 percent, to 51,017 units. But now rent would become positive, albeit at a low level, RM0.4 million. In reality, the rent would probably be higher, given that the effort index used in the model, and hence the model's estimates of total costs, are biased upward.

Actual catch in 1991 was 355,725 units in the commercial fishery, close to the *MEY* level, but only 43,543 units in the traditional fishery, well below the *MEY* level. Why was the 1991 catch in the traditional fishery so much lower than the predicted *MEY* level, when the actual and predicted *MEY* levels of effort were so similar? This is perhaps a sign that the fishery has not yet recovered from overfishing in the 1970s and early 1980s.[19] The great disparity between landings and catch in 1991 (Figure 6.5), due to the rising proportion of Grade III fish, supports this hypothesis. It indicates that the composition of fish stocks has changed substantially. Whether the change is permanent, or whether the fishery will eventually recover and once again yield a greater proportion of higher-valued species, is a dynamic question that the model cannot answer. Due to the low catch level, rent in 1991 was estimated to be negative. The upward bias in the divisia effort index was surely partly responsible as well.

CONCLUSIONS

Fishing effort rose in west coast fisheries during the 1960s due to the introduction of a new technology, trawling. Initially, the government concentrated not on controlling fishing effort but rather on reducing the conflict between trawlers and traditional fishermen. In fact, the government promoted traditional fishermen's involvement in commercial fishing through subsidy programs and LKIM's commercial fishing activities. These actions further increased fishing effort. By the 1970s, several indicators pointed to the existence of biological and economic overfishing: catch exceeding estimated *MSY* levels, dramatic declines in *CPUE*, a rising proportion of trash fish, and rates of return no greater than the opportunity cost of capital.

With the 1981 Fisheries Licensing Policy and the 1985 Fisheries Act, the government for the first time placed substantial weight on controlling fishing effort in inshore waters. In offshore waters, it continued to emphasize increased effort and production. Our analysis of catch and effort during the 1980s determined that effort indeed fell in the traditional fishery following the introduction of the 1981 Fisheries Licensing Policy, from levels that were well above *MEY* at the beginning of the 1980s. In the commercial fishery, effort rose above *MSY* as well as *MEY* in the mid-1980s, but it declined thereafter. The decline coincided with the introduction of the 1985 Fisheries Act. By the end of the decade, levels of effort in both fisheries were close to *MEY*.

The Department of Fisheries must continue controlling effort to keep it at these desired levels, through continuation of such measures as the moratorium on licenses for boats below 40 GRT in Zones A and B. In the traditional fishery, the fact that the proportion of lower-valued fish in landings was still rising at the end of the period suggests that even lower levels of effort, below what are statically optimal, may be necessary for a while for the fishery to recover fully from historical overfishing. Strict enforcement of existing rules on minimum mesh size and bans on pair and beam trawlers are important in this regard.

Unlike *MSY*, *MEY* is not fixed by biological factors alone. Its position also depends on fish price, which affects the position of the total revenue curve in Figure 6.2, and the unit cost of fishing effort, which affects the position of the total cost curve. Hence, the optimal level of fishing effort in future years will depend on trends in these two factors. Malaysia's growing population and rising per capita income will continue to raise demand for fish and put upward pressure on fish prices. Increased production from aquaculture and higher imports will help relieve the pressure, but not necessarily entirely. A higher level of effort might therefore be justified. The future trend in unit costs is less clear. The country's rising per capita income will increase the opportunity cost of labor, and its continuing industrialization will provide an increasing array of investment opportunities for capital. For given levels of fishing technology, these factors will raise the unit cost of fishing effort and reduce increases in effort, as they did in the 1980s when many traditional fishermen took up alternative occupations. But advances in technology are inevitable. What is uncertain is the extent to which they will outweigh anticipated increases in labor and capital costs. If they do, then the effort-raising effects of higher fish prices will be reinforced on the cost side, and effort should increase. If they do not, then optimal effort could be either higher or lower than it is today. In any event, the Department of Fisheries needs to continue monitoring fish prices, fishing costs, and fishing technology and to revise regulations affecting fishing effort as necessary.

Even if fishing effort should be increased at some point in the future, the increase in fishing power associated with technological advances probably implies that the number of fishing vessels should be decreased. For this reason, the recent decline in the number of traditional fishermen does not mean that overfishing cannot recur. If the number of fishermen falls to half its original level, but the fishing power of the vessels operated by the remaining fishermen rises by more than a factor of two, then fishing effort will rise. Technological advances are desirable from an economic standpoint, as they reduce the cost of fishing, but they imply that the Department of Fisheries cannot regulate fishing effort simply on the basis of number of licenses issued in different zones. This is the core of the regulatory approach under the Fisheries Licensing Policy and the Fisheries Act; it is pragmatic, and, given the degree of overfishing in the early 1980s, it was perhaps the most appropriate approach at that time.

An alternative, more sophisticated approach would be to introduce tradable catch quotas. Under this system, the department would set overall annual quotas on the catch of different species in different zones and then allocate these quotas among fishermen either administratively or, better, by auction. Fishermen would be allowed to buy and sell quota amounts among themselves after the initial allocation. This system would shift the focus of regulatory efforts from fishing effort to fish catch, which is more directly of interest from the standpoint of management of fishery resources. It would leave it to the market to determine the appropriate number and size of vessels for the given annual allowable catch. If fishing power increases, the number of vessels (or the length of time they were operated) would necessarily decrease to keep catch at the allowable level. This system would promote economic efficiency in the sector (maximization of rents) and encourage technological development, as fishermen with the lowest costs would be able to pay more for fishing quotas and thus would come to dominate the sector. It obviously requires an effective monitoring system to ensure that fishermen catch no more than their quota, which is more difficult than simply ensuring that all vessels are licensed. But if this monitoring challenge can be met, the system has many desirable features.

In the event that higher labor and capital costs outweigh all other factors, and fishing effort should be decreased, the challenge facing the government will be to resist the temptation to use subsidies to maintain production. Given the historical weight that the government has placed upon production-related objectives such as foreign exchange earnings and employment, and given as well the Department of Fisheries' probable desire to avoid being viewed as the overseer of a declining sector, there would undoubtedly be suggestions that the government should provide subsidies to support to the sector. These suggestions should be resisted, as they would inevitably reduce the sector's net contribution to the country's economy. Success in fisheries management is measured in terms of size of rents, not level of production.

The need to be concerned about rents, and not just production, is a point that has apparently received little attention in discussions about development of the country's deep-sea fishery, which is regarded as the sector's new frontier. Open-access rent dissipation can occur in offshore as well as inshore waters. The results in *Economic analysis of catch and efforts in west coast fisheries during the 1980s* indicated that the commercial fishery in Zones B through D on the west coast was already economically (and biologically) overfished in the mid-1980s. Jomo's (1991) skepticism about the general prospects for developing deep-sea fisheries in the country were mentioned earlier. If substantial deep-sea resources are indeed available, the lesson of the west coast experience is that effort (or catch, if tradable quotas are introduced) must be controlled when those resources are developed. The *Sixth Malaysia Plan*'s emphasis on raising deep-sea production suggests that the government needs to take this lesson more seriously. Uncontrolled expansion of fishing in offshore waters could deplete fish stocks and dissipate available rents, just as trawlers depleted the inshore waters of the west coast during the 1960s and 1970s.

APPENDIX 6: BIOECONOMIC MODEL OF WEST COAST FISHERIES

The bioeconomic model is based on the classic Gordon-Schaefer model (Clark 1976), which assumes that growth of the fish stock is a quadratic function of the level of the stock:[20]

$$G_t = r \times B_t - r/k \times B_t^2 \qquad (A6.1)$$

where G_t is growth, B_t is stock (biomass), r and k are positive parameters, and the subscript t is an index of time. The carrying capacity is k, the maximum value that B_t can reach. The maximum proportional growth rate (G_t/B_t) is r, i.e., the rate if the carrying capacity is infinite. Equation A6.1 yields an inverted U-shaped growth curve.

The change in fish stock from one period to the next is determined by the difference between growth and catch (C_t):

$$B_t - B_{t-1} = G_{t-1} - C_{t-1}$$

or:

$$B_t = B_{t-1} + G_{t-1} - C_{t-1}. \qquad (A6.2)$$

Catch is assumed to be an increasing function of stock and effort:

$$C_t = f(B_t, E_t).$$

This is the production function for the fishery. For a given level of effort, the catch will be larger when stock is larger ($\partial f/\partial B > 0$); for a given level of stock, the catch will be larger when effort is greater ($\partial f/\partial E > 0$).

It is standard to assume that the increase in catch diminishes as the level of biomass or effort increases ($\partial^2 f/\partial B^2 < 0$; $\partial^2 f/\partial E^2 < 0$). A function that can show these properties is the Cobb-Douglas:

$$C_t = \alpha_0 B_t^{\alpha_B} E_t^{\alpha_E}. \qquad (A6.3)$$

For the properties to hold, α_B and α_E must be positive and less than one. As should be the case, equation A6.3 predicts that catch equals zero when either biomass or effort equals zero.

Although data on catch and effort are readily available in Malaysia, data on fish stocks are not. Therefore, equation A6.3 cannot be estimated directly. However, equations A6.1 through A6.3 can be manipulated to derive an equation that involves only current and lagged values of catch and effort. In order, the manipulations are:

1) substitute equation A6.1 into equation A6.2 to eliminate G_t;
2) solve equation A6.3 for B_t;

3) lag the expression derived in step 2 and then substitute it into the expression derived in step 1 to eliminate B_{t-1};

4) substitute the expression derived in step 3 into equation A6.3 to eliminate B_t.

This procedure yields:

$$C_t = \alpha_0 \times [(1+r)(C_{t-1}/\alpha_0/E_{t-1}{}^{\alpha_E})^{1/\alpha_B} - r/k \times \qquad \text{(A6.4)}$$
$$(C_{t-1}/\alpha_0/E_{t-1}{}^{\alpha_E})^{1/\alpha_B} - C_{t-1}]^{\alpha_B} \times E_t{}^{\alpha_E}.$$

The parameters α_0, α_B, α_E, r, and k can be estimated by nonlinear least squares.

We obtained poor results when we estimated equation A6.4. Most parameters were either statistically insignificant, had the wrong sign, or were unreasonably large or small. The results discussed in the section *Bioeconomic model: results* are for a simpler version of the model. We made two simplifying assumptions. First, we assumed that catch equals growth in every year, which implies that the fishery adjusts to a new equilibrium within one year:

$$C_t = G_t$$

or, substituting equation A6.1:

$$C_t = r \times B_t - r/k \times B_t^2. \qquad \text{(A6.5)}$$

This replaced equation A6.2. Second, we assumed that both exponents in the Cobb-Douglas production function equal one:

$$C_t = \alpha_0 B_t E_t. \qquad \text{(A6.6)}$$

This replaced equation A6.3.

We then solved equation A6.6 for B_t, substituted the result into equation A6.5, and solved for C_t to obtain:

$$C_t = k \times \alpha_0 \times E_t - k \times \alpha_0^2/r \times E_t^2$$

or:

$$C_t = \beta_1 E_t - \beta_2 E_t^2. \qquad \text{(A6.7)}$$

Under the two simplifying assumptions, the bioeconomic model therefore reduces to a simple quadratic relationship between catch and effort, as in Figure 6.1.

We estimated equation A6.7 over the period 1981 to 1991. We obtained the following results:

Commercial fishery
Catch = $-23654800 + 12103 \times$ *Effort* $- 1.52 \times$ *Effort²*
      (2.01)   (2.05)   (2.08)
$R^2 = 0.401$, *S.E.R.* $= 59199$, *Durbin-Watson statistic* $= 1.80$

Traditional fishery
Catch = − 70608 + 16.7 × Effort − 0.000536 × Effort²
    (0.960   (1.46)   (1.22)
R² = 0.598, S.E.R. = 5541, Durbin-Watson statistic = 1.65.

Shown in parentheses are t-statistics. Although equation A6.7 does not include an intercept, we included intercepts in the regression equations to ensure that the mean of the error terms was zero. Moreover, we were interested in the relationship between catch and effort within the sample range, not at extreme values such as zero (the theoretical intercept). The Durbin-Watson statistics indicate that we can reject the hypothesis of serial correlation at the 5 percent level in both equations.

As expected, the coefficients on effort and effort-squared are positive and negative, respectively, in both regressions. Both are significant at the 10 percent level for the commercial fishery. For the traditional fishery, neither is individually significant at this level, but jointly they are. Effort and effort-squared are highly correlated in the traditional fishery, causing the estimated standard errors to be large. Moreover, when the regression for the traditional fishery was run without the intercept, β_1 was significant at the 1 percent level and β_2 was significant at the 10 percent level.

If p_t equals fish price (from the divisia price index) and w_t equals annual average total cost (from the divisia cost index), annual resource rent is given by:

$$p_t C_t - w_t E_t.$$

Substituting equation A6.7 for C_t and taking the derivative with respect to E_t, we find that the *MEY* level of fishing effort is given by:

$$E_t^{MEY} = (p_t \beta_1 - w_t)/(2p_t \beta_2)$$

or:

$$E_t^{MEY} = \beta_1/(2\beta_2) - w_t/(2p_t \beta_2). \qquad (A6.8)$$

This equation predicts the optimal effort for given values of p_t and w_t. E_t^{MEY} is higher for higher levels of p_t but lower for higher levels of w_t. Once E_t^{MEY} is determined by solving equation A6.8, the corresponding optimal catch can be determined by substituting E_t^{MEY} into equation A6.7. This is how we determined the *MEY* values in Tables 6.3 and 6.4.

The first term in equation A6.8 is the *MSY* effort level, which is determined by setting the derivative of equation A6.7 with respect to E_t equal to zero:

$$E_t^{MSY} = \beta_1/(2\beta_2). \qquad (A6.9)$$

Examination of equation A6.8 indicates that as long as $w_t > 0$ and p_t is less than infinity, which in practice is always the case, $E_t^{MSY} > E_t^{MEY}$: production at the MSY level involves excessive fishing effort.

NOTES

1 In fact, Munro and Chee (1978, p. 9) suspected that E_{OA} occurred to the left of E_{MSY} in the fisheries in Pulau Pinang and Kedah in late 1960s and early 1970s.

2 Labon (1974) based this projection not only on population growth but also on rising per capita consumption due to rising income. Indeed, per capita food fish consumption rose from 27 kg to 40 kg from 1971 to 1981 (Labon 1974, MAJUIKAN 1981).

3 For example, the catch of one traditional gear, the *pukat payang* (a sunken bag with warps that are shaken to scare fish into the bag), "is said to have dropped off dramatically with the introduction of trawling" (Gibbons 1976, p. 101).

4 The success of mesh-size regulations depends, of course, on how well they are enforced. Jahara (1988, p. 97) commented that "noncompliance with the minimum mesh size regulation is not uncommon."

5 As it turned out, the government did not explicitly adopt either of these funding mechanisms.

6 The movement out of fishing was analogous to the movement out of smallholder agriculture that led to idle land. See Chapter 5.

7 Export earnings from fishery commodities reached a high of RM630 million in 1990. This was less than 1 percent of the country's total export earnings.

8 We did not model catch and effort for Zones B through D separately, due to a lack of data on landings by zone.

9 For 1989 and 1990, landings by grade were calculated by aggregating data in Table 7.1, "Landings of Marine Fish by Gear Group and Species, West coast, Peninsular Malaysia" in Jabatan Perikanan (1991). For other years, data were aggregated either from corresponding tables in other issues of this bulletin or from data provided by the Department of Fisheries.

10 For 1989 and 1990, data were taken from Table 7.3, "Value of Marine Fish Landings by Gear Group and Grade of Fish, Peninsular Malaysia," in Jabatan Perikanan (1991). Note that the data are for all of Peninsular Malaysia, not just the west coast. Data for other years were taken from corresponding tables in earlier issues of the bulletin or from additional materials provided by the department.

11 The margins were 14 percent for Grade I, 21 percent for Grade II, 37 percent for Grade III, 14 percent for prawns, and 37 percent for trash fish. Margins for the first four grades were based on comparison of species-level, wholesale and ex-vessel prices reported in Jabatan Perikanan (1991). The margin for trash fish was assumed to be equal to that for Grade III fish.

12 More precisely, it weights changes in the logarithms of landings by the revenue shares of the different categories.

13 Sources of data are those described in notes 9 through 11.

14 This could be a result of the limited sample. More than 90 percent of the estimates fell within the period 1985 to 1988.

15 Within the traditional category, the higher cost for hooks and lines was surprising. According to the studies, boats using this gear did tend to be larger, but the sample size was small and perhaps unrepresentative. Fortunately, the divisia effort index was not very sensitive to the cost estimate for hooks and lines, because this gear represented a small share of licenses in the traditional fishery.

16 Regression analysis showed that the trends were statistically significant for catch in the

commercial fishery and catch and effort in the traditional fishery. For commercial effort, the coefficient on the time trend was positive but not significant.

17 We ignored "errors in variables" problems resulting from the upward bias in the divisia effort indices.

18 The negative rent indicates that the open-access equilibrium is to the left of the MSY equilibrium, confirming Munro and Chee's (1978) suspicions for Penang and Kedah (see note 1). At 1991 prices and costs, the open-access equilibrium occurs at 12,007 units of effort.

19 This implies that a fundamental assumption of the model, that the fishery adjusts instantaneously to a new equilibrium (see Appendix 6), is violated. That the assumption is not strictly true is not surprising; the important issue is the degree to which it is violated.

20 More sophisticated models, which account for the age structure of the fish population, can be estimated if sufficiently detailed data are available. This was not the case for Malaysia. For an exposition of such models, see Deriso (1980) and Schnute (1985). For evaluations of their empirical performance, see Roff (1983) and Deacon (1989).

7

Freshwater

INTRODUCTION

Because Malaysia is located in the humid tropics, most of the country receives abundant rainfall throughout the year. There is a true dry season only in the extreme northwest of the Peninsula. Most rivers are perennial (Uzir 1988, p. 158). Nevertheless, rainfall and river flows can vary substantially during the year even in wet areas. For example, rainfall is much heavier on the east coast of the Peninsula during the northeast monsoon (approximately October to January). Throughout the country, rainfall tends to occur in short, heavy showers. Given the country's relatively small size and the steep terrain of its interior, rivers tend to be short and swift. Hence, rainfall runs off into the sea quickly.

The government of Malaysia commissioned the first comprehensive study of the country's freshwater resources in the late 1970s. The study, which was conducted by the Japan International Cooperation Agency (JICA), was completed in 1982. Table 7.1 shows the country's hydrological balance as reported in the study (JICA 1982a, p. 99). Most rainfall ends up as surface runoff (57 percent), although a significant portion is transpired by plants or lost to evaporation (36 percent). Groundwater recharge accounts for only a small portion (6 percent). The study estimated that the country's total water consumption[1] for irrigation, domestic (household) uses, and industrial uses was 8.7 billion cubic meters in 1980 (JICA 1982a, p. 11), or less than 2 percent of annual runoff.

In spite of consumption's small volume compared to runoff, water is a scarce resource in Malaysia for at least three reasons. First, although rain falls freely from the heavens, water that is consumed is not a free good. Costs must be incurred to capture, store, distribute, and, if the use is industrial or domestic, treat it. Raw water, like any resource in its natural state, has attributes that

---

G. Sivalingam was a coauthor of this chapter.

Table 7.1 *Hydrological balance in Malaysia (billion cubic meters per year)*

| Region | Rainfall | Distribution | | |
		Surface runoff	Evapo-transpiration	Groundwater recharge
Peninsular Malaysia	320	147	153	20
Sabah	194	113	67	14
Sarawak	476	306	140	30
Malaysia	990	566	360	64

Source: JICA (1982b, p. 99).

affect its usefulness to humans, for example salinity, turbidity, odor, taste, and appearance. It can also carry diseases: the World Health Organization "considers that provision of a safe and convenient water supply is the single most important activity that could be undertaken to improve the health of people living in rural areas" (Meerman 1979, p. 197, citing the World Bank). Water must undergo a production process to make it suitable for human use, just as timber must be processed or fish must be caught.

Production costs related to storage are particularly important in Malaysia. Because rainfall is not evenly spread during the year and runoff is so rapid, on average only about 10 percent of annual runoff is available for human use in undeveloped river basins, that is those without reservoirs or other storage works (JICA 1982a, p. 12). Much of the annual runoff occurs as floods in the wet season and peak flows following rainstorms (JICA 1982a, p. S–3). An even smaller percentage is available during droughts, which occurred about every five years during the 1960s and 1970s.

Moreover, most rainfall in Malaysia occurs in the least densely populated parts of the country: Sabah, Sarawak, and the east coast of the Peninsula (Uzir 1988, p. 158). Malaysia shares this characteristic of a skewed spatial distribution of freshwater resources with many other Asian countries (Asian Development Bank 1991, p. 227). The JICA study defined "water-stress basins" as river basins in which water consumption was at least 10 percent or more of surface runoff (JICA 1982b, p. 29). It estimated that 18 of 41 river basins in the Peninsula and 7 river basins in Sabah and Sarawak exceeded this threshold. All but one of the river basins in the Peninsula were on the more densely populated and relatively drier west coast. In the absence of reservoirs, most of the country's population would face chronic water shortages.

Building and operating reservoirs and associated works in a water supply system require capital, labor, and other economic resources that have competing uses. The scarcity value of treated water derives partly from the scarcity value of the nonnatural resources that are necessary to produce it. In this sense water is no different than minerals, timber, fish, or other natural resources that are nature given, but not free in an economic sense.

Second, water is scarce in that there is a finite number of locations in the country suitable for reservoirs and a finite (though slowly rechargeable) stock of groundwater. The cost of water from potential supply sources varies, and decisions must be made as to which sources to tap. If the least-cost sources are not selected, or if the user cost of groundwater is ignored and groundwater resources are depleted too rapidly (see Chapter 2 for a discussion of user cost), the country incurs unnecessary costs. Moreover, water development decisions are usually irreversible. Damming a river to create a reservoir causes an essentially permanent loss of alternative uses of the flooded valley. This opportunity cost must be considered when deciding on the economic feasibility of a water development project.

Finally, in addition to these two supply-side reasons, water is scarce on the demand side because its consumption by one user makes it effectively unavailable to others. By drawing water from a tap, one household prevents others from using that volume of water. By diverting water for irrigation, farmers prevent that water from being used for downstream domestic and industrial purposes. Even when water is returned to a stream following use—for example, through a municipal sewerage system—contamination usually prevents it from being reused directly. Developing Malaysia's physically abundant water resources in a way that generates net benefits and is cost-effective is only half of the country's water management challenge. It must also allocate the water thereby produced to the most valuable uses. The supply and demand sides are, of course, interrelated. For example, if water consumption is approaching the capacity limit of the existing supply system but water is not allocated efficiently among users, then reallocating water might make more sense than expanding the supply system.

Economic development raises water demand, and this raises the scarcity value of water. The economic stakes involved in making water supply and demand decisions become higher and higher. Demand for irrigation water rises due to expansion of crop area and development of irrigation works to permit more intensive cultivation. Demand by industrial users rises due to growth in the manufacturing sector, which requires water for processing. Demand by households rises due to population growth and increases in per capita income, which enable more households to afford indoor plumbing and raise water consumption due to the acquisition of flush toilets, washing machines, and other household appliances and facilities.

Water demand in Malaysia has risen since independence for all these reasons. The government accelerated irrigation development in the early 1960s to enhance self-sufficiency in rice and to permit double-cropping (Uzir

1988, Wan 1988). Irrigated paddy area reached 329,000 ha in 1980 (JICA 1982b, p. 28). The manufacturing sector grew from 14 percent of GDP in 1970 to 27 percent in 1990. Population grew by more than 2 percent per year from 1970 to 1990, and per capita GDP by about 4 percent in real terms (Ministry of Finance, *Economic Report* (various issues), Kuala Lumpur).

The JICA study estimated that water consumption in 1980 totaled 7.4 billion cubic meters for irrigation and 1.3 billion cubic meters split evenly between industrial and domestic uses (JICA 1982a, p. 11). It forecast that these amounts would rise to 9.0 and 2.6 billion cubic meters in 1990, with the industrial share of the latter increasing to 56 percent by the year 2000. These forecasts were identical to consumption levels for 1990 reported in the *Sixth Malaysia Plan 1991–1995* (p. 336).

This chapter examines how Malaysia managed the rising demands on its water resources during the 1970s and 1980s. It focuses on demand by industrial and domestic users, that is demand for treated, piped water. Although irrigation is the largest single use of water in the country, focusing on industrial and domestic uses makes sense for several reasons. First, irrigation is more a regional than a national water management issue. Irrigation is limited primarily to rice-growing areas in the northern states of the Peninsula. In 1982, 92 percent of the irrigated area in the country was in Peninsular Malaysia (Khan et al. 1992). About a third of the area was in a single irrigation scheme, the Muda Agricultural Development Authority scheme in Kedah and Perlis (Wan 1988). Most of the remaining area was in other parts of these states or in Kelantan and Terengganu (Khan et al. 1992).

Second, there is little evidence that withdrawals of water for irrigation have had a significant impact on the availability of water for industrial and domestic uses. Irrigation schemes tend to be located in river basins separate from those where industrial and population centers are found. The northern states are among the least industrialized and urbanized in the Peninsula. Distance reduces the feasibility of transfers of water from river basins with major irrigation schemes to those with major urban centers. Only in the Muda basin is there apparently significant competition between irrigation and piped-water users. Water from the upper reaches of the Sungai[2] Muda is diverted to the Muda scheme, while water from the lower reaches provides water for the town of Sungai Petani in Kedah and is one source of water for Penang (Wan 1988).

Third, water demand by domestic and industrial users has been rising more rapidly than demand for irrigation.[3] Consumption by domestic and industrial users doubled from 1980 to 1990, whereas consumption for irrigation increased by only one-fifth. Moreover, the number of industrial and domestic users of water is many times greater than the number of paddy farmers, and the difference is rising. Finally, for these and other reasons, federal and state governments increasingly view irrigation as a lower-priority water use than domestic and industrial consumption. This was stated explicitly in the *Fifth Malaysia Plan 1986–1990* (p. 477).

Official figures indicate that production of piped water increased dramatically from 1970 to 1990, rising from less than 1 billion liter-days in 1970 to 5 billion liter-days in 1990. The increase reflected not only rising consumption due to the increases in industrial activity, population, and income discussed earlier, but also the extension of piped water to areas that previously lacked it. Both the number of people and the percentage of the population with access to piped water—that is, in households with private water connections or in villages with standpipes—increased sharply from 1970 to 1990. By 1990, 66 percent of the rural population and 96 percent of the urban population had access to piped water. The former was about equal to the average for developing countries, while the latter was somewhat higher (World Bank 1992, Figure 2.2).

The increased production required substantial expansion of the country's water supply capacity. This chapter looks particularly closely at system expansions and related long-run supply-side issues. It considers whether the benefits of system expansions exceeded the costs, and whether the least-cost supply sources were developed first. At the core of the analysis is an evaluation of how well water tariffs functioned as indicators of the scarcity value of water.

The next section, *Economics of water resource development*, reviews economic concepts related to the long-run development of water resources. *Water resource development in Malaysia* reviews and evaluates the development of water resources in Malaysia during the last two decades. Finally, *Conclusions* discusses implications of the analysis for water management in coming decades.

ECONOMICS OF WATER RESOURCE DEVELOPMENT

Economies of scale and concern about natural monopolies have led most countries to make public agencies or regulated utilities responsible for water supply. Water rates, or tariffs, are usually determined administratively rather than by a market mechanism. Nevertheless, like any economic good, water is utilized at the economically efficient level when the cost of the last unit supplied (the marginal cost) is just equal to the benefits of the use to which that unit is put (the marginal benefit).

Figure 7.1 illustrates efficient water utilization at the aggregate level (for example, a region serviced by a single water supply system). The demand curve shows consumers' marginal willingness to pay, which is the economic measure of the benefits of water consumption. The supply curve shows the marginal costs of withdrawing raw water from natural water bodies, treating it, and distributing it. The efficient level of water utilization, Q^*, is determined by the intersection of the demand and supply curves. Below Q^*, willingness to pay exceeds marginal costs. Water utilization should be increased, because the incremental supply costs are more than offset by the incremental consumption benefits. Above Q^*, marginal costs exceed willingness to pay. Water utilization should be reduced, because the costs of supplying units of water above Q^* exceed the value of the water to consumers.

The intersection of the supply and demand curves determines not only the efficient utilization level, but also the efficient water tariff, P^*. Faced with a tariff equal to P^*, consumers will consume an amount of water exactly equal to Q^*. At this tariff level, the water agency can cover the costs of each unit of water supplied, up to and including Q^*.[4]

Figure 7.1 depicts the water demand curve as a downward-sloping line. Water consumption falls when the water tariff rises, and rises when it falls. That is, water consumption responds to changes in price in the same way as consumption of any other commodity. This characterization is at odds with the "engineering" approach to water management, which assumes that per capita consumption of water is fixed and independent of price (Hanke 1970, Hanke and Davis 1973). Under the engineering approach, water management is purely a supply-side exercise: system expansions are the only way to cope

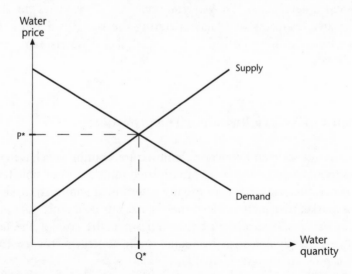

Figure 7.1   Efficient utilization of water resources

with rising demand. The characterization of water demand in Figure 7.1 is also at odds with the "basic needs" approach of many governments, which assumes that households require a fixed quantity of water for essential household activities and have no scope for adjusting their water usage.

Empirical evidence contradicts the assumption of the engineering and basic needs approaches. Many studies of municipal water demand have determined that consumption does indeed respond to the water tariff, that higher tariffs induce households to use water more conservatively (Gibbons 1986; Hanke 1978, cited in Hanke 1982; see also Hanke 1970). Most of the studies have been conducted in North America. Gibbons (1986, Table 1-1) reviewed twelve studies conducted from the early 1960s to 1980 in the United States and Canada. The studies reported price elasticities ranging from -0.02 to -1.38. That is, a 1 percent increase in the tariff would decrease water consumption by 0.02 to 1.38 percent. The median estimate was -0.51. Most of the studies combined in-house use and "sprinkling" use (watering plants and other outdoor uses); those that separated out in-house use found that the elasticities for it were substantially lower, around -0.2 to -0.3. Hanke (1982), interpreting the available evidence, concluded that the elasticity for in-house use was around -0.15 (a 1 percent increase in the tariff reduces water consumption by 0.15 percent). Recently, a series of studies sponsored by the World Bank in Brazil, Nigeria, Zimbabwe, Pakistan, and India and by USAID in Haiti, Kenya, and Tanzania have confirmed that water prices also affect household water consumption in developing countries (World Bank Water Demand Research Team 1993). This finding is consistent with a much earlier cross-sectional study of average water consumption in forty cities in the developing world, also sponsored by the World Bank, which estimated a price elasticity of -0.4 (Meroz 1968).

Apparently only one study, by Katzman (1977), has estimated price elasticities for water demand in Malaysia. Katzman analyzed water consumption by 167 households in Pulau Pinang from May 1970 to November 1975. The households were of four types: rich urban, shophouses (combined residential and business use of water), poor urban (squatters), and poor rural. In May 1973, water tariffs increased for all users. Based on a statistical analysis of water consumption before and after the tariff increase, he concluded that the elasticity ranged from -0.1 to -0.2, depending on the type of household. This is consistent with Hanke's (1982) estimate of -0.15. Not all of the estimates were statistically significant, however, so their reliability is somewhat questionable. That water consumption in Pulau Pinang is sensitive to price received additional support in a more recent survey conducted by Goh (1990). Sixty-seven percent of the 1,510 households surveyed responded that they would reduce water consumption if the tariff increased by 20 percent.

Goh did not ask them how much they would reduce consumption, however, so it is not possible to use his survey results to estimate the price elasticity.

Because water supply is capital-intensive, requiring the construction of reservoirs, treatment plants, and distribution systems, the relevant marginal cost for analyzing the efficiency of water development is long-run marginal cost. This includes capital (fixed) costs as well as operating (variable) costs.[5] Saunders and Warford (1976) recommended calculating long-run marginal cost by dividing the discounted total costs of a prospective supply scheme by the discounted amount of additional water it will provide.[6] That is, long-run marginal cost equals the unit cost of water supplied by the scheme, where the unit cost includes both capital and operating costs.

The long-run marginal cost curve for a given region is therefore a step function, with each step corresponding to a particular water supply scheme. The length of a step is determined by the capacity of the scheme, and the height by the unit cost. Figure 7.2 shows such a curve. Potential supply sources are ranked on the horizontal axis from least to most expensive per unit of water supplied. A units are available from the least-cost source, perhaps withdrawals from a nearby river. The next most expensive source, which perhaps involves the construction of an upstream reservoir, provides B units. The most expensive source, which perhaps represents the transfer of water from another river basin, provides C units.

The fact that capital costs occur toward the start of a water supply project means that long-run marginal costs are strongly influenced by the discount

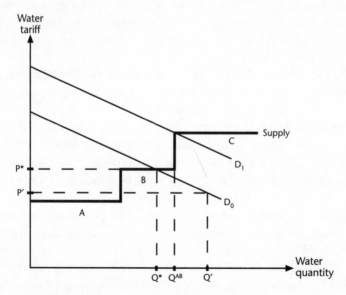

Figure 7.2   Efficient expansion of a water supply system

rate. Long-run marginal costs increase as the discount rate increases, because the weight placed on future units of water supplied diminishes. In effect, capital costs are spread over fewer units of water. A higher discount rate indicates that the opportunity cost of capital is higher: the loss of output in the economy due to capital being invested in water supply projects rather than other projects is higher. Long-run marginal costs are also higher when the leakage rate of the system is higher: both capital and operating costs are spread over fewer units of water actually delivered and sold to consumers.

The water agency can determine whether development of new sources is justified by examining the supply and demand curves. Suppose that sources A and B have been developed, and that the water agency wants to determine whether it should develop source C. Furthermore, suppose that the demand curve is given by D_0, and that demand is not expected to shift. For example, D_0 could represent demand in a mature urban area with a stable industrial base and a stable population. The efficient utilization level is, as in Figure 7.1, determined by intersection of the demand curve and the marginal cost curve. The intersection occurs partway along the step for source B, at Q^*. Expansion is not justified because the capacity of source B is not fully utilized at the efficient utilization level.

Expansion should occur only if the demand curve shifts outward (i.e., toward the right). Rising population or per capita consumption (in response to rising income) could cause this to happen. Suppose that demand is expected to shift outward to D_1 and intersect the step for source C in ten years. The expansion is then justified, and it should be timed so that production from source C begins in ten years. At that point, consumers' willingness to pay will match the unit cost of water from source C. Earlier development would result in the misallocation of investment funds.

Returning to the initial situation and demand curve D_0, the actual consumption level depends on the water tariff. Consumers will use water up to the point where the amount they pay for it (the water tariff) equals the amount they are willing to pay (the marginal benefit, given by D_0). Hence, consumption will be at Q^* only if the water tariff equals the long-run marginal cost of source B. This is the efficient water tariff, P^*. Consumption will be too low—water is underutilized—if the tariff is above this level, and too high—water is overutilized—if it is below. The former case illustrates the rationale for supplying water by public agencies or regulated private companies: a monopolist would be expected to price water above its marginal cost, in order to earn monopoly rents.

A water agency cannot directly observe the water demand curve. Is there any way to determine whether water resources are being developed efficiently without knowing the demand curve? Fortunately, the answer is yes.[7] The fact that consumption adjusts so that willingness to pay equals the water tariff indicates that one simply needs to check whether the marginal supply source is self-financing. The supply source is self-financing if the tariff equals the long-run marginal cost, and if this is the case, marginal cost and willingness to pay must be equal, since both equal the tariff.

Raising water tariffs to cover the costs of developing new water resources is not politically popular. Its impacts on the poor usually raise particular concerns. Governments often justify keeping the cost of water low for poorer households not only on equity grounds, but also to prevent the spread of water-borne diseases. They fear that epidemics could break out if the poor do not have access to and cannot afford treated piped water. For these reasons, governments often set water tariffs below long-run marginal costs (Rogers 1992).

Although health-related reasons for subsidized consumption are compelling, below-cost water can lead to excessive use of water and pressure on the water agency to expand the supply system when expansion is not economically justified. Consider the very low water tariff, P', in Figure 7.2. The amount of water consumers wish to consume, Q', is determined by the intersection of P' with D_0. Because only sources A and B have been developed, the water agency can supply water only up to Q^{AB}. Physical shortages of water occur; water does not always flow when users turn on the tap.

From an economic perspective, the appropriate response by the water agency is unambiguous: reduce consumption by raising the water tariff from P' to P^* so that the tariff equals the marginal cost of source B. But raising the tariff would probably be politically less popular than keeping the tariff low and developing source C to furnish the additional water. The latter response would have negative consequences for both consumers and the water agency, however. The low tariff benefits consumers in a narrow sense by making water cheaper, but its overall impact is to make them worse off. A low tariff reduces the costs of water consumption, but the costs of supplying the water still must be paid. Since the water supply system is not self-financing, these costs must be financed by taxes on other activities. In the aggregate, consumers are made worse off because the amount they are willing to pay for the subsidized water they consume is less than the amount they pay directly (through water tariffs) and indirectly (through other taxes). Because much of the payment may be indirect, they might be unaware of how much they are truly paying for water. The additional taxes also create distortions in other sectors.

Preventing the water agency from directly covering costs through water tariffs places its financing at the whim of the budget process. If its budget allocation is too low, it might be forced to cut costs by reducing expenditure on maintenance. This eventually affects the quality of service, as treatment plant equipment and pipelines begin to break down. This creates a vicious circle: the agency's service suffers because of low tariffs, and the poor service makes consumers reluctant to pay higher tariffs for what they expect will continue to be poor service. If the water agency is severely underfunded, it might be unable to extend the water supply system to some sections of the community. The subsidization of existing users, who are typically more affluent urban dwellers, prevents the extension of supplies to new users, who are typically poorer people in rural areas or in squatter settlements in and near cities. In this sense, low tariffs do not necessarily promote equity objectives. The Asian Development Bank (1991) has pointed out that the underpricing of water "taxes the general public, including the poor, to subsidise wasteful water uses by the affluent" (p. 257). It argued that "both equity and efficiency objectives could be served by progressive water charges that reflect long-run marginal supply costs" (p. 257).

A pragmatic response to political pressures would be for the water agency to adopt an increasing block-rate tariff structure. Ensuring that water is utilized efficiently requires only that water be priced correctly at the margin. In Figure 7.2, the tariff for the last unit of water consumed must equal the marginal cost of supply from source B. Other units of water could be priced at a lower level. At the household level, the water tariff could increase with the amount of water consumed. For example, the tariff could be low for an amount estimated to be the minimum necessary for basic household activities,[8] and higher for amounts above this, which would reflect less essential uses. The poor could still obtain the water they need for drinking, cooking, and washing at a low price, while the rich would pay a premium for water used in their gardens and the like. This progressive pricing structure might reduce the political consequences of raising the marginal water tariff. Tariffs could be varied not only by quantity of consumption but also by type of user. Those who are viewed as being able to pay more could be required to pay more. For example, industries might be charged more than households, and urban households might be charged more than poorer, rural ones.

One attractive feature of increasing block-rate tariffs is that they can be set so that supply costs are covered exactly and the water agency earns no more than a normal profit margin. In Figure 7.2, a uniform tariff equal to the marginal cost of supply from source B would result in the agency earning supranormal profits on the first A units sold, as their unit cost is less than the cost from source B. Limiting the profits of regulated utilities—avoiding the natural monopoly problem—is in fact one of the chief motivations for block-rate pricing in developed countries (Tietenberg 1988, p. 205).

WATER RESOURCE DEVELOPMENT IN MALAYSIA

Institutions

The federal constitution of Malaysia makes water a state matter.[9] The states have full jurisdiction over the use of rivers within their boundaries, and there are few rivers that cross state boundaries. Each state has its own Water Supply Enactment for the development and protection of water resources and catchment areas.

Water sections within the Public Works Department (Jabatan Kerja Raya) or separate water supply departments (Jabatan Bekalan Air) are responsible for water supply in most states, but a few states have more commercially-oriented water boards (JKR and Bina Runding 1989, p. 1). Water is the responsibility of public works departments in Kedah, Kelantan, Pahang, Perlis, and Sarawak, and water supply departments in Johor, Negeri Sembilan, Perak, Sabah, Selangor, and Terengganu. The Federal Public Works Department has jurisdiction over the Federal Territory of Labuan, while the Selangor Water Supply Department is responsible for the Federal Territory of Kuala Lumpur. Melaka and Pulau Pinang have Water Boards, as do two towns in Sarawak, Kuching and Sibu.

The Federal Public Works Department provides technical advice and consultation to the states, including general guidelines on how water resources should be developed. It also coordinates all water supply projects funded by the federal government. These projects are typically earmarked in the country's five-year plans. The Economic Planning Unit (EPU) of the Prime Minister's Department evaluates proposals, and the Ministry of Finance disburses funds.

States are responsible for the costs of operating and maintaining water systems, including those in FELDA schemes,[10] as well as for financing their share of projects cofinanced by the federal government and any projects they finance on their own. Since the late 1970s most projects have involved some degree of federal financing (JKR and Bina Runding 1989, p. 2–2; *Fourth Malaysia Plan 1981–1985*, p. 337; Asian Development Bank 1986, p. 10).

Besides the Federal Public Works Department and the state-level agencies, several other agencies are also involved in water projects (JKR 1992, p. 7).[11] The federal Ministries of Works, Rural Development, Land and Cooperative Development, and Health have responsibility for the provision of treated water to various target groups. The Ministry of Works designs and implements water projects in regional development areas (Asian Development Bank 1986, p. vi) and special projects, such as the Antah Biwater Rural Water Supply project. The Ministry of Rural Development plans and coordinates federal rural water supply projects. The Ministry of Land and Cooperative

Development administers federal grants and loans for building treatment plants and distribution systems in FELDA schemes and regional development schemes like Kejora, Kesedar, Dara, Jengka, and Ketengah. The Ministry of Health works with state governments to provide community water supplies to prevent the spread of communicable diseases in selected areas, under the Rural Environmental Sanitation Programme. The federal government fully covers the capital costs of projects under this program (JICA 1982a, p. 39).

Expansion of the water supply system

The increase in water supply from 1970 to 1990 required substantial public investment. Public expenditure on water projects rose from less than RM200 million under the *First Malaysia Plan 1966–1970* to nearly RM2.5 billion under the *Fifth Malaysia Plan 1986-1990.*[12] It increased sharply under the *Fourth Malaysia Plan 1981–1985,* nearly quadrupling compared to the level under the *Third Malaysia Plan 1976–1980,* and it continued to increase, albeit at a slower rate, under the *Fifth Plan.* The year 1980 therefore separates decades of lower and higher public expenditure on water resource development.

In 1970 Malaysia had 204 treatment plants, which supplied piped water to about 4.5 million people. These were impressive figures compared to 1960, when there were only 140 water treatment plants supplying water to 2.7 million people. The output of water increased at an average annual rate of 6.7 percent, from 0.381 billion liter-days in 1960 to 0.744 billion liter-days in 1970. Although the increase in production was impressive, much of the population still did not have access to piped water in 1970, particularly in rural areas and in Sabah and Sarawak (Table 7.2). In 1970, 61 percent of the rural population lacked access, compared to only 17 percent of the urban population. The percentage in rural areas was, however, much less than the average in developing countries, 85 percent (Meerman 1979, p. 197, citing the World Bank).

Much of the financing for large-scale water projects in the decade following independence was provided by international financial institutions such as the World Bank and the Asian Development Bank (*First Malaysia Plan,* p. 162; *Second Malaysia Plan,* p. 217). One reason for difficulties in supplying piped water to rural areas was the disinclination of donors to finance small treatment plants suitable for sparsely populated rural areas. Because the government's financial resources were limited, small-scale rural water projects could not be carried out during the *First Malaysia Plan 1966–1970* (p. 116).

Expenditure under the *Second Malaysia Plan 1971–1975* was only slightly

Table 7.2   *Piped water supply coverage (percentage of population)*

Region	Year	Rural	Urban	Total
Peninsular Malaysia	1970	39	83	46
	1980	47	91	59
	1990	72	93	81
Sabah	1970	—[b]	95	—
	1980	18	99	—
	1990	47	96	64
Sarawak	1970	13	90	—
	1980	25	93	—
	1990	52	100	57
Malaysia	1970[a]	39	83	46
	1980	43	89	59
	1990	66	96	78

Sources: Malaysia Plans; JICA (1982a).
[a] Peninsular Malaysia only.
[b] Data not available.

higher than under the *First Malaysia Plan,* and a higher proportion of the funding was allocated to urban projects. The *Third Malaysia Plan 1976–1980* stated that "the rural water supply programme was accelerated during the latter part of the SMP [Second Malaysia Plan] period," but the Asian Development Bank (1986, p. 17) judged that "public expenditure on rural water supply up until 1975 was insignificant." Most water projects, other than those in FELDA schemes, were financed by state governments rather than the federal government (*Second Malaysia Plan,* p. 217). The output of water increased at an average annual rate of 9.6 percent, to 1.2 billion liter-days in 1975. Although water supply programs in FELDA schemes were expanded and the federal government provided financing for equipment needed by rural water projects (*Third Malaysia Plan,* pp. 377–378), coverage continued to lag in rural areas, as well as in Sabah and Sarawak. Sixty percent of the total population in Peninsular Malaysia had access to piped water in 1975, compared to only 30 percent in Sabah and 39 percent in Sarawak (*Third Malaysia Plan,* pp. 377–378).

Total public expenditure on water supply increased by about three times between the *Second* and *Third Plans,* due to an acceleration of rural and regional water supply projects (*Fourth Malaysia Plan,* p. 337). The amount spent on rural systems (including FELDA schemes) equaled the amount spent on urban systems (*Fourth Malaysia Plan,* p. 342). The increased emphasis on rural water supply reflected the objectives of the New Economic Policy (NEP). Most *bumiputera* and most of the poor were in rural areas. The increase in expenditure reflected not only the government's willingness to expand the role of the public sector to implement the NEP, but also an increase in the means to do so: the development of the country's petroleum resources and the first OPEC oil shock substantially raised federal revenues after the early 1970s (see Chapter 1).

According to the Asian Development Bank (1986, p. 23), the federal government's approach to providing piped water to rural areas consisted mainly of financing extensions from existing urban water supply systems. In some rural areas, however, new water resources were developed and new treatment plants were constructed. Despite the increased emphasis on rural water supply, and despite a more than doubling of water treatment capacity between 1975 and 1980, by the end of the *Third Plan* period a majority of the rural populations in Peninsular Malaysia, Sabah, and Sarawak—53 percent, 82 percent, and 75 percent, respectively—still lacked access to piped water. Access in urban areas was not a serious problem, as more than 90 percent of the urban population had access. A survey of Peninsular Malaysia households conducted by Meerman (1979, Table 9.4 and p. 208) found that households were more likely to have piped water if their income was higher, if they were in larger towns, if they were Chinese or Indian, and if they were not in the four northern, and more rural, states of Kedah, Kelantan, Perlis, and Terengganu.

Substantial though it was, the increase in public expenditure on water projects between the *Second* and *Third Plans* was dwarfed by the increase between the *Third* and *Fourth Plans.* Expenditure under the *Fourth Plan* reached nearly RM2 billion. As a result of the increased expenditure, water supply capacity increased by 1.6 billion liter-days from 1980 to 1985, compared to 1.4 billion liter-days from 1975 to 1980. The percentage of the total population with access to piped water jumped to 71 percent by 1985.

The *Fourth Plan* continued to place emphasis on expansion of rural water supplies (p. 339). The increase in coverage for the rural population was particularly large. The proportion of the rural population in Peninsular Malaysia without access to piped water fell to less than half (46 percent) by 1985. The proportions remained above half in Sabah and Sarawak (62 and 67 percent, respectively), but they registered sharp decreases compared to 1980. The unserved rural areas were typically those that were too remote and too inaccessible to permit connections to existing urban systems (*Mid-Term Review of the Fourth Malaysia Plan*, p. 387). More than 90 percent of the urban populations in all states except Kelantan and Terengganu had access to piped water by 1985.

The *Mid-Term Review of the Fourth Malaysia Plan* contains perhaps the clearest statement of the government's water supply philosophy under the NEP: "Water is one of the basic needs and it is the objective of the government to provide safe water to all" (p. 337). To assist in developing a strategy to achieve this objective, toward the end of the *Third Plan* period the government commissioned the JICA *National Water Resources Study*. The study was initiated in October 1979, and completed in 1982. It presented a water supply development program for the remaining two decades of the century. It estimated that the required public development expenditure for this program was, at 1980 price levels, RM14.2 billion (JICA 1982b, p. 123). Estimated expenditure under the *Fifth* and *Sixth Plans* alone was RM4.7 billion and RM5.1 billion, respectively.

Put simply, the study recommended a massive dam-building program. It proposed forty-five new dams (JICA 1982a, p. 26) and stated that "water storage development or the development of water source[s] has to be undertaken on a much bigger scale than in the past" (JICA 1982a, p. 24). The study's enthusiasm for supply expansion is perhaps best captured by a comment about the development of water resources for energy generation: "*All* known hydropower potential of 1,026 MW in Peninsular Malaysia should be developed in view of minimizing dependence on fossil fuels" (JICA 1982a, p. S-6; emphasis added). The need to expand supply capacity was apparently the message that came through most clearly to the government. The principal comment in the *Fifth Malaysia Plan 1986–1990* about the JICA study was: "The study recommended the construction of more storage dams to retain high flows during wet seasons for release in dry seasons" (p. 473).

Expenditure under the *Fourth Plan* was comparable to the level recommended by the JICA study, but actual expenditure under the *Fifth Plan* and planned expenditure under the *Sixth Plan* were only about half the recommended levels. The gap appears to have two explanations. First, in the mid-1980s a growing debt burden and recession prompted the government to rein in public expenditure. Second, the cost of developing water resources turned out to be higher than anticipated due to rising input costs and the increasing remoteness of remaining undeveloped water resources (*Fifth Malaysia Plan*, p. 473; Asian Development Bank 1986, p. 10; JKR and Bina Runding 1989, p. 2-2). Marginal capital costs of system expansions during the 1970s and 1980s can be crudely calculated by dividing the total public expenditure on water projects during each decade by the increase in water supply capacity. This calculation yields estimates of RM0.44 per liter-day for 1970–1980 and RM1.10 per liter-day for 1980–1990.[13]

Despite public expenditure being lower than recommended by the JICA study, production nevertheless increased more rapidly during the 1980s than the 1970s. Capacity increased even more rapidly, so that by 1990 the excess capacity in the entire system was about 25 percent. In 1987, there were 354 treatment plants and 903 reservoirs in the country (JKR and Bina Runding 1989, p. 1); in 1990, there were 43 dams developed for water supply, irrigation, or flood control (*Sixth Malaysia Plan*, p. 326). Both the number of people and the percentage of the population with access to piped water also increased more rapidly during the 1980s. Much of the increase in coverage was due to the launching of a special program in 1986 to accelerate development of water systems in rural areas (*Sixth Malaysia Plan*, p. 330). By 1990, about half of the rural populations even in Sabah (47 percent) and Sarawak (52 percent) had access to piped water (*Sixth Malaysia Plan*, p. 332–333).

The *Second Outline Perspective Plan 1991–2000*, indicated that the government's commitment to providing piped water to rural areas would continue: " specific programmes will be undertaken to improve accessibility to basic amenities . . . to upgrade the quality of life, especially of the rural poor. Since inaccessibility to piped and hygienically treated water is largely a rural problem, special focus will be on removing factors impeding physical and economic accessibility of the rural households to water supply" (p. 147). In a similar vein, a recent report of the Federal Public Works Department announced that "Great efforts are being made by the government to supply drinking water to nearly all the population by the year 2010" (JKR 1992, p. 12).

Self-financing

The extension of piped water to so much of the Malaysian population since independence has undoubtedly brought benefits in terms of increased convenience and improved health and quality of life. It was an expensive undertaking, however, involving the expenditure of RM8 billion in public funds earmarked in the six *Malaysia Plans* covering the years 1966 to 1995 and an unknown amount of additional funds for other projects. If the water supply projects were self-financing, then, as discussed in *Economics of water resource development*, their benefits surely exceeded their costs. On the other hand, if the projects were not self-financing, some of them might not have been economically justified. They should either have been postponed or not implemented at all.

Anecdotal evidence and the analysis of available data indicate that many projects were not self-financing. The *Malaysia Plans* and consultants' reports repeatedly claim that the government favored self-financing, but beginning with the *Third Plan* the government quite clearly placed more emphasis on expanding supplies than on ensuring that supply schemes were self-financing. The overriding objective was to provide inexpensive water to as much of the population as possible. The government hoped that low-cost water would help raise living standards in rural areas and help reduce the incidence of rural poverty (*Third Malaysia Plan*, p. 379). Cost considerations were secondary.

The *First Plan* stated, "At present water charges do not cover the capital and operating costs of water supply schemes. In many cases the supply of water has been heavily subsidised by the government" (p. 161). It declared that this situation would not continue: "In view of the growth in the level of private incomes, heavy subsidisation of water supply development is no longer necessary. In the future water supplies like other utility services will be expected to be self-supporting as in the case in many countries, including even the developing countries." In the late 1960s and early 1970s, however, most states charged uniform tariffs set equal to suspiciously even amounts. For example, all states in Peninsular Malaysia except Melaka, Perak, and Pulau Pinang charged domestic users a flat RM1 per 1000 gallons (*Second Malaysia Plan*, p. 220). The tariffs were apparently not based on long-run marginal costs, which surely varied across states.

The *Third Plan* reiterated a general commitment to self-financing—"the entire [water supply] programme will be implemented, as far as possible, on a self-supporting basis through appropriate tariffs for various categories of users" (p. 382)—but it expanded federal subsidization of water projects. The federal government already provided outright grants for the construction of water supply systems in FELDA and regional development schemes (*Second Malaysia Plan*, p. 220). Starting in 1977, the federal government provided grants to cover in full the capital costs not only of water projects in these schemes but also of all federally approved water projects in the so-called budget deficit states, Kedah, Kelantan, Melaka, Perlis, and Terengganu (*Fourth Malaysia Plan*, p. 337; Asian Development Bank 1986, p. 17). In "nondeficit" states, the federal government was only slightly less generous: it provided grants to cover two-thirds of the capital costs, and low-interest loans at concessionary rates to cover the remaining third. As a result, states needed to set tariffs only high enough to cover operating costs and to make payments on no more than one-third of the capital costs of new schemes.

Despite the financial support from the federal government, all states increased their tariffs during the *Fourth Plan* period, "In view of the increased capital cost of water supply projects and the rising operation and maintenance costs" (*Fifth Malaysia Plan*, p. 473). Several introduced an increasing block-rate structure. The guiding principles for the block-rate structure were: 1) to provide a "cross-subsidy for domestic users by industrial users," by charging industrial users more than domestic users; 2) to charge "higher rates for higher consumption to discourage wastage"; and 3) to reduce costs for poor households, by setting the size of the lowest-priced block equal to a "life line quantum to be charged at a very low rate to meet the 'ability to pay' criteria for the low-income group" (JKR and Bina Runding 1989, p. 6–2). The life-line approach was intended to ensure that the poor had sufficient quantities of piped water at affordable prices to meet basic household needs.

State representatives met at the federal Public Works Department in the early 1980s to agree on broad guidelines for determining blocks and tariff rates (JKR and Bina Runding 1989, p. 6–6). The guidelines recommended three blocks for domestic consumption. The lowest-priced one was to be set equal to 20m³ per month, the assumed average consumption of poor families. The tariff rate on this block was to be set so that the monthly payment would work out to be about 4 percent of monthly household income for households on the poverty line (JKR and Bina Runding 1989, p. 6–2). A 4 percent "ability to pay" criterion is a rule of thumb often used by the World Bank (JKR and Bina Runding 1989, p. 6-2; World Bank Water Demand Research Team 1993). Tariffs were to increase by 50 percent from one block to the next. In the case of industrial users, the guidelines recommended a flat rate (no blocks). The tariff for industrial users was to be set equal to twice the average for domestic users.

Writing just before the tariff revision, JICA claimed that, "Although public water supply projects are supposed to be self-financing, in the great majority of cases, water charges only cover the operation and maintenance expenditure and do not cover the cost of capital works" (JICA 1982a, p. 38). It claimed that the "Pinang Water Authority, Kuching, and Sibu Water Boards are among the few self-paying concerns" (JICA 1982a, p. 38). In spite of these observations, the JICA study essentially recommended that no action be taken. It endorsed the general principle that the "entire costs of a public project should be paid by the beneficiaries rather than depending on general tax revenue collected from tax payers" (JICA 1982a, p. S–7), but it concluded that, for the ambitious water supply program it proposed, "the self-financing operation may not be practicable due to increasing burden for repayment of heavy loans and interests [sic]. In such a case, it may be necessary to consider providing grant[s] to partly finance public water supply projects" (JICA 1982a, p. 41). It added that, "in respect of rural water supply projects, federal grant[s] for such projects should be continued for the time being in view of [the] low level [of] income in the rural areas" (JICA 1982a, p. 41).[14] The study placed the provision of water before the costs of doing so.

The JICA study estimated that, overall, the annualized benefits of its recommended water supply program exceeded the annualized costs by 10 to 18 percent (JICA 1982b, p. 123). The fact that it endorsed subsidization of particular projects, however, suggests that not all elements of the program were financially viable. Information in the JICA report was sufficiently detailed to enable us to determine how many of the proposed supply schemes were self-financing at prevailing tariff rates. Table 21 in the report (JICA

1982b, p. 113) gave the net supply capacity and total construction cost of all proposed water projects. We excluded single-use irrigation schemes. This left forty-one schemes related to piped water supply. We assumed that construction of a scheme would take five years, that the lifetime of a scheme was fifty years, and that the relevant discount rate (the cost of borrowing to the water agency) was 8 percent. We based these assumptions on information in JICA (1982a, 1982b) and JKR and Bina Runding (1989). We drew estimates of state-specific nonrevenue water rates from JKR and Bina Runding (1989). Nonrevenue water is treated water that either does not reach consumers or, if it is consumed, is not paid for (JKR and Bina Runding 1989, p. 3-7). Water may not reach consumers due to leakage in storage, treatment, and distribution systems; overflows at reservoirs and treatment plants; and losses incurred during the flushing of water mains, the backwashing of filters, and other operational activities. Water may not be paid for due to its provision free of charge for certain uses, such as firefighting, or due to underregistration by water meters, failure to read all meters or bill all customers, and illegal use.

Together, this information and these assumptions enabled us to calculate the long-run marginal capital cost of each scheme.[15] We added to each the state-specific operating cost, drawn from JKR and Bina Runding (1989). The sum gave us an estimate of the long-run marginal cost of each scheme.

To check whether a scheme was self-financing, we needed to compare the long-run marginal cost to the average water tariff. We selected tariffs for 1987, the year when schemes initiated in 1982 would have begun operating. We used information on the domestic and industrial shares of water consumption (reported in JKR and Bina Runding 1989) to calculate weighted average tariffs. A scheme was self-financing only if the average tariff was at least as large as the long-run marginal cost.

Figure 7.3 displays the results in the form of a scatter plot. Each cross (+) represents an individual water supply scheme. The vertical axis gives the average water tariff, and the horizontal axis gives the long-run marginal cost. Both are expressed in ringgit per cubic meter, at 1980 price levels. The dashed diagonal line indicates equivalence between tariffs and marginal costs. One-third of the schemes—fourteen—were to the right of this line and were therefore not self-financing. These schemes were not viable at 1987 tariff rates. They were economically justified only if benefits related to flood control, recreation, fishing, and other nonconsumptive uses offset the losses related to water supply. They were not justified on the basis of water supply alone.

In spite of the tariff revision in the early 1980s, just a few years later the Asian Development Bank (1986) commented that although "it is the government's intention that water be sold to the public, and that the revenue from

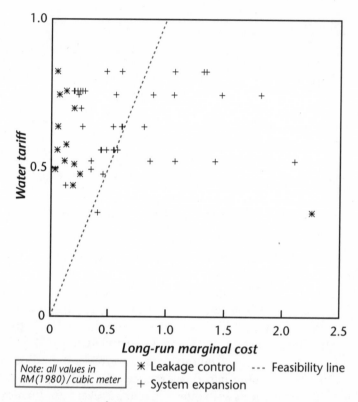

Figure 7.3   Feasibility of supply options

the sale of water cover the cost of operating and maintaining water supplies and repaying loans" (p. 10), "the revision of the water rates is not keeping pace with increased costs" (p. 21). A study of tariff rates in the late 1980s (JKR and Bina Runding 1989) confirmed this. It found that states were unable to cover not only capital costs but also maintenance costs: "The budgetary allocations for operation and maintenance are generally sufficient to provide for satisfactory operation but for only minimal maintenance" (p. 10). Although states were making emergency repairs, "In most states, no provision is made for the replacement of old pipes and equipment" (p. 10). It projected that, from 1991 to 1995, water supply agencies in "virtually all states will not recover sufficient revenue from present tariffs and would therefore continue to be operating in deficit" (p. 4). It recommended that "the rates charged should just make

Table 7.3   *Selected water tariffs in Selangor by end use (ringgit per cubic meter)*

Use	Block	Period 1984–88	1989–90	1991
Domestic	All	0.27		
	A		0.38 (0–20 m^3)	0.42 (0–15 m^3)
	B		0.57 (21–45 m^3)	0.65 (16–40 m^3)
	C		0.85 (45 m^3)	1.05 (40 m^3)
Industrial		0.55	1.04	1.20
Government		0.26	0.65	0.80

Note: Block quantities refer to monthly consumption. Minimum payments also apply.

operations (including loan servicing) self-financing, without cross-subsidy from other sectors" (p. 6–3).

We obtained and analyzed detailed data on a major system expansion in the state of Selangor to investigate further the impact of tariff revisions.[16] Table 7.3 shows water tariffs for principal users in Selangor from 1984 through 1991. The Selangor Waterworks Department raised the tariffs and introduced an increasing block-rate structure in 1989, and it raised the tariff rates again in 1991 and simultaneously reduced the quantity in the lowest-priced block. These revisions were intended to raise revenue to finance several water supply projects (JKR and Bina Runding 1989, p. 6–8). The major projects were construction of remaining works for the Semenyih dam, the largest water supply project in the country (Asian Development Bank 1986, p. 16); new works on the Sungai Selangor, including the Beletak dam; and new mains for extending the distribution system. The projects were to be implemented from 1985 to 2010 and would increase water supply capacity by 1.9 billion liter-days. Capital expenditures were to be financed by loans from the federal government, at an annual interest rate of 7.5 percent.

The feasibility study for the expansion estimated the water tariffs necessary to cover loan payments and operating costs. The study considered two scenarios, which differed in terms of assumptions about nonrevenue water rates. In one scenario, the nonrevenue water rate was assumed to be 24 percent in 1985, falling to 20 percent by 1995. In the other, more pessimistic scenario, the initial rate was assumed to be 30 percent, but it was still assumed to fall to 20 percent by 1995.

The study found that the average water tariff necessary for self-financing was about RM0.63/m^3 in both scenarios (at 1985 price levels).[17] Differentiated by use, the tariff was RM0.50/m^3 on domestic users and RM1.17/m^3 on industrial users. These tariff rates were about twice the levels in 1984 (see Table 7.3). Hence, the schemes were not viable at the time they were initiated. Most of the increased capacity, however, was not scheduled to come on stream until 1990 or later. A more appropriate comparison is therefore with 1991 water tariffs. Deflated to 1985 price levels by using the consumer price index, these tariffs were RM0.57/m^3 for domestic users[18] and RM1.05/m^3 for industrial users. Their weighted average, RM0.66/m^3, was slightly above the self-financing tariff rate reported in the study. At the higher 1991 water tariffs and the assumed nonrevenue water rates, the expansion was indeed justified.

To sum up, some, but not all, of the water development projects implemented during the 1970s and 1980s failed the self-financing test. The long-run marginal costs of the projects exceeded the tariffs water users paid. The proportion of nonviable projects increased beginning in the *Third Plan* period due to increased federal subsidization.

Consequences of underpricing water

What were the consequences of pricing water below the costs of supplying it? The discussion in *Economics of water resource development* suggests several potentially negative impacts. On the demand side, low tariffs reduced the financial incentive for users to conserve water.[19] In the data supporting Figure 7.3, operating costs accounted for about half of median long-run marginal costs: RM0.21/m^3 out of RM0.43/m^3, at 1980 price levels.[20] If tariffs covered only operating costs, as evidence indicates often was the case, they needed to be doubled to cover total costs. At the price elasticities cited in *Economics of water resource development*, -0.1 to -0.4, doubling tariffs would have reduced water consumption by 10 to 40 percent and made some of the expansion in water supply capacity unnecessary.

On the supply side, the underpricing had up to four negative consequences. First, if projects were truly uneconomic even after adding in benefits related to flood control, recreation, fishing, and other uses aside from water supply, then the underpricing reflected a misallocation of investment capital. The potential misallocation associated with the supply schemes proposed by JICA that were not self-financing (see Figure 7.3) was greater than the relative number of the schemes indicated. The fourteen schemes that were not self-financing tended to be the largest ones. The aggregate capital cost of these schemes was RM4.7 billion (1980 price levels). This was more than three-fourths of the total capital cost of all forty-one proposed schemes, RM6.0 billion.

Second, underpricing reduced water supply agencies' funds for investing in system expansions. This probably had little impact before the mid-1980s, given the federal government's generosity in providing grants and low-interest loans. The government did not have the funds to subsidize water supply indefinitely, however. After the *Fourth Plan* period, the tighter federal budget resulted in public expenditure on water supply not rising as rapidly as the JICA study recommended. If some of the projects that were not implemented were those to the left of the feasibility line in Figure 7.3, then insufficient investment was made in the capacity necessary for meeting the country's future water demands.

Third, the federal government's willingness to underwrite much of the cost of water projects, which was instrumental in enabling states to underprice water, and the government's emphasis on expanding supplies instead of ensuring that projects were self-financing apparently contributed to excessively costly projects, particularly in rural areas. The Asian Development Bank (1986, p. 23) was particularly critical of the common practice of servicing rural areas by subsidizing the extension of pipelines from distant urban areas. It claimed that, "Although there may occur some cases where extensions may be economically sound, alternative solutions to extending existing systems generally are not considered, and economic evaluation of rural extensions is not usually undertaken." It argued that "more than 90 per cent of proposed extension schemes have exceedingly high per capita costs," and that "villages and small urban centers have simpler and less costly water supply systems."

The Bank suggested that "because quantities of water required by such communities are not large, it may be possible to make use of the ground water as a source of water" (p. 23). Ironically, the *Second Plan* (p. 219) had cautioned that "proposals for extensions and new supplies to serve isolated areas . . . require further detailed study as to the availability of cheaper sources, especially in the form of groundwater." At the time of the *Second Plan*, there had been "no systematic investigation into possibilities of groundwater sources" (p. 219). In the *Mid-Term Review of the Fourth Malaysia Plan*, published in 1984, the government announced that it planned to promote groundwater as a source of water in rural areas. It set targets of 5,208 wells with hand pumps, 1,283 wells with reticulation systems, and 51 gravity water supply schemes, which would serve 300,000 people (p. 342). Two years later, however, the Asian Development Bank (1986, p. 24) judged that "groundwater sources are still seldom used."

The costs of rural water supply projects might also have been unduly increased by the government's policy of providing individual connections at the household level. Meerman (1979, p. 208) argued that "it might conceivably make sense to provide more multi-family standpipes where settlement patterns permit these." Even at the subsidized water prices, he found that "many poor families who can choose often choose not to have piped and treated water," because of its cost (p. 207); "at present charges, it would appear that perhaps more than a third of the poverty population is priced out of the market even if such water were available" (p. 208). Offering water through means other than individual connections might have reduced supply costs and better matched rural households' valuation of water as indicated by their willingness to pay. The need to match the type of water service to households' willingness to pay is a lesson emphasized by the World Bank Water Demand Research Team's (1993) analysis of World Bank and USAID experience with rural water supply projects.

Fourth, and probably most important, the underpricing and rapid expansion led to a neglect of maintenance. The federal government subsidized expansion of the water supply system, but not its maintenance. FELDA rubber and oil palm schemes provide particularly extreme examples: states were obliged to provide water free of charge for five to seven years and therefore could not generate any revenue to cover operating and maintenance costs (Asian Development Bank 1986, p. 21). The great expansion in the country's water supply system left the states with large systems to manage, but political pressure made it difficult for them to set tariffs high enough to cover the full costs of running the systems.

Simply managing the implementation of new projects distracted state and federal agencies from maintenance and quality control. A 1989 report coauthored by the federal Public Works Department (JKR) commented that "significant recent increases in the number of new connections . . . [have been] focussing JKR's attention on meeting growth in demand rather than increase [sic] in efficiency of operation" (JKR and Bina Runding 1989, p. 11). It added, "The concept of pipeline rehabilitation/replacement (which is an essential part of the asset management of any water supply authority) has been identified as lacking in JKR short and long term planning strategies" (p. 4). The rapid development of FELDA schemes resulted in "poor workmanship in pipelaying and consumer tapping coupled with poor operation" (JKR and Bina Runding, p. 2).

The neglect of maintenance caused the nonrevenue water rate to rise. Several studies have stated that a well-run water supply system in Malaysia should have a nonrevenue water rate of around 20 percent (JICA 1982a, p. 27; Asian Development Bank 1986, p. 22; JKR and Bina Runding 1989, p. 6-6). Table 7.4 shows that the nonrevenue water rate rose steadily after the late 1970s. The *First, Second,* and *Third Plans* did not discuss the issue of nonrevenue water, perhaps because the rate then was apparently not much above the minimum thought possible. In 1978, the national rate was estimated at a modest amount above the 20 percent figure, 26 percent (JKR and Bina Runding 1989, p. 2). A couple of years later, JICA (1982a, p. 27) estimated that

Table 7.4   *Estimated nonrevenue water rates (percentage of production of treated water)*

Year	Average	Range across states
1978	26	
1982		Up to 30
Early 1980s		Up to 45
1983	32	18–58
1987	43	20–61

Sources: See text.

"water losses in most public water supply systems are as high as 30%."[21] It suggested reducing the rate through rehabilitation of the distribution system. In the *Mid-Term Review of the Fourth Malaysia Plan* (published in 1984 but apparently based on information available as of early 1983), the government suggested that the system of water supply management needed revamping to reduce the amount of nonrevenue water (p. 341). It estimated that the non-revenue water rate was as high as 45 percent in some states. By 1983, the estimated average rate had risen to 32 percent (Asian Development Bank 1986, p. 22; JKR and Bina Runding 1989, p. 2). It ranged from lows of 18 percent in Pulau Pinang, 21 percent in Terengganu, and 22 percent in Melaka, to highs of 53 percent in Kedah and 58 percent in Perlis.

Evidence that the rate was rising prompted the government to commission a special report on the problem, in order to estimate the magnitude of the losses more accurately, to determine their causes, and to suggest management and policy responses. The report, *Non-Revenue Water Control Study & Development of a Control Programme for Malaysia*, was prepared by the Federal Public Works Department with assistance from a local consulting firm, Bina Runding Sdn. Bhd. (JKR and Bina Runding 1989). The report estimated that the average nonrevenue water rate had jumped all the way to 43 percent by 1987 (p. 2). Pulau Pinang still had the lowest rate, at 20 percent, while Kedah had the highest, at 61 percent. In FELDA schemes, the average rate was 60 percent. Following the report, the Public Works Department set up a Non-revenue Water Unit in its Water Supplies Branch and began a pilot study on control measures in Perlis (JKR 1992, p. 10).

The report determined that leakage was the major cause of nonrevenue water, accounting for three-fourths of the total (p. 2). Hence, one-third (32 percent) of the treated water produced in the country never reached consumers. Meter underregistration was a distant second cause, accounting for one-fifth of the total. Household water meters should be replaced every three to seven years (depending on type), but 49 percent of the meters in the country in 1987 were more than five years old. Nearly 6 percent had stopped working altogether. Moreover, more than half of the production meters at treatment plants were no longer operating.

Miscellaneous causes—incomplete revenue collection, firefighting, operational activities—accounted for the remainder of the nonrevenue water (5 percent). The Asian Development Bank (1986, p. 20) had earlier attributed incomplete revenue collection to shortage of personnel, especially accountants and meter readers; lack of discipline among meter readers; reluctance by workers to disconnect service to nonpaying customers; and outmoded billing equipment.

The JKR and Bina Runding report estimated the economic losses associated with leakage in each state by multiplying the volume of leakage times the unit cost of leakage. The latter was the sum of unit operating costs and unit capital costs. That is, it was an estimate of the long-run marginal cost of the water. The estimates of unit cost of leakage averaged RM0.209/m³ in Peninsular Malaysia and RM0.330/m³ in Sabah and Sarawak. Losses in 1987 totaled RM95 million in Peninsular Malaysia and RM11 million in Sabah and Sarawak, for a total of RM106 million (p. 5–3). This was about one-fifth of average annual public development expenditure on water supply projects under the *Fifth Plan* (*Sixth Malaysia Plan*, p. 343). The report estimated that an economically viable control program could recover 29 percent of the losses in Peninsular Malaysia and 36 percent in Sabah and Sarawak, for a total of RM33 million (p. 5–4).

The report also estimated gross revenue losses in each state due to meter underregistration, by multiplying the underregistered volume times the average tariff rate. These losses totaled RM72 million in Peninsular Malaysia and RM6 million in Sabah and Sarawak, for a total of RM78 million. It estimated that these losses could be fully recovered through replacement of old or broken meters.

Obviously, the revenue losses due to both leakage and meter underregistration reduced the funds that state water supply agencies could use to finance expansions and improvements in water supply systems. Underpricing therefore created a vicious circle: low tariffs reduced revenue, which forced water supply agencies to skimp on maintenance; but the reduced expenditure on maintenance caused leakage and meter underregistration to worsen, which reduced revenue even more.

At the same time that nonrevenue water reduced states' investment funds, leakage forced them to consider developing new water resources to offset the water being lost to leakage. At a leakage rate of 32 percent, the effective supply capacity of the country's water supply system in 1990 was reduced by 2.1 billion liter-days. This is not much less than the forecast increase in annual consumption between 1990 and 1995, 2.8 billion liter-days. Even if the leakage were only reduced to 20 percent, the effective increase in capacity, 0.8 billion liter-days, would still be equivalent to almost a third of the increase in consumption. The *Sixth Malaysia Plan* noted that reducing the nonrevenue water rate would "reduce the pressure to develop new [water] sources" (p. 333).

There was yet another layer of effects. By reducing the amount of treated water that could actually be sold, leakage and meter underregistration reduced the viability of proposed water projects. We took this effect into account in preparing the estimates of long-run marginal costs plotted in Figure 7.3, whereas JICA, in its appraisal of the same projects, assumed that the nonrevenue water rate was only 20 percent. JICA therefore overestimated the net annual benefits of its recommended water supply program.

The feasibility study of the Selangor system expansion also assumed nonrevenue water rates—20 to 24 percent or 20 to 30 percent, depending on the scenario—that were on the low side of estimated values for the state in 1983, 29 percent (Asian Development Bank 1986, p. 22), and 1987, 45 percent (JKR and Bina Runding 1989, Figure 3.7). For the system expansion to be self-financing at the 1987 nonrevenue water rate, water tariffs needed to be about 10 percent higher than their actual values in 1991.[22] Similarly, JKR and Bina Runding (1989, p. 4) found that even if all states were able to reduce their nonrevenue water rates to 20 percent, "for the period 1991-1995 at least six States [would] need to increase or make adjustments to their tariff systems to generate sufficient revenue just to pay for operational and investment costs."

The Asian Development Bank (1986, p. 10) noted that in most states "no provision is made . . . for the undertaking of a leakage detection program to reduce the volume of unaccounted-for water." JKR and Bina Runding (1989, p. 5) estimated that the first ten years of such a program would cost RM41 million in development expenditure, partly because "comprehensive mapping records . . . are deficient in many states" (p. 3), and RM208 million in operating costs, including the costs of replacing faulty meters. To determine the economic viability of this program, we estimated the long-run marginal cost of the water that this effort would save for each state, and compared the result to the average tariff rate in the state in 1987. Results are plotted as the stars (*) in Figure 7.3. In all cases but one the stars are to the left of the feasibility line, indicating that the programs were viable. The one star to the right of the line is for Pulau Pinang, which had the lowest nonrevenue water rate in 1987 and would be expected to gain less from an additional leakage control program. The stars are generally further to the left than the crosses, which represent the recommended JICA water supply schemes. In the late 1980s, therefore, reducing leakage through leakage control programs was generally a lower-cost means of increasing water supply than developing additional water resources. This is not to say that no system expansion was necessary to keep pace with rising water consumption—as discussed above, reducing the nonrevenue water rate to 20 percent would cover only one-third of the projected consumption increase from 1991 to 1995—but a control program could have eliminated the need for some water development projects and should have been implemented before some others were initiated.

Conclusions

Water demand increased rapidly in Malaysia during the 1970s and 1980s. The expansion of supply capacity to meet this demand was heavily subsidized by the federal government, particularly after the introduction of the NEP. This enabled states to maintain low water tariffs, which was attractive for political reasons. As operating costs and the costs of water resource development rose, however, water supply agencies found it increasingly difficult to cover maintenance costs. The neglect of maintenance led to a worsening problem of nonrevenue water, which weakened water supply agencies' financial positions and forced them to expand systems further to offset the water lost to leakage. Subsidization also discouraged conservation by water consumers, and it led in some instances to the selection of unduly expensive water supply options, particularly in rural areas. In short, water was not treated as a scarce resource. The costs of disregarding the scarcity value of water can only be expected to escalate in the future, as population, income, industrial activity, and therefore consumption continue to rise.

Recently, there is evidence of a shift in government policy in favor of pricing water at its scarcity value. In the early 1990s, the federal government changed its policy for financing water projects, eliminating grants for projects in urban areas, and limiting grants for projects in rural areas to no more than 20 percent of the cost (*The Star* 1993). The *Sixth Malaysia Plan* (p. 340) stated that willingness to pay should be used as the main criterion for pricing water: "The high investment cost associated with the development of the sector will require cost recovery and tariff structures to be analyzed in conjunction with the consumers' affordability and willingness to pay." The word *affordability* indicates that although the government favors more efficient water pricing, it is at the same time cautious of the consequences, particularly for poor households. This would seem to be a problem easily resolved by appropriate structuring of increasing block-rate tariffs, which by 1991 were used to price water for domestic consumers in all states except Sabah.

The need to generate sufficient investment funds will become even more critical in the future. We noted earlier that long-run marginal costs apparently more than doubled between the 1970s and 1980s. Further increases are likely, because the development of remaining water resources will increasingly involve interbasin transfers, either within states or between states (*Fifth Malaysia Plan*, p. 477; *Sixth Malaysia Plan*, pp. 327, 337; *Second Outline Perspective Plan*, p. 147). Of the 45 dams proposed by the JICA study, 13 were related to interbasin transfers within states and 5 to interstate transfers. By the end of the 1980s, many parts of the country had, in effect, reached step *C* in Figure 7.2. A distribution system that facilitated interbasin transfers might even eliminate the need for new water resource development in some basins by enabling the country to make better use of its existing capacity. Treatment plant capacity exceeded production by 31 percent in 1990 and was projected to exceed it by 35 percent in 1995 (*Sixth Malaysia Plan*, p. 331).

Schemes involving interbasin and, to a lesser extent, interstate transfers already exist. During the *Fourth Plan* period, the Arau dam project was completed to transfer water from Kedah to Perlis. Similarly, the Gemencheh dam was built to transfer water from Negri Sembilan to Melaka. Additional interstate transfers are hindered by not only their economic costs, which full-cost pricing could help overcome, but also by institutional obstacles. Water-surplus states are, not surprisingly, reluctant to agree to arrangements that they perceive weaken their property rights over water, in particular their control over the quantities and prices sold (Vatikiotis 1991). In 1991 the cabinet established a National Water Council, coordinated by the Minister of Works, to address this and other issues related to interstate transfers.

Malaysia's experience with three types of water supply agencies at the state level gives some indication of the types of institutional arrangements that promote efficient water management. As mentioned earlier, the JICA study (1982a, p. 38) noted that the water boards in Pulau Pinang, Melaka, and Kuching and Sibu in Sarawak were among the few water supply agencies that were self-financing. Pulau Pinang and Melaka had two of the three lowest nonrevenue water rates in 1983 (Asian Development Bank 1986, p. 22), and these two states plus Sarawak had three of the four lowest nonrevenue water rates in 1987 (JKR and Bina Runding 1989, Figure 3.11). This evidence of better performance is not surprising. Water boards are operated on a commercial basis (JKR and Bina Runding, 1989, p. 2-2). They recognize that revenue lost to leakage, meter underregistration, and incomplete collection worsens their financial performance. They have an incentive to invest in maintenance and repair activities and to improve collection efforts, if necessary by raising tariffs to cover additional expenses. Public works departments and water supply departments, on the other hand, are governed by more rigid regulations and have less authority to set water tariffs.

What is more surprising is that the commercial orientation of water boards has not necessarily led them to charge higher water tariffs. In fact, Pulau Pinang had the lowest water tariffs in Malaysia in 1991, even though it is a water-stress state (according to JICA 1982a). Nearly 80 percent of the residents in Pulau Pinang surveyed by Goh (1990) responded that they were satisfied with the tariffs charged. Tariffs in Melaka, Kuching, and Sibu were in the middle of the pack compared to other states. The greater efficiency of the water boards, physically evident in their lower nonrevenue water rates and higher collection rates, enabled them to reduce the cost of water to consumers.

Experience in other countries also indicates that making water supply agencies more commercially-oriented improves the efficiency of water services. In China, reforms that bestowed a greater degree of financial autonomy on provincial water management agencies resulted in water being priced closer to its actual cost, increased conservation, and made the service more reliable (Asian Development Bank 1991, p. 247).

The government has promoted privatization of certain water supply functions as a means of enhancing efficiency. The *Fifth Malaysia Plan* announced that "privatization of the construction, operation, and maintenance of public utilities will be given due consideration" (p. 479). This reflected a broader government policy "to privatise as many services as are practicable in order to: (i) relieve the government of the financial and administrative burden in undertaking and maintaining a vast and constantly expanding network of services and (ii) capitalise on the efficiency of the private sector to increase productivity" (JKR 1992, p. 18).

Since water resources are under state jurisdiction, water supply projects can be privatized only with the approval of state governments, and only after close consultation with EPU. Three methods of privatization have been adopted by the government in the water sector: management and service contracts, build-operate-transfer (BOT) contracts, and a combination of BOT and management contracts (Subramaniam 1992). The government initiated the privatization of water supply projects during the *Fifth Plan* period, with projects in Labuan and Selangor (*Mid-Term Review of the Fifth Malaysia Plan* 1989, p. 229). All contracts so far have been for the operation and management of treatment plants. Privatization contracts for the construction of storage and treatment plants and distribution systems have not yet been offered. The federal government has also encouraged industries to play a larger role in constructing plants to treat water for their own use (*Sixth Malaysia Plan* 1991, p. 342). This is an idea suggested by the JICA study a decade earlier (JICA 1982a, p. S–5).

The *Sixth Malaysia Plan* declared that "in the future, more water supply projects will be privatized. . . . studies will be undertaken on projects to be privatized to ensure that the affordability of consumers and competitiveness of industrial users will be safeguarded" (p. 340). As in the case of willingness to pay, the word *affordability* signals that the distributional impacts of privatization concern the government. Water tariffs for industrial users are a particularly sensitive issue. When Kedah attempted to raise water tariffs for industrial users in the early 1990s, the Ministry of International Trade and Industry described the increases as "indiscriminate" and unfavorable to its goal of attracting foreign investment. The Ministry succeeded in convincing the state government to make the increase smaller than planned.

The need to regulate tariff setting by water supply agencies is legitimate, even in the absence of privatization, given that unregulated water supply agencies could potentially exercise monopoly power and price water above long-run marginal costs. During the 1970s and 1980s in Malaysia, however, the problem was quite the opposite: prices were below long-run marginal costs. To the extent that this remains the case, restraining tariff increases is not in the long-run interests of either domestic or industrial water consumers in Malaysia.

NOTES

1 Some favor the term *usage* over *consumption*, as human activities change the location and quality of water but do not alter its molecular composition. We use *consumption* because it is the term employed most commonly in the Malaysian literature.

2 *Sungai* means "river" in Bahasa Malaysia.

3 This is true even in the Sungai Muda basin (JICA 1982b, p. 28).

4 The marginal cost-pricing rule described here is not the same as the accountant's cost-recovery method for setting prices, which is based on historical costs. The problem with the cost-recovery method is that prices and costs do not remain constant; hence, historical costs do not reflect current scarcity values. Marginal cost pricing, on the other hand, is based on the current opportunity cost of resources and hence reflects current scarcity values.

5 In theory, marginal cost should also include the opportunity cost of water: the forgone benefits of water in other uses (e.g., fishing, if extraction reduces streamflow to a trickle) or at other points in time (e.g., the user cost associated with depletion of groundwater resources). We ignore this component here, as it does not appear to be very large in Malaysia.

6 Saunders and Warford note that this is a "practicable approximation." In theory, the average incremental cost calculated by this method equals true long-run marginal cost only when the water supply system is utilized at full capacity.

7 For simplicity, the following comments ignore the issue of the likelihood that potential users will actually hook up to and use municipal water services when the system is expanded into a new area. The failure of potential users to do so in many developing countries is discussed by the World Bank Water Demand Research Team (1993).

8 Whittington (1992) has pointed out, however, that increasing block rates can be regressive when poor households share a common tap while wealthier households can afford separate connections.

9 Water used for irrigation is on the Concurrent List: it is a joint responsibility of state and federal governments (Uzir 1988, p. 167).

10 The FELDA (Federal Land Development Authority), which is responsible for the development of most government-sponsored agricultural schemes.

11 In the case of private agricultural estates, the owners are responsible for funding all water projects within the estate and for supplying treated piped water to people living on the estate.

12 These values are in nominal terms. The plans do not give a year-by-year breakdown of spending, so it is not possible to deflate the figures. Inflation in Malaysia from 1970 to 1990 was modest, averaging 4.5 percent per year (based on the GDP deflator).

13 These estimates are in nominal terms, so they overstate the real increase.

14 Similarly, it recommended that the government should set water rates in irrigation schemes only high enough to cover operation and maintenance costs, due to the low income of farmers (JICA 1982a, p. 43).

15 If TCC is the total capital cost of a scheme, NRW is the nonrevenue water rate, Q is the annual quantity of water treated, and i is the discount rate, then the long-run marginal capital cost is given by:

$$\frac{TCC}{(1 - NRW) \times Q/i \times [(1 + i)^{-5} - (1 + i)^{-55}]}$$

16 Jabatan Bekalan Air Selangor generously provided the data from the feasibility study for the projects.

17 Results in the study indicated that a domestic rate of RM0.50/m^3 and an industrial rate of RM1.17/m^3 would yield internal rates of return of 7.6 percent in the first scenario and 8.0 percent in the second. These rates of return are close to the loan rate of 7.5 percent, and so the estimated domestic and industrial rates can be taken as approximate break-even rates. The study assumed that consumption shares were 0.81 for domestic consumption and 0.19 for commercial/industrial. Hence, the weighted-average break-even rate was RM 0.63/m^3.

18 The average domestic tariff in 1991 was assumed to equal the tariff for the middle block (Block B) in Table 7.3, 0.65 ringgit per cubic meter.

19 Uzir (1988, p. 165) commented that low prices have led to inefficient water use in irrigation schemes.

20 These estimates include adjustments for nonrevenue water. Without the adjustments, the estimates would be lower.

21 The situation was even worse in irrigation schemes: "the efficiency of water use scarcely exceeds 50%" (JICA 1982a, p. 27).

22 This estimate is based on reworking the data in the JBA Selangor feasibility study. We assumed that the domestic consumption share was 0.81 and the industrial share was 0.19 (these were the shares used in the feasibility study), and that the industrial water tariff would be twice the domestic tariff (JKR and Bina Runding 1989, p. 6–6).

8

Pollution and Economic Development

INTRODUCTION

Information in Chapter 1 indicated that several indicators of environmental quality worsened in Malaysia during the 1970s and 1980s, when both population and per capita income grew rapidly. On the surface, this is not surprising. A larger population means more people discharging pollutants into the air and water. Higher per capita income might be expected to result in greater pollution discharge per person, particularly when manufacturing accounts for much of the increase in income, as was the case in Malaysia during the 1970s and 1980s. The total human impact on the environment, which by definition is the product of population times per capita environmental impact, would seem necessarily to rise.

Grossman and Krueger (1991) and other economists have argued, however, that the relationship between economic development and pollution is not so simple. A simple *scale* effect does indeed suggest that economic growth increases pollution. If output rises, but the structure of the economy and environmental policies remain the same—for example, simply more of the same types of factories, facing the same pollution-control regulations, are built—then pollution emissions would rise proportionately.

Three other factors can conceivably offset this effect, however. First, the *composition* of economic output inevitably changes with development. Hettige et al. (1992, p. 479) decomposed economic development into three stages, which vary in their pollution intensity. In the first stage, the economy is dominated by agriculture, agroprocessing, and light manufacturing (e.g., assembly), which have a relatively low pollution intensity. Next comes heavy industry, which has high pollution intensity. Finally, the economy shifts toward high-technology industries and services, which are again relatively low in pollution intensity. In sum, pollution per unit of output first rises and then falls as these structural changes occur.

Second, one would expect a country's *technology* to become more advanced with development. Improvements in processing technology can reduce pollution indirectly by reducing consumption of inputs (raising physical efficiency), while improvements in pollution-control technologies can reduce emissions directly. Pollution discharge by a traditionally heavily polluting industry can fall as output rises if the increase in output comes from factories that use more modern, less polluting processes.

Third, increases in income resulting from economic growth might raise public demand for improved environmental quality and thereby result in more stringent *environmental policies*. Economists agree that demand for environmental quality is positively correlated with income. Of course, much environmental damage could still occur if public demand rises slowly or if the government does not respond with effective policies.

Recent cross-country empirical research by Grossman and Krueger (1991) and others suggests that, for certain pollutants anyway, the net effect of these four factors has in practice been an inverted U-shaped relationship between pollution and per capita GDP. That is, pollution worsens up to an income threshold, or turning point, but thereafter it diminishes. There is a trade-off between income and environmental quality below the turning point, but both rise after income passes this point. Because the relationship is analogous to the famous one between income inequality and average income level proposed by Simon Kuznets (1955), it has been dubbed the "environmental Kuznets curve."

Arrow et al. (1995) emphasized that the existence of this relationship in a cross-sectional sample of countries does not imply that the turning points are in any way "optimal." Countries below the turning points could well be suffering substantial welfare losses by not taking more aggressive action to reduce pollution. They also emphasized that the curve's existence does not imply that economic growth alone will be sufficient to cause pollution to start falling once a country's income passes the turning point. It is entirely possible for a country to continue to suffer worsening pollution if it fails to enforce existing environmental policies, ignores public demands for a better quality environment, or subsidizes the use of polluting inputs. In the absence of appropriate policies, the structural changes and improved technologies that typically accompany economic development might not be enough to slow and eventually reduce pollution.

This chapter investigates whether the relationship between pollution and development in Malaysia has been consistent with the environmental Kuznets curve hypothesis. It begins by reviewing cross-country studies on this relationship. Next, it uses the results of these studies to generate predictions for the Malaysian case. It then tests these predictions via statistical analyses of Malaysian monitoring data. The chapter concludes by highlighting the implications of these results for future pollution trends in the country.

CROSS-COUNTRY STUDIES OF THE POLLUTION/DEVELOPMENT RELATIONSHIP

Empirical research on the pollution/development relationship consists of just a handful of studies. We will review four in some detail here.[1] Key findings are summarized in Table 8.1.

Ambient environmental quality

Grossman and Krueger (1991; G&K) conducted their study in response to controversy over the environmental impacts of the North American Free Trade Agreement. Environmentalists opposed to the Agreement argued that freer trade and investment between the United States and Mexico would

Table 8.1 *Per capita GDP turning points estimated by cross-country studies (purchasing power parity estimates, 1985 price levels)*

	Grossman & Krueger (1991)[a]	Shafik & Bandyopadhyay (1992)	Selden & Song (1994)[b]
		US$/person	
I. Ambient air quality			
TSP	None[c]	3,280	
SO_2	5,257	3,670	
II. Ambient water quality			
Fecal coliform count		1,375[d]	
Dissolved oxygen concentration		None[c]	
III. Air pollution emissions[e]			
Per capita TSP			9,811
Per capita SO_2			10,681
Per capita NOx			12,041
Per capita CO			6,241

[a] Random-effects estimates, for regressions with median values of pollutants as dependent variables and trade intensity included as explanatory variables.

[b] Random-effects estimates for SO_2 and fixed-effects estimates for others, for regressions without population density, which was not statistically significant at the 5 percent level.

[c] Concentration declines continually with income.

[d] Beyond US$11,400, the count rises.

[e] Estimates by Panayotou (1993) are omitted, as they are not in purchasing power parity terms.

increase pollution emissions in Mexico by increasing economic activity in Mexico and inducing U.S. firms to shift manufacturing facilities to Mexico, where environmental regulations were less stringent and enforced less aggressively.

G&K estimated statistical relationships between ambient air quality and per capita GDP from 1977 to 1988 in a sample of urban areas in four to thirty two countries (depending on the pollutant). The air-quality data were collected by the World Health Organization and the United Nations Environment Programme under the Global Environmental Monitoring System. They consisted of daily (in most cases) concentrations of two major air pollutants, TSP (total suspended particles) and SO_2.[2] G&K used annual median or 95th percentile (peak) concentrations of the pollutants as the dependent variables in their regressions. They drew their estimates of per capita GDP from the Penn World Table (Mark 5), which adjusts ordinary per capita GDP for differences in price levels between countries (Summers and Heston 1991). The Penn World Table reports these "purchasing power parity" estimates in U.S. dollars at 1985 international price levels. In addition to per capita GDP, raised to the first, second, and third powers (to allow for nonlinear effects), G&K included urban population density and several other explanatory variables.[3]

G&K found that both median and 95th percentile concentrations of the two pollutants were related to per capita GDP at an extremely high level of statistical significance. We will review just the results for median concentrations;[4] the results for 95th percentile concentrations are quite similar. For SO_2, the relationship was cubic (all three powers of per capita GDP were significant), but within the income range in the sample it had an inverted U shape. The turning point was US$5,257 (Table 8.1).[5] In the case of TSP, median concentrations declined continually as per capita GDP rose.[6] Population density had a statistically significant impact on SO_2 levels—as expected, it raised them—but not on TSP levels.

The relationship between ambient air quality and economic development was thus not simply a negative one for either pollutant. In the case of SO_2, the most polluted countries tended to be neither the poorest nor the richest, but the newly industrializing ones in the middle. For TSP, air quality improved continually with income.

As Arrow et al. (1995) cautioned, these findings do not imply that the estimated turning points are necessarily the lowest that could or should have been achieved. Indeed, some countries in the sample had declining pollution levels even before they passed the estimated turning points. Moreover, developing countries today might face turning points lower than the values estimated by G&K, which reflect historical levels of technology. Industrial equipment imported by developing countries tends to be newer and less polluting, on average, than the existing capital stock in developed countries (Hettige et al. 1992). This, along with improved policies, probably explains why G&K found that after controlling for the effects of changes in income, population density, and other explanatory variables, the median concentrations of TSP and SO_2 were declining at annual rates of 2.26 and 1.77 $\mu g/m^3$ (micrograms per cubic meter), respectively.

Another of G&K's results illustrates more directly the importance of policies. Among the explanatory variables in their regressions was a dummy variable indicating whether a country's government was communist. The estimated coefficient on this variable was highly significant and large for both pollutants, indicating that communist countries were more polluted than noncommunist countries at the same income level.[7] This is not surprising. Former communist governments in Eastern Europe and the former Soviet Union had some of the most stringent environmental standards in the world, but they failed to enforce them, fearing the impact on industrial output. The closed nature of the communist political system stifled public concerns about the lack of enforcement. The amount of pollution generated by the industries was increased by the fact that they received the highest subsidies in the world for many polluting inputs, especially energy.

The second study, by Shafik and Bandyopadhyay (1992; S&B), was a background paper for the World Bank's 1992 *World Development Report*. S&B's methodology was similar to G&K's: panel data on environmental indicators for a sample of countries were regressed on per capita GDP (in purchasing power parity terms, and raised to up to the third power) and other explanatory variables.[8] S&B did not, however, include variables related to population. Their data sets were larger, involving up to 149 countries for periods as long as 1960–1990.

Like G&K, S&B analyzed ambient urban levels of SO_2 and TSP. For both, they found that the relationship with per capita GDP was given by an environmental Kuznets curve. The turning point for SO_2, US$3,670, was similar to G&K's. The turning point for TSP was slightly lower, US$3,280. After controlling for changes in income, concentrations of both pollutants showed statistically significant downward trends of 5 percent and 2 percent per year, respectively. This is qualitatively consistent with G&K's results.

S&B also analyzed two indicators of ambient river water quality: concentration of dissolved oxygen and fecal coliform count.[9] Neither followed an environmental Kuznets curve. The former worsened continually as per capita GDP rose. S&B speculated that this might be because the consequences of oxygen depletion are not felt in the areas that discharge oxygen-depleting pollutants, thus diminishing the pressure for a policy response. For example, oxygen depletion may be of little concern to urban dwellers who do not swim or fish in rivers that pass through the cities they live in. The estimated relationship for fecal coliform had an inverted U shape for incomes up to US$11,400, with a turning point of just US$1,375. For incomes above US$11,400, however, the relationship turned upward. S&B doubted that the upward turn was a statistical artifact.

S&B emphasized that their Kuznets-style results do not imply that countries will automatically "grow out of" environmental problems. They argued that rising per capita GDP is a proxy for various changes that tend to be associated with economic growth. They noted that these changes include stronger environmental policies and increased expenditure on pollution abatement and environmental clean up.

Pollution emissions[10]

Selden and Song (1994; S&S) analyzed air pollution emissions instead of ambient air quality, arguing that the former provide a more accurate measure of air pollution at the national level. Ambient air quality can vary greatly within a country, yet data on it tend to be collected from monitoring stations located disproportionately in urban areas. Emissions data, on the other hand, usually reflect all major pollution sources in a country, regardless of location.[11]

S&S (p. 148) cited four reasons to expect turning points for national air-pollution emissions to be higher than turning points for ambient air quality in urban areas:

(i) urban air quality is of the most immediate importance from a public health perspective (justifiably increasing the attention it receives from policy makers); (ii) improvements in urban air quality can be achieved at relatively low cost compared to reductions in aggregate emissions (for instance, requiring taller smokestacks would reduce urban pollution at relatively low cost, but would not reduce aggregate emissions); (iii) rising land rents tend to cause industry to move out of urban areas as economies develop; and (iv) urban residents have incomes that are high relative to the national average (so that they may have disproportionate political clout).

They tested this hypothesis by: 1) regressing per capita emissions on per capita GDP, measured in purchasing power parity terms and raised to the first, second, and third powers (as in G&K), national population density, and dummy variables for period of time; and 2) comparing the estimated turning points, if there were any, to those in G&K.

S&S analyzed two of the same pollutants as G&K and S&B, SO_2 and TSP, and also NO_x and carbon monoxide (CO). Carbon monoxide results from the incomplete combustion of fossil fuels, especially by motor vehicles. It interferes with the uptake of oxygen by red blood cells and can cause severe illness, even death. S&S's data were three-year means for 1973 to 1975, 1979 to 1981, and 1982 to 1984. The number of countries ranged from fifteen to thirty, depending on the pollutant and the time period.

S&S found statistically significant relationships between per capita emissions and per capita GDP for all pollutants except CO, and the relationships all had inverted U shapes.[12] As hypothesized, the turning point for SO_2 was higher than in G&K and S&B, and the turning point for TSP was higher than in S&B. All the turning points were in the vicinity of US$10,000, with the turning point for NO_x being the highest. This figure is comparable to the dividing line between upper-middle-income and high-income countries in 1988, approximately US$9,400 (in purchasing power parity terms; see Summers and Heston 1991 and World Bank 1992).[13] Population density was not significant at the 5 percent level for any of the pollutants. For SO_2 only, emissions were lower from 1982 to 1984 than in the two earlier periods after taking into account changes in incomes. This is consistent with G&K's and S&B's results for this pollutant.

S&S's findings lend support to G&K's and S&B's conclusion that economic growth and environmental improvement can coincide in the long run. They also indicate, however, that this coincidence has historically occurred at the national level only after countries have attained income levels typical of developed countries. But this does not mean that the turning points cannot be reduced. The first and fourth reasons cited by S&S for expecting turning points to be lower in urban areas were policy related. This suggests that policies that have helped reduce air pollution in urban areas could potentially be applied nationally at an earlier stage than has historically been the case.

The fourth study is by Panayotou (1993, 1995). Like S&S, he analyzed per capita emissions of SO_2, TSP, and NO_x. The sample was a cross-section of 55 developed and developing countries. Data were drawn from the OECD *State of the Environment* and other sources, as well as estimates constructed from data on consumption of fossil fuels. He investigated the pollution/development relationship by regressing the natural logarithm of per capita emissions on per capita GDP and per capita GDP squared (also in log form). Like S&S, he found that emissions of all three followed an environmental Kuznets curve. The estimated turning points were considerably lower, however, at US$3,000, US$4,500, and US$5,500, respectively. One explanation may be the fact that Panayotou used ordinary GDP, not purchasing power parity estimates. For this reason, the estimates are not comparable.

The Pollution/Development Relationship in Malaysia

Predictions based on cross-country studies

Malaysia's per capita GDP in purchasing power parity terms (1985 price levels) was US$4,727 in 1988 (Summers and Heston 1991) and US$7,110 in 1992 (according to International Monetary Fund estimates quoted by Jasin 1993). These values can be compared to those in Table 8.1 to predict which side of the turning points the country should be on for the various environmental indicators.

Consider indicators of air quality first. By 1988, Malaysia's per capita GDP had already passed the turning points estimated by S&B for ambient concentrations of SO_2 and TSP in urban areas, and it was nearing the turning point for ambient SO_2 estimated by G&K. By 1992, it had passed the latter turning point. Urban air quality as measured by the concentrations of these pollutants should therefore have been improving, if Malaysia was following the environmental Kuznets curves estimated by the studies. On the other hand, S&S's results predict that per capita country-level emissions of SO_2, TSP, and NO_x were still rising in 1992.

Of course, the country's future economic growth rate will determine how quickly it reaches S&S's turning points. At the inaugural meeting of the Malaysian Business Council on February 28, 1991, Prime Minister Mahathir proclaimed the objective of Malaysia becoming a "fully developed country" by the year 2020 (Mahathir 1991). Even if Malaysia indeed attains the income level of US$9,400 cited above by 2020, S&S's results predict that per capita emissions of SO_2, TSP, and NO_x will still be rising.

Turning to indicators of water quality, by 1988 Malaysia's per capita GDP had already passed the turning point estimated by S&B for fecal coliform count. Dissolved oxygen concentrations should still have been declining, however, and should continue to decline beyond 2020, as S&B found no evidence of a turning point.

The studies therefore predict that rising per capita GDP in Malaysia in the late 1980s and early 1990s should have had varying impacts on environmental quality. Ambient air quality in urban areas should have been improving, while per capita air-pollution emissions at the national level should have been worsening. Some indicators of water quality should have been improving, while others should have been deteriorating. The accuracy of these predictions depends on how closely the relationships between pollution and income in Malaysia correspond to the "average" ones estimated by the studies. The following sections test the predictions by analyzing Malaysian data on air and water pollution. Details of the statistical methods and results are presented in Appendix 8.

Air pollution

Data on air-pollution emissions are more limited in Malaysia than data on ambient air quality. Since 1987, the Department of Environment (DOE) has estimated annual emissions of five pollutants: particulates, sulfur oxides (SO_x), nitrogen oxides, carbon monoxide, and hydrocarbons (DOE 1992).[14] It derives the estimates by multiplying data on the level of polluting activities (e.g., fossil fuel consumption) by factors that predict the quantity of emissions per unit of the activity. Table 8.2 shows the DOE's estimates by major source categories. Although total emissions fluctuated substantially from 1987 to 1991, they tended to be higher at the end of the period than at the beginning, except in the case of SO_x. The sharp drop in emissions of SO_x was due to reduced emissions by power plants (Table 8.2), which switched from fuel oil to natural gas as domestic production of natural gas rose. This is an example of the sort of technological change that can cause relationships based on historical data to exaggerate the impact of economic growth on pollution emissions.

Evidence for this and other pollutants indicates that the country's rapid growth during the late 1980s did not raise pollution emissions as much as the relationships estimated by S&S predict. We calibrated their relationships to predict per capita Malaysian emissions in 1987 perfectly, given the country's per capita GDP in that year. Then, we predicted per capita emissions in 1991 by inserting 1991 per capita GDP into the calibrated relationships. Table 8.3 shows the results. Actual per capita emissions rose between 1987 and 1991 for all pollutants except SO_x,[15] although the rises were small for NO_x and CO. In all cases, however, actual per capita emissions in 1991 were much smaller than the predicted values. Per capita emissions of air pollutants increased less rapidly in Malaysia than predicted for a country at its income level.

The data series on emissions were so short that we did not attempt to relate them to per capita GDP. The second category of data, which pertains to ambient air quality, covered a longer period and enabled us to conduct that type of analysis. Ambient air-quality data are most comprehensive for TSP.[16] The Malaysian Meteorological Service (MMS) began collecting data on TSP in 1977 from two monitoring stations, in Petaling Jaya and Tanah Rata (in the Cameron Highlands). By 1991, it had established an additional thirteen stations.[17] The DOE established its own system of TSP monitoring stations in 1985, with stations in Georgetown, Kuala Terengganu, and two in Kuala Lumpur. By 1991, it had established thirty two additional ones and closed the original Georgetown station.[18]

We obtained data on mean annual readings for all stations except five of the DOE stations.[19] The first question we asked was whether the data

Table 8.2   *Principal sources of air pollution emissions (thousands of metric tonnes)*

			Source			
			Stationary			
Pollutant	Year	Mobile	Power plants	Other[a]	Open burning	Total
Particulates	1987	3	1	10	6	21
	1988	3	2	33	4	43
	1989	4	2	23	7	36
	1990	5	3	26	14	48
	1991	4	3	24	32	62
SO_x	1987	3	195	54	0	252
	1988	3	182	63	0	248
	1989	3	30	34	0	68
	1990	3	31	42	0	77
	1991	4	32	37	2	75
NO_x	1987	36	42	26	1	105
	1988	36	37	24	2	98
	1989	29	38	24	1	92
	1990	43	40	29	1	114
	1991	47	38	29	4	119
CO	1987	506	0	5	30	541
	1988	476	0	3	22	501
	1989	511	2	2	7	522
	1990	551	3	8	12	575
	1991	596	1	6	33	636
HC	1987	24	2	6	17	48
	1988	24	2	2	16	44
	1989	26	0	2	3	31
	1990	28	1	2	6	37
	1991	30	3	6	30	69

Source: DOE (1992).
[a] Industrial fuel, industrial processes, households. No data on industrial processes in 1987.

showed any overall trend over time: Did TSP concentrations rise, fall, or remain constant? We approached this question in two ways. First, we calculated the annual mean reading across a subsample of monitoring stations consisting of the twenty-one stations for which data were available in at least five consecutive years.[20] We limited the subsample to those stations to reduce the potential bias associated with new monitoring stations being located in areas that were, on average, either more or less polluted than the areas with existing stations. Table 8.4 shows the results. The mean reading was substantially higher from 1983 to 1991 than from 1977 to 1982, and it rose sharply at the end of the period. In fact, in 1991 it exceeded the 90 µg/m³ recommended standard. The table also shows the number of stations whose annual mean exceeded the recommended standard. In most years,

Table 8.3 *Actual and predicted per capita air pollution emissions (in kilograms)*

Pollutant	Actual[a]		Predicted[b]
	1987	1991	1991
Particulates	1.3	3.4	10.5
SO_x	15.3	4.1	29.5
NO_x	6.4	6.5	12.1
CO	32.8	34.9	39.6

[a] Calculated by dividing estimates of total emissions in DOE (1992) by national population.
[b] Calculated by inserting estimates of Malaysian per capita GDP into relationships estimated by Selden and Song (1994).

the annual mean violated the standard at 25 to 50 percent of the stations. The percentage rose fairly steadily from 1980 to 1991.

The data in Table 8.4 suggest that particulate pollution worsened after the early 1980s, but they are not entirely free of potential biases. Thirteen of the twenty-one stations in the sample were established after 1984, and nine of those were located in industrial, commercial, or traffic areas. This was a higher proportion than for the eight stations established earlier. In light of this, we also statistically estimated trends in the annual mean readings for each of the twenty-one stations by regressing the natural logarithms of the readings on a time trend (year) and an intercept. This approach gave

Table 8.4 *Annual mean TSP concentration across monitoring stations with at least five consecutive years of readings*

Year	Number of stations	Mean ($\mu g/m^3$)	Number of stations violating standard	Percentage of violations
1977	2	62.3	1	50
1978	3	59.5	1	33
1979	3	57.1	1	33
1980	5	46.5	0	0
1981	7	47.7	0	0
1982	7	45.6	1	14
1983	8	69.7	2	25
1984	8	53.9	2	25
1985	11	70.6	3	27
1986	18	80.5	5	28
1987	20	71.4	5	25
1988	21	63.7	5	24
1989	21	67.6	7	33
1990	21	78.9	9	43
1991	18	93.4	9	50

the average annual percentage change in the readings. We found that the readings showed no statistically significant trend at almost all of the stations, eighteen.[21] Taken at face value, this suggests that the increase in the annual mean concentration across the twenty-one stations was primarily due to the siting of new stations in more polluted areas, not to actual increases in ambient concentrations. This inference is probably not correct, however. The estimated trends were positive for most stations and substantially larger than zero in many instances. Their statistical insignificance probably simply reflected the few degrees of freedom in many regressions. Of the three stations with statistically significant trends, two had positive trends and one was negative. The fact that the percentage of stations violating the standard rose from 1986 to 1991 (Table 8.4), when the overall number of stations did not change significantly, offers additional evidence that concentrations actually increased.

The next step was to estimate the relationship between TSP concentration and income. We hypothesized that TSP concentration was related to an intercept that varied across monitoring stations and a common term given by the product of population density and per capita pollution impact. We measured population density by the value in the administrative district where a monitoring station was located. We defined per capita pollution impact as a function of per capita GDP in the state where the station was located and a time trend (i.e., year).[22] The time trend was a proxy for changes over time due to factors other than income. We estimated three versions of the model: in the first, per capita GDP was raised to the first power (the linear model); in the second, it was raised up to the second power (the quadratic model); and in the third, it was raised up to the third power (the cubic model). Given that the monitoring stations were located in a more diverse set of locations (i.e., rural as well as urban areas) than in the cross-country data set analyzed by S&B, we expected that the turning point, if any, would be higher than S&B's estimate.

The cubic model had the best statistical properties. All coefficients in it were statistically significant at the 5 percent level. Figure 8.1 shows the relationship between TSP concentration and per capita GDP according to this model, with population density and year set equal to their mean values in the sample.[23] The curve has neither the continually declining form estimated by G&K nor the inverted U shape estimated by S&B. It rises continually, although its slope does diminish up to an inflection point at RM6,300. Thereafter, however, it gets steeper. If there is a turning point for TSP concentration in Malaysia, it appears to be at a much higher level than S&B's study predicts. The turning point estimated by that study, US$3,280 at 1985 international prices, is equivalent to only RM2,689 at 1978 Malaysian prices.[24] This is below even the inflection point in Figure 8.1.

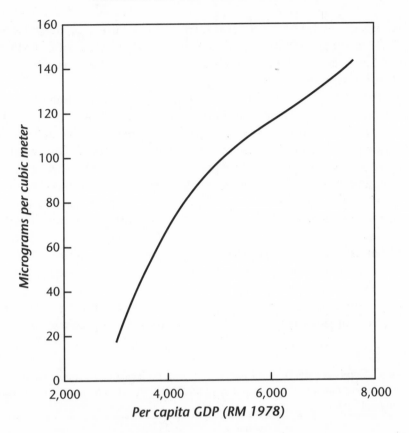

Figure 8.1   Estimated TSP relationship

Although the curve depicted in Figure 8.1 is the opposite of what G&K found in a cross-country context, it is plausible in the Malaysian context. Agriculture tends to be a more important sector of the Malaysian economy in lower-income states. In these states, open burning during land conversion and replanting of tree crops has historically been a major source of particulate pollution.[25] In higher-income states, industrial processing and the burning of industrial and municipal wastes are more important. The curve perhaps shows that the rate of increase in TSP concentration temporarily diminishes as agricultural expansion slows down, but it then accelerates as emissions related to manufacturing and waste disposal rise.

The curve is consistent with the increase in per capita emissions in Table 8.3, as emissions are the prime determinant of ambient concentrations.[26] It is also consistent with S&S's estimated turning point for per capita emissions, US$9,811 at 1985 international prices, which equals approximately RM8,042 at 1978 Malaysian price levels, and is greater than any of the per capita GDP values in the sample.

The impacts of per capita GDP and other explanatory variables on TSP concentrations at the average monitoring station are shown in Table 8.5. The impacts are presented in elasticity form: the percentage change in TSP concentration per 1 percent increase in per capita GDP or population density or one-year passage of time. The impact of per capita GDP was of course positive, and it was more than proportionate: economic growth not only worsened particulate pollution, it worsened it by nearly a factor of two. An increase in population density also raised TSP concentration, though less than proportionately.

In contrast, the simple passage of time decreased the concentration substantially and partially offset the impacts of increases in the other two variables. This result is qualitatively consistent with, although larger than, the negative residual trends detected by G&K and S&B. It is also consistent with per capita emissions of particulates being lower than predicted by S&S's

Table 8.5 *Estimated impacts of a 1 percent change in per capita GDP, population density, and residual trend on air and water quality at the average monitoring station in Malaysia (percentages)*

	Per capita GDP[a]	Population density[b]	Residual trend[c]
I. Air quality (1977–1991)			
Ambient TSP	+1.87	+0.47	−9.14
II. Water quality (1978–1991)[d]			
Ambient BOD[e]	0	+0.25	−3.97
Ambient COD[f]	0	0	0
Ambient ammoniacal nitrogen	+1.10	+0.17	−2.49
Ambient suspended solids	Turning point at RM5,764 (1978 price levels)	-97.05	−5.11
Ambient pH	+0.04	−0.004	0

Note: A positive value indicates that an increase in the variable causes the level of the environmental indicator to rise. This indicates deteriorating environmental quality in all cases except possibly pH. A negative value indicates the opposite relationship.

[a] At the state level (RM, 1978 price levels).

[b] Number of people per hectare. For air quality, at the district level; for water quality, at the state level.

[c] The impact pertains to the passage of one year.

[d] Based on data for Peninsular Malaysia only.

[e] BOD—biochemical oxygen demand.

[f] COD—chemical oxygen demand.

relationship (Table 8.3). The explanation is not clear, but it could relate to increasingly effective enforcement of air-pollution regulations by the DOE. Relevant regulations include the 1977 Motor Vehicle (Control of Smoke and Gas Emissions) Rules, which contained provisions related to black smoke emissions from diesel-powered vehicles, and the 1978 Environmental Quality (Clean Air) Regulations, which contained provisions related to the open burning of rubbish and the emission of dark smoke from industrial premises.

Water quality

The DOE established its first water-quality monitoring stations in 1978, almost a decade before it began monitoring air quality.[27] By 1991, it had expanded the system to include 555 monitoring stations on 87 major rivers throughout the country. At each station, it measured the levels of as many as 52 water-quality parameters (DOE 1992, Appendix 4.7).[28] As mentioned in Chapter 1, it was most concerned about five parameters: biochemical oxygen demand (BOD), chemical oxygen demand (COD), ammoniacal nitrogen (NH_3N), suspended solids, and pH. BOD, COD, ammoniacal nitrogen, and suspended solids are all measured in milligrams per liter, which is equivalent to parts per million (ppm), while pH is a logarithmic index that ranges from 0 (acidic) to 14 (alkaline).

We obtained data on mean annual levels of the five parameters in all forty seven major river basins in Peninsular Malaysia from 1978 to 1991.[29] As in the case of TSP, the first question we asked was whether the parameters exhibited any trends over time. For most river basins, the readings covered all or nearly all of the period.[30] Hence, the annual mean reading across the river basins is less likely to be biased than in the case of the overall mean reading for TSP. Figure 8.2 shows the Peninsula-wide annual means, expressed in index form to allow easier comparisons across pollutants. Two exhibited no apparent trends: ammoniacal nitrogen and pH. Two more, BOD and suspended solids, declined during the first half of the period and were more or less stable thereafter. Only COD worsened, and then only in the second half after improving in the first half. Overall, the indices suggest that some improvements in water quality occurred, but only during the first half of the period.

Of course, aggregate values can disguise important differences within the country. We therefore also examined readings for individual river basins. Figure 8.3 shows the percentage of river basins whose annual mean parameter values violated the proposed interim national water quality standards for class IIA and class IIB rivers (see Table 1.6). Rivers violating these standards were too polluted to serve as a source of drinking water via conventional treatment

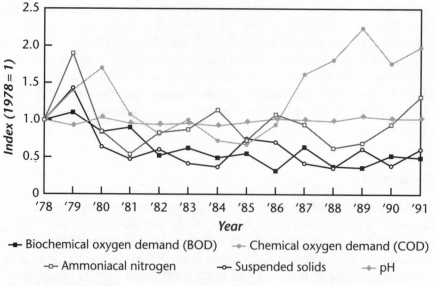

Figure 8.2   Annual means, water quality parameters

methods, too polluted to support sensitive aquatic species, and too polluted to permit body contact during recreational use (DOE 1992, Appendix 4.10). These standards provide an appropriate reference point, as violations of them indicate a level of pollution with potentially significant economic consequences. For all parameters except BOD, the mean annual readings violated the standards in at least half of the river basins in most years. The annual violation rate was generally between 20 and 30 percent of river basins for BOD, compared to 30 to 60 percent for ammoniacal nitrogen, 50 to 75 percent for COD and suspended solids, and 40 to 80 percent for pH. The violations for pH were overwhelmingly due to excess acidity. By all measures, but especially COD, ammoniacal nitrogen, suspended solids, and pH, many rivers in the Peninsula were polluted to a degree likely to have significant economic consequences.

We also statistically estimated the trends in readings for individual river basins. As in the case of TSP, we regressed the natural logarithms of the readings on a time trend (year) and an intercept. Table 8.6 summarizes the results. Water quality was unchanged in most rivers according to all parameters, which is broadly consistent with the aggregate trends in Figure 8.2. Improvements outnumbered declines in water quality for BOD and, especially, suspended solids, but not for COD. These results are broadly consistent

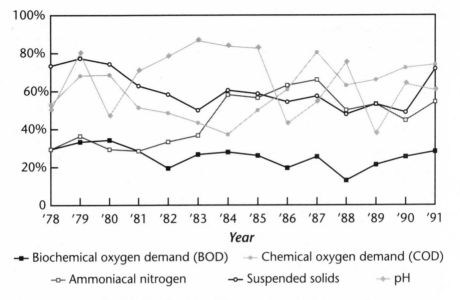

Figure 8.3   River basins violating Class IIA/IIB water quality standards

with changes over time in the percentage of river basins violating class IIA/IIB standards (Figure 8.3). The greatest deterioration was for ammoniacal nitrogen: statistically significant positive trends occurred in more than double the number of rivers with statistically significant negative trends. This too is consistent with the trends in violation percentages. Nitrogenous wastes tend to be alkaline when dissolved in water, so it is not surprising that the results for pH show no rivers becoming acidic and several becoming more alkaline.

To analyze the role of socioeconomic factors in causing these trends, we estimated relationships analogous to those for TSP.[31] Table 8.5 shows the estimated impacts.[32] Per capita GDP had a statistically significant impact on ammoniacal nitrogen, suspended solids, and pH, but not on BOD or COD. For both ammoniacal nitrogen and pH, higher income was associated with higher levels of the parameters (less acidity in the case of pH). Urbanization and industrial expansion associated with the country's income growth probably explain the impact on ammoniacal nitrogen, as municipal and industrial sewage capacity did not keep pace.[33] As noted above, increased discharge of nitrogenous wastes due to these reasons could explain the impact on pH. Only for suspended solids was there evidence of an environmental Kuznets curve. The turning point, RM5,700, was comparable to the per capita GDP of more indus-

Table 8.6   *Trends in annual mean values of water-quality parameters, by river basin*
(Peninsular Malaysia only)

Parameter	Number of rivers with positive trends	Number of rivers with negative trends	Number of rivers with no trend
BOD[a]	4	6	37
COD[b]	7	5	35
Ammoniacal N[c]	12	5	30
Suspended solids	0	6	41
pH	9	0	38

Note: Trends were analyzed by regressing the natural logarithm of each water-quality parameter in a given river basin on a constant and the year of the reading. A 5 percent significance level was used in testing whether the coefficient on the year variable was statistically different from zero.
[a] BOD—biochemical oxygen demand.
[b] COD—chemical oxygen demand.
[c] N—nitrogen.

trialized states in 1991. These are states where less land clearing for agriculture, and thus less erosion, was occurring.

Population density had a significant impact on BOD, ammoniacal nitrogen, pH, and suspended solids, with higher population densities being associated with worse water quality as measured by BOD and ammoniacal nitrogen, better quality as measured by suspended solids, and less acidic water as measured by pH. The impacts on ammoniacal nitrogen and pH probably again reflect sewage discharge, which rises with population. This probably also explains the impact on BOD. The lack of an impact on COD is not surprising, as COD is related more to industrial effluent than to domestic sewage. The impact on suspended solids might reflect population density acting as a proxy for urbanization: with urbanization, large-scale land clearing for agriculture declines. The magnitude of the impact given in Table 8.5, however, is not plausible.

The residual trends were significant and negative for BOD, ammoniacal nitrogen, and suspended solids. Had per capita GDP and population density remained constant, water quality as measured by these parameters would have improved. Policy-related factors are probably the explanation, at least for the first two parameters. In 1978, right at the start of the period analyzed, the DOE introduced regulations to reduce BOD discharge by crude palm-oil mills, the major source of BOD pollution at that time. As discussed in detail in Chapter 10, the regulations have been spectacularly successful. Regarding ammoniacal nitrogen, despite shortcomings in the country's sewerage system, the percentage of the population without access to any sanitary facility dropped from 10.2 to 6.3 percent during the Fifth Malaysia Plan (*Sixth Malaysia Plan 1991–1995*, p. 335).

S&B did not analyze any of these five parameters, but they did analyze dissolved oxygen concentration, which they found declined continually with income (Table 8.1). This would correspond to a positive impact of income on BOD. The fact that our analysis found no such impact suggests that the BOD/development relationship in Malaysia was fundamentally different than in the average country. This is probably due to the dominance of palm-oil mills as a BOD source, at least before the Crude Palm-Oil regulations were fully implemented.

CONCLUSIONS

Cross-country studies have identified statistically significant descriptive relationships between pollution and per capita GDP. In several cases, these relationships have an inverted U shape, suggesting that pollution in many developing countries will get worse before it gets better. The studies emphasize, however, that the relationships are not solely a consequence of changes in the scale and composition of economic activity or the level of technology. Improved environmental policies and enforcement efforts, in response to rising public demand for better environmental quality, are crucial. Improvements in environmental quality are attainable at lower income levels than the studies indicate if governments make the right policy moves.

Malaysian monitoring data were available for several of the pollutants included in the cross-country studies, providing an opportunity to test the studies' predictions. Per capita emissions of four air pollutants, TSP, SO_x, NO_x, and CO, did not rise as rapidly as predicted. In fact, in the case of SO_x they fell, and for NO_x and CO they scarcely rose. Only for TSP was there a fairly steady increase. This is consistent with the country being below the predicted turning point for emissions of this pollutant. Contradicting the environmental Kuznets curve hypothesis, however, ambient TSP concentrations rose continually with per capita GDP. This effect, along with the increasing effect of population density, offset the effect of a negative residual trend.

The negative residual trend for TSP might reflect increasingly effective policies to control air pollution. Even if it does, it is unlikely to be strong enough to prevent ongoing deterioration in ambient air quality. At rates of growth in population and per capita GDP forecast by *The Second Outline Perspective Plan*, the elasticities in Table 8.5 imply that the average TSP concentration will rise by about three-quarters of a percentage point per year from 1991 to 2000.[34] In the absence of a stronger policy response, Malaysia's air will be substantially more polluted by particulates in coming years than it was in 1991. Ambient TSP concentrations in that year already violated the recommended Malaysian standard at half of the monitoring stations. Worse, the violation rate had been rising since the early 1980s.

There is less overlap between Malaysian data and cross-country studies in the case of ambient water quality. Moreover, the results of analyses of the Malaysian data varied considerably across pollution parameters, with evidence of an environmental Kuznets curve only for suspended solids. The risk of future deterioration in water quality seems greatest for ammoniacal nitrogen, whose level rose with both per capita GDP and population density. For BOD, as well as for ammoniacal nitrogen and suspended solids, negative residual trends might indicate more effective environmental protection efforts. Despite the negative residual trends, and the Kuznets relationship for suspended solids, a substantial proportion of rivers—more than half in most years for COD, ammoniacal nitrogen, suspended solids, and pH—were polluted throughout the period at levels likely to have significant economic impacts.

Two differences between the predictions of cross-country studies and the actual empirical relationship between pollution and development in Malaysia are most interesting from a policy standpoint: first, the fact that ambient TSP concentrations did not stabilize and decline in the way predicted by the studies, and second, the fact that ambient BOD concentrations did not rise with income as expected. The former raises the issue of the economic impacts of high concentrations of TSP, while the latter raises the issue of the country's policies to control BOD pollution. The next two chapters examine these two issues in depth.

APPENDIX 8: ANALYSIS OF AMBIENT ENVIRONMENTAL QUALITY AND DEVELOPMENT

We analyzed the relationship between environmental quality and socioeconomic factors by estimating the following model:

$$Q_{it} = \alpha_i + P_{it} \times (\beta_P + \beta_Y Y_{it} + \beta_{YY} Y_{it}^2 + \beta_{YYY} Y_{it}^3 + \beta_t t).$$

Y is per capita GDP, and P is population density. For Y, i indicates the state where the monitoring station was located; for P, i indicates administrative district in the case of TSP and state in the case of water-quality parameters. The model assumes that environmental quality is determined by the product of population density and per capita environmental impact (the term in parentheses), which itself is a function of per capita GDP and year.

The model can be rewritten as:

$$Q_{it} = \alpha_i + \beta_P P_{it} + \beta_Y P_{it} Y_{it} + \beta_{YY} P_{it} Y_{it}^2 + \beta_{YYY} P_{it} Y_{it}^3 + \beta_t P_{it} t.$$

We estimated two versions of this equation. The fixed-effects version treated differences in the intercepts (the α_is) as due to deterministic factors, while the random-effects version treated the differences as due to stochastic factors. See Judge et al. (1985) for a discussion of differences between the two versions. We determined the preferred version by testing the null hypothesis that the

Table A8.1 *Regression results for TSP: fixed effects*

		Cubic	Quadratic	Linear
I.	Coefficient estimates[a]			
	Intercept[b]			
	Population density	+1609	+1398	+682
		(462)***	(0.0359)***	(388)*
	Population density × Per capita GDP	+0.0248	+0.00674	+0.00171
		(0.00824)***	(0.00182)***	(0.000376)***
	Population density × Per capita GDP^2	-0.365×10^{-5}	-0.352×10^{-6}	
		(0.147×10^{-5})**	(0.125×10^{-6})***	
	Population density × Per capita GDP^3	$+0.194 \times 10^{-9}$		
		(0.864×10^{-10})**		
	Population density × Year	-0.835	-0.715	-0.349
		(0.234)***	(0.230)***	(0.194)*
II.	R^2	0.176	0.153	0.116
III.	Number of observations	232	232	232

[a] Standard errors are in parentheses under the coefficient estimates. *** means that estimate is significantly different from zero at the 1 percent level; ** means that estimate is significantly different from zero at the 5 percent level; * means that estimate is significantly different from zero at the 10 percent level.

Table A8.2   *Regression results for BOD (biochemical oxygen demand): random effects.*

	Cubic	Quadratic	Linear
I. Coefficient estimates[a]			
Intercept	+2.11	+2.59	+2.74
	$(0.981)^{**}$	$(0.933)^{***}$	$(0.914)^{***}$
Population density	+164	+152	+162
	$(61.0)^{***}$	$(60.6)^{**}$	$(59.2)^{***}$
Population density × Per capita GDP	−0.00551	−0.000356	+0.000169
	(0.00343)	(0.000759)	(0.000172)
Population density × Per capita GDP^2	$+0.109 \times 10^{-5}$	$+0.501 \times 10^{-7}$	
	(0.678×10^{-6})	(0.709×10^{-7})	
Population density × Per capita GDP^3	-0.668×10^{-10}		
	(0.434×10^{-10})		
Population density × Year	−0.0779	−0.0760	−0.0814
	$(0.0309)^{**}$	$(0.0310)^{**}$	$(0.0301)^{***}$
II. R^2		0.024	0.0190.018
III. Number of observations	542	542	542

  [a] Standard errors are in parentheses under the coefficient estimates. *** means that estimate is significantly different from zero at the 1 percent level; ** means that estimate is significantly different from zero at the 5 percent level; * means that estimate is significantly different from zero at the 10 percent level.

Table A8.3   *Regression results for COD (chemical oxygen demand): random effects*

	Cubic	Quadratic	Linear
I. Coefficient estimates[a]			
Intercept	+65.1	+64.5	+69.8
	$(14.9)^{***}$	$(13.9)^{***}$	$(13.3)^{***}$
Population density	+114	+136	+365
	(1101)	(1085)	(1070)
Population density × Per capita GDP	−0.00927	−0.0163	+0.00105
	(0.0603)	(0.0139)	(0.00293)
Population density × Per capita GDP^2	$+0.262 \times 10^{-6}$	$+0.169 \times 10^{-5}$	
	(0.121×10^{-4})	(0.132×10^{-5})	
Population density × Per capita GDP^3	$+0.925 \times 10^{-10}$		
	(0.778×10^{-9})		
Population density × Year	−0.0451	−0.0503	−0.187
	(0.555)	(0.554)	(0.543)
II. R^2		0.005	0.0050.002
III. Number of observations	541	541	541

  [a] Standard errors are in parentheses under the coefficient estimates. *** means that estimate is significantly different from zero at the 1 percent level; ** means that estimate is significantly different from zero at the 5 percent level; * means that estimate is significantly different from zero at the 10 percent level.

Table A8.4   *Regression results for ammoniacal nitrogen: random effects*

	Cubic	Quadratic	Linear
I. Coefficient estimates[a]			
Intercept	+0.681	+0.620	+0.740
	(0.295)[**]	(0.282)[**]	(0.284)[***]
Population density	+17.7	+19.0	+27.3
	(16.9)	(16.8)	(16.4)[*]
Population density $\times$ Per capita GDP	+0.000380	−0.000264	+0.000161
	(0.000952)	(0.000208)	(0.484×10^{-4})[***]
Population density $\times$ Per capita GDP^2	-0.888×10^{-7}	$+0.404 \times 10^{-7}$	
	(0.187×10^{-6})	(0.193×10^{-7})[**]	
Population density $\times$ Per capita GDP^3	$+0.828 \times 10^{-11}$		
	(0.119×10^{-10})		
Population density $\times$ Year	−0.00916	−0.00930	−0.0140
	(0.00857)	(0.00857)	(0.00834)[*]
II. R^2	0.044	0.043	0.034
III. Number of observations	542	542	542

[a] Standard errors are in parentheses under the coefficient estimates. *** means that estimate is significantly different from zero at the 1 percent level; ** means that estimate is significantly different from zero at the 5 percent level; * means that estimate is significantly different from zero at the 10 percent level.

Table A8.5   *Regression results for suspended solids: random effects*

	Cubic	Quadratic	Linear
I. Coefficient estimates[a]			
Intercept	+146	+142	+126
	(27.2)[***]	(25.5)[***]	(24.2)[***]
Population density	+6325	+6472	+5821
	(2050)[***]	(2021)[***]	(1996)[*]
Population density $\times$ Per capita GDP	+0.105	+0.0594	+0.00592
	(0.112)	(0.0259)[**]	(0.00541)
Population density $\times$ Per capita GDP^2	-0.146×10^{-4}	-0.523×10^{-5}	
	(0.224×10^{-4})	(0.247×10^{-5})[**]	
Population density $\times$ Per capita GDP^3	$+0.610 \times 10^{-9}$		
	(0.145×10^{-8})		
Population density $\times$ Year	−3.30	−3.34	−2.94
	(1.03)[***]	(1.03)[***]	(1.01)[***]
II. R^2	0.025	0.024	0.017
III. Number of observations	541	541	541

[a] Standard errors are in parentheses under the coefficient estimates. *** means that estimate is significantly different from zero at the 1 percent level; ** means that estimate is significantly different from zero at the 5 percent level; * means that estimate is significantly different from zero at the 10 percent level.

Table A8.6   *Regression results for pH: random effects*

	Cubic	Quadratic	Linear
I. Coefficient estimates[a]			
Intercept	+6.20	+6.22	+6.23
	$(0.0735)^{***}$	$(0.0702)^{***}$	$(0.0673)^{***}$
Population density	+0.981	−0.401	−0.348
	(7.21)	(7.11)	(7.12)
Population density × Per capita GDP	−0.000269	-0.614×10^{-5}	$+0.318 \times 10^{-4}$
	(0.000327)	(0.754×10^{-4})	$(0.166 \times 10^{-4})^{*}$
Population density × Per capita GDP^2	$+0.573 \times 10^{-7}$	$+0.368 \times 10^{-8}$	
	(0.655×10^{-7})	$(0.707 \times 10^{-8})^{**}$	
Population density × Per capita GDP^3	-0.345×10^{-11}		
	(0.421×10^{-11})		
Population density × Year	−0.000311	+0.000178	+0.000103
	(0.00362)	(0.00361)	(0.00362)
II. R^2	0.192	0.191	0.190
III. Number of observations	443	443	443

[a] Standard errors are in parentheses under the coefficient estimates. *** means that estimate is significantly different from zero at the 1 percent level; ** means that estimate is significantly different from zero at the 5 percent level; * means that estimate is significantly different from zero at the 10 percent level.

random effects were uncorrelated with the explanatory variables (the Hausman test). The random-effects version was preferred unless the null hypothesis was rejected at a significance level of 5 percent.

We also estimated restricted forms of the equation that assumed that per capita environmental impact was just a quadratic or a linear function of per capita GDP ($\beta_{YYY} = 0$ or $\beta_{YYY} = \beta_{YY} = 0$, respectively). Tables A8.1 through A8.6 show the preferred results. The fixed-effects version was preferred for TSP, while the random-effects versions were preferred for the water-quality parameters. The results in Table 8.5 are for the cubic model in the case of TSP, the quadratic model in the case of suspended solids, and the linear model in all other cases.

NOTES

1 A fifth study, by Hettige et al. (1992), analyzed the relationship between per capita GDP and toxic intensity of manufacturing, as measured by total pounds of toxic pollutants discharged into the environment. They calculated the latter for a sample of eighty countries during 1960–88 by using U.N. data on output by industrial sector and U.S. data on pounds of toxic discharge per dollar of sectoral output. The estimated relationship had an inverted U shape.
2 G&K also analyzed dark matter (smoke), which is not monitored by air-quality stations in Malaysia.
3 The general form of the estimated equations was:

$$Q_{it} = \alpha_i + \beta_Y Y_{it} + \beta_{YY} Y_{it}^2 + \beta_{YYY} Y_{it}^3 + \beta_Z Z_{it},$$

where Q_{it} is air quality in urban area i at time t, Y_{it} is per capita GDP, Z_{it} is a vector of other explanatory variables, and α and β are parameters. Other explanatory variables, aside from population density, included trade intensity (sum of exports and imports divided by GDP), a linear time trend, and dummy variables for the country's government (communist or not), location of the urban area (on coast, near desert), location of monitoring station within the city (city center or suburban), land use near the station (industrial, commercial, or residential), and monitoring method (if it differed across stations for a given pollutant).

4 These are the results in column 3 of Tables 2 and 4 in G&K.

5 The curve turned upward at very high levels of income. G&K questioned the significance of the upturn, due to the small number of countries with very high income levels in the sample.

6 This finding was not very robust. When G&K changed the specification from random effects to fixed effects (see Table 5 in their paper), they obtained the opposite result: TSP levels rose continualy with income.

7 By 107.81 $\mu g/m^3$ for TSP and 12.64 $\mu g/m^3$ for SO_2.

8 Unlike G&K, S&B entered the income variables in logarithmic form.

9 The results discussed here are from Table 1 in S&B. As mentioned in Chapter 4, S&B also examined annual rates of deforestation.

10 Not discussed here is an analysis by S&B of per capita emissions of carbon (not carbon monoxide). The relationship with income was an environmental Kuznets curve, but the turning point was not reached until a per capita GDP level of US$7 million.

11 Emissions data also suffer shortcomings. In particular, they tend to be calculated by multiplying estimates of industrial output times engineering-based estimates of emissions factors, instead of being measured directly.

12 Statistical tests rejected the significance of per capita GDP cubed, so the relationships were purely inverted U shapes, unlike G&K's relationship for SO_2.

13 Two countries classified by the World Bank as high income, Ireland and Spain, had incomes below US$9,400 in 1988, and two classified as upper middle income, Oman and Saudi Arabia, had incomes above.

14 The report of the Klang Valley Environmental Improvement project, which was funded by the Asian Development Bank, contained partial estimates of emissions of these pollutants in the Klang Valley during 1985 (Government of Malaysia and Asian Development Bank 1987).

15 S&S state that their relationship is for SO_2, not SO_x. However, technical notes in their data source, World Resources Institute (1991), indicate that the data pertain to SO_2 for some countries and SO_x for others.

16 More limited data are collected by both the DOE and the Malaysian Meteorological Service (MMS) on dust fallout and its chemical composition (e.g., lead content). In addition, the MMS began collecting data on PM_{10} at some of its monitoring stations in the late 1980s. The DOE followed suit at a few of its stations in the early 1990s. It announced plans in the 1991 *Environmental Quality Report* to begin monitoring ambient concentrations of SO_2 and other gaseous pollutants. At the time of writing, the only monitoring of these pollutants was being conducted by Prof. Azman Zainal Abidin of Universiti Pertanian Malaysia. Some of his monitoring results were reported in DOE (1992).

17 Bayan Lepas (Pulau Pinang), Bukit Kledang (Perak), Senai (Johor), Kuching, Lawa Mandau (Sabah), Perai (Pulau Pinang), Bukit Tinnggi (Pahang), Tawau (Sabah), Bintulu (Sarawak), Melaka, Kuala Terengganu, Alor Setar, and Labuan.

18 Sg. Petani (Kedah); Seberang Prai, Bukit Mertajam, Butterworth, Kepela Batas, and George-town (Pulau Pinang); two stations in Ipoh; Petaling Jaya; Shah Alam; four in Kuala Lumpur; Port Dickson and Senawang (Negeri Sembilan); Melaka; Air Keroh (Melaka); four in Johor

Bahru; Pasir Gudang (Johor); four in Kuantan; Kuala Terengganu; two in Kemaman (Terengganu); two in Kuching; and Kota Kinabalu.

19 The three in East Malaysia, and one each in Ipoh and Johor Bahru. These stations were opened recently, so their omission did not cause much data to be excluded from the analysis. We also excluded data for the station in Labuan, which opened in 1991, because of the peculiar status of this island (geographically part of Sabah, but administered as a Federal Territory). We express our gratitude to the DOE and the MMS for providing the data.

20 Ten MMS stations (Petaling Jaya, Tanah Rata, Bayan Lepas, Bukit Kledang, Senai, Lawa Mandau, Kuching, Perai, Bukit Tinggi, and Tawau) and eleven DOE stations (Seberang Prai, Butterworth, Kepela Batas, Petaling Jaya, Shah Alam, four in Kuala Lumpur, one in Kuantan, and Kuala Terengganu).

21 A 5 percent significance level was employed.

22 With income raised to up to the third power, the model was given by:

$$Q_{it} = \alpha_i + P_{it} \times (\beta_P + \beta_Y Y_{it} + \beta_{YY} Y_{it}^2 + \beta_{YYY} Y_{it}^3 + \beta_t t),$$

where Q is concentration, i indicates monitoring station/administrative district/state, t indicates year, Y is per capita GDP, and P is population density. We estimated both fixed-effects and random effects versions of the model. See Appendix 8.

23 The relationship is plotted only up to the highest income in the sample, RM7,553 (for Kuala Lumpur/Selangor, in 1991).

24 For 1988, the ratio of Malaysia's per capita GDP in purchasing power parity terms (U.S. dollars at 1985 international prices) to its per capita GDP in ringgit (at 1978 Malaysian prices) was 1.22.

25 These sources are not included in the estimates for open burning in Table 8.2, which include only municipal and industrial burning.

26 The stock of TSP in the atmosphere changes from one period to the next due primarily to the difference between emissions and assimilation. The rate of assimilation is determined by meteorological factors and is relatively constant over time. The stock is also affected by pollution that drifts into the country from neighboring countries. In recent years, forest fires in Indonesia have been an important source of particulate pollution affecting the west coast of the Peninsula (see Chapter 9).

27 The earliest stations were on the Sungai Kedah, Merbok, Muda, Perai, Jejawi, Kerian, Selangor, Kelang, Linggi, Muar, Pahang, Kemaman, Paka, Dungun, Setiu, and Golok in Peninsular Malaysia.

28 The Drainage and Irrigation Department (DID) also has a system of monitoring stations on major rivers. Most of the stations monitor streamflow, but more than 50 in Peninsular Malaysia also monitor suspended sediment levels. The DID established its first suspended-sediment station in 1971 in Selangor, and several more in Pahang in 1974. We did not include the DID data series in the analysis because they were incomplete in many years.

29 We express our appreciation to the DOE for providing the data.

30 For example, for BOD, readings were available for 17 river basins in 1978, 21 in 1979, 30 to 35 (depending on the year) from 1980 to 1983, and 43 to 47 from 1984 to 1991. Coverage was comparable for other parameters, with the exception of pH in 1978 and 1979, when readings were available for only 2 and 5 river basins, respectively.

31 In contrast to the TSP analysis, population density was defined at the state level instead of the district level, because water pollution could be a consequence of activities in upstream districts. Most rivers in the Peninsula pass through more than one district but not more than one state.

32 The results are for the linear regressions (random effects) in the case of BOD, COD, ammoniacal nitrogen, and pH, and the quadratic regression (also random effects) in the case of suspended solids. These are the results that we regarded as best in terms of coefficient significance and goodness of fit. Full regression results are presented in Appendix 8.

33 The government announced a major project in 1992 to upgrade and expand the country's sewage system.

34 The *Plan* forecasts that per capita GDP will rise by 4.7 percent per year and population by 2.3 percent per year. Combining these rates with the elasticities in Table 8.4 yields:

$$1.87 \times 4.7 + 0.47 \times 2.3 - 9.14 = 0.73 \text{ percent per year.}$$

9

Air Pollution and Health

INTRODUCTION

The evidence of high ambient TSP concentrations rising with population and the economy does not, on its own, provide sufficient justification for more vigorous pollution abatement efforts. Pollution abatement is not free, and it is economically justified only if it generates benefits that are at least as great as its costs. Abatement costs are usually reasonably well understood, at least for individual pollution sources, as they typically involve direct expenditures on equipment and personnel. Benefits, on the other hand, almost always relate to nonmarket impacts spread over many individuals, many economic activities, and an extended period of time. Although they may be large in the aggregate, they might nevertheless be unrecognized.

A growing body of empirical evidence indicates that it can be a mistake to assume that the benefits of air pollution abatement are negligible. Reducing air pollution can provide benefits to many sectors of the economy and society: it can reduce maintenance expenditures for buildings and other structures if the pollutants are, like sulfur dioxide, corrosive; raise crop yields if the pollutants are, like ozone, physiologically damaging to plants; and provide a healthier and more productive work force if the pollutants increase the incidence of respiratory and cardiovascular diseases, as many, like particulates do (Tietenberg 1988, Table 15.1; World Resources Institute 1992, notes to Tables 24.5 and 24.6). Health-related benefits are often particularly large. The Los Angeles metropolitan area in the United States has been the subject of some of the best-known attempts to quantify such benefits in monetary terms. Krupnick and Portney (1991) estimated that an ambitious 1989 plan to reduce ambient concentrations of particulates and ozone to the U.S. government's national ambi-

---

Chang Yii Tan was a coauthor of this chapter.

ent air-quality standards would generate US$3 billion in health benefits related to reduced mortality and morbidity (nonfatal illnesses). This was more than US$600 per household in the metropolitan area. The aggregate benefit estimate rose to US$4 billion when the value of reductions in materials damage was included. A later study by Hall et al. (1992) raised the "best estimate" of health benefits to US$9.8 billion, with an upper bound of US$21.5 billion.[1]

Without some information on the magnitude of the benefits of pollution abatement, it is impossible to determine the level of abatement that provides the greatest net benefits to society. Figure 9.1 illustrates how an environmental agency can determine this level if it has information on both the costs and benefits of abatement. The horizontal axis shows the aggregate level of abatement, which rises from zero units (uncontrolled pollution discharge) to 100 units (no pollution discharge). The vertical axis shows the cost or benefit of abating an incremental unit of pollution. One would generally expect that the first unit of pollution can be abated through measures that are not very sophisticated and not very costly. As abatement rises, however, abating an additional unit becomes more and more expensive. The rising incremental costs of abatement are depicted by the upward-sloping marginal cost curve, MC.

The opposite relationship should hold for incremental benefits. For example, consider an air pollutant with multiple effects. At low concentrations (i.e., high levels of abatement), it might affect visibility but have insignificant

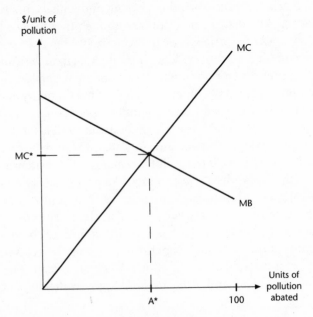

Figure 9.1   Determining the optimal abatement level

impacts on human health and physical structures. At medium concentrations, its impacts on visibility would intensify, and in addition its impacts on human health, mainly morbidity impacts, might become significant. At high concentrations, these two effects might intensify further, with mortality becoming a more important component of health impacts, and damage to physical structures might become significant as well. Under this pattern of cascading effects, a unit of pollution abatement generates greater benefits when the air is very dirty than when it is very clean. Such declining incremental benefits are depicted by the downward-sloping marginal benefit curve, *MB*.

The intersection of the two curves determines the optimal level of abatement, A^*. Up to this level, the benefits of each incremental unit of abatement exceed the costs. Although abatement might impose substantial costs on the polluting industry, up to A^* it provides benefits to society that are even greater. At A^*, marginal benefits and marginal costs are exactly equal. Pollution abatement beyond A^* is not justified because the marginal costs exceed the marginal benefits.

According to Krupnick and Portney (1991), the planned level of abatement in Los Angeles was probably to the right of this point. They estimated that the annual cost of the plan would be US\$13 billion, more than three times their aggregate benefits estimate. But Los Angeles, despite its severe pollution problem, is an area that has already taken various steps to reduce pollution. That the costs of additional action there are so high is perhaps not surprising. A more favorable ratio of benefits to costs would be expected in places that are earlier on in their pollution abatement efforts, so that marginal benefits are large relative to marginal costs. Developing countries and economies in transition often fall into this category. For example, a study by Cofala et al. (1991, cited in World Bank 1992, pp. 71–72) of particulate pollution in the Polish town of Tarnobrzeg found that the economic benefits related to reduced mortality, morbidity, and materials damage exceeded the costs of pollution abatement by up to 70 percent.

This chapter examines the benefits side of the ledger for air-pollution abatement in Malaysia. It focuses on one particular benefit: the value of lives saved by reducing ambient concentrations of TSP to the recommended Malaysian standard. TSP is the focus because studies conducted in other countries, including those by Krupnick and Portney (1991) and Hall et al. (1992) for Los Angeles, indicate that reducing exposure to elevated concentrations of particulates is often the source of the greatest benefits of air pollution abatement. The next section, *Valuing lives saved*, begins by summarizing epidemiological evidence on the link between ambient TSP concentrations and life expectancy. It then discusses how the benefits of reduced mortality can be quantified in monetary terms. *Development of air pollution policies* reviews the development of air pollution policies in Malaysia, paying particular attention to TSP and the extent to which information on its health impacts has shaped policies. Next, *Mortality-related benefits in urban areas in Malaysia in 1991* presents an application of the methods described in section *Valuing lives saved* to urban areas in Malaysia. In *Conclusions,* we compare the estimated benefits to available information on the costs of air pollution abatement.

VALUING LIVES SAVED

Valuing health benefits is relatively straightforward, at least conceptually. First, one needs to relate the reduction in pollution to some measure of improved health, for example lives saved. This requires a "dose-response" parameter for that measure. Second, one must value a unit change in the health measure. The aggregate value of health benefits is then just the product of the quantities calculated in those two steps. Below, we discuss these two steps in some detail for the case of TSP.

Estimating the number of lives saved

Estimating the number of lives saved by reducing ambient TSP concentrations to a target level involves three steps. First, the difference between existing TSP concentrations and the target level is multiplied by a dose-response parameter to calculate the relative impact on the mortality rate. The dose-response parameter gives the relative decrease in the crude mortality rate that occurs when the TSP concentration declines by one $\mu g/m^2$. For example, a parameter value of 0.0007 indicates that a one $\mu g/m^3$ reduction in the TSP concentration causes the crude mortality rate to decrease by 0.07 percent. If the difference between actual and target concentrations is, say, $30\mu g/m^3$, then achieving this reduction can be expected to reduce the crude mortality rate by 2.1 percent (30 $\mu g/m^3$ times 0.07 percent). Next, this relative impact is multiplied by the crude mortality rate to calculate the absolute reduction in the rate. To continue the example, if the crude mortality rate was 0.5 percent before the decline in TSP, it would be 0.0105 percentage points lower afterward (0.5 percent times 2.1 percent). Finally, this percentage is multiplied by the population exposed to arrive at the number of lives saved. If the population is 1 million, then the 30 $\mu g/m^3$ reduction saves 105 lives (1 million times 0.0105 percent).

Ideally, the calculations should use estimates of TSP concentrations at a disaggregated local level, age- and sex-specific mortality rates, and information on differences in exposure by age, sex, and daily habits. The study by Hall et al. (1992) provides an example of a study that went to great lengths to model exposure and its impacts carefully.

Numerous epidemiological studies conducted since the early 1970s have estimated dose-response parameters for particulates. Most have been conducted in the United States and, to a lesser extent, other developed countries. Freeman (1982a,b), Evans et al. (1984), and Ostro (1992a,b) have reviewed this substantial literature. Some of the studies have analyzed particulates as measured by TSP, while others have analyzed particular portions of the particulate spectrum defined by particle diameter (e.g., PM_{10}) or chemical composition (e.g., sulfates, SO_4^{2-}). With few exceptions, the studies have found that particulates have a statistically significant impact on mortality rates. That is, after controlling for other factors, mortality rates are lower in areas with lower ambient particulate concentrations. The life expectancies of children and elderly people with respiratory problems, and asthmatics of all ages, appear to be particularly sensitive to particulate concentrations.

All the studies covered in the reviews listed above have been conducted in the temperate zone, but they have covered a wide range of cities and towns. Despite the variation in the urban areas analyzed, and thus the inevitable variation in the characteristics of the particulates to which the populations were exposed, the studies have reported remarkably similar mortality impacts. Table 9.1 summarizes estimates from some of the better-known studies. The difference between the lowest and highest estimates, a factor of approximately five, is surprisingly small considering the different areas and time periods analyzed, the different methods used, and the different definitions of particulates employed.

The robustness of the estimated dose-response parameters has led to their being used to predict particulate-related mortality in areas where existing studies are not available, including the Czech Republic (Industrial Economics and Sullivan Environmental Consulting 1992), Mexico City (Margulis 1991), and Jakarta (Ostro 1992a). Parameter estimates drawn from the literature were also used in the two studies of Los Angeles (Krupnick and Portney 1991, Hall et al. 1992).

Waller and Swan (1992; see also Dockery and Schwartz 1992) have cautioned that applying dose-response parameters to an area other than the one where the original epidemiological study was conducted is inappropriate when the physical and chemical composition of the particulates differs substantially. For example, one of the few studies to examine differences in particulate composition found that particulates from industrial sources, such as steel mills and coal-fired power plants, had a greater impact on mortality than did airborne soil particles (Ozkaynak and Thurston 1987). Another

Table 9.1   *Dose-response parameters for TSP and mortality*

Study	Location	Parameter[a]
Schwartz & Marcus (1990, Table 2)	London	0.000172[b]
Schwartz & Marcus (1990, Table 3)	London	0.000188[b]
Ozkaynak & Thurston (1987, Table IV, row 4)	SMSAs[c] in U.S.	0.000353[d]
Evans et al. (1984, Table 11, row 1)	Review	0.000367[e]
Evans et al. (1984, Table 18)	SMSAs in U.S.	0.000376[e]
Schwartz & Dockery (1992b, Table 2)	Steubenville, U.S.	0.000381
Lave (1972, Table 6.2, row 5)	SMSAs in U.S.	0.000449[f]
Ostro (1992a, lower bound)	Review	0.000479
Evans et al. (1984, Table 11, row 2)	Review	0.000500[e]
Ozkaynak & Thurston (1987, Table IV, row 3)	SMSAs in U.S.	0.000506[g]
Lave & Seskin (1979, Table 3, column 6)	SMSAs in U.S.	0.000509[h]
Schwartz (1991, Table 3)	Detroit, U.S.	0.000546
Schwartz & Dockery (1992a)	Philadelphia, U.S.	0.000661
Ostro (1992a, central estimate)	Review	0.000682
Lave & Seskin (1979, Table 3, column 8)	SMSAs in U.S.	0.000792[h]
Dockery et al. (1992, Table 2, row 1)	St. Louis, U.S.	0.000825[i]
Ozkaynak & Thurston (1987, Table IV, row 2)	SMSAs in U.S.	0.000843[j]
Dockery et al. (1992, Table 2, row 1)	E. Tennessee, U.S.	0.000880[d,i]
Ostro (1992a, upper bound)	Review	0.000891

[a] Change in the crude mortality rate per 1 $\mu g/m^3$ increase in ambient TSP concentration.

[b] Study analyzed particulates measured by British Smoke, not TSP. Original estimate from study was converted by assuming that mean of daily deaths in London was 280 (from Figures 1 and 2), mean of British Smoke was 174 (calculated from Table 1), and conversion factor was 0.55 (Ostro 1992b).

[c] SMSAs—Standard Metropolitan Statistical Areas.

[d] Original estimate was not significantly different from zero at the 5 percent level.

[e] Calculated from original estimate by assuming a crude mortality rate of 0.9 percent.

[f] Calculated from original estimate by using the mean crude mortality rate in the sample, 0.913 percent.

[g] Study analyzed inhalable particles (diameter 15 microns), not TSP. Original estimate was converted by using the mean crude mortality rate in the sample, 0.8487 percent, and a conversion factor of 0.613 (based on data reported in study).

[h] Calculated from original estimate by assuming a crude mortality rate of 0.913 percent, from earlier study by Lave (1972).

[i] Study analyzed PM_{10} (diameter 10 microns), not TSP. Original estimate was converted by using a conversion factor of 0.55 (based on information in study).

[j] Study analyzed fine particles (diameter 2.5 microns), not TSP. Original estimate was converted by using the mean crude mortality rate in the sample, 0.8487 percent, and a conversion factor of 0.298 (based on data reported in study).

concern is related to the fact that the physiological mechanism linking exposure to particulates and mortality has not yet been determined. Until a convincing mechanism is identified, the epidemiological studies are open to the criticism that their demonstration of correlation does not prove that particulates are the actual cause of higher mortality rates.[2] If the underlying cause is something else, dose-response parameters defined in terms of TSP exposure might not provide reliable predictions outside the area studied.

In spite of these concerns, the accumulating epidemiological evidence has led some environmental scientists in the United States to conclude that mortality due to particulates could be the greatest environmental health problem facing the country, causing 50,000 to 60,000 premature deaths annually (Hilts 1993). The World Bank (1992, p. 52) estimated that 300,000 to 700,000 lives per year could be saved in developing countries if particulate concentrations were reduced to the annual average level recommended by the World Health Organization (WHO). Moreover, increased mortality is not the only health consequence of exposure to elevated TSP concentrations. Several epidemiological studies conducted in the United States have found that particulates have a statistically significant impact on morbidity (Dockery et al. 1989; Krupnick et al. 1990; Ostro 1983, 1987, 1990; Ostro and Rothschild 1989; Pope et al. 1991).[3] Increased risk of morbidity creates economic costs related to efforts to reduce exposure (for example, by purchasing household air filters or staying indoors during heavily polluted days), expenditure on medication and health care, lost earnings due to illness, and reductions in welfare due to pain and suffering (Freeman 1985).

Valuing a statistical life

Placing a monetary value on lives saved is more difficult and, for obvious reasons, more controversial than predicting the number saved. Economists have employed two basic approaches. The first is the human capital approach, which estimates the value of human beings simply as factors of production (Hufschmidt et al. 1983, pp. 183-191). When a person dies prematurely, the economy loses the output that person would have generated over the remainder of his or her working life. If earnings reflect a person's marginal value product of labor, as economic theory predicts they should, then the gain to the economy of saving the life of a productive person is the discounted sum of that person's earnings up to retirement age.

Three special cases are worth highlighting. If a person has already retired or is not gainfully employed (e.g., is an invalid), then his or her life has no value under this method. If, however, a person voluntarily chooses not to work for a cash income but nevertheless does provide economically valuable services (e.g., a housewife), then the person's lifetime earnings are valued the same as those of someone employed in the cash economy. The assumption is that the services provided by the person are, at the margin, the same in value as the marginal value product of someone employed in the cash economy. Otherwise, the person would not have chosen to stay out of the cash economy. Finally, if a person has not yet entered the work force, then he or she has an entire lifetime of productive services to contribute. These earnings are discounted, however, by the number of years until the person enters the workforce. This means that the younger a child, the lower the value placed on his or her life. At a 10 percent discount rate and a work-force entry age of twenty years, the capitalized lifetime earnings of a newborn are less than a sixth as large as those of a twenty-year-old receiving the same future earnings.

By treating people as factors of production no different than machines, and by placing low or no value on the lives of the retired, the disabled, and the very young, the human capital approach has been rightly criticized on ethical grounds. It can also be criticized on purely economic grounds. According to welfare economics theory, the true value of any good or service in monetary terms is the maximum amount a person is willing to pay for it. At first, this line of reasoning might appear to be broadly consistent with the human capital approach: assuming perfect capital markets, the most a person could pay to save his or her life would be the discounted sum of his or her future lifetime earnings, supplemented by any accumulated wealth. But people usually face not a certainty that they will die if they expose themselves to some environmental hazard, but rather a higher probability that they will die. Hence, the correct measure of willingness to pay to save a life is willingness to pay to reduce the risk of death, not to avert certain death. Probability is in fact explicit in the dose-response parameters in Table 9.1: the parameters predict the relative decrease in the mortality rate, but they do not predict which particular individuals in an exposed population will be saved if environmental quality improves. That is, they predict statistical lives saved (Schelling 1968).

Due to the element of probability, willingness to pay for reductions in risk can exceed capitalized lifetime earnings. Suppose a person can pay $1,000 to reduce the risk of dying by 0.1 percent. The payment might be, for example, the difference in prices between two houses that are identical in all respects except one: one house is in an area with better air quality. If the person purchases the more expensive house, he reveals that he places a value of at least $1,000,000—the price differential divided by the reduction in risk—on his life. This could well exceed the person's capitalized lifetime earnings.

Common sense would suggest that willingness to pay for reductions in risk should indeed exceed a person's capitalized lifetime earnings. Earnings enable a person to purchase and consume priced goods, but of course material consumption is not the only aspect of life that people value. To continue enjoying those other aspects, and to avoid the pain and suffering that might attend death, a rational person would be willing to pay more than his or her capitalized lifetime earnings to save his or her life in a statistical sense. As Schelling (1968, p. 128) put it, "life as well as livelihood is at stake."

Unlike earnings, willingness to pay for reduced risks cannot be observed directly. It must either be inferred from people's behavior, as in the example above or through studies of the wage premium that workers in riskier jobs receive, or estimated via contingent valuation surveys, in which individuals respond to questions about a hypothetical situation involving specific risks and actions to reduce those risks.[4] Fisher et al. (1989) reviewed estimates from studies based on these approaches in the United States, where most such studies have been conducted. They concluded that US$1.6 million and US$8.5 million were empirically defensible lower- and upper-bound estimates of the value of a statistical life in the United States, at 1986 price levels. These values are approximately 100 to 500 times as large as per capita GNP in the U.S. in 1986. A more recent reviews by Viscusi (1992, 1993) gave a somewhat narrower range, US$3 to 7 million (at December 1990 price levels).

DEVELOPMENT OF AIR POLLUTION POLICIES IN MALAYSIA

It was mentioned in Chapter 1 that water pollution, not air pollution, was of greater concern initially to the Department of Environment. In the early 1970s, air quality was not considered to be an issue except in localized areas where uncontrolled emissions prompted nuisance complaints by nearby residents. It is therefore not surprising that the government did not act immediately on a recommendation in a 1975 World Bank report to develop ambient standards for several air pollutants, including particulates (World Bank 1975).

In the absence of accepted ambient standards, the DOE's early air-pollution control efforts necessarily emphasized emissions standards: the amount of pollution discharged by particular sources. The third set of regulations introduced by the DOE—following, within a few months, the Environmental Quality (Prescribed Premises) (Crude Palm Oil) Regulations and the Environmental Quality (Licensing) Regulations—was the Motor Vehicles (Control of Smoke and Gas Emissions) Rules, which took effect on December 22, 1977. Unlike the other two, it was promulgated under the 1958 Road Traffic Ordinance, not the Environmental Quality Act. It aimed at reducing visibly dirty exhaust ("black smoke") discharged by motor vehicles. This was the most obvious type of vehicular air pollution, and it was the main source of particulates discharged by motor vehicles. It was a particular problem with diesel engines that were not well tuned. Under the Rules, the DOE, with the Road Transport Department and the traffic police, could randomly stop vehicles, check for violations of the prescribed standard,[5] and fine the offenders.

Emissions standards for particulates, along with other air pollutants, were extended to stationary sources the following year with the introduction of the Environmental Quality (Clean Air) Regulations, which took effect on October 1, 1978. The Regulations were mainly a response to the rising number of industrial pollution sources as the country's manufacturing sector expanded (Tan 1982). They introduced phased-in standards, with new facilities expected to comply immediately with the most stringent standard, standard C, while existing facilities were given two years to comply with standard A, which for particulate emissions was 50 percent higher than standard C for most sources, and another year to comply with standard B, which was 20 percent higher (Ong et al. 1987). The intention was to set standards that the majority of facilities could attain without undue financial difficulty; indeed, the proposed standards were discussed with industry (e.g., the Federation of Malaysian Manufacturers) before being approved. As in the case of the "Black Smoke" Rules, the Regulations targeted the most obvious sources, such as asphalt and cement plants. They required that certain highly polluting industrial facilities be located at least 1,000 m from residential areas, unless the DOE granted a waiver. Such facilities included those discharging smoke as dark or darker than specified standards[6] or particulates at a rate above 0.5 kg/hr.

The Regulations also included guidelines pertaining to the third major source of particulate emissions, open burning of agricultural and municipal wastes. Like dirty exhaust and emissions from asphalt and cement plants, this was an obvious source. The guidelines did not include penalties for noncompliance; instead, they left this issue to state and local authorities to decide, under their by-law procedures. Moreover, parties unable to comply with the guidelines could file for a contravention license from the DOE.

Within the DOE, both the "Black Smoke" Rules and the Clean Air Regulations were primarily motivated by concerns about the health impacts of air pollution (Tan 1993). The effectiveness of emissions standards as a means of managing health impacts is diminished, however, when they are not formulated on the basis of an understanding of how emissions interact with other factors to determine the ambient concentrations to which human populations are exposed. One such factor is distance from emissions sources. The 1,000-m siting provision in the Clean Air Regulations was a pragmatic recognition of this fact. Weather and topography are other important factors. (Sham 1992). Rainfall "scavenges" particulates from the air, while inversion layers and mountain ranges can trap pollution in an area for extended periods. Understanding the interactions between emissions and these factors was impeded in Malaysia in the 1970s by the sheer lack of air-quality data. Permanent monitoring stations were not established until 1976 when, under the WHO's Global Environmental Monitoring System, the Malaysian Meteorological Service (MMS) established stations in Petaling Jaya and Tanah Rata to record concentrations of TSP and SO_2 (Perkhidmatan Kajiuaca Malaysia n.d.). Regular readings became available the next year. The DOE also began monitoring air quality in 1977, but only through sporadic, short-term measurements (Sham n.d.). It did not establish a permanent monitoring system until the mid-1980s.

In the absence of a solid information base, the DOE had little choice but to base emissions standards on those in other countries. In the 1970s, this by and large meant industrialized countries in the temperate zone. During the preparation of the Clean Air Regulations, the DOE reviewed emissions standards in Australia, the United Kingdom, the United States, and also Singapore. Sham (1992) has pointed out, however, that atmospheric ventilation in midlatitude regions is better than in the equatorial region. Hence, all else being equal, emissions standards set at the same level as in industrialized countries would be expected to result in worse ambient air quality in Malaysia.

Several episodes of persistent, peak particulate concentrations drew attention to the possible health consequences of poor air quality. "Haze" episodes had been noted as early as the 1960s on the west coast of the Peninsula, especially in the Klang Valley, during the drier months of June to September. The first episode to attract substantial attention occurred in September 1982. It was ultimately attributed to a combination of forest fires in Sumatra, southwesterly winds, and lack of rain, as was a subsequent episode in April 1983. These two episodes "made headlines and created a great deal of discussion in the media" (Sham et al. 1991). They led to a proposal for ambient standards of 50 $\mu g/m^3$ in nonindustrial areas and 100 $\mu g/m^3$ in industrial areas, which apparently was not officially accepted (Sham, n.d.).

The haze episodes also prompted one of the first attempts at an environmental epidemiology study in the country. Mahathevan (1985) examined trends in outpatient cases for respiratory illnesses at government hospitals and selected clinics in the Klang Valley during January 1982 to March 1984. During that period doctors in Petaling Jaya had reported a rising number of patients complaining of respiratory disorders, and they had attributed this to increased air pollution. Mahathevan concluded, however, that "there has been no marked increase in respiratory diseases among both children and adults" (p. 12). He apparently reached this conclusion by visually inspecting the data, not by analyzing it statistically.

The next haze episode was more intense and did not coincide with forest fires in Indonesia (Tsuruoka 1990). TSP concentrations in the Klang Valley during August 1990 reached the astonishingly high figure of 785 $\mu g/m^3$ (Sham 1992). This was more than an order of magnitude higher than the maximum concentration consistent with protecting human health according to the U.S. Environmental Protection Agency, 60 $\mu g/m^3$ (Tietenberg 1988, Table 15.2). The haze led the MMS to convene an expert group to study its causes (Sham et al. 1991) and the Ministry of Health to investigate its health impacts (Ministry of

Health, n.d.). The expert group attributed the haze to a combination of particulate emissions and meteorological conditions that prevented dispersion. It referred to extensive open burning in areas south and west of the Klang Valley in Selangor, Negeri Sembilan, and Melaka. Estimated particulate emissions from open burning were particularly high in 1990 (Table 8.2).[7]

The Ministry of Health study was conducted by its Occupational Health Unit. The study investigated whether monthly admissions and outpatient cases for asthma, conjunctivitis, and all respiratory diseases at the three major government hospitals in the Klang Valley were positively correlated with mean monthly TSP concentrations from 1985 to 1990 or mean monthly PM_{10} concentrations from 1987 to 1990.[8] It found that the relationship was not statistically significant in twenty-one of the twenty-four cases analyzed. In the three where it was, the relationship was negative, suggesting, paradoxically, that pollution improved health. The study concluded that "no firm conclusion could be drawn" (p. 11).

The failure of that study and, before it, the Mahathevan study to detect a significant relationship between particulate concentrations and morbidity is not surprising. Detecting morbidity impacts requires a much finer level of analysis than Mahathevan's casual-observation approach or the Ministry of Health's study of aggregate demand for health care services. The U.S.-based studies cited in *Estimating the number of lives saved* monitored the health of a large sample of individuals at two-week intervals over an extended period of time. This enabled the researchers to collect information on personal traits and habits that affected individuals' susceptibility to pollution-related illnesses—for example, age, occupation, and smoking habits—as well as detailed information on the nature and severity of any symptoms that occurred. It also enabled them to investigate lagged and cumulative effects of exposure to elevated pollution concentrations, as morbidity impacts are not necessarily instantaneous. The possibility of a lagged response was not investigated by the Ministry.

Although anecdotal evidence is often misleading, it is worth noting that disorders that have been linked to particulates by epidemiological studies in the United States increased markedly in Malaysian urban areas during the 1980s. The number of asthma patients admitted to the Klang General Hospital increased from 1,000 in 1985 to 2,150 in 1990, and the Perak Medical and Health Services Department recorded a 79 percent increase in the number of asthma cases in the late 1980s (*The Sunday Star*, October 11, 1992). Over a longer period, 1962 to 1988, upper respiratory tract infections as a cause of first attendance at government clinics in Peninsular Malaysia rose from 16.0 percent of total cases to 43.2 percent, according to annual reports of the Ministry of Health.

In response to the haze, the Cabinet ordered stricter enforcement of pollution-control regulations (Sham et al. 1991). Enforcement of the "Black Smoke" Rules and Clean Air Regulations had in many instances been weak, due to inadequate enforcement resources and low fines (Sham 1992). Compliance with the "Black Smoke" Rules rose from 70 percent in 1979 to 87 percent in 1987, but it declined every year afterward. By 1991, it had fallen to 77 percent (DOE 1992). At the end of the 1980s, some 90 percent of all contravention licenses issued by the DOE were for open burning (Sham 1992). The liberal issuance of contravention licenses for open burning in part reflected pressure by local and state authorities and land development agencies.

Even with strict enforcement, a regulatory approach based on emissions standards is fated to result in greater pollution discharge if the number of sources increases, unless the standards are made more stringent. The overview in Chapter 1 and the emissions data in Chapter 8 indicated that all sources of particulates increased in Malaysia during the 1970s and 1980s. The number of licensed motor vehicles in the country nearly doubled every five years between 1970 and 1985, rising from 669,200 to 4,010,430 (IPT 1992). It reached nearly 5 million in 1990. The number of industrial sources rose as the manufacturing sector expanded, particularly after the mid-1980s economic liberalization. Rising land conversion (at least until the mid-1980s) and rising populations generated more waste to dispose, typically by burning. In response to these developments, in the early 1990s the DOE initiated a review of the emissions standards contained in the "Black Smoke" Rules and Clean Air Regulations. These standards had not changed since the regulations were introduced. Revised standards had not been issued at the time of writing.

Another haze episode occurred the following year, in October 1991 (Cheang et al., n.d.; Vatikiotis 1991; Yong 1992). This time, the TSP concentration reached a peak of 489.7 $\mu g/m^3$ at the MMS monitoring station in Petaling Jaya. A preliminary report by the MMS attributed the haze primarily to forest fires in both Sumatra and Kalimantan (Cheang et al., n.d.), as did a local Ph.D. dissertation (Yong 1992). Unlike previous episodes, this one affected most of the Peninsula, not just the west coast, and also western Sarawak. This is consistent with forest fires in Kalimantan playing a role. But local factors undoubtedly contributed. For example, emissions from the open burning of municipal waste were at the highest levels ever estimated (Table 8.2).[9] As a belated response to the 1975 World Bank recommendation, the DOE completed a study on the ambient TSP standard just before the 1990 and 1991 haze episodes. The study recommended an annual average of 90 ug/m³ and a daily average of 260 $\mu g/m^3$, with 1995 as the target year for compliance. In 1991, the DOE, with assistance from the Japan International

Cooperation Agency, initiated a project to determine how emissions levels would need to change to achieve this standard in the Klang Valley (JICA 1991).

MORTALITY-RELATED BENEFITS IN URBAN AREAS IN MALAYSIA IN 1991

Even if one ignores the exceptionally high readings during the haze episodes, the upward trend in the national average TSP reading and the increasing proportion of readings above the recommended standard (Table 8.4) suggest that compliance with the recommended standard will not be easy and could entail substantial costs. It is therefore important to have some evidence on the magnitude of the expected benefits of compliance.

We applied the methods discussed in *Valuing lives saved* to value mortality-related benefits in 1991 in four urban areas: the Klang Valley, Penang, Ipoh, and Johor Bahru. We focused on mortality, which was ignored by the Mahathevan (1985) and Ministry of Health (n.d.) studies, because studies such as Krupnick and Portney (1991) and Hall et al. (1992) have found that the mortality impacts of reductions in particulate concentrations are usually economically more important than the morbidity impacts. We will return to this last point in the final section. We defined the Klang Valley as Wilayah Persekutuan[10] Kuala Lumpur, Majlis Daerah[11] Petaling, and Majlis Daerah Klang; Penang as Majlis Daerah Timur Laut and the Local Authority Areas of Butterworth and Perai; Ipoh as the area administered by Majlis Bandaraya[12] Ipoh; and Johor Bahru as the area administered by Majlis Perbandaran[13] Johor Bahru. These are the four largest urban areas in the country. In 1991, they accounted for about one quarter of the total population of Peninsular Malaysia.

We chose 1991 as the year for the analysis because it was a census year and because more TSP monitoring stations were operating in the four urban areas in that year than in the previous census year of 1980.[14] Moreover, a major survey on earnings in the four urban areas was conducted just one year earlier (Lee 1990), and a Household Income Survey was conducted by the Economic Planning Unit two years earlier. The fact that it was a year with a haze episode indicates that the benefits might be greater than in an "average" year. As indicated in the last section, however, haze episodes came with increasing frequency in the 1980s (compared to the 1970s) and were not entirely due to exogenous events like forest fires in Indonesia. Moreover, the 1991 haze affected only one month of the year, and so its effects were diluted on an annual basis. Annual mean TSP concentrations in the Klang Valley in 1991 were not tremendously higher than in preceding years (Figure 1.11), including 1990 when the haze was attributed to local causes.

Estimating the number of statistical lives saved

Table 9.2 shows 1991 annual mean readings for the DOE and MMS monitoring stations that were included in the analysis. There are a few other monitoring stations in the four areas, but 1991 data for them were incomplete. Because the number of stations in each area was so low, we did not attempt to model the variation in TSP concentration within each area. Instead, we took the average of the annual mean readings for the stations in each area as the exposure level.[15] Data in Table 9.2 indicate that annual mean readings violated the recommended standard at all stations but one. The difference between the annual average of these means and the target ranged from about a quarter of the target in Johor Bahru to about half in the Klang Valley and Penang.

No epidemiological studies on air pollution and mortality have been con-

Table 9.2   *Mean annual TSP levels in urban areas of Malaysia in 1991 in μ/m^3*

Urban area	Station[a]	Reading
Klang Valley	Petaling Jaya (MMS)	99.90
	SIRIM, Shah Alam (DOE)	117.64
	Kuala Lumpur City Hall (DOE)	126.56
	Johnson & Johnson, Petaling Jaya (DOE)	145.61
	Pudu Post Office, Kuala Lumpur (DOE)	188.36
	Average	135.61
Penang	AIA Building, Georgetown (DOE)	117.50
	Perai (MMS)	129.90
	ITI Prai Industrial Estate, Seberang Prai (DOE)	142.45
	Bagan Ajam Clinic, Butterworth (DOE)	166.70
	Average	139.14
Ipoh	Asean Rare Earth, Lahat Road (DOE)	120.54
Johor Bahru	Mara Institute of Skill Learning (DOE)	80.74
	Telecoms Interchange Center (DOE)	106.82
	Tampoi Police Station (DOE)	146.08
	Average	111.21

Source: Data files provided by the Malaysian Meteorological Service and the Department of Environment.
[a] Monitoring agency is given in parentheses.
MMS—Malaysian Meteorological Service
DOE—Department of Environment.

ducted in Malaysia. In the absence of direct estimates, we used 0.0007 as a point estimate of the dose-response parameter. This value is essentially the central estimate in Ostro's (1992a) review (see Table 9.1). In contrast, quite detailed data on mortality rates were available. A publication by the Department of Statistics, *Jadual Hayat Ringkas Semenanjung Malaysia (Abridged Life Tables Peninsular Malaysia), 1981-1989*, contained mortality rates disaggregated by age group (in five-year increments) and gender. The rates gave the probability that a person of a given age would die within five years. We used the rates reported for 1989, converting them to annual rates.[16] For males, the rates increased from age five forward; for females, from age ten. Rates for males were approximately 50 to 100 percent larger than rates for females from age ten forward. The rates were reported for the Peninsula as a whole; they were not disaggregated by urban area. Hence, we assumed that rates were identical across the four urban areas.

We obtained data on male and female populations in each urban area from the relevant *Preliminary Count Reports* of the 1991 census. The Klang Valley had the highest population, 2,185,051 people, followed by Penang at 485,194, Ipoh at 382,633, and Johor Bahru at 328,646. The Klang Valley and Johor Bahru had slightly more males than females, while the other two urban areas had slightly more females. At the time of writing, the Department of Statistics had not compiled 1991 population estimates by age group. We assumed that the percentage of the population in each age group was the same as in the 1980 census. According to the 1980 estimates, the populations in Ipoh and Penang were significantly older: the percentage of the population above age forty was 22.3 percent in Ipoh and 23.4 percent in Penang, compared to only 16.4 percent in Johor Bahru and 17.3 percent in the Klang Valley. Together with the fact that mortality rates rise with age after age five (for males) and age ten (for females), this implies that a given reduction in the TSP concentration would save more statistical lives per capita in Ipoh and Penang than in Johor Bahru and the Klang Valley.

Table 9.3 shows the estimated number of statistical lives that would have been saved if TSP concentrations in 1991 had not exceeded the recommended standard. The total across the four areas was 468.5, which represents 3.0 percent of the total number of deaths that occurred in the four areas in 1991. This percentage is comparable to the range of percentages reported by the World Bank for TSP-related mortality in urban areas in the developing world, 2 to 5 percent (World Bank 1992, p. 52). Due to differences in mortality rates between the sexes, the number of male lives saved was one-quarter to two-fifths higher than the number for females. The Klang Valley and Penang accounted for most of the lives saved, which is to be

Table 9.3 *Statistical lives saved by age group and sex by reducing ambient TSP*
concentrations to the recommended Malaysian standard in 1991

	Klang Valley		Penang		Ipoh		Johor Bahru	
Age	*M*	*F*	*M*	*F*	*M*	*F*	*M*	*F*
0–14	20.6	15.9	4.2	3.4	2.3	1.9	1.6	1.2
15–39	29.0	14.1	6.1	3.2	2.8	1.5	2.0	1.0
40–59	31.6	19.0	10.2	6.5	4.5	2.9	2.2	1.3
60+	95.3	78.1	33.8	29.4	16.9	14.8	6.5	5.2
Total	176.5	127.1	54.3	42.4	26.4	21.0	12.2	8.6

expected given the larger populations and higher TSP concentrations in those two areas.

Human capital estimates

Most of the lives saved—about two-thirds—were for people below age five or above age sixty. This has a great impact on value estimates from the human capital approach. The average entry age into the labor force in Malaysia is about fifteen years, while the average retirement age is sixty years.[17] Hence, the capitalized lifetime earnings of a child below age five must be discounted by at least an additional ten years, while the capitalized lifetime earnings of individuals above age sixty are assumed to equal zero. Hence, under the human capital approach most of the lives saved are valued at zero or a low amount.

For age groups below sixty years, we calculated lifetime earnings as follows. First, we obtained estimates of monthly earnings[18] by male and female workers in 1990 from Lee's (1990) survey of companies in the four areas. This was a reverse tracer study that covered "semi-skilled and skilled occupations and a range of industries thought likely to play major roles in the future development of the country" (Lee 1990). Given the forward-looking nature of the human capital approach, this choice of occupations and industries was appropriate. The estimates were not disaggregated by area. The estimates of mean earnings were RM922 for males and RM541 for females. The difference in earnings is large, and it is amplified in the final benefit estimates by the higher proportion of males among the statistical lives saved.

Second, we multiplied the monthly earnings estimates by twelve to convert to an annual basis, and by 1.063 percent to approximate the rise in wages between 1990 and 1991 (6.3 percent was the rate of increase in per capita GDP between the two years). We used the resulting values as the estimates of annual earnings in Penang and Johor Bahru. We increased them by 25 percent to estimate earnings in the Klang Valley, and we decreased them by the same amount to estimate earnings in Ipoh. We based these adjustments on differences in manufacturing earnings in the four areas reported by Richardson and Soon (1990) for 1985 and on differences in per capita incomes of urban households in the states where the urban areas are located, as reported in the 1989 Household Income Survey.[19] The final estimates of average annual 1991 earnings were, for the Klang Valley, RM14,701 for males and RM8,626 for females; for Penang, RM11,761 and RM6,901; for Ipoh, RM8,821 and RM5,176; and for Johor Bahru, RM11,761 and RM6,901.

Third, we assumed that annual earnings would rise up to retirement at a constant rate of 4 percent per year in real terms. This is between the actual per capita GDP growth rate experienced from 1970 to 1990, 3.7 percent per year, and the rate projected in the Second Outline Perspective Plan (OPP2) between 1991 and 2000, 4.7 percent per year. We ignored unemployment and disability: we assumed that every death below retirement age was the death of an economically productive person. This assumption is broadly consistent with the tight labor market in Malaysia in the late 1980s and early 1990s, but it might not hold in the future if the country suffers prolonged periods of less than full employment.

Finally, we capitalized lifetime earnings for remaining working years up to retirement by using discount rates of 4 and 10 percent. The former is comparable to the real return on fixed deposits in Malaysia, while the latter is at the lower end of the range of discount rates used by the Economic Planning Unit in project appraisal (Veitch 1986). For a fresh, fifteen-year-old entrant into the labor force, the capitalized value ranged from a low of RM136,332 for a female in Ipoh whose earnings were discounted at 10 percent, to a high of RM661,557 for a male in the Klang Valley whose earnings were discounted at 4 percent.

Table 9.4 presents the estimates of the value of lives saved according to the human capital approach. The aggregate estimates for the four areas combined were RM22.6 million and RM58.5 million for the 10 percent and 4 percent discount rates, respectively. These are equivalent to 0.08 percent and 0.2 percent, respectively, of the 1991 value of GDP in the manufacturing sector in the Federal Territory of Kuala Lumpur and the states of Selangor, Pulau Pinang, Johor, and Perak combined. Most of the benefits, about three-fourths for both discount rates, occurred in the Klang Valley.

Willingness-to-pay estimates

As discussed in the section Valuing a statistical life, the human capital approach understates willingness to pay, which is a better measure of the economic

Table 9.4 *Economic benefits of reducing ambient TSP concentrations to the recommended Malaysian standard in 1991 (million RM)*

Approach	Klang Val ley	Penang	Ipoh	Johor Bahru	Total
I. Human capital					
10% discount rate	17.1	3.4	1.2	0.9	22.6
4% discount rate	44.7	8.3	3.0	2.5	58.5
II. Willingness to pay	576.8	183.7	90.1	63.1	913.7

benefit of reduced mortality risks. We estimated this measure by multiplying Malaysia's 1991 per capita GDP times the ratio of the midpoint of Viscusi's (1992, 1993) range of estimates for the United States, US$5 million, to per capita GDP in the United States. It is reasonable to expect willingness to pay to be related to income, and Viscusi (1993, p. 1930) offers some evidence to support a proportional relationship. Margulis (1991) suggested using this approach in his study of particulate pollution in Mexico City, although in the end he applied only the human capital approach, and Ostro (1992a) applied it in his study of particulate pollution in Jakarta. Krupnick (1993) has warned, however, that transferring estimates of willingness to pay from one location to another can lead to large errors even when both locations are in the same country. It is therefore best to regard our estimates as being no more than indicative of the willingness to pay for mortality risk reductions in Malaysia.

This procedure gave an estimate of RM1,900,000 per statistical life saved. Multiplying this by the total number of statistical lives saved yielded an estimated total benefit of nearly 1 billion ringgit (Table 9.4). This figure is equivalent to 0.7 percent of Malaysia's GDP in 1991 and 62 percent of the federal government's operating expenditure in the health sector in that year. It converts to about US$0.3 billion. For comparison, Ostro (1992a) estimated mortality benefits of US$0.1 to 0.2 billion per year for reductions in TSP concentrations in Jakarta,[20] and Krupnick and Portney (1991) and Hall et al. (1992) estimated US$2 billion and US$6.4 billion per year, respectively, in Los Angeles.

Soon after completing this analysis, we obtained the results of a similar analysis conducted independently by the World Bank (1993). The Bank's analysis focused on the same four urban areas, and it too estimated the benefits of reducing TSP concentrations to 90 $\mu g/m^3$ in 1991. It predicted a considerably higher number of lives saved, however, 1,300. There are four reasons to suspect that this prediction is too high. First, the Bank used the total populations of the states of Pulau Pinang, Perak, and Johor as the exposed populations instead of just the urban populations. This vastly over-estimated exposure in the three states. It more than offset the fact that the Bank excluded all urban areas in the Klang Valley other than Kuala Lumpur. Second, the Bank used only readings of TSP from the DOE monitoring stations, which tend to be located in the most polluted areas. Table 9.2 shows that readings from the two stations operated by the MMS that were included in our analysis tended to be lower than those from the DOE stations. Third, the Bank included readings from some stations that only operated during heavily polluted periods of the year. This led to an extraordinarily high, and incorrect, annual mean for Perak of more than 200 µg/m³. As noted earlier, we included only stations with readings for the entire year. Fourth, the Bank implicitly assumed that the population age structure in the four urban areas was identical to the national age structure. In fact, the national age structure includes higher proportions in older age groups, and thus more people with higher mortality rates.

Despite these differences, the Bank's estimate of the total benefit of the statistical lives saved based on the willingness-to-pay approach was remark-ably similar to ours, RM1.023 billion. The explanation is that the Bank used a much lower value per statistical life, RM768,750.

CONCLUSIONS

Reducing ambient TSP concentrations to 90 µg/m³, the recommended Malaysian standard, would have saved nearly five hundred lives in the four largest urban areas of the country in 1991. This would have added some RM20 to 60 million (in present value terms) to national output and raised human welfare by nearly RM1 billion. The benefits would have been even greater, of course, if the recommended standard were more stringent. In fact, the WHO recommends a standard of 75 µg/m³.

These estimates understate the benefits of TSP reductions even for the recommended Malaysian standard, as they exclude the benefits of reduced morbidity. The ratio of total health-related benefits (mortality plus morbid-ity) to the benefits of reduced mortality was 1.12 in Hall et al.'s (1992) study of Los Angeles, 1.35 in Krupnick and Portney's (1991) study of Los Angeles, 1.37 in the World Bank (1993) study of the four Malaysian urban areas, 1.77 in Margulis's (1991) study of Mexico City,[21] and 2.36 to 2.53 in Ostro's (1992a) study of Jakarta. Morbidity benefits in the World Bank study included reduced numbers of hospital admissions for respiratory disorders, emergency room visits, restricted activity days, bronchitis cases in children, and asthma attacks. These ratios suggest that the total health-related benefits of reductions in TSP concentrations in the four urban areas in Malaysia could have been up to about twice as large as the mortality-related estimates in Table 9.4.

Available cost estimates suggest that the benefits of reduced mortality alone would justify a more aggressive effort to reduce particulate pollution. Chan (1990) conducted a "rough assessment" of the costs of attaining an "acceptable level of environmental quality" in Malaysia. His assessment covered a broad class of air and water pollutants, not just particulates. He estimated costs by applying international estimates of pollution abatement costs relative to sectoral value added, from Walter (1975), to a simplified version of the 1983 Malaysian national input-output table.[22] He did not state how the "acceptable level" compared to either actual pollution concentrations in the country or recommended Malaysian standards, but given his source of information on abatement costs, it was probably similar to standards recommended by the WHO. As noted earlier, these are somewhat more stringent than the recommended Malaysian standards, at least in the case of TSP. For 1991, Chan estimated the aggregate abatement costs of reducing air and water pollution to the "acceptable level" to be 1.2 percent of GDP. If the costs of TSP reduction accounted for even half this figure, which is unlikely, they would still be less than the willingness-to-pay benefit estimate of 0.7 percent of GDP for just mortality impacts. The World Bank (1993) reported an aggregate cost figure even lower than Chan's, 0.3 to 0.6 percent of GDP in 1992, by extrapolating more recent data from Japan and the United States.

The comprehensive pollution abatement programs costed by Chan and the World Bank would, of course, generate aggregate benefits in addition to those related to TSP. Although epidemiological evidence of an impact on mortality is weaker for most other air pollutants, sulfur dioxide, nitrogen oxides, ozone,[23] hydrocarbons, carbon monoxide, and lead all have well-established morbidity impacts (Tietenberg 1988, Table 15.1; World Resources Institute 1992, notes to Tables 24.5 and 24.6). The impacts include respiratory diseases (sulfur dioxide, nitrogen oxides, ozone, hydrocarbons); cardiovascular diseases (sulfur dioxide, carbon monoxide, ozone); and impaired mental and physical development of infants and children (carbon monoxide, lead). Published studies by Lim et al. (1983, 1985) found that mothers in urban areas of Malaysia had higher concentrations of lead in their blood and breast milk than mothers in less polluted rural areas, and unpublished work by Dr. Zailina Hashim of the Nutrition and Community Health Department at Universiti Pertanian Malaysia found that these and other sources of exposure had negative impacts on children's health (Noraini 1993). Although ambient lead concentrations fell at most monitoring stations in Kuala Lumpur and Selangor from 1988 to 1991 (see Chapter 1), the benefits of reducing concentrations by another 90 percent in 1991 would have totaled RM1.1 billion, according to the World Bank (1993). This estimate includes both mortality and morbidity impacts, and it is based on techniques similar to those employed in this chapter.

In sum, the economic benefits of reducing ambient TSP concentrations in Malaysia to the recommended $90\mu g/m^3$ standard in 1991 apparently would have exceeded the costs. Whether an even greater reduction in TSP would have been justified is less clear, although this could well be the case. The World Bank (1993) estimated that reducing the concentration in the four urban areas by an additional 30 $\mu g/m^3$, to 60 $\mu g/m^3$, would have generated an additional RM605 million in benefits.[24] Reducing the standard to that level would have been justified only if the increase in abatement costs were no greater. The Bank rightly emphasized that the magnitude of abatement costs depends very much on the structure of pollution policies and regulations, as some policies and regulations can achieve a given pollution reduction at a lower cost than others. We turn to a discussion of this issue in the next chapter. The focus is on water pollution, specifically organic pollution from palm-oil mills, where there is a much richer policy and regulatory experience to analyze than in the case of air pollution.

NOTES

1 The lower bound estimate was US$5.0 billion.

2 See Lave and Seskin (1979) for a discussion of the issue of causality.

3 A few have failed to find evidence of a statistically significant relationship. See Atkinson and Crocker (1992), Gerking and Stanley (1986), and Portney and Mullahy (1986).

4 Mitchell and Carson (1989) is a standard reference on the contingent valuation method.

5 50 Hartridge smoke units.

6 No. 1 or 2 on a Ringelmann Chart, depending on the source.

7 Recall that the statistics on open burning in Table 8.2 exclude the burning of agricultural wastes.

8 The hospitals included in the study were Kuala Lumpur General Hospital, University Hospital, and Tengku Ampuan Rahimah General Hospital in Kelang.

9 The 1991 haze episode reportedly prompted another government study of health impacts, which we were unable to obtain.

10 Federal Territory.

11 Administrative District.

12 City Council.

13 Municipal Council.

14 The year 1970 was also a census year, but, as discussed in *Development of air pollution policies*, the first air-quality monitoring stations were not established until the late 1970s.

15 According to a local atmospheric chemist, Dr. Azman Zainal Abidin of the Universiti Pertanian Malaysia, our assumption that TSP concentrations were more or less uniform within the areas analyzed was reasonable. In the case of Jakarta, Ostro (1992a) was able to use data on emissions to model isopleths (contours) of ambient TSP concentrations and thus estimate local variations in actual exposure levels.

16 In the case of the sixty-five-year age bracket, we used the expected number of remaining years of life for the group, which the publication also reported.

17 The retirement age for government employees is fifty-five years, but many government employees obtain jobs in the private sector after leaving their posts.

18 This is not the same as monthly salary, which excludes benefits and allowances. Earnings provide a better measure of a worker's marginal value product.

19 Data from the Survey were provided by the Economic Planning Unit.

20 Converted from values given in Ostro's Tables 4 through 6 using the conversion factor on p. 23 of his report.

21 Unlike the other studies, Margulis valued reductions in mortality using the human capital approach, which understates the economic value of saving a statistical life. Hence, the ratio from his study is biased upward compared to the others.

22 Labys (1980) used a similar approach to estimate the costs of pollution abatement in resource-based sectors in Malaysia. He applied cost parameters from studies conducted in the United States to mid-1970s Malaysian data for two commodity sectors, tin mining and sawmilling. For tin mining, he estimated that the imposition of pollution controls comparable to those for mining in the United States would decrease production by 1.85 percent, but the impact of this on profits would be largely offset by a price increase of 1.76 percent. For sawmilling, he estimated that profits would be reduced by 2.8 to 8.6 percent.

23 Ozone is formed by chemical reactions involving nitrogen oxides and hydrocarbons, both of which are emitted primarily by motor vehicles. Studies on the health impacts of ozone include Dickie and Gerking (1991), Gerking and Stanley (1986), Kinney and Ozkaynak (1991), Krupnick et al. (1990), Ostro (1990), Ostro and Rothschild (1989), and Portney and Mullahy (1986).

24 The dose-response model employed by the World Bank (1993) for TSP is linear, so the benefits function does not show diminishing marginal returns, unlike the MB curve in Figure 9.1.

10

Water Pollution Control

INTRODUCTION

Most of Malaysia's pollution-control regulations are based on command-and-control principles.[1] They typically establish mandatory standards, expressed as allowable concentrations of specified pollutants per unit of flue gas or wastewater, on pollution discharge. These standards are usually uniform across different sources of a given pollutant. The regulations authorize the Department of Environment (DOE) to monitor pollution sources and to fine sources that violate the standards. If the violations are sufficiently large, the DOE can suspend a source's operating license. The regulations typically require stationary pollution sources to submit pollution-control plans to the DOE for approval. The DOE's policy is to require sources to use the "best practicable means" of controlling pollution.

Command and control is the standard approach in most countries, not just Malaysia. Economists have for many years criticized it for making pollution-reduction efforts unnecessarily costly.[2] Their chief criticisms pertain to uniform discharge standards and requirements to use best available pollution-control technology (technological standards). When abatement costs differ across pollution sources, the minimization of aggregate abatement costs (cost-effectiveness) requires that the lowest-cost sources bear relatively more of the burden of abatement and the highest-cost sources bear relatively less. This is impossible under uniform standards, which require the same level of abatement by all sources. Best available pollution-control technology may be "best" from an engineering standpoint, but it is often quite expensive. The same amount of pollution reduction may be achievable at a lower cost through changes in an industry's manufacturing processes (pollution preven-

---

Khalid Abdul Rahim was a coauthor of this chapter.

tion) rather than end-of-pipe pollution control. A good example is to switch from high-sulfur coal or fuel oil as a fuel source to natural gas, as Malaysia has done, instead of installing flue-gas desulfurization equipment.

Although the command-and-control approach dominates Malaysia's environmental regulations, it does not do so exclusively.[3] Two notable exceptions are the Crude Palm Oil and Raw Natural Rubber Regulations. In neither case did the initial regulations impose mandatory, uniform standards or specify the specific abatement technology to be employed. Instead, they levied a charge on the pollution that crude palm-oil and rubber mills discharged, and they left it to the mills to choose their abatement level and means of abatement. This pollution-charge approach is one of the alternatives to command-and-control that economists typically advocate.

More information is available on the performance of the Crude Palm Oil Regulations. It indicates that they have been spectacularly successful in reducing pollution discharge. In the early 1970s, crude palm-oil (CPO) mills were probably the worst source of water pollution in the country (Maheswaran and Singam 1977). Untreated palm-oil effluent, which consists of nontoxic organic wastes, depletes the concentration of oxygen in freshwater as it decomposes. Environmental scientists measure oxygen-depleting potential by tonnes of biochemical oxygen demand, or BOD.[4] The magnitude of BOD pollution from industrial sources is perhaps most easily grasped by expressing it in terms of the number of people whose raw sewage would generate as much BOD. In 1975, the BOD load discharged by CPO mills was equivalent to the BOD load in the raw sewage of 12 million people (Figure 10.1). This was equivalent to the entire population of the country.

By 1985, however, the population-equivalent BOD load fell to only 80 thousand people. This provides a direct explanation for the declining BOD concentrations in Peninsular Malaysia's rivers discussed in Chapter 8. The more than hundredfold reduction in the population-equivalent BOD load would be remarkable under any circumstances. What makes it especially so is that it occurred during a period when the number of CPO mills more than doubled and the industry's output of crude palm oil more than tripled. This growth solidified Malaysia's position as the largest producer and exporter of palm oil in the world.

The indisputable success of the Crude Palm Oil Regulations in reducing pollution discharge without stalling industrial growth calls for closer examination. On the surface, it appears to provide a striking illustration of the advantages of pollution charges over mandatory uniform standards. It turns out, however, that the Regulations were not without command-and-control features. For example, discharge standards became mandatory after the first year of the Regulations. To draw sound lessons from the Regulations, one

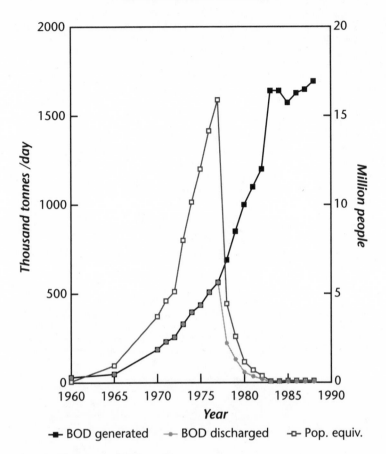

Figure 10.1   BOD load from CPO mills

must determine how much of the credit for the Regulations' performance the pollution charges deserve. These lessons are of potentially great importance to the country: ensuring that it does not pay more for pollution control than necessary would help facilitate the government's goal that the country be "fully developed" by 2020 (Mahathir 1991).

To provide background for those unfamiliar with the economics of pollution control, the next section discusses differences between the uniform standards approach and alternative approaches favored by economists. The section *Palm-oil effluent charges in Malaysia* then reviews the development of the palm-oil effluent problem, the Regulations, and the industry's response to them. Evidence on the role of the pollution charges is highlighted. *Cost savings of the effluent charges in the Sungai Johor* basin presents an economic analysis of the cost-effectiveness of the Regulations compared to alternative regulatory approaches, for the case of mills on the Sungai Johor. This river

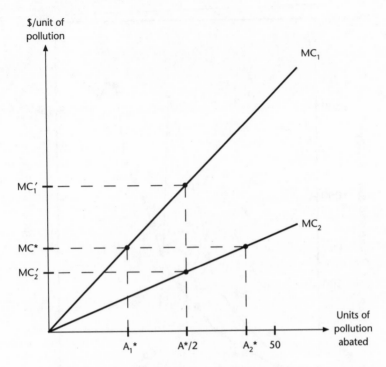

Figure 10.2   Minimizing the cost of pollution abatement

basin has the largest concentration of CPO mills in the country and was particularly badly polluted among major river basins in the Peninsula (Chapter 8). *Conclusions* summarizes the major lessons of the country's experience with the Crude Palm Oil Regulations.

THE ECONOMIC APPROACH TO POLLUTION CONTROL[5]

Uniform standards versus economic instruments

Pollution abatement costs include both direct expenditure to reduce the generation of pollutants in the first place (pollution prevention) or to reduce their concentration in discharged wastes (pollution control), and the indirect costs of curtailing industrial activity to reduce the amount of pollution generated. From an economic perspective, pollution should be abated only if the benefits of abatement outweigh the costs. Two questions arise immediately.

First, how can an environmental agency determine the optimal level of abatement? Second, once that level is determined, how can the agency design policies that achieve it most cost-effectively?

The analytics of the first question were discussed in the last chapter. The second question becomes relevant once the desired abatement level has been chosen. How can this level be achieved at minimum cost? Economic theory predicts that the answer is generally *not* to require individual polluters to achieve the same level of abatement. To see why this is the case, suppose that there are two pollution sources in a particular river basin. The two sources—call them mills—are identical in all respects except that mill 2's abatement costs are lower than mill 1's. For example, if abatement requires the construction of ponds for treating wastewater, mill 1's costs might be higher because it owns less land. The difference in costs is shown in Figure 10.2 by mill 2's marginal cost curve, MC_2, being below mill 1's curve, MC_1, at all levels of abatement.[6] In the absence of abatement effort, each mill discharges fifty units of pollution.

Suppose that the environmental agency has decided that the optimal aggregate abatement level is A^* units. Furthermore, following a command-and-control approach, it has decided to achieve this target by imposing a uniform standard that requires both mills to abate $A^*/2$ units. At this level of abatement, mill 1's marginal cost, MC_1' exceeds mill 2's, MC_2'.

The difference in marginal abatement costs implies that there is a way to maintain aggregate abatement at A^* units but reduce aggregate abatement costs: by allowing mill 1 to abate one less unit and requiring mill 2 to abate one more. Since mill 1 abates one fewer unit and mill 2 one more, aggregate abatement does not change. The reduction in mill 1's abatement costs, MC_1', is greater than the increase in mill 2's, MC_2', however, so aggregate abatement costs drop. Reallocating abatement effort would cause costs to keep dropping until the mills' marginal abatement costs were equalized at MC^*. At this point, mill 1 abates less than mill 2, A_1^* versus A_2^*.

There are therefore two fundamentally different approaches to pollution control. One approach, the uniform standards approach, requires mills' abatement levels to be identical but allows their marginal abatement costs to vary. The other, the economic approach, equalizes mills' marginal costs but allows their abatement levels to vary. Both approaches achieve the same aggregate level of abatement, but the economic approach does so at a lower aggregate abatement cost.

The magnitude of the difference in costs between the two approaches depends on both the absolute and relative levels of the marginal cost curves. If marginal abatement costs are low, so is the absolute magnitude of potential savings. If the curves are very similar across pollution sources, the potential for cost savings is small. The savings become greater as the discrepancy between the curves increases.

The economic approach might appear to be more difficult to implement. Figure 10.2 appears to imply that the environmental agency needs not only to choose an overall abatement level, but also to assign differentiated effluent standards in such a way that the marginal abatement costs are equalized. This conclusion overlooks the fact that standards are not an environmental agency's only regulatory device. In addition, there are two economic instruments that can be used to implement the economic approach. One, the pollution charge, is a price-based instrument. The other, the tradeable pollution permit, is quantity based.

A pollution charge can be viewed as a tax on unabated pollution, although its primary purpose is not to raise revenue. Faced with the same pollution charge, mills will abate at levels with identical marginal costs. Consider Figure 10.2 again. Suppose that both mills face a pollution charge equal to MC^*. Mill 1 will decide to abate no more and no less than A_1^*: if it abates less, it saves on abatement costs, but these savings are more than offset by the pollution charge on the additional unit of pollution it discharges; if it abates more, it saves on the pollution charge, but this is more than offset by the increase in abatement costs. For analogous reasons, mill 2 suffers a net loss if it abates at any level other than A_2^*. Because mill 1 abates less, it winds up paying a higher total pollution fee, $(50-A_1^*)MC^*$, than does mill 2, $(50-A_2^*)MC^*$.

If the pollution charge were set at a level other than MC^*, the mills' marginal costs would still be equalized, but the aggregate abatement level would differ from A^*. The practical challenge with a pollution charge, therefore, is to set it at just the right level that achieves the target abatement level. Since environmental agencies do not have perfect knowledge about mills' marginal cost curves, a pollution charge provides less assurance than a uniform standard that the abatement target will be hit.

In theory, the environmental agency could revise the charge repeatedly until it achieves the target abatement level, but in practice this could be difficult. Moreover, even if the charge achieved the target initially, it would need to be revised over time to offset inflation and to adjust for changes in the number of mills, their processing capacity, and abatement technology. For example, if the charge stayed constant but the number of mills increased, aggregate pollution discharge would also increase.

Aside from cost-effective abatement, two features of a pollution charge should be attractive to an environmental agency. First, the charge generates revenue. Of course, whether the revenue flows to the agency or to the treasury depends on institutional arrangements. Second, the charge creates an incentive for pollution-control innovation and thereby induces mills to increase abatement voluntarily. Suppose that mill 2 developed an abatement technology that lowered its marginal cost curve. It would be rewarded not only through a reduction in its abatement costs, but also through a reduction in its total pollution fee: it would discharge less pollution because its marginal cost curve would now intersect the pollution charge at a point further to the right. If instead the mill faced a standard at $A^*/2$, it would benefit from the reduced abatement costs, but it would have no incentive to abate more than $A^*/2$. Moreover, if a mill feared that the improved technology would prompt the environmental agency to make the standard more stringent, it might attempt to hide the innovation.

On the other hand, pollution charges are a mixed blessing to the industry. They save the industry money by reducing aggregate abatement costs, and they reward mills that develop lower-cost abatement technologies. Being a charge, however, they impose an additional cost on the industry. The total cost burden on the industry is higher than under uniform standards if payments of pollution charges exceed the reduction in aggregate abatement costs. In practice, this is usually the case.

Tradeable pollution permits can overcome many of the disadvantages of pollution charges. Under this approach, the environmental agency determines the total amount of pollution to be discharged into a river. Ideally, this amount corresponds to the optimal $100 - A^*$ units. The agency then allocates this amount among mills, via permits that each grant the right to discharge one unit of pollution. Mills can buy and sell the permits freely. If the market for the permits is competitive, the market-clearing price for the permits will be exactly the same as the value of the optimal pollution charge, MC^*. To see why this is so, suppose that mills 1 and 2 were each granted permits for half the optimal total, $50 - A^*/2$ units. If each mill used all the permits it was granted, each would abate at $A^*/2$. Mill 1's marginal costs would be MC_1', and mill 2's would be MC_2'. In this situation, both would benefit if mill 2 sold one permit to mill 1, as long as the price was above MC_2' and below MC_1'. After selling the permit, mill 2 would need to abate an additional unit, but it would be better off because the price it received from selling the permit would be higher than the incremental abatement cost (MC_2'). Mill 1 would be better off because the cost savings from abating one less unit (MC_1') would be greater than the price it paid for the permit.

Permits would be traded from mill 2 to mill 1 until there were no mutual gains from further trades. This would occur when mill 1 abates at A_1^* and mill 2 at A_2^*. At this point, the difference between their marginal abatement costs would be eliminated, so no further arbitrage would be possible.

Because tradeable permits fix the total pollution load, inflation does not affect their impact on pollution reduction. Inflation simply affects the price of a permit. The total number of permits does not need to be refigured when mills enter or leave the industry: to enter, a mill must purchase permits from existing mills; if a mill leaves, the price of permits simply falls because of lower demand. To an environmental agency, these characteristics offer advantages compared to the uncertain and changing impacts of pollution charges.

Tradeable permits do not raise revenue if they are granted free of charge, but they do if they are auctioned. Charging for the permits, however, mitigates one of their political advantages over pollution charges: they do not impose an additional cost on the industry if they are granted free of charge. In fact, they represent new assets for mills. Tradeable permits also reward innovation: the development of lower-cost abatement technologies enables mills to free up permits for sale to other mills.

Disadvantages of tradeable permits include a possibly heavier administrative burden for the environmental agency. Moreover, tradeable permits do not work well when transaction costs are high relative to the potential gains from trade, or when the trading market is not competitive.[7]

Experience with economic instruments

Several countries have implemented environmental regulations based on either pollution charges or tradeable permits.[8] In most cases, the economic instruments have not been applied in the pure form described in the preceding section. They are usually combined with existing standards and other command-and-control regulations to form a hybrid system.

Pollution charges have been applied most extensively in Europe, and primarily to water pollution (effluent charges). Czechoslovakia, France, Hungary, Italy, Germany, and the Netherlands have all employed effluent charges. France and the Netherlands instituted effluent charges in 1969, while some parts of Germany have had them for decades. Most countries link payment of the charge to a standard: pollution sources are required to comply with a minimum standard, and they pay the charge on any additional pollution they discharge.

Effluent charges in most countries were introduced as revenue-raising devices, for example to finance wastewater treatment facilities, not to induce cost-effective pollution abatement. They are typically set at low levels. Consequently, they have tended to have a minor impact on polluters' behavior. In the Netherlands, however, charges are much higher than in France or Germany, and increases in their levels have been correlated with decreases in pollution discharge.

Tradeable permits, mainly for air pollutants (emissions trading), have been tried primarily in the United States. Hahn (1989) reported only four existing applications of tradeable permits, and three were in the United States.[9] Best-known is the Emissions Trading Program, which was introduced by the U.S. Environmental Protection Agency in 1974 to deal with a variety of air pollutants. The only example of tradeable permits for water pollution is the Transferable Discharge Permits program on the Fox River in Wisconsin, which was introduced in 1981 and was targeted at reducing BOD.

Unlike effluent charges, tradeable permits programs have been motivated by the desire to reduce aggregate abatement costs. In practice, thin markets (too few polluting sources) and heavy restrictions have limited the number of trades and thus the magnitude of cost savings. For example, although the first trade under the Fox River program occurred in 1982, no more had been made as of 1989 (Hahn 1989). On the other hand, despite the fact that trading under the Emissions Trading Program was more limited than anticipated, it had saved industries an estimated US$1 to 12 billion in abatement costs by the mid-1980s (Hahn 1989).

Tietenberg (1988, Table 18.1) summarized the results of simulation studies that compared the costs of controlling water pollution by uniform standards to the costs under approaches based on economic instruments. BOD was the targeted pollutant in all the studies. Aggregate costs under uniform standards were higher by as little as 12 percent and by as much as 213 percent, with the median difference being 54 to 62 percent. He separately reported estimates from a well-known simulation study of the Delaware River estuary (Kneese and Bower 1968), which estimated that costs under uniform standards would be about 200 percent higher than costs under the least-cost option based on economic instruments.

The cost savings of actual programs involving economic instruments have probably been lower than these simulation studies predict, both because economic instruments have generally not been implemented in pure form and because of the institutional problems mentioned earlier. For example, O'Neil (1983, cited in Hahn 1989) estimated that the Fox River program could save US$7 million a year, but with only one trade to its credit it certainly has not done this. Russell (1979) concluded that in practice, "effluent charges have only one unambiguous advantage—they tend to force environment-saving innovation." Tietenberg (1988, p. 416) agreed that a chief benefit of greater reliance on economic instruments in the United States would be to overcome the "technological stagnation" associated with approaches based on uniform standards.

PALM-OIL EFFLUENT CHARGES IN MALAYSIA

Development of the palm-oil pollution problem

Like most of Malaysia's leading crops, the oil palm, *Elaeis guineensis*, is an exotic. It is native to Africa and was first planted commercially in Malaysia in 1917 (Khera 1976). Only minor expansion of the crop occurred during the next five decades, due to high returns to the principal competing crop, rubber. The plantation sector's shift toward oil palm began in the 1960s, when rubber prices began a prolonged decline and the government enacted various policies to promote agricultural diversification. Most expansion occurred in Peninsular Malaysia.

Oil-palm fruits produce two commercially valuable oils. The mesocarp (middle layer) of the fruit produces palm oil, an all-purpose vegetable oil. The nut or kernel yields a smaller amount of palm kernel oil. Fruit bunches must be harvested as soon as they are ripe and processed within twenty-four hours. CPO mills are therefore usually located in or adjacent to plantations. By the early 1970s, the processing needs of the plantations had led to the establishment of a large number of moderately sized mills scattered around the countryside.

CPO mills utilize a primarily mechanical processing technology (Aiken et al. 1982, Ma et al. 1982). They tend to be located on watercourses, because they require about one tonne of water to process one tonne of fresh fruit bunches (Aiken et al. 1982). Palm-oil effluent is a mixture of wastes generated at three points: when the bunches are sterilized using steam to loosen the fruits and to arrest the formation of free fatty acids; when residual oil is separated from other components of the sludge from the clarification tank, where palm oil is decanted; and when palm kernels are processed. Mills generate 2.5 tonnes of effluent for every tonne of CPO produced (Ma et al. 1980, 1982).

CPO mills in Malaysia in the early 1970s disposed of effluent by discharging it, untreated, into the nearest body of water (Ma et al. 1980). When there were only a handful of mills in the country, the environmental impacts of this disposal method were minor. Effluent consists mainly of dissolved organic compounds. At low concentrations, these compounds are readily decomposed by naturally occurring microbes. Between 1965 and 1975, however, the output of CPO grew at a literally exponential rate, as oil-palm plantations in converted rubber estates and government-sponsored land development schemes began reaching maturity. Because the mills were dispersed, within a very short time they became the major source of water pollution in most major river basins in the Peninsula.

Pollution problems were caused mainly by the depletion of dissolved oxygen as the effluent decomposed. Tonne for tonne, the oxygen-depleting potential of palm-oil effluent is one hundred times as great as that of domestic sewage (Maheswaran and Singam 1977). When oxygen concentrations fall to very low levels, decomposition is taken over by anaerobic bacteria, which release hydrogen sulfide, ammonia, and other compounds (Maheswaran and Singam 1977, Shamsudin and Jimat 1981). These compounds are extremely malodorous and are toxic to fish (Shamsudin and Jimat 1981). By mid-1977, "42 rivers in Malaysia were so severely polluted that freshwater fish could no longer survive in them" (Aiken et al. 1982). At that time, fish provided a significant share of the protein in the diets of rural Malays (Aiken et al. 1982, Maheswaran et al. 1980).

Rivers and streams also provided the major source of drinking water for rural Malaysians in the 1970s (Ong et al. 1987). Water from anaerobic, effluent-clogged rivers was unsuitable for human consumption, forcing villagers in some areas to dig wells (Aiken et al. 1982). Rivers were also the site of intakes for municipal water supplies for most cities and towns. Pollution caused by palm-oil effluent raised the costs of treating water to meet municipal standards (Maheswaran et al. 1980). For these various reasons, CPO mills were the major source of water pollution complaints to the government from 1974 to 1978 (Ho 1987).

Structure of the Crude Palm Oil Regulations

By the early 1970s, pollution caused by palm-oil effluent had become a difficult issue that the government could not ignore. Effluent discharge was already large, and it was growing. The combined area of immature and newly cleared plantations was comparable to the area already in production. But the government could not simply shut down the palm-oil industry, which was a principal engine of the country's economic growth and diversification. Palm-oil exports were nearly 15 percent of the country's total export earnings in 1975 (IMF 1991). Government agencies like the Federal Land Development Authority (FELDA) had made substantial investments in land development schemes based on oil palm, and these schemes were a principal means by which the government was attempting to fight rural poverty.[10] FELDA's oil-palm schemes represented two-fifths of the area of new agricultural land developed in Peninsular Malaysia from 1965 to 1975 (Ministry of Agriculture, various issues).

The government's first step was to pass the Environmental Quality Act (EQA) in 1974. Pollution from palm-oil mills was not the sole factor motivating the passage of the EQA—for example, rubber mills were also a major source of water pollution—but it was arguably the most important one. The

EQA authorized the DOE to "prescribe" certain industrial premises, that is to require them to obtain a license before they could operate, and to attach conditions related to pollution control. In determining the license conditions, the EQA directed the DOE to consider factors related to the economic costs of pollution abatement (*Environmental Quality Act, 1974 (Act 127)*, part III, section 11):

(a) whether it would be practicable to adopt the existing equipment, control equipment, or industrial plant to conform with the varied or new condition;
(b) the economic life of the existing equipment, control equipment, or industrial plant; . . .
(d) the estimated cost to be incurred by the licensee to comply with the varied or new condition.

The EQA did not similarly require the DOE to consider the economic benefits of pollution abatement, but it did direct the DOE to consider "the quantity or degree of cut-back of emission . . . to be achieved by the varied or new condition."

The DOE began the process of formulating license conditions by forming an expert committee with representatives from both industry and government (Maheswaran and Singam 1977). The committee's assignment was to investigate possible treatment technologies and to advise the DOE on regulations that were "not only environmentally sound but also sensible within the framework of economic feasibility and available technology" (Ong et al. 1987, p. 37).

The passage of the EQA, the establishment of the DOE, and the formation of the committee convinced the palm-oil industry that the government was intent on reducing pollution from palm-oil effluent. The industry therefore initiated research on effluent treatment technologies. No treatment system for the effluent existed, but systems for treating similar types of organic waste had been developed in industrialized countries (Wood 1977). These systems typically involved a series of treatment ponds that provided proper conditions for growing bacteria that could decompose the waste. Water containing the waste got cleaner and cleaner as it proceeded from one pond to the next. The industry's research strategy was to adapt one of these systems and thereby avoid the high costs involved in designing a treatment system from scratch.

Within two years, the industry's research and development efforts were sufficiently promising to convince the DOE that it did not need to wait much longer to invoke its licensing authority. On July 7, 1977, the DOE announced the Environmental Quality (Prescribed Premises) (Crude Palm Oil) Regulations (Maheswaran 1984). The Regulations imposed standards on eight parameters of palm-oil effluent, with BOD being the key one. The Regulations required CPO mills to apply for an operating license every year. In their application, mills needed to describe their systems for treating and discharging effluent. The DOE could reject a mill's application if it disapproved of the proposed treatment system. Every three months mills also needed to file "quarterly returns" in which they reported the amount of effluent discharged and its BOD concentration, based on tests by independent laboratories.

The DOE announced that the standards would be made increasingly stringent over four years (Table 10.1). Standard A would take effect on July 1, 1978. Existing mills were therefore given a one-year grace period to construct treatment systems. From Standard A to Standard D, mills would be required to reduce the BOD concentration from 5,000 parts per million (ppm)—one-fifth the level in untreated effluent (PORIM 1986)—to 500 ppm. The DOE informed the industry that Standard D would not necessarily be the final and most stringent one (Maheswaran and Singam 1977).

Some industry representatives complained that the Regulations were too stringent (Thillaimuthu 1978). An engineer with one of the largest plantation companies argued: "What is quite clear at this stage is that there is no single generally applicable solution [i.e., treatment system] that is proven on a large scale, over an acceptable period of time. . . . There can be little doubt that the limits for discharge will be very difficult to meet, except at cost incompatible with the economics of operating a mill, unless there are unforeseen advances in technology" (Wood 1977). The DOE responded to these complaints by pointing to three provisions that eased the burden of the Regulations. First, in granting the one-year grace period and phasing in the standards over four years, it recognized that the industry needed time to construct treatment facilities, to gain experience operating them, and in other ways to move from experiment to practice. The DOE might have wanted to reduce the industry's pollution discharge more rapidly, but it recognized that the only way many mills could have complied with more stringent standards would have been by

Table 10.1 *BOD (biochemical oxygen demand) standards for palm-oil effluent*

Standard[a]	Date effective	Level (ppm)[b]
A	July 1, 1978	5,000
B	July 1, 1979	2,000
C	July 1, 1980	1,000
D	July 1, 1981	500
E	July 1, 1982	250
F	July 1, 1984	100

Source: DOE (1985).
[a] Standards A–D were announced in the 1977 Crude Palm Oil Regulations.
[b] ppm—parts per million (mg/l).

shutting down. Given the importance of the industry, this was not a politically feasible option.

Second, the DOE did not make the BOD standard mandatory in the first year. It recognized that many mills did not have treatment systems in place, and that others could substantially reduce their pollution discharge even if they fell short of achieving the standard. For example, a mill that reduced its BOD concentration from the 25,000 ppm typical of untreated effluent to "only" 15,000 ppm would have nevertheless reduced the BOD load it discharged by 40 percent. Given the time needed to construct a treatment system, such a mill could well be on its way to full compliance with the standard.

Instead, the DOE used a novel feature of the EQA to relate the size of the annual license fee to a mill's effluent discharge. The licensing provisions in the EQA authorized the DOE to vary the size of the license fee for prescribed premises according to (*Environmental Quality Act*, part III, section 17): "(a) the class of premises; (b) the location of such premises; (c) the quantity of wastes discharged; (d) the pollutant or class of pollutants discharged; (e) the existing level of pollution."

The regulations invoked provision (c), which gave the DOE the latitude to make the license fee equivalent to an effluent charge. Mills could choose the least-cost option: either treating effluent to reduce the BOD load in their effluent, or paying a higher license fee.

The Regulations made the license fee the sum of two parts, a flat processing fee of RM100 and a variable effluent-related fee. If the mill discharged effluent onto land, the effluent-related fee was linked simply to the quantity of effluent, with the mill required to pay RM0.05 per tonne. If it discharged effluent into a watercourse, the effluent-related fee was more complicated and was linked to the BOD load in the effluent. Mills were required to pay RM10 per tonne of BOD for concentrations up to the standard, and RM100 per tonne of BOD above the standard. For example, an average-sized mill that discharged 90,000 tonnes of effluent a year with a BOD concentration of 15,000 ppm would owe a basic fee of RM4,500 (90,000 tonnes times 5,000 ppm times RM10/tonne) and an excess fee of RM90,000 (90,000 tonnes times the difference between 15,000 ppm and 5,000 ppm, times RM100/tonne). In effect, the regulations imposed a dual effluent-charge system, with the charge being higher above the standard than below to induce compliance.[11]

An interesting feature of the system is that it involved an element of self-enforcement. The DOE calculated the fees on the basis of information on projected effluent volume and BOD levels for the forthcoming year reported by mills in their license applications.[12] The quarterly returns and unannounced site visits provided means for the DOE to check that the estimates were reasonably accurate. A minimum payment applied: mills had to pay an effluent-related license fee of at least RM150, even if the calculated value was less.

The DOE did not set the charges by determining the marginal benefits of effluent abatement at the optimal level. The DOE's officers, none of whom were economists, were more uncertain about the level of the charges than any other part of the Regulations. In the end, the DOE set the charges at levels that it judged would provide some financial incentive for the industry to reduce its pollution discharge without being onerous.

Third, the DOE recognized that ongoing research and development were necessary for addressing the effluent disposal problem. Therefore, it included in the regulations a provision authorizing it to reduce the license fee for mills conducting research on effluent treatment. Section 17 of the regulations stated: "If the Director-General [of the DOE] is satisfied that research on effluent disposal or treatment of a kind or scale that is likely to benefit the cause of environmental protection is being or to be carried out at any pre-scribed premises, he may, with the approval of the Minister, completely or partially waive any effluent-related amount payable by virtue of [the license-fee] regulation." In effect, the DOE allowed the industry to retain some of the revenue that it otherwise would have had to pay out in effluent charges.

Two features of the regulations reveal the DOE's reasons for imposing efflu-ent charges. The first is the minimum payment. Given that the effluent charge for watercourse disposal was RM10 per tonne of BOD, the minimum payment removed the incentive for mills to reduce watercourse discharge below 15 tonnes of BOD: they had to pay RM150 even if their actual abatement level was lower. The DOE was apparently unaware of this effect. The second is the mandatory standard after the first year. Once the standard was mandatory, the DOE could suspend or cancel the license of any mill that violated the standard. It retained the effluent charges, however, with the excess charge being applied to mills whose violations were not considered serious enough to merit license suspension. For example, the DOE might apply the excess charge to a mill that was in the process of constructing a treatment system.

These features indicate that the DOE viewed the effluent charges less as a means of promoting cost-effective abatement than as a means of reinforcing a system of uniform standards. The minimum payment made the Regulations less than a pure effluent-charge system in the first year, by reducing the incentive effect of the basic charge. The mandatory standard made the Regu-lations even less like a pure system in following years, by reducing mills' flexibility in making abatement decisions. These features were attractive from DOE's point of view because the former guaranteed that licensing would generate a minimum amount of revenue, while the latter guaranteed that mills would reduce their BOD discharge by a minimum amount.

Performance of the Regulations

The DOE was somewhat disappointed with the performance of the Regulations during the first year (Maheswaran et al. 1980). On the positive side, it collected a substantial amount of revenue from license fees, RM2.8 million, as many mills chose to pay the excess charge rather than meet the standard. Most important to the DOE, the average mill reduced its discharge of BOD by about two-thirds. Although this was an impressive reduction, the DOE had expected the average mill to meet the standard and thereby reduce its discharge by about 80 percent. The DOE's high expectations were not met because so many mills opted to pay the excess charge.

The DOE could have responded by raising the basic and excess charges, since the charges were apparently too low to induce, on average, compliance with the BOD standard.[13] Instead, as discussed above, the regulations committed it to making Standard B and subsequent standards mandatory. The DOE signaled its willingness to take strong measures to enforce the standard almost immediately. In November, 1979, it suspended the license of a mill on the Sungai Langat in the state of Selangor. From 1981 to 1984, it took similar action against twenty-seven mills (DOE 1985).

After the first year, the motivation to comply with the standard was therefore not the excess charge, but rather the risk of being shut down for violating the mandatory standard. It follows that the standard, not the excess charge, deserves most of the credit for the rapid reduction in the aggregate BOD load discharged during the initial years of the regulations (Figure 10.1). One might argue that the excess charge deserves two-thirds of the credit because the BOD load dropped by about two-thirds during the first year, before the standard was mandatory. This argument is not very convincing, however. More likely, the load dropped so much because mills were building systems capable of meeting the more stringent, mandatory standards that the regulations had announced would immediately follow Standard A.

It is nevertheless possible that the basic charge had some residual impact on BOD levels after the first year. An average-sized mill discharging 90,000 tonnes of effluent annually would discharge a BOD load of 180 tonnes if it complied with Standard B, 90 tonnes if it complied with Standard C, and 45 tonnes if it complied with Standard D. Given the basic charge of RM10 per tonne, its effluent-related license fee would be RM1800, RM900, and RM450, respectively. These amounts were larger than the minimum license fee, RM150. Depending on its marginal abatement cost curve, an average-sized mill could save up to RM1650, RM750, and RM300, respectively, by voluntarily decreasing its BOD concentration to 167 ppm, at which concentration it would owe the minimum fee (90,000 tonnes times 167 ppm times RM10).

During the second year of the regulations, the average mill reduced its daily discharge of BOD to about half the level during the first year. Although this still did not match the DOE's expectation (Maheswaran et al. 1980), the discrepancy between performance and expectation was narrowing. The treatment pond system was proving to be effective at an operational scale. In just two years, the regulations had reduced the population-equivalent of the pollution load from 15.9 to 2.6 million people (Figure 10.1), despite a 50 percent increase in CPO production.

The BOD load continued declining in succeeding years. The industry's efforts to improve treatment technologies were given a boost in 1980 when the government established the Palm Oil Research Institute of Malaysia (PORIM). A survey conducted by PORIM and the Rubber Research Institute of Malaysia (RRIM) in 1980–1981 found that 90 percent of the forty mills surveyed were discharging effluent with a BOD concentration below Standard D (500 ppm), and that 40 percent were achieving a BOD concentration below 100 ppm (Ma et al. 1982). Most of the mills were using the ponding system, although seven were using tank digestion systems developed to overcome land constraints.

Although the basic charge is one possible explanation for the mills beating the standard, it probably does not explain why so many achieved concentrations below 100 ppm. As mentioned above, the basic charge gave an average-sized mill an incentive to reduce its concentration down to, but not below, 167 ppm. An alternative explanation is that the mills expected the DOE to impose even more stringent standards, as it had indicated it might when it announced the regulations, and that they had therefore constructed systems to meet these anticipated standards, not Standards A through D. If so, they guessed right: the PORIM/RRIM survey and other evidence of ongoing improvements in treatment technology led the DOE to announce more stringent fifth- and sixth-generation standards in the early 1980s (Table 10.1). In fact, under Standard F, the DOE included a provision allowing it to impose a special standard of 20 ppm on mills upstream from intakes for water supply systems.

By the mid-1980s, the population-equivalent of the industry's BOD load dropped to the nearly insignificant level of less than 100,000 people (Figure 10.1). In 1991, the DOE randomly monitored 112 of the 265 CPO mills in Malaysia and found that 75 percent were complying with Standard F (DOE 1992). The industry's ability to reduce its BOD discharge to such low levels was facilitated not only by improvements in treatment technology, but also by the development, by it and by PORIM, of various commercial byproducts made from palm-oil effluent (Ong et al. 1987, Khalid and Wan Mustafa 1992). As early as 1977, a Danish company perceived a market opportunity in the forthcoming regulations and began marketing a process to convert separator sludge into animal feed (Jorgensen 1977). By 1982, ten large pig and poultry farms were using palm-oil meal in their feed mixes (Jorgensen 1982). Mills that discharged effluent onto land found that it had a fertilizing effect (Maheswaran and Singam 1977, Ma et al. 1980). This enabled many plantations to eliminate their purchases of fertilizers (Ma et al. 1980, Yusof and Ma 1992). One company saved an estimated RM390,000 per year on its fertilizer purchases (Tam et al. 1982). In 1982, three mills with tank digesters were recovering methane, which comprises 60–70 percent of the gases generated during anaerobic digestion, and using it to generate electricity for mill use (Ma 1993, Ong et al. 1987). The industry has discussed selling electricity generated from the "biogas" to the National Electricity Board (Lim et al. 1984). One analysis found that the payback period for the investment required to build an integrated fertilizer/biogas recovery system was only 3.1 years (Quah et al. 1982). In 1984, four mills found uses for all their effluent and consequently had zero discharge (Maheswaran 1984).

Although the industry expanded after the Regulations were implemented and was able to turn some of the effluent into commercially viable products, it did incur costs due to the regulations. Capital costs accounted for most of the costs associated with treatment systems. Excluding the cost of land, estimates of capital costs ranged from RM330,000 for a ponding system to RM600,000 to 950,000 for systems involving tanks (Khalid and Wan Mustafa 1992, citing various sources). By 1984, mills other than those owned by FELDA had spent an estimated RM100 million to construct and operate treatment systems (Lim 1984). Relative to the industry's total production costs, however, treatment costs were low: only 0.2 percent in 1983, according to one estimate (Chooi 1984).

The regulations might not have impaired overall competitiveness of the processing sector of the palm-oil industry, but they did affect the distribution of economic returns within the industry (Khalid 1991, Khalid and Braden 1993). Most of Malaysia's output of crude and refined palm oils was, and is, sold in an extremely competitive world market for fats and oils.[14] This prevented mills from passing much of the costs of effluent treatment onto consumers. Instead, they shifted the costs upstream to oil-palm growers, who had no sales outlet aside from CPO mills, by reducing the price they paid for fresh fruit bunches. Ultimately, palm-oil growers bore two-thirds to three-fourths of the costs. Cumulative losses in producer surplus[15] from 1982 to 1986, relative to the value of output during the same period, were only 1.2 percent for CPO mills and 4.7 percent for refined palm-oil mills, but 44 percent for growers.

Cost Savings of the Effluent Charges in the Sungai Johor Basin

Although the effluent charges probably had only a minor impact on the industry's aggregate BOD load after the first year, they still might have generated some cost savings. The basic charge gave mills flexibility to adjust their BOD concentrations between the floor created by the minimum effluent-related license fee and the ceiling imposed by the mandatory standard, while the excess charge gave the DOE an alternative to shutting down mills that violated the standard only temporarily.

We estimated the potential magnitude of these cost savings for the case of mills on the Sungai Johor. In 1991, this river had sixteen mills, more than any other river in the country, and it received the largest aggregate BOD load. We restricted our analysis to the ten mills that discharged effluent into the river instead of onto land. All used the standard ponding system to treat their effluent.

Most of the mills were established several years after the regulations came into force. To control for the standard they faced, we analyzed their abatement behavior from 1984 to 1991, when only Standard F applied. Half of the mills were established during this period. Treatment technologies were well established by this time, so mills' behavior was unlikely to have been affected by uncertainties related to effluent treatment.

Appendix 10 provides details of the analysis. The general approach was: 1) to estimate a system of marginal cost curves—one curve for each mill—corresponding to the mill-level curves in Figure 10.2; and 2) to use these curves to simulate abatement behavior in response to both a uniform standard and an effluent charge, which yielded the same aggregate reduction in the BOD load as the standard. From the simulation results we calculated aggregate abatement costs under the two pollution-control options. The simulated effluent charge was a pure effluent charge: unlike the actual charges, it did not vary according to the BOD level, and there was no minimum license fee. Hence, the simulation results indicated the aggregate abatement cost savings that the ten mills would have enjoyed if they had faced a pure effluent charge instead of a uniform standard. The simulated savings therefore provide an upper bound on the magnitude of the cost savings that the actual charges provided.

The DOE provided data for the analysis from the mills' annual license applications and quarterly returns. The quarterly returns report tonnes of effluent discharged each month and BOD concentrations during the first week of each month. We converted these to quarterly estimates by summing the effluent estimates and weighting the BOD estimates by the quantity of effluent. We calculated quarterly BOD abatement by multiplying tonnes of effluent times the difference between 25,000 ppm, the mean concentration of BOD in untreated effluent, and the actual concentration. This corresponds to the quantity variable, A, in the marginal cost curves in Figure 10.2.

We treated the quantity of effluent as an exogenous variable. This is a reasonable assumption, since CPO production, and therefore effluent generation, is largely determined by the ripening of palm-oil fruits, which is subject to climatic and biological factors beyond mills' control. Hence, we assumed that mills minimized abatement costs purely by selecting the BOD concentration of the fixed amount of effluent they discharged. In practice, mills do not have precise control over the BOD concentration, but they can influence it through the amount of residual oil and solids they allow in untreated effluent entering the treatment system, by the length of time they retain effluent in the various treatment ponds, and by the effort they put into maintaining the ponds (primarily to prevent buildup of suspended solids and sludge).To estimate the marginal cost curves we also needed data on the marginal costs at actual abatement levels, as well as on other variables that might be expected to affect abatement costs. Regarding the latter, we obtained data on processing capacity utilization from the license applications and quarterly returns. One might expect abatement costs to rise with capacity utilization, assuming that the capacity of a mill's treatment system is proportional to its processing capacity.

Unfortunately, no direct data on treatment costs were available. In line with the discussion in the section *Uniform standards versus economic instruments*, we assumed that mills were rational cost-minimizers that abated up to the point where the marginal abatement cost equaled the marginal effluent charge they actually paid. If they complied with the standard, we set the marginal cost equal to the basic charge; if they violated it, we set it equal to the excess charge. Out of the 172 quarterly observations in the data set, mills complied with the standard in about half of the quarters. We deflated the charges using the GDP deflator (1978 price levels). Although the charges were constant in nominal terms, due to inflation they were lower in 1991 than in 1984. At 1978 price levels, the values in 1991 were RM6.66 for the basic charge and RM66.62 for the excess charge.

The estimation results confirmed that marginal abatement costs were positively and significantly related to both abatement level and capacity utilization. In spite of the minimum effluent-related license fee and the mandatory standards, the effluent charges evidently had a significant impact on mills' abatement decisions. On average, a 10 percent increase in abatement resulted in a 4.3 percent increase in the marginal cost. It was therefore meaningful to proceed with the simulation of cost savings.

We simulated the cost savings at average 1991 values for effluent discharge and capacity utilization.[16] As discussed in the section the *Uniform standards versus economic instruments*, the difference in aggregate abatement costs between effluent charges and uniform standards depends on the magnitude of differences between mills' marginal cost curves. In the simulation model, mills' marginal cost curves differed for three reasons: the amount of effluent they treated (which affected their abatement level), their capacity utilization, and the intercepts of their marginal cost curves, which were allowed to vary across mills. All three factors varied substantially. Average quarterly tonnes of effluent and capacity utilization varied by factors of nearly ten. Differences in the intercepts implied that, at given levels of effluent and capacity utilization, the marginal abatement cost for the lowest-cost abater was 49 percent below the average for the mills, while that for the highest-cost abater was 95 percent above. These differences suggest that cost savings from effluent charges could potentially be large.

Table 10.2 shows results of simulations of the uniform standard. We simulated four standards, ranging from 5,000 ppm (Standard A) to 100 ppm (Standard F). The aggregate BOD load dropped from 1,029 tonnes under the 5,000 ppm standard to only 21 tonnes under the 100 ppm standard. Aggregate abatement costs rose sharply when the standard dropped from 5,000 ppm to 1,000 ppm, but more modestly as the standard dropped even further. This reflected not only diminishing differences between the four standards analyzed (4000 ppm, 500 ppm, and 400 ppm), but also the inelasticity of the marginal cost curve: marginal costs increased less and less rapidly as abatement rose. For each standard, the difference between the marginal cost for the mill with the lowest marginal cost curve (that is, the marginal cost corresponding to MC_2') and the marginal cost for the mill with the highest curve (MC_1') was more than RM30. The ratio of highest to lowest was on the order of five to six, which is comparable to what O'Neil (1980, cited in Tietenberg

Table 10.2 *Simulated abatement costs for uniform standards: crude palm-oil mills on Sungai Johor, average quarter in 1991*

	Standard (ppm)[a]			
	5000	1000	500	100
Aggregate discharge (tonnes of BOD)[b]	1029	206	103	21
Minimum marginal cost	RM6.51	RM7.03	RM7.10	RM7.15
Maximum marginal cost	RM37.62	RM40.67	RM41.03	RM41.31
Aggregate abatement costs[c]	RM67,117	RM87,065	RM89,666	RM91,763

[a] ppm—parts per million.
[b] BOD—Biochemical oxygen demand.
[c] Sum of areas under marginal cost curves.

1988) reported in a simulation study of BOD abatement on the Fox River in the United States. These differences suggest that effluent charges might generate sizeable cost savings.

Table 10.3 shows the effluent charges corresponding to each standard and the abatement costs associated with them.[17] All the charges were much greater than the 1991 basic charge and much lower than the 1991 excess charge. This implies that in 1991, the basic charge alone would not have achieved the aggregate abatement level of even Standard A, while the excess charge alone would have achieved an abatement level even higher than Standard F. The DOE probably did not need to make the standards mandatory after the first year: the excess charge would have provided sufficient incentive for the industry to meet the standards on average.

In the presence of only effluent charges, however, abatement levels would have varied greatly across mills. Under the lowest charge, RM29, only four mills discharged BOD with concentrations exceeding 100 ppm, but those that did violated it by a great amount. One had a BOD concentration of 14,098 ppm. At higher effluent charges, only two mills exceeded 100 ppm. These results suggest that a pure effluent-charge system would induce most mills to reduce their BOD discharge to very low levels, but it might possibly create local pollution problems in the vicinity of the few mills that continued to discharge effluent with high BOD concentrations.

Table 10.3 Simulated abatement costs for effluent charges: crude palm-oil mills on Sungai Johor, average quarter in 1991

| | Effluent charge | | | |
	RM29.03	RM37.57	RM39.00	RM40.15
Aggregate discharge (tonnes of BOD)[a]	1029	206	103	21
Mills exceeding 100 ppm	4	2	2	1
Minimum concentration (ppm)	0	0	0	0
Maximum concentration (ppm)	14,098	5,064	3,243	1,711
Aggregate abatement costs[c]	RM 57,632	RM 84,250	RM 88,184	RM91,451
Cost savings: absolute terms[d]	RM9,485	RM2,815	RM1,482	RM312
Cost savings: relative terms[e]	1.165	1.033	1.017	1.003
Aggregate effluent fees	RM29,848	RM7,735	RM4,022	RM824
Total cost to mills[f]	RM87,480	RM91,985	RM92,206	RM92,275

[a] BOD—biochemical oxygen demand.

[b] ppm—parts per million.

[c] Sum of areas under marginal cost curves.

[d] Aggregate abatement costs for the uniform standard minus aggregate abatement costs for the corresponding effluent charge.

[e] Aggregate abatement costs for the uniform standard divided by aggregate abatement costs for the effluent charge.

[f] Sum of aggregate abatement costs and aggregate effluent fees.

As expected, aggregate abatement costs were lower in all cases compared to the uniform standards. The savings were greater in both absolute and relative terms at lower abatement levels (less stringent standards), but they were modest even there: about RM1,000 per mill at the RM29 effluent charge. Differences were still detectable between the 100 ppm standard and the RM40 effluent charge, but they were tiny: about RM30 per mill. The effluent charges generated very low cost savings when abatement levels were high.

From the standpoint of total costs—abatement costs plus effluent charges—the industry would actually be better off under a uniform standard. Aggregate abatement costs under this approach were less than the sum of aggregate abatement costs and aggregate effluent fees under an effluent charge. The effluent charges would more than offset the industry's savings on abatement costs.

Conclusions

Malaysia's Crude Palm Oil Regulations were not equivalent to a pure effluent charge system. They most closely resembled a pure system in their first year, when the BOD standard was not mandatory. They were more complicated even then, however, in that the level of the charge depended on whether or not the BOD concentration of a mill's effluent exceeded the standard. Mills' abatement decisions were also affected by the provision for payment of a minimum fee. In being linked to a standard and being motivated by objectives other than cost-effective pollution control, the palm-oil effluent charges were similar to effluent charge systems implemented in other countries.

Malaysia's experience with the Regulations offers several lessons for pollution control efforts in the country. The most general, and most important, is that pollution abatement and industrial expansion can occur simultaneously. The government need not be reluctant to address the pollution problems of leading industries, as indeed it was not in the case of the palm-oil industry. Output of the industry expanded as rapidly after 1978 as before.

A facilitating factor was that CPO mills' concerns about excessive abatement costs proved to be unfounded. One reason was the mills' ability to shift the costs of the regulations onto oil-palm growers. Another, which reduced instead of simply shifted costs, was technology. Research and development efforts softened the potential trade-off between pollution abatement and industrial expansion. The ponding system was relatively inexpensive, especially in terms of operating costs, and mills were able to develop numerous byproducts from the effluent. The credit for research and development provided an incentive to investigate these technologies, and the low value of the basic charge made it easier for mills to finance their implementation from internal resources.

The research credit and the low value of the basic charge were critical in gaining industry support of the regulations. They reflected the industry's influence on the expert committee that proposed draft regulations to the DOE. Industry representation on this committee helped ensure that the structure and timing of the regulations took into account the costs the regulations imposed on the industry and offered the industry flexibility in responding to them. The risk in this arrangement, of course, was that industry could have "captured" the DOE and weakened the regulations to the point of ineffectiveness. The government's commitment to solving the palm-oil effluent problem prevented this from happening.

The government's commitment was illustrated most strikingly by its well-publicized actions to suspend the operating licenses of mills that violated the regulations. Such actions, coupled with the minimum fee requirement and, especially, the imposition of mandatory standards after the first year, strongly suggest that the risk to a mill of having its operating license suspended, not the financial incentive created by the effluent charges, was primarily responsible for the reduction in BOD discharge. This was probably true even in the first year, as the mandatory standards were preannounced, and mills knew they had just a one-year grace period. The impact of the charges was weakened subsequently by inflation, which might explain why treatment technology has advanced little since the early 1980s (Ma 1993).

Mandatory standards also reduced the ability of the charges to promote cost-effective abatement. Simulation results for the Sungai Johor suggest that the increased cost to the industry was small, because the difference in marginal costs across mills was low in absolute terms. The simulation results understated the cost impacts, however, because they measured only short-run marginal costs (operating costs). The estimated marginal cost curves were for mills' existing treatment systems, which were constructed to meet Standard F. If in reality mills had faced an effluent charge rather than a mandatory standard, mills could have saved on capital costs as well as operating costs by altering the design of their treatment systems.

The simulation results also illustrate a potential environmental risk associated with effluent charges: charges can result in local pollution problems when pollutants do not disperse readily. The simulation results indicated that some mills would discharge effluent with a BOD concentration well above historical standards if they faced a pure effluent charge. Although it is possible to design a cost-effective system of "ambient charges" whose levels vary across pollution sources and are linked to local ambient conditions (Tietenberg

1988, pp. 320-326), such a system is information intensive and difficult to administer. In essence, it is not much different from a system of mill-specific effluent standards,[18] which offers an environmental agency greater certainty about pollution abatement.

In sum, Malaysia's experience with the Crude Palm Oil regulations is by no means a straightforward testament to the advantages of economic instruments over command-and-control regulations. The regulations had many aspects of the latter. These aspects undermined the charges' advantages related to cost-effectiveness and technology development, but they minimized the risk of continued pollution problems downstream from high-cost mills. The economics of this trade-off are not clear, as neither the effluent charges nor the standards were chosen by comparing marginal abatement costs and marginal abatement benefits. The regulations undeniably led to a massive reduction in the BOD load in the country's rivers, but it is possible that the reduction was either too big or too little, or that it occurred too quickly or too slowly.

Appendix 10: Estimation and Solution of the Simulation Model for CPO Mills on the Sungai Johor

As discussed in the section *Cost savings of the effluent charges in the Sungai Johor basin*, we assumed that marginal abatement costs for mills on the Sungai Johor equaled the marginal effluent charges they paid:

$$CHARGE = f(ABATE). \tag{A10.1}$$

CHARGE is the effluent charge and *f* is the marginal cost curve, which is a function of the BOD load abated, *ABATE*. *CHARGE* equals the basic charge for concentrations less than the standard, and the excess charge for concentrations above.

Estimating the marginal cost curve was complicated by characteristics of the data on effluent charges. When a mill's BOD concentration exactly equals the standard, its marginal cost does not necessarily equal the basic charge. The mill would pay a marginal effluent charge of RM10 per tonne, but its marginal cost could be as high as RM100 per tonne. The marginal cost is bounded by the basic and excess charges, but its precise value cannot be determined.

We dealt with this problem by defining the data set in two ways. The first, full panel included all the data. As it turned out, in no case did the quarterly BOD concentration exactly equal the standard. The second, partial panel excluded data for which the standard fell within a range defined as the quarterly BOD concentration plus or minus two standard deviations. We calculated the standard deviation using the three monthly estimates for each quarter, and we calculated it separately for each mill and each quarter.[19] The full panel included a total of 172 quarterly observations, while the partial one included 86 observations. Both panels were unbalanced: there were differing numbers of observations for the mills, because some mills were older than others. The partial panel included data on only nine of the mills.

A second complication related to the possible lack of comparability between the marginal cost curves for BOD concentrations above and below the standard. An unusually large harvest is perhaps the most common reason for temporary violations of the standard. The size of the harvest affects the output of crude palm oil, which in turn affects the amount of effluent to be treated. When the amount is large, a mill might be forced to move the effluent through the treatment system more rapidly than usual, and this results in a higher BOD level. This implies that the mill's marginal cost curve has shifted temporarily upward. We included capacity utilization, the ratio of CPO output to processing capacity, in equation A10.1 to reflect this shift.

A third complication related to the amount of variation in the effluent charges. If the charges vary little over time, then estimation of equation A10.1

will not yield meaningful results. The basic and excess charges were set at RM10 and RM100 per tonne in the regulations, and they have remained the same since. In spite of this, there was substantial variation in the data on the charges, for two reasons. First, the basic and excess charges differ by a factor of ten. Second, although each charge has remained constant in nominal terms, its real value has decreased due to inflation. Malaysia has an excellent record in controlling inflation, but nevertheless the real value of the charges, determined by dividing them by the GDP deflator (base year of 1978), fell by more than 30 percent between 1978 and 1991.

We converted equation A10.1 into a form that could be econometrically estimated through the following steps. We assumed that the quarterly total variable cost (*TVC*) of operating a treatment system was a Cobb-Douglas function of the BOD load abated (*ABATE*) and capacity utilization (*CAP*):

$$TVC_{it} = EXP(\alpha_i) \times ABATE_{it}^{\beta+1} \times CAP_{it}^{\gamma}/(\beta+1). \qquad \text{(A10.2)}$$

EXP is the exponential function (the mathematical constant e raised to the power indicated in parentheses); α, β, and γ are parameters to be estimated, and i and t are subscripts distinguishing data by mill and time period, respectively. Note that α was allowed to vary across mills. We will say more about this below. Equation A10.2 indicates that total variable costs equal zero when there is no abatement, which makes sense. *ABATE* was defined as:

$$ABATE_{it} = EFF_{it} \times (0.025 - CONC_{it}) \qquad \text{(A10.3)}$$

where *EFF* is the amount of effluent discharged and *CONC* is the BOD concentration of the effluent. The number 0.025 represents 25,000 ppm, the average BOD concentration of untreated effluent.

A mill selects the value of *CONC* that minimizes the sum of total variable costs related to effluent treatment, given by equation A10.2, and effluent discharge, which equals the total effluent charge (*TF*, for total fees):

$$TF_{it} = CHARGE_t \times EFF_{it} \times CONC_{it}. \qquad \text{(A10.4)}$$

CHARGE is the effluent charge per tonne of BOD load. If we sum the expressions on the right-hand sides of equations A10.2 and equation A10.4, substitute equation A10.3 to eliminate *ABATE*, and take the derivative with respect to *CONC*, we obtain:

$$CHARGE_t = EXP(\alpha_i) \times ABATE_{it}^{\beta} \times CAP_{it}^{\gamma}. \qquad \text{(A10.5)}$$

The mill abates up to the point where the effluent charge (the left-hand side) equals the marginal treatment cost (the right-hand side). This demonstrates that the general form of equation A10.1 is valid.

Taking the natural logarithm of each side of equation A10.5 converts it into a linear expression that is more readily estimated:

$$ln(CHARGE_t) = \alpha_i + \beta \times ln(ABATE_{it}) + \gamma \times ln(CAP_{it}) + \epsilon_{it}. \quad (A10.6)$$

This equation includes an error term, ϵ, which we assumed was independently and identically distributed (i.i.d.) across mills and time periods.

The proper procedure for estimating equation A10.6 depends on the characteristics of the intercept α_i (Judge et al. 1985, Chapter 13). If α_i reflects purely fixed differences between mills—for example, permanent differences related to the scale or design of their treatment systems—then equation A10.6 can be estimated by ordinary least squares (OLS), with a different intercept included for each mill. The estimated intercepts equal the α_is. This is the *fixed-effects*, or *dummy-variable*, *model*.

On the other hand, α_i might reflect random differences between mills. The values of α_i might be drawn from a common distribution with a mean of α^*, with differences among them being due to a random error term, μ_i:

$$\alpha_i = \alpha^* + \mu_i. \quad (A10.7)$$

The mean of μ_i is zero. This implies that equation A10.6 can be rewritten as:

$$ln(CHARGE_t) = \alpha^* + \beta \times ln(ABATE_{it}) + \gamma \times ln(CAP_{it}) + (\epsilon_{it} + \mu_i). \quad (A10.8)$$

The error term now has two components, ϵ_{it} and μ_i. Hence, this model is called the *error-components*, or *random-effects*, *model*.

Using OLS to estimate equation A10.8 yields inefficient estimates of α^* and β: the standard errors of the OLS coefficient estimators are larger than necessary, because they ignore information on the non-i.i.d. nature of the error term. Moreover, estimates of the standard errors of the coefficients are biased, because OLS estimators of coefficients' standard errors assume that error terms are i.i.d. Efficient estimation of equation A10.8 requires generalized least squares.

Following estimation, the random effect μ_i for each mill can be estimated by the formula:

$$\mu_i = \{\Sigma \; [ln(CHARGE_t) - \alpha^* - \beta \times ln(ABATE_{it}) \quad (A10.9)$$
$$- \gamma \times ln(CAP_{it})]\} \times \sigma_\mu^2/(T_i\sigma_\mu^2 + \sigma_\epsilon^2).$$

The term in curly brackets is the sum of the residuals for the mill in question (here, α^*, β, and γ are estimates of the coefficients), σ_μ^2 and σ_ϵ^2 are the estimated variances of μ_i and ϵ_{it}, respectively, and T_i is the number of observations on the mill.

A chi-squared test can assist in choosing between the models (Hausman 1978). The null hypothesis is that the random effects are uncorrelated with the explanatory variables on the right-hand side of equation A10.8. If the test fails to reject this hypothesis, then the random-effects model is preferred: it provides more efficient coefficient estimates than does the fixed-effects model. If one rejects the hypothesis, however, then the fixed-effects model is preferred: its coefficient estimates are inefficient but unbiased, whereas those of the random-effects model are biased.

Table A10.1 presents the results of estimating the fixed-effects model (equation A10.6) and the random-effects model (equation A10.8) for both panels. The table also includes results for a third model, identical to equation A10.6 except that the α_is are constrained to have the same value. These results are for OLS with a common intercept (ordinary OLS).

Results for each model differed relatively little between the samples. This is a satisfying result: it suggests that effluent charges did indeed equal marginal costs for observations in the larger sample. Since the larger sample includes not just more data but data on all the mills, we regarded estimates based on it as the preferred estimates. Ordinary OLS, fixed-effects, and random-effects estimates of β and γ were fairly similar, indicating that the estimates of the coefficients were fairly robust. The estimates of β and γ were significantly different from zero at the 1 percent level in the OLS and random-effects models; only γ was significant, at the 5 percent level, in the fixed-effects model.

We used an F test to test the null hypothesis that the mill-specific intercepts in the fixed-effects model were identical. Failure to reject this hypothesis would indicate that the fixed-effect model is not statistically different from the ordinary OLS model. The value of the test statistic was 4.94 (10 and 160 degrees of freedom), which rejected the null hypothesis at the 1 percent level

Table A10.1 *Estimates of parameters in the marginal cost curve for abatement by mills on the Sungai Johor*

	Full panel			Partial panel		
	OLS[a]	FE[b]	RE[c]	OLS[a]	FE[b]	RE[c]
ß	0.488***	0.316	0.427***	0.571***	0.295	0.413**
	(0.092)	(0.211)	(0.150)	(0.116)	(0.196)	(0.159)
γ	0.694***	0.412**	0.487***	0.844***	0.276	0.388**
	(0.128)	(0.168)	(0.149)	(0.131)	(0.178)	(0.157)

Note: ß is the exponent on abatement, and γ is the exponent on capacity utilization. ** and *** indicate parameter estimates that are significantly different from zero at the 5 percent and 1 percent levels, respectively. Standard errors are in parentheses.

[a] OLS—ordinary-least-squares estimates, with the intercept (not shown) constrained to be the same across mills.

[b] FE—fixed-effects estimates.

[c] RE—random-effects estimates.

(critical value of approximately 2.47). Hence, the values of the α_is did differ between the mills.

We used the chi-squared test to determine whether it was more appropriate to treat the differences in the α_is as resulting from fixed or random effects. The value of the chi-squared statistic (2 degrees of freedom) was 1.86, which meant that we failed to reject the null hypothesis of no correlation between the random effects and the explanatory variables at even a 10 percent level (critical value of 4.61). Hence, the random-effects estimates were preferred.

The random effects estimates of β and γ for the full panel were both positive, as expected: marginal costs rose with abatement level and capacity utilization. The value of β was less than one, which, given the Cobb-Douglas form, indicates that the marginal cost curve was inelastic: a 10 percent increase in abatement raised the marginal cost by 4.3 percent. The estimate of γ was also less than one.

To simulate a uniform standard, we used equation A10.3 to predict the amount of abatement for a given value of CONC, and then we substituted the result into equation A10.2 to predict total variable costs of abatement. We knew the parameter values in equation A10.2 from estimating equation A10.8. We set the values of EFF and CAP equal to their average values in 1991.[20] The exponential value of each random effect—$EXP(\mu_i)$, which is part of $EXP(\alpha_i)$ in equation A10.2—was calculated using equation A10.9.

To simulate an effluent charge, we first solved equation A10.5 for CONC and constrained it to predict only nonnegative values:

$$CONC_{it} = POS\{0.025 - [CHARGE_t/EXP(\alpha_i)/CAP_{it}^\gamma]^{1/\beta}/EFF_{it}\}. \quad (A10.10)$$

POS is a mathematical operator which sets CONC equal to zero if the expression in curly brackets is negative. The calculated value of CONC was then substituted into equation A10.2, and simulation proceeded as in the case of the uniform standard.

NOTES

1 Regulations promulgated under the 1974 Environmental Quality Act include the 1977 Crude Palm Oil Regulations, the 1978 Raw Natural Rubber Regulations, the 1978 Clean Air Regulations, the 1979 Sewage and Industrial Effluents Regulations, the 1985 Control of Lead Concentration in Motor Gasoline Regulations, the 1987 Motor Vehicle Noise Regulations, and the 1989 Scheduled Wastes Regulations (DOE 1992). Regulations promulgated under the 1958 Road Traffic Ordinance include the 1977 Motor Vehicle (Control of Smoke and Gas Emissions) Rules.

2 Kneese and Schultze (1975), Tietenberg (1988, 1990), and Hahn (1989) provide information on the debate over pollution-control strategies in the United States.

3 Institute for Advanced Studies (1992) provides a concise discussion of the scope for economics-oriented approaches to environmental management in Malaysia.

4 BOD is the total amount of oxygen that microorganisms consume while decomposing organic waste. For example, 1 liter of wastewater with a BOD of 5,000 mg/l will consume 5,000 mg of oxygen as decomposition occurs.

5 This section draws upon Tietenberg (1988, 1990) and Cropper and Oates (1992).

6 The aggregate marginal cost curve in Figure 9.1, MC, equals the horizontal sum of MC_1 and MC_2.

7 A classic paper by Weitzman (1974) pointed out that the choice between pollution charges and tradeable permits is influenced by uncertainty about the marginal benefits and marginal costs of pollution abatement. Tradeable permits are the preferred instrument when the marginal benefits curve is steeper than the marginal cost curve, and pollution charges are preferred when the marginal cost curve is steeper.

8 This section draws on reviews by Hahn (1989), Tietenberg (1988, 1990), and Cropper and Oates (1992).

9 More recently, the United States introduced a trading scheme for sulfur dioxide emissions.

10 Aiken et al. (1982) have commented that the schemes were "one of the most successful forms of rural land development in the Third World."

11 Czechoslovakia and Italy have used similar dual effluent-charge systems (Tietenberg 1988, 1990).ↀIn the case of Italy, the charge was, as in Malaysia, "mainly devised to encourage polluters to achieve provisional effluent standards as soon as possible" (Tietenberg 1990, p. 20). The ratio of the excess charge to the basic charge in Italy was nine, very similar to the ratio in Malaysia.

12 Effluent charges in France are also based on expected levels of discharge (Hahn 1989).

13 The impact of the charges was probably not as weak as it appeared; many mills had simply not yet completed their treatment systems.

14 By 1985, Malaysia exported mainly refined palm oil.

15 Roughly speaking, producer surplus is analogous to short-term profits.

16 We used average values for 1989 for one mill, because data were not available for 1991.

17 The estimated effluent charges also indicate the trading price for tradeable permits if that system were employed instead of effluent charges. See the section *Uniform standards versus economic instruments.*

18 Standard F can be viewed as a crude system of mill-specific standards, given the special standard for mills upstream from a water intake.

19 We also considered excluding data on mills whose quarterly BOD discharge was less than 3.75 tonnes. This is the quarterly equivalent of the annual 15 tonnes associated with the minimum effluent-related license fee. Such mills' marginal costs could be below the basic charge. Excluding these data, however, would have reduced the number of observations in the partial panel to only twenty-eight and entirely eliminated half the mills. We judged that the potential increase in accuracy in measuring the marginal costs was not worth this massive loss of data.

20 We used 1989 values for mill 7, because data were not available for 1991.

11

Conclusions

This book has examined natural resource and environmental policy issues at both the macroeconomic level (Chapters 2 and 8) and the sectoral level (the remaining chapters). Malaysia's efforts to address these issues during the 1970s and 1980s offer lessons that are useful for future policy making not only within the country but also in other developing countries. This chapter highlights those lessons, organized around the four questions raised at the end of Chapter 1.

WHAT WERE THE LINKS BETWEEN NATURAL RESOURCES AND ECONOMIC GROWTH?

The analysis in Chapter 2 estimated that resource rents from minerals and timber were equivalent to about a third of gross domestic investment during the 1970s and 1980s. The actual contribution of resource rents was probably substantially higher, as the analysis ignored land rents. (Fishing was not a major source of rents, as the sector was small compared to mining and logging and, as noted in Chapter 6, suffered from open-access rent dissipation.) The ratio of rents to investment changed little during the period, despite the country's rapid industrialization. Similarly, resource-based revenue remained a principal source of revenue for the federal government and state treasuries, especially in Sabah and Sarawak. These features indicate that Malaysia still needed to be concerned about making adequate investments to offset resource depletion in the early 1990s, when it was much more industrialized. Natural resources were still providing much of the financial support for the economy.

According to the analyses of both net investment and NDP, Malaysia as a nation succeeded in using investible funds from resource rents and other sources to build up stocks of physical capital that more than offset the depletion of mineral and timber resources. Net investment, adjusted for depletion of minerals and timber, was positive in all years but one, and adjusted NDP rose at 2.9 percent per year. These results imply that Malaysia not only benefitted immediately from natural resource utilization but will also benefit in the long term. This contrasts with the experience of most resource-rich developing countries, which have tended to suffer from a boom-and-bust growth pattern. Had the analysis included human capital, Malaysia's sustainability prospects would have appeared even brighter. The lesson is that sustainability has more to do with resource rents and investment than the physical rate of resource depletion. Though blessed with natural resources, Malaysia was more than geologically fortunate. It also made policy decisions that made it attractive to domestic and foreign investors.

At the regional level, the findings were even more positive for Peninsular Malaysia. For Sabah and Sarawak, however, they were not very reassuring. Neither state invested enough in physical capital to offset resource depletion as the production of minerals and timber expanded in the 1980s. Adjusted NDP declined in Sarawak toward the end of the period and was scarcely higher in either state at the end of the period than in the mid-1970s. Relative to the federal government, both state governments fared poorly in terms of both capturing resource rents (contrast petroleum, which is federally managed, to timber, which is managed by the states) and allocating revenue from resources and other sources toward development expenditure (as opposed to operating expenditure). The two states appear to have been following the boom-and-bust path typical of resource-rich regions. To switch paths, both need to introduce policies that result in higher levels of public and private investment.

Were Natural Resources Managed to Maximize Net Benefits?

Although Chapter 2 presented estimates of rent capture for minerals and timber, it did not consider whether resource management was optimal. Chapters 3 through 7 offered insights into this issue. They told a mixed story, with examples of both successes and failures occurring in most sectors. Consider the success stories first. Malaysia's petroleum-sharing contracts did an outstanding job of retaining resource rents within the country while attracting investment by international oil companies, which provided essential capital and technology. The government demonstrated flexibility in restructuring the contracts when lower oil prices made revisions necessary for attracting new investment in exploration and development. Without new investment, there would have been no new rents to capture.

In the forest sector, prospects for sustained flows of timber rents and other benefits were greatly enhanced in Peninsular Malaysia by the establishment of the Permanent Forest Estate. Of course, much forest was lost before the establishment of the Permanent Forest Estate. Even here, however, there was a success story. Forests in Peninsular Malaysia were converted mainly to tree-crop plantations, which are evidently a sustainable land use, thanks in large part to the country's investment in agricultural research. This contrasts with the situation in many other tropical countries, where the end result of deforestation has been unproductive, degraded land. Although forest-related values were sacrificed in the conversion process, Peninsular Malaysia gained a lasting source of economic benefits in return.

Over time, some agricultural land, mainly rubber and padi smallholdings, went out of production for various reasons. Although the performance of programs to rehabilitate this land was decidedly mixed, in some cases they succeeded in overcoming land fragmentation and other institutional factors that caused otherwise economically viable smallholdings to be idled. In this way, they enabled the land to begin generating a flow of rents again.

In marine fisheries, rents were made to flow again through the 1981 Fisheries Licensing Act and related actions by the Fisheries Department to reduce fishing effort. Abundant evidence indicates that traditional west coast fisheries were economically overfished by the 1970s. As a result of the implementation of better control measures, effort in traditional fisheries was remarkably close to the maximum economic yield level by the late 1980s. The same was apparently true for commercial fisheries, even though fishing effort in them increased.

During the 1970s and 1980s, Malaysia dramatically increased the percentage of urban and rural households with access to treated, piped water. Some states and municipalities apparently did so in a self-financing manner, by setting average water tariffs equal to average long-run supply costs. This ensured that the benefits of water supply were at least as large as the costs. These same states and municipalities tended to have higher revenue collection rates and lower leakage rates, as they were better able to maintain their water supply systems and, because they were financially more autonomous, had a stronger incentive to collect revenue. This experience indicates that a resource as valuable as water should not, and need not, be given away for free or at subsidized rates.

Although direct government actions played an essential role in these success stories, in several instances they were assisted by unrelated, but fortuitous, socioeconomic developments. For example, reductions in deforestation and traditional fishing effort in Peninsular Malaysia owed much to the region's rapid economic growth and diversification. Superior employment opportunities raised production costs in traditional activities as labor flowed out of rural areas, resulting in less land clearing and less demand for fishing licenses. Although state governments could in principle still excise areas from the Permanent Forest Estate for development, reduced returns to agricultural expansion diminished this threat. In such ways, economic development lessened the pressure on the country's resource base. It did so as well in smallholder agriculture, although the consequence, idle land, tended to be viewed more as a problem than an opportunity to return the land to forest or other natural uses.

Despite these successes, several opportunities to improve resource management and thereby generate additional economic benefits were either missed or not acted upon as quickly as they could have been. These opportunities were typically related to externalities: costs that resource users imposed on other users or other segments of Malaysian society. A prime example is the dissipation of fishery rents from the mid-1960s into the early 1980s, when fishing effort was subject to little control. Each additional fishing vessel increased fishing costs for existing vessels, due to the depletion of fish stocks, but license fees did not reflect this cost. A second example is the loss of biodiversity in the country's shrinking lowland forests. The value of this loss is unknown but potentially enormous, and it was ignored during the great burst of land conversion from the mid-1960s to the mid-1980s. Land development agencies and private estates were not required to compensate the public for this loss.

To varying degrees these problems still exist. The open-access problem diminished in west coast inshore fisheries in the 1980s with the introduction of the Fisheries Licensing Act, but it remains for deep-sea fisheries. The closing of the agricultural frontier in Peninsular Malaysia and the establishment of the Permanent Forest Estate are positive developments for biodiversity protection, but land conversion continues in Sabah and Sarawak, and logging continues to degrade the biodiversity value of remaining lowland forests in the Peninsula.

In addition to their immediate costs, depletion of fisheries and loss of biodiversity affected future options for resource use. Depleted traditional fisheries did not recover immediately, and extinction of species is irreversible. There were many other examples of potentially large, long-run costs of resource-related decisions. The overconsumption of resource rents in Sabah and Sarawak, which could cause future residents of those states to suffer lower standards of living than the current population enjoys, provides a macro example. Although the petroleum production-sharing contracts did a superb job of retaining resource rents within the country, the government's desire for immediate revenue might have caused the rate of extraction to be too rapid under the *Fourth Malaysia Plan 1981-1985*, thus diminishing the capitalized value of the country's oil reserves. In the forest sector, high rates of logging damage and lingering uncertainties about the best silvicultural system for hill forests raise the risk that current timber production is at the expense of future harvests.

At the root of most of these problems were classic failures of markets to deal efficiently and equitably with unpriced goods and the preferences of future generations. In many cases, however, the government's own policies inadvertently caused or exacerbated the problems. The idle land issue was associated with two such policy failures. First, policy-induced rigidities in land markets were one reason economically valuable land went out of production. Second, government programs to rehabilitate land that was no longer economically valuable for agriculture led to the wastage of hundreds of million ringgit per Malaysia Plan. In the forest sector, log export restrictions intended to promote domestic wood processing led to the sacrifice of resource rents worth hundreds of million ringgit annually in Peninsular Malaysia, thus reducing economic value added in the forest sector. The underpricing of freshwater in some states led to insufficient funds for maintenance, which caused service to deteriorate and leakage rates to rise. The annual economic cost of water lost to leakage was above a hundred million ringgit in the late 1980s; the cost of proposed water supply projects, some of which would not have been necessary had leakage rates been lower, ran into the billions.

Why were policies that were so costly implemented? One reason is simply that the magnitude of the costs was not known. Even the mere existence of certain costs was probably not obvious. Examples include the rehabilitation of idle land that appeared underutilized but in fact was no longer economically valuable for agriculture, and the promotion of local wood processing through policies that reduced the value of the wood itself.

The main reason, however, was the government's emphasis on maximizing physical production instead of maximizing net economic benefits. This emphasis was most evident in the fisheries sector, and it was acknowledged in papers authored by officials in the Fisheries Department. Until the 1980s, the department's goal was to raise fish catch, not to manage the resource. The expansion of logging into the hill forests before the development of a proven silvicultural system for those forests indicates that the Forestry Department, too, emphasized production over management, although in fairness its authority to restrict harvests was extremely limited. The interest of state treasuries in short-term revenue from logging, and the consequent persistent discrepancy between the Forestry Department's scheduled annual allowable coupe and the actual area harvested, was another manifestation of the production focus. The apparent influence of revenue targets on petroleum production levels and the near obsession with keeping agricultural land in production were mentioned above. In most cases, water management focused on expansion of supply instead of self-financing, improved maintenance, and demand-side management.

By ignoring the cost side, the emphasis on production was bound to lead to economic inefficiencies. It contributed to the development of a blind spot with regard to the long-run costs of resource depletion. The government worsened the situation through two types of actions. First, it not only encouraged production through easy terms of entry for resource users, but it also directly and indirectly subsidized users. Direct subsidies included those paid out to padi farmers to keep them farming and to fishermen to upgrade their vessels and gear. Both categories of subsidies were high by world standards. Indirect subsidies included low royalties paid by timber concessionaires, artificially depressed prices of logs enjoyed by domestic wood processors, the subsidized costs of FELCRA's tree-crop rehabilitation programs, and water tariffs that were below long-run costs.

Second, the government became directly involved in production through integrated timber complexes, state-level land development schemes,[1] and LKIM's fishing fleet. Most of these ventures generated a double loss: they failed financially, requiring subsidies to stay in operation, and they contributed to excessive resource depletion. These and similar public enterprises were one factor that dimmed Sabah's and Sarawak's prospects for sustainable development. Although some subsidies were scaled back during the mid-1980s fiscal crisis, and many public enterprises were privatized in the late 1980s and early 1990s, not all were.

Subsidies and public enterprises were often motivated by distributional objectives viewed as consistent with one or both prongs of the NEP. Subsidies for fishermen and padi farmers, FELCRA's programs for rubber smallholders, and below-cost water were all viewed as contributing to the fight against poverty. Since most traditional fishermen, smallholders, and rural poor were *bumiputera*, these subsidies were also consistent with the NEP's emphasis upon upgrading the economic status of the *bumiputera*. However, these subsidies were inconsistent with the NEP's goal of eliminating the identification of race with economic function, as fishing and smallholder agriculture were the very occupations that were most closely associated with *bumiputera*. Integrated timber complexes and LKIM's fishing fleet were intended to bring *bumiputera* into commercial sectors of the economy. Unfortunately, subsidies made fishermen worse off in the long run by exacerbating the open-access problem, the underpricing of water eroded the quality of service that the urban and rural poor received, and public enterprises needed to be profitable to create a viable *bumiputera* business class in the resource sectors. Subsidies that kept uneconomic padi and tree-crop land in production were short-term palliatives that diverted government resources from alternative programs that could have had a greater impact on poverty reduction.

The point is not that governments should not be concerned with distributional issues; indeed they must, particularly in ethnically heterogeneous countries like Malaysia. Rather, it is that they must be well informed about the full costs of distributionally motivated policies, so that they can avoid adopting policies that are unlikely to achieve either equity or efficiency goals. Unfortunately, many resource-related subsidy programs and state-owned commercial ventures failed on both counts. Had better information on the full costs of resource depletion been available, perhaps some of the policies might have been redesigned to achieve their distributional goals better while minimizing their resource-related costs. For example, fishermen and padi farmers could have received direct income support instead of subsidies tied to continued activity in traditional sectors, or they could have been granted stronger property rights over the resources they used (e.g., through transferable fishing rights or the creation of land banks). In other cases, however, the policies were probably doomed from the start. Although Malaysia pursued a "redistribution with growth" policy at the macroeconomic level, within the resource sectors the policy was better termed "redistribution with *short-term* growth."

Political considerations aside from those associated with the NEP also played a role in the emphasis on production. Resource producers and consumers—timber concessionaires, owners of wood-processing mills, smallholders, fishermen, households and industries that consume water—comprised politically important constituencies, which demanded policies and programs that benefitted them. Examples of political factors affecting resource management include selection criteria for settlers in some state development schemes, which contributed to the idle land problem; election-year pressure to increase the number of fishing licenses, which led to a sharp rise in fishing effort in 1989 after several years of declines; and pressure to keep water tariffs low to satisfy households and industries. The absence of a competitive process for allocating timber concessions made the system prone to political patronage, which had equity impacts if not efficiency impacts. The patronage element in the timber sector also increased the pressure to keep timber fees low, thus depressing state revenues.

For these various reasons, it will surely not be easy for the government to shift away from physical production as the objective of resource management and toward net economic benefits instead. But the cost estimates cited above indicate that shifting in this direction would yield significant returns. A reasonable first step would be to phase out the various subsidies that have resulted in both economic inefficiency and resource degradation. The benefits provided by these subsidies are short-term and are smaller than their long-term costs. At the same time, the government should continue privatizing public enterprises in resource-based industries. As noted for marine fisheries, bureaucracies are inherently ill suited to the management of risky commercial ventures involved in resource extraction.

Although the public sector should continue to recede from resource production, it should not leave decisions to a completely unregulated private sector. The government must play a role in directing market behavior toward socially desirable outcomes. This means enacting policies that create incentives for producers and consumers to recognize and respond to the full costs of their decisions. Various suggestions for creating such incentives were proposed in the concluding sections of the preceding chapters. They include strengthening timber concession tenure, so that concessionaires have an incentive to manage concessions as valuable renewable assets instead of one-time mines; instituting a land bank to reduce rigidities in the market for agricultural smallholdings; introducing a system of transferable fishing quotas, to encourage technological innovation while maintaining effort at levels that maximize economic yield; and introducing commercial principles to water agencies that are currently not operating according to them, to ensure that willingness to pay for water matches the costs of supplying it and to create incentives to conserve water. In these and other ways, market forces can be harnessed to serve the interests of both economic development and natural resource management.

A more market-oriented approach to resource management could accommodate the distributional considerations that have historically been so important in Malaysia. For example, participation in timber auctions could occasionally be restricted to companies with a minimum percentage of *bumiputera* ownership or a specified maximum size. Existing fishermen could be "grandfathered" into a quota system by being granted all or some of the initial block of quotas. Block-rate tariffs could continue to be used to ensure that minimum amounts of water are available at affordable prices to low-income households.

A market-oriented approach would also offer fiscal and macroeconomic benefits. Phasing out subsidies and unprofitable public enterprises would alleviate pressure on the expenditure side of state and federal budgets. Policies to require resource users to pay in full for resource depletion would bolster the revenue side. The tendering of timber concessions, which has already been introduced in several states in Peninsular Malaysia, and fishing quotas if they are not "grandfathered," could raise significant amounts of revenue. So could increases in water tariffs. This revenue could be used to finance enhanced programs related to education, research and development, infrastructure, and other public sector activities that help ensure sustainability. It would also enable the Ministry of Finance and state treasuries to reduce distortionary taxes, such as corporate and personal income taxes and excise taxes on goods and services, which reduce incentives to work, produce, and save. By definition, rents can be fully taxed without sacrificing economic efficiency. The replacement of distortionary taxes by neutral or distortion-eliminating charges and fees related to natural resources could boost economic growth. If such opportunities are recognized and acted upon, Malaysia's natural resources can make an even greater contribution to the country's future development than they have in the past.

WHAT WERE THE LINKS BETWEEN ECONOMIC DEVELOPMENT AND ENVIRONMENTAL QUALITY?

Chapter 8 analyzed trends in air and water pollution and how they were affected by economic growth and population. Emissions increased for most air pollutants between 1987, when the Department of Environment began estimating emissions, and 1991. They decreased only in the case of sulfur dioxide. Data on ambient air quality cover a longer period of time, extending back to 1977, but only for TSP. Consistent with the upward trend in particulate emissions, the national average TSP reading was higher after the mid-1980s than before; the proportion of monitoring stations reporting violations of the recommended Malaysian standard also increased. Interpretation of these findings is complicated, however, by the fact that many of the monitoring stations added in the mid-1980s were in relatively more polluted areas. Nevertheless, it is likely that ambient TSP concentrations rose.

The only extensive data on water pollution are for ambient concentrations, with readings covering most of the period from 1978 to 1991 in most river basins. Mean readings across river basins for BOD, COD, and suspended solids showed a break in trends around the mid-1980s: they decreased (water quality improved) up to that point for all three parameters, but they showed no clear trend thereafter for BOD and suspended solids, and they increased for COD. They showed no overall trend for ammoniacal nitrogen and pH. The percentage of rivers violating class IIA/IIB standards showed similar trends for BOD, COD, and suspended solids, but it increased sharply for ammoniacal nitrogen and decreased for pH. The relative number of positive and negative trends in readings for the five parameters at the river basin level was consistent with this evidence of improving or unchanging water quality in terms of BOD, suspended solids, and pH and deteriorating quality in terms of ammoniacal nitrogen and, during the second half of the period, COD.

In sum, it appears that air pollution emissions generally increased, ambient air quality as measured by TSP concentrations worsened, and ambient water quality worsened according to some parameters and improved according to others. Cross-country studies have detected statistical evidence linking such changes to changes in income. For air pollution, Malaysia's performance was better than the studies predicted for emissions but worse for ambient quality. Emissions of nitrogen oxides, carbon monoxide, and particulates increased less rapidly than predicted, and the decrease in sulfur dioxide emissions was the opposite of what was predicted. On the other hand, econometric analysis of Malaysian data found that ambient TSP concentrations rose continually with per capita GDP. This contradicted the results of the cross-country studies, which predicted that TSP concentrations should start declining after a country passes a relatively low income threshold. Hence, economic growth apparently had a more negative impact on ambient TSP concentrations in Malaysia than in the average country at its income level, despite the country's better performance in terms of emissions.

Cross-country studies have paid less attention to water pollution. One pertinent finding is that dissolved oxygen concentration declines with income, which implies that BOD concentration should rise. Econometric analysis of Malaysian data determined that this was not the case: there was no statistically significant relationship between per capita GDP and BOD concentration. Per capita GDP did affect ammoniacal nitrogen concentrations and pH, causing both to rise. It was associated with rising concentrations of suspended solids up to a turning point but declining concentrations thereafter. Economic growth was therefore associated with worsening water quality according to some parameters (ammoniacal nitrogen, suspended solids below the turning point) and improving water quality according to others (pH, suspended solids above the turning point).

In some instances, population growth reinforced the effects of economic growth. Ambient concentrations of TSP in the air and ammoniacal nitrogen in the water rose with population density, and concentrations of suspended solids in the water fell. Although per capita GDP did not affect BOD concentrations in the water, rising population density caused it to increase.

Was Environmental Quality Managed to Maximize Net Benefits?

In several cases, government actions prevented certain pollution problems from being worse. The most obvious example is the Crude Palm Oil Regulations, which dramatically reduced BOD discharge by palm-oil mills in just a few years. Another example is the decision to switch from fuel oil to natural gas in the power sector, which, although not motivated by environmental considerations, reduced sulfur dioxide emissions nonetheless. Indirect evidence of the positive impact of government actions comes from the econometric analyses of the air- and water-quality monitoring data. After accounting for the effects of population density, the residual trend in BOD concentrations was negative, which is consistent with the direct evidence on the effectiveness of the Crude Palm Oil Regulations. Residual trends were also negative for concentrations of TSP in the air and concentrations of ammoniacal nitrogen and suspended solids in the water.

As in the case of natural resources, government actions were not the only factors contributing to pollution reductions. The acceptability of the Crude Palm Oil Regulations was enhanced by relatively strong markets for palm-oil products, at least until the recession of the mid-1980s, and by the structure of the industry, which enabled mills to shift a significant portion of the regulatory costs onto oil-palm growers. The switch toward low-sulfur natural gas was made possible by the discovery of the country's offshore gas fields. The deceleration of land conversion was probably one reason the levels of suspended solids in rivers declined as states achieved higher income levels.

Despite these policy and nonpolicy factors, air and water quality in much of the country was low from the late 1970s into the early 1990s relative to recommended Malaysian environmental quality standards. TSP concentrations violated the recommended guideline at an increasing proportion of air-quality monitoring stations during the 1980s, reaching 50 percent in 1991. The much more limited data on airborne concentrations of gaseous pollutants revealed violations in the early 1990s for sulfur dioxide, nitrogen oxides, and carbon monoxide in urban and industrial areas during peak pollution periods (Chapter 1). Readings on COD, ammoniacal nitrogen, pH, and suspended solids violated the proposed interim national water-quality standards in at least half of the river basins in Peninsular Malaysia in most years from 1978 to 1991, and in about a quarter of the river basins for BOD.

A comparison of the cases of palm-oil effluent and particulates suggests that the characteristics of pollution problems strongly influenced the vigor and effectiveness of the government's policy response. Palm-oil effluent had a finite number of obvious, similar sources, and it affected a well-defined group, downstream villagers, in fairly predictable and obvious ways. For these reasons, it was more amenable to solution by targeted, uniform regulations. In contrast, particulates are emitted by multiple sources of very different types: vehicles, industries, open burning. The impacts of emissions from any single source is heavily influenced by terrain and weather conditions. Even the simple presence of particulate pollution is not always readily evident; it attracted widespread attention in Malaysia only during "haze" episodes. Both palm-oil effluent and particulates caused negative externalities, but the externalities, their causes, and their effects were more obvious in the case of palm-oil effluent. It is not surprising that the Department of Environment dealt first with the most obvious sources of particulate emissions, through the "Black Smoke" Rules. It is also not surprising that responses to even less obvious air pollutants such as sulfur dioxide, nitrogen oxides, and carbon monoxide, and water pollutants like ammoniacal nitrogen and excess acidity, were slow in coming.

The analysis of health impacts in Chapter 9 demonstrated, however, that less obvious pollution problems are not necessarily economically unimportant. In 1991, the life-expectancy benefits of reducing TSP concentrations to the recommended Malaysian standard had an estimated value on the order of RM1 billion. Adding the value of reductions in morbidity might have doubled this figure. Although the benefits of improved water quality were not quantified in this book, the high rate of violations of class IIA/IIB standards implies that improvements might have brought significant benefits in terms of reduced costs of water treatment, higher freshwater fish catch, and greater recreational usage.

These benefits went unrealized because, in the absence or inadequacy of policies to address pollution externalities, producers and consumers did not face the full costs of their actions. Before the introduction of the Crude Palm Oil Regulations, palm-oil mills did not have to pay for the use of the country's rivers as a sewer for their effluent. Similarly, operators of motor vehicles, industrial facilities, land development schemes, and waste dumps did not have to pay for the use of the atmosphere as a waste sink for their emissions of particulates and other air pollutants.

As in the case of natural resources, economic principles can be used to design policies that compel producers and consumers to pay for the pollution they discharge. The effluent charges included in the Crude Palm Oil Regulations were one of the earliest applications of this approach anywhere in the world. Although charges on pollution are the most direct means of applying the "polluter pays principle," others exist, including tradable pollution permits (discussed in Chapter 10) and charges on polluting inputs (for example, setting the price of leaded petrol above that for unleaded petrol). The market-based pollution approach offers fiscal advantages analogous to those of resource taxes, by generating government revenue through the taxation of bads instead of goods or, in the case of tradable permits, by auctioning rights to use the environment's assimilative capacity.

In many developing countries, government action against pollution problems, whether through economic or more conventional regulatory approaches, is impeded by not only uncertainty about the benefits of pollution abatement but also concerns about the impact of regulations on industrial performance. The most important lesson of the Crude Palm Oil Regulations is that such concerns are often unjustified. Output and exports of crude palm oil and investment in new mills all expanded after the Crude Palm Oil Regulations were introduced. Moreover, the cost of pollution abatement to industry depends very much on the policy approach chosen. A key advantage of market-based approaches is that they tend to be more cost-effective: they achieve a given improvement in environmental quality at the lowest aggregate abatement cost, thus minimizing the burden on industry. In the case of the Crude Palm Oil Regulations, the use of effluent charges did indeed result in cost savings, although they were small due to the characteristics of the abatement technology (low marginal costs) and the strengthening of command-and-control features of the regulations after their first year.

If in certain cases there is indeed a trade-off between industrialization and protection of environmental quality, then it is in Malaysia's best interest to opt for environmental protection whenever it generates positive net benefits. A better-quality environment provides economic benefits that are just as legitimate as the more tangible ones associated with economic growth. These benefits were apparently comfortably in excess of the costs of pollution abatement in the case of particulates. By failing to act more forcefully to reduce particulate pollution, Malaysia suffered a substantial welfare loss. The estimates of per capita NDP in Chapter 2 ignored this loss, as well as other direct welfare losses stemming from air and water pollution and other forms of environmental degradation (e.g., traffic congestion and loss of amenity values). For these reasons, the well-being of the average Malaysian did not increase as rapidly during the 1970s and 1980s as the per capita NDP estimates indicated.

A statement in *The Second Outline Perspective Plan (OPP2), 1991–2000* suggests that the government recognized the need to address pollution problems more effectively than in the past if it hoped to take full advantage of opportunities to enhance its citizens' welfare. The *OPP2* highlighted eight ways in which the National Development Policy would aim at more balanced development than under the NEP. The final one was "ensuring that in the pursuit of economic development adequate attention is given to the protection of the environment and ecology so as to maintain the long term sustainability of the country's development as well as the quality of life" (Mahathir 1991, p. 21). Although economic growth can incidentally improve some aspects of environmental quality, in most instances public policies are needed to prevent environmental degradation from partially or wholly offsetting the benefits brought by growth. Whether the country's experience under the

National Development Policy will compare favorably with the statement in the *OPP2* is largely dependent on the policy choices the government makes in the remaining few years of the century. Economic principles are of great value in making those choices.

NOTES

1 Federal land development schemes generally earned acceptable rates of return.

Bibliography

PREFACE

Abdul Rahman bin Jamal. 1993. "Economic development and the environment in Malaysia: issues and considerations." In *Economic Development and the Environment in ASEAN Countries*, ed. P. Koomsup. The Economic Society of Thailand, Bangkok.

Aiken, S.R., C.H. Leigh, T.R. Leinbach, and M.R. Ross. 1982. *Development and Environment in Peninsular Malaysia*. McGraw-Hill, Singapore.

Asian Development Bank. 1990. *Economic Policies for Sustainable Development*. Asian Development Bank, Manila.

Behrman, J., and T.N. Srinivasan, eds. 1995. *Handbook of Development Economics, vol. 3A*. North-Holland, Amsterdam.

Brookfield, H., ed. 1994. *Transformation with Industrialization in Peninsular Malaysia*. Oxford University Press, New York.

Chenery, H., and T.N. Srinivasan. 1988. *Handbook of Development Economics, vols. 1 and 2*. North-Holland, Amsterdam.

Cleary, M., and P. Eaton. 1992. *Borneo: Change and Development*. Oxford University Press, Singapore.

Dasgupta, P., and K.G. Mäler. 1991. "The environment and emerging development issues." In *Proceedings of the World Bank Annual Conference on Development Economics, 1990*. World Bank, Washington, D.C.

Earl of Cranbrook. 1988. *Key Environments: Malaysia*. Pergamon Press, Oxford.

EPU (Economic Planning Unit). 1993. *Malaysian National Conservation Strategy: Towards Sustainable Development*, 4 vols. Economic Planning Unit, Kuala Lumpur.

Goh, K.C. 1982. "Environmental impacts of economic development in Peninsular Malaysia: A review." *Applied Geography* 2:3–16.

Malaysian Institute of Economic Research. 1990. "Economic policies for sustainable development: Implementing the Brundtland Commission in Malaysia." Malaysian Institute of Economic Research, Kuala Lumpur.

Ong, A.S.H., A. Maheswaran, and A.N. Ma. 1987. "Malaysia." In *Environmental Management in Southeast Asia*, ed. L.S. Chia. Faculty of Science, National University of Singapore.

Sham Sani. 1993. *Environment and Development in Malaysia: Changing Concerns and Approaches*. Institute of Strategic and International Studies, Kuala Lumpur.

Vincent, J.R., and Yusuf Hadi. 1991. "Deforestation and agricultural expansion in Peninsular Malaysia." *Development Discussion Paper No. 396*. Harvard Institute for International Development, Cambridge, Mass.

———. 1993. "Malaysia." In *Sustainable Agriculture and the Environment in the Humid Tropics*, ed. Committee on Sustainable Agriculture and the Environment in the Humid Tropics, National Research Council. National Academy Press, Washington, D.C.

World Bank. 1993. "Malaysia: managing costs of urban pollution." *Report No. 11764-MA*. Country Department I, East Asia and Pacific Region. World Bank, Washington, D.C.

Yip,Y.H. 1969. *The Development of the Tin Mining Industry of Malaya*. University of Malaya Press, Kuala Lumpur.

CHAPTER 1: NATURAL RESOURCES AND THE ENVIRONMENT IN THE MALAYSIAN CONTEXT

Bruton, H.J., in collaboration with G. Abeysekera, N. Sanderatne, and Zainal Aznam Yusof. 1992. *Sri Lanka and Malaysia: The Political Economy of Poverty, Equity, and Growth*. Oxford University Press for the World Bank, New York.

Chai, H.C. 1964. *The Development of British Malaya, 1896–1909*. Oxford University Press, Kuala Lumpur.

Courtenay, P.P. 1972. *A Geography of Trade and Development in Malaya*. G. Bell and Sons, London.

Department of Environment. 1981. *Environmental Quality Report 1980*. Ministry of Science, Technology, and the Environment, Kuala Lumpur.

———. 1984. *Environmental Quality Report 1983*. Ministry of Science, Technology, and the Environment, Kuala Lumpur.

———. 1992. *Environmental Quality Report 1991*. Ministry of Science, Technology, and the Environment, Kuala Lumpur.

———. 1993. *Environmental Quality Report 1992*. Ministry of Science, Technology, and the Environment, Kuala Lumpur.

———. 1994. *Environmental Quality Report 1993*. Ministry of Science, Technology, and the Environment, Kuala Lumpur.

EPU (Economic Planning Unit). 1980. *Land Resources Report of Peninsular Malaysia*. Economic Planning Unit, Kuala Lumpur.

INTAN (National Institute of Development Administration). 1994. *Malaysian De-*

velopment Experience: Changes and Challenges. National Institute of Development Administration, Kuala Lumpur.

Jabatan Pertanian. Various issues. *Agricultural Statistics of Sarawak.* Kuching.

Jomo, K.S. 1990. *Growth and Structural Change in the Malaysian Economy.* Macmillan, London.

Kementerian Pertanian. 1992. *Statistical Handbook, Agriculture: Malaysia 1990.* Kementerian Pertanian, Kuala Lumpur.

Kementerian Perusahaan Utama. 1992. *Perangkaan Barangan Utama: Perhutanan.* Kementerian Perusahaan Utama, Kuala Lumpur.

Khoo, S.G. 1995. *Population and Housing Census of Malaysia 1991: General Report of the Census, vol. 1.* Department of Statistics, Kuala Lumpur.

Lim, C.Y. 1967. *Economic Development of Modern Malaya.* Oxford University Press, Kuala Lumpur.

Lim, D. 1973. *Economic Growth and Development in West Malaysia, 1947–70.* Oxford University Press, Kuala Lumpur.

Sachs, J.D., and A.M. Warner. 1995. "Natural resource abundance and economic growth." *Development Discussion Paper No. 517a.* Harvard Institute for International Development, Cambridge, Mass.

Seksyen Banci and Perangkaan, Bahagian Ekonomi Pertanian. 1990. *Agricultural, Livestock, and Fisheries Statistics for Management, Malaysia (1980–1988).* Kementerian Pertanian, Kuala Lumpur.

Snodgrass, D.R. 1980. *Inequality and Economic Development in Malaysia.* Oxford University Press, Kuala Lumpur.

Umikalsum Haji Mohd. Nor. 1991. *Fiscal Federalism in Malaysia, 1971–1987.* Ph.D. dissertation. Faculty of Economics and Administration, University of Malaya, Kuala Lumpur.

Wong, I.F.T. 1971. *The Present Land Use of West Malaysia (1966).* Ministry of Agriculture and Lands, Kuala Lumpur.

World Bank. 1992. *World Development Report 1992: Development and the Environment.* Oxford University Press, New York.

———. 1994. *World Development Report 1994: Infrastructure for Development.* Oxford University Press, New York.

World Resources Institute. 1992. *World Resources 1992–93.* Oxford University Press, New York.

Young, K., W.C.F. Bussink, and P. Hasan. 1980. *Malaysia: Growth and Equity in a Multiracial Society.* Johns Hopkins University Press for the World Bank, Baltimore.

Chapter 2: Natural Resources and Economic Sustainability

Abang Helmi bin Tan Sri Ikhwan. 1993. "Diversifying the Sarawak economy: challenges and changing role of the statutory bodies as catalyst for change and progress." Paper presented at International Conference on Sarawak, April 26–27, Kuching, Sarawak.

Bartelmus, P., E. Lutz, and S. Schweinfest. 1993. "Integrated environmental and economic accounting: A case study for Papua New Guinea." In *Toward Improved Accounting for the Environment*, ed. E. Lutz. World Bank, Washington, D.C.

Brown, S., L. Iverson, and A. Lugo. 1991. "Land-use and biomass changes of forests in Peninsular Malaysia during 1972–1982: Use of GIS analysis." In *Effects of Land-Use Change on Atmospheric CO_2 Concentrations: Southeast Asia as a Case Study*, ed. V. Dale. Springer-Verlag, New York.

Chung, K.S. 1984. "Costs of logging in hill and swamp forests of Sarawak: 1979, 1980 & 1981." Forestry Department, Kuching, Sarawak.

Dasgupta, P.S., and G.M. Heal. 1979. *Economic Theory and Exhaustible Resources*. James Nisbet & Co./Cambridge University Press, Welwyn, U.K.

Dasgupta, P.S., and K.G. Mäler. 1991. "The environment and emerging development issues." In *Proceedings of the World Bank Annual Conference on Development Economics 1990*. The World Bank, Washington, D.C.

Department of Statistics. 1988. *National Accounts Statistics: 1988*. Department of Statistics, Kuala Lumpur.

———. Various issues. *Industrial Surveys*. Kuala Lumpur.

———. Various issues. *Report of the Financial Survey of Limited Companies*. Kuala Lumpur.

Devarajan, S., and R.J. Weiner. 1990. "Natural resource depletion and national income accounting." *Development Discussion Paper No. 332*. Harvard Institute for International Development, Cambridge, Mass.

El Serafy, S. 1989. "The proper calculation of income from depleting natural resources." In *Environmental Accounting for Sustainable Development*, eds. Y.J. Ahmad., S. El Serafy, and E. Lutz. The World Bank, Washington, D.C.

El Serafy, S., and E. Lutz. 1989. "Environmental and resource accounting: An overview." In *Environmental Accounting for Sustainable Development*, eds. Y.J. Ahmad et al.

EPU (Economic Planning Unit). 1993. *Malaysian National Conservation Strategy: Towards Sustainable Development. Vol. 4: Natural Resource Accounting*. Economic Planning Unit, Prime Minister's Department, Kuala Lumpur.

FAO (Food and Agriculture Organization). 1973. "A national forest inventory of West Malaysia, 1970–72." *FO:DP/MAL/72/009, Technical Report No. 5*. Food and Agriculture Organization, Rome.

FAO/UNEP (United Nations Environment Program). 1981. "Tropical Forest Resources Assessment Project: Forest resources of tropical Asia." *UN 32/6.1301-78-04, Technical Report No. 3*. FAO, Rome.

Foo, L., and B. Ramasamy. 1991. "A macro-economic analysis of the oil industry in Malaysia." In *Oil and Economic Development*, ed. S. Sadri. Forum Publications, Kuala Lumpur.

Gillis, M. 1988. "Malaysia: Public policies and the tropical forest." In *Public Policies and the Misuse of Forest Resources*, ed. R. Repetto and M. Gillis. Cambridge University Press, Cambridge, U.K.

Golay, F.H. 1976. "Southeast Asia: The 'colonial drain' revisited." In *Southeast Asian History and Historiography: Essays Presented to D.G.E. Hall*, ed. C.D. Cowan and O.W. Wolters. Cornell University Press, Ithaca, N.Y.

Hartwick, J.M. 1977. "Intergenerational equity and the investing of rents from exhaustible resources." *American Economic Review* 67(5):972–74.

———. 1990. "Natural resources, national accounting, and economic depreciation." *Journal of Public Economics* 43(3):291–304.

———. 1993. "Forestry economics, deforestation, and national accounting." In *Toward Improved Accounting for the Environment*, ed. E. Lutz.

Hartwick, J.M., and A. Hageman. 1993. "Economic depreciation of mineral stocks and the contribution of El Serafy." In *Toward Improved Accounting for the Environment*, ed. E. Lutz. The World Bank, Washington, D. C.

Hartwick, J.M., and N.D. Olewiler. 1986. *The Economics of Natural Resource Use*. Harper & Row Publishers, New York.

Hendrix, K. 1990. "Vanishing forest fells a way of life." Los Angeles Times. March 18.

Hotelling, H. 1931. "The economics of exhaustible resources." *Journal of Political Economy* 39:137–75.

Hough, G.V. 1986. "Internal problems impede progress." *Petroleum Economist* 53(May):177–79.

Ibu Pejabat Perhutanan, Semenanjung Malaysia (Forestry Department Headquarters, Peninsular Malaysia). 1987. "Inventori Hutan Nasional II, Semenanjung Malaysia: 1981–1982." Ibu Pejabat Perhutanan, Semenanjung Malaysia, Kuala Lumpur.

IMF (International Monetary Fund). 1992. *International Financial Statistics 1991*. International Monetary Fund, Washington, D.C.

Ismail Muhd. Salleh. 1993. "Development trends of public enterprises in Malaysia." *Borneo Review* 4(1):37–59.

Jomo, K.S., ed. 1990. *Undermining Tin: The Decline of Malaysian Pre-eminence*. Forum Publications, Petaling Jaya, Malaysia.

Khalil bin Datu Haji Jamalul. 1992. "Government linked agencies and corporations: Issues, challenges, and strategies for the 1990s." *Borneo Review* 3(2):180–208.

Kumar, R. 1986. *The Forest Resources of Malaysia: Their Economics and Development*. Oxford University Press, Singapore.

Landefeld, J.S., and J.R. Hines. 1985. "National accounting for non-renewable natural resources in the mining industries." *Review of Income and Wealth* 31(1):1–20.

Mäler, K.G. 1986. "Comment on R.M. Solow." *Scandinavian Journal of Economics* 88(1):151–52.

———. 1991. "National accounts and environmental resources." *Environmental and Resource Economics* 1:1–15.

————. Personal communication. October 20.

Markandya, A., and D. Pearce. 1988. "Environmental considerations and the choice of the discount rate in developing countries." *Environment Department Working Paper No. 3.* The World Bank, Washington, D.C.

Ministry of Finance. 1992. *Economic Report 1992/93.* Ministry of Finance, Kuala Lumpur.

Nordhaus, W.D., and J. Tobin. 1972. "Is growth obsolete?" In *Fiftieth Anniversary Colloquium, vol. 5.* National Bureau of Economic Research, New York.

Pang, T.W. 1989. "Economic growth and development in Sabah: 25 years after independence." In *Sabah: 25 Years Later,* ed. J.G. Kitingan and M.J. Ongkili. Institute for Development Studies (Sabah), Kota Kinabalu.

————. 1993. Personal communication. September 27.

Pearce, D.W., and G.D. Atkinson. 1993. "Capital theory and the measurement of sustainable development: An indicator of 'weak' sustainability." *Ecological Economics* 8:103–108.

Peskin, H.M. 1989. "Accounting for natural resource depletion and degradation in developing countries." *Environment Department Working Paper No. 13.* The World Bank, Washington, D.C.

Pura, R. 1990. "Battle over forest rights in Sarawak pits ethnic groups against wealthy loggers." *Asian Wall Street Journal.* February 26.

Repetto, R., W. Magrath, M. Wells, C. Beer, and F. Rossini. 1989. *Wasting Assets: Natural Resources in the National Income Accounts.* World Resources Institute, Washington, D.C.

Repetto, R., W. Cruz, R. Solorzano, R. de Camino, R. Woodward, J. Tosi, V. Watson, A. Vasquez, C. Villabos, and J. Jimenez. 1991. *Accounts Overdue: Natural Resource Depreciation in Costa Rica.* World Resources Institute, Washington, D.C.

Sesser, S. 1991. "Logging the rainforest." *The New Yorker* (May 27):42–67.

Solow, R.M. 1986. "On the intergenerational allocation of exhaustible resources." *Scandinavian Journal of Economics* 88(2):141–56.

————. 1992. "An almost practical step toward sustainability." Invited lecture on the occasion of the fortieth anniversary of Resources for the Future. Resources for the Future, Washington, D.C.

Star (newspaper). 1991. "Concession said to be a political patronage," September 12. Kuala Lumpur.

Stauffer, T.R. 1986. "Accounting for 'wasting assets': Measurements of income and dependency in oil-rentier states." *Journal of Energy and Development* 11(1):69–93.

Sulaiman bin Haji Noordin. 1977. "A method of forest revenue assessment based on inventory data." *Malaysian Forester* 40(3):144–59.

Teo, P.C. 1966. "Revision of royalty rates." *Malayan Forester* 29(4):254–58.

Thang, H.C. 1986. "Selective Management System: Concept and practice." Forestry Department Headquarters, Peninsular Malaysia, Kuala Lumpur.

————. 1987. "Forest management systems for tropical high forest, with special reference to Peninsular Malaysia." *Forest Ecology and Management* 21:3–20.

Toh, M. 1991. "The legislative framework for petroleum development in Malaysia: a case study of the production-sharing contract." LL.M. paper, Harvard Law School, Cambridge, Mass.

Umikalsum Haji Mohd. Nor. 1991. *Fiscal Federalism in Malaysia, 1971–1987.* Ph.D. dissertation. Faculty of Economics and Administration, University of Malaya, Kuala Lumpur.

van Tongeren, J., S. Schweinfest, E. Lutz, M. Gomez Luna, and G. Martin. 1993. "Integrated environmental and economic accounting: A case study for Mexico." In *Toward Improved Accounting for the Environment,* ed. E. Lutz. World Bank, Washington, D.C.

Veitch, M.D. 1986. *National Parameters for Project Appraisal in Malaysia. Vol. 3: Summary of Estimation Procedures.* Regional Economics Section, Economic Planning Unit, Prime Minister's Department, Kuala Lumpur.

Vincent, J.R. 1990. "Rent capture and the feasibility of tropical forest management." *Land Economics* 66(2):212–23.

————. 1991. Unpublished analysis conducted for the World Bank.

————. Vincent, J.R. 1992. "A simple, nonspatial modeling approach for analyzing a country's forest-products trade policies." In *Forestry Sector Analysis for Developing Countries,* ed. R. Haynes, P. Harou, and J. Mikowski. *Special Report No. 10.* Center for International Trade in Forest Products, College of Forest Resources, University of Washington, Seattle.

Vincent, J.R., Awang Noor Abd. Ghani, and Yusuf Hadi. 1993. "Economics of timber fees and logging in tropical forest concessions." Unpublished manuscript. Harvard Institute for International Development, Cambridge, Mass.

Vincent, J.R., and Yusuf Hadi. 1993. "Malaysia." In *Sustainable Agriculture and the Environment in the Humid Tropics,* ed. National Research Council. National Academy Press, Washington, D.C.

Vincent, J.R., T. Panayotou, and J.M. Hartwick. 1995. "Resource depletion and sustainability in small open economies." *Environment Discussion Paper No. 8.* Harvard Institute for International Development, Cambridge, Mass.

Ward, M. 1982. *Accounting for the Depletion of Natural Resources in the National Accounts of Developing Countries.* Organization for Economic Cooperation and Development Center, Paris.

Weitzman, M.L. 1976. "On the welfare significance of national product in a dynamic economy." *Quarterly Journal of Economics* 90(1):156–62.

World Bank. 1991. "Malaysia: forestry subsector study." Report No. 9775-MA (draft). Washington, D.C.

————. 1992. *World Development Report 1992: Development and the Environment.* World Bank, Washington, D.C.

————. 1995. *Monitoring Environmental Progress: A Report on Work in Progress.* World Bank, Washington, D.C.

Yip Y.H. 1969. *The Development of the Tin Mining Industry of Malaya.* University of Malaya Press, Kuala Lumpur.

CHAPTER 3: PETROLEUM

Adelman, M.A. 1986a. "Oil producing countries' discount rates." *Resources and Energy* 8(December):309–29.

————. 1986b. "Scarcity and world oil prices." *Review of Economics and Statistics* 68:387–97.

————. 1990. "Mineral depletion, with special reference to petroleum." *Review of Economics and Statistics* 72(1):1–10.

Adelman, M.A., and M. Shahi. 1989. "Oil development-operating cost estimates, 1955–85." *Energy Economics* 11(1):2–10.

Adelman, M.A., and G.L. Ward. 1980. "Worldwide production costs for oil and gas." In *Advances in the Economics of Energy and Resources,* vol. 3, ed. J.R. Moroney. Jai Press, Greenwich, Conn.

Oxford Analytica Daily Brief. 1995. "Malaysia: oil complacency." (An electronic information service). October 5.

Arief, S., and R. Wells. 1985. *A Report on the Malaysian Petroleum Industry.* Rosecons, for the Southeast Asia Research and Development Institute, Balmain, Australia.

Auty, R.M. 1990. *Resource-Based Industrialization: Sowing the Oil in Eight Developing Countries.* Clarendon Press, Oxford.

Baharuddin Ali. 1992. "Development of petrochemical industry in Malaysia." Background paper prepared for National Conservation Strategy. World Wildlife Fund Malaysia, Petaling Jaya.

Bank Negara Malaysia. 1991. *Annual Report 1990.* Kuala Lumpur.

Barrows. 1995. *World Fiscal Systems for Oil.* A report supported by the World Bank. World Bank, Washington, D.C.

Blitzer, C.R., D.M. Lessard, and J.L. Paddock. 1984. "Risk-bearing and the choice of contract forms for oil exploration and development." *Energy Journal* 5(1):1–28.

Conrad, R., S. Shalizi, and J. Syme. 1990. "Issues in evaluating tax and payment arrangements for publicly owned minerals." *Policy Research and External Affairs Working Paper, WPS 496.* World Bank, Washington, D.C.

ECAFE (Economic Commission for Asia and the Far East). 1959. "The prospects for petroleum in the Federation of Malaya." In *Proceedings of the Symposium on the Development of Petroleum Resources of Asia and the Far East.* United Nations, Bangkok.

EPU (Economic Planning Unit). 1993. *Malaysian National Conservation Strategy:*

Towards Sustainable Development, vol. 4: Natural Resource Accounting. Economic Planning Unit, Kuala Lumpur.

Emerson, C. 1985. "Mining taxation in Malaysia." *Singapore Economic Review* (April):34–55.

Energy Information Administration. 1984. *The Petroleum Resources of Malaysia, Brunei, and Indonesia.* U.S. Department of Energy, Washington, D.C.

Foo, L., and B. Ramasamy. 1991. "A macro-economic analysis of the oil industry in Malaysia." In *Oil and Economic Development*, ed. S. Sadri. Forum Publications, Petaling Jaya.

Garnaut, R., and A. Clunies Ross. 1993. *Taxation of Mineral Rents.* Oxford University Press, New York.

Hough, G.V. 1986. "Internal problems impede progress." *Petroleum Economist* 53(May):177–79.

Jasin, A.K. 1995. "Peaceful, prosperous Asia better for all." *New Sunday Times* (Kuala Lumpur), May 21, p. 15.

Meyanathan, S., and R.J.G. Wells. 1982. "Petroleum products pricing in Malaysia." *Kajian Ekonomi Malaysia* 19(1):46–54.

Meyer, A.S. 1986. "The Peruvian petroleum industry: Analysis of contract and tax systems." Discussion paper, University of Konstanz.

Ministry of Finance. 1991. *Economic Report 1990/91.* Kuala Lumpur.

Nordhaus, W.D. 1992. "Lethal model 2: The limits to growth revisited." *Brookings Papers on Economic Activity* 2:1–43.

Rozali bin Mohamed Ali. 1992. "Energy." Background paper prepared for National Conservation Strategy. World Wildlife Fund Malaysia, Petaling Jaya.

Segal, J. 1982. "An expensive prospect." *Far Eastern Economic Review* (December 3):109–10.

Siddayao, C.M. 1978. *The Off-Shore Petroleum Resources of South-East Asia.* Oxford University Press, Kuala Lumpur.

———. 1980. *The Supply of Petroleum Reserves in South-East Asia.* Oxford University Press, Kuala Lumpur.

———. 1988. "Energy policy issues in developing countries: Lessons from ASEAN's experience." *Energy Policy* (December):608–20.

Subramaniam, A. 1982. *Petroleum Income Tax in Malaysia.* Malayan Law Journal, Kuala Lumpur.

Toh, M. 1991. "The legislative framework for petroleum development in Malaysia: A case study of the production-sharing contract." LL.M. paper, Harvard Law School, Cambridge, Mass.

Umikalsum Haji Mohd. Noh. 1991. *Fiscal Federalism in Malaysia, 1971–1987.* Ph.D. dissertation. Faculty of Economics and Administration, University of Malaya, Kuala Lumpur.

Veitch, M.D. 1986. *National Parameters for Project Appraisal in Malaysia. Vol. 3:*

Summary of Estimation Procedures. Regional Economics Section, Economic Planning Unit, Prime Minister's Department, Kuala Lumpur.

Wan, L.F. 1984. "Resource depletion rent and its implications on optimal depletion in selected oil producing countries in Southeast Asia." *Malaysian Journal of Agricultural Economics* 1(1):32–57.

Widjadono, P. 1993. "The comparison of petroleum contractual systems in Asia Pacific." In Proceedings of Society of Petroleum Engineers (SPE) Asia Pacific Oil & Gas Conference & Exhibition, Singapore, February 8–10. SPE, Richardson, Texas.

World Bank. 1991. "Malaysia: Gas utilization study." *Report No. 9645-MA.* World Bank, Washington, D.C.

Chapter 4: Forests

A.M.b.Hj.M.S. 1963. "Regional notes: Federation of Malaya." *Malayan Forester* 26 (October):298–99.

Abdul Ghaffar bin Hamid. 1972. "The impact of land clearance for agriculture on forestry." *Malayan Forester* 35(1):47–53.

Aiken, R.S., and C.H. Leigh. 1992. *Vanishing Rain Forests: The Ecological Transition in Malaysia.* Clarendon Press, Oxford.

Allen, J.C., and D.F. Barnes. 1985. "The causes of deforestation in developing countries." *Annals of the Association of American Geographers* 75(2):163–84.

Malayan Forester. 1959. Editorial. 22(3):187–190.

———. 1960a. Editorial. 23(1):1–3.

———. 1960c. Editorial. 23(3):144–46.

———. 1960d. Editorial. 23(4):248–49.

———. 1961. Editorial. 24(4):243–45.

———. 1962a. Editorial. 25(1):1–2.

———. 1962b. Editorial. 25(2):114–16.

———. 1962c. Editorial. 25(3):181–84.

———. 1963a. Editorial. 26(3):78–80.

———. 1963b. Editorial. 26(3):138–39.

———. 1964a. Editorial. 27(1):1–2.

———. 1964b. Editorial. 27(2):78–80.

———. 1964c. Editorial. 27(3):186–87.

———. 1964d. Editorial. 27(4):295–96.

———. 1965a. Editorial. 28(2):80–81.

———. 1965b. Editorial. 28(3):155–57.

———. 1965c. Editorial. 28(4):263.

———. 1966. Editorial. 29(2):53–55.

———. 1967a. Editorial. 30(2):80–81.

———. 1967b. Editorial. 30(3):162–63.

———. 1968a. Editorial. 31(1):1–2.

———. 1968b. Editorial. 31(2):72–73.

———. 1968c. Editorial. 31(3):155–56.

———. 1969a. Editorial. 32(1):1–2.

———. 1969b. Editorial. 32(2):141–42.

———. 1970a. Editorial. 33(1):1–2.

———. 1970b. Editorial. 33(2):124–25.

———. 1970c. Editorial. 33(3):201–03.

———. 1970d. Editorial. 33(4):279–81.

———. 1971a. Editorial. 34(2):82–83.

———. 1971b. Editorial. 34(3):162–64.

———. 1971c. Editorial. 34(4):255–57.

———. 1972a. Editorial. 35(1):1–3.

———. 1972b. Editorial. 35(2):92–93.

———. 1972c. Editorial. 35(3):143.

Malaysian Forester. 1973a. Editorial. 36(1):1–2.

———. 1973b. Editorial. 36(2):76–77.

———. 1978. Editorial. 41(3):209–10.

———. 1980. Editorial. 43(1):1.

———. 1983. Editorial. 46(3):286–89.

———. 1984. Editorial. 47(4):252–54.

———. 1986. Editorial. 49(3):206–07.

———. 1993b. "Department to urge review of logging concession deals." January 12.

———. 1993c. "Logging rights for ruler." April 18.

Appanah, S., and G. Weinland. 1990. "Will the management systems for hill dip-terocarp forests, stand up?" *Journal of Tropical Forest Science* 3(2):140–58.

———. 1991. "Letter to the Editor." *Journal of Tropical Forest Science* 4(3):270–72.

———. 1993. *Planting Quality Timber Trees in Peninsular Malaysia. Malayan Forest Record No. 38.* Forest Research Institute Malaysia, Kepong, Kuala Lumpur.

Asian Development Bank. 1984. "Appraisal of the compensatory forestry sector project in Malaysia." *Report No. MAL:Ap-53.* Asian Development Bank, Manila.

Azam Aris. 1993a. "Overhaul timber concession system." *New Straits Times.* February 1.

———. 1993b. "State govts urged to change timber concession policies." *New Straits Times.* February 10.

Bernama. 1993. "Halim: Timber tenders above board." *New Straits Times.* May 24.

Bilsborrow, R.E. 1992. "Population, development and deforestation: Some recent evidence." Paper prepared for United Nations Expert Group Meeting on Population, Environment and Development, January 20–24, New York. *IESA/P/AC/34/6*. Population Division, Department of International Economic and Social Affairs, United Nations, New York.

Bilsborrow, R.E., and M.E. Geores. 1991. "Population, land use and the environment in developing countries: What can we learn from cross-national data?" Paper prepared for National Academy of Sciences Workshop on Population and Land Use, December 4–5. National Academy of Sciences, Washington, D.C.

Binkley, C.S., and J.R. Vincent. 1988. "Timber prices in the U.S. south: Past trends and outlook for the future." *Southern Journal of Applied Forestry* 12:15-18.

Brookfield, H. 1994a. "Change and the environment." In *Transformation with Industrialization in Peninsular Malaysia*, ed. H. Brookfield. Oxford University Press, New York.

Brookfield, H. 1994b. "The end of the 'resource frontier'." In *Transformation with Industrialization in Peninsular Malaysia*, ed. H. Brookfield.

Brookfield, H., F.J. Lian, L. Kwai-Sim, and L. Potter. 1990. "Borneo and the Malay Peninsula." In *The Earth as Transformed by Human Action*, ed. B.L. Turner II, W.C. Clark, R.W. Kates, J.F. Richards, J.T. Matthews, and W.B. Meyer. Cambridge University Press, Cambridge, U.K.

Brown, K., and D.W. Pearce, eds. 1994. *The Causes of Tropical Deforestation*. University College London Press, London.

Brown, S., L. Iverson, and A.E. Lugo. 1991. "Land use and biomass changes of forests in Peninsular Malaysia during 1972–1982: Use of GIS analysis." In *Effects of Land-Use Change on Atmospheric CO_2 Concentrations: Southeast Asia as a Case Study*, ed. V. Dale. Springer-Verlag, New York.

Cheah, L.C. 1991. "Letter to the Editor." *Journal of Tropical Forest Science* 4(1):96–99.

Chong, P.W. 1972. "Secondary Wood Processing Industries." *Malayan Forester* 35(3):175–185.

Choong, A., and S. Kuttan. 1992. "Illegal logging: State-owned companies biggest culprits." *New Straits Times*. November 25.

Clawson, M. 1979. "Forests in the long sweep of American history." *Science* 204:1168–74.

Cropper, M., and C. Griffiths. 1994. "The interaction of population growth and environmental quality." *American Economic Review* 84(2):250–54.

EPU (Economic Planning Unit). 1980. *Land Resources Report of Peninsular Malaysia, 1974/1975*. Prime Minister's Department, Kuala Lumpur.

———. 1993. *Malaysian National Conservation Strategy, Vol. 4: Natural Resource Accounting*. EPU, Kuala Lumpur.

FAO/UNDP (Food and Agriculture Organization/United Nations Development Program). 1973. "A national forest inventory of West Malaysia, 1970–72." *FO:DP/MAL/72/009, Technical Report No. 5*. Food and Agriculture Organization, Rome.

FAO/UNEP (United Nations Environment Program). 1981. "Tropical Forest Resources Assessment Project: Forest resources of tropical Asia." *UN 32/6.1301-78-04, Technical Report No. 3.* FAO, Rome.

Fisher, A.C., J.V. Krutilla, and C.J. Cicchetti. 1972. "The economics of environmental preservation: A theoretical and empirical analysis." *American Economic Review* 62(3):605–19.

Harris, L.D. 1989. *The Fragmented Forest.* University of Chicago Press, Chicago.

Hartman, R. 1976. "The harvesting decision when a standing forest has value." *Economic Inquiry* 14:52–58.

Harun bin Ismail. 1976. "The performance of integrated timber complexes and their impact on the socio-economic development in Peninsular Malaysia." Paper presented at the Sixth Malaysian Forestry Conference, Kuching, Sarawak.

Hisham Abdullah. 1992. "Fix quota for ruler's timber concession." *New Straits Times.* December 28.

Hisham Mahzan and Shamsul Akmar. 1992. "Rulers' privy purses ample." *New Straits Times.* December 19.

Hyde, W.F., and R.A. Sedjo. 1992. "Managing tropical forests: Reflections on the rent distribution discussion." *Land Economics* 68(3):343–50.

Ibu Pejabat Perhutanan, Semenanjung Malaysia (Forestry Department Headquarters, Peninsular Malaysia). 1987. "Inventori Hutan Nasional II, Semenanjung Malaysia: 1981–1982." Ibu Pejabat Perhutanan, Semenanjung Malaysia, Kuala Lumpur.

Ismail Ali. 1966. "A critical review of Malayan silviculture in the light of changing demand and form of timber utilization." *Malayan Forester* 29(4):228–33.

———. 1974. "The potential of Malaysian forest resources for industry and trade development." *Malaysian Forester* 37(3):142–151.

Ismail Muhd. Salleh. 1993. "Development trends of public enterprises in Malaysia." *Borneo Review* 4(1):37–59.

Ismail bin Johari and Low, B.H. 1972. "The role of integrated timber complexes in national development with particular reference to Trengganu." *Malayan Forester* 35(3):158–66.

Jasin, A. Kadir. 1992. "Of Western conspirators and local *kembiri politik.*" *New Straits Times.* December 27.

Juhaidi Yean Abdullah. 1992. "Tighter rules on logging." *New Straits Times.* December 26.

Kanapathy, V. 1986. "Forest land use and management: A review of the Compensatory Forest Plantation Programme." Technical report prepared for the Forestry Department Headquarters, Peninsular Malaysia. Institute for Strategic and International Studies, Kuala Lumpur.

Kathirasen, A. 1992. "Keng Yaik: Pressure from palace." *New Straits Times.* December 18.

Kementerian Perusahaan Utama (Ministry of Primary Industries). 1992. *Perangkaan Barangan Utama: Forestry.* Kementerian Perusahaan Utama, Kuala Lumpur.

Khairun Nazirah. 1992. "Lim: Illegal logging in Pahang area." *New Straits Times.* December 14.

Krishnamoorthy, M., K. Vijiyan, and Sufi Yusoff. 1993. "Loggers fined RM24m." *New Straits Times.* January 29.

Krutilla, J.V. 1991. "Environmental resource services of Malaysian moist tropical forests." Mimeo.

Kumar, R. 1986. *The Forest Resources of Malaysia: Their Economics and Development.* Oxford University Press, Singapore.

Lee, H.L. 1978. *Public Policies and Economic Diversification in West Malaysia, 1957–1970.* Penerbit Universiti Malaya, Kuala Lumpur.

Lee, H.S. 1982. "The development of silvicultural systems in the hill forests of Malaysia." *Malayan Forester* 45(1):1–9.

Lee, P.C. 1968. "The implications of the land capability classification on forest reservation in West Malaysia." *Malayan Forester* 31(2):74–77.

Lee, P.C., and W.P. Panton. 1971. *First Malaysia Plan Land Classification Report.* Economic Planning Unit, Kuala Lumpur.

Lian, K.K. 1966. "The future of the sawmilling and plywood industries in West Malaysia." *Malayan Forester* 24(4):245–50.

Lim, H.F. 1991. "Knowledge and use of forest produce as traditional medicine: The case of the forest dwelling communities." In *Medicinal Products from Tropical Rain Forests*, ed. Khozirah Shaari, Azizol Abd. Kadir, and Abd. Razak Mohd. Ali. Forest Research Institute Malaysia, Kepong.

Lim H.F., and Jamaluddin Ismail. 1994. *The Uses of Non-Timber Forest Products in Pasoh Forest Reserve, Malaysia. FRIM Research Pamphlet No. 113.* Forest Research Institute Malaysia, Kepong.

Lindsay, H. 1989. "The Indonesian log export ban: An estimation of foregone export earnings." *Bulletin of Indonesian Economic Studies* 25(2):111–21.

MacArthur, R.H., and E.O. Wilson. 1967. *The Theory of Island Biogeography.* Princeton University Press, Princeton, N.J.

Menon, K.P.V. 1976. "History and development of forestry and forest industries in Malaysia." *FRI Bibliographies No. 4.* Forestry Research Institute Malaysia, Kepong.

MIDA/UNIDO (Malaysian Industrial Development Authority/U.N. Industrial Development Organization). 1985. *Medium and Long Term Industrial Master Plan, Malaysia, 1986–1995, Vol. 2, part 4: Wood-Based Industry.* Malaysian Industrial Development Authority, Kuala Lumpur.

Mohd. Shahwahid Haji Othman. 1985a. "Determining an economic cutting regime for the tropical rainforest." *Malayan Forester* 48(1):57–74.

———. 1985b. "Production and input-use efficiency in the sawmilling industry of Peninsular Malaysia." *Pertanika* 8(2):203–14.

———. 1986. "Production and input-use efficiency in the plywood manufacturing industry of Peninsular Malaysia." *Jurnal Produktiviti* 1(1):41–50.

———. 1989. "Foregone export earnings from West Malaysian log export restriction: A counterfactual exercise." *Malaysian Journal of Agricultural Economics* 6(1):52–69.

———. 1990. "A preliminary economic valuation of wetland plant species in Peninsular Malaysia." Asian Wetlands Bureau, Manila.

———. 1992. "Rural communities' utilisation of wetland species and perception towards development and conservation of Southeast Pahang swamp forests." *Publication No. 78*, Asian Wetlands Bureau, Manila.

———. 1994. "A look at non-wood forest resources—rattan." *Options* 9(2):11–12.

Mohd. Shahwahid Haji Othman, and Nik Mustapha R.A. 1991. "Economic valuation of wetland plant, animal and fish species of Tasek Bera, and residents' perceptions on development and conservation." *Publication No. 77*, Asian Wetlands Bureau, Manila.

Mok, S.T. 1977. "Forest management strategies for sustained maximum socio-economic benefits." *Malayan Forester* 40:14–26.

Muhammad Jabil. 1972. "Bumiputera participation in the timber industry." *Malayan Forester* 35(3):167–74.

Myers, N. 1980. *Conversion of Tropical Moist Forests.* National Research Council, Washington, D.C.

National Forest Council. 1991. Minutes of tenth meeting, held April 4, 1991.

New Straits Times. 1993a. "ACA gets list of 15 logging firms." June 7.

Norazlin, Y. 1990. "Utilization of wetland plant species by local communities—results of an interview survey of communities near wetland areas in Peninsular Malaysia." *Publication No. 67b*, Asian Wetlands Bureau, Manila.

Nordhaus, W.D. 1994. *Managing the Global Commons: The Economics of Climate Change.* MIT Press, Cambridge, Mass.

Palloni, A. 1992. "Methodologies for generalizations from micro studies: An illustration from the literature in deforestation." Unpublished manuscript. Center for Demography and Ecology, University of Wisconsin, Madison, Wisc.

Palo, M. 1987. "Deforestation perspectives for the tropics: A provisional theory with pilot applications." In *The Global Forest Sector: An Analytical Perspective,* ed. by M. Kallio, D.P. Dykstra, and C.S. Binkley. John Wiley & Sons, Chichester, U.K.

Panayotou, T. 1993. "Empirical tests and policy analysis of environmental degradation at different stages of economic development." *Working Paper No. WEP 2-22/WP.238.* International Labour Office, Geneva.

———. 1995. "Environmental degradation at different stages of economic development." In *Beyond Rio: The Environmental Crisis and Sustainable Livelihoods in the Third World,* ed. I. Ahmed and J.A. Doeleman. Macmillan Press Ltd., London.

Panayotou, T., and S. Sungsuwan. 1989. "An econometric study of the causes of tropical deforestation: The case of northeast Thailand." *Development Discussion Paper No. 284.* Harvard Institute for International Development, Cambridge, Mass.

Paris, R., and I. Ruzicka. 1991. "Barking up the wrong tree: The role of rent appropriation in sustainable tropical forest management." *ADB Environment Office Occasional Paper No. 1.* Asian Development Bank, Manila.

Poh, L.Y. 1991. "Country paper: Malaysia." Paper prepared for Regional Expert Consultation on Non Wood Forest Products in the Asia-Pacific Region. Bangkok.

Poh, L.Y., Mohd. Shahwahid Haji Othman, and J. Saroni. 1994. *Bamboo Industry Research in Peninsular Malaysia.* Forestry Department Headquarters, Peninsular Malaysia, Kuala Lumpur.

Ramayah, J. 1993. "War on illegal logging." *New Straits Times.* January 28.

Ramayah, J., and Tengku Sarifuddin. 1993. "Move to control timber concessions." *New Straits Times.* February 4.

Repetto, R., and M. Gillis, eds. 1988. *Public Policies and the Misuse of Forest Resources.* Cambridge University Press, Cambridge, U.K.

Ross, M.L. 1996. *The Political Economy of Boom-and-Bust Logging in Indonesia, the Philippines, and East Malaysia, 1950–94.* Ph.D. dissertation. Department of Politics, Princeton University, Princeton, NJ.

Rudel, T.K. 1989. "Population, development, and tropical deforestation: A cross-national study." *Rural Sociology* 54(3):327–38.

Sabry Shariff, and Sufi Yusoff. 1993. "Army to check illegal logging." *New Straits Times.* August 10.

Salleh Mohd. Nor. 1972. "Proposals for a permanent forest estate for West Malaysia." *Malayan Forester* 35(4):269–84.

Scotti, R. 1990. "Estimating and projecting forest area at global and local level: A step forward." Paper prepared for Forest Resources Assessment 1990. Food and Agriculture Organization, Rome.

Sedjo, R.A., and K.S. Lyon. 1990. *The Long-Term Adequacy of World Timber Supply.* Resources for the Future, Washington, D.C.

Setten, G.G.K. 1962. "The need for a forest estate in Malaya." *Malayan Forester* 25:184–99.

Shafik, N., and S. Bandyopadhyay. 1992. "Economic growth and environmental quality: Time-series and cross-country evidence." *World Development Report Working Paper WPS 904.* The World Bank, Washington, D.C.

Shamsul Akmar. 1992. "Lim: Overlogging by Kelantan." *New Straits Times.* November 14.

———. 1993a. "Illegal logging due to unwanted interference." *New Straits Times.* August 25.

———. 1993b. "Timber for 'Tengku Wong'." *New Straits Times.* May 28.

Southgate, D., R. Sierra, and L. Brown. 1991. "The causes of tropical deforestation in Ecuador: A statistical analysis." *World Development* 19(9):1145–51.

Star (newspaper). 1991. "Concession said to be a political patronage." September 12.

Sulaiman bin Haji Noordin. 1977. "A method of forest revenue assessment based on inventory data." *Malayan Forester* 40(3):144–59.

Tang, H.T. 1974. "A brief assessment of the regeneration systems for hill forests in Peninsular Malaysia." *Malayan Forester* 37(4):263–70.

———. 1987. "Problems and strategies for regenerating dipterocarp forests in Malaysia." In *Natural Management of Tropical Moist Forests*, ed. F. Mergen and J.R. Vincent. Yale University, School of Forestry and Environmental Studies, New Haven, Conn.

Tang, H.T., and Wan Razali Mohd. 1981. "Report on growth and yield studies in inland mixed indigenous forests in peninsular Malaysia." Photocopy. Forestry Department Headquarters, Peninsular Malaysia, Kuala Lumpur.

Teo, P.C. 1966. "Revision of royalty rates." *Malayan Forester* 29(4):254–58.

Thang, H.C. 1986. "Selective management system: Concept and practice (Peninsular Malaysia)." Photocopy. Forest Management Unit, Forestry Department Headquarters, Peninsular Malaysia, Kuala Lumpur.

———. 1987. "Forest management systems for tropical high forest, with special reference to Peninsular Malaysia." *Forest Ecology and Management* 21:3–20

Umikalsum Haji Mohd. Nor. 1991. *Fiscal Federalism in Malaysia, 1971–1987*. PhD. dissertation. Faculty of Economics and Administration, University of Malaya, Kuala Lumpur.

Unit Ekonomi, Ibu Pejabat Perhutanan. n.d. (a). *Perangkaan Perhutanan, Semenanjung Malaysia: 1971–1978*. Ibu Pejabat Perhutanan, Kuala Lumpur.

———. n.d. (b). *Perangkaan Perhutanan, Semenanjung Malaysia:1979–1986*. Ibu Pejabat Perhutanan, Kuala Lumpur.

———. n.d. (c). *Perangkaan Perhutanan, Semenanjung Malaysia: 1986–1990*. Ibu Pejabat Perhutanan, Kuala Lumpur.

Veitch, M.D. 1986. *National Parameters for Project Appraisal in Malaysia, vol. 3: Summary of Estimation Procedures*. Regional Economics Section, Economic Planning Unit, Prime Minister's Department, Kuala Lumpur.

Vijiyan, K. 1993. "Police uncover illegal logging operations." *New Straits Times*. August 14.

Vincent, J.R. 1986. "Growth of the forest products industry in Malaysia: 1961-85." *Malayan Forester* 49(3):223–40.

———. 1990. "Rent capture and the feasibility of tropical forest management." *Land Economics* 66(2):212–23.

———. 1992a. "A simple, nonspatial modeling approach for analyzing a country's forest-products trade policies." In *Forestry Sector Analysis for Developing Countries*, comp. R.W. Haynes, P. Harou, and J. Mikowski. *CINTRAFOR Special Report 10*. College of Forest Resources, University of Washington, Seattle.

———. 1992b. "The tropical timber trade and sustainable development." *Science* 256(5064):1651–55.

———. 1993. "Managing tropical forests: Comment." *Land Economics* 68(3):313–18.

Vincent, J.R., and C.S. Binkley. 1992. "Forest-based industrialization: A dynamic perspective." In *Managing the World's Forests*, ed. N. Sharma. Kendall/Hunt Publishing Company, for The World Bank, Dubuque, Iowa.

Vincent, J.R., W.J. Lange, and H.D. Seok. 1992. "Labor demand by forest products industries: A review." *Research Paper FPL-RP-510.* Forest Products Laboratory, U.S. Forest Service, Madison, Wisconsin.

Vincent, J.R., and Yusuf Hadi. 1991. "Deforestation and agricultural expansion in Peninsular Malaysia." *Development Discussion Paper No. 396.* Harvard Institute for International Development, Cambridge, Mass.

———. 1993. "Malaysia." In *Sustainable Agriculture and the Environment in the Humid Tropics,* ed. Committee on Sustainable Agriculture and the Environment in the Humid Tropics, National Research Council. National Academy Press, Washington, D.C.

Wan Razali Wan Mohd. 1989. "Summary of growth and yield studies in tropical mixed forests of Malaysia." *Forest Research Institute Malaysia Reports* 59:16–38.

Wan Sabri Wan Mansor. 1987. "Forest Recreation Use Patterns, User Behavior, and Recreational Value in Malaysia." Ph.D. dissertation. University College of North Wales, Bangor, Wales.

Whitmore, T.C. 1988. "Forest types and forest zonation." In *Key Environments: Malaysia,* ed. Earl of Cranbrook. Pergamon, Oxford.

Wong, I.F.T. 1971. *The Present Land Use of West Malaysia (1966).* Ministry of Agriculture and Lands, Kuala Lumpur.

World Resources Institute. 1992. *World Resources 1992–93: A Guide to the Global Environment.* Oxford University Press, New York.

Wyatt-Smith, J. 1988. "Letter to the Editor." *Journal of Forest Ecology and Management* 24:219–23.

CHAPTER 5: AGRICULTURAL LAND

Abdul Rahim bin Rahmat. 1981. "Strategi dan cara-cara perlaksanaan pembangunan tanah terbiar." Working paper in *Lapuran Pemulihan Tanah-Tanah Sawah Terbiar, Jilid 1,* Pasukan Petugas Tanah Terbiar. Kementerian Pertanian, Kuala Lumpur.

Amriah Buang. 1988. "The Malays' idle agricultural land: An Islamic dilemma and a problem of modernization." Paper presented at the Third International Islamic Geographical Conference, August 28–September 1, Genting Highlands, Malaysia.

———. 1989. "Dinamiks penglibatan akar umbi dalam pembangunan tanah pertanian terbiar: Teladan dari Sg. Raya—Bukit Tembok, Negeri Sembilan." Paper presented at Bengkel Penyelidikan IRPA/UKM/Pertama, September 2–3, Melaka, Malaysia.

Malayan Forester. 1968. Editorial. 31 (April):72–73.

———. 1970. Editorial. 33 (July): 201–203.

Appanah, S., and G. Weinland. 1993. *Planting Quality Timber Trees in Peninsular Malaysia. Malayan Forest Record No. 38.* Forest Research Institute Malaysia, Kepong.

Barlow, C.S. 1978. *The Natural Rubber Industry: Its Development, Technology, and Economy in Malaysia.* Oxford University Press, Kuala Lumpur.

———. 1984. "Institutional and policy implications of economic change: Malaysian rubber, 1950–1983." Unpublished manuscript. Department of Economics, Research School of Pacific Studies, Australian National University, Canberra.

Brookfield, H. 1994a. "Change and the environment." In *Transformation with Industrialization in Peninsular Malaysia*, ed. H. Brookfield. Oxford University Press, New York.

———. 1994b. "Land use and rural employment changes since 1966." In *Transformation with Industrialization in Peninsular Malaysia*, ed. H. Brookfield.

Burrows, J. 1980. "Idle land and poverty." Mimeo. Ministry of Agriculture, Kuala Lumpur.

Cabinet Committee on Agriculture. 1984. *National Agricultural Policy.* Government Printer, Kuala Lumpur.

Campbell, R.B., W.D. Sorenson, S.T. Chew, and C.Y.Wong. 1985. "Study on the restructuring and modernization of smallholder agriculture in Malaysia." Report prepared for the Asian Development Bank and the Government of Malaysia. Development Alternatives, Inc., Washington, D.C.

Clawson, M. 1979. "Forests in the long sweep of American history." *Science* 204:1168–74.

Courtenay, P.P. 1986. "The dilemma of Malaysian padi policy." *Australian Geographer* 17:178–85.

EPU (Economic Planning Unit). 1980. *Land Resources Report of Peninsular Malaysia.* Kuala Lumpur.

Edwin, J. 1993. "From idle land to profitable forest." *New Straits Times.* June 15.

Fadzim Othman. 1990. "Land-abandonment in the rice sector in West Malaysia: A case study of the Muda and Kemubu irrigation schemes." Ph.D. dissertation. University of Wisconsin, Madison, Wisc.

FELCRA (Federal Land Consolidation and Rehabilitation Agency). n.d. "Land rehabilitation and consolidation: FELCRA's experience." Unpublished paper. Kuala Lumpur.

Fujimoto, A. 1991. "Evolution of rice farming under the New Economic Policy." *The Developing Economies* 29(4):432–54.

Gates, W.B., Jr., T.J. Goering, and D.H. Keare. 1967. "The role of land in the economic development of West Malaysia, 1966–1985." Unpublished paper. Economic Planning Unit, Kuala Lumpur.

Gibbons, D.S., et al. 1981. *Land Tenure in the Muda Irrigation Area—Final Report, Part 2: Findings.* Universiti Sains Malaysia, Penang.

Gibbons, E.T., and Mohd. Ariff Hussein. 1986. "Revitalizing Peninsular Malaysia's agriculture: Some areas of scope for better performance." Paper presented at Malaysian Economic Association seminar, Kuala Lumpur. Mimeo.

Guyot, D. 1971. "The politics of land: Comparative development in two states of Malaysia." *Pacific Affairs* 44(3):368–89.

Hart, J.F. 1968. "Loss and abandonment of cleared farm land in the eastern United States." *Annals of the Association of American Geographers* 58(3):417–40.

———. 1984. "Cropland change in the United States, 1944–78." In *The Resourceful Earth*, ed. J.L. Simon and H. Kahn. Basil Blackwell, Oxford.

Hill, R.D. 1982. *Agriculture in the Malaysian Region.* Akademiai Kiado, Budapest.

International Fund for Agricultural Development. 1990. "General identification report." *Report No. 0291-MA.*

Jabatan Pertanian. 1988. "Banci petani 1982–86." Mimeo. Kuala Lumpur.

———. 1992. *Laporan Banci Petani 1990, Jilid 1.* Jabatan Pertanian, Kuala Lumpur.

Kementerian Pertanian. 1980. *Lapuran Pebangunan Tanah-Tanah Terbiar.* Pasukan Petugas bagi Mengusahakan Tanah-Tanah Terbiar, Kuala Lumpur.

———. 1981. *Lapuran Pebangunan Tanah-Tanah Sawah Terbiar, Jilid 1.* Pasukan Petugas Tanah Terbiar, Kuala Lumpur.

———. 1983. *Statistical Handbook, Agriculture: 1980.* Kementerian Pertanian, Kuala Lumpur.

———. 1988. *Statistical Handbook, Agriculture: 1985.* Kementerian Pertanian, Kuala Lumpur.

———. 1989. "Ringkasan executive lapuran keberkesanan program pemulihan tanah terbiar Semenanjung Malaysia." Bahagian Ekonomi Pertanian, Kuala Lumpur.

———. 1990. *Statistical Handbook, Agriculture: 1988.* Kementerian Pertanian, Kuala Lumpur.

———. 1993. *Statistical Handbook, Agriculture: 1990.* Kementerian Pertanian, Kuala Lumpur.

Khera, H.S. 1976. *The Oil Palm Industry of Malaysia.* Penerbit Universiti Malaya, Kuala Lumpur.

Lembaga Pertubuhan Peladang. n.d. "Program pemulihan tanah sawah terbiar." Bahagian Pembangunan, Kuala Lumpur.

———. 1991. "Program pemulihan tanah sawah terbiar: Status dan program RME." Cawangan Pengurusan Ladang, Bahagian Pembangunan, Kuala Lumpur.

Lim, T.G., and R. Phillips. 1992. "Livestock farmers in Malaysia: Key issues in development." *Kajian Malaysia* 10(2):18–38.

Loh, K.W. 1988. *Beyond the Tin Mines: Coolies, Squatters, and New Villagers in the Kinta Valley.* Oxford University Press, Singapore.

Mehmet, O. 1986. *Development in Malaysia.* Croom Helm, London.

Ministry of Agriculture. 1993. *The National Agricultural Policy, 1992–2010: Policy Statement.* Ministry of Agriculture, Kuala Lumpur.

Mohd. Fuad Mat Jali. 1989. "Perancangan dan pembangunan tanah terbiar di Selangor: Kajian projek pembangunan bersepadu barat laut Selangor." In *Prosiding, Bengkel IRPA UKM 1.* Penerbit Universiti Kebangsaan Malaysia, Bangi.

Mohd. Ghazali Mohayiddin, and Abdul Aziz Abdul Rahman. 1989. "Malaysian agriculture in the year 2000: Towards a structural adjustment." In *Malaysian Agricultural Policy: Issues and Directions*, ed. Fatimah Mohd. Arshad et al. Centre for Agricultural Policy Studies, Universiti Pertanian Malaysia, Serdang.

Mohd. Helmi bin Mohd. Hussain. 1980. "Masaalah perundangan dalam pembangunan tanah terbiar." Mimeo. Jabatan Tanah dan Galian Persekutuan, Kuala Lumpur.

Mustapha Juman. 1980. "Peranan Felcra dalam pembangunan tanah secara in situ termasuk tanah terbiar." Mimeo. Jabatan Tanah dan Galian Persekutuan, Kuala Lumpur.

Nasaruddin Arshad and Zulkifly Hj. Mustapha. 1986. "National agricultural policy in relation to agricultural development in Malaysia: Some observations." *Jurnal Antropologi dan Sosiologi* 14.

Parti Gerakan Rakyat Malaysia. 1986. *Into the Mainstream of Development*. Parti Gerakan Rakyat Malaysia, Kuala Lumpur.

Pazim @ Fadzim Othman. 1992. "Land-abandonment in the rice sector in West Malaysia." *Malaysian Journal of Economic Studies* 29(1):51–68.

Perunding Bersatu Sdn. Bhd. 1988. "Land tenure in Pahang State." Unpublished report. Kuala Lumpur.

Prime Minister's Department. n.d. *Report of The Cabinet Committee on National Agricultural Policy, part II, vol. I.* Prime Minister's Department, Kuala Lumpur.

RISDA (Rubber Industry Smallholders' Development Authority). 1983. *Banci Pekebun Kecil Getah Semenanjung Malaysia 1977: Analisa Profail Sosio-Ekonomi Kemiskinan dan Penvertaan Dalam Rancangan RISDA Lapuran Akhir.* Rubber Industry Smallholder's Development Authority, Kuala Lumpur.

Selvadurai, S. 1963. *Census of Agriculture, Federation of Malaya. Preliminary Report Number Sixteen: Estates.* Ministry of Agriculture and Cooperatives, Kuala Lumpur.

Shand, R.T., and Mohd. Ariff Hussein. 1989. "Directions of Malaysian agriculture and policy alternatives: A question of linkages." In *Malaysian Agricultural Policy: Issues and Directions*, ed. Fatimah Mohd. Arshad et al.

Sivalingam, G. 1993. *Malaysia's Agricultural Transformation*. Pelanduk Publications, Petaling Jaya.

Suhaini Aznam. 1991. "Law of the land." *Far Eastern Economic Review* (August 15): 21.

Syed Hussain Wafa. 1972. "Land development strategies in Malaysia: an empirical study." *Kajian Ekonomi Malaysia* 9(2):1–28, 10(2):1–50.

Timmer, C.P. 1988. "The agricultural transformation." In *Handbook of Development Economics, vol. 1*, ed. H. Chenery and T.N. Srinivasan. North-Holland, Amsterdam.

Unit Penyelidikan Sosio-Ekonomi. 1988. "Draf laporan kajian kekesanan projek mini estet padi." Jabatan Perdana Menteri, Kuala Lumpur.

Vincent, J.R., and Yusuf Hadi. 1991. "Deforestation and agricultural expansion in Peninsular Malaysia." *Development Discussion Paper No. 396.* Harvard Institute for International Development, Cambridge, Mass.

————. 1993. "Malaysia." In *Sustainable Agriculture and the Environment in the Humid Tropics*, ed. National Research Council. National Academy Press, Washington, D.C.

Wan Ibrahim Wan Daud. 1982. "Pertubuhan peladang dan tanah terbiar." Paper presented at Farmers Convention, August 8, Kuala Pilah, Negeri Sembilan.

Wong, C.Y. 1995. Personal communication. May 24.

Wong, I.F.T. 1971. *The Present Land Use of West Malaysia (1966)*. Ministry of Agriculture and Lands, Kuala Lumpur.

World Bank. 1980. *Malaysia: Selected Issues in Rural Poverty*. World Bank, Washington, D.C.

————. 1984. "Sector report, Malaysia: Incentive policies in agriculture, vol. 1: Overview of issues and recommendations." *Report No. 4792-MA*. Country Programs Department, East Asia and Pacific Region, World Bank, Washington, D.C.

————. 1988. "Sector report, Malaysia: Review of the rice industry." *Report No. 7395-MA*. Agriculture Operations Division, Country Department II, Asia Region, World Bank, Washington, D.C.

————. 1990. "Project completion report, Malaysia: Felcra 1 Project (Loan 2013-MA)." *Report No. 8653*. Agricultural Operations Division, Country Department II, Asia Region, World Bank, Washington, D.C.

————. 1992. "Staff appraisal report, Malaysia: Third Felcra land development project." *Report No. 10372-MA*. Agricultural Operations Division, Country Department I, East Asia and Pacific Region, World Bank, Washington, D.C.

Zulkifly Hj. Mustapha. 1983. "Public investments and the development of Malaysian agriculture." In *The Malaysian Economy and Finance*, ed. Sritua Arif and Jomo K.S. Rosecons, Balmain, Australia.

————. 1989. "The evolution of Malaysian agricultural development policy, issues and challenges." In *Malaysian Agricultural Policy: Issues and Directions*, ed. Fatimah Mohd. Arshad et al.

Zulkifly Hj. Mustapha, and Shaik Mohd. Noor Alam. 1985. "Idle agricultural land in Peninsular Malaysia: Problems and opportunities." *Malaysian Journal of Agricultural Economics 2(1)*:36–53.

CHAPTER 6: MARINE FISHERIES

Anderson, E.N., Jr. 1987. "A Malaysian tragedy of the commons." In *The Question of the Commons*, ed. B.J. McCay and J.M. Acheson. University of Arizona Press, Tucson.

Aron, W., D. Fluharty, D. McCaughran, and J.F. Ross. 1993. "Fisheries management" (letter to the editor). *Science* 261:813–14.

Ch'ng, K.L. 1983. "Management of marine capture fisheries in Malaysia: Issues and problems." Paper presented at the International Conference on the Development and Management of Tropical Living Aquatic Resources. Serdang, Selangor, Malaysia, August 2–5.

Clark, C.W. 1976. *Mathematical Bioeconomics: The Optimal Management of Renewable Resources.* John Wiley & Sons, New York.

Deacon, R.T. 1989. "An empirical model of fishery dynamics." *Journal of Environmental Economics and Management* 16(2):167–83.

Deriso, R.B. 1980. "Harvesting strategies and parameter estimation for an age-structured model." *Canadian Journal of Fisheries and Aquatic Sciences* 37(2):268–82.

Elliston, G.R. 1980. "Some problems in the future development of the marine fishing industry." In *The Malaysian Fisheries: A Diminishing Resource.* Consumer Association of Penang, Penang.

Fredericks, L.J., Sulochana Nair, and Jahara Yahaya. 1985. "Cost structure and profitability of small-scale fisheries in Peninsular Malaysia." In *Small-Scale Fisheries in Asia: Socio-Economic Analysis and Policy*, ed. T. Panayotou. International Development and Research Council, Ottawa.

Gibbons, D.S. 1976. "Public policy towards fisheries development in Peninsular Malaysia: A critical review emphasizing Penang and Kedah." *Kajian Ekonomi Malaysia* 13(1&2):89–121.

Goh, C.T. 1976. "The fishing conflict in Penang and Perak: Personal memoir." *Kajian Ekonomi Malaysia* 13(1&2):17–25.

Gordon, H.S. 1954. "Economic theory of a common-property resource: The fishery." *Journal of Political Economy* 62:124–42.

Gulland, J.A. 1974. *The Management of Marine Fisheries.* Bristol, U.K.

Institut Penyelidikan Perikanan and Cawangan Perancang dan Sistem, Maklumat Pengurusan Perikanan. n.d. "Kajian biologi dan kos dan pulangan pukat jerut ikan berlampu dan tidak berlampu yang dijalankan di perairan pantai barat Semenanjung Malaysia dari Jun hingga Oktober 1988." Department of Fisheries, Kuala Lumpur.

Ishak Shaari, and Y.T. Chang. 1986. "Impact of new technology on the lives of fishing communities in peninsular Malaysia." Fakulti Ekonomi, Universiti Kebangsaan Malaysia, Bangi.

Jabatan Perikanan. n.d. "Dayamaju ekonomi laut dalam di perairan, Semenanjung Malaysia." Jabatan Perikanan, Kuala Lumpur.

———. Various issues. *Perangkaan Tahunan Perikanan.* Ministry of Agriculture, Kuala Lumpur.

———. 1989. "Kajian kos dan pulangan perkakas-perkakas tradisional di Semenanjung Malaysia, 1988." Jabatan Perikanan, Kuala Lumpur.

———. 1991. *Perangkaan, Tahunan Perikanan 1990.* Ministry of Agriculture, Kuala Lumpur.

Jahara Yahaya. 1976. "Some implications of the fishermen's subsidy scheme in Peninsular Malaysia." *Kajian Ekonomi Malaysia* 13(1&2):72–80.

———. 1977. "The socio-economic impacts of the trawler industry in Malaysia." *Occasional Paper Series No. 5.* Faculty of Economics and Administration, University of Malaya, Kuala Lumpur.

————. 1981. "Development of capture fisheries: Lessons from MAJUIKAN's experience." *Marine Policy* 5(4).

————. 1984. "An economic analysis of fisheries production—with specific reference to the multi-species trawl fishery of Terengganu, Malaysia." *Kajian Ekonomi Malaysia* 21(1):1–17.

————. 1988. "Fishery management and regulation in Peninsular Malaysia: Issues and constraints." *Marine Resource Economics* 5:83–98.

Jahara Yahaya, and R.J.G. Wells. 1982. "A case study of costs and earnings of three gears in the Terengganu fishery, Malaysia." *Developing Economies* 20(1):73–99.

Jomo, K.S. 1991. *Fishing for Trouble: Malaysian Fisheries, Sustainable Development and Inequality. Occasional Papers and Reports, No. 3.* Institute for Advanced Studies, University of Malaya, Kuala Lumpur.

Jorgenson, D.W., and Z. Griliches. 1971. "Divisia index numbers and productivity measurement." *Review of Income and Wealth* 17(2):227–29.

Khoo, K.H. 1976. "Optimal utilization and management of fishery resources." *Kajian Ekonomi Malaysia* 13(1&2):40–50.

————. 1980. "Implementation of regulations for domestic fishermen." In *Law of the Sea*, ed. F.J. Christy. Manila.

Kusairi Mohd. Noh, and S.Y. Tai. 1988. "The development of the Malaysian offshore fishery: Some issues and problems." In *Malaysian Agricultural Policy: Issues and Directions*, ed. Fatimah Mohd. Arshad et al. Centre for Agricultural Policy Studies, Universiti Pertanian Malaysia, Serdang.

Labon, A. 1974. "Malaysian long-term fisheries development plan until 1995." *SCS/DEV/73/10.* South China Sea Fisheries Development and Coordinating Programme, Food and Agriculture Organization, Rome.

Ludwig, D., R. Hilborn, and C. Walters. 1993. "Uncertainty, resource exploitation, and conservation: Lessons from history." *Science* 260:17,36.

MAJUIKAN. 1981. "Fisheries in Malaysia: Sector status and issues." *MAJUIKAN Policy Review Working Paper No. 1.* Lembaga Kemajuan Ikan Malaysia, Kuala Lumpur.

Ministry of Agriculture. 1979. "Penilaian sekim subsidi nelayan Semenanjung Malaysia." Mimeo. Kuala Lumpur.

Mohamed Mazlan bin Jusoh. 1972. "Survey of resources and economics of catches by boats 10–25 tons in Kedah waters." Mimeo. Department of Fisheries, Alor Setar.

Mohd. Shaari bin Sam Abdul Latiff. 1976. "Demersal fish resources surveys and problems of fisheries resource management." *Fisheries Bulletin* No. 15, part 1. Ministry of Agriculture, Kuala Lumpur.

Munro, G.R., and K.L. Chee. 1978. *The Economics of Fishing and the Developing World: A Malaysian Case Study.* University of Malaya Press, Kuala Lumpur.

Ooi, J.B. 1990. *Development Problems of an Open-Access Resource: The Fisheries of Peninsular Malaysia. Occasional Paper No. 86.* Institute of Southeast Asian Studies, Singapore.

Pathansali, D. 1976. "Assessment of potential yields from the coastal marine fisheries resource of Malaysia." *Fisheries Bulletin* No. 15, part 3. Ministry of Agriculture, Kuala Lumpur.

———. 1977. "Some observations on catch and effort of commercial and research trawlers with estimate of yield." *Fisheries Bulletin.* Ministry of Agriculture, Kuala Lumpur.

Rabihah Mahmood, C.F. Lim, and Zaini bin Baharuddin. 1989. "Perusahaan perikanan laut dalam di Malaysia dari segi kos dan pulangan bagi bot 70 GRT dan ke atas" (Deep-sea fishing industries in Malaysia, by cost and return for boats of 70 GRT and above). Department of Fisheries, Kuala Lumpur.

Roff, D.A. 1983. "Analysis of catch/effort data: A comparison of three methods." *Canadian Journal of Fisheries and Aquatic Sciences.* 40(9):1496–1506.

Schaefer, M.B. 1957. "Some considerations of population dynamics and economics in relation to the management of marine fisheries." *Journal of the Fisheries Research Board of Canada* 14:669–81.

Schnute, J. 1985. "A general theory for analysis of catch and effort data." *Canadian Journal of Fisheries and Aquatic Sciences.* 42(3):414–29.

Shahrom bin Abdul Majid. 1984. "Controlling fishing effort: Malaysia's experience and problems." *FAO Fisheries Report No. 289, Supplement 3:319–27.* Food and Agriculture Organization, Rome.

———. 1992. "Coastal fisheries management in Malaysia." Paper presented at Food and Agriculture Organization/Japan Expert Consultation on the Development of Community-Based Coastal Fishery Management Systems for Asia and the Pacific, June 8–12, 1992, Kobe, Japan. Food and Agriculture Organization, Rome.

Soong, M.K. 1964. "Trawling in Singapore and the states of Malaya and the problem raised." Paper presented at Indo-Pacific Fisheries Council, 11th Session, October 1964, Kuala Lumpur.

Tan, J. 1993. "Helping fishermen to go for other jobs." *New Straits Times.* October 4.

World Bank. 1982. "Malaysia: A review of fisheries policies and programs." Draft. Agriculture Division 5, East Asia and Pacific Projects Department, World Bank, Washington, D.C.

Yap, C.L. 1973. "Overexpansion in the trawler industry with specific reference to the Dindings District of West Malaysia." *Kajian Ekonomi Malaysia* 10(2).

———. 1976. "Fishery policies and development with special reference to the West coast of Peninsular Malaysia from the early 1900s." *Kajian Ekonomi Malaysia* 13(1&2):7–16.

CHAPTER 7: FRESHWATER

Asian Development Bank. 1986. *Malaysia Water Supply and Sanitation Sector Profile.* Water Supply Division, Asian Development Bank, Manila.

———. 1991. *Asian Development Outlook.* Economics and Development Resource Centre, Asian Development Bank, Manila.

Gibbons, D.C. 1986. *The Economic Value of Water.* Resources for the Future, Washington, D.C.

Goh, K.C. 1990. "Aspects of domestic water consumption on Penang Island." *Malaysian Journal of Tropical Geography* 21(1):35–42.

Hanke, S.H. 1970. "Demand for water under dynamic conditions." *Water Resources Research* 6(5):1253–61.

———. 1978. "A method of integrating engineering and economic planning." *Journal of the American Water Works Association* (September).

———. 1982. "Economic aspects of urban water supply: Some reflections on water conservation policies." *CP-82-91.* International Institute for Applied Systems Analysis, Laxenburg, Austria.

Hanke, S.H., and R.K. Davis. 1973. "Potential for marginal cost pricing in water resource management." *Water Resources Research* 9(4):808–25.

JICA (Japan International Cooperation Agency). 1982a. *National Water Resources Study, Malaysia. Main Report, vol. 1: Master Action Plan.* Japan International Cooperation Agency, Tokyo.

———. 1982b. *National Water Resources Study, Malaysia. Main Report, vol. 2: Water Resources Development and Use Plan.* Japan International Cooperation Agency, Tokyo.

JKR (Jabatan Kerja Raya, Malaysia). 1992. *Malaysian Water Supply: General Information.* Cawangan Bekalan Air, Ibu Pejabat JKR, Kuala Lumpur.

JKR (Jabatan Kerja Raya, Malaysia) and Bina Runding Sdn. Bhd. 1989. *Non-Revenue Water Control Study & Development of a Control Programme for Malaysia. Phase 1 Final Report: Text & Appendices.* Cawangan Bekalan Air, Ibu Pejabat JKR, Kuala Lumpur.

Katzman, M.T. 1977. "Income and price elasticities of demand for water in developing countries." *Water Resources Bulletin* 13(1):47–55.

Khan, N., Ismail Yaziz, Wan Norazmin Wan Sulaiman, and S. Kanthaswamy. 1992. "Freshwater resources." Background paper for Malaysia National Conservation Strategy. Institut Pengajian Tinggi, University of Malaya, Kuala Lumpur.

Meerman, J. 1979. *Public Expenditure in Malaysia: Who Benefits and Why.* Oxford University Press, New York.

Meroz, A. 1968. "A quantitative analysis of urban water demand in developing countries." *Working Paper No. 17.* Economics Department, The World Bank, Washington, D.C.

Rogers, P. 1992. "Comprehensive water resources management: A concept paper." *Policy Research Working Paper, Water and Sanitation, WPS 879.* Infrastructure and Urban Development Department, The World Bank, Washington, D.C.

Saunders, R.J., and J.J. Warford. 1976. *Village Water Supply.* Johns Hopkins University Press, Baltimore. (Sections reprinted in *Pricing Policy for Development Management*, ed. G.M. Meier. Johns Hopkins University Press, Baltimore, 1983.)

Subramaniam, V. 1992. "Privatisation of water supplies the—Malaysian experience." Mimeo. Jabatan Bekalan Air, Selangor, Kuala Lumpur.

Teerink, J.R., and M. Nakashima. 1993. "Water allocation, rights, and pricing: Examples from Japan and the United States." *Technical Paper No. 198*. World Bank, Washington, D.C.

Tietenberg, T.H. 1988. *Environmental and Natural Resource Economics*, 2d ed. Scott, Foresman and Company, Glenview, Ill.

Uzir Abdul Malik. 1988. "An appraisal of water use policy in the agricultural sector of Malaysia." In *Malaysian Agricultural Policy: Issues and Directions*, ed. Fatimah Mohd. Arshad et al. Centre for Agricultural Policy Studies, Universiti Pertanian Malaysia, Serdang, and Malaysian Agricultural Economics Association, Kuala Lumpur.

Vatikiotis, M. 1991. "Water pressure: States rights may be diluted." *Far Eastern Economic Review.* July 18, p. 22.

Wan, L.F. 1988. "Land and water resource policies for agricultural development in the Kedah/Perlis/Penang region." In *Malaysian Agricultural Policy: Issues and Directions*, ed. Fatimah Mohd. Arshad et al.

Whittington, D. 1992. "Possible adverse effects of increasing block water tariffs in developing countries." *Economic Development and Cultural Change*: 41(1):75–87.

World Bank. 1992. *World Development Report 1992: Development and the Environment.* Oxford University Press, Oxford.

World Bank Water Demand Research Team. 1993. "The demand for water in rural areas: Determinants and policy implications." *World Bank Research Observer* 8(1):47–70.

CHAPTER 8: POLLUTION AND ECONOMIC DEVELOPMENT

The Economist. 1992/1993. "Don't green the GATT." (December 26, 1992–January 8, 1993):13–14.

Arrow, K., B. Bolin, R. Costanza, P. Dasgupta, C. Folke, C.S. Holling, B.O. Jansson, S. Levin, K.G. Mäler, C. Perrings, and D. Pimentel. 1995. "Economic growth, carrying capacity, and the environment." *Science* 268:520–21.

Birdsall, N., and D. Wheeler. 1992. "Trade policy and industrial pollution in Latin America: Where are the pollution havens?" In *International Trade and the Environment*, ed. P. Low. *Discussion Paper No. 159.* World Bank, Washington, D.C.

Dean, J. 1992. "Trade and the environment: A survey of the literature." Background paper prepared for the *1992 World Development Report.* World Bank, Washington, D.C.

DOE (Department of Environment, Malaysia). 1992. *Environmental Quality Report 1991*. Ministry of Science, Technology, and the Environment, Kuala Lumpur.

Government of Malaysia and Asian Development Bank. 1987. *Report of Klang Valley Environmental Improvement Project*, 3 vol. Government of Malaysia and Asian Development Bank, Manila.

Grossman, G.M., and A.B. Krueger. 1991. "Environmental impacts of a North American Free Trade Agreement." *NBER Working Paper No. 3914*. National Bureau of Economic Research, Cambridge, Mass.

Hettige, H., R.E.B. Lucas, and D. Wheeler. 1992. "The toxic intensity of industrial production: Global patterns, trends, and trade policy." *American Economic Review* 82(2):478–81.

Jasin, A. Kadir. 1993. "Other shots." *New Straits Times*, May 23.

Kuznets, S. 1955. "Economic growth and income inequality." *American Economic Review* 45(1):1–28.

Lopez, R. 1994. "The environment as a factor of production: The effects of economic growth and trade liberalization." *Journal of Environmental Economics and Management* 27(2):163–84.

Lucas, R.E.B., D. Wheeler, and H. Hettige. 1992. "Economic development, environmental regulation, and the international migration of toxic industrial pollution: 1960–1988." In *International Trade and the Environment*, ed. P. Low.

Low, P., and A. Yeats. 1992. "Do 'dirty' industries migrate?" In *International Trade and the Environment*, ed. P. Low.

Mahathir bin Mohamad. 1991. "Malaysia: The way forward (Vision 2020)." National Printing Department, Kuala Lumpur.

Panayotou, T. 1993. "Empirical tests and policy analysis of environmental degradation at different stages of economic development." *Working Paper No. WEP 2-22/WP.238*. International Labour Office, Geneva.

―――. 1995. "Environmental degradation at different stages of economic development." In *Beyond Rio: The Environmental Crisis and Sustainable Livelihoods in the Third World*, ed. I. Ahmed and J.A. Doeleman. Macmillan Press Ltd., London.

Selden, T.M., and D. Song. 1994. "Environmental quality and development: Is there a Kuznets curve for air pollution emissions?" *Journal of Environmental Economics and Management* 27(2):147–62.

Shafik, N., and S. Bandyopadhyay. 1992. "Economic growth and environmental quality: Time-series and cross-country evidence." *World Development Report Working Paper WPS 904*. World Bank, Washington, D.C.

Smith, K.R. 1987. *Biofuels, Air Pollution, and Health: A Global Review*. Plenum Press, New York.

Summers, R., and A. Heston. 1991. "The Penn World Table (Mark 5): An expanded set of international comparisons, 1950–1988." *Quarterly Journal of Economics* 61(2):327–68.

World Bank. 1992. *World Development Report 1992: Development and the Environment.* Oxford University Press, Oxford.

World Resources Institute. 1991. *World Resources 1990–91: A Guide to the Global Environment.* Oxford University Press, New York.

———. 1992. *World Resources 1992–93: A Guide to the Global Environment.* Oxford University Press, New York.

Chapter 9: Air Pollution and Health

Atkinson, S.E., and T.D. Crocker. 1992. "Econometric health production functions: Relative bias from omitted variables and measurement error." *Journal of Environmental Economics and Management* 22(1):12–24.

Chan, H.C. 1990. "The environment: pressures of high growth." Paper prepared for MIER (Malaysian Institute of Economic Research) 1990 National Outlook Conference, December 5–6, Kuala Lumpur.

Cheang, B.K., C.P. Leong, S.H. Ooi, and Abdul Malek bin Tusin. n.d. "Haze episode: October 1991." Unpublished report. Malaysian Meteorological Service, Petaling Jaya.

Cofala, J., T. Lis, and H. Balandynowicz. 1991. *Cost-Benefit Analysis of Regional Air Pollution Control: Case Study for Tarnobrzeg.* Polish Academy of Sciences, Warsaw.

DOE (Department of Environment). 1992. *Environmental Quality Report 1991.* Ministry of Science, Technology, and the Environment, Kuala Lumpur.

Dickie, M., and S. Gerking. 1991. "Willingness to pay for ozone control: Inferences from the demand for medical care." *Journal of Environmental Economics and Management* 21(1):1–16.

Dockery, D.W., and J. Schwartz. 1992. "Response to Waller and Swan." *American Journal of Epidemiology* 135(1):23–25.

Dockery, D.W., J. Schwartz, and J.D. Spengler. 1992. "Air pollution and daily mortality: Associations with particulates and acid aerosols." *Environmental Research* 59:362–73.

Dockery, D.W., F.E. Speizer, D.O. Stram, et al. 1989. "Effects of inhalable particles on respiratory health of children." *American Review of Respiratory Disease* 139:587–94.

Evans, J.S., T. Tosteson, and P.L. Kinney. 1984. "Cross-sectional mortality studies and air pollution risk assessment." *Environment International* 10:55–83.

Fisher, A., L.G. Chestnut, and D.M. Violette. 1989. "The value of reducing risks of death: A note on new evidence." *Journal of Policy Analysis and Management* 8(1):88–100.

Freeman, A.M., III. 1982a. *Air and Water Pollution Control: A Benefit-Cost Assessment.* John Wiley, New York.

———. 1982b. "The health implications of residual discharges: A methodological overview." In *Explorations in Natural Resource Economics*, ed. V.K. Smith and J.V. Krutilla. Johns Hopkins University Press, Baltimore.

———. 1985. "Methods for assessing the benefits of environmental programs." In *Handbook of Natural Resource and Energy Economics, vol. 1*, ed. A.V. Kneese and J.L. Sweeney. North-Holland, Amsterdam.

Gerking, S., and L.R. Stanley. 1986. "An economic analysis of air pollution and health: The case of St. Louis." *Review of Economics and Statistics* 68(1):115–21.

Hall, J.V., A.M. Winer, M.T. Kleinman, F.W. Lurmann, V. Brajer, and S.D. Colome. 1992. "Valuing the health benefits of clean air." *Science* 255 (February 14):812–17.

Hilts, P.J. 1993. "Industrial soot is found to be a sinister urban killer." *International Herald Tribune*. July 20.

Hufschmidt, M.M., D.E. James, A.D. Meister, B.T. Bower, and J.A. Dixon. 1983. *Environment, Natural Systems, and Development: An Economic Valuation Guide*. Johns Hopkins University Press, Baltimore.

Industrial Economics, Inc., and Sullivan Environmental Consulting, Inc. 1992. *Project Silesia: Comparative Risk Screening Analysis*. Report prepared for Technical Workgroup, Ostrava, Czechoslovakia, and U.S. Environmental Protection Agency (EPA). U.S. Environmental Protection Agency, Washington, D.C.

IPT (Institut Pengajian Tinggi). 1992. "Report for project on planning for environmentally sound development in Malaysia." Prepared for United Nations Environment Program, University of Malaya, Petaling Jaya.

JICA (Japan International Cooperation Agency). 1991. "Malaysia: Air quality management study for Kelang Valley region" (inception report). Department of Environment, Kuala Lumpur.

Kinney, P.L., and H. Ozkaynak. 1991. "Associations of daily mortality and air pollution in Los Angeles County." *Environmental Research* 54:99–120.

Krupnick, A.J. 1993. "Benefit transfers and valuation of environmental improvements." *Resources* 110:1–7.

Krupnick, A.J., W. Harrington, and B. Ostro. 1990. "Ambient ozone and acute health effects: Evidence from daily data." *Journal of Environmental Economics and Management* 18(1):1–18.

Krupnick, A.J., and P.R. Portney. 1991. "Controlling urban air pollution: A benefit-cost assessment." *Science* 252(April 26):522–28.

Labys, W.C. 1980. "Interactions between the resource commodity sector, the developing economy, and the environment: The case of Malaysia." *Report No. LCD/13*. United Nations Conference on Trade and Development, Geneva.

Lave, L.B. 1972. "Air pollution damage: Some difficulties in estimating the value of abatement." In *Environmental Quality Analysis: Theory and Method in the Social Sciences*, ed. A.V. Kneese and B.T. Bower. Johns Hopkins University Press, Baltimore.

Lave, L.B., and E.P. Seskin. 1979. "Epidemiology, causality, and public policy." *American Scientist* 67(2):178–86.

Lee, K.H. 1990. "Report of the reverse tracer study of workers." Report prepared under the UNDP/ILO Malaysian Human Resources Development Plan Project (*MAL/87/015*). Economic Planning Unit, Kuala Lumpur.

Lim, H.H., Z. Domala, and H.E. Khoo. 1983. "Lead concentrations in breast milk of Malaysian urban and rural mothers." *Archives of Environmental Health* 38(4).

Lim, H.H., C.N. Ong, Z. Domala, W.O. Phoon, and H.E. Khoo. 1985. "Blood lead levels in Malaysian urban and rural pregnant women." *The Society of Community Medicine* 99:23–29.

Mahathevan, R. 1985. "Air quality and health." Paper presented at Seminar Keadaan Kualiti Alam Sekeliling 1985, July 8–11, Asia-Pacific Development Centre, Kuala Lumpur.

Margulis, S. 1991. "Back of the envelope estimates of environmental damage costs in Mexico." *Internal Discussion Paper, Report No. IDP-0104*. Latin America and the Caribbean Region, World Bank, Washington, D.C.

Ministry of Health. n.d. "Health implications of haze: Preliminary report." Unpublished report prepared for National Main Committee on Haze. Kuala Lumpur.

Mitchell, R.C., and R.T. Carson. 1989. *Using Surveys to Value Public Goods: The Contingent Valuation Method*. Resources for the Future, Washington, D.C.

Noraini Shariff. 1993. "Lead pollution stunts children's growth." *New Straits Times*. August 16, p. 34.

Ong, A.S.H., A. Maheswaran, and A.N. Ma. 1987. "Malaysia." In *Environmental Management in Southeast Asia*, ed. L.S. Chia. Faculty of Science, National University of Singapore.

Ostro, B.D. 1983. "The effects of air pollution on work loss and morbidity." *Journal of Environmental Economics and Management* 10(4):371–82.

———. 1987. "Air pollution and morbidity revisited: A specification test." *Journal of Environmental Economics and Management* 14(1):87–98.

———. 1990. "Associations between morbidity and alternative measures of particulate matter." *Risk Analysis* 10(3):421–27.

———. 1992a. "Estimating the health and economic effects of particulate matter in Jakarta: A preliminary assessment." Paper presented at the Fourth Annual Meeting of the International Society for Environmental Epidemiology, August 26–29, Cuernavaca, Mexico.

———. 1992b. "Generic estimates of the economic effects of criteria air pollutants: A review and synthesis." Paper prepared for the World Bank, Washington, D.C.

Ostro, B.D., and S. Rothschild. 1989. "Air pollution and acute respiratory morbidity: An observational study of multiple pollutants." *Environmental Research* 50(2):238–47.

Ozkaynak, H., and G.D. Thurston. 1987. "Associations between 1980 U.S. mortality rates and alternative measures of airborne particle concentration." *Risk Analysis* 7(4):449–61.

Perkhidmatan Kajicuaca Malaysia. n.d. *Ringkasan Tahunan Pemerhatan Pencemaran Udara 1989.* Perkhidmatan Kajicuaca Malaysia, Kuala Lumpur.

Pope, C.A. III, D.W. Dockery, J.D. Spengler, and M.E. Razienne. 1991. "Respiratory health and PM$_{10}$ pollution: A daily time-series analysis." *American Review of Respiratory Disease* 144(3):668–74.

Portney, P.R., and J. Mullahy. 1986. "Urban air quality and acute respiratory illness." *Journal of Urban Economics* 20:21–38.

Richardson, R., and L.Y. Soon. "Wage trends and structures in Malaysia." Report prepared under the UNDP/ILO Malaysian Human Resources Development Plan Project (*MAL/87/015*). Economic Planning Unit, Kuala Lumpur.

Schelling, T.C. 1968. "The life you save may be your own." In *Problems in Public Expenditure Analysis,* ed. S.B. Chase, Jr. Brookings Institution, Washington, D.C.

Schwartz, J. 1991. "Particulate air pollution and daily mortality in Detroit." *Environmental Research* 56(2):204–13.

Schwartz, J., and D.W. Dockery. 1992a. "Increased mortality in Philadelphia associated with daily air pollution." *American Review of Respiratory Disease* 145(3):600–604.

———. 1992b. "Particulate air pollution and daily mortality in Steubenville, Ohio." *American American Journal of Epidemiology* 135(1):12–19.

Schwartz, J., and A. Marcus. 1990. "Mortality and air pollution in London: A time-series analysis." *American Journal of Epidemiology* 131:185–94.

Sham Sani. n.d. "Atmospheric pollution in Malaysia." Mimeo. Institute of Strategic and International Studies (ISIS) Malaysia, Kuala Lumpur.

———. 1992. *Environment and Development in Malaysia.* Institute of Strategic and International Studies (ISIS) Malaysia, Kuala Lumpur.

Sham Sani, B.K. Cheang, C.P. Leong, and S.F. Lim. 1991. "The August 1990 haze in Malaysia with special reference to the Klang Valley region." *Technical Note No. 49.* Malaysian Meteorological Service, Kuala Lumpur.

Syed Muhammad Hooi dan Binnie. 1989. *Development of Criteria and Standards for Air Quality, 3 vols.* Department of Environment, Kuala Lumpur.

Tan M.L. 1982. "Air pollution in Malaysia: Problems, perspectives, and control." In *Development and the Environmental Crisis: A Malaysian Case Study.* Consumer Association of Penang, Malaysia.

———. 1992. Personal communication.

Tietenberg, T.H. 1988. *Environmental and Natural Resource Economics,* 2d ed. Scott, Foresman and Company, Glenview, Ill.

Tsuruoka, D. 1990. "Merchants of gloom." *Far Eastern Economic Review* (September 20):12–13.

Vatikiotis, M. 1991. "Official fog: Countrywide haze sparks alarm and health fears." *Far Eastern Economic Review* (November 14):24.

Veitch, M.D. 1986. *National Parameters for Project Appraisal in Malaysia, vol. 3: Summary of Estimation Procedures*. Regional Economics Section, Economic Planning Unit, Kuala Lumpur.

Viscusi, W.K. 1992. *Fatal Tradeoffs: Public and Private Responsibilities for Risk*. Oxford University Press, New York.

———. 1993. "The value of risks to life and health." *Journal of Economic Literature* 31(4):1912–46.

Waller, R.E., and A.V. Swan. 1992. "Particulate air pollution and daily mortality." *American Journal of Epidemiology* 135(1):20–22.

Walter, I. 1975. *International Economics of Pollution*. MacMillan, London.

World Bank. 1975. "Malaysia environment and development: Report to the Government of Malaysia." Mimeo. Economic Planning Unit, Kuala Lumpur.

———. 1992. *World Development Report 1992: Development and the Environment*. Oxford University Press, Oxford.

———. 1993. "Malaysia: Managing costs of urban pollution." *Report No. 11764-MA*. World Bank, Washington, D.C.

World Resources Institute. 1992. *World Resources 1992–93: A Guide to the Global Environment*. Oxford University Press, New York.

Yong, W. 1992. *The Occurrence of Haze in the Klang Valley: A Case Study of the October 1991 Haze Episode*. M.Sc. thesis, Dept. of Environmental Science, Universiti Pertanian Malaysia, Serdang.

Chapter 10: Water Pollution Control

Aiken, R.S., C.H. Leigh, T.R. Leinbach, and M.R. Moss. 1982. *Development and Environment in Peninsular Malaysia*. McGraw-Hill International Book Company, Singapore.

Chooi, C.F. 1984. "Ponding system for palm oil mill effluent treatment." In *Proceedings of the Workshop on Review of Palm Oil Mill Effluent Technology vis-à-vis Department of Environment Standard (PORIM Workshop Proceedings No. 9)*. Palm Oil Research Institute of Malaysia, Bandar Baru Bangi, Malaysia.

Cropper, M.L., and W.E. Oates. 1992. "Environmental economics: A survey." *Journal of Economic Literature* 30(2):675–740.

DOE (Department of Environment, Malaysia). 1985. *Environmental Quality Report 1981–84*. Kuala Lumpur.

———. 1992. *Environmental Quality Report 1991*. Kuala Lumpur.

Hahn, R.W. 1989. "Economic prescriptions for environmental problems: How the patient followed the doctor's orders." *Journal of Economic Perspectives* 3(2):95–114.

Hausman, J.A. 1978. "Specification tests in econometrics." *Econometrica* 46:1251–72.

Ho, Y.C. 1987. "Control and management of pollution of inland waters in Malaysia." *Arch. Hydrobiol. Beih.* 28:547–56.

Institute for Advanced Studies. 1992. "Market based instruments and other financial arrangements for environmentally sound development." Summary report for second session of National Workshop on Environmentally Sound Development, October 22–23, Institute for Advanced Studies, University of Malaya, Kuala Lumpur.

IMF (International Monetary Fund). 1991. *International Financial Statistics 1990.* IMF, Washington, D.C.

Jorgensen, E.V., Inc. 1977. "Palm oil sludge—a profitable investment" Mimeo. Department of Environment, Malaysia, Kuala Lumpur.

Jorgensen, H.K. 1982. "The U.P. decanter-drier system for reduction of palm oil effluent." In *Proceedings of Regional Workshop on Palm Oil Mill Technology and Effluent Treatment (PORIM Workshop Proceedings No. 4).* Palm Oil Research Institute of Malaysia, Bandar Baru Bangi, Malaysia.

Judge, G.G., W.E. Griffiths, R.C. Hill, H. Lutkepohl, and T.C. Lee. 1985. *The Theory and Practice of Econometrics,* 2d ed. John Wiley & Sons, New York.

Khalid Abdul Rahim. 1991. "Internalization of externalities: Who bears the cost of pollution control?" *The Environmentalist* 11(1):19–25.

Khalid Abdul Rahim, and J.B. Braden. 1993. "Welfare effects of environmental regulation in an open economy: The case of Malaysian palm oil." *Journal of Agricultural Economics* 44(1):25–37.

Khalid Abdul Rahim, and Wan Mustafa Wan Ali. 1992. "External benefits of environmental regulation." *The Environmentalist* 12(4):277–85.

Khera, H.S. 1976. *The Oil Palm Industry of Malaysia.* Penerbit Universiti Malaya, Kuala Lumpur.

Kneese, A.V., and B.T. Bower. 1968. *Managing Water Quality: Economics, Technology, Institutions.* Johns Hopkins University Press, Baltimore.

Kneese, A.V., and C.L. Schultze. 1975. *Pollution, Prices, and Public Policy.* The Brookings Institution, Washington, D.C.

Lim, K.H. 1984. "Problems of implementation by MOPGC members." In *PORIM Workshop Proceedings No. 9.*

Lim, H.K., S.K. Quah, D. Gillies, and B.J. Wood. 1984. "Palm oil effluent treatment and utilization in Sime Darby plantations—the current position." In *PORIM Workshop Proceedings No. 9*

Ma, A.N. 1992. Personal communication. November 27.

Ma, A.N., Yusof Basiron, and Mohd. Nasir Amiruddin. 1980. "The interdependence of economic development and environmental quality in South East Asia: Malaysia as a case study." Unpublished manuscript. Palm Oil Research Institute of Malaysia, Bandar Baru Bangi, Malaysia.

Ma, A.N., C.S. Chow, C.K. John, Ahmad Ibrahim, and Z. Isa. 1982. "Palm oil mill effluent treatment—a survey." In *PORIM Workshop Proceedings No. 4.*

Mahathir bin Mohamad. 1991. "Malaysia: The way forward (Vision 2020)." National Printing Department, Kuala Lumpur.

Maheswaran, A. 1984. "Legislative measures in the control of palm oil mill effluent discharge." Mimeo.

Maheswaran, A., and G. Singam. 1977. "Pollution control in the palm oil industry—promulgation of regulations." *Planter* 53:470–76.

Maheswaran, A., Abu Bakar Jaafar, and G. Singh. 1980. "Water quality management in Malaysia." Paper presented at *The Interdependence of Economic Development and Environmental Quality in South-East Asia Symposium*, August 5–7, Miami University, Oxford, Ohio. Department of Environment, Malaysia, Kuala Lumpur.

Ministry of Agriculture. Various years. *Statistical Handbook, Agriculture: Malaysia.* Ministry of Agriculture, Kuala Lumpur.

O'Neil, W. 1980. *Pollution Permits and Markets for Water Quality.* Ph.D. dissertation. University of Wisconsin, Madison, Wisc.

———. 1983. "The regulation of water pollution permit trading under conditions of varying streamflow and temperature." In *Buying a Better Environment: Cost-Effective Regulation Through Permit Trading*, ed. E. Joeres and M. David. University of Wisconsin Press, Madison, Wisc.

Ong, A.S.H., A. Maheswaran, and A.N. Ma. 1987. "Malaysia." In *Environmental Management in Southeast Asia*, ed. L.S. Chia. National University of Singapore Press, Singapore.

PORIM (Palm Oil Research Institute of Malaysia). 1986. "Environmental quality and standard." Paper prepared for 8th Palm Oil Mill Engineer/Executives Training Course, April 25. Palm Oil Research Institute of Malaysia, Bandar Baru Bangi, Malaysia.

Quah, S.K., K.H. Lim, D. Gillies, B.J. Wood, and J. Kanagaratnam. 1982. "Sime Darby POME treatment and land application systems." In *PORIM Workshop Proceedings No. 4.*

Russell, C.S. 1979. "What can we get from effluent charges?" *Policy Analysis* 5(2):155–80.

Shamsudin Hj. Abd. Latif, and Jimat Bolhassan. 1981. "Report on study of the impact of the effluent discharge from Trengganu Development Management Berhad (TDMB) palm oil mill on the water quality of Sg. Ransan, Sg. Tebak, and Sg. Kemaman." *WPC-031/B-38/SR-05/81*. Department of Environment, Malaysia, Kuala Lumpur.

Tam, T.K., H.K. Yeow, and Y.C. Poon. 1982. "Land application of palm oil mill effluent (POME)—H&C experience." In *PORIM Workshop Proceedings No. 4.*

Thillaimuthu, J. 1978. "The environment and the palm oil industry: A new solution—the incineration of sludge." *Planter* 54:228–36.

Tietenberg, T.H. 1988. *Environmental and Natural Resource Economics*, 2d ed. Scott, Foresman and Company, Glenview, Ill.

————. 1990. "Economic instruments for environmental regulation." *Oxford Review of Economic Policy* 6(1):17–33.

Weitzman, M.L. 1974. "Prices vs. quantities." *Review of Economic Studies* 41(4):477–91.

Wood, B.J. 1977. "A review of current methods for dealing with palm oil effluents." *Planter* 53:477–95.

Yusof Basiron and A.N. Ma. 1992. "Current status of environmental management and regulations in the palm oil industry in Malaysia." Unpublished manuscript. Palm Oil Research Institute of Malaysia, Bandar Baru Bangi, Malaysia.

CHAPTER 11: CONCLUSIONS

Mahathir bin Mohamad. 1991. *The Second Outline Perspective Plan (OPP2), 1991–2000.* Speech in Dewan Rakyat, June 17. Government Printing Office, Kuala Lumpur.

Contributors

Principal Authors

Dr. Jeffrey R. Vincent is a Fellow at the Harvard Institute for International Development. He is a resource economist with ongoing research interests related to tropical forestry policy issues, national income accounts and the environment, and environmental management in newly industrializing and transition economies. He was a resident researcher at the Institute of Strategic and International Studies (ISIS) Malaysia during 1992–1993, when the core of the research for this book was conducted.

Dr. Rozali Mohamed Ali is currently Executive Director of Commerce Asset-Holding Berhad, Malaysia. He was formerly Assistant Director-General at ISIS Malaysia, heading the Bureau of Science, Technology, Energy, Natural Resources, and Environment and the Center for Environmental Studies. He has particular interest and experience in energy issues and international environmental issues.

Other Contributors

Mr. Chang Yii Tan is Director of PE Research, a Malaysian consulting firm. His area of expertise is environmental assessment and economic evaluation of development projects. He is coauthor of Chapter 9, "Air Pollution and Health."

Dr. Jahara Yahaya is a Professor in the Faculty of Economics and Administration at the University of Malaya. Her area of expertise is fishery economics and management. She is coauthor of Chapter 6, "Marine Fisheries."

Dr. Khalid Abdul Rahim is an Associate Professor in the Faculty of Economics and Management at Universiti Pertanian Malaysia. His area of expertise is environmental economics. He is coauthor of Chapter 10, "Water Pollution Control."

Dr. Lim Teck Ghee is Regional Advisor in Poverty Alleviation at the United Nations Economic and Social Commission for Asia and the Pacific (ESCAP). His areas of expertise include the political economy of rural development. He is coauthor of Chapter 5, "Agricultural Land."

Dr. Anke Sofia Meyer is an economist with the World Bank. Her area of expertise is energy economics and policy. She is coauthor of Chapter 3, "Petroleum."

Dr. Mohd. Shahwahid Haji Othman is an Associate Professor in the Faculty of Economics and Management at Universiti Pertanian Malaysia. His area of expertise is forest economics and policy. He is coauthor of Chapter 4, "Forests."

Dr. G. Sivalingam is a Professor in the Faculty of Economics and Administration at the University of Malaya. His areas of expertise are corporate finance and public policy. He is coauthor of Chapter 7, "Freshwater."

Index

The terms in this index are alphabetized on a letter-by-letter basis. Page references followed by an italic *f* or *t* (e.g. 27*t)* indicate a figure or table respectively. Page references followed by *n* and a number indicate an endnote (e.g. 101*n1).*

A

Abang Helmi, 56
aboriginal groups *(Orang asli),* 6, 144
acid rain, 23
adat inheritance laws, 171
Adelman, M. A., 97–98
Africa, 107
Agenda 21, 26
agricultural labor
   demographic data, 160
   inheritance laws, 171
   opportunity costs, 153, 168–169
   outmigration of, 159–160
agricultural land
   history of, 5, 5*t,* 151–156
   illegal clearing and use, 176–177
   inheritance laws, 171
   soil depletion, 35–36, 52
   use surveys, 119, 152*t,* 160–161
agriculture. *See also specific state*
   air pollution from, 279 *(See also* air pollution)
   as a land-use priority, 25, 105–106
   economic concepts about, 111–113
   growth in, 1, 10, 156
   idle land *(See* idle land)
   introduction of plantation, 8
   mechanization, 172
   public sector development of, 13, 155, 164*t*
   share of gross domestic product, 16*f*

   state government role expanded, 155
   water pollution from, 17 *(See also* water pollution)
Aid to the Fishing Industry Scheme, 195
Aiken, R. S., 142
air pollution. *See also specific substance*
   abatement
      benefits of, 295–296
      enforcement of regulations, 307
      modeling optimal level, 296–297
   economic consequences, 53
   increases in, 17, 20, 22–23
   monitoring, 2, 291*n16*
   policy development, 303–308
   relationship to economic development
      cross-country studies, 269–273
      estimates compared to predictions, 275–277, 277*t,* 278–279
      predictions for Malaysia, 274, 285–286
   sources of, 21, 276*t*
"Ali-Baba" syndrome, 138–139
Allen, J. C., 112
amenity forests, defined, 118
ammoniacal nitrogen. *See* nitrogen, ammoniacal
Anderson, E. N., Jr., 191–192, 195, 199, 202–203
Anglo-Saxon Petroleum Company, 80
Antah Biwater Rural Water Supply project, 244
Aquitane Petroleum, 85
Arau dam, 262
Arief, S., 76, 80, 82, 100

Arrow, K., 268, 270
Article 76(1), 25
Asam Paya (oil) Field, 101*n1*
Asian Development Bank, 243, 245–247, 252, 256, 259–260
Australia, 89
automobile industry, 12

B

Bajau (ethnic group), 6
Bandyopadhyay, S., 112, 271
Bank Bumiputera, 71*n29*
Bank Pertanian Malaysia, 155, 158, 170, 196
Barnes, D. F., 112
Barrows, 89, 100
Bartelmus, P., 34
Beletak dam, 254
Bidayuh (ethnic group), 6
Bilsborrow, R. E., 113
Bina Runding Sdn. Bhd., 252, 258–260
Binkley, C. S., 128
biochemical oxygen demand (BOD)
    described, 17, 349*n4*
    in the Sungai Kelang, 19, 21*t*
    load from crude palm-oil mills, 321*f*
    relationship to economic development, 288*t*
    standards regulating
        cost comparisons modeled, 337–341
        effectiveness of, 334–336
        imposition of, 330–331, 331*t*, 332–333
        proposed interim national, 21*t*
    trends in Malaysian rivers, 281–286
bioeconomic model of fisheries management, 185–187, 227–230
biological diversity. forests and, 143–144, 150*n65*
biotechnology, 144
bird species, extinction, 143
"Black Smoke" Rules, 303–304, 307
Blitzer, C. R., 90, 97
boat buy-backs, 209
Boat Ownership Scheme, 201
BOD. *See* biochemical oxygen demand
Borneo, 3
Brazil, water tariffs, 239
Brookfield, H., 124, 142–143
Brown, S., 116, 144
Brunei, 51, 73, 89
bumiputera (indigenous population groups)
    as an ethnic group, 7
    favored under oil production-sharing
        contracts, 84

goals and achievements under the New
        Economic Policy, 11, 14
    land policy and, 155, 158–159
    population by region, 7*t*
    rural-urban drift (outmigration), 174–175
    timber industry licenses, 138–140
    under the *Second Malaysia Plan*, 74
Burrows, J., 158

C

capital consumption allowance. *See also* physical
        capital
    estimating national and regional, 68–69
carbon dioxide emissions, from deforestation and
        degradation, 144
carbon monoxide pollution
    health effects of, 23, 272–273
    increases in, 23
    official estimates in Malaysia, 275, 276*t*
    relationship to economic development
        cross-country studies, 269*t*, 272–273
        estimates compared to predictions, 277*t*
Central Borneo Company, 80
Chan, H. C., 315
Chee, K. L., 188, 190, 193–194, 197–198, 202–203, 220
chemical oxygen demand (COD)
    described, 18
    in the Sungai Kelang, 19, 21*t*
    proposed interim national standards, 21*t*
    relationship to economic development, 288*t*
    trends in Malaysian rivers, 281–284
China, 89, 263
Chinese (Malaysian)
    fishing industry activities, 182, 189, 193
    historic economic activity of, 10
    New Villages, 176, 179*n25*
    population data, 6, 7*t*
    start of immigration, 9
chlorofluorocarbons, 26
Chong, P.W., 137
Christians, 6
Chung, K. S., 65
Cicchetti, C. J., 145
cocoa cultivation, 151, 152*t*
coconut cultivation, 9, 152*t*
COD. *See* chemical oxygen demand
Cofala, J., 297
coffee cultivation, 9
colonial period, 8–10

Commission on Sustainable Development (UNCED), 26
communist countries, 271
Concurrent List (legislative powers), 24–25, 184
consumption
    maximum sustainable, 37
    natural resource rents and, 30–33
    strategy for sustaining, 50–51
Continental Oil, 81, 85
Continental Shelf Act (1966), 81
Conventions on Climate Change and Biodiversity, 26
CO pollution. *See* carbon monoxide pollution
Costa Rica, 35–38, 52
Courtenay, P. P., 159, 172–173
Cropper, M., 112
crude oil. *See under* petroleum industry
Crude Palm Oil Regulations, 320, 341, 343
Czechoslovakia, 326

D

dams, 248, 262
Dasgupta, P. S., 37, 39
deep-sea fishing, 209–210, 225
deficit, under the New Economic Policy, 13
deforestation
    by time period
        colonial period, 8–9
        during the 1980s, 121–122
        from 1970 to 1990, 43
    definition, 109
    documented by Forest Inventories I and II, 116–117, 119
    economic development and, 122–123, 123*f,* 124
    economic fundamentals of, 110, 110*f,* 112–113
    land development and, 106
    Malaysia compared to Asia, 119
    population changes and, 122, 148*n29*
    public policies assessed, 141–145
    regression model, 146
Democratic Action Party, 7
Department of Agriculture, 25, 158, 174
Department of Environment (DOE)
    air pollution
        contravention licenses, 307
        early efforts to control, 303–304
        emission estimates, 275, 276*t*
        monitoring stations and efforts, 275, 291*n16,* 304–305, 309*t*
        reports, 17, 20

standards, 19–21, 284, 305, 307–308
        authority and responsibility, 319, 330
    water pollution
        effectiveness of regulation, 333, 335–336
        monitoring stations, 281
        regulations developed, 330–333
Department of Fisheries
    authority and responsibility, 25, 183–184
    enforcement efforts strengthened, 207
    overfishing, 183, 201, 204
    subsidy program, 196, 199
Department of Mines, 25
Department of Statistics, 41, 44, 58, 69, 310
Devarajan, S., 38
developing countries
    cost/benefit analysis of reducing air pollution, 297
    deforestation and development, 112–113, 122
    resource rents and economic diversification, 31–32
    risk aversion of, 97
    water, 237, 239, 245
development
    colonial period, 8–10
    environmental quality and
        lessons from Malaysia, 360–364
        links in Malaysia, 359–360
    expenditure compared to resource-based revenue, 53, 54*f*
    stages and pollution intensity, 267–268 (*See also* pollution)
Dipterocarpaceae, 107
Drainage and Irrigation Department, 158
drainage and irrigation expenditures, 164*t*
Dulang (oil) Field, 88
Durio zibethinus, durian (tree), 144
dustfall measurements, 22

E

Earth Summit (1992, Rio de Janeiro), 26, 109
economic development. *See* development
Economic Planning Unit (EPU), 40, 52, 91, 143, 244, 263
economic sustainability
    achieved in Malaysia, 50–52
    gross domestic product flawed as a measure of, 38–40
    natural resource rents and
        linkages in Malaysia, 351–352
        studies of, 35–36
        theory, 30–35
    net national income and, 36–37

economic sustainability (*continued*)
  resource depletion and
    analytic method for assessing, 40
    estimating resource consumption allow-
      ances, 40–44
    regional analysis, 47–50
    resource rents compared to gross investment,
      44–45, 45*f,* 46
economy
  at the start of independence, 10
  colonial period, 8–10
  expansion and structural changes, 11
  peasant, 155–156
education, 51, 174–175
effluent charges. *See* pollution charge
Elaeis guineensis, oil palm, 328
electric utilities, 13
Elf Aquitane, 87, 89
Elliston, G. R., 202
El Serafy, S., 41
Emergency (Essential Powers) Ordinance, 82–83
Emerson, C., 95, 99–100
emissions trading. *See* pollution permits, tradeable
Emissions Trading Program, 327
employment, 10, 51, 175, 182, 193
energy consumption, 16–17
Energy Information Administration, 76
environmental impact assessment, mandated, 26
environmental Kuznets curve, defined, 268
environmental management, 8, 23–25
environmental organizations, scrutiny by, 26
environmental quality. *See also* pollution
  adjusting gross domestic product for, 38–39,
    52–53
  development and
    lessons from Malaysia, 360–364
    links in Malaysia, 359–360
  government concern with, 23
  legislative protection of, 25
  monitoring, start of, 2
Environmental Quality Act (1974)
  regulations promulgated under, 348*n1*
  scope and intention, 25–26, 329–330
Environmental Quality (Clean Air) Regulations
  (1978), 281, 303, 307
Environmental Quality (Licensing) Regulations
  (1977), 303
Environmental Quality (Prescribed Premises)
  (Crude Palm Oil) Regulations (1977), 303,
    330
Environmental Quality Report (1980), 17
Environmental Quality Report (1983), 21
Environmental Quality Report (1984), 20

Environmental Quality Report (1992), 23
Environmental Quality Report (1993), 23
EPU (Economic Planning Unit), 40, 52, 91, 143,
  244, 263
Erb West (oil) Field, 81
erosion and soil depletion, 35–36, 52, 143
Esso, 81–82, 85, 87–88, 95
ethnic groups
  by region, 7*t*
  history of, 6
  politics and economics of, 7, 10
  tensions among, 11, 82, 177
Europe, deforestation in, 112
Evans, J. S., 299
Exclusive Economic Zone (EEZ) Act, 207–208
export processing zones, development of, 11
exports
  at the start of independence, 10
  compared to other countries, 12*t*
  diversification, 11
  federal-state allocation of revenue, 24
  fishing, earnings from, 192–193, 230*n7*
  growth and changes in, 1, 3*f,* 17*f*
  manufacturing, 74
  oil, 17*f,* 74–75
  palm oil, 1, 17*f,* 52, 329
  price variability in, 95, 96*t*
  timber and logs
    demand for, 106–107, 133–134
    importance of, 1, 17*f*
    pricing and export policy, 135
    restrictions, 133–134
extinction, deforestation and, 143

F

Fadzim Othman, 160
FAO. *See* U.N. Food and Agriculture Organization
Farmer's Organization Authority, 155, 163,
  169–170
fecal coliform count, 269*t,* 271
Federal Agricultural Marketing Authority, 158
Federal Land Consolidation and Rehabilitation
  Authority (FELCRA), 155, 163–167
Federal Land Development Authority (FELDA)
  agricultural expansion under, 106, 329
  establishment, 13
  expanded and given broader mandates, 155
  water projects, 246, 257–258
Federal List (legislative powers), 24
Federated Malay States Waters Enactment of
  1920, 25

Federation of Malaysia
  before independence, 8–10
  departments and ministries *(See specific department, specific ministry)*
  dependence on oil, 97
  development expenditure compared to resource-based revenue, 53–54, 54*f*
  economic base at independence, 1
  economic plans *(See specific plan)*
  ethnic groups in, 6, 7*t*
  formation, 1, 7
  geography, 3, 4*f*, 5
  government
    allocation of power between federal and state, 24–25
    description and organization of, 7–8
    environmental leadership, 23–24
    spending increase, 13
  population, 6, 6*t*, 13*t*
FELCRA (Federal Land Consolidation and Rehabilitation Authority), 155, 163–167
FELDA. *See* Federal Land Development Authority
Fifth Malaysia Plan 1986–1990
  oil exploration, 102*n26*
  overfishing, 203, 205, 209
  privatization of public utilities, 263
  public-sector land development, 14*f*, 175
  sewerage system, 284
  water priorities and expansion, 237, 245, 248, 263
fine particulates (PM), monitoring started, 22
First Malaysia Plan 1966–1970
  fishing goals, 190
  minerals, 73
  public-sector land development, 14*f*
  water spending, 245–246, 250, 257
Fisher, A., 303
Fisher, A. C., 145
Fisheries Act, 25, 190, 207, 223
Fisheries Industry Development Authority (LKIM), 196, 199–201, 205, 209
Fisheries Licensing Policy, 201, 205, 223
Fisheries Research Institute, 202
Fishermen Resettlement Program, 209
Fishermen's Subsidy Scheme, 195–196, 199, 208
fishing. *See also specific state*
  allocation of tax revenue from, 24
  authority and management over, 183–184
  bioeconomic model of fisheries management, 185–187, 227–230
  commercial stocks, 184–185

conflicts, 194–195
depletion
  evidence of, 201–204, 223
  examples and issues, 36, 52, 189
  policy responses to, 204–210
economics of
  analysis, 210–223
  concepts, 185–189
  implications for the future, 223–226
government assistance to, 13, 195–201, 223
gross domestic product, 1, 16*f*, 52
history and overview, 181–185
licensed boats and fishermen, 184, 184*t*, 192–193, 197, 198*f*, 206, 213
mechanization and trawling, 189–195
production, 15, 15*f*, 184*t*, 190, 194, 201
traditional, described, 182
flood protection, 164*t*
food supply, fishing and, 182, 192
Ford Foundation report (1963), 13
foreign investment, 9, 11–12
Forest Administration Report (1958), 105
Forest Industries Development project, 125
Forest Inventories, 116–117, 117*t*, 119, 122
Forest Research Institute, 107
Forestry Department (federal)
  authority and responsibility, 25
  effort to restrain logging, 136
  effort to stabilize timberland base, 106, 124–126
  land-use policy struggles, 105, 113–116, 119–120, 165, 167
  promotion of domestic processing, 133–134, 137–139
  recreational use of forests, 142–145
  staffing, 107
Forestry Research Institute Malaysia, 175
forests. *See also* deforestation; timber and logging; *specific state*
  as a source of government revenue, 24
  cleared during the colonial period, 8–9
  development history, 105–109
  economic concepts about, 109–113
  harvest recommendations, 106
  land use for over time, 5, 5*t*, 6
  Malaysia's described, 107
  minor products, 142, 144
  national policy
    complications in Malaysia, 108
    development and promulgation of, 25, 117–121
    Interim Forest Policy, 113–114

forests (*continued*)
  land-use survey and inventory, 115–116, 116*t*, 119
  use classification scheme, 114–115, 132
  nontimber value of, 113, 124, 142–145
  silviculture research, 107, 147*n*10, 147*n*12
  state authority over, 106
Fourth Malaysia Plan 1981–1985
  petroleum industry, 86, 98, 100
  public-sector land development, 14*f*, 156
  water system and spending, 245, 247–248
  water tariffs and financing, 250
Fox River (Wis.) Transferable Discharge Permit
    program, 327, 339
France, 326
Freeman, A. M., 299
freshwater. *See* water
Fujimoto, A., 160, 167

G

gambier, cultivation, 154
Gemencheh area, 9
Gemencheh dam, 262
Geores, M. E., 113
Georgetown. *See* Pulau Pinang
Germany, 326
Gibbons, D. S., 190, 192–193, 208
global warming, 26
Goh, C. T., 193–194, 201, 208
Goh, K. C., 239–240, 263
Gordon, H. S., 185
Griffiths, C., 112–113
gross domestic product (GDP)
  adjustment theories assessed, 38–39
  as a measure of economic welfare and
      sustainability, 30
  compared to net domestic product, 36–37, 46,
      47*f*, 50
  exports as a percentage of, 10, 73
  federal spending as a percentage of, 13
  fishing, 182
  growth in, 2*f*, 11
  manufacturing, 11, 236
  per capita, 46, 47*f*, 236
  pollution (*See* pollution, relationship to
      economic development)
  primary sectors, 1, 2*f*, 16*f*, 18*f*
gross fixed capital formation. *See also* physical
    capital
  regional analysis of, 47–50
  trends in Malaysia, 44, 45*f*-46*f*

gross fixed investment. *See* gross fixed capital
    formation
gross investment. *See* gross fixed capital formation
Grossman, G. M., 267–271
groundwater sources and recharge, 233, 234*t*, 256
Gulf War, 35
Gulland, J. A., 205
Gunung Kinabalu, 5–6
Guyot, D., 167

H

Hageman, A., 41
Hahn, R. W., 327
Hall, J. V., 296–297, 299, 308, 313–314
*Handbook on Integrated Environmental and
    Economic Accounting* (United Nations), 34
Hart, J. F., 174
Hartman, R., 145
Hartwick, John, 30, 32, 37, 41
Hartwick's Rule
  applying, 33–36, 45
  explained, 30–33
  for a nonrenewable resource, 31*f*
Harun Ismail, 139–140
Hati, water tariffs, 239
hazardous waste regulation, 26
Heal, G. M., 37
health
  air pollution, risks from, 21, 23, 299
  air pollution abatement, benefits of, 295–297
  environmental epidemiology study, 305–306
heavy industry, government investment in, 11–12
heavy metals, airborne, 23
Hettige, H., 267
"high-grading"
  defined, 80
  induced by oil production-sharing contracts,
      92–94
Hinduism, 6
Hines, J. R., 34
Hong Kong, 1, 12*t*
Hose, Charles, 80
Hotelling rent
  converting total resource rents to, 58–59
  defined, 31
  economic sustainability and, 32
  forestry, 61–63
  oil, 60*f*
  predicting, 41
Hotelling's Rule, 41
human capital

changes in Malaysia, 51
difficulty of measuring, 33
economic theory explained, 301–302
Hartwick's Rule and, 32
Hungary, 326
Hussein Onn, 194
Hyde, W. F., 128
hydrocarbon pollution, 275, 276*t*

I

Ibam timber complex, 139–140
Iban (ethnic group), 6
idle land
benefits of, 175
estimated amount, 156–157, 160–163, 163*t*, 173
fragmentation, 171–172, 176
issues summarized, 152–154, 173
Malaysia compared to other countries, 173–174
origin and definition of term, 152, 161–162
padi land rehabilitation, 158, 167–170
perception of, as a problem, 154–160
policy response, overview, 163–164
rehabilitation expenditures, 164*t*
socioeconomic and institutional problems,
170–173, 176
tree-crop land rehabilitation, 164–167
illegal logging, 130
income
correlation with demand for environmental
quality, 268
per capita, 46, 47*f*, 124
rural/urban disparity, 10
Income Tax Ordinance (1947), 81
India, 239
Indians, 6, 7*t*, 10, 176
Indonesia
export comparisons, 11, 12*t*
fish consumption, 182
impact of immigration from, 47
natural resource depletion study, 35, 52
net domestic product estimate, 37
oil, 83, 85, 89
industrialization, 12–13, 174
Industrial Master Plan, 140
Industrial Surveys (Malaysia Department of
Statistics), 41, 58
inflation, 1970–1990, 265*n12*
inframarginal rent, defined, 31
inheritance laws, 171
Integrated Agricultural Development Projects,
164*t*

integrated timber complexes (ITCs), 133,
137–141
Interim Forest Policy, 113–114, 124, 142
International Financial Statistics (IMF 1992), 68
investment. *See also* gross fixed capital formation;
net investment in reproducible capital
foreign, 9, 11–12
heavy industry, 11–12
natural resource rents and, 30–33
overseas, 51
Ipoh, 9, 309*t*, 310
irrigation and drainage
colonial period, 9
government support for, 13, 235
irrigation volume and forecast, 236
jurisdiction over water used for, 264*n9*
Islam, 6, 171
island biogeography theory, 143, 150*n65*
Ismail Ali, 139
Ismail bin Johari, 140
Ismail Muhd. Salleh, 56
Italy, 326

J

Jabatan Kerja Raya (JKR) (Public Works
Department), 244, 249, 252, 257–260
*Jadual Hayat Ringkas Semenanjung Malaysia
(Abridged Life Tables Peninsular Malaysia),
1981–1989* (Dept. of Statistics), 310
Jahara Yahaya, 195, 197, 204, 207
Japan International Cooperation Agency (JICA),
233–234, 236, 248, 251–252, 255–258, 260,
262–263, 307–308
Jengka timber complex, 139–140
jobs. *See* employment
Johor
land use, 9, 163*t*
railroad extended to, 9
royal family's role, 7
state development schemes, 167
water, jurisdiction, 244
Johor Bahru, 13, 309*t*, 310
Jomo, K. S., 181, 210, 225

K

Kadazan (ethnic group), 6
Kajian Ekonomi Malaysia, 181
Katzman, M. T., 239
Kayan (ethnic group), 6

Kedah
    farm mechanization, 172
    influence of geography on development, 10
    irrigation, 236
    padi land use, 163*t*
    railroad extended to, 9
    royal family's role, 7
    trawling in, 191, 193–194
    water, 244, 247, 250, 258, 262, 264
Kelang. *See* Klang
Kelantan
    idle land in, 162
    influence of geography on development, 10
    padi land use, 163*t*
    royal family's role, 7
    timber fees, 127
    water, 244, 247, 250
Kelantan State Land Development Authority
        (KSLDA), 167
Kenya, 239
Kenyan (ethnic group), 6
Kerian (district in Perak), 9
Khalil bin Datu Haji Jamalul, 56
Khoo, K. H., 205–206
Kinta Valley, 29
Kiribati, 29
Klang, 12
Klang General Hospital, 306
Klang River (Sungai Kelang), 19–20, 21*t*
Klang Valley
    air pollution, 22, 305–309
    industrialization, 12
    population, 310
    total suspended particulates, 22*f*, 309*t*
Krueger, A. B., 267–271
Krupnick, A. J., 295, 297, 313–314
Krutilla, J. V., 144–145
Kuala Lumpur
    air pollution, 22*f*, 23, 315
    start of urbanization, 9
    water, jurisdiction, 244
    mentioned, 7
Kuching Water Board, 251, 262–263
Kumar, R., 126, 140
Kuwait, 35, 51, 86
Kuznets, Simon, 268

L

Labuan Exploration Company, 80
Labuan (Federal Territory), 7, 244, 263
Landefeld, J. S., 34

land rent
    defined, 110
    factors influencing, 111–112
land use. *See also specific use*
    as a source of water pollution, 18
    by region over time, 5*t*
    classification scheme, 114–115
    colonial period, 8–10
    government authority over, 8
    priorities set by legislation, 25
    private ownership, 9
    public-sector, 13, 14*f*
Land Use Capability Classification Act (1966), 25
lead, 23, 315
Lee, H. L., 119
Lee, K. H., 311
Leigh, C. H., 142
Lembaga Kemajuan Ikan Malaysia (LKIM)
        (Fisheries Industry Development Authority),
        196, 199–201, 205, 209
Levy, Walter, 81
Lian, K. K., 135
Lim, H. H., 315
liquefied natural gas (LNG), 15, 15*f*
living standard, investment strategy for
        developing countries, 31–32
LKIM (Lembaga Kemajuan Ikan Malaysia)
        (Fisheries Industry Development Authority),
        196, 199–201, 205, 209
logging. *See* timber and logging
Los Angeles, 295, 297, 313–314

M

Mahathevan, R., 305–306, 308
Mahathir Mohamad, 8, 14, 274
Main Range, 10, 107
MAJUIKAN (Lembaga Kemajuan Ikan Malaysia)
        (Fisheries Industry Development Authority),
        196, 199–201, 205, 209
Malacca. *See* Melaka
Malayan Forester, 142
Malayan Uniform System (MUS)
    assumptions questioned, 131–132
    explained, 105
    limitations of, 107
    modified, 126
Malay Peninsula. *See* Peninsular Malaysia
Malay Reservation Enactment, 172
Malays (ethnic group), 6, 10
Malaysia. *See* Federation of Malaysia

Malaysian Agricultural Research and Development Institute, 158
Malaysian Business Council, 14, 274
Malaysian Chinese Association, 7
Malaysian Economic Association, 181
Malaysian Indian Congress, 7
Malaysian Industry Development Authority (MIDA), 140
Malaysian Meteorological Service (MMS), 21, 275, 291n16, 304–307, 309t
Malaysia Plans. *See specific plan name*
Mäler, K. G., 32, 37, 39
Mali, 38
manufacturing
    air pollution and, 303–304
    export earnings surpass oil, 74
    foreign investment in, 12
    growth, 11, 236
    water pollution and, 18
Margulis, S., 313–314
marine fisheries. *See* fishing
Maritime Fisheries Regulations, 191, 201
Medium and Long Term Industrial Master Plan for the Wood-Based Industry, 140
Meerman, J., 247, 256
Melaka
    agricultural land ownership in New Villages, 176
    colonial period, 8
    household income from padi schemes, 168
    padi land use, 163t
    water
        interstate transfers, 262
        jurisdiction, 244
        losses, 258
        tariffs and financing, 250, 262–263
Melanau (ethnic group), 6
meranti (trees), 127–128, 132–134
mersawa (trees), 133
MEW (measure of economic welfare), defined, 39
Mexico, 36, 39, 269–270
Mexico City, 313–314
Meyer, A. S., 90
Mid-Term Review of the Fourth Malaysia Plan 1981–85, 247, 256, 258
Mid-Term Review of the Second Malaysia Plan 1971–75, 74
Mid-Term Review of the Third Malaysia Plan 1976–1980, 86
mineral resource consumption allowance
    by region, 59–61
    calculating, 58–61
    in Malaysia, 40–43, 43f, 44

mining and quarrying
    as a land-use priority, 25
    gross domestic product percentage, 16f
    growth in, 1
Mining Enactment of 1929, 25
Ministry of Agriculture
    adopts activist role in development, 155, 157
    idle-land, definition and survey of, 161–162
    rehabilitation of idle padi land, 158, 164, 167–170
    responsibility and authority, 25
Ministry of Finance, 244
Ministry of Health, 244–245, 305–306, 308
Ministry of Land and Cooperative Development, 244–245
Ministry of Land and Regional Development, 155, 158
Ministry of Primary Industries, 25
Ministry of Rural Development, 155, 158, 244
Ministry of Science, Technology, and Environment, 25
Ministry of Works, 244, 262
Miri (oil) Field, 73, 80, 101n1
MMS (Malaysian Meteorological Service), 21, 275, 291n16, 304–307, 309t
Mobil, 81
Mohd. Shaari, 194, 202
Mohd. Shahwahid, 132, 137, 144
morbidity, 296, 306
mortality rates, 310
Motor Vehicle (Control of Smoke and Gas Emissions) Rules (1977), 281, 303
motor vehicles, number of, 307
Muda Agricultural Development Authority, 160, 236
Munro, G. R., 188, 190, 193–194, 197–198, 202–203, 220
Murut (ethnic group), 6
MUS. *See* Malayan Uniform System
Muslims, 6
Myers, N., 109

N

National Agricultural Policy, 157–158, 175–176
National Conservation Strategy, 143–144
National Development Policy (1991–2000), 14
National Forest Policy, 25, 118–119, 121, 124, 134, 139, 142
National Forestry Act, 25, 120–121, 127, 130
National Forestry Council, 117–118, 120, 126, 129–130, 140

National Front *(Barisan Nasional)*, 7
National Land Code, 155, 162
National Land Council, 118
National Oil Depletion Policy, 86
National Padi and Rice Authority, 155, 171
National Trust Fund, established, 71*n29*
National Water Council, 262
Nation Water Resources Study, 248
natural gas, 61, 103*n43*
natural gas royalties, 24
natural resource accounting, 33–35
natural resource rents
    defined, 27, 30–31
    economic sustainability and
        gross domestic product, 38–40
        linkages in Malaysia, 351–352
        net national income, 36–37
        studies of, 35–36
        theory, 30–35
    federal and state allocation and use, 53–54, 54*f*,
      55
    public and private investments and, 53
    trends in Malaysia, 44, 45*f*
natural resources. *See also specific type*
    authority over and fees, 8, 24–25
    colonial period, 8–10
    management lessons from Malaysia, 352–359
    production, 1, 15–16
    value of changes in (*See* resource consumption
      allowance)
Negeri Sembilan
    household income from padi schemes, 168
    land use during the colonial period, 9
    padi land use, 163*t*
    royal family's role, 7
    tapioca planting, 9
    water, 244, 262
NEP. *See* New Economic Policy
net domestic product (NDP). *See also specific state*
    by region, 49*f*
    compared to gross domestic product, 36–37,
      46, 47*f*, 50
    interpreting, 37
    per capita, 46, 47*f*, 49*f*
Netherlands, 326
net investment (in reproducible capital)
    per capita, 46*f*, 48*f*
    regional analysis of, 47–48, 48*f*
    trends in Malaysia, 44–45, 46*f*
net national income, calculating, 36–37
net present value (NPV)
    assumptions used for analysis of petroleum
      industry, 90–91

    assumptions used for analysis of timber
      industry, 131
    contractor share under oil production-sharing
      contracts, 92*t*
net-price method, defined, 35
New Economic Policy (NEP)
    environmental quality trends during,
      17–23
    goals of, 11, 106
    integrated timber complexes, 139
    introduction of, 74
    land development, 106, 116, 155
    natural resource use trends during, 15–16
    overview of, 11–14
    rural water supply, 246–247
New Villages, 176, 179*n25*
New Zealand, 89
Nigeria, 239
Nik Mustapha, 144
nitrogen, ammoniacal
    described, 18
    in the Sungai Kelang, 19–20, 21*t*
    proposed interim national standards, 21*t*
    relationship to economic development,
      analytical model, 289*t*
    trends in Malaysian rivers, 281–284
nitrogen oxide pollution
    effects of, 23
    official estimates in Malaysia, 275, 276*t*
    relationship to economic development
      cross-country studies, 269*t*, 272–273
      estimates compared to predictions, 277*t*
      predictions for Malaysia, 274
nongovernmental organizations, 26
Non-Revenue Water Control Study & Development
    of a Control Programme for Malaysia, 258
Nordhaus, W. D., 39, 98, 144
North America, deforestation in, 112
North American Free Trade Agreement (NAFTA),
    269
Norway, petroleum depletion, 35
NO_x pollution. *See* nitrogen oxide pollution

O

offshore oil and gas deposits, allocation of tax
    revenue from, 24
oil-palm cultivation. *See* palm oil
oil refining. *See* petroleum industry
O'Neil, W., 327, 339
Ooi, J. B., 181, 190, 192, 201–202, 204–205, 208

OPEC (Oil Producing and Exporting Countries), 74, 86
Orang asli (aboriginal groups), 6, 144
Ostro, B. D., 299, 313–314
overfishing. *See* fishing, depletion
overseas investment, role of, 51
Oxford Analytica Daily Brief, 89

P

Padi Cultivators Act, 172
padi land
   cultivation on Peninsular Malaysia, 151, 152*t*, 163*t*
   irrigated, 236
   rehabilitation of idle, 158, 167–170
   small farm size, 172
Pahang
   development expenditure compared to
      resource-based revenue, 54
   integrated timber complexes in, 139–140
   New Villages, 176
   padi land use, 163*t*
   royal family's role, 7
   timber fees, 127–128
   water, jurisdiction, 244
Pakistan, 239
palm oil
   exports, 1, 17*f*, 52, 329
   growth in output, 156, 329
   oil-palm cultivation, 13, 151, 152*t*
   rate of return earned, 115
palm oil effluent
   commercial uses for developed, 336
   development of the pollution problem,
      328–329
   pollution regulations
      cost comparisons modeled, 337–341
      effectiveness of, 334–336
      introduced, 284
      structure of, 320, 329–331, 331*t*, 332–333
      volume, 320, 328
Palm Oil Research Institute of Malaysia
   (PORIM), 335
Panayotou, T., 113, 273
Pang, T. W., 49, 51, 56
Papua New Guinea, 36, 39
Paris, R., 128
particulates. *See* total suspended particulates
Pathansali, D., 201
Patricia (oil) Field, 81
peasant economy, 155–156
Penan (ethnic group), 6

Penang
   fishing conflicts, 195
   population, 310
   total suspended particulates, 309*t*
Peninsular Malaysia
   colonial period, 9, 56
   consumption allowance
      mineral, 61
      timber, 64–65
   economic sustainability in, 50
   ethnic groups, 7*t*
   fishing
      conflicts, 194–195
      depletion of stocks, 183, 185, 201–204
         policy responses to, 204–210
      development on the West Coast, 189–210
      economic analysis of catch and effort,
         210–223
      government assistance, 195–200
      licensed boats and fishermen, 184*t*, 197,
         198*f*, 206, 213
      pretrawling period, 189–190
      production, 184, 184*t*, 194
      trawling period, 190–195
   forests and timber
      deforestation, 122–123, 123*f*, 124, 141
      export policy, 135
      harvest, 19*f*
      inventory, 116–117, 117*t*, 119
      issues, 108–109
      land use for, 152*t*
      log prices, 130–131, 135
      Permanent Forest Estate in, 119–120, 121*t*
      processing mills, 135
      status at independence, 106
   geography, 3, 4*f*, 5
   industrialization, 12
   irrigation, 236
   land use, 5*t*, 115–116, 116*t*, 152*t*
      idle land, 156–157, 161–162, 163*t*
   oil, 73–74, 81–82, 102*n*12
   per capita data, 48, 48*f*, 49, 49*f*, 123–124
   population and migration, 6*t*, 13*t*, 159–160
   rainfall, 234, 234*t*
   respiratory disorders, 306
   revenue from natural resource-related taxes, 55,
      55*t*, 133
   water
      losses, 259
      piped supply, 246, 246*t*, 247
      pollution trends, 17–18, 281–283, 284*t*
      tariffs and financing, 250
pepper, cultivation, 154

Perak
    agricultural land ownership in New Villages,
        176
    fishing conflicts, 195
    integrated timber complexes in, 139
    land use during the colonial period, 9
    padi land use, 163t
    per capita gross domestic product, 29
    respiratory disorders, 306
    royal family's role, 7
    trawling in, 191, 193–194
    water, 244, 250
Perlis
    farm mechanization, 172
    household income from padi schemes, 168
    influence of geography on development, 10
    irrigation, 236
    National Forestry Act application in, 120
    padi land use and rehabilitation, 163t, 168
    royal family's role, 7
    water, 244, 247, 250, 258, 262
Permanent Forest Estate
    additions to, 120–121
    establishment, 25, 117–119
    in Peninsular Malaysia, 121t
    logging from 1981 to 1995, 127
    primary motivation for, 124
    protective forests in, 142–143
    state authority regarding, 121
    mentioned, 136
Persian Gulf states, oil dependence of, 97
Pertamina, 83–84
Petaling Jaya, 22f, 23, 275, 304–305
petroleum depletion, 35–36
Petroleum Development Act, 24, 71n29, 76,
    82–83
Petroleum Income Tax, rate, 99
Petroleum Income Tax Act (1967), 81
Petroleum Income Tax Amendment Act (1977), 85
petroleum industry
    characteristics of Malaysian crude oil, 75
    economics of extraction, 78–79, 79f, 80
    exploration and development, 75–76, 78f, 86,
        102n26
    exports, 17f, 74–75
    history in Malaysia, 73–76, 80–82
    Hotelling rent, 60f
    Malaysian contracts compared to other
        Asia-Pacific region countries, 88–89
    median field size, 93
    price collapse, 12
    production-sharing contracts

comparison of first- and second-generation,
    88t
economic analysis of, 89–98
first-generation, 82–86, 86t, 87
second-generation, 87–89
refinery output and capacity, 75
reserves, defined, 101n2
reserves and production, 15, 15f, 16, 74–76, 77f,
    100
taxation of, 81
Petroleum Mining Act, 81–82
Petroleum Mining Rules (1968), 81
petroleum revenue
    as a government revenue source, 24, 54
    federal and state contention over, 55
    growth in, 75–76
    production-sharing contracts
        analytic method described, 89–91
        first-generation, 84–86, 86t, 88t
        government rent capture through, 89, 91–92
        high grading, 92–94
        risk sharing, 94–98
        second-generation, 87–88, 88t, 89
        strategic considerations, 98–101
Petroliam Nasional Berhad. See Petronas
Petronas Carigali
    establishment, 84, 88
    production-sharing contracts and, 87
Petronas (national oil company)
    establishment and authority of, 24, 76, 82–85,
        87
    estimate of reserves, 76, 77f
    production-sharing contracts, 88–89
    use of earnings from, 71n29
pH
    analytical model for relating to economic
        development, 290t
    described, 18
    in the Sungai Kelang, 19–20, 21t
    proposed interim national standards, 21t
    trends in Malaysian rivers, 281–284
Philippines
    economics of oil production in, 85
    export comparisons, 11, 12t
    fish consumption, 182
    impact of immigration from, 47
    low-cost timber exhausted, 107
    oil contracts, 89
physical capital, 31–33. See also gross fixed capital
    formation
Pinang Water Authority, 251
political parties, description and organization of, 7
political patronage, 128–129, 167

pollution. *See also specific substance; specific type*
  abatement, economic principles of
    economic instruments approach, 320, 322*f,*
      323–327
    lessons from Malaysia's experience, 341–342
    overview, 319–320
    simulation model comparing costs, 337–341,
      344–348
    uniform standard approach, 319, 322*f,*
      323–324, 327
  control mandated, 26
  monitoring efforts, start of, 2
  overview and history of Malaysian regulations,
    319–321
  relationship to economic development
    analytical model described, 287–290
    cross-country studies, 269–273, 290*n1*
    factors influencing, 267–268
    gross domestic product, 268–269, 269*t,*
      270–273, 279–280, 280*t,* 283–284
    predictions for Malaysia, 274
    regulation and enforcement, 268, 271, 273,
      284–285
pollution charge
  cross-country experiences, 326–327
  explained, 324–326
pollution permits, tradeable
  cross-country experiences, 324–327
  explained, 324–326
population, 6*t,* 13*t,* 159, 236, 310
PORIM (Palm Oil Research Institute of
  Malaysia), 335
Port Dickson, 9
Portney, P. R., 295, 297, 308, 313–314
Port Swettenham (Port Klang), 9
Port Weld (Kuala Sepeting), 9
poverty
  among fishermen, 182, 199
  drop in rate of, 14, 156, 165
  for rural areas, 182
  linked to idle land, 157
privatization, 13, 263
production-sharing contracts (PSCs). *See under*
  petroleum industry
productive forests, defined, 118
productive reserves (forest), defined, 113–114
protective forests, defined, 118
protective reserves (forest), defined, 113
Public Works Department (Jabatan Kerja Raya)
  (JKR), 244, 249, 252, 257–260
Pulau Pinang
  air pollution from lead, 23
  development as a harbor, 8
  export processing zone established, 11
  industrialization, 12–13
  land use during the colonial period, 9
  padi land use, 163*t*
  trawling, 191, 193–194, 203
  water
    consumption, 239
    jurisdiction, 244
    losses, 258, 260
    tariffs and financing, 250, 262–263
purse seine, introduction, 189

Q

quality of life, no pricing mechanism for, 38
quarrying. *See* mining and quarrying

R

racial tensions. *See* ethnic groups, tensions among
railroads, building of, 9
rainfall, 233, 234*t*
Raw Natural Rubber Regulations, 320
Rembau area, 9
Repetto, R., 34–38, 52
Report of the Financial Survey of Limited
  Companies (Malaysia Department of
  Statistics), 44, 69
reservoirs, 248
resource consumption allowance
  calculating
    minerals, 58–61
    summarized, 33–35
    timber, 61–67, 68*f*
  defined, 33
  estimating for Malaysia, 40–43, 43*f,* 44
resource depletion. *See* economic sustainability;
  specific resource
resource rents. *See* natural resource rents
respiratory disorders, 305–306
rice, self-sufficiency goal, 157, 175
rice farming, 13, 156
Rice Lands Enactment, 172
Richardson, R., 312
RISDA (Rubber Industry Smallholders'
  Development Authority), 155, 163
river basins, 234
rivers, 17, 19–20, 244, 281
Road Traffic Ordinance, 303
Royal Dutch Shell Company, 80
royal families, 7, 128

RRIM (Rubber Research Institute of Malaysia), 335
rubber
  colonial period, 9
  cultivation on Peninsular Malaysia, 151, 152t, 163
  exports, 1, 17f, 52
  growth in latex production, 156
  move to reduce dependence on, 13
  pollution regulations, 320
  rate of return earned, 115
Rubber Industry Smallholders' Development Authority (RISDA), 155, 163
Rubber Research Institute of Malaysia (RRIM), 335
Rudel, T. K., 113
Rural Environmental Sanitation Programme, 245
Russell, C. S., 327
Ruzicka, I., 128

S

Sabah
  colonial development, 10
  consumption allowance
    mineral, 60–61
    timber, 65, 68f
  economic sustainability, 50, 53, 57
  ethnic groups, 6, 7t
  Fisheries Department, 25, 184
  fishing, 184t
  Forestry Department, 25, 108
  forests and logging, 19f, 108, 135
  geography, 3, 4f, 5–6
  gross fixed capital formation, 47
  land use, 5t
  oil, 73–74, 76, 80–83
  per capita, net domestic product, 49, 49f, 50
  per capita, net investment, 48, 48f
  population, 6t, 13t
  rainfall and distribution, 234, 234t
  revenue from natural resource-related taxes
    authority over, 24
    compared to public investment, 53–54, 54f
    petroleum, 55
    timber, 54–55, 55t, 56
    use of, 56, 133
  water
    jurisdiction, 244
    losses, 259
    quality, 18
    supply, 245–246, 246t, 247, 249

Sabah Shell, 85
Salleh Mohd. Nor., 116
Sarawak
  colonial development, 10
  consumption allowance
    mineral, 60–61
    timber, 65–66, 68f
  economic sustainability in, 50, 53, 57
  ethnic groups, 6, 7t
  fishing, 184, 184t
  Forestry Department, 25, 108
  forests and logging, 19f, 108
  geography, 3, 4f, 5
  gross fixed capital formation, 47
  land use, 5t
  natural gas production, 61
  net investment, per capita, 48f
  oil, 73–74, 76, 80–82
  per capita, net domestic product, 49, 49f, 50
  per capita, net investment, 48
  population, 6t, 13t
  rainfall and distribution, 234, 234t
  revenue from natural resource-related taxes
    authority over, 24
    compared to public investment, 53–54, 54f
    petroleum, 55
    timber, 54–55, 55t, 56
    use of, 56, 133
  water
    jurisdiction, 244
    losses, 259
    piped supply, 245–246, 246t, 247, 249
    quality, 18
    tariffs and financing, 262
Sarawak Shell, 80, 82, 85
Saudi Arabia, oil reserves, 86
saw mill industry. *See* timber
sawnwood. *See* timber
Schaefer, M. B., 185
Schelling, T. C., 302
Seberang Prai (costal strip of Pulau Pinang), 9
Second Malaysia Plan 1971–1975
  fishing program, 200
  minerals, 73
  public-sector land development, 13, 14f
  water spending, 245–247, 256–257
Second Outline Perspective Plan 1991–2000, 249, 285, 312
Sedjo, R. A., 128
Selangor
  air quality in, 315
  farm mechanization, 172
  forest policy, 118, 175

land use during the colonial period, 9
padi land use and rehabilitation, 163*t*, 168
per capita income, 124
royal family's role, 7
water
    jurisdiction, 244
    privatization of supply projects, 263
    tariffs, 254, 254*t*
Selangor Waterworks Department, 254
Selden, T. M., 272–273
Selective Management System (SMS), 126,
    131–132
Seligi (oil) Field, 87
Semarang (oil) Field, 81
Semenyih dam, 254
Seremban, 9
sewerage system, 284
Shafik, N., 112, 271
Shah Alam, 22*f*, 23
Shahrom bin Abdul Majid, 202, 204–208, 210
Sham Sani, 305
Shell, 80, 82, 85, 88, 95
Sibu Water Board, 251, 262–263
Siddayao, C. M., 81, 85, 87
Singapore
    export comparisons, 12*t*
    history, 7–8
    Malaysian log exports to, 134
    natural resource comparison, 1
    railroad extended to, 9
Sivalingam, G., 176
Sixth Malaysia Plan 1991–1995
    deep-sea fishing, support for, 210, 226
    petroleum industry, 88
    public-sector land development, 14*f*, 122,
        175
    response to overfishing, 205, 209
    water priorities and expansion, 248, 260–261,
        263–264
smallholding sector
    demographic data, 160
    development expenditure, 164, 164*t*
    development policy and, 13, 155–156
    inheritance laws and, 171
    land rehabilitation program and, 165–167
SMS (Selective Management System), 126,
    131–132
SO$_2$. *See* sulfur dioxide
Socio-Economic Research Unit, 168
soil conservation, as a nontimber value of forests,
    143
Solow, R. M., 32–33, 37, 53
Song, D., 272–273

Soon, L. Y., 312
South Korea, 1, 12*t*
spice trade, 8
state enterprises, management of, 56
State List (legislative powers), 24–25
Statistics on Primary Commodities: Forestry
    (Ministry of Primary Industries), 64
Stauffer, T. R., 35, 41
steel industry, 12
Straits Settlements, 8–9
stumpage value, defined, 111
substitutability, 32
sugar cane, 8–9
Sulaiman bin Haji Noordin, 128
sulfates, sources of, 21
sulfur dioxide pollution
    health and environmental effects, 23
    monitoring started, 304
    relationship to gross domestic product
        cross-country studies, 269*t*, 270–273
        predictions for Malaysia, 274
sulfur oxide pollution
    official estimates in Malaysia, 275, 276*t*
    relationship to economic development, 277*t*
Sungai Johor
    palm-oil pollution in, 322, 337–341
    pollution control costs, simulation model,
        344–348
Sungai Kelang (Klang River), 19–20, 21*t*
Sungai Muda, 236
Sungai Selangor, 254
Sungsuwan, S., 113
surface runoff (water), 233, 234*t*
suspended solids (in water)
    described, 18
    in the Sungai Kelang, 19, 21*t*
    proposed interim national standards, 21*t*
    relationship to economic development, 289*t*
    trends in Malaysian rivers, 281–284
sustainability. *See* economic sustainability
Swan, A. V., 299
Syed Hussain, 167

T

Taiping, colonial period, 9
Taiwan, 1
Tamana (oil) Field, 81
Taman Negara (national park), 142, 144–145
Tamils, 6
Tan, J., 209
tanah pusaka (inheritance land), 171

Tanah Rata, 304
Tanzania, water tariffs, 239
Tapah Road, 9
tapioca, 8–9, 154
Tapis (oil) Field, 102*n12*
Tarnobrzeg (Poland), 297
technology
  biology based, 144
  developing countries, 270–271
  pollution control, 268, 341–342
  pollution prevention, 268, 319–320
telecommunications utilities, 13
Telok Anson (Telok Intan), 9
temporary occupation licenses (TOL), 177
Teo, P. C., 128
Terengganu
  development expenditure compared to
    resource-based revenue, 54
  geography, 10
  oil
    discovery, 73, 81
    production, 61
    revenue, 76
  padi land use, 163*t*
  political patronage, 167
  royal family's role, 7
  timber fees, 127
  water, 244, 247, 250, 258
Thailand
  deforestation and development, 113
  export comparisons, 11, 12*t*
  fish consumption, 182
  natural resource depletion study, 38
  oil contracts, 89
Third Malaysia Plan 1976–1980
  development policy, 155
  environmental improvement and protection,
    17, 23
  fishing development, 196, 200
  government spending, 13
  objectives for the oil sector, 74–75
  public-sector land development, 14*f,* 156
  water system and spending, 245–248, 250, 255,
    257
Tietenberg, T. H., 327
timber and logging. *See also* forests; *specific state*
  as a percentage of gross domestic product, 16*f*
  as a revenue source for government, 54–55, 55*t*
  depletion (*See* timber depletion)
  exports (*See under* exports)
  government authority over, 8
  illegal logging, 130
  losses, 43

production, 1, 15, 15*f,* 16, 19*f*
promotion of domestic processing, 133–136,
    139–141
rents
  captured by private and political interests,
    56, 128
  policy impact on, 129, 132, 136–137
  tax evasion, 71*n31*
resource consumption allowance
  calculating, 61–67, 68*f*
  Hotelling rent, 61–63, 68*f*
  in Malaysia, 40, 42–43, 43*f,* 44
  Peninsular Malaysia, 64–65, 68*f*
  physical accounts described, 63–64
  regional comparisons, 66–67
  Sabah, 65, 68*f*
  Sarawak, 65–66, 68*f*
timber depletion
  awareness of, 124–125
  international studies of, 35–36
  licensing policies, 125–133
  promotion of domestic processing and,
    133–141
  public policies assessed, 141–145
Timber Profits Tax, 71*n31*
tin
  as a source of government revenue, 24
  colonial period, 9, 56
  exports, 1, 17*f*
  outflow of rents from, 56–57
  production, 15, 15*f,* 29
Tobin, J., 39
TOL (temporary occupation licenses), 177
total suspended particulates (TSP)
  ambient concentrations
    epidemology studies, 298–300, 300*t,* 301
    monetary value of reducing, 301–303,
      308–312, 313*t,* 314–316
    willingness-to-pay estimates, 312–314
  health risks associated with, 21
  in the Klang Valley, 22, 22*t,* 305–307, 309
  monitoring system, 275, 304
  official estimates, 276*t,* 277, 277*t,* 278, 309*t*
  relationship to economic development
    analytical model described, 287*t*
    estimates compared to predictions, 275–277,
      277*t,* 278, 279*t,* 280
  relationship to gross domestic product
    cross-country studies, 269*t,* 270–273
    predictions for Malaysia, 274, 285
  sources of, 21, 292*n26,* 305, 307
  violations of proposed standard, 20–22
tourism, forests and, 142, 144

toxic waste, 26
tradeable pollution permits, 324–326
trash fish, 203
trawling. *See under* fishing
TSP. *See* total suspended particulates

U

Umikalsum Haji Mohd. Nor., 127
U.N. Conference on the Law of the Sea (1980), 207
U.N. Food and Agriculture Organization (FAO), 107, 116, 120, 125, 201
U.N. Industrial Development Organization (UNIDO), 140
UNCED (United Nations Conference on the Environment and Development) (1992), 26, 109
UNDP (United Nations Development Programme), 116, 120
United Malays National Organization, 7
United Nations, 34, 36, 39
United Nations Conference on the Environment (1972), 26
United Nations Conference on the Environment and Development (UNCED) (1992), 26, 109
United Nations Development Programme (UNDP), 116, 120
United States
    abandonment of agricultural land, 174
    air pollution reduction benefits estimated, 295–297
    monetary value of a statistical life, 303
    North American Free Trade Agreement, 269–270
    pollution permits, 327
Universiti Pertanian Malaysia, 210, 315
University of Malaya, 22
urban land use, 5*t*, 152*t*
USAID (United States Agency for International Development), 239, 257
user cost
    defined, 31–32
    estimating, 33–34

V

Veitch, M. D., 41
Vincent, J. R., 122, 128, 136–137, 143
Viscusi, W. K., 303, 313

W

"Wallace Line," 107, 147*n8*
Waller, R. E., 299
Walter, I., 315
water
    consumption, 17, 233, 236
    demand for, 236
    development and allocation issues, 234–236, 261–264
    distribution issues and coverage, 234, 246*t*
    economics of supply and demand, 237–243
    jurisdiction, 244
    nonrevenue losses and cost, 241, 257–258, 258*t*, 260
    policy inefficiencies, 53
    pollution (*See* water pollution)
    production, 237, 245–246, 248
    rainfall, 233, 234*t*
    system expansion, 237, 245–249
    treatment plants, 245, 248
water pollution
    forests and prevention of, 143
    increase in, 17–18
    in the Sungai Kelang, 19–20, 21*t*
    monitoring, 2, 17, 281
    relationship to economic development
        cross-country studies, 269–273
        predictions for Malaysia, 274, 286
    sources and extent of, 18, 329
    standards used, 21*t*
    trends, 281–284
"water-stress" basins, defined, 234
water tariffs
    and system financing, 249–255, 261–264
    consequences of inadequate, 255–261
    effect of changes in, 239
    social and political issues, 242–243
Weiner, R. J., 38
Weitzman, M. L., 36–37
welfare economics theory, explained, 302
Wells, R., 76, 80, 82, 100
West Lutong (oil) Field, 81
WHO. *See* World Health Organization
Widjadono, P., 88–89
wildlife, 24, 142–143, 145
Wisconsin, 327
Wong, C. Y., 176
Wong, I. F. T., 115
Wood Mackenzie, 91, 98
World Bank
    air pollution reduction
        analysis of benefits, 301, 313–316

World Bank (*continued*)
   recommendations, 303, 307
  farm income and rural poverty, 165–166
  fishing industry
    depletion, 203–204, 206
    subsidies, 196–197, 200, 208
    trawling impact on jobs, 193
  land bank support, 177
  natural resources depletion studies, 36, 39
  padi land rehabilitation, 167–168
  water
    projects, 245
    tariffs, 239, 251, 257
World Health Organization (WHO)
  Global Environmental Monitoring System, 304
  particulate concentrations, 301, 314
  sulfur dioxide standard, 23
  water in rural areas, 234
World Resources Institute, 124

Y

Yap, C. L., 197
Yusuf Hadi, 122, 143

Z

Zailina Hashim, 315
Zimbabwe, water tariffs, 239